Exploring digitally-mediated communication with corpora

Digital Linguistics

Edited by
Andreas Witt

Volume 2

Exploring digitally-mediated communication with corpora

Methods, analyses, and corpus construction

Edited by
Louis Cotgrove, Laura Herzberg and Harald Lüngen

DE GRUYTER

The Open Access version of this publication was funded by the Leibniz Association's Open Access Publishing Fund for the promotion of scientific research.

ISBN 978-3-11-143259-5
e-ISBN (PDF) 978-3-11-143401-8
e-ISBN (EPUB) 978-3-11-143433-9
ISSN 2751-1278
DOI https://doi.org/10.1515/9783111434018

Library of Congress Control Number: 2025936015

Bibliographic information published by the Deutsche Nationalbibliothek
The Deutsche Nationalbibliothek lists this publication in the Deutsche Nationalbibliografie; detailed bibliographic data are available on the internet at http://dnb.dnb.de.

Cover image: piranka/E+/Getty Images
Printing and binding: CPI books GmbH, Leck

www.degruyterbrill.com
Questions about General Product Safety Regulation:
productsafety@degruyterbrill.com

MIX
Papier | Fördert gute Waldnutzung
FSC® C083411

Table of contents

Louis Cotgrove, Laura Herzberg, and Harald Lüngen

From CMC to DMC: Digital writing beyond the keyboard

1 Terminology

The prevalent terminology for denoting interpersonal communication facilitated by digital media is, at the time of writing, 'Computer-Mediated Communication' (CMC), a term that gained prominence in the 1980s, supplanting the earlier descriptor, "computerized conferencing," initially introduced in 1978 (see Hiltz and Turoff 1978/1993: xix). CMC was adopted to encompass "any system that uses the computer to mediate communication among human beings". The initialism CMC became widely used as informal digital communication methods like online message boards emerged. Nevertheless, since the mid-2000s, scholars have contested the appropriateness of the term CMC for at least three reasons:

1. Microprocessor-based communication has evolved beyond traditional keyboard-centric interactions. It now encompasses a diverse array of modalities, including auditory, visual, and audio-visual means. Moreover, contemporary communication often integrates multiple modes and media, employing combinations of text, images, and audio elements (see Jucker and Dürscheid 2012: 4–8). Additionally, haptic feedback, characterized by vibrations, has become an integral component of this communicative paradigm.
2. The scope of CMC practices has expanded beyond what is considered as a 'computer'. A variety of devices such as mobile phones, tablets, and wearable technology are all used to communicate, redefining the conventional understanding of computing in this context (see Carr 2020).
3. Linguistic features traditionally associated with CMC extend beyond computer and internet devices. Instances of such features are evident in non-computer, non-internet communication, exemplified by activities like sending SMS using a mobile phone (see Herring 2007).

Louis Cotgrove, Leibniz-Institute for the Germany Language (IDS), Mannheim, Germany, e-mail: cotgrove@ids-mannheim.de
Laura Herzberg, Leibniz-Institute for the Germany Language (IDS), Mannheim, Germany, e-mail: herzberg@ids-mannheim.de
Harald Lüngen, Leibniz-Institute for the Germany Language (IDS), Mannheim, Germany, e-mail: luengen@ids-mannheim.de

https://doi.org/10.1515/9783111434018-001

Authors have attempted to reconcile these discrepancies by expanding the definition of CMC or suggesting alternative terms. For example, Herring (2007) defined CMC as "text-based human-human interaction mediated by networked computers or mobile telephony",[1] but the focus on text-based communication in this definition excludes the other modes mentioned in point 1, such as audio-based technology. Other suggestions for new terminology have included "electronic language" (Collot and Belmore 1996: 13), "electronically-mediated communication" (Baron 2008: xii), "internet-mediated communication" (Yus 2011), and "electronic communication" (Herring 2012), and even simply "Mediated Communication" (Carr 2020).

According to Carr (2020: 10), the term Computer-Mediated Communication (CMC) poses a broader epistemological challenge due to the widespread mediation of communicative experiences by "omnipresent digital tools". Carr suggests that any terminological framework should be inclusive of the extensive array of communication devices, moving beyond the historical association of "technology tethered to a desk by a cord" (Carr 2020: 10). The proposition of "Mediated Communication" (MC) by Carr serves to de-emphasise the centrality of computers and underscores the importance of the mediation process itself, suggesting a "technology-agnostic approach" (Carr 2020: 17), assuming a detachability of language from the medium. However, this perspective may encounter challenges as human-to-human interaction exhibits variations even among similar platforms (e.g., WhatsApp vs Telegram), not to mention sites with differing communicative motivations (e.g., WhatsApp vs YouTube), thereby questioning the effectiveness of this approach.

Another term which instead refers to the environments and platforms where CMC occurs is *Social Media*. Unlike CMC, the term is also used outside linguistics. Cann et al. (2011: 7) define social media as "Internet services where the online content is generated by the users of the service". In the subsequent explanations they name two features which we also regard as defining:

Firstly, social media services emerged in the first decade of the 21st century following technological advances that allowed the easy and dynamic exchange of user-generated content, including platforms like MySpace and Facebook, referred to as "Web 2.0". Before that, to publish content online (i.e., Web 1.0), an individual would need knowledge of HTML, to have access to a web server and to be able to deploy files on it, something that was possible only for a few private individuals.

Secondly, social media serve one or more of the following three functions: communication (such as in blogs and chat messengers), collaboration (e.g., wikis, google docs), or the sharing and consuming of multimedia content (e.g., YouTube, Insta-

1 Some definitions of CMC also include human-machine interaction (HMI), although in this paper, we focus on human-human interaction.

gram). Similarly Kaplan and Haenlein (2010) defined social media as a "group of Internet-based applications that build on the ideological and technological foundations of Web 2.0, and that allow the creation and exchange of User Generated Content". As social media are based on the World Wide Web i.e. built on HTML and HTTP, the term excludes earlier genres of CMC that relied on other internet protocols such as Internet Relay Chat (IRC), Usenet News, or email – or SMS, which is not based on the internet at all but on mobile telephony.

Personal homepages, business and institutional websites, or platforms with a focus on transactions such as the trading of products are also excluded from classification as social media as their primary focus is not on communication, collaboration and content sharing. Although these other web genres might offer components with social media functions such as commenting or reviewing, this is neither their main focus nor a defining feature.

While there may be some generalisable linguistic characteristics across various communicative technologies, the specific platform often remains a crucial consideration for any linguistic analysis. The term 'Mediated Communication' presents a potentially more future-proof alternative compared to a mere substitution of 'computer' with a technologically specific term like 'microprocessor,' as ongoing technological advancements may also render such descriptors obsolete. However, the term 'Mediated Communication' is inherently broad, encompassing mediums like air, water, and copper coil through which communication occurs, leading to a potential lack of precision and reduced utility. As per the title of this collection and in this chapter, we suggest the term 'Digitally Mediated Communication' (DMC) (see Yao and Ling 2020), akin to the German expression "digital vermittelte Kommunikation" (Androutsopoulos and Busch 2020: 137). This term is characterized by its device-agnostic nature and explicitly highlights the technologically-mediated nature of communication, unlike the similar phrase "digital communication" (Tagg 2015; Georgakopoulou and Spilioti 2016).

2 The development of DMC

Novel linguistic practices have been a central focus of DMC scholarship from the very beginning of the field in the late 1970s. For example, Carey (1980), identified emergent graphemic methods of communicating emotion when using "computer conferencing systems", such as "vocal spelling" (the repetition of graphemes to represent prosody). However, these novel practices have not been limited to graphemic features, developments have occurred in almost all aspects of language, including grammar and interaction, particularly following the increased access to digital communication methods in the late 1990s and early 2000s, which saw a huge increase in Digital Writing by ordinary users.

2.1 Interaction in DMC

One of the earliest frameworks designed for the analysis of interactive facets within DMC was introduced by Collot and Belmore (1996: 15–18). This framework applied the multidimensional-multi-feature model (MD-MF), initially formulated by Biber (1988), to scrutinize discourse and interaction in digital "speech situations". Notably, research on DMC interaction has frequently drawn upon methodologies from Conversation Analysis (e.g., Schegloff and Sacks 1973; Hutchby and Wooffitt 1998). These studies often concentrate on various aspects including turn-taking (Herring 1999; Riva 2002; Kessler 2008; Bou-Franch et al. 2012; Androutsopoulos and Tereick 2016; Meredith 2019), examinations of openings and closings (Kessler 2008; Meredith 2019) and topic structure and shift (Herring 1999; Herring et al. 2013; Dowell et al. 2017).

2.1.1 Styles and modes of DMC

From very early on in DMC scholarship, it was acknowledged that different modes of DMC (e.g. email, chat) produced not just different linguistic features, but also different interactive styles, as noted in Werry (1996), often related to the synchronicity of the mode of communication (Frehner 2008: 168). More synchronous communication has been characterised as more dialogical with rapid alternation of turns (Crystal 2008), containing more topic shift (Herring 1999; Herring et al. 2013), as well as lexical features that represent openings and closings (e.g. "hi") (Kessler 2008). Within German and English-language DMC, Siever et al. (2005), Wirth (2005), and Kessler (2008) have suggested that more synchronous situations encourage language economisation and the representation and approximation of spoken features in a written form (sometimes referred to in German-language work as conceptual orality, see Section 3.2).

However, there is also evidence that the link between the synchronicity of a DMC mode and the choice of certain linguistic and interactive features is not this straightforward. Dürscheid (2005) and Gibson (2008) both demonstrated that openings and closings, characteristic of synchronous communication, were also widely used in both email and Virtual Learning Environments (VLEs), which had been considered asynchronous. Similarly, Androutsopoulos (2015) demonstrated that communication between participants on *Facebook* (on a user's profile page, or 'wall') can exhibit qualities of both asynchronous and synchronous communication, in that posts may be responded to almost immediately, after several hours or after days, yet the comments, regardless of the time gap, contain examples of features characteristic of synchronous communication, such as ellipsis, see Figure 1:

Dee: Sitze jetzt in der schön warmen bahn & wünsche mein schwesterherz @ M weiterhin einen schönen schlaf & süße träume♥

Dee: Am now sitting in the warm train & wishing my dear sister @ M a lovely sleep & sweet dreams♥

Figure 1: Facebook status update, adapted from Androutsopoulos (2015: 194).

2.1.2 Identity in DMC

In addition to research on the structural aspects of DMC interaction, a significant proportion of scholarship also deals with social aspects of interaction features, especially concerning user identity (or anonymity) and the construction of online communities (for a discussion of anonymity, pseudonymity, and online identity, see Döring 2010). Herring (2019: 31–32) notes that the first online communities were interest-based and this is discussed in early scholarship, which examined, for example, newsgroups for political discussion (Gruber 1997; Jones 1998; Papacharissi 2004), mailing lists for hobbies and interests (Bell and Hübler 2001; Dresner and Herring 2010; Erickson 1999), and MUDs for role-playing games (Danet 1998; Kendall 1998; Nakamura 2002; Utz 2000). Despite the popular hope that the newfound online anonymity might lead to a socially equal space (Herring 1996a), research found that it often resulted in "uninhibited verbal behavior," characterized by swearing, insults, name-calling, and hostile comments (Kiesler et al. 1984: 1129). This behaviour was identified as indicative of masculine posturing (Jones 1998: 59). Notably, the "pre-web" period of DMC (1983–1993) was primarily populated by white men from the USA and the UK, although a noticeable "increase in female users" was observed from the early 1990s (Herring 2019: 39).

The perceived rise in female users prompted a focus on the socially gendered aspects of DMC, becoming a prominent theme in 1990s scholarship and continuing as an essential topic. Scholars applied developments in offline sociolinguistic research to analyse discourses in online communication. Studies explored tendencies of men to use assertive language, swearing, and sarcasm, while women were found to employ cooperative language, hedges, apologies, and questions (e.g., Herring 1992 1996b 1996a; Savicki et al. 1996; Schwartz et al. 2013). Additionally, researchers examined potential gendered differences in DMC-specific linguistic features. Some proposed that emoticons, like < :) >, and punctuation marks were characteristic of women's language in DMC (Baron 2004; Parkins 2012; Schwartz et al. 2013; Waseleski 2006; Witmer and Katzman 1997; Wolf 2000). However, Huffaker and Calvert (2005), in a study of blogs, found no gender-based differences in lexical choice, and noted that (young) men used more emoticons than women. Furthermore, Hilte et al. (2020) suggested that age may play a more crucial role in determining the emotional expressiveness of DMC texts, with younger individuals using more expressive features.

2.1.3 Gender in DMC

The increased availability of substantial DMC data since the mid-2010s has facilitated more sophisticated approaches to analysing emoticons and emoji, among other linguistic features. For instance, Fladrich and Imo (2020) utilized the *MoCoDa2* corpus of German-language *WhatsApp* conversations to investigate the use of specific emoji as indicators of gender identity.[2] Figure 2 presents an example of emoji usage in a male group chat.

Figure 2: *MoCoDa2 WhatsApp* chat, adapted from Fladrich and Imo (2020: 113).

The study revealed significant differences in the top 20 emoji used by women and men in both mixed and single-gender settings. A growing body of research has adopted larger-scale computational linguistic methodologies, such as machine learning algorithms, to explore emoji use with the objective of discerning the gender identity of users (e.g., Chen et al. 2018; Jaeger et al. 2018; T. Koch et al. 2020). However, these analyses predominantly operate within the framework of a binary understanding of gender, potentially reflecting limitations in the technical features

2 https://www.reddit.com/r/funny/comments/1buvwm4/you_had_one_job_calendar_makers (last accessed 14 February 2025).

of the data sources, such as Twitter or *WhatsApp*, which may not provide mechanisms for users to express non-binary gender identities.

The increase of research on gender led to an expansion in the late 2000s of analyses of other social dimensions of identity. This included investigations into how language is employed to construct and sustain communities, as well as explore sexual, regional, and ethnic identities. Such online communities have been termed "speech communities" following Gumperz' (2009: 66) definition as "any human aggregate characterized by regular and frequent interaction by means of a shared body of verbal signs". Alternatively, Gruzd et al. (2011) favoured the term "imagined communities" (from B. Anderson 1983), describing groups with shared interests or identity who may not necessarily interact directly. Varis and van Nuenen (2017: 478) noted that online communities do not necessitate "temporal and spatial co-presence," challenging established notions of community, instead describing online communities as "translocal".

2.1.4 Sociolinguistics of DMC

In the late 2000s, there was a shift from generalized linguistic variation research, such as binary gender language differences, towards analysing the active construction of identities in online contexts, although the earliest research on this topic stems from Turkle (1995). The concept of 'doing' identity originates from gender research by West and Zimmerman (1987: 125), which posits that gender is "a routine accomplishment embedded in every interaction," implying that it is not an inherent, unchangeable property but a socially constructed and "performed" aspect (Butler 2006: 187). This conceptualization of gender has been extended to other social identities, such as ethnicity (i.e., "acts of identity" Le Page and Tabouret-Keller 1985; "ethnifying" Lytra 2016) and youth ("doing youth" Neuland 2003; Walther 2018).

In the field of sociolinguistics, this approach to language and identity aligns with what Eckert (2012) has termed "Third Wave Variationist" sociolinguistics. This entails examining how language variation is employed to construct meaning, identity, and style, recognizing these aspects as inherently "mutable" (Eckert 2012: 94). Within DMC scholarship, researchers such as Blashki and Nichol (2005), Milani and Jonsson (2011), and Heritage and Koller (2020) have analysed linguistic features in online men's communities, investigating how language is used to shape heterosexual masculinities. This includes the creation of a 'geek' identity and the promotion of discourses involving sexism and misogyny.

Other studies, such as Dmitrow-Devold (2017) on the gendered performances of teenaged girls in blogs, Mackenzie (2018) on the performance of motherhood in online forums, and Willem et al. (2019) on sexist and classist language expressing sexualized stereotypes of women, delve into diverse facets of identity construction through language.

Other sociolinguistic investigations in DMC have explored the role of language to perform ethnicity. For instance, E. Chun and Walters (2011) investigated the use of humor to construct Arab and East Asian identities, while E. W. Chun (2013) explored the use of stereotypically 'Black' language as part of Asian-American identities. Multilingualism has also been a focal point in DMC scholarship on language and ethnicity, particularly in studies of online diasporic websites (e.g. Lo 1999; Androutsopoulos 2006; Paolillo 2011; Wiese 2015; Hinrichs 2018). This includes phenomena like "codeswitching" between the language of the country of residence and 'heritage' languages. More recently, research has examined the use of multiple linguistic resources within the same communicative act, referred to as "translanguaging" (García and Li 2014). Alternative terms for similar concepts have included "codemeshing" (Canagarajah 2011) and "metrolingualism" (Pennycook and Otsuji 2015).

2.2 Beyond "written orality"

The early research perspective portrayed DMC as "neither simply speech-like nor simply written-like" (Yates 1996: 46), with language forms in DMC analysed as representing or emulating spoken language. Common terms for this style of writing included "typed conversations" (Storrer 2001), "typed dialogue" (Dürscheid and Brommer 2016) or "written colloquial speech" (Kilian 2001). This discourse often employed the framework of "orality" and "literality" (*Mündlichkeit* and *Schriftlichkeit*), which explores the interplay between spoken and written language (P. Koch and Oesterreicher 1985; Ong 1982; see Söll and Hausmann 1980). The influential *Nähe-Distanz Modell* ('Proximity-Distance model'), developed by Koch and Oesterreicher (1985) and later refined in Koch and Oesterreicher (2007), is depicted in Figure 3 and has served as a cornerstone since the 1990s for analyzing DMC (Beißwenger and Pappert 2020; e.g., Günther and Wyss 1996; Schlobinski 2005).

The model posits a spectrum where spoken (oral) and literal (graphic) language reside at opposite ends, each associated with distinct characteristics that define their 'conception.' Conceptually, 'oral' language is characterized as dialogical, expressive, and spontaneous, while 'literal' language is seen as monological, objective, and reflective. Importantly, the 'conception' is independent of the medium, whether the language is produced orally or graphically.

Despite the typical association of oral features with oral language production and literal features with written language, the model acknowledges that conceptually oral features can manifest in written language, and vice versa. Table 1 illustrates examples of each of the four combinations between concept and medium. Given the prevalence of conceptually oral features in Digital Writing, DMC was widely perceived to occupy a middle ground between "literality and orality" (Bader 2002).

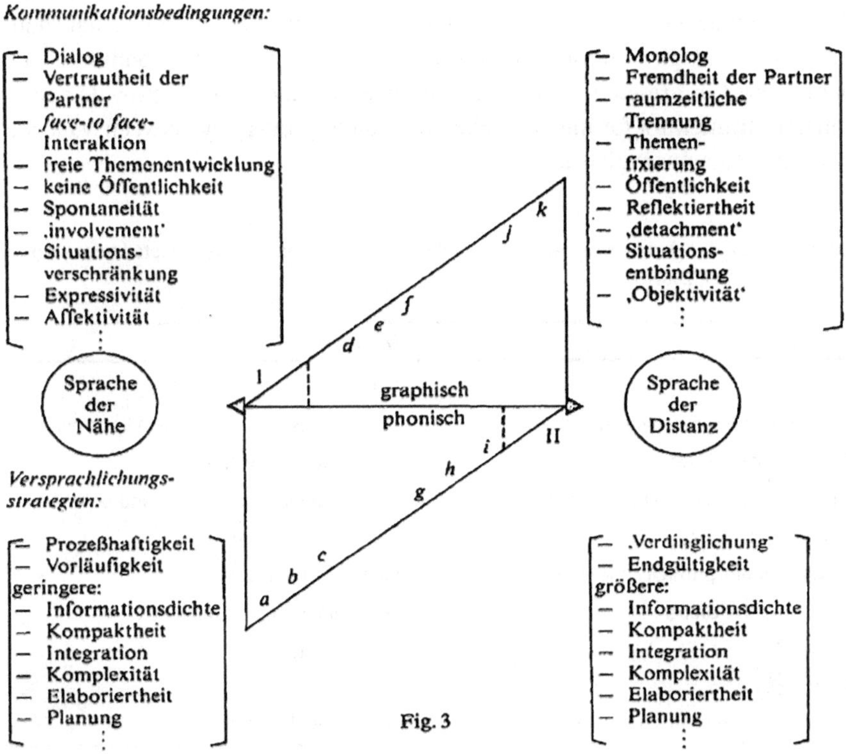

Figure 3: The Proximity-Distance model (Koch and Oesterreicher 1985: 23).

Table 1: Examples of the combinations between conception and medium based on the Proximity-Distance model, adapted from Kilian (2010 [2001]: 69).

		Medium	
		Graphic	**Phonic**
Conception	*Oral*	< nehm wa mal an >	[ne:mwɐma'an]
	Literal	< nehmen wir einmal an >	[ne:mən‿wɪɐ̯‿aɪnmal‿an]

Since the initial publication of the *Nähe-Distanz Modell*, there has been extensive discourse regarding its application to DMC, leading to several proposed revisions (e.g. Dürscheid 2003; Ágel and Hennig 2006; Schlobinski 2006a; Landert and Jucker 2011; for a fuller analysis of the revisions see Cotgrove 2024), each trying to account for the rapid communicative developments in DMC in this period (i.e., the transition from Web 1.0 to Web 2.0). Koch and Oesterreicher (2007: 351) even adapted their own model to account for the criticism, and integrated their original conditions and strategies into a unified group of ten pairs termed "communicative parameters," as presented in Table 2. This consolidation aimed to provide a more coherent framework for understanding the nuanced interplay between *Nähe* and *Distanz* in communicative acts.

Table 2: Updated communicative parameters of the Proximity-Distance model, adapted from Koch and Oesterreicher (2007: 351).

Proximity	**Distance**
Private	Public
Familiarity with conversational partner	Unfamiliarity with conversational partner
Strong emotional involvement	Low emotional involvement
Influenced by situation and/or actions	Disassociation from situation and/or actions
Referential proximity	Referential distance
Spatio-temporal proximity (face-to-face)	Spatio-temporal distance
Communicative cooperation	No communicative cooperation
Dialogicity	Monologicity
Spontaneity	Reflectedness
Unrestricted evolution of topic/theme	Fixed topic/theme

However, Koch and Oesterreicher's update, as well as some of the suggested revisions, have been criticised by Androutsopoulos (2007), who contended that many of the stylistic distinctions between spoken and written language were determined by (a lack of) technology. For instance, any email exchange, while asynchronous, can function quasi-synchronously due to technological advancements in internet speed and text input capabilities. Similarly, Storrer (2013: 354) argued that "characteristic stylistic features are not tied to the medium [...] or a particular social network" and emphasized that "writers adapt their writing style to the respective communicative setting and the appropriate linguistic conventions".

2.2.1 Towards a new literality

These critiques reflect a growing body of scholarly recognition that the *Nähe-Distanz* model is just one of many potential frameworks for analysing specific features of Digitally Mediated Communication (DMC). Androutsopoulos (2007) advocated for terms like "neue Schriftlichkeit" ('new literality'), initially coined by Haase et al. (1997: 81), and later "digitale Schriftlichkeit" ('digital literality'). As DMC ceased to be considered 'new,' these terms were introduced to acknowledge potential distinctions between digital and traditional forms of writing, although the ubiquity and volume of DMC also calls the usefulness of such distinctions into question. However, these new terms provide a reframed analysis of digital features that transcends the constraints of the *Nähe-Distanz* model, which, as noted by Dürscheid (2016b: 386), "was never designed for this purpose [the analysis of Digital Writing]". Dürscheid (2016b: 386) went on to argue that the "new communicative forms, particularly chat," make it almost impossible to integrate DMC "within the continuum of *Nähe* and *Distanz*".

Echoing this sentiment, Androutsopoulos (2007) and later Saxalber and Micheluzzi (2018) concurred that the linguistic features of DMC cannot simply be treated as "a medial transposition of the aspects of spoken language" (Androutsopoulos 2007: 81). This perspective contrasts with much of the older research, which viewed Digital Writing as an "emulated" form of spoken language (see Siever et al. 2005: 7). Moreover, even if certain linguistic themes and features are common across DMC, the diverse array of online platforms and communication opportunities introduces significant linguistic variations within and across platforms, including the differing modalities to which users respond, e.g. a picture or video, and the surrounding text, such as in Figures 4 and 5, with Reddit and YouTube. These linguistic features are dynamic, evolving, diverging, and converging, necessitating ongoing research (Androutsopoulos 2011). While the *Nähe-Distanz* model contains a list of useful dimensions and characteristics that can be used to analyse communicative situations, it falls short as a comprehensive solution for DMC, and certainly not as an over-generalised, one-dimensional model.

Figure 4: Youtube comment section (extract) taken from the Channel "The Dodo".[3]

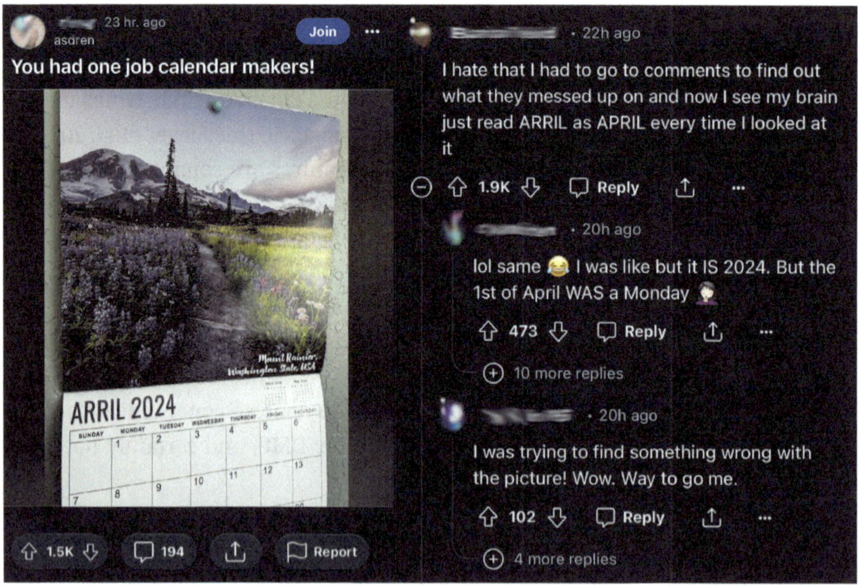

Figure 5: Reddit comment section (extract) taken from the posting "You had one job calendar makers!"[4] in the Subreddit "r/funny".

3 https://www.tiktok.com/@ristoripa/video/7344349526293024033 (last accessed 14 February 2025).
4 https://www.tiktok.com/@ristoripa/video/7344349526293024033 (last accessed 14 February 2025).

2.3 Further frameworks for analysing DMC

A subset of DMC pertaining to the lexical, graphemic, and morphosyntactic choices within written language is referred to as 'Digital Writing', following Androutsopoulos (2018: 741–742), i.e., the graphical characters chosen to be transmitted by an author and how they interplay with DMC conventions, including orthographic norms. Early studies in this area often emphasized the "stylistic distinctiveness" (Crystal 2006: 31) and "colloquial" linguistic features of digital writing (Hentschel 1998: 3.2.1), including abbreviations, acronyms (e.g. Werry 1996: 53–56; Kilian 2001), obscenities (e.g. Diekmannshenke 2000: 144), non-standard syntax (Kilian 2001), and emoticons such as < :) > (e.g. Runkehl et al. 1998: 11–12; Wolf 2000). In the context of the German language, a significant portion of research explored the use of "inflectives," verb stems enclosed in punctuation to signify actions, e.g., < *grins* >, conveying a grinning expression in face-to-face conversation (e.g., see Hentschel 1998; Schlobinski 2001; Siever 2006).

Many features identified in prior research on digital writing have been examined within the framework of conceptual orality. These encompassed interjections, terms of address (e.g., *hey*), hedging, filler words (e.g., *err*) (Bader 2002; see Storrer 2001), dialect words, slang, and other elements that perhaps would not typically appear in formal written language. Other conceptually oral graphemic features include phonetic spelling (< playa > instead of < player >), the use of 'shouting capitals' (e.g., < WHAT >), and the extended repetition of letters (< noooooooo >) (Androutsopoulos 2003; see Kilian 2001; Soffer 2010). Figure 6 contains examples of these features in an email.

DU BIST SOOOOOOOOOOOOOOOOOOO
LIIIIIIIEEEEEEEEEEEBBBBBBB!!!!

knuddeldrückumarmkussgeb
Der NAME-Server hat heut absolut was gegen mich! Ich kann nich mehr einloggen: Da kommt immer ein Meldung mit Server-Errror *schluchzheul* Es tut mir echt leid!!!!!!!!!!!!! ICH FIND DAS SO GEMEIN!!!!!!!!!!

YOU ARE SOOOOOOOOOOOOOOOOOOO
SWEEEEEEEEEEEEEEEEETTT!!!!
hug hug hug kiss
The NAME server has absolutely something against me today! I can't log in anymore: There is always a message with server error *sob cry* I'm really sorry!!!!!!!!!!!!!
I THINK IT'S SO MEAN!!!!!!!!!!

Figure 6: Email exchange, adapted from Androutsopoulos (2003: 183).

An initial attempt to move away from conceptual orality was made by Androutsopoulos (2003, 2007, 2011), who reframed the interpretation of shouting capitals and the repetition of graphemes as “compensation practices” for face-to-face communication, which is more than just orality. Another set of features that resists easy classification is the use of emoji and emoticons. Initially interpreted as compensation for facial expressions in face-to-face communication, as they represent human faces (Beck 2010; Beißwenger and Pappert 2019; Dresner and Herring 2010; Hilte et al. 2019; Hougaard and Rathje 2018; Kavanagh 2019; see Miyake 2007; Thompson and Filik 2016), the functions of emoji and emoticons remain a subject of significant debate within DMC scholarship. According to Albert (2015: 3), “emoticons in written language today cannot be described as a compensation strategy”; instead, they “have evolved into abstract, symbolic signs” used to modify how a message should be received, i.e. modifying the illocutionary force of a message (see Cotgrove 2024). Similarly, Herring (2013: 8) argues that emoji and emoticons are not solely compensatory but can also be employed ludically as part of “language play”.

2.3.1 Graphostylistics

In addition to conceptual orality and compensation, Androutsopoulos (2007: 81–83) posited two additional frameworks for analyzing linguistic features within Digital Writing: “graphostylistics,” building on prior work by Sassen (2000) and Schlobinski (2001); and “language economisation” (see Siever 2006). Graphostylistics, also known as “graphic variation” (Spitzmüller 2013) or “graphomatic microvariation” (Dürscheid 2016a), involves the “manipulation of visually represented language without correspondence to phonics,” i.e., stylizing writing in a visual and often playful manner (Androutsopoulos 2007: 83). This can include phonetic spellings, e.g., < kul > for < cool > (Dürscheid 2016a: 496), alternating upper and lower case letters (e.g., < aWeSoMe >, for *awesome*) to communicate irony; and grapheme substitution, e.g., < gr8 > to represent < great > and < cu > for < see you >. Such stylization has been utilized by commenters as a graphemic strategy to express aspects of their identity within their Digital Writing.

Stylisations like < gr8 > and < cu > are also often categorized as ‘language economisation’, representing the use of graphemic strategies to “shorten a message form” in response to technological and financial barriers (Androutsopoulos 2011: 149; also see Ferrara et al. 1991: 19; Schlobinski 2006b; Siever 2006).

In Digital Writing, scholars have classified ellipsis and the use of phonetic and colloquial spellings as language economisation strategies (Crystal 2008; Dürscheid 2005; Kessler 2008; e.g., Siever et al. 2005; Wirth 2005), wherein specific linguistic features are intentionally omitted or abbreviated to save time, space, and sometimes money (as in the case of SMS exchanges where users are charged per 160-character text). With the proliferation of smartphones and more affordable data packages, SMS exchange in Europe has significantly decreased, replaced using messaging clients such as *WhatsApp* and *Facebook Messenger*. Consequently, the financial and spatial constraints of fitting a message into as few characters as possible have largely vanished, although some language economisation features, along with other non-standard graphemic practices, persist in more recent communication channels as stylistic choices. For example, the phonetic respelling of < u > for < you > (Rotne 2018: 900), referred to by Berg (2020) as a "democratisation of orthography". However, discussions often arise regarding whether children's use of such forms negatively impacts their writing ability or is a conscious stylistic choice (Androutsopoulos and Busch 2021; see Kleinberger Günther and Spiegel 2006).

2.3.2 Metacommunication

One area of DMC that is not as widely researched is the examination of the paralinguistic or metacommunicative functions conveyed by non-lexical signs – conventions that express emotion or tone or signify certain sociocultural information between interlocutors. While Androutsopoulos's framework, as elaborated earlier, has proven valuable for a holistic analysis of digital writing, it requires adaptation for studying the metacommunicative functions of graphemic features in digital writing.

For instance, studies on "digital punctuation" by young German speakers explored how punctuation marks can serve metacommunicative functions (Androutsopoulos and Busch 2021; Rinas and Uhrová 2016), including the indexing of specific identities (Androutsopoulos 2018, 2020). In Figure 7, a planned expansion can be interpreted by the usage of elliptical points in the initial position, which can be interpreted as a cohesive device.

Luisa: Ach Quatsch stört mich nie :)
'Oh that [if your place is a mess] doesn't bother me at all :)'

Luisa: ... bei anderen :D in meiner wg treibt mich das zur Weißglut aber das ist ein anderes Thema 😜 *'... as long as it's not my place :D the mess in my dorm drives me crazy but that's a different issue* 😜 *'*

Figure 7: Self-selection strategy in WhatsApp, imitating floor keeping strategies from spoken conversation, adapted from Beißwenger et al. (2023: 35).

Metacommunicative devices and other functions have also been explored within emoji usage in digital writing, as demonstrated by the “Face with Tears of Joy” emoji in Figure 8 in a TikTok comment which here modifies the illocutionary force of the proposition. Emoji use in metacommunication has seen a dramatic uptake since 2015 (see Pavalanathan and Eisenstein 2015; Ljubešić and Fišer 2016; Evans 2017; Beißwenger and Pappert 2019; Dainas and Herring 2020).

Figure 8: TikTok comment section of video “pov: trying to play it cool while waiting for your takeaway”.[5]

Figure 9: Variation of animoji (top two rows) and memoji (bottom two rows), adapted from Herring, Dainas, Lopez Long et al. (2020).

Figure 10: The “kappa” Twitch emote, one of the most popular emotes, signalling irony (Cotgrove 2025: 232).

5 https://www.tiktok.com/@ristoripa/video/7344349526293024033 (last accessed 14 February 2025).

A further current research area relates to the investigation of graphical features specific to various platforms, such as personalized bitmoji on *SnapChat* (Danesi 2016: 60–61), augmented-reality animoji on iOS, see Figure 9 (Herring, Dainas, Lopez Long et al. 2020; Herring, Dainas, Long et al. 2020), and emotes on *Twitch*, see Figure 10 (Barbieri et al. 2017).

The ubiquitous yet rapidly-developing nature of DMC means that even attempts to generalise communicative practices across digital spaces are short-lived, let alone attempts to establish comparisons with oral language practices. Instead, fine-grained approaches to specific aspects, platforms or modes of DMC can be more useful for future research, as they analyse digital linguistic practices within their specific contexts. Corpus-based approaches, such as the 19 chapters in this edited collection, are particularly beneficial for providing these contexts, as they are based on authentic data, and highlight the diverse and complex practices within DMC.

3 What to expect from this volume

Five chapters in this edited collection focus specifically on different linguistic features and phenomena in digitally mediated communication (DMC). They offer linguistic perspectives from Turkish, English, German and Chinese and cover different sites of DMC, including YouTube, Reddit, WhatsApp and other web texts.

The chapter "Utilizing Text Dispersion Keyword Analysis on Informational Description and Opinion Web Registers of Turkish" by Selcen Erten and Veronika Laippala examines the linguistic differences between different web registers in Turkish, with a particular focus on the information description and opinion registers. The research questions are how these registers differ linguistically and what insights these differences provide into the linguistic landscape of the Turkish web. The study uses the *Turkish Corpus of Online Registers* (TurCORE) and applies Text Dispersion Keyword Analysis (TDK) to examine 481 informational texts and 215 opinion texts, analysing keyword dispersion to identify distinctive linguistic features across these registers.

Staying within generalised web corpora, the chapter titled "'Also ehrlich' – From adjectival use to interactive discourse marker" by Lothar Lemnitzer and Antonia Hamdi examines the evolving use of the German word *ehrlich* from its traditional adjectival meaning ("honest") to its function as an interactive discourse marker. The research questions focus on identifying the specific function of *ehrlich* in its non-traditional use and the contexts that trigger this function. The study uses various corpora, including the *Digitales Wörterbuch der deutschen Sprache* (DWDS) and the *Deutsches Referenzkorpus* (DeReKo), and applies both quantitative and qualitative analyses to explore the linguistic patterns of *ehrlich* in different modes of communication, from written texts to spoken dialogues.

Also focusing on a particular feature of DMC is "Digital Punctuation from a Contrastive Perspective: Corpus-based Investigations of Ellipsis Points in German and Chinese Messaging Interactions" by Michael Beißwenger, Sarah Steinsiek and Yinglei Zang, which examines the use of ellipsis points in German and Chinese messaging interactions. The chapter looks at how ellipsis points function in digital communication and whether these functions are consistent across languages. The research questions focus on the pragmatic functions of ellipsis points in WhatsApp and WeChat messages and their origins in written traditions. The authors adopt a corpus-based approach, analysing randomised samples from the *MoCoDa2* corpus for German and a dataset of WeChat interactions for Chinese.

A further study of the variation of DMC features is provided in the chapter "A Multivariate Register Perspective on Reddit": Exploring Lexicogrammatical Variation in Online Communities" by Florian Frenken, which investigates linguistic variation within Reddit's subcommunities, called subreddits, using a geometric multivariate approach. The research questions focus on whether subreddits exhibit distinct lexicogrammatical features that qualify them as subregisters of Reddit, and how these features align with their contextual and functional differences. The study uses systemic functional theory to analyse 42 lexicogrammatical features across texts from 33 subreddits, revealing overlapping clusters that reflect contextual similarities and differences. This approach aims to improve our understanding of linguistic variation in online communities and the wider internet landscape.

An analysis of features beyond lexicogrammatical processes can be found in the chapter "Novel Methods of Intensification in Young People's Digitally-Mediated Communication" by Louis Cotgrove, which examines creative intensification strategies in German YouTube comments written by young people. It explores how these strategies modify the quality of elements in sentences. The research questions focus on identifying and classifying novel methods of intensification in youth DMC outside of traditional lexicogrammatical categories. The chapter uses data from the *NottDeuYTSch* corpus, a collection of 33 million tokens from YouTube comments. Methods include categorising intensification into morphological, syntactic, graphemic and typographic strategies, revealing how digital communication creatively develops linguistic conventions.

Five chapters deal with the construction of DMC corpora, from data collection via legal and representational issues to converting and preparing corpora for exchange and for use in corpus analysis systems to distributing corpora via corpus analysis platforms or repositories. They cover such diverse DMC sources as twitter, instant messaging/private chat data, multimodal human-robot interaction, SUD datasets, and audio data extracted from video sharing sites.

In the first chapter in this group, entitled "Collecting minority language data from Twitter (X): a case study of Karelian", Ilia Moshnikov and Eugenia Rykova introduce a Karelian Twitter (meanwhile known as X) corpus as a first DMC corpus of Karelian and as a case study of data collection for an endangered minority language. Karelian is a finno-ugric language closely related to Finnish and nowadays spoken by some 20,000 to 25,000 speakers in Russia and Finland. The authors describe their methods for identifying tweets in Karelian which is erroneously classified as Finnish by many LID systems and scraping them from the web. Tweets in the resulting corpus are also tagged for one of four Karelian dialects using the recent HeLi-OTS tool. The 2,625 Twitter posts of the corpus are also characterised according to the most prolific users and accordings to the most prominent topics discussed in them. The contribution showcases data collection and linguistic annotation for a DMC corpus of an endangered and underresourced language.

Aris Xanthos, Lliana Doudot, Prakhar Gupta introduce a corpus of instant messages in their chapter "What's new Switzerland? Collecting and sharing half a million WhatsApp message in French". This novel corpus builds on the famed What's up Switzerland project, the French part of which it continues temporally for the years since 2015, while also improving on the methods and procedures developed in the former project. The chapter describes the collection, preparation, and publishing of the data with special focus on the improved anonymisation (de-identifying) method for chat messages. The resulting corpus contains over 500,000 messages and more than 3,2 million tokens and is one of the few current efforts to construct corpora of private chat or instant messaging.

The third chapter in this group by Anne Ferger, André Frank Krause and Karola Pitsch is entitled "A Workflow for Creating, Harmonizing, and Analyzing Multimodal Interaction". It is based on the authors' experiences in the MoMoCorp project (Data reuse of multimodal and multisensorial corpora) and its data of human-robot interaction in a museum. MuMuCorp shares many features with DMC, but additionally produced audio-visual data, robot log files from speech recognition and synthesis, and sensor data with motion captures. The authors present their corpus construction workflow with linguistic annotation, quality assurance using GitLab continuous integration tests (CI) and further consistency checks, and TEI export based on the ISO 24624-2016 standard for transcription of speech and CMC-core, as well as export to R dataframes.

The fourth chapter in this group, by Dimitri Niaouri, Bruno Machado Carneiro, Michele Linardi and Julien Longhi is dedicated to online SUD deduction and entitled "Machine Learning is heading to the SUD (Socially Unacceptable Discourse) analysis: from Shallow Learning to Large Language Models to the rescue, where do we stand?". The authors constructed a unified SUD corpus from 13 publicly available datasets to fine-tune and evaluate pre-trained LLMs. They performed an extensive evaluation of 12 SOTA models and provide a comparative analysis of three model families, namely Shallow Learning Models (SLMs), Masked Language Models (MLMs), and Causal Language Models (CLMs). Finally, they enhance model explainability by employing certain visualisation techniques to the top performing models.

The final chapter in this group is "An Automatic Pipeline for Processing Streamed Content: New Horizons for Corpus Linguistics and Phonetics" by Steven Coats. It introduces the novel, notebook-based Video Phonetics Pipeline (ViPP) which facilitates the extraction and analysis of audio and transcript data from video and streaming platforms such as YouTube or TikTok using the python library yt-dlp, the Montreal Forced Aligner, Praat-Parselmouth and other python libraries. The utility of the pipeline is demonstrated by a consideration of diphthong trajectories in contemporary North American English.

Three chapters focus on digital identities and linguistic variation in online interactions. The chapter "Incel Data Archive: A Multimodal Comparable Corpus for Exploring Extremist Dynamics in Online Interaction", Selenia Anastasi, Tim Fischer, Florian Schneider and Chris Biemann examine the dynamics of extremist discourse within incel communities, focusing on their migration from mainstream social networks into independent ecosystems. The research questions address the contextualisation of online violent behaviour and the influence of local culture on the dissemination of extremist narratives. The authors use a multimodal and bilingual corpus in Italian and English and draw on Computer Mediated Discourse research to analyse forum-based interactions. The study aims to provide insights into the construction of incel ideology and cross-cultural differences in extremist discourse.

Another analysis of negative behaviour, albeit in a completely different context, is "Not an expert, but not a fan either. A corpus-based study of negative self-identification as epistemic index in web forum interaction" by Eva Triebl, which examines the linguistic micro-management of identity in online contexts through corpus-based pragmatic analyses of negative self-identifiers (NSIs) in British web discussion forums. The research questions focus on the categories of identification, the co-texts in which NSIs are used, and their implications for identity performance in informal web forum interactions. The study uses qualitative and quantitative analyses of 936 instances of NSIs collected from publicly available English language UK web forums to explore their forms, functions and contextual uses.

"Individual Linguistic Variation in Social Media" by Tatjana Scheffler, explores the impact of various factors on individual linguistic variation in DMC. The research questions focus on how topic, register and individual user characteristics interact with the medium of social media to influence linguistic expression. The chapter adopts a case study approach, constructing a DMC corpus to analyse linguistic variation across different social media platforms within the same group of authors. Methods include the collection and analysis of large-scale DMC corpora, highlighting the importance of controlling for factors to accurately study intra-author variation.

A further three chapters in this edited collection focus specifically on different features and phenomena of the linguistics of inclusion and discrimination. Firstly, the chapter "Computer-Mediated Communication to Facilitate Inclusion: Digital Corpus Analysis on Disability Diversity on Social Media" by Annamária Fábián and Igor Trost outlines a study that focuses on digital language use related to disability and inclusion, specifically on social media. This research analyses a Twitter corpus of 2,559 German tweets containing 61,249 tokens using the hashtags *#Behinderung* ('disability') and *#Inklusion* ('inclusion') from December 2020. The study explores the lexicon and co-occurrences of words related to disability and inclusion, aiming to provide insights into how these concepts are discussed online. The paper also discusses how data-mining tools like *AntConc* and *SentiStrength* can be used for lexicon and sentiment analysis.

Secondly, in the study "The representation of the Jew as enemy in French public Telegram channels within an identitarian-conspiratorial milieu" by Laura Gärtner, the author examines antisemitic conspiracy theories that gained traction during the Covid-19 pandemic, portraying Jews as manipulative puppet-masters controlling global events. The study focuses on the spread of these ideas through the internet and social networks, particularly within conspiracy and identitarian movements. A corpus of 90,000 messages from ten Telegram channels, collected between January 2018 and May 2022, is analyzed to detect linguistic patterns used to describe Jews in conspiratorial narratives. The analysis is grounded in the frameworks of Construction Grammar (CxG) and discourse formulae, integrating approaches from both fields, which have previously been developed independently.

Finally, the study by Rachel McCullough, Daniel Drylie, Mindi Barta, Cass Dykeman, and Daniel Smith titled "CoDEC-M: The multi-lingual manosphere subcorpus of the Corpus of Digital Extremism and Conspiracies". This chapter addresses the spread of extremist ideas between English- and Russian-speaking communities against the backdrop of a movement defined by loneliness and isolation: the incel ("involuntary celibate") movement. The study introduces *CoDEC-M*, a subcorpus of the larger *Corpus of Digital Extremism and Conspiracies* (CoDEC), which focuses on language used in non-English manosphere communities. Using *Sketch Engine*, the authors compare the top twenty keywords and bigrams in the English and Russian sections of *CoDEC-M*.

In the last of the thematic groups, two chapters investigate patterns of online interaction using Wikipedia's talk pages as a database. Talk pages offer a rich, multilingual, and freely accessible source of data for studying online interactions on a large scale.

The chapter "The negotiation of pronominal address on talk pages of the German, French, and Italian Wikipedia" by Carolina Flinz, Eva Gredel, and Laura Herzberg explores the use of social deixis, specifically pronominal address, in the context of DMC, with a focus on the German, French, and Italian versions of Wikipedia. The study examines two types of Wikipedia talk pages: article talk pages, where encyclopedic content is discussed, and user talk pages, where individual contributors' actions are reviewed. Using multilingual corpora from the Leibniz Institute for the German Language, the authors investigate how users negotiate formal and informal address pronouns (e.g., German *Sie* vs. *du*, French *vous* vs. *tu*, Italian *L/lei* vs. *tu*) in these discussions, showcasing the complexity, fluidity and variation of pronominal address in DMC.

The study "Investigating extreme cases in Wikipedia talk pages: some insights on user behaviours" by Ludovic Tanguy, Céline Poudat, and Lydia-Mai Ho-Dac focuses on extreme and marginal behaviors observed on Wikipedia talk pages. Using a dataset of 4 million threads from the English and French Wikipedia, the authors analyze structural aspects of the discussions on the one hand, and subsets of extreme cases for closer analysis on the other hand. By developing a typology, containing features such as highly prolific users, excessively long threads (measured by duration, number of posts, or participant count), and monologues, of these extreme cases, the authors aim to uncover patterns that shed light on both expected and unexpected interactions between Wikipedia contributors.

4 Thanks and acknowledgements

The editors would like to thank everyone who has contributed to the success of this volume: the chapter authors for their insightful and impactful contributions and the anonymous reviewers for their thorough and constructive feedback. We are indebted to the Leibniz Open Access Publishing Fund for its support in making the book openly accessible. We are grateful to the past and present editors at De Gruyter for their assistance in all matters great and small, and to the series editor, Andreas Witt, for his support in the publication of this volume. The editors accept full responsibility for all mistakes and shortcomings in this volume.

This chapter is based on work within Text+, funded by the Deutsche Forschungsgemeinschaft (DFG, project number 460033370) as part of the German National Research Data Infrastructure (NFDI e.V.). The authors thank the funding bodies and acknowledge the contributions of all supporting institutions and individuals.

References

Ágel, Vilmos & Mathilde Hennig. 2006. Überlegungen zur Theorie und Praxis des Nähe- und Distanzsprechens. In Vilmos Ágel & Mathilde Hennig (eds.), *Überlegungen zur Theorie und Praxis des Nähe- und Distanzsprechens*, 179–214. Tübingen: Max Niemeyer Verlag. https://www.degruyter.com/document/doi/10.1515/9783110936063.179/html (last accessed 14 February 2025).

Albert, Georg. 2015. Semiotik und Syntax von Emoticons. *Zeitschrift Für Angewandte Linguistik* 62 (1), Article 1. https://doi.org/10.1515/zfal-2015-0001.

Anderson, Benedict R. 1983. *Imagined communities: Reflections on the origin and spread of nationalism.* London: Verso.

Anderson, Jeffrey. F., Fred. K. Beard & Joseph. B. Walther. 2010. Turn-taking and the local management of conversation in a highly simultaneous Computer-Mediated Communication system. *Language@Internet 7.*

Androutsopoulos, Jannis. 2003. Online-Gemeinschaften und Sprachvariation. Soziolinguistische Perspektiven auf Sprache im Internet. *Zeitschrift Für Germanistische Linguistik 31*, 173–197. https://doi.org/10.1515/zfgl.2004.002.

Androutsopoulos, Jannis. 2006. Multilingualism, diaspora, and the Internet: Codes and identities on German-based diaspora websites. *Journal of Sociolinguistics 10*, 520–547. https://doi.org/10.1111/j.1467-9841.2006.00291.

Androutsopoulos, Jannis. 2007. Style online: Doing Hip-Hop on the German-speaking web. In Peter Auer (ed.), *Style and social identities: Alternative approaches to linguistic heterogeneity*, 279–317. Berlin & New York: De Gruyter.

Androutsopoulos, Jannis. 2011. Language change and digital media: A review of conceptions and evidence. In Tore Kristiansen & Nikolas Coupland (eds.), *Standard languages and language standards in a changing Europe*, 145–161. Oslo: Novus Press.

Androutsopoulos, Jannis. 2015. Networked multilingualism: Some language practices on Facebook and their implications. *International Journal of Bilingualism 19* (2), Article 2. https://doi.org/10.1177/1367006913489198.

Androutsopoulos, Jannis. 2018. Digitale Interpunktion: Stilistische Ressourcen und soziolinguistischer Wandel in der informellen digitalen Schriftlichkeit von Jugendlichen. In Arne Ziegler (ed.), *Jugendsprachen: Aktuelle Perspektiven Internationaler Forschung*, 721–748. Berlin & Boston: De Gruyter.

Androutsopoulos, Jannis. 2020. Auslassungspunkte in der schriftbasierten Interaktion. In Jannis Androutsopoulos & Florian Busch (eds.), *Register des Graphischen*, 133–158. Berlin & Boston: De Gruyter. https://doi.org/10.1515/9783110673241-006.

Androutsopoulos, Jannis & Busch, Florian. 2021. Digital punctuation as an interactional resource: The message-final period among German adolescents. *Linguistics and Education 62*. https://doi.org/10.1016/j.linged.2020.100871.

Androutsopoulos, Jannis & Florian Busch (eds.), 2020. *Register des Graphischen: Variation, Interaktion und Reflexion in der digitalen Schriftlichkeit.* Berlin & Boston: De Gruyter.

Androutsopoulos, Jannis & Jana Tereick 2016. YouTube: Language and discourse practices in participatory culture. In Alexandra Georgakopoulou & Tereza Spilioti (eds.), *The Routledge handbook of language and digital communication*, 354–370. Abingdon: Routledge.

Bader, Jennifer. 2002. Schriftlichkeit und Mündlichkeit in der Chat-Kommunikation. *NetWorx 29*. https://doi.org/10.15488/2920.

Barbieri, Francesco, Luis Espinosa-Anke, Miguel Ballesteros, Juan Soler & Horacio Saggion. 2017. Towards the understanding of gaming audiences by modeling Twitch emotes. *Proceedings of the 3rd Workshop on Noisy User-Generated Text*, 11–20. https://doi.org/10.18653/v1/W17-4402.

Baron, Naomi S. 2004. See you online: Gender issues in college student use of Instant Messaging. *Journal of Language and Social Psychology 23*, 397–423. https://doi.org/10.1177/0261927X04269585.

Baron, Naomi. S. 2008. *Always on: Language in an online and mobile world*. New York: Oxford University Press.

Beck, Klaus. 2010. Soziologie der Online-Kommunikation. In Wolfgang Schweiger & Klaus Beck (eds.), *Handbuch Online-Kommunikation*, 15–35. Wiesbaden: VS Verlag für Sozialwissenschaften.

Beißwenger, Michael & Steffen Pappert. 2019. *Handeln mit Emojis: Grundriss einer Linguistik kleiner Bildzeichen in der WhatsApp-Kommunikation*. Duisburg: Universitätsverlag Rhein-Ruhr.

Beißwenger, Michael & Pappert, Steffen. 2020. Small Talk mit Bildzeichen. *Zeitschrift Für Literaturwissenschaft Und Linguistik 50* (1), 89–114. https://doi.org/10.1007/s41244-020-00160-5.

Beißwenger, Michael, Marcel Fladrich, Wolfgang Imo & Evelyn Ziegler. 2020. Die Mobile Communication Database 2 (MoCoDa 2). In Konstanze Marx, Henning Lobin & Alex Schmidt (eds.), *Deutsch in Sozialen Medien: Interaktiv – multimodal – vielfältig*, 349–352. Berlin & Boston: De Gruyter.

Beißwenger, Michael, Eva Gredel, Lena Rebhan & Sarah Steinsiek. 2023. Ellipsis points in messaging interactions and on Wikipedia talk pages. In Louis Cotgrove, Laura Herzberg, Harald Lüngen & Ines Pisetta (eds.), *Proceedings of the 10th International Conference on CMC and Social Media Corpora for the Humanities*, University of Mannheim, 40–46. https://ids-pub.bsz-bw.de/frontdoor/index/index/docId/12095 (last accessed 14 February 2025).

Bell, Diana. C. & Mike T. Hübler. 2001. The virtual writing center: Developing ethos through mailing list discourse. *The Writing Center Journal 21* (2), 57–78. https://doi.org/10.7771/2832-9414.1453.

Berg, Kristina. 2020. Variation im digitalen Schreiben. In Jannis Androutsopoulos & Florian Busch (eds.), *Register des Graphischen*, 53–66. Berlin & Boston: De Gruyter. https://doi.org/10.1515/9783110673241-003.

Biber, Douglas. 1988. *Variation across speech and writing*. New York: Cambridge University Press.

Blashki, Katherine & Sophie Nichol. 2005. Game geek's goss: Linguistic creativity in young males within an online university forum (94/\/\3 933k'5 9055oneone). *Australian Journal of Emerging Technologies and Society 3* (2), 71–80.

Bou-Franch, Patricia, Lorenzo-Dus, Nuria & Blitvich, Pilar G.-C. 2012. Social interaction in YouTube text-based polylogues: A study of coherence. *Journal of Computer-Mediated Communication 17* (4), 501–521. https://doi.org/10.1111/j.1083-6101.2012.01579.

Butler, Judith. 2006. *Gender Trouble: Feminism and the subversion of identity*, 2nd edition. New York: Routledge.

Canagarajah, Suresh. 2011. Codemeshing in academic writing: Identifying teachable strategies of translanguaging. *Modern Language Journal 95*, 401–417. https://doi.org/10.1111/j.1540-4781.2011.01207.

Cann, Alan, Dimitriou Konstantia & T. Hooley. 2011. Social Media: A guide for researchers. London: Research Information Network.

Carey, John. 1980. Paralanguage in computer mediated communication. *Proceedings of the 18th Annual Meeting on Association for Computational Linguistics*, 67. https://doi.org/10.3115/981436.981458.

Carr, Caleb. T. 2020. CMC Is Dead, Long live CMC!: Situating Computer-Mediated Communication scholarship beyond the Digital Age. *Journal of Computer-Mediated Communication 25* (1), 9–22. https://doi.org/10.1093/jcmc/zmz018.

Chen, Zhenpeng , Lu, Xuan, Ai, Wei, Li, Huaron, Mei, Qiaozhu & Liu, Xuanzhe. 2018. Through a gender lens: Learning usage patterns of emojis from large-scale Android users. *Proceedings of the 2018 World Wide Web Conference*, 763–772. https://doi.org/10.1145/3178876.3186157.

Chun, Eliane & Keith Walters. 2011. Orienting to Arab orientalisms: Language, race, and humor in a YouTube video. In Crispin Thurlow & Kristine R. Mroczek (eds.), *Digital discourse: Language in the new media*, 251–273. New York: Oxford University Press.
Collot, Milena & Nancy Belmore. 1996. Electronic language: A new variety of English. In Susan C. Herring (ed.), *Computer-Mediated Communication: Linguistic, social, and cross-cultural perspectives*, 13–28. Amsterdam: John Benjamins.
Cotgrove, Louis. 2025. *Abogeil! The language of German teens on YouTube*. amades 63. Mannheim: IDS-Verlag.
Crystal, David. 2006. *Language and the internet*, 2nd edition. New York: Cambridge University Press.
Crystal, David. 2008. Texting. *ELT Journal 62* (1), 77–83. https://doi.org/10.1093/elt/ccm080.
Dainas, Ashley R. & Susan C. Herring. 2020. Interpreting emoji pragmatics. In Chaoqun Xie, Francisco Yus & Hartmund Haberland (eds.), *Approaches to internet pragmatics: Theory and practice*, 107–144. Amsterdam: John Benjamins.
Danesi, Marcel. 2016. *The semiotics of emoji: The rise of visual language in the age of the internet*. London: Bloomsbury Publishing.
Danet, Brenda. 1998. Text as mask: Gender, play, and performance on the internet. In Steven G. Jones (ed.), *Cybersociety 2.0: Revisiting Computer-Mediated Communication community*, 129–158. London: SAGE.
Diekmannshenke, Hajo. 2000. Die Spur des Internetflaneurs: Elektronische Gästebücher als neue Kommunikationsform. In Caja Thimm (ed.), *Soziales im Netz: Sprache, Beziehungen und Kommunikationskulturen im Internet*, 131–155. Wiesbaden: Westdeutscher Verlag.
Dmitrow-Devold, Karolina. 2017. Performing the Self in the Mainstream: Norwegian girls in blogging. *Nordicom Review 38* (2), 65–78. https://doi.org/10.1515/nor-2016-0391.
Döring, N. 2010. Sozialkontakte online: Identitäten, Beziehungen, Gemeinschaften. In Wolfgang Schweiger & Klaus Beck (eds.), *Handbuch Online-Kommunikation*, 159–183. Wiesbaden: VS Verlag für Sozialwissenschaften.
Dowell, Nia M. M., Cristopher Brooks, Vitomir Kovanović, Srećko Joksimović & Dragan Gašević. 2017. The Changing Patterns of MOOC Discourse. *Proceedings of the Fourth (2017) ACM Conference on Learning @ Scale*, 283–286. https://doi.org/10.1145/3051457.3054005.
Dresner, Eli & Susan C. Herring. 2010. Functions of the nonverbal in CMC: Emoticons and illocutionary force. *Communication Theory 20* (3), 249–268. https://doi.org/10.1111/j.1468-2885.2010.01362.
Dürscheid, Christa. 2003. Medienkommunikation im Kontinuum von Mündlichkeit und Schriftlichkeit. Theoretische und empirische Probleme. *Zeitschrift für Angewandte Linguistik 38*, 37–56.
Dürscheid, Christa. 2005. Email – verändert sie das Schreiben? In Torsten Siever, Peter Schlobinski & Jens Runkehl (eds.), *Websprache.net: Sprache und Kommunikation im Internet*, 85–97. Berlin & New York: De Gruyter.
Dürscheid, Christa. 2016a. Graphematische Mikrovariation. In Ulrike Domahs & Beatrice Primus (eds.), *Handbuch Laut, Gebärde, Buchstabe*, 492–510. Berlin & Boston: De Gruyter.
Dürscheid, Christa. 2016b. Nähe, Distanz und neue Medien. In Helmuth Feilke & Mathilde Hennig (eds.), *Zur Karriere von ›Nähe und Distanz‹*, 357–386. Berlin & Boston: De Gruyter. https://doi.org/10.1515/9783110464061-013.
Dürscheid, Christa & Sarah Brommer. 2016. Getippte Dialoge in neuen Medien. Sprachkritische Aspekte und linguistische Analysen. *Linguistik Online 37*, 9.
Eckert, Penelope. 2012. Three waves of variation study: The emergence of meaning in the study of sociolinguistic variation. *Annual Review of Anthropology 41*, 87–100. https://doi.org/10.1146/annurev-anthro-092611-145828.
Erickson, Thomas. 1999. Persistant conversation: An introduction. *Journal of Computer-Mediated Communication* 4 (4). https://doi.org/10.1111/j.1083-6101.1999.tb00105.

Evans, Vyvyan. 2017. *The Emoji Code. How smiley faces, love hearts and thumbs up are changing the way we communicate*. London: Michael O'Mara Books Limited.
Ferrara, Kathleen, Hans Brunner & Greg Whittemore. 1991. Interactive written discourse as an emergent register. *Written Communication* 8 (1), 8–34. https://doi.org/10.1177/0741088391008001002.
Fladrich, Marcel & Wolfgang Imo. 2020. ♀ J = ♂ J? Oder: Das Gelächter der Geschlechter 2.0: Emojigebrauch in der WhatsApp-Kommunikation. In Konstanze Marx, Henning Lobin & Axel Schmidt (eds.), *Deutsch in Sozialen Medien: Interaktiv – multimodal – vielfältig*, 95–122. Berlin & Boston: De Gruyter. https://doi.org/10.1515/9783110679885-006.
Frehner, Carmen. 2008. *Email, SMS, MMS: The linguistic creativity of asynchronous discourse in the new media age*. Bern: Peter Lang.
García, Ofelia & Wei Li. 2014. *Translanguaging: Language, bilingualism and education*. London: Palgrave Macmillan.
Georgakopoulou, Alexandra & Tereza Spilioti (eds.), 2016. *The Routledge handbook of language and digital communication*. New York: Routledge.
Gibson, Will. 2008. Intercultural Communication Online: Conversation analysis and the investigation of asynchronous written discourse. *Forum Qualitative Sozialforschung/Forum: Qualitative Social Research 10*.
Gruber, Helmut. 1997. Themenentwicklung in wissenschaftlichen E-mail-Diskussionslisten. Ein Vergleich zwischen einer moderierten und einer nichtmoderierten Liste. In Rüdiger Weingarten (ed.), *Sprachwandel durch Computer*, 105–128. Wiesbaden: Westdeutscher Verlag.
Gruzd, Anatoliy, Barry Wellman & Yuri Takhteyev. 2011. Imagining Twitter as an imagined community. *American Behavioral Scientist 55* (10), 1294–1318. https://doi.org/10.1177/0002764211409378.
Gumperz, John J. 2009. The speech community. In Alessandro Duranti (ed.), *Linguistic anthropology: A reader*, 2nd edition, 66–73. Malden: Wiley-Blackwell.
Günther, Ulla & Eva L. Wyss. 1996. E-mail-Briefe-eine neue Textsorte zwischen Mündlichkeit und Schriftlichkeit. In Ernest Hess-Lüttich, Werner Holly & Ulrich Püschel (eds.), *Textstrukturen im Medienwandel*, 61–86. Lausanne: Peter Lang.
Haase, Martin, Huber, Michael, Krumeich, Alexander & Rehm, Georg. 1997. Internetkommunikation und Sprachwandel. In Rüdiger Weingarten (ed.), *Sprachwandel durch Computer*, 51–85. Wiesbaden: Westdeutscher Verlag.
Hentschel, Elke. 1998. Communication on IRC. *Linguistik Online* 1. https://doi.org/10.13092/lo.1.1084.
Heritage, Frazer & Veronika Koller. 2020. Incels, in-groups, and ideologies: The representation of gendered social actors in a sexuality-based online community. *Journal of Language and Sexuality* 9 (2), 152–178. https://doi.org/10.1075/jls.19014.her.
Herring, Susan. C. 1992. Gender and participation in computer-mediated linguistic discourse. Washington, D.C.: ERIC Clearinghouse on Languages and Linguistics. https://homes.luddy.indiana.edu/herring/participation.1992.pdf (last accessed 14 February 2025).
Herring, Susan. C. 1996a. Gender and democracy in computer-mediated communication. In Rob Kling (ed.), *Computerization and controversy: Value conflicts and social choices*, 2nd edition, 476–489. San Diego: Academic Press.
Herring, Susan. C. 1996b. Bringing familiar baggage to the new frontier: Gender differences in computer-mediated communication. In Victor Vitanza (ed.), *CyberReader*, 144–154. Boston: Allyn & Bacon.
Herring, S. C. 1999. Interactional coherence in CMC. *Journal of Computer-Mediated Communication 4*. https://doi.org/10.1111/j.1083-6101.1999.tb00106.
Herring, S. C. 2007. A faceted classification scheme for computer-mediated discourse. *Language@Internet 4* (1). http://www.languageatinternet.org/articles/2007/761 (last accessed 14 February 2025).

Herring, Susan. C. 2012. Grammar and Electronic Communication. In Carol A. Chapelle (ed.), *The encyclopedia of applied linguistics*. Hoboken: Blackwell.

Herring, Susan. C. 2013. Discourse in Web 2.0: Familiar, reconfigured, and emergent. In Deborah Tannen & Anna M. Trester (eds.), *Discourse 2.0: Language and new media*, 1–26. Washington: Georgetown University Press.

Herring, Susan. C. 2019. The coevolution of computer-mediated communication and computer-mediated discourse analysis. In Patricia Bou-Franch & Pilar G.-C. Blitvich (eds.), *Analyzing digital discourse: New insights and future directions*, 25–67. Cham: Springer International Publishing.

Herring, Susan C., Ashley Dainas, Holly Lopez Long & Ying Tang. 2020. Animoji adoption and use: Gender associations with an emergent technology. https://doi.org/10.36190/2020.03.

Herring, Susan C., Ashley R. Dainas, Holly Lopez Long & Ying Tang. 2020. Animoji performances: "Cuz I can be a sexy poop". *Language@Internet. 18*.

Herring, Susan. C., Dieter Stein & Tuija Virtanen (eds.), 2013. *Pragmatics of computer-mediated communication*. Berlin & Boston: De Gruyter.

Hilte, Lisa, Walter Daelemans & Reinhild Vandekerckhove, . 2020. Lexical patterns in adolescents' online writing: The impact of age, gender, and education. *Written Communication 37* (3), 365–400. https://doi.org/10.1177/0741088320917921.

Hilte, Lisa, Reinhild Vandekerckhove & Walter Daelemans, . 2019. Expressive markers in online teenage talk. *Nederlandse Taalkunde 23* (3), 293–323. https://doi.org/10.5117/NEDTAA2018.3.003.HILT.

Hiltz, Starr. R. & Murray Turoff. 1993. *The network nation: Human communication via computer*, 2nd edition. Cambridge: MIT Press.

Hinrichs, Lars. 2018. The Language of diasporic blogs. In Cecelia Cutler & Unn Røyneland (eds.), *Multilingual youth practices in Computer Mediated Communication*, 186–204. Cambridge: Cambridge University Press. https://doi.org/10.1017/9781316135570.011.

Hougaard, Tina T. & Marianne Rathje. 2018. Emojis in the Digital Writings of Young Danes. In Arne Ziegler (ed.), *Jugendsprachen: Aktuelle Perspektiven Internationaler Forschung*, 773–806. Berlin: De Gruyter.

Huffaker, David A. & Sandra L. Calvert. 2005. Gender, identity, and language use in teenage blogs. *Journal of Computer-Mediated Communication 10*. https://doi.org/10.1111/j.1083-6101.2005.tb00238.

Hutchby, Ian & Robin Wooffitt. 1998. *Conversation analysis: Principles, practices, and applications*. Cambridge: Polity.

Jaeger, Sara R., Yixun Xia, Pui-Yee Lee, Denise C. Hunter, Michelle K. Beresford & Gastón Ares. 2018. Emoji questionnaires can be used with a range of population segments: Findings relating to age, gender and frequency of emoji/emoticon use. *Food Quality and Preference 68*, 397–410. https://doi.org/10.1016/j.foodqual.2017.12.011.

Jones, Steven. 1998. *Cybersociety 2.0: Revisiting Computer-Mediated Communication community*. Thousand Oaks, California; London: SAGE.

Jucker, Andreas H. & Christa Dürscheid. 2012. The linguistics of keyboard-to-screen communication. A new terminological framework. *Linguistik Online 56* (6/12), Article 6/12. https://doi.org/10.5167/uzh-67310.

Kaplan, Andreas & Michael Haenlein. 2010. Users of the world, unite! The challenges and opportunities of Social Media. *Business Horizons 53*, 59–68. https://doi.org/10.1016/j.bushor.2009.09.003.

Kavanagh, Barry. 2019. Exploration of Kaomoji, Emoji, and Kigō. In Elena Giannoulis & Lukas R. A. Wilde (eds.), *Emoticons, Kaomoji, and Emoji: The transformation of communication in the Digital Age*, 148–167. New York: Routledge.

Kendall, Lori. 1998. Meaning and identity in "cyberspace": The performance of gender, class, and race online. *Symbolic Interaction 21*, 129–153. https://doi.org/10.1525/si.1998.21.2.129.

Kiesler, Sara, Jane Siegel & Timothy W. McGuire 1984. Social psychological aspects of Computer-Mediated Communication. *American Psychologist 39*, 1123–1134. https://doi.org/10.1037/0003-066X.39.10.1123.
Kilian, Jörg. 2001. T@stentöne. Geschriebene Umgangssprache in computervermittelter Kommunikation. Historisch-kritische Ergänzungen zu einem neuen Feld der linguistischen Forschung. In Michael Beißwenger (ed.), *Chat-Kommunikation. Sprache, Interaktion, Sozialität & Identität in synchroner computervermittelter Kommunikation*, 55–78. Stuttgart: Ibidem.
Kleinberger Günther & Carmen Spiegel. 2006. Jugendliche schreiben im Internet: grammatische und orthographische Phänomene in normungebundenen Kontexten. In Christa Dürscheid & Jürgen Spitzmüller (eds.), *Perspektiven der Jugendsprachforschung- Trends and developments in youth language research*, 101–115. Lausanne: Peter Lang.
Koch, Peter & Wulf Oesterreicher. 1985. Sprache der Nähe–Sprache der Distanz. *Romanistisches Jahrbuch 36*, 15–43. https://doi.org/10.1515/9783110244922.15.
Koch, Peter & Wulf Oesterreicher. 2007. Schriftlichkeit und kommunikative Distanz. *Zeitschrift Für Germanistische Linguistik 35*, 346–375. https://doi.org/10.1515/zgl.2007.024.
Koch, Timo & Peter Romero & Clemens Stachl. 2020. Age and gender in language, emoji, and emoticon usage in Instant Messages. https://doi.org/10.31234/osf.io/92ydh.
Landert, Daniela & Andreas H. Jucker 2011. Private and public in mass media communication: From letters to the editor to online commentaries. *Journal of Pragmatics 43* (5), 1422–1434. https://doi.org/10.1016/j.pragma.2010.10.016.
Le Page, Robert B. & Andrée Tabouret-Keller. 1985. *Acts of identity: Creole-basedaApproaches to language and ethnicity*. Cambridge: Cambridge University Press.
Ljubešić, Nikola & Darja Fišer. 2016. A global analysis of emoji usage. *Proceedings of the 10th Web as Corpus Workshop*, 82–89. https://doi.org/10.18653/v1/W16-2610.
Lo, Adrienne. 1999. Codeswitching, speech community membership, and the construction of ethnic identity. *Journal of Sociolinguistics 3*, 461–479. https://doi.org/10.1111/1467-9481.00091.
Lytra, Vally. 2016. Language and ethnic identity. In Siân Preece (ed.), *The Routledge handbook of language and identity*, 131–145. New York: Routledge.
Mackenzie, Jai. 2018. *Language, gender and parenthood online: Negotiating motherhood in Mumsnet talk.* New York: Routledge.
Meredith, Joanne. 2019. Conversation analysis and online interaction. *Research on Language and Social Interaction 52* (3), 241–256. https://doi.org/10.1080/08351813.2019.1631040.
Milani, Tommaso M. & Rickard Jonsson. 2011. Incomprehensible language? Language, ethnicity and heterosexual masculinity in a Swedish school. *Gender and Language 5* (2), Article 2. https://doi.org/10.1558/genl.v5i2.241.
Miyake, Kazuko. 2007. How young Japanese express their emotions visually in mobile phone messages: A sociolinguistic analysis. *Japanese Studies 27* (1), 53–72. https://doi.org/10.1080/10371390701268646.
Nakamura, Lisa. 2002. *Cybertypes: Race, ethnicity, and identity on the Internet*. New York: Routledge.
Neuland, Eva. 2003. Doing Youth: Zur medialen Konstruktion von Jugend und Jugendsprache. In Eva Neuland (ed.), *Jugendsprache – Jugendliteratur – Jugendkultur*, 261–274. Lausanne: Peter Lang.
Ong, Walter J. 1982. *Orality and literacy*. New York: Routledge.
Paolillo, John. 2011. "Conversational" codeswitching on Usenet and Internet Relay Chat. *Language@Internet 8* (3), Article 3.
Papacharissi, Zizi. 2004. Democracy online: civility, politeness, and the democratic potential of online political discussion groups. *New Media & Society 6*, 259–283. https://doi.org/10.1177/1461444804041444.

Parkins, Rosin. 2012. Gender and emotional expressiveness: An analysis of prosodic features in emotional expression. *Griffith Working Papers in Pragmatics and Intercultural Communication 1* (5), 46–54.

Pavalanathan, Umashanthi & Jacob Eisenstein. 2015. Emoticons vs. emojis on Twitter: A causal inference Approach. *CoRR*. https://doi.org/10.48550/arXiv.1510.08480.

Pennycook, Alastair & Emi Otsuji. 2015. *Metrolingualism: Language in the city*. New York: Routledge.

Rinas, Karsten & Veronika Uhrová. 2016. Perioden mit Smileys. Zum Verhältnis von Emoticons und Interpunktion. *Linguistik Online 75* (1). https://doi.org/10.13092/lo.75.2519.

Riva, Giuseppe. 2002. The sociocognitive psychology of Computer-Mediated Communication: The present and future of technology-based interactions. *CyberPsychology & Behavior 5* (6), 581–598. https://doi.org/10.1089/109493102321018222.

Rotne, Lene. 2018. "I don't have time for tits". An investigation of Italian and Danish adolescents' writing on Facebook and in school essays. In Arne Ziegler (ed.), *Jugendsprachen: Aktuelle Perspektiven Internationaler Forschung*, 891–914). Berlin & Boston: De Gruyter.

Runkehl, Jens, Peter Schlobinski & Torsten Siever. 1998. Sprache und Kommunikation im Internet. *Muttersprache 108*, 97–109.

Sassen, Claudia. 2000. Phatische Variebilität bei der Initiierung von Internet-Relay- Chat-Dialogen. In Caja Thimm (ed.), *Soziales im Netz: Sprache, Beziehungen und Kommunikationskulturen im Internet*, 89–108. Wiesbaden: Westdeutscher Verlag.

Savicki, Victor, Dawn Lingenfelter & Merle Kelley. 1996. Gender language style and group composition in internet discussion groups. *Journal of Computer-Mediated Communication 2*. https://doi.org/10.1111/j.1083-6101.1996.tb00191.

Saxalber, Annemarie & Miriam Micheluzzi. 2018. Facebook-Sprachgebrauch im Kontext von innerer Mehrsprachigkeit in Südtirol. In Eva Neuland, Benjamin Könning & Elisa Wessels, *Jugendliche im Gespräch*, 277–298. Lausanne: Peter Lang.

Schegloff, Emanuel A. & Harvey Sacks. 1973. Opening up closings. *Semiotica 8* (4). https://doi.org/10.1515/semi.1973.8.4.289.

Schlobinski, Peter. 2001. * knuddel-zurueckknuddel-dich-ganzdollknuddel*: Inflektive und Inflektivkonstruktionen im Deutschen. *Zeitschrift Für Germanistische Linguistik 29* (2), 192–218. https://doi.org/10.1515/zfgl.2001.013.

Schlobinski, Peter. 2005. Mündlichkeit/Schriftlichkeit in den Neuen Medien. In Ludwig Eichinger & Werner Kallmeyer (eds.), *Standardvariation: Wie viel Variation verträgt die deutsche Sprache?*, 126–142. Berlin & New York: De Gruyter.

Schlobinski, Peter. 2006a. Die Bedeutung digitalisierter Kommunikation für Sprach- und Kommunikationsgemeinschaften. In Peter Schlobinski (ed.), *Von *hdl* bis *cul8r*: Sprache und Kommunikation in den neuen Medien: Vols. Thema Deutsch*, 26–37. Berlin: Dudenverlag.

Schlobinski, Peter (ed.). 2006b. *Von *hdl* bis *cul8r*: Sprache und Kommunikation in den neuen Medien: Vols. Thema Deutsch*. Berlin: Dudenverlag.

Schmidt, Gurly. 2000. Chat – eine kommunikative Gattung. In Caja Thimm (ed.), *Soziales im Netz: Sprache, Beziehungen und Kommunikationskulturen im Internet*, 109–130. Wiesbaden: Westdeutscher Verlag.

Schwartz, H. Andrew, Johannes C. Eichstaedt, Margaret L. Kern, Lukasz Dziurzynski, Stephanie M. Ramones, Megha Agrawal, Achal Shah, Michal Kosinski, David Stillwell, Martin E. P. Seligman & Lyle H. Ungar. 2013. Personality, gender, and age in the language of Social Media: The open-vocabulary approach. *PLOS ONE 8* (9), e73791. https://doi.org/10.1371/journal.pone.0073791.

Siever, Torsten. 2006. Sprachökonomie in den "Neuen Medien". In Peter Schlobinski (ed.), *Von *hdl* bis *cul8r*: Sprache und Kommunikation in den neuen Medien: Vols. Thema Deutsch*, 71–88. Berlin: Dudenverlag.

Siever, Torsten, Peter Schlobinski & Jens Runkehl. 2005. *Websprache.net: Sprache und Kommunikation im Internet*. Berlin & New York: De Gruyter.

Soffer, Oren. 2010. "Silent orality": Toward a conceptualization of the digitaloOral features in CMC and SMS texts. *Communication Theory 20* (4), 387–404. https://doi.org/10.1111/j.1468-2885.2010.01368.

Söll, Ludwig & Franz J. Hausmann. 1980. *Gesprochenes und geschriebenes Französisch*. Berlin: E. Schmidt.

Spitzmüller, Jürgen. 2013. *Graphische Variation als soziale Praxis: Eine soziolinguistische Theorie skripturaler ›Sichtbarkeit‹*. Berlin & Boston: De Gruyter.

Storrer, Angelika. 2001. Getippte Gespräche oder dialogische Texte? Zur kommunikationstheoretischen Einordnung der Chat-Kommunikation. In Andrea Lehr, Matthias Kammerer, Klaus-Peter Konerding, Angelika Storrer, Caja Thimm & Werner Werner (eds.), *Sprache im Alltag*, 439–465. Berlin & New York: De Gruyter.

Storrer, Angelika. 2013. Sprachstil und Sprachvariation in sozialen Netzwerken. In Barbara Frank-Job, Alexander Mehler & Tilmann Sutter (eds.), *Die Dynamik sozialer und sprachlicher Netzwerke: Konzepte, Methoden und empirische Untersuchungen an Beispielen des WWW*, 331–366. Wiesbaden: Springer.

Tagg, Caroline. 2015. *Exploring digital communication: Language in action*. New York: Routledge. https://doi.org/10.4324/9781315727165.

Thompson, Dominic & Ruth Filik. 2016. Sarcasm in written communication: Emoticons are efficient markers of intention. *Journal of Computer-Mediated Communication 21* (2), 105–120. https://doi.org/10.1111/jcc4.12156.

Turkle, Sherry. 1995. *Life on the screen*. New York: Simon and Schuster.

Utz, Sonja. 2000. Social information processing in MUDs: The development of friendships in virtual worlds. *Journal of Online Behavior*.

Varis, Pila & Tom van Nuenen. 2017. The Internet, language, and virtual interactions. In Ofelia García, Nelson Flores & Massimiliano Spotti (eds.), *The Oxford handbook of language and society*, 473–488. New York: Oxford University Press.

Walther, Diana. 2018. "Doing Youth" – Zur Erweiterung einer Theorie der Jugendspracheforschung. In Arne Ziegler (ed.), *Jugendsprachen: Aktuelle Perspektiven Internationaler Forschung*, 25–48. Berlin: De Gruyter.

Waseleski, Carol. 2006. Gender and the use of exclamation points in Computer-Mediated Communication: An analysis of exclamations posted to two electronic discussion lists. *Journal of Computer-Mediated Communication 11*, 1012–1024. https://doi.org/10.1111/j.1083-6101.2006.00305.

Werry, Christopher C. 1996. Linguistic and interactional features of Internet Relay Chat. In Susan C. Herring (ed.), *Computer-Mediated Communication: Linguistic, social, and cross-cultural perspectives*, 47–63. Amsterdam: John Benjamins.

West, Candace & Don H. Zimmerman. 1987. Doing gender. *Gender & Society 1* (2), 125–151. https://doi.org/10.1177/0891243287001002002.

Wiese, Heike. 2015. "This migrants' babble is not a German dialect!": The interaction of standard language ideology and "us"/'them'dichotomies in the public discourse on a multiethnolect. *Language in Society 44* (3). https://doi.org/10.1017/S0047404515000226.

Willem, Cilia, Núria Araüna & Iolanda Tortajada. 2019. Chonis and pijas: Slut-shaming and double standards in online performances among Spanish teens. *Sexualities 22* (4), 532–548. https://doi.org/10.1177/1363460717748620.

Wirth, Uwe. 2005. Chatten. Plaudern mit anderen Mitteln. In Torsten Siever, Peter Schlobinski & Jens Runkehl (eds.), *Websprache.net: Sprache und Kommunikation im Interne*, 67–84. Berlin & New York: De Gruyter.

Witmer, Diane F. & Sandra L. Katzman. 1997. On-line smiles: Does gender make a difference in the use of graphic accents? *Journal of Computer-Mediated Communication 2*. https://doi.org/10.1111/j.1083-6101.1997.tb00192.

Wolf, Alecia. 2000. Emotional expression online: Gender differences in emoticon use. *CyberPsychology & Behavior 3*, 827–833. https://doi.org/10.1089/10949310050191809.

Yao, Mike. Z. & Rich Ling. 2020. "What Is Computer-Mediated Communication?" An introduction to the special issue. *Journal of Computer-Mediated Communication 25* (1), 4–8. https://doi.org/10.1093/jcmc/zmz027.

Yates, Simeon J. 1996. Oral and written linguistic aspects of computer conferencing. In Susan C. Herring (ed.), *Computer-Mediated Communication: Linguistic, social, and cross-cultural perspectives*. Amsterdam: John Benjamins.

Yus, Francisco. 2011. *Cyberpragmatics: Internet-mediated communication in context*. Amsterdam: John Benjamins.

Selcen Erten-Johansson and Veronika Laippala

Utilizing Text Dispersion Keyness on Turkish web registers: The case of Informational Description and Opinion

Abstract: Registers, such as news reports, frequently asked questions (FAQs), and opinion blogs, serve as indicators of linguistic variation that reflect the linguistic characteristics of digital environments. Understanding registers occurring on the web, known as web registers, is crucial in today's digital age. However, despite the abundance of linguistic data available on the internet, a notable gap in knowledge regarding the origins and the linguistic analyses of web registers remains. This especially applies to less-explored non-Indo-European languages. This study focuses on the Turkish web, drawing data from the Turkish Corpus of Online Registers (TurCORE) (Erten-Johansson et al. 2024). The linguistic characteristics of the Informational Description register comprising 481 texts and the Opinion register comprising 215 texts were examined using Text Dispersion Keyword Analysis (Egbert and Biber 2019). The findings highlight disparities not only in discoursal but also in linguistic features between the two registers. Moreover, notable variations in linguistic characteristics were found within each register, notwithstanding their shared objective or subjective discourse. By shedding light on the similarities of and differences between the characteristics of these registers, particularly within the context of a less studied non-Indo-European language, this research contributes to a more comprehensive understanding of language use in the digital environment.

Keywords: web registers, linguistic variation, Turkish Corpus of Online Registers (TurCORE), register analysis, Informational Description, opinion, Text Dispersion Keyword Analysis

Selcen Erten-Johansson, University of Turku, Finland, e-mail: selcen.s.erten@utu.fi
Veronika Laippala, University of Turku, Finland, e-mail: veronika.laippala@utu.fi

https://doi.org/10.1515/9783111434018-002

1 Introduction

The internet is a primary source for seeking and sharing information, with language playing a crucial role in expressing subjective opinions alongside objective descriptions. Understanding linguistic variations, particularly in web contexts, involves understanding how registers – for example, whether a text is informational or opinionated – affect language use and the interpretation of the text. However, analyzing web data poses challenges owing to the absence of essential metadata pertaining to, for example, text purpose or the factual versus opinionated nature of the content (Biber, Egbert, and Davies 2015). This makes the identification of registers on the web and the analysis of their linguistic characteristics difficult.

Prior studies on web registers have mostly focused on text collections with only few different registers, limiting our understanding of linguistic attributes across different registers. The creation of the Corpus of Online Registers of English (CORE) (Egbert, Biber, and Davies 2015) and similar corpora such as FinCORE for Finnish (Laippala et al. 2019; Skantsi and Laippala 2023), SweCORE for Swedish and FreCORE for French (Repo et al. 2021) have expanded our register knowledge, particularly in terms of natural language processing (NLP) and register identification. Despite this progress, CORE remains the only corpus among these corpora that has undergone extensive linguistic analysis, highlighting a research gap for languages like Turkish – a language characterized by its agglutinative nature and rich morphology. To address this gap, the Turkish Corpus of Online Registers (TurCORE) (Erten-Johansson et al. 2024) was developed following the principles established for CORE. In their study, Erten-Johansson et al. (2024) identified all the existing registers on the Turkish web and provided brief descriptions for each. In particular, they analyzed news reports, interactive discussions and recipes from linguistic and cultural standpoints. Since there is limited knowledge about the other registers in TurCORE, this study focuses on examining the linguistic characteristics of the Informational Description and Opinion registers, with a particular focus on descriptive and legal texts versus reviews and opinion blogs. We apply Text Dispersion Keyword Analysis proposed by Egbert and Biber (2019) to investigate how the Informational Description and Opinion registers are presented in Turkish.

Our research questions are as follows:

1. How do Informational Description versus Opinion serve the main registers' communicative purpose when analyzed using Text Dispersion Keyness?
2. What semantic and grammatical characteristics are prevalent in the sub-registers 'description of a thing/person' and 'legal terms and conditions' versus 'review' and 'opinion blog'?

The article proceeds with a review of the current literature on registers in Section 2 followed by the methodology in Section 3. The findings are detailed in Section 4.1 and 4.2. Finally, Section 5 summarizes the article's main points.

2 Previous work

Linguistic research has increasingly emphasized the importance of language use context, particularly when investigating variations in text with different communicative purposes (e.g., Biber 1986; Biber and Conrad 2001). Various terms including *style*, *genre*, and *register* have been used to denote these linguistic variations (Biber and Conrad 2009). As noted by Seoane and Biber (2021), although style and genre traditionally found their roots in literary studies, their scope has expanded to encompass non-literary variations. Aligning with the framework developed over the last three decades (e.g., Biber 1995; Biber et al. 1999; Biber and Conrad 2009), we define registers as a language variety associated with a particular situation of use, including communicative purposes. They are characterized by their typical grammatical features that reflect their linguistic attributes. These features inherently serve a functional purpose when considered from a register perspective, suggesting that linguistic features tend to recur in a register as they are well-suited for the intended purpose and situational context of the register (Biber and Conrad 2009).

Research has typically used pre-defined registers and limited collection of texts, mainly in Indo-European languages to study the linguistic characteristics of registers. For instance, Karapetjana and Lokastova (2015) analyzed the linguistic features of maritime e-mails written by chief engineers, revealing written and spoken registers that created a hybrid form of language use. More recently, Li et al. (2021) explored an academic Question & Answer platform, identifying that certain linguistic characteristics such as second-person pronouns in questions have a positive effect on response quantity, whereas linguistic characteristics such as first-person pronouns have the opposite effect.

Multi-dimensional Analysis has frequently been employed in register studies. For instance, Berber-Sardinha (2018) examined register variation across samples extracted from blogs, webpages, social media platforms and e-mails. Berber-Sardinha (2022) also employed a multi-dimensional perspective to investigate register variation on social media platforms such as Facebook, X (formerly Twitter), Instagram, Reddit, Telegram, and YouTube. Both studies revealed distinct linguistic characteristics among registers. In a similar vein, Liimatta (2019, 2022) extensively explored register variation through a multi-dimensional perspective on the social media platform Reddit. The former study analyzed the *online subjective production*, *informational style*, and *instructional focus* dimensions, revealing patterns of register variation within Reddit. The latter study delved into the impact of registers on comment lengths, considering that the same text length may have different functions in different registers.

These studies have contributed to the field of online register studies, particularly in the context of English. However, it is important to note that they have primarily focused on pre-defined registers, failing to encompass the entire spectrum of registers that can be found online. The introduction of CORE (Egbert, Biber, and Davies 2015) marked a notable advancement in this regard, as it addressed the need for the comprehensive coverage of registers and linguistic variations on the internet without relying on pre-established categories. Furthermore, Biber and Egbert (2018) conducted extensive analyses using CORE data and examined a wide range of lexico-grammatical features.

Although CORE (Egbert, Biber, and Davies 2015) represents a major advancement in exploring register variation, and Biber and Egbert's (2018) work has contributed to the linguistic analyses of registers, the pivotal roles played by non-Indo-European languages, which have received less attention in register studies, is important. Turkish, an agglutinative language, has a wide range of suffixes with distinctive features. Most multi-syllabic words in Turkish are complex, resulting in lengthy words that could be translated to entire sentences in English (Lewis 2001). The primary mechanism for word formation in Turkish is suffixation, where a new word is formed by attaching a suffix to the end of a root. A considerable number of suffixes can be affixed to a root. Derivational suffixes creating new words typically precede inflectional suffixes, which provide grammatical information such as case, person, and tense (Göksel and Kerslake 2005: 43).

Previous studies on register variation in Turkish have primarily focused on specific registers. For instance, Özyıldırım (2011) investigated legislative language and compared it with various registers, concluding that it is the least narrative in comparison with research articles, men's/women's magazines, newspaper feature articles and television commercials. Koçak (2013) examined the lexico-grammatical and discoursal features of Turkish cooking recipes from two cookery books published in 1974 and 2011 to investigate whether any linguistic and discoursal differences existed between them. The findings revealed that although the recipes in the two books show similar discoursal characteristics, such as explicit reference discourse, they differ in terms of their linguistic features, including the use of the second-person pronoun. News articles and editorials have also been studied. Çarkoğlu, Baruh and Yıldırım (2014) explored news articles and editorial columns collected from various newspapers to investigate press-party parallelism in the 2011 national elections and found out linguistic variations across the newspapers. Using a genre-based approach, Aksan and Aksan (2015) examined the differences between informative and imaginative texts with Turkish multi-word units. They identified distinct lexical patterns and linguistic features prevalent in fiction and non-fiction texts. For instance, person references were frequently found in fictional imaginative texts, whereas they appeared much less often in non-fiction informative ones.

Similar to many studies conducted for English, these investigations have focused on pre-defined registers and restricted collection of texts without covering linguistic variations in their entirety. This underscores the need for developing a corpus that encompasses the linguistic variations present in Turkish web content and analyzing their linguistic characteristics. The creation of the Turkish Corpus of Online Registers (TurCORE) and in-depth analyses of various registers within it such as news reports, interactive discussions, and recipe texts (Erten-Johansson et al. 2024) address this need, thereby highlighting the necessity to explore the Informational Description and Opinion registers within the Turkish web.

3 Methodology

3.1 TurCORE

The compilation, cleaning, and annotation processes of TurCORE are presented in Erten-Johansson et al. (2024). TurCORE comprises texts randomly sampled from the CommonCrawl dataset that contains web documents. The corpus contains 2,780 unique web texts, comprising 1,026,253 tokens. The average token length of the texts varies, from a minimum of 203 to a maximum of 1,431 (Erten-Johansson et al. 2024). As noted by Erten-Johansson et al. (2024), the cleaning process involved fetching the documents in HTML format from the URLs, followed by boilerplate removal with Trafilatura (Barbaresi 2021), and deduplication using Onion (Pomikalek 2011). Next, manual annotation was performed on Prodigy (https://prodi.gy, last accessed 14 February 2025). The process involved collaboration between a supervisor and a trained annotator with a corpus linguistics background.

In TurCORE, a taxonomy based on that of CORE (Egbert, Biber, and Davies 2015) and FinCORE (Laippala et al. 2019; Skantsi and Laippala 2023) was utilized to cover the full range of online registers. However, this taxonomy was simplified, by excluding registers that were found to be low-frequent and vaguely defined in previous studies (Biber, Egbert, and Davies 2015; Skantsi and Laippala 2023). The adapted taxonomy was developed in a hierarchical manner. This enabled the identification of the basic situational characteristics for each web document by classifying them into main register categories, which then led to the development of specific *sub-reg-*

isters. The taxonomy used for the Turkish data recognizes 9 main registers along with a total number of 24 sub-registers (Erten-Johansson et al. 2024). The main registers are Informational Persuasion, Narrative, Informational Description, Machine-translated, Opinion, How-to/Instruction, Interactive Discussion, Spoken, and Lyrical. The documents assigned to more than one category were annotated as hybrids.

This study centers on the examination of the main registers Informational Description and Opinion, along with their sub-registers. The Informational Description register delivers factual details, whereas the Opinion register provides subjective and interpretive content. Understanding their linguistic expressions is crucial for distinguishing between them on the internet.

The Informational Description register comprises 481 texts, totaling 196,624 tokens, whereas the Opinion register comprises 215 texts, with 107,828 tokens in total. Table 1 illustrates the total number of texts, the token counts, and the distributions of each sub-register within its corresponding main register. Texts that do not exhibit the specific characteristics of a sub-register are labelled as 'other.' Percentage was calculated in terms of the number of texts.

Table 1: Registers and sub-registers with counts of texts and tokens.

Sub-register of Informational Description (IN)	**No. of texts**	**No. of tokens**	**Percentage (%) in IN**
Description of a thing/person	124	46,273	25.77
Legal terms and conditions	105	52,059	21.82
Encyclopedia article	18	7,979	3.74
FAQs	6	2,447	1.24
Research article	4	1,693	0.83
Other	224	86,173	46.56
Total	**481**	**196,624**	**99.96**
Sub-register of Opinion (OP)	**No. of texts**	**No. of tokens**	**Percentage (%) in OP**
Review	66	20,933	30.69
Opinion blog	58	32,351	26.97
Advice	46	17,122	21.39
Religious blog/sermon	29	26,695	13.48
Other	16	10,727	7.44
Total	**215**	**107,828**	**99.97**

The 'other' sub-register within Informational Description constitutes about half of the Informational Description register. Although this finding is intriguing, it falls outside the scope of this study and would necessitate separate research. Nevertheless, we can state that a variety of informational and descriptive texts such as descriptive reports, course materials, test papers, and meeting minutes are classified under this sub-register.

3.2 Text dispersion keyword analysis

Scott (1997: 236) defines keywords as words that occur with notable frequency in a target corpus compared to a reference corpus. The notion of keyness employs a comparison of a target corpus and a reference corpus to assess the "aboutness" of a text or corpus (Baker 2004: 347). Traditionally, keyness has been determined using log-likelihood statistics (Scott and Tribble 2006), which approached the concept of keyness through frequency. This calculation is called the standard frequency keyword analysis. Although the analysis aims to identify statistically significant words within a collection of texts (Scott 1997; Scott and Tribble 2006), it often overlooks how these words are spread across different texts. Standard frequency keyword analysis operates under the assumption of corpus homogeneity, where words are evenly distributed across the corpus. However, corpus frequency keywords are often abundant in a corpus but not widely dispersed across its texts (Egbert and Biber 2019), marking them inadequate in representing the domain of the corpus in question.

Content-distinctiveness and content-generalizability serve as criteria for assessing the effectiveness of keyword analysis. Content-distinctiveness refers to the strength of the relationship between a keyword and the discourse domain of the target corpus, whereas content-generalizability pertains to the degree to which a keyword represents the discourse across the entire target corpus (Egbert and Biber 2019: 78–79). Content-distinctive keywords should better typify the target discourse domain relative to other domains, whereas content-generalizable keywords should be representative of the entire target corpus. In pursuit of greater content-distinctiveness and content-generalizability, as "keywords should be used by many different writers/speakers.", Egbert and Biber (2019) introduced Text Dispersion Keyword (TDK) Analysis. TDK uses text rather than the corpus as the unit of observation. The frequency of word repetition is not crucial, as words that are repeated often hold significance within a specific text but not necessarily across the entire corpus (Egbert and Biber 2019: 83). In TDK analysis, word frequency is disregarded; and instead, keyword lists are generated based on word dispersion across texts. It has demonstrated its suitability for register studies with large corpora and surpasses traditional frequency-based methods in terms of effectiveness (Gries 2021).

To create the reference corpus, we incorporated all texts from various registers, excluding those from the target register. For instance, when conducting TDK analysis on legal texts, our target corpus comprised all legal texts, and our reference corpus comprised all texts of TurCORE except legal texts. Following the creation of the reference and target corpora, we utilized Python scripts to extract the keywords associated with each sub-register. After identifying the keywords, we categorized those from the sub-registers with highest number of texts. They are 'description of a thing/person' and 'legal terms and conditions' under the main register of Informational Description and 'review' and 'opinion blog' under the main register of Opinion. The keywords were grouped into semantic and grammatical categories based on their semantic and functional similarities. Grammatical categories were established based on the observation that certain linguistic features tend to co-occur in texts owing to their interconnected functions (Biber and Egbert 2018: 46). Semantic categorization involved allocating each identified word into relevant semantic categories. Consistent with Egbert and Biber's (2019) methodology, we examined the top 100 keywords for each register.

4 Findings

We define the sub-registers of Informational Description in Section 4.1. and those of Opinion in Section 4.2. using examples from their top keywords. The top 20 keywords provide sufficient information to illustrate the aboutness of each register. The top 20 Turkish keywords for each register, along with their English translations, are provided in Appendices A and B.

Section 4.1.1. offers a detailed examination of 'description of a thing/person' and Section 4.1.2. delves into 'legal terms and conditions.' Similarly, Section 4.2.1 provides detailed analyses of 'review' and Section 4.2.2. focuses on 'opinion blog.' The analyses entail grouping the top 100 text dispersion keywords of each register into semantic and grammatical categories. Appendix C shows all abbreviations used in grammatical annotations.

4.1 Informational Description

The primary aim of the Informational Description register is to describe or explain information. Authors are typically not specified in the texts of this register. The output can vary depending on the text – from carefully written texts like 'legal terms' to unedited ones such as 'description of a thing' (Skantsi and Laippala 2023:

14). A notable characteristics of Informational Description texts is their factual or factually expressed essence.

Below, we cover all sub-registers of Informational Description. As is the case with all keywords, a single Turkish word can often correspond to multiple words in English (Biber 1995). For this reason, when translated into English, the original single-word keywords might be expressed as several words.

The 'description of a thing or person' sub-register involves the depiction of a thing or a person. In TurCORE, this register was observed to predominantly describe a thing rather than a person, with a focus on medical topics indicated by keywords such as *tedavisi* 'treatment of', *enfeksiyonlar* 'infections', *belirtileri* 'symptoms of', *hastalarda* 'in the patients', *hastalık* 'disease', *bağırsak* 'intestine' and *ilaçlar* 'medications.' One of the most frequent keywords *vardır* 'there is/are' highlights a distinctive characteristic. The suffix *-DIr* is a generalizing modality marker in Turkish grammar (Göksel and Kerslake 2005: 80), commonly used to emphasize a generalization or statement of principle in the content being described.

The 'legal terms and conditions' sub-register concerns any topic related to legality where the author is not mentioned (Skantsi and Laippala 2023). One of the notable features of this register, which makes the text easily identifiable, is its official context-specific and formal words (Özyıldırım 2011), such as *işbu* 'hereby', *kanunu* 'act of', *maddesinde* 'in the article of' and *yetkili* 'authorized' that we identified within the top 20 keywords. Specific to online data, privacy policies and cookie descriptions are often present in this register (Biber and Egbert 2018), expressed via the keywords *bilgilerin* 'of data', *kişisel* 'personal' and *korunması* 'protection of'. In the Turkish data, a notable group of words also pertain to the delivery of purchases and the return policy of products, as the keywords *iade* 'return', *kargo* 'cargo' and *kargoya* 'to cargo' exemplify.

A prime example of 'encyclopedia articles' found on the internet is Wikipedia, whose format is the same across languages, making the articles easily identifiable (Biber and Egbert 2018). A considerable number of encyclopedia articles in Turkish feature biographical descriptions, evident from keywords such as *doğdu* 'was born' and *doğmuştur* 'was born'. In addition, temporal markers such as years *1972, 1989* and *2004*, phrases like *yılında* 'in the year of' and geographic location names such as *Ankara* and *Berlin* reflect time- and place-related words typically used in biographical descriptions.

TurCORE has a scarcity of texts categorized as 'FAQs' and 'research articles', necessitating a cautious approach to their interpretation. Nevertheless, FAQs typically comprise a list of commonly asked questions regarding a particular subject, which is typically accompanied by answers, structured in a question-and-answer format (Asheghi, Sharoff, and Markert 2016; Biber and Egbert 2018). FAQs predominantly address products or services offered on a website, with responses usually provided by company personnel (Skantsi and Laippala 2023), as observed via the top 20 keywords *hazırlıyoruz* 'we are preparing' that suggests product readiness and *sitelerimizi* 'our sites' that indicates website affiliation.

'Research articles' are a form of academic writing detailing a research study, including the motivation for the study, the methodologies employed, and the research findings. They are typically written by an individual or a group of authors affiliated with an academic institution, and are intended for an audience of specialists (Biber and Egbert 2018). On the Turkish web, although infrequent, research articles seem to mainly pertain to medical research, evident from keywords such as *sendromu* 'syndrome of', *coronavirüsler* 'coronaviruses', *algınlığından* 'from the delusion of' and *akciğerlere* 'to the lungs.' Technical terminology such as *nanopartiküller* 'nanoparticles', *iğnesiz* 'mutic' and *nebulizatör* 'nebulizer' was also observed.

4.1.1 Description of a thing or person

In this semantic grouping and the subsequent ones for other registers, variations in keywords that do not affect the meaning or the sentence structure, have been disregarded, and only the nominative-cased noun is used for semantic categorization. For instance, keywords like *tedavisi* 'treatment of' and *tedavisinde* 'in the treatment of' are simplified to *tedavi* 'treatment' and displayed as one keyword instead of three.

Based on the top 100 text dispersion keywords, description of a thing/person texts are categorized into semantic groups of medicine and physiology, description, higher education, time, and other, as illustrated in Table 2.

In texts concerning the description of a thing/person, the presence of keywords related to description and time is expected owing to the communicative purpose of such texts. In Turkish texts, keywords were observed within both the description and time-related semantic categories. However, the inclusion of keywords categorized under the groups of medicine and physiology and higher education seems to reflect the annotation process, which distinguishes description of a thing/person from encyclopedia articles (Erten-Johansson et al. 2024). Although the current register predominantly features description of things rather than persons, these descriptions often pertain to diseases and treatments, as well as to universities and faculties.

Most keywords associated with the description of a thing/person texts in Turkish are nouns, followed by adjectives, verbs, numerals, and adverbs. However, from a more Turkish-specific perspective, they fall under the main categories of copular marker formed with the suffix *-DIr* and aorist with *-(A/I)r*, and adjectives, as seen in Table 3.

Modality is concerned with whether a situation is presented as a directly known fact or in some other way. The modality marking system in Turkish enables differentiation between statements that reflect the speaker's direct experience, knowledge, or observation, and those that make assertions of more general, theoretical ideas, or convey assumptions or hypotheses. Among the various modalized expressions, the markers indicating generalization, general rule, or statement of principle are the aorist forms *-(A/I)r* in verbal sentences and the generalizing modality marker *-DIr* in nominal sentences (Göksel and Kerslake 2005: 294–295). In the description of a thing/person sub-register, both forms were observed within the top 100 keywords. Examples such as *vardır* 'there is/are', *nedir* 'what is' and *denir* 'is called' in Table 3 illustrate this, aligning with the descriptive nature of this register.

Table 2: Semantic categories of description of a thing/person with examples.

medicine and physiology	description	higher education	time	other
treatment	there is/are	faculty	2005	announcement
infection	has gotten	university	2007	south
symptom	personifies	undergraduate	2009	film
patient	is directing	class	1997	
disease	what is	title	1991	
series	is seen	graduate	1973	
medications	can be seen	edu	when it is	
history	that is seen	sciences	generally	
apo	indicates	career		
psychotherapy	is available	program		
addiction	they pass	literature		
cell	is called	school		
pain	was born			
receptor	must be done			
histamin	widespread			
auditory	married			
chronic	apparent			
genetic	general			
doctor	expression			
immunity	character			
therapy	family			
hereditary	civil servant			
contagious	child			
disorder	in women			
incidence	role			
diagnosis	in Anatolia			
examination				

medicine and physiology	description	higher education	time	other
physique				
intestine				
tooth				
bone				
kidney				
body				

In Turkish, adjectives have the flexibility to function as nouns and adverbs. When employed as a noun, their identification is straightforward owing to the case markers attached to the noun. However, pinpointing their function as adverbs may not be as straightforward. Nonetheless, by checking the concordance lines, we observed a considerable number of adjectives that can also function as adverbs in description of a thing or person texts, some of which are illustrated in Table 3. Göksel and Kerslake (2005) classify adjectives into two main groups based on whether they contain a productive derivational suffix. Although both types were present within the top 100 keywords of this sub-register, we included those with a derivational suffix in Table 3 to demonstrate the influence of grammar on adjective formation. For instance, the suffix *-GIn* forms *yaygın* 'widespread' from the verb *yay-* 'spread', and *belirgin* 'apparent' from the verb *belir-* 'appear'. Similarly, the suffix *-sAL* forms *kalıtsal* 'hereditary' from the noun *kalıt* 'gene'. Although the function of these keywords may not immediately be apparent without examining concordance lines, the inclusion of adjectives that can also serve as nouns and adverbs in this register enriches descriptions of things or persons by offering detailed characteristics.

Table 3: Grammatical categories of description of a thing/person with samples.

Grammatical category	Keyword in English	Keyword in Turkish	Grammatical annotation
copular marker -DIr and aorist -(A/I)r	there is/are what is is called	var-dır ne-dir de-n-ir	existent + -DIr what+ -DIr say +pass+ -(A/I)r
adjective	widespread apparent hereditary	yay-gın belir-gin kalıt-sal	spread+ -GIn appear+ -GIn gene+ -sAl

4.1.2 Legal terms and conditions

The top 100 keywords of Turkish legal texts were semantically classified into the categories of legality, coordination/relation, online shopping, data protection, number and other, as Table 4 illustrates.

Legal texts are recognizable by their extensive use of formal language, comprising technical legal terms that typically require specialized knowledge for comprehension (Özyıldırım 2011: 85). The keywords grouped under the semantic categories of legality and coordination/relation support the presence of this formal and official terminology. However, it is noteworthy that certain keywords related to the internet, such as data protection and online shopping, which may not require specialized expertise, are also prominent in these texts. Upon manually examining concordance lines, we observed that certain keywords categorized as number, such as *otuz* 'thirty', are commonly used in online shopping texts, referring to the thirty-day period within which the customer can return a product. The presence of legal documents on the internet, intended not only for specialists but also for potential consumers or website users, appears to challenge the conventional perception of legislative language.

Table 4: Semantic categories of legal terms and conditions with examples.

legality	coordination/ relation	online shopping	data protection	number	other
legitimate	thereunder	return	personal	numbered	responsible
accordment	that is designated	cargo	data	no	written
hereby	within	order	protection	6698	registered
act	anticipated	delivery	privacy	third	cancellation
article	pursuant to	address	processing	thirty	responsibility
court	determinated	mail	reserved		cannot be used
commitment	on the basis of	firm	unpermitted		that you are
abolitionary	that might arise	customer	mischief		
legislation	that originates	product	copyright		
declaration	provided that	membership			
obligation	in case of	site			
outher	inflicting	www			
execution	expounded	com			
feasance	regarding				
compatibility	appurtenant				
prerogative	concerned				
parties	with intendments				
demand	or				
right					
contract					
authorized					

We observed patterns of relative clauses, passive voice structures, and plural nouns in legal texts, as seen in Table 5.

Table 5: Grammatical categories of legal terms and conditions with samples.

Grammatical category	Keyword in English	Keyword in Turkish	Grammatical annotation
relative clause	that might arise that originates	doğ-abil-ecek kaynaklan-an	arise+psb+part originate+part
passive voice	that is designated on the basis of cannot be used	belirt-il-en dayan-ıl-arak kullan-ıl-a-maz	designate+pass+part base+pass+cv use+pass+psb+neg.aor
plural noun	obligations parties data	yükümlülük-ler taraf-lar veri-ler	obligation+pl party+pl datum+pl

The relative clause structure in Turkish is a complex adjectival construction where a modifying clause precedes the head (Kornfilt 1997). The most common type of relative clause is marked by the suffix *-(y)An, -DIk,* or *(y)-AcAk,* corresponding to various relative pronouns including who, which, that, whom, whose and where in English (Göksel and Kerslake 2005). In legal documents, we identified these relative clause structures, and found the *-(y)An* suffix as the most common. The prevalence of various relative clauses in legal documents indicates the aim for precision and unambiguousness within the legal context. The frequent use of relative clauses in legal texts underscores their role in conveying messages that are clearly defined and aimed to be correctly understood in legal discourse.

Another commonly observed structure among the top 100 keywords in legal documents is the passive voice. Some instances of passive voice were embedded within structures featuring non-finite verbs forms such as *belirtilen* 'that is designated' and *dayanılarak* 'on the basis of', whereas others occur finite verb forms such as *kullanılamaz* 'cannot be used', as seen in Table 5. The frequent presence of passive voice in various verb forms seems to indicate an intent to maintain a formal tone. Passive voice serves to centers the attention on actions and consequences without attributing to a specific person or entity.

The plural form in Turkish is created by adding the suffix *-lAr* to the noun. In legal documents, we observed the frequent use of plural nouns such as *yükümlülükler* 'obligations', *taraflar* 'parties' and *veriler* 'data', indicating that legal terms apply to multiple entities, individuals, and situations. This reflects the generalizable nature of legal discourse, where rules are designed to be broadly applicable. The frequent use of plural-marked nouns for generalizations is both anticipated and intriguing, given the objectives of precision and unambiguousness inherent in legal documents.

4.2 Opinion

The Opinion register expresses subjective viewpoints based on the personal opinions of an individual author or a group of authors (Biber and Egbert 2018). In some cases, the author is mentioned by a pseudonym or by their actual name (Skantsi and Laippala 2023). Below, we explore each sub-register of Opinion with their top 20 keywords.

'Review' entails the evaluations of a product or service written by an individual on a personal, institutional, or commercial website. Although the author may claim to have expertise regarding the product or service under review, they often may have only used the product or service (Biber and Egbert 2018). Reviews hold considerable influence on consumers' purchasing decisions online (Wang et al. 2023). This might explain why the review register emerged as the most prevalent sub-register of Opinion on the Turkish web. Turkish reviews were found to commonly evaluate various forms of media such as films, documentaries, books, and games, with specific mentions such as *Spinoza* and *Minecraft*.

'Opinion blog', a sub-register specific to the internet, serves as a platform for individuals to publicly share personal viewpoints, often involving evaluations and stances. They are commonly written by non-professional authors. According to Biber and Egbert (2018: 107), opinion blogs are one of the least well-defined registers owing to their diverse nature, encompassing a broad spectrum of texts that may not clearly exhibit opinionated elements. Although this register typically includes politics-related topics and may even be written by political figures (Skantsi and Laippala 2023), politics did not emerge as a prominent theme on the Turkish web. This could be attributed to the fact that during the annotation process, texts related to politics were often categorized under Informational Persuasion, indicating an intent to persuade rather than simply express opinion (Erten-Johansson et al. 2024).

'Advice' involves offering recommendations based on personal opinion with the aim of prompting action to solve a particular problem (Biber and Egbert 2018). Often, the authors remain anonymous but claim expertise regarding the problem and its solution. The focus lies on the thoughts and emotions of the reader (Skantsi and Laippala 2023), who could be anyone seeking guidance on addressing a particular problem. In Turkish advice texts, the guidance offered to readers is reflected through keywords related to second-person markers, such as *kendinizi* 'yourselves', *size* 'to you', *yaşamınızda* 'in your life', *unutmayın* 'don't you forget' and *olabilirsiniz* 'you might be.' In addition, keywords such as *nasıl* 'how' and *dikkat* 'caution' indicate the provision of guidance intended to lead to actions in this register.

'Religious blog/sermon' comprises texts of denominational religious nature, excluding those merely describing a religion (Biber and Egbert 2018). Typically authored by individuals, these texts are often hosted on institutional websites, and some of the website visitors are regular followers. Despite being based on beliefs and opinions, the discourse within religious blog/sermon often adopts an informational description framework, which complicates its communicative purposes (Biber and Egbert 2018). Furthermore, the complexity of this register arises from the occasional inclusion of narrative elements such as stories. Nevertheless, a consistent feature of this register is the utilization of context-specific religious terminology, as observed in Turkish with keywords such as *Allah, Muhammad, peygamber* 'prophet', *namaz* 'prayers', *Hz* 'His holiness' and *ahirette* 'in the afterlife'.

4.2.1 Review

The top 100 keywords found in Turkish review texts were semantically categorized into groups of evaluation, (background) description, material, feature, name and other, as Table 6 illustrates.

A large number of the keywords identified in reviews pertain to the material under review, such as a film, game, or book, providing detailed descriptions and mentioning associated features. In line with this observation, specific names such as the title of a website informing users about new technology *Teknolojioku* or the seventh season of a series *s7* were noted. These items are assessed using various evaluation-related keywords, such as *açıkçası* 'frankly', *düşünülmüş* 'thought-out' and *yargılıydım* 'I was prejudiced.' It is notable that many of the keywords of this register demonstrate close semantic connections with each other, enhancing and complementing their meanings.

In Turkish reviews, we did not observe frequently repeating grammatical patterns, aligning with Biber and Egbert's (2018: 123) findings for English. However, the categories in Table 7 display certain Turkish-specific grammatical features in the context of reviews.

Table 6: Semantic categories of reviews with examples.

evaluation	(background) description	material	feature	name	other
impression	it addresses to	film	layers	Spinoza	honor
frankly	it points at	documentary	model	Minecraft	I will not mention
black	it comes about	book	differences	Sigma	questioning
rationalist	when I saw	game	features	Nurdan	in seasons
shattered	it leaves	cover	vibe	Teknolojioku	living creatures
as much as	in the town	skirt	android	Franz	thought
thought-out	of the town	image	pixel	auto	audience
can be provided	it catches	life	dialogue	news	2010
what we understand	that I used	series	weight	a0	punch
I was biased	from the building	religion	version	s7	
stance	that I know		visual	v1	
which does not resemble	that s/he takes on				
unuseful	identity				
driven	to the front				
fictional	role				
views	I had used				
publicity					
masterpiece					
prominent					
my interest					

Table 7: Grammatical categories of reviews with samples.

Grammatical category	Keyword in English	Keyword in Turkish	Grammatical annotation
negative adjectivals	unuseful irrelevant which does not resemble	kullanış-sız alaka-sız benze-me-yen	use+ *-sIz* relevance+ *-sIz* resemble+neg+ *-(y)An*
adjectives with perfect participle	shattered thought-out	parçala-n-mış düşün-ül-müş	shatter+pass+part think+pass+part
accusative case marked noun	the film the book the documentary	film-i kitab-ı belgesel-i	film+acc book+acc documentary+acc

Adjectives or words functioning as adjectives (adjectivals) within the top 100 keywords were not notably prevalent in Turkish reviews. However, most of the adjectives found were constructed either with the suffix *-sIz* or with the negative marker

-mA. The suffix *-sIz* expresses absence or lack, and is translatable as 'less', 'without' and 'lacking' (Johanson 2021: 489). Illustrated in Table 7, adjectives such as *kullanışsız* 'useless' and *alakasız* 'irrelevant' are examples of the pattern where the suffix *-sIz* is added to the nouns *kullanış* 'usage', and *alaka* 'relevance.' The keyword *benzemeyen* 'which does not resemble' functions as an adjectival, formed with negation marker *-mA* followed by the relative clause marker *-(y)An*. It is noteworthy that despite the limited number of adjectives, the subjectivity in reviews tends to be negative. However, we are cautious not to draw generalizing conclusions from individual words.

Another group of adjectives was found to be formed with the perfect participle. In Turkish, the suffix *-mIş* serves functions, including inference and perception (Johanson 2021: 653). The keywords *parçalanmış* 'shattered' and *düşünülmüş* 'thought-out' exemplify the role of this suffix as an indicator of perfect participle. The inference and perception functions of the suffix are in line with the nature of reviews, which involve evaluations of a product or service based on the reviewer's experiences.

In Turkish reviews, we observed a greater prevalence of nouns than of adjectives. These nouns varied in their grammatical cases, with one group showing a consistent pattern: the accusative case. The accusative case is used to mark the definite object of a verb, indicating an object specified by its identity as a name or title, or one that has been previously mentioned, such as the use of the definite article in English (Lewis 2001: 35). In reviews, both functions of the accusative case on the object are evident, especially when reviewers assess products or services, as exemplified by the keywords *filmi* 'the film', *kitabı* 'the book' and *belgeseli* 'the documentary'.

4.2.2 Opinion blog

The top 100 keywords extracted from Turkish opinion blog texts were categorized into semantic groups of stance, opinion and evaluation, identity, topics and concepts, action and activity, and other. Table 8 displays these categories.

We observed that the keywords related to opinion blog displayed a more diverse distribution than the keywords from other registers. Accordingly, we created the semantic groups by combining related categories, such as opinion and evaluation, or topics and concepts. Words categorized under stance were found to express negativity, certainty and uncertainty, and probability and improbability, all indicating the markings of stance. In addition, we identified a large number of words belonging to the category other in this register. The lack of clear-cut semantic categories and the presence of numerous keywords in the other category in Turkish opinion blogs reinforces the observation by Biber and Egbert (2018) regarding the diverse nature of opinion blogs, which cover a wide range of textual content.

Table 8: Semantic categories of opinion blogs with examples.

stance	opinion and evaluation	identity	topics and concepts	action and activity	other
never	I think	who	thing, stuff	to start	mi (a question particle)
but	you are right	s/he, it	pain	to hold	what
not	by thinking	I	life	to do, make	this
maybe	in my opinion	ourselves	happiness	to say	mu (a question particle)
must be	there is/are	individual	years	dance	that it is
in fact	when you look at	my	society	to study, work	how
if only	I say	others	wisdom	to write	because
no, nothing	that I know	man	decisions	writing	homeland
already, anyway	regularly	person	words	to show	then
should/must be	let's not be bothered			sharing	I want
so that				to give	to be
if it happened				to cover	ya (a clitic)
while				to lose	mı (a question particle)
a little					there
like that					that
accordingly					full of
işte (a discourse marker)					team
even					lessons
of course					modern-day
cannot be					the yes sayers
in vain					
a bit					
again					

We observed a relatively frequent pattern of pronouns in opinion blogs, some of which are shown in Table 9. These include *ben* 'I', *benim* 'my' and *kendimize* 'to ourselves'. Most of the pronouns are in first-person singular form, with some also appearing in first-person plural form. This aligns with the subjective nature of opinion blogs, which reflect the personal viewpoints of the bloggers. In Turkish, subject pronouns can be omitted, as the verbs are marked with person suffixes. Despite this, the subject pronoun *ben* 'I' was identified as one of the most frequent keywords within the top 100. This could be attributable to blogger's intentions to emphasize their personal opinion or to introduce a new topic of discussion in the opening sentence of a paragraph. (Göksel and Kerslake 2005: 241–242).

Modalized utterances are of various kinds, and encompass different functions such as assumptions or hypotheses, possibility or necessity statements, or expressions of desire or willingness for an event or state to occur (Göksel and Kerslake 2005: 294–295). For instance, as demonstrated in Table 9, the keyword *başlarız* 'we would start' indicates an assumption or hypothesis, *olmalı* 'it should/must be' signifies necessity, and *takılmayalım* 'let's not be bothered' exemplifies willingness. The diverse array of modals found in opinion blog appears to reflect the subjective nature of this register, enabling the author to convey their viewpoints by employing a variety of personal perspectives.

Table 9: Grammatical categories of opinion blogs with samples.

Grammatical category	Keyword in English	Keyword in Turkish	Grammatical annotation
pronouns	I	ben	I
	I have, my	ben-im	I+gen
	to ourselves	kendimiz-e	ourselves+dat
modality	we would start	başla-r-ız	start+aor+1P
	let's not be bothered	takıl-ma-yalım	be bothered+neg+opt+1P
	it should/must be	ol-malı	be+nec3S
imperfective aspect	I think	düşün-üyor-um	think+impf+1S
	I want	ist-iyor-um	want+impf+1S
	I am saying	d-iyor-um	say+impf+1S

Considering that aspect expresses a viewpoint from which a situation is presented, the imperfective aspect typically refers to actions or events that are ongoing, habitual, or continuous without any endpoint. In Turkish opinion blogs, we identified several verbs expressed in imperfective aspect. For instance, *düşünüyorum* 'I think', *istiyorum* 'I want' and *diyorum* 'I am saying' are keywords expressed in the imperfective aspect, which is consistent with the content of opinion blogs. This usage of imperfective aspect appears to give a sense of continuous engagement with the topic under discussion. Further, it contributes to a more conversational tone, possibly enhancing the blog's relatability to the reader.

5 Conclusion

In this article, we examined the Informational Description and Opinion registers of TurCORE created by Erten-Johansson et al. (2024). The analysis revealed that Informational Description serves as a register for objectively presenting information, whereas Opinion represents a domain where individuals express subjective viewpoints, in line with Biber and Egbert (2018) and Skantsi and Laippala (2023).

Within Informational Description in Turkish, we found that the 'description of a thing/person' and 'legal terms and conditions' sub-registers exhibit similarities in their descriptive content but differ in their linguistic characteristics. Descriptions typically rely on nouns and adjectives supported by generalizing modality markers. In contrast, texts of 'legal terms and conditions' are distinguishable not only by their vocabulary but also by their frequent use of specific grammatical structures such as the relative clause and passive voice. These linguistic features serve to enhance precision and formality in legal discourse, characteristics not commonly found in descriptions of things or persons. Moreover, legal texts can encompass online-specific contexts, a feature not always observed in descriptions.

Our findings reveal that the sub-registers within Opinion, such as 'review' and 'opinion blog', share similarities owing to their subjective content. However, notable differences exist between the two. Reviews predominantly center around products or services and are authored by individuals who used the products or service. This sub-register is characterized by an abundance of evaluation words reflecting subjective assessment. In contrast, opinion blogs cover a wide range of topics, making them less well-defined. They predominantly express personal viewpoints with emphatic stances, adopting a conversational tone through the frequent use of modality and imperfective aspect markers.

Informational Description and Opinion represent distinct registers, each characterized by unique linguistic features. In today's digital age, where information is sought and shared primarily online, distinguishing between informative content and opinion-based material to enhance media literacy is essential. We anticipate that the work by Erten-Johansson et al. (2024) along with the research presented in this study, will contribute to future studies on the linguistic characteristics of web-based communication in less studied non-Indo-European languages.

6 Funding

The study was funded by the Eino Jutikkala Fund of the Finnish Academy of Science and Letters.

7 Acknowledgements

We thank our anonymous reviewers for their time in reading the manuscript and providing valuable feedback.

References

Aksan, Mustafa & Yeşim Aksan. 2015. Multi-word expressions in genre specification. *Dil ve Edebiyat Dergisi* 12 (1), 1–42.
Asheghi, Nouhsin Rezapour, Serge Sharoff & Katja Markert. 2016. Crowdsourcing for web genre annotation. *Language Resources and Evaluation* 50 (3), 603–641.
Baker, Paul. 2004. Querying keywords: Questions in difference, frequency, and sense in keyword analysis. *Journal of English Linguistics* 32 (4), 346–359.
Barbaresi, Adrien. 2021. Trafilatura: A web scraping library and command-line tool for text discovery and extraction. In Proceedings of the 59th Annual Meeting of the Association for Computational Linguistics and the 11th International Joint Conference on Natural Language Processing: System Demonstrations. 122–131.
Berber-Sardinha, Tony. 2018. Dimensions of variation across Internet registers. *International Journal of Corpus Linguistics* 23 (2), 125–157.
Berber Sardinha, Tony. 2022. A text typology of social media. *Register Studies* 4 (2), 138–170.
Biber, Douglas. 1986. Spoken and written textual dimensions in English: Resolving the contradictory findings. *Language* 62 (2), 384–414.
Biber, Douglas. 1995. *Dimensions of register variation: A cross-linguistic perspective.* Cambridge: Cambridge University Press.
Biber, Douglas & Susan Conrad. 2001. *Variation in English: Multi-Dimensional studies*. London: Routledge.
Biber, Douglas & Susan Conrad. 2009. *Register, genre, and style*. Cambridge: Cambridge University Press.
Biber, Douglas & Jesse Egbert. 2018. *Register variation online*. Cambridge: Cambridge University Press.
Biber, Douglas, Jesse Egbert & Mark Davies. 2015. Exploring the composition of the searchable web: A corpus-based taxonomy of web registers. *Corpora* 10 (1), 11–45.
Biber, Douglas, Stig Johansson, Geoffrey Leech, Susan Conrad & Edward Finegan. 1999. *The Longman grammar of spoken and written English.* London: Longman.
Çarkoğlu, Ali, Lemi Baruh & Kerem Yıldırım. 2014. Press-party parallelism and polarization of news media during an election campaign: The case of the 2011 Turkish elections. *The International Journal of Press/Politics* 19 (3), 295–317.
Egbert, Jesse & Douglas Biber. 2019. Incorporating text dispersion into keyword analyses. *Corpora* 14 (1), 77–104.
Egbert, Jesse, Douglas Biber & Mark Davies. 2015. Developing a bottom-up, user-based method of web register classification. *Journal of the Association for Information Science and Technology* 66 (9), 1817–1831.
Erten-Johansson, Selcen, Valtteri Skantsi, Sampo Pyysalo & Veronika Laippala (2024). Linguistic variation beyond the Indo-European web: Analyzing Turkish web registers in TurCORE. *Register Studies* 6 (1), 60–90.
Göksel, Aslı & Celia Kerslake. 2005. *Turkish: A comprehensive grammar.* London & New York: Routledge.

Gries, Stefan. 2021. A new approach to (key) keyword analysis: Using frequency, and now also dispersion. *Research in Corpus Linguistics* 9 (2), 1–33.

Johanson, Lars. 2021. *Turkic*. Cambridge: Cambridge University Press.

Karapetjana, Indra & Jelena Lokastova. 2015. Register of electronic communication at sea. *Baltic Journal of English Language, Literature and Culture* 5, 52–61.

Koçak, Aslıhan. 2013. *A comparative register analysis of the language of cooking used in Turkish recipes* MA thesis. Ankara: Hacettepe University.

Kornfilt, Jaklin. 1997. *Turkish*. London & New York: Routledge.

Laippala, Veronika, Roosa Kyllönen, Jesse Egbert, Douglas Biber & Sampo Pyysalo. 2019. Toward multilingual identification of online registers. In *Proceedings of the 22nd Nordic Conference on Computational Linguistics*, 292–297. Turku, Finland: Linköping University Electronic Press.

Lewis, Geoffrey. 2001. *Turkish grammar*. Oxford: Oxford University Press

Li, Lei, Anruze Li, Xue Song, Xinran Li, Kun Huang & Edwin M. Ye. 2021. Characterizing response quantity on academic social Q&A sites: A multidiscipline comparison of linguistic characteristics of questions. *Library Hi Tech* 41 (3), 921–938.

Liimatta, Aatu. 2019. Exploring register variation on Reddit. A multi-dimensional study of language use on social media website. *Register Studies* 1 (2), 269–295.

Liimatta, Aatu. 2022. Do registers have different functions for text length? A case study of Reddit. *Register Studies* 4 (2), 263–287.

Özyıldırım, Işıl. 2011. A comparative register perspective on Turkish legislative language. In Tarja Salmi-Tolonen, Iris Tukiainen & Richard Foley (eds.), *Law and language in partnership and conflict*. Turku: Oikeustieteiden tiedekunta Lapin yliopisto.

Pomikalek, Jan. 2011. *Removing boilerplate and duplicate content from web corpora*. Dissertation. Brno: Masaryk University.

Repo, Liina, Valtteri Skantsi, Samuel Rönnqvist, Saara Hellström, Mika Oinonen, Anna Salmela, Douglas Biber, Jesse Egbert, Sampo Pyysalo & Veronika Laippala. 2021. Beyond the English web: Zero-shot cross-lingual and lightweight monolingual classification of registers. In *Proceedings of the 16th Conference of European Chapter of the Association for Computational Linguistics: Student Research Workshop*, Kiev, 21–23 April.

Scott, Mike. 1997. PC analysis of key words – and key words. *System* 25 (2), 233–245.

Scott, Mike & Christopher Tribble. 2006. *Textual patterns: Keywords and corpus analysis in language education*. Amsterdam: John Benjamins.

Seoane, Elena & Douglas Biber. 2021. Corpus-based approaches to register variation. In Douglas Biber & Elena Seoane (eds.), *Corpus-based approaches to register variation*, 1–18. John Benjamins Publishing.

Skantsi, Valtteri & Veronika Laippala. 2023. Analyzing the unrestricted Web: The Finnish corpus of online registers. *Nordic Journal of Linguistics* 1 (1), 1–31.

Wang, Yiru, Xun Xu, Christina A. Kuchmaner & Ran Xu. 2023. But it was supposed to be healthy! How expected and actual nutritional value affect the content and linguistic characteristics of online reviews for food products. *Journal of Consumer Psychology* 33 (4), 743–761.

Appendices

Appendix A: Top 20 keywords of the sub-registers of Informational Description

Sub-register	Text Dispersion Keywords (Top 20)
Description of a thing/person	*tedavisi* 'treatment of' *enfeksiyonlar* 'infections' *enfeksiyonun* 'of the infection' *belirtileri* 'symptoms of' *fizik* 'physique' *rol* 'role' *hastalarda* 'in the patients' *2005* *hastalık* 'disease' *vardır* 'there is/are' *fakültesi* 'faculty of' *yaygın* 'widespread' *bağırsak* 'intestine' *ifadeyle* 'with expression' *dizisinde* 'in the series of' *ilaçlar* 'medications' *öykü* 'history' *kadınlarda* 'in women' *2007* *almıştır* 'has gotten'
Legal terms and conditions	*iade* 'return' *sayılı* 'numbered' *yasal* 'legitimate' *uyarınca* 'thereunder' *sözleşmesi* 'contract of' *işbu* 'hereby' *belirtilen* 'designated' *bilgilerin* 'of data' *kişisel* 'personal' *kargo* 'cargo' *kanunu* 'act of' *no* 'number' *6698* *korunması* 'protection of' *maddesinde* 'in the article of' *kanun* 'act' *verilerin* 'data of'

Sub-register	Text Dispersion Keywords (Top 20)
Legal terms and conditions (continued)	*kargoya* 'to cargo' *maddesi* 'article of' *yetkili* 'authorized'
Encyclopedia article	*doğdu* 'was born' *1972* *2004* *1988* *silmeden* 'wraparound' *evrenselliğe* 'to universality' *1989* *doğmuştur* 'was born *adlı* 'with the name of' *rock* 'rock' *yılında* 'in the year of' *almıştır* 'has gotten' *düze* 'dose' *filmleriyle* 'with the films of' *Ankara* *Mayıs* 'May' *2003* *Berlin* *kimdir* 'who is' *çini* 'tile'
FAQs	*hazırlıyoruz* 'we are preparing' *inceleyebilir* 's/he can examine' *başvurarak* 'by consulting' *araması* 'searching of' *bulunabilir* 'can be found' *yönlendirme* 'guidance' *çatlatma* 'fracturing' *pod* 'pod' *yurdumuz* 'our homeland' *sgkya* 'to sgk (social security institution)' *alkantra* 'alcantara' *coil* 'coil' *kargolanır* 'is shipped' *likitleri* 'liquids of' *iğnesinden* 'from the needle of' *klomen* 'klomen' *dansite* 'density' *lamine* 'laminated' *süngeri* 'the sponge' *sitelerimizi* 'our sites'

Sub-register	Text Dispersion Keywords (Top 20)
Research article	*sendromu* 'syndrome of' *etkilerini* 'the effects of' *araştırmak* 'to search' *frekans* 'frequency' *frekanslı* 'with frequency' *polariteli* 'with polarity' *coronavirüsler* 'coronaviruses' *ailesidir* 'is the family of' *polarite* 'polarity' *algınlığından* 'from the delusion of' *mers* 'mers' *virüsleridir* 'are the virus of' *zarflı* 'enveloped' *rmit* 'rmit' *akciğerlere* 'to the lungs' *nanopartiküller* 'nanoparticles' *iğnesiz* 'mutic' *nebulizatör* 'nebulizer' *kimyaya* 'to chemistry' *yeo* 'yeo'

Appendix B: Top 20 keywords associated with the sub-registers of Opinion

Sub-register	Text Dispersion Keywords (Top 20)
Review	*izlenim* 'impression' *açıkçası* 'frankly' *filmde* 'in the film' *belgeselin* 'of the documentary' *kitapta* 'in the book' *a0* *android* 'android' *filmleri* 'films of' *modelin* 'of the model' *filmi* 'the film' *kitabı* 'the book' *izleyiciye* 'to the audience' *oyunla* 'with game' *modeli* 'model of' *Spinozanın* 'of Spinoza' *izleyiciyi* 'the audience'

Sub-register	Text Dispersion Keywords (Top 20)
Review (continued)	*siyahi* 'black'
	hocalarım 'my gowns men'
	Minecraft
	şerefi 'honor of'
Opinion blog	*mi* (a question particle)
	şey 'thing, stuff'
	ne 'what'
	hiç 'never'
	ama 'but'
	kim 'who'
	o 'he/she/it/that'
	bunu 'this'
	değil 'not'
	belki 'maybe'
	insanın 'of the person'
	düşünüyorum 'I think'
	mu (a question particle)
	yıllar 'years'
	olduğunu 'that it is'
	olmalı 'should/must be'
	diye 'so that'
	olsa 'if it happened'
	oysa 'but/while'
	biraz 'a bit'
Advice	*burcu* 'zodiac of'
	kendinizi 'yourselves'
	burç 'zodiac'
	size 'to you'
	yaşamınızda 'in your life'
	duygusal 'emotional'
	nasıl 'how'
	yorumu 'interpretation of'
	dikkat 'caution, attention'
	insanlar 'people'
	olacaktır 'will happen'
	olabilir 'might happen'
	unutmayın 'don't you forget'
	gerekiyor 'it is necessary'
	olabilirsiniz 'you might be'
	olun 'be' (in imperative form)
	günlük 'daily'
	aşk 'love'
	yaparken 'while you do'
	sevdiğiniz 'that you love'

Sub-register	Text Dispersion Keywords (Top 20)
Religious blog/sermon	*Allah* *ey* (an interjection used in poetic contexts) *peygamber* 'prophet' *suresi* 'surah of' *Allahın* 'of Allah' *ayet* 'verse' *Bakara* 'Baqarah' *namaz* 'prayers' *onu* 'him/her' *onun* 'his/her' *Muhammed* 'Muhammad' *ona* 'to him/her' *insanın* 'of the person *Allaha* 'to Allah' *Hz* 'His holiness' *iman* 'faith' *Allahı* 'Allah' *ahirette* 'in the afterlife' *inkâr* 'denial' *dua* 'prayer'

Appendix C: Abbreviations in grammatical annotations

acc	accusative case	opt	optative
aor	aorist	part	participle
cv	converb	pass	passive
dat	dative case	pl	plural
gen	genitive case	psb	possibility
impf	imperfective	1P	first person plural
nec	necessity	1S	first person singular
neg	negative	3S	third person singular

Lothar Lemnitzer and Antonia Hamdi

"Also ehrlich" – From adjectival use to interactive discourse marker

Abstract: In this paper, we will take a closer look at the German word *ehrlich*. Traditionally, it is seen and described as an adjective. However, this word, as we will demonstrate using corpus data, is now being used frequently, and in combination with other words, as an interactive unit or discourse marker. As such, it is typically used in spoken or written dialogues, while having lost central aspects of its original meaning. In addition to the use with adverbs (for example with *mal*), the characteristic postposition of punctuation marks (such as colons or commas) and its syntactic isolation, these units have undergone pattern-like consolidation. Our findings are based on a variety of corpora, ranging from written medium and monological mode of communication to transcripts of spoken dialogues. We will outline how the exemplary quantitative and qualitative findings we are presenting here can be generalized and captured lexicographically as well as used as a case of data-driven exercise in the classroom.

Keywords: interactive unit, discourse marker, face work, German language, discourse analysis

1 Introduction

The German word *ehrlich* traditionally signifies a trait of human character (en: 'honest') as well as a trait of human activity and its result (en: 'fair' as in 'she acted fairly towards me' or 'a fair deal'). This type of usage is also registered in dictionaries of contemporary German.

Over the last decades, the word has gained additional functions while becoming more and more devoid of its original meaning. Besides its frequent use as an adjective, it is frequently used as an interactive unit nowadays, typically in genres of spoken language and computer-mediated communication, but also in written corpora where dialogues are cited or reported. It co-occurs with a small set of (modal) adverbs. We base these findings on a quantitative analysis of the DWDS and IDS corpora, covering a range of the last forty years, wherefore these corpora are sufficiently large.

Lothar Lemnitzer, Berlin-Brandenburg Academy of Sciences and Humanities, e-mail: lemnitzer@bbaw.de
Antonia Hamdi, University of Duisburg-Essen, e-mail: antonia.hamdi@uni-due.de

https://doi.org/10.1515/9783111434018-003

One of these collocations, *ehrlich gesagt* (en: 'frankly speaking'), has already been subject of linguistic investigations. For example, Stoltenburg (2009) described the use of this phrase to establish politeness in discourse. It allows speakers to distance themselves from former utterances and possible consequences for them (2009: 275–276). Imo describes the phrase as an element of the comment adverb class (2012: 70), as well as the Duden Grammar (Kunkel-Razum 2005: 594). Additionally, Wich-Reif has described it as more or less fixed, a phrase with which recurring communicative actions are mastered (2019: 191).

In this paper, we will broaden the perspective and describe some other collocations with *ehrlich* in the framework of *interactional linguistics* (cf. Imo and Lanwer 2019) and investigate their interactional function(s).

In Section 2, we will state our research questions and set them in relation to central theoretical concepts, on which our interpretation of the data is based. In Sections 3 and 4, the main part of this paper, we will describe our database (corpora of various kinds) and our quantitative analyses (Section 3). Examples from the corpora are presented and discussed in Section 4. In Section 5, we will present perspectives for future work: Firstly, we want to show the potential for lexicography. We will broaden the scope and present a way to describe such elements more comprehensively in a general dictionary of contemporary German (5.1). Secondly, we will show the potential of teaching interactive units in the classroom (5.2).

2 The research question and related concepts

In our daily use of German as native speakers and our use of interactive social media, we stumbled across a frequent use of the word *ehrlich* in contexts which do not support its usual meaning(s) as a qualitative adjective (en: 'honest', 'fair'), as we will demonstrate with the following example (all examples are translated into English using DeepL with post-editing of the result):

(1) *Sonst könnte ich mich ja auf irgendein Buch von Fomenkos "Neuer Chronologie" berufen, der behauptet, dass das Mittelalter komplett erfunden wurde.* ***Mal ehrlich****, wie viele Quellen mit Polen hast du übergangen, bevor du auf diesen Mist gestoßen bist?*
'Otherwise, I could refer to some book by Fomenko's "New Chronology", which claims that the Middle Ages were completely invented. Honestly, how many sources with Poland did you ignore before you came across this rubbish?'
Voevoda 17:33, 9. Jul. 2007 (CEST) (WDD19/P0027.16804 Diskussion:Polnisch-Russischer Krieg 1609–1618)

Three aspects are striking in the shown example, which is taken from the Wikipedia discussion pages: (1) the position: *ehrlich* precedes a rhetorical question, (2) the combination: *ehrlich* is surrounded by the particle "mal" and a comma, and (3) the function: *ehrlich* does not modify a reference noun (phrase) as an attributive adjective, which would thus describe the modified word or phrase qualitatively. We decided to take a closer look at such constructions (i.e. Adverb + the word *ehrlich*).

From this first intuitive observation, two questions arose that we decided to investigate further with the use of several corpora:

a) What is the specific function of the word *ehrlich* when used in the non-traditional way?
b) Which are the typical contexts of the word that "trigger" this particular function?

We will base our quantitative as well as qualitative analysis on the framework of interactional linguistics.

Nowadays, interactional Linguistics are seen as an established sub-discipline of theoretical as well as applied linguistics. It originates in the work of Elizabeth Couper-Kuhlen and Margret Selting (Selting and Couper-Kuhlen 2000; Couper-Kuhlen and Selting 2001) and gained ground particularly in the linguistics community in Europe (cf. Lindström 2009).

Interactional Linguistics investigates language in use quantitatively as well as qualitatively, viewing language as an activity to obtain certain goals rather than a (semiotic) system. In the past, studies have been carried out on various linguistic levels such as the consolidation of prosodic patterns, rhetorical-semantic routines, sequential patterns and, finally, syntactic patterns.

Recent investigations have shown that during interactions, recurrent patterns emerge that become more and more stable and lexicalized over time – grammatical constructions and idiomatic expressions are typical linguistic means to realise these communicative functions. Günthner (2009: 403) uses the term "sedimentierte Muster" ('sedimented patterns'). Such patterns are typically not syntactically integrated, they are an optional "add on" to the proposition(s) and operate on a metapragmatic level (cf. Torres Cajo 2017: 225). In interactional contexts, such units usually have a pivot role ("Scharnierfunktion", according to Auer 2023: 263), i.e. they not only announce a continuation of the thread by the speaker/writer, but they also recommit to the previous context (cf. Helmer and Deppermann 2017: 135).

In contrast to recent studies that are based on (samples of) spoken language only, we will be using corpora of written text and computer-mediated communication as well. Recent research has shown that interactive units are not only reserved for spoken language in the media, but that the norms and characteristics of spoken language can increasingly be found in written language in general (cf. Imo 2013: 94).

Leaning on Imo and Lanwer (2019), we will present a detailed qualitative analysis based on a small sample of patterns from these corpora.

In this framework, the research aims to investigate language in use, both quantitatively and qualitatively. Language is viewed as an activity to obtain certain goals rather than a (semiotic) system.

Our interpretation of the examples (Section 4) will be based on a theory of face work, a concept that has been introduced by Brown and Levinson (1987: 61, 101). Face work can be defined as a set of strategic behaviours by which people attempt to maintain both their own dignity (*face*) and that of the people with whom they are dealing. In the context of our work, we will narrow down the concept to verbal interaction. In particular, we will introduce face threatening and face saving actions or strategies as part of verbal interactions.

3 Quantitative Data Analysis

Using corpora of the "Digitales Wörterbuch der deutschen Sprache" (DWDS, www.dwds.de, cf. Geyken et al. 2017) and the corpus collection "Deutsches Referenzkorpus" (DeReKo) at the Leibniz-Institute for German language (IDS), we looked at co-occurrences of *ehrlich* with some other adverbs. As a result of a first investigation of these co-occurrence patterns, we decided to focus on four of them: *aber ehrlich*, *also ehrlich*, *ganz ehrlich* and *mal ehrlich*.

Table 1 shows the corpora that we have consulted for this study. We used the corpora of the DWDS via the query engine DWDS/DDC, the corpora of the DeReKo via CosmasIIweb (https://cosmas2.ids-mannheim.de/cosmas2-web/faces/investigation/queryString.xhtml) and the "Forschungs- und Lehrkorpus Gesprochenes Deutsch" (FOLK) via the "Datenbank für Gesprochenes Deutsch" (DGD, https://dgd.ids-mannheim.de). For the formulation of our corpus queries, we included characteristics of interactive units that appear in syntactically isolated position. The patterns occur either as a complete sentence or in front of a sentence, followed by a delimiter (comma, colon etc.). The respective search patterns are: a) for DWDS/DDC: `"@Aber WITH $.=0 @ehrlich $p={'$,' '$.' '$:'}"` and b) for COSMASII: `(aber /+1w,Max (ehrlich /0w,Max ,)) or ((aber /+1w,Max (ehrlich /0w,Max .)) or (aber /+1w,Max (ehrlich /0w,Max :))).`

Table 1: Description of the corpora that have been used for this study, size (column 2) in million tokens.

Name and abbreviation	Size	Description	Documentation
Reference and Newspaper corpora (R/N)	2993	A collection of freely available news and reference corpora = written mode/monologic communication style	https://www.dwds.de/d/korpora/dwdsxl
Webmonitor (WM)	3701	An up-to-date collection of web sources of various kinds = written mode/monologic	https://www.dwds.de/d/korpora/webmonitor
Wikipedia Discussion pages (WDD19)	416	A collection of Wikipedia discussion pages = written mode/dialogic	https://www.ids-mannheim.de/digspra/kl/projekte/korpora/archiv/wp/
Blogs (B)	107	A corpus of blogs = towards written mode/slightly dialogic	https://zwei.dwds.de/d/korpora/blogs
Movie Subtitles (MST)	75	A collection of movie subtitles = scripted spoken mode/dialogic	https://zwei.dwds.de/d/korpora/untertitel
Forschungs- und Lehrkorpus Gesprochenes Deutsch (FOLK)	3	A collection of speech transcripts = spoken/dialogic	https://agd.ids-mannheim.de/folk.shtml

The corpora cover a large spectrum regarding the medium/mode (written vs. spoken), as well as communication style (monologic vs. dialogic). The Wikipedia Discussion pages corpus, as well as the Blogs corpus, represent the genre of computer-mediated communication with its unique combination of written medium and (partially) dialogic communication style (for this concept, cf. Beißwenger 2016; Herzberg 2022: 42–44). On the other hand, the FOLK corpus, though rather small, represents authentic spoken language.

Table 2 shows the normalized frequencies of the four patterns over the six corpora that are listed in Table 1.

Table 2: Normalized frequencies of the four patterns over the six corpora (parts per million).

Pattern	R/N	WM	WDD19	B	MST	FOLK
Aber ehrlich 'but to be honest'	0,006	0,027	0,18	0,21	0,27	2,42
Also ehrlich 'honestly'	0,003	0,008	0,29	0,18	1,03	1,82
Ganz ehrlich 'quite honestly'	0,053	0,611	1,02	2,654	3,171	7,87
Mal ehrlich 'to be honest'	0,023	0,21	2,91	1,52	0,98	2,72

To guarantee comparability, figures in this table are given as "parts per million" (ppm). According to this, the phrase *Mal ehrlich* appears roughly once per million words in the MST corpus. The figures of the FOLK corpus should be analysed with care. Firstly, the corpus is very small in comparison to the other corpora. Secondly, there are no punctuation signs in transcripts of spoken utterances. We therefore decided to broaden the query (i.e. a query that does not include punctuation) and in return, received more false positives, corpus citations that are not relevant for our investigations and that had to be removed from the data sample. Finally, we obtained ~50 true positives for *ganz ehrlich* and fewer than 20 true positives for the other patterns from the FOLK corpus.

The order of the corpora/columns in Table 2 is from written/monologic to spoken/dialogic. It can be derived from the data that there is a kind of "invisible borderline" that separates the first two corpora (columns 2 and 3) from the rest (columns 4–7). This nicely matches our intuition that these patterns are typical for a dialogic communication style, regardless of the medium. As you will see from the examples that are presented in the following section, even in the typical newspaper text, many occurrences are of a dialogic nature as they are part of direct or reported speech.

One goal of this cross-corpus quantitative analysis was to select (and present in this paper) prototypical examples of the use of these phrases as interactional units as a basis for the qualitative analysis, in other words: to switch from distant reading to close reading.

4 Qualitative Analysis – Presentation and Discussion of examples

In the following, we will present two or three examples for each pattern from the data and a qualitative interpretation of each one. These examples are, in our opinion, prototypical for the use of these phrases. From there, we will derive a description of the function(s) of each interactive unit.

Interactive units of the here described type instantiate three types of relations, two of them at textual level, the third at discourse level:

1. a backward relation (directed to preceding sentences or to sentences in the broader context of the conversation);
2. a forward relation to an assertion or argument of the speaker/writer. The interactive unit sets the tone in which the following statement should be perceived by the interaction partner(s).

3. a reference to the assumed perception of the object of the discourse of the interaction partner(s). The interactive unit can be seen as a kind of "invitation" to recalibrate this perception of the discourse object.

With the use of these (as well as many other) interactive units, speakers establish a link between a preceding proposition (of the partner in the dialogue or discussion) and their own response to that proposition. Therefore, these interactive units are of the responsive type. We will deliberately include as much context as needed in each of the following examples to highlight the specific role and function of the interactive unit.

With the following examples we will show and illustrate the two main functions of these responsive interactive units:

1. They can be used to steer a conversation in a certain direction (a direction that is possibly not expected by the other participant(s), e.g. in example 2)
2. They can be used to express the attitude of a speaker to previously uttered propositions and to express an interpersonal relation (see examples 6 and 9).

While the first function is common for all four patterns, they differ in the second function. We will show this in the following.

4.1 *Ganz ehrlich*

We will present three examples for the use of *ganz ehrlich* as an interactive unit. Example 2 is part of an interview for a newspaper.

(2) *Haben Sie früher auch in der letzten Reihe geknutscht, oder war das Kino für Sie dafür zu unromantisch?* ***Ganz ehrlich****? Ich habe früher auch im Kino rumgemacht.*
'Did you once use the back row for smooching, or was the movie theater too unromantic for you? Honestly? I used to make out at the movies too.'
(R/N, Berliner Zeitung, 29.12.2005)

In this example, the speaker makes a confession of what he has done in his earlier days. The speaker is looking for the interviewer's understanding and tolerance for his behaviour. The function of the interactive unit can be interpreted as a face saving action. Also, the rest of the answer maintains an atmosphere of familiarity, e.g. the informal register of the verb *rummachen* (*'make out'*).

(3) *Häufig sagen mir bis dahin unbekannte Menschen, das sei aber ein schöner Name.* ***Ganz ehrlich****: tut jedes Mal ein bisschen gut. Viele fragen mich auch, wie ich zu meinem Namen gekommen bin.*
'People I've never met before often tell me that it's a nice name. Honestly, it does me good every time. Many people also ask me how I got my name.'
(WM: Business Insider, 2024-02-18)

Example 3 is part of an interview for a newspaper, in which the speaker confesses to the interviewer (and the reading public) that he likes to be flattered for his interesting first name. As demonstrated in example 2, this can be interpreted as a face saving action in favour of the speaker himself.

(4) *Weniger Lehrer, mehr Schüler.* ***Ganz ehrlich****, das ist kein zukunftsfittes Bildungssystem. Das sind keine Klassen, wie wir sie uns wünschen, Herr Finanzminister!*
'Fewer teachers, more pupils. Honestly, that is not an education system fit for the future. These are not the classes we want, Mr. Finance Minister!'
(R/N: Rede von Andreas Schieder, 22.03.2018)

In example 4, a formal speech of a politician, the speaker frankly rejects a proposal made by the finance minister, presumably a political opponent. The proposition that is referred to is introduced by the speaker himself. The addressee of this face threatening action might be present or not. In any way, he is not able to respond directly.

Ganz ehrlich is not only the most frequent of the four patterns, but also the one with the largest functional variety.

Firstly, it can be used literally, where *ganz* is used to intensify the modified adjective, *ehrlich*, as demonstrated in the following example:

(5) *Der ist großartig, der Bus.*
Ganz ehrlich*, er gefällt dir?*
Ja, ich liebe ihn
'It's great, the bus.
Honestly, you like it?
Yes, I love it'
(MST: Californication – I'll Lay My Monsters Down, 2013)

The adjective *ehrlich* is semantically (maximally) charged insofar that a mode of complete honesty is asked for. This can be seen as the basic sense of this pattern, whereas in the other senses or usages, the phrase has become semantically opaque.

Secondly, it can be used to introduce a personal confession that might not be what is expected by the dialogue partner, very often an interviewer, see examples 2 and 3 above. If used in this function, it would often be, but not always, followed by a question mark (example 2) or a colon (example 3).

Thirdly, it can be used as an interactive unit that marks (complete) disagreement with what has been said before or with what is currently at issue. Example 4 above and example 6 are clear cases. If used in this function, the phrase would typically be followed by a comma (examples 4 and 6).

(6) ***Ganz ehrlich,*** *ich habe es wirklich satt, mich hier mit IP-Adressen rumzuschlagen, die fortwährend den Artikel fälschen. Zum kommentarlos zurückgesetzten Edit gebe ich hier eine Quelle an. Das ist das letzte Mal, dass ich wegen zigfach belegter Tatsachen diskutiere. Google ist Dein Freund und ein Buch zu lesen würde auch einmal nicht schaden.*
‘Honestly, I’m really tired of dealing with IP addresses that constantly falsify the article. I’ll provide a source for the edit that was reset without comment. This is the last time I discuss facts that have been proven umpteen times over. Google is your friend and reading a book wouldn’t hurt either’
(WDD19/B0070.77872 Diskussion:Bayernpartei/Archiv/1)

In these two examples (4 and 6), *ganz ehrlich* opens and simultaneously marks dissent. By using honesty as a strategy of courtesy and a social norm, the speaker intends to maintain social norms in a situation of disagreement and potential conflict in this particular interaction.

The propositions in examples 4 and 6 are face threatening actions. It is characteristic that in the context in which these propositions have been made, the addressee of this action is not present or at least cannot respond directly. *Ganz ehrlich* can therefore be interpreted to down tone the respective proposition(s) by reference to shared social norms (of courtesy etc.).

4.2 *Aber ehrlich*

In the following, we will present two examples for the use of *aber ehrlich* as an interactive unit, one from a Wikipedia discussion page and one from a newspaper. Example 8 is an instance of reported speech, something that can be found frequently in newspapers. The originally spoken utterance is transformed into the written medium. One result of this transformation is the punctuation that would not occur in a faithful transcription of a spoken utterance, a comma in example 8.

(7) *Du betonst zu recht die Teamarbeit hier; ja, jeder kann und darf diesen Artikel verbessern.* ***Aber ehrlich:*** *Wenn dein Tonfall hier symptomatisch für deine Arbeits- und Argumentationsweise ist, prophezeie ich dir keine lange Zukunft hier.*
'You rightly so emphasize teamwork here; yes, everyone can and may improve this article. But honestly, if your tone of voice here is symptomatic of the way you work and argue, I don't predict a long future for you here.'
(WDD19/D0100.30875 Diskussion:Dürkopp Typ P 16.)

In example 7, the speaker initially agrees with the discussion partner but continues with criticising his/her style of discussion. The phrase *aber ehrlich* opens a face threatening action. The phrase also marks the transition from courtesy to conflict.

(8) *Auf die Frage, ob es ihn nicht störe, dass dieser Golfstaat die LGBT+-Symbole aus den Stadien und Straßen verbannt hat, sagte er: „Man muss anerkennen, dass Katar diese WM sehr gut organisiert hat. (...) Aber es stimmt, es gibt (hier) noch vieles zu regeln, es gibt viele Länder, wo noch vieles zu regeln ist.* ***Aber ehrlich****, seien wir jetzt erst mal glücklich.*
'When asked whether it didn't bother him that this Gulf state had banned LGBT+ symbols from the stadiums and streets, he said: "You have to acknowledge that Qatar has organized this World Cup very well. (...) But it's true, there is still a lot to regulate (here), there are many countries where there is still a lot to regulate. But honestly, let's be happy for now.'
(R/N: WM-Euphorie in Frankreich: Liebe zu zwei Teams. TAZ Verlags- und Vertriebs GmbH, 2022-12-15)

In this example, a Moroccan soccer player characterizes the sceptical remark of an interviewer as being irrelevant in the situation of just having won a game and refuses to answer it. The interactive unit marks the rhetorical move from accepting the matters that are mentioned by the interviewer to rejecting them as irrelevant (a face threatening action). The soccer player explicitly seeks the understanding of the interaction partner, the interviewer, by using the inclusive *wir* ('we').

Aber ehrlich opens a statement of the participant that is face threatening for the dialogue partner and not very polite. *Aber ehrlich* thus not only serves as a link to a previous proposition of the discussion partner, but also introduces a kind of face saving strategy: the (admittedly) face threatening statement that follows the interactive unit is mitigated by it in a way of maintaining a respectful tone of communication (example 8). Consequently, we can assign the function of establishing or maintaining an atmosphere of respect as the core function of this phrase.

In the phrase *aber ehrlich*, the word *aber* (`'but'`) preserves the contrastive function that it has if used as a subordinate conjunction.

4.3 *Also ehrlich*

In the following, we present two examples for the use of *also ehrlich* as an interactive unit, one from a Wikipedia discussion page and one from (the transcript of) a film dialogue.

(9) *Bleibt die Aussage, der Artikel sei oberflächlich und mit nicht verarbeiteter Primär- und Sekundärliteratur vollgestopft.* ***Also ehrlich:*** *Wenn man sich nicht die Mühe macht, Probleme wirklich herauszuarbeiten und zunächst auf der Artikel-Disk zur Diskussion zu stellen, dann erwarte ich wenigstens, dass man sich mit der Artikel-Historie auseinandersetzt und herauszufinden versucht, wer die Autoren waren, wie deren Vorgehensweise zu beurteilen ist und was das über die Qualität des Artikels aussagt.*
'What remains is the statement that the article is superficial and crammed with unprocessed primary and secondary literature. Honestly: If you don't make the effort to really work out problems and first put them up for discussion on the article disk, then I at least expect you to deal with the history of the article and try to find out who the authors were, how their approach is to be judged and what that says about the quality of the article.'
(WDD19/A0055.03746 Diskussion:Atlantis/Archiv/012)

In example 9, the speaker rejects the criticism that has been uttered by the other participant. The face threatening action aims at the competence of the interaction partner, which is put into question. Along with the competence, the right of the interactive partner to utter criticism is challenged.

(10) *Ich weiß genau, wovon ich rede.* ***Also ehrlich,*** *diese Bemerkung war sexistischer als alles, was ich von Dir gehört hab, seit wir hier sind.*
'I know exactly what I'm talking about. Honestly, that comment was more sexist than anything I've heard from you since we've been here.'
(MST: Baby Shower, 2011)

In example 10, the speaker bluntly criticizes a remark of the interaction partner. This remark is challenged as being in stark contrast to the speaker's expectations as well as the (implicit) social norm. This criticism is a face threatening action that is even intensified by the interactive unit.

With *also ehrlich*, a previous opinion, proposal etc. is rejected and is in many cases contrasted with the opinion, proposal etc. that the speaker claims to be the (more) appropriate one. The latter is the core of the proposition that follows the initial phrase. *Also ehrlich* is the most blunt and direct reaction to the challenged proposal, it intensifies the face threatening function of the following proposition. There is an undertone of indignation connected with that impression.

4.4 *Mal ehrlich*

In the following, we present three examples for the use of *mal ehrlich* as an interactive unit, one from a Wikipedia discussion page, one from (the transcript of) a film dialogue (scripted speech). The third is a transcript of an authentically spoken dialogue.

(11) *Dieser Abschnitt sollte komplett gelöscht werden!* ***Mal ehrlich****: ist es wirklich enzyklopädisch interessant, dass es in Altena eine Firma für"Flies- und Wischtücher" gibt ? Ich finde es nur lächerlich.*
'This section should be deleted completely! Honestly: is it really encyclopaedically interesting that there is a company for "tile and wiping cloths" in Altena? I just find it ridiculous.'
(WDD19: Erledigt. -- Bubo 23481; 23:17, 26. Jan. 2007 (CET) GrummelMC 11:45, 17. Mai 2007 (CEST) 2019)

In example 11, the speaker enforces his own request to remove a passage from a Wikipedia article. He (or she) does so by (rhetorically) challenging the relevance. This is face threatening to the interaction partner who proposed to add this passage. The pure proposition might be regarded as being a face threat. The interactive unit down tones this threat by inviting the interaction partner to reconsider his/her proposal.

(12) *Die Gastfreundlichkeit unseres Volkes wird ausgenutzt, und wir haben es zugelassen.* ***Mal ehrlich****, wie oft seid ihr vor Wut an die Decke gegangen, wenn ihr Politiker im Fernsehen seht, die vormittags von Integration reden und wie wichtig es sei, unsere neuen Nachbarn zu unterstützen, die es so schwer haben, aber uns drücken sie dann am Nachmittag eine Steuererhöhung rein.*
'The hospitality of our people is being exploited and we have allowed it to happen.Honestly, how many times have you gone ballistic with rage when you see politicians on TV talking about integration in the morning and how important it is to support our new neighbours who are having such a hard time, but then they push a tax increase on us in the afternoon.'
(MST: Alacrán enamorado, 2013)

In example 12, the speaker elaborates the attitude of the interaction partner and poses the rhetorical question of when they have experienced political decisions that ignited their rage. In this conversation, the interactive unit is used to ask for a stronger support of the speaker's xenophobic attitude (that has been mentioned before) and can be seen as an invitation to recalibrate the attitude towards the matters that are at issue.

(13)	*0239*	*AF*	*(ah/ja) sieh[t ma ja]*
	0240	*IR*	*[nee also* ***jetz] ma ehrlich*** *kann er sich das leisten eigentlich*
	0241		(0.91)
	0242	*GW*	*hm*
	0239	*AF*	*(ah/yes) you can see that]*
	0240	*IR*	*[no, so now] honestly, can he actually afford it*
	0241		*(0.91)*
	0242	*GW*	*hm*

(transcript FOLK_E_00287_SE_01_T_02)

In example 13, the speaker utters his doubts whether another person – who is probably not a participant in the conversation – can afford something. Again, this can be considered as an invitation to reconsider the topic that is introduced before (someone having done an expensive transaction).

With the use of *mal ehrlich*, the speaker's proposition typically has the form of a rhetorical question that (indirectly) challenges the proposition that is addressed (as doubtful, useless, superfluous etc.). On the one hand, this phrase is close to the core meaning of *ehrlich*, as it could be rephrased with *be honest, face the facts*. On the other hand, it belongs to the group of constructions that assumes the role of a comment. Imo (2012: 80–83) uses the terms "Projektorkonstruktion" or "Kommentarphrase". We are, however, not aware of an English equivalent for these terms.

Mal ehrlich expresses the mildest form of challenge. That the proposition takes the form of a rhetorical question indicates that it is addressed not only to the other participant of the dialogue, but to a broader audience (example 13). The speaker indirectly asks for approval of his/her position by the audience.

The interactive units that we have presented so far are used to organise the discourse by linking two propositions. The proposition that is referred to might be present and explicitly uttered as part of the conversation, or it might only be cited and referred to by the speaker (see example 2).

Semantically, the phrase signals that a previous proposal or the person who uttered it is challenged. The core proposition of the conversation is typically a face threatening action, and the interactive unit operates on it (intensifying or down toning).

The semantics core of the adjectival part *ehrlich* is devoid in such constructions. The phrase conveys a particular attitude of the speaker (in short: being honest) or an indirect request to the dialogue partner to recalibrate the view that has been expressed before. They realise a meta-pragmatic framing of the proposition that corresponds well with the syntactically non-integrated position – typically the sentence initial position.

Most of these interactive units can be seen as part of a face threatening or face saving action of the speaker. As such, it establishes a particular relation between the speaker and the addressee(s). That goes beyond the semantic content of the proposition that the interactive unit refers to. In general, the validity and coherence with a discursive world that has been established by the interacting dialogue partners is at stake here.

There are, of course, other, less prototypical examples with this phrase. In the following, we will show this with the phrase *mal ehrlich*. In this example, the phrase is addressed to a statement of the speaker himself (or herself). The primary function is to put more emphasis to this proposition.

(14) *Es ist nichts los in Rostock.* ***Mal ehrlich****, das Leben pulsiert nicht gerade in den Straßen.*
'Nothing happens in (city of) Rostock. Really, life on the streets is all but vibrating.'
(B: Kunstnacht in der östlichen Altstadt. Heuler – Online-Ausgabe Des Studierendenmagazin In Rostock, ~2011-05-11)

5 Conclusion: lessons learned so far and future applications

With *ehrlich*, we have examined one lexical unit that is frequently and recurrently being used, in combination with other (modal) adverbs, in dialogic functions. The key word of the phrase(s) is becoming more and more devoid of its core meaning(s), it can, in some cases, be substituted with other words (e.g. *aber echt, echt mal* en: 'really, for real') while the main function(s) of the phrase(s) do not differ much. All of these unit(s) lose semantic content while gaining pragmatic force.

5.1 Lessons learned

In the following, we will present two insights that we obtained during the planning of our experiments and the data analysis.

Firstly, it turned out to be a good decision to select a wider range of corpora, with different media (written, spoken) and communication styles (monologic, dialogic). Spoken language, dialogic corpora might be the first choice for our subject of investigation. However, they are still very small nowadays, the relevant data are sparse and might not qualify for quantitative analyses. Written corpora, which are much larger, also contain dialogical sequences, e.g. in the form of reported speech. Table 1 above shows that, while interactive units are more typical for spoken language, the larger written corpora provide us with samples that are large enough to generate reliable quantitative results.

Secondly, we considered that interactive units typically occur in syntactically isolated positions. The search queries were designed accordingly. Still, we have to be aware of false negatives. In our studies, this can be examples which are otherwise relevant but are missing something, e.g. the closing punctuation sign (comma, colon ...). For our analysis of the FOLK corpus of spoken language, we have designed our queries differently, leaving out the closing punctuation signs. Such signs do not occur in transcripts of spoken language. The downside of this approach is that it results in a high number of false positives, which must then be manually removed. Nevertheless, that step was not too time-consuming.

5.2 Future research and applications

In future research, we will investigate whether these interactive units are fixed, invariably expressions or if they allow variation and/or phrase internal extension. We investigated this question with the four pattern that we analysed above: *aber ehrlich, also ehrlich, mal ehrlich, ganz ehrlich.*

We queried some of the corpora for positional variation and possible extensions. The results are listed in Table 3. We present the absolute numbers of occurrences over all corpora. A more precise analysis, listing the distribution over the corpora, is not necessary and can be left to further studies.

Table 3: Variation and extension, findings from the corpora.

	Pattern	R/N	WM	WDD19	B	MST
1	Ehrlich mal	1	1	20	0	0
2	Ganz ehrlich mal	0	3	1	0	0
3	Also ehrlich mal	0	1	1	1	1
4	Also mal ehrlich	17	12	102	16	4
5	Aber mal ehrlich	128	472	200	93	11
6	Mal ganz ehrlich	18	140	88	43	11
7	Aber ganz ehrlich	25	780	56	44	6
8	Also ganz ehrlich	2	39	46	15	1

The figures in lines 1–3 of Table 3 show that phrase internal variation in the form of permutation of its elements (e.g. *mal ehrlich → ehrlich mal*) is rare or does not occur at all. This finding is in line with our analysis that, as a routine formulae, these patterns are fixed phrases or, in the words of Günthner (2009), 'sediments'.

From the figure in lines 4–8 we can infer that extensions are possible and occur at a (modestly) high frequency. They can be seen as "competing" with the shorter phrases. Their function, in contrast to those shorter phrases, has yet to be determined.

For the patterns that are listed in lines 4–8, we retrieved examples from the corpora. A first look at the resulting excerpts gives us the impression that these extended interactive units cumulate the functions of the corresponding simpler phrases (e.g.: *Aber mal ehrlich* = *Aber ehrlich* + *Mal ehrlich*) – see examples 15 and 16.

(15) *Der Körper verbraucht, sobald er in Bewegung ist, immer gleich viele Kalorien. Kälte lässt uns nur dann mehr Kalorien verbrennen, wenn wir anfangen zu zittern und die Muskeln dadurch in zusätzliche Bewegung kommen.* ***Aber mal ehrlich****: Wer zittert schon beim Sport?*
'The body always burns the same number of calories as soon as it is in motion. Cold only makes us burn more calories when we start to shiver and the muscles start to move more. But let's be honest: who shivers during sport?'
(WM: Verbrennen wir bei Kälte mehr Kalorien? 10 Mythen rund zum Winter. SWR3, 2024-01-11)

In example 15, the relevance of the previous proposition is challenged (indicated by "Aber") and a rhetorical question follows (indicated by "mal", which is the prototypical opener of a rhetorical question, see above, Section 4.4).

(16) *Hab ich gelesen.* ***Aber mal ehrlich:*** *wer weiß am Ende noch, was am Anfang gesagt wurde? Hier wird nicht mehr artikelbezogen diskutiert, sondern hier werden politische Ansichten und Spekulationen über politische Ansichten breitgewalzt, ohne dass das zu einem Ergebnis führen kann.*
'I read it. But let's be honest: who knows at the end what was said at the beginning? This is no longer an article-related discussion, but a place where political views and speculation about political views are being rolled out, without this being able to lead to a result.'
(WDD19/A0079.49026 Diskussion:Alternative für Deutschland/Archiv/011)

In example 16, the process of article production is challenged as being too time-consuming and cumbersome. The means of doing this is a rhetorical question, which is signalled by the word *mal.*

It might also be the case that one of the adverbs does not add to but modify the other part of the phrase (e.g.: *Mal (aber ehrlich),* see example 17).

(17) *Das ideale Mittel gegen Akne – Trotz dieser kleinen Nachteile ist die Zinksalbe ein wirklich vielseitiges Produkt, vor allem weil sie sehr gut verträglich ist. Allerdings sollten Sie keine Wunder von heute auf morgen erwarten, vor allem nicht bei schwerer Akne.* ***Aber mal ehrlich****, ein bisschen Geduld hat noch niemandem geschadet.*
'The ideal remedy for acne – Despite these minor disadvantages, zinc ointment is a really versatile product, mainly because it is very well tolerated. However, you shouldn't expect miracles to happen overnight, especially if you have severe acne. But let's be honest, a little patience never hurt anyone.'
(WM: Zinksalbe gegen Pickel: Schnell und effektiv zu klarer Haut. Arch Media Group, 2024-01-18)

The speaker challenges the attitude of impatience of the interaction partner towards a particular therapy. That might be regarded as face threatening. This threat is down toned by the insertion of the word *mal.*

A deeper investigation into extended patterns should be considered in further research.

With our sample analysis as a starting point, we would like to broaden our view. For future research, we would like to apply the topic of interactive units as well as our approach to analyse them and place them into two different contexts: a) a broader lexical description of such units, e.g. in the context of an established dictionary of contemporary German; b) an application of this lexical field in the classroom, addressing learners of German as a first and second language.

5.2.1 Interactive units as a task for lexicography

Dictionaries of contemporary German should register discursive function(s) of *ehrlich* (these are currently missing, to the best of our knowledge, in all of the larger dictionaries). The appropriate use of interactive units is difficult to grasp for learners of German (both as first and second language). They must be understood well, and their correct use is a sign for a near-native command of the language.

The Digital Dictionary of the German Language (DWDS) has started to add such elements as independent entries, see for example: example: 1) https://www.dwds.de/wb/aber%20hallo and 2) https://www.dwds.de/wb/i%20wo. However, this has not yet been done systematically. The first step of this task would be to establish a list of such multi-word lexical units.

An important first step is therefore to find a way how to create an inventory of interactive units. Can we find further bigrams, trigrams etc. of words that assume the same functional roles, i.e. as interactive (responsive) units? The collection of interactive units in corpora is not an easy task.

The application of well-established methods and tools for the detection of collocational patterns proved not to be appropriate for this particular task. Firstly, both parts (in the case of binary constructions) of interactive units are themselves frequent and highly ambiguous. Secondly, the parts of interactive units are adjacent, while the parts of collocations are not (in most of the cases). Thirdly, statistical methods such as Mutual information and LogDice are not sensitive to combinations of highly frequent words. A look at the DWDS's *Word Profile* proves these assumptions to be correct. This tool lists only *mal ehrlich* as significant co-occurrence for the word *ehrlich*. In addition, such statistics produce too many false positives: significant co-occurrences which are irrelevant for our purposes.

A promising alternative is pattern-based analysis. The idea is to break down the characteristics of interactive units to be syntactically isolated into search queries on the corpora using their query languages. In DWDS/DDC for the corpora of the DWDS, we can formulate the search query "`$p=ADV WITH $.=0 $p=ADJ* $p={'$,' '$.'}`" – to be interpreted as "retrieve patterns of adverb in sentence-initial position, followed by an adjective followed by a clause or sentence delimiter (comma, semi-colon, full stop etc.)”. We will surely get many false positives, but sorting the data by their frequency of occurrence will help to find the interesting patterns. The DWDS/’DDC query *COUNT ("$p=ADV WITH $.=0 $p=ADJ* $p={'$,' '$.'}") #BY[$w, $w+1] #DESC_COUNT* will sort the patterns by their frequency of occurrence. In response to a remark of one of the reviewers, we would like to point out that our search queries rely on the part-of-speech annotation of the underlying corpora. The word *aber* is classified, in these corpora, either as a conjunction or as an adverb. One might challenge the grammatical appropriateness of such a classification and the underlying scheme, i.e. the Stuttgart-Tübingen Tagset (STTS) for written text. However, it does not influence the recall of the retrieval negatively.

As a test case for our approach, we accessed the Reference and Newspaper Corpus (R/N, abbreviations taken from Table 1), the blogs corpus (B) and the Movie Subtitle Corpus (MST) with these search queries. In Tables 4–6, we present the most frequent patterns in these corpora, together with their absolute frequency.

Table 4: Syntactically isolated ADV-ADJ chunks in the reference and newspaper corpus (the seven most frequent patterns).

1.	12115	Sehr	richtig
2.	11669	Sehr	gut
3.	8378	Bitte	schön
4.	5598	Sehr	wahr
5.	4311	Schon	gut
6.	3471	Also	gut
7.	2270	Nun	gut

Table 5: Syntactically isolated ADV-ADJ chunks in the blogs corpus (the five most frequent patterns).

1.	594	Sehr	schön
2.	560	Nun	gut
3.	485	Ganz	einfach
4.	284	Ganz	ehrlich
5.	243	Sehr	gut

Table 6: Syntactically isolated ADV-ADJ chunks in the Movie Subtitle Corpus (the eight most frequent patterns).

1.	4208	Schon	gut
2.	3173	Sehr	gut
3.	3061	Also	gut
4.	2099	Ganz	ruhig
5.	934	Sehr	schön
6.	754	Hier	lang
7.	663	Ganz	genau
8.	649	Nun	gut

In all of the corpora we have queried, the phrase *nun gut* ('well then') appears prominently (at rank 3, 7 and 8 respective). In the following, we will focus on this prominent pattern.

This interactive unit seems to initiate (and signal) a change of topic, and it signals an acceptance, a positive attitude towards what has been talked about before. Besides, many examples have a tone of resignation.

(18) *Aber wenig später war ich an meiner Foto-Location angekommen und hatte nur noch eine Sorge: wo sind denn bitte die Wolken hin, die vorhin noch geflogen sind? Ein Blick in die andere Richtung und ein "na toll " entgleiste mir.* ***Nun gut****, hab ja kaum noch Zeit und diese Szene muss jetzt aufgenommen werden, dann eben auch ohne Wolken.*
'But a little later I arrived at my photo location and only had one worry: where had the clouds gone that were still flying earlier? A glance in the other direction and a "great" escaped me. Well, there's hardly any time left and this scene has to be photographed now, even without clouds.'
(Blogs: splitt-it.de, 2023-06-29)

Corpus queries of this kind and complexity are probably not easy to reproduce on larger corpus collections and their respective search engines. We therefore recommend performing the first exploratory step on the smaller DWDS corpora and to follow this up with more detailed data collection requests afterwards.

5.2.2 Interactive units as a topic in the classroom

Furthermore, responsive interactive units can be used in teaching German as first and second language. They can serve to illustrate the function of such linguistic entities (discourse markers, in general) to maintain an atmosphere of politeness and respect even in confronting situations (face saving). This is particularly important in digitally mediated communication where the participants do not see or even know each other. We can imagine to present and analyze such formulae as *mal ehrlich* in connection with types of argumentation, in particular such with indirect or normative arguments (cf. Schurf and Wagener 2016: 303). Teachers can also introduce them as a part of a toolkit of "modalizers" (cf. https://de.frwiki.wiki/wiki/Modalisateur) in the context of teaching/learning strategies of argumentation. They can raise awareness for the special, non-propositional function of these elements that is in many cases overlooked or even misinterpreted by students. In particular, the examples from the Wikipedia corpus provide illustrative material for this teaching goal (for example Hug 2017). Such teaching models are in the spirit of a didactic move in Germany towards the integration of (corpora of) authentic language into the classroom. In Germany, on the federal level, such guidelines are called "Bildungsstandards". To learn more about the current discussion on the national level in Germany cf. https://www.kmk.org/themen/qualitaetssicherung-in-schulen/bildungsstandards.html. It is also conceivable that the teacher generates data or teaching material from the corpora and analyses it in class with the learners. Contrasting examples with and without these patterns could be one way of analyzing the effect of such interactive units.

As a result of such analyses, students are able, after having investigated authentic examples with these phrases, to understand the strategic reference to politeness as a concept that underlies or frames this type of discourse, and, more generally, as a reference to a socially shared and accepted value that underlies this kind of discourse.

In addition, German lessons at school can focus more on the word *ehrlich* itself by examining its (changed) semantics in such contexts and its relationship to other words, as we have also focused on here. Then, for example, the functional contribution of intensifiers such as *ganz* can form one subject of the lesson.

References

Auer, Peter. 2021. Genau! Der auto-reflexive Dialog als Motor der Entwicklung von Diskursmarkern. In Beate Weidner, Katharina König, Wolfgang Imo & Lars Wegner (eds). 2021. *Verfestigungen in der Interaktion. Konstruktionen, sequenzielle Muster, kommunikative Gattungen*, 263–294. Berlin & Boston: De Gruyter.

Beißwenger, Michael. 2016. Praktiken in der internetbasierten Kommunikation. In Arnulf Deppermann, Helmuth Feilke & Angelika Linke (eds.), *Sprachliche und kommunikative Praktiken*, 279–311. Berlin & Boston: De Gruyter.

Brown, Penelope & Stepen C. Levinson. 1987. *Politeness: Some universals in language usage.* Vol. 4. Cambridge : Cambridge University Press.

Couper-Kuhlen, Elizabeth & Margret Selting. 2001. *Studies in Interactional Linguistics*. Amsterdam: John Benjamins.

Geyken, Alexander, Adrien Barbaresi, Jörg Didakowski, Bryan Jurish, Frank Wiegand & Lothar Lemnitzer. 2017. Die Korpusplattform des „Digitalen Wörterbuchs der deutschen Sprache" (DWDS). *Zeitschrift für germanistische Linguistik* 45 (2). 327–344.

Günthner, Susanne. 2009. Konstruktionen in der kommunikativen Praxis. Zur Notwendigkeit einer interaktionalen Anreicherung konstruktionsgrammatischer Ansätze. *Zeitschrift für germanistische Linguistik* 37 (3). 402–426.

Helmer, Henrike & Arnulf Deppermann. 2017. ICH WEIß NICHT zwischen Assertion und Diskursmarker: Verwendungsspektren eines Ausdrucks und Überlegungen zu Kriterien für Diskursmarker. In Hardarik Blühdorn, Arnulf Deppermann, Henrike Helmer, Thomas Spranz-Fogasy (eds.), *Diskursmarker im Deutschen. Reflexionen und Analysen*, 131–156. Göttingen: Verlag für Gesprächsforschung.

Hug, Michael. 2017. „Es sollte vielleicht ..." – Modalisieren beim argumentativen Schreiben. *Praxis Deutsch* 262. 50–59.

Imo, W. 2012. Wortart Diskursmarker?. In Björn Rothstein (ed.). *Nicht-flektierende Wortarten*. Berlin & Boston: De Gruyter, pp. 48–88

Imo, Wolfgang 2013. *Sprache-in-Interaktion: Analysemethoden und Untersuchungsfelder*. Berlin & Boston: De Gruyter.

Imo, Wolfgang & Jens Philipp Lanwer. 2019. *Interaktionale Linguistik. Eine Einführung*. Heidelberg: Springer Verlag.

Kunkel-Razum, Kathrin & Dudenredaktion. 2005. *Duden Band 4: Die Grammatik*. Mannheim: Bibliographisches Institut & F. A. Brockhaus AG.

Lemnitzer, Lothar & Nils Diewald. 2022. Abfrage und Analyse von Korpusbelegen. In Michael Beißwenger, Lothar Lemnitzer & Carolin Müller-Spitzer. *Forschen in der Linguistik. Eine Methodeneinführung für das Germanistik-Studium*, 374–390. Stuttgart: utb Fink.

Lindström, Jan. 2009. Interactional Linguistics. In Sigurd D'hondt, Jan-Ola Östman, J.A. & Jef Verschueren (eds.), *The pragmatics of interaction*, 96–103. Amsterdam: John Benjamins.

Schurf, Bernd & Andrea Wagener. 2016. *Texte, Themen und Strukturen. Deutschbuch für die Oberstufe. Nordrhein-Westfalen*. Berlin: Cornelsen.

Selting, Margret & Couper-Kuhlen, Elizabeth. 2000. Argumente für die Entwicklung einer ‚interaktionalen Linguistik'. *Gesprächsforschung – Online-Zeitschrift zur verbalen Interaktion* 1, 76–95.

Stoltenburg, Benjamin. 2009. Was wir sagen, wenn wir es „ehrlich" sagen... Äußerungskommentierende Formeln bei Stellungnahmen am Beispiel von „ehrlich gesagt". In Susanne Günthner & Jörg Bücker (eds.), *Grammatik im Gespräch*, 249–280. Berlin & Boston: De Gruyter.

Storrer, Angelika & Laura Herzberg. 2022. Alles okay! Korpusgestützte Untersuchungen zum Internationalismus OKAY. In Michael Beißwenger, Lothar Lemnitzer & Carolin Müller-Spitzer. *Forschen in der Linguistik. Eine Methodeneinführung für das Germanistik-Studium*, 37–59. Stuttgart: utb Fink.

Torres Cajo, Sarah. 2017. „das is SO lächerlich; ohne SCHEISS jetz ma" – Zur affektiven Äußerungsmodalisierung durch *ohne Scheiß*-Konstruktionen im gesprochenen Deutsch. *Gesprächsforschung* 18. 223–240.

Wich-Reif, Claudia. 2019. „Ehrlich gesagt" und Verwandtes – Emotionen und Routineformeln. In Iwona Bartoszewicz, Joanna Szczęk & Artur Tworek (eds.), *Linguistische Treffen in Wrocław, Vol. 16 (II)*, 191–210. Wrocław Neisse. https://doi.org/10.23817/lingtreff.16-14 (last accessed 14 March 2024).

Sarah Steinsiek, Michael Beißwenger, and Yinglei Zang

Digital punctuation from a contrastive perspective: Corpus-based investigations of ellipsis points in German and Chinese messaging interactions

Abstract: In this chapter, we examine the usage of ellipsis points (EP) in German and Chinese messaging interactions. After outlining the characteristics of EP usage in written standard German, we first present the results of a study which describes practices of EP usage in German WhatsApp interactions based on a randomized sample from the MoCoDa2 corpus. We present a typology of pragmatic functions of EP in WhatsApp interactions that has been derived from our findings and discuss how the practices of EP usage in these data originate from traditions of writing that can be found in, for instance, literary prose. In a second step, we adopt our functional typology for the investigation of a dataset of WeChat interactions between Chinese students and describe the commonalities and differences of EP usage in German and Chinese. The goal of this second study is to determine to what extent the EP functions established for German messaging interactions can be utilized for the analysis of EP usage in Chinese as a typologically different language which uses punctuation marks that have been adopted from Western languages. The results of this study add to the knowledge base i) on the adaptation of punctuation marks for interaction-oriented writing in different languages and ii) on practices in CMC discourse from a contrastive perspective.

Keywords: CMC, messaging, German, Chinese, WhatsApp, WeChat, pragmatics, practices, punctuation, ellipsis points

1 Introduction

In the past two decades there has been a growing interest of linguistics in the pragmatics of written interactional discourse in computer-mediated communication

Sarah Steinsiek, University of Duisburg-Essen, e-mail: sarah.steinsiek@uni-due.de
Michael Beißwenger, University of Duisburg-Essen, e-mail: michael.beisswenger@uni-due.de
Yinglei Zang, University of Duisburg-Essen, e-mail: yinglei.zang@stud.uni-due.de

https://doi.org/10.1515/9783111434018-004

(CMC). This chapter adds to the pragmatic knowledge on how interlocutors adapt to the affordances of written interpersonal communication in the digital sphere by an examination of the usage of ellipsis points (henceforth: *EP*) in messaging interactions. The reported work builds on previous research on EP as elements of (1) the standard writing system and (2) in CMC. We compare randomized samples from corpora of messaging interactions for German (WhatsApp) and Chinese (WeChat).

In a first study, we derive a typology of pragmatic functions of EP from the analysis of a randomized sample (N=108) extracted from the Mobile Communication Database (MoCoDa2) and discuss to what extent the "novel" practices of EP usage found in text messaging interactions originate from traditions of writing. In a second study, we investigate whether the typology from study 1 is also suitable for the analysis of a random sample of Chinese WeChat messages (N=107). The results of both studies illustrate the flexibility of the writing tradition to be adapted to new domains of communication and social interaction for two languages from distinct, non-related language families with different writing systems which both have a defined character and a prescriptive norm for marking ellipses in the written standard text.

Our study is motivated by the observation that there seem to be common practices of EP usage across languages and cultures. The introductory Examples (1)–(4)[1] show that "non-canonical" usage of EP can be found in messaging interactions in different Indo-European languages. The practices underlying the EP occurrences in the examples will be defined in Section 5.

The first example is an extract from a German WhatsApp interaction between Muriel and Julia, who are friends and fellow students. Julia offers to proofread one of Muriel's texts, which is why Muriel asks Julia how much time she has. Because Muriel has been struggling to get in the "flow" (see #294), Julia tries to encourage her (see #300). After correcting a typo in a previous message (see #302), Muriel adds the discourse marker "You know..." (see #304), which – in combination with the message-final EP – serves to indicate that Muriel assumes that she doesn't have to further explain why she texted Julia the single letter "K" (see #303). Instead, Julia is "made responsible" to infer that Muriel did not type the letter "K" by mistake but intentionally in order to correct the typing error in "Thanjs".

1 Examples (2), (3) and (4) were donated by speakers of the represented languages, for which we are very grateful.

(1) German (MoCoDa2, #y91fl)

Muriel:	Bis wann kannste heut abend?	**#297 14:01**
translation	‘How much time you got tonight?’	
Julia:	Weiß nicht, die Kinder sind nicht da und ich kann ausschlafen. Ich kann bis 23 Uhr oder so.	**#298 14:14**
translation	‘Don’t know, the kids aren’t home and I can sleep in. Probably until about 11 o‘clock.’	
Julia:	😁	**#299 14:14**
Julia:	Du schaffst das!!! 👊	**#300 14:15**
translation	‘You got this!!! 👊’	
Muriel:	Cool	**#301 15:28**
Muriel:	Danje!!	**#302 15:28**
translation	‘Thanjs!!’	
Muriel:	K	**#303 15:35**
Muriel:	Du weißt schon...	**#304 15:35**
translation	‘You know...’	

Example (2) shows four Polish WhatsApp messages written by a mother to ask her German-speaking niece for help with the translation of a text her son Antoś has to write for school. The first message contains a file, Antoś’s Polish text that needs to be translated into German. In the following messages, his mother formulates her request and explains the problem (see #2, #3). By using message-final EP in message #3, she imitates a self-selection strategy in that she subsequently adds further details on her son’s writing task in message #4. Another possible interpretation is that she is implying that her niece knows why she cannot help her son with the translation (perhaps because of language barriers) and there is no need for further explanation:

(2) Polish

Antoś’s mother:	[Antoś’s Polish text]	**#1 21:01**

Antoś's mother:	Kochana mam do Ciebie ogromna prośbę – czy mogłabyś mi to przetłumaczyć na niemiecki	**#2 21:02**
translation	'My dear, I have a big favor to ask – could you translate this [= Antoś's text sent in the previous message] into German for me'	
Antoś's mother:	Antoś ma na środę opisać swój dzień, a ja mu raczej nie pomogę....	**#3 21:04**
translation	'Antoś is supposed to describe his day until Wednesday and I probably won't be able to help him....'	
Antoś's mother:	To musi być napisane prostymi słowami, Antoś napisał to po polsku, a jutro będziemy próbowali to przetłumaczyć, ale Twoja pomoc byłaby dla nas ogromnym ułatwieniem. Dziękuje Ci bardzo z gory ❤❤❤❤❤❤❤❤❤❤❤	**#4 21:06**
translation	'It's supposed to be written in simple words, Antoś wrote it in Polish, and tomorrow we will try to translate it, but your support would be a great help for us. Thanks in advance' ❤❤❤❤❤❤❤❤❤❤❤	

In Example (3), two French students discuss the attendance policy of a university class they are both attending. After student A states that she hopes not to get into trouble for being absent (see #1), student B expresses some doubts (see #2). The text-medial EP create the impression that student B pauses and ponders after the utterance "I don't know" – subsequently, she objects that the "mcc" (modalités de contrôle des connaissances = knowledge management modalities) says that a "ue" (unité d'enseignement = teaching unit) is in fact confirmed by attendance:

(3) French

Student A:	Ok merci j'espère que ça va pas nous porter préjudice de pas y être	**#1 17:41**
translation	'Ok thanks I hope it won't be that bad for us that we won't be present'	
Student B:	Je sais pas... du coup j'ai vu dans le mcc que l'ue se validait à la presence	**#2 17:42**

translation	'I don't know... I did read in the mcc that the ue is confirmed by attendance'	
Student B:	Mais jsp ce que ça veut dire	**#3 17:42**
translation	'But I don't know what that means'	
Student B:	Si genre 1 absence ça passe ou pas	**#4 17:43**
translation	'Whether like 1 absence is ok or not'	

In Example (4), a Russian student asks her tutor to postpone a scheduled German lesson (see #1). Message #1 contains two EP usages: The first one serves as a means of segmentation, similar to a comma. However, it also creates the impression that the student hesitates to ask her tutor whether they could move the lesson to a later time. The second EP usage, which follows a direct speech act that can be interpreted as a face threatening act[2] (see Brown and Levinson 2007), establishes conditional relevance in that it elicits a response from the recipient. At the same time, it serves to mitigate the potential face threat in combination with the crying face emoji:

(4) Russian

Student:	Здравствуйте! Мне ужасно не удобно...но меня пригласили на день рождение 👉👈 Сможем ли мы позаниматься после 7??... 😭	**#1 21:51**
translation	'Hello! I'm very sorry to ask...but I was invited to a birthday party 👉👈 Could we move the lesson to a time after 7??... 😭'	
Tutor:	Здравствуй! Не проблема) В пол 8?	**#2 21:52**
translation	'Hello! No worries) Half past 7?'	
Student:	Даа!	**#3 21:52**
translation	'Yess!'	

The examples show that EP are used in similar practices across different Indo-European languages, which is most likely due to the fact that punctuation conventions

2 According to Brown and Levinson (2007), a *face-threatening act* is an act or utterance that can potentially be considered inconvenient or even impolite by an addressee and, thus, threatens their positive self-concept (= *positive face*) or autonomy (= *negative face*).

> were first developed in the early Middle Ages for writing Latin. The Scriptures, the liturgy and the heritage of the past were transmitted to the West in Latin texts; Latin became the language of scholarship and diplomacy, and acquired a privileged role in the recording of information. Because many had to learn Latin as a foreign language, there was a need for conventions which made it easier to read. Over the centuries these conventions of written language were gradually augmented and refined, and, where necessary, modified to meet the needs of different European languages (Parkes 1992: 1).

However, examples of these practices can also be found in languages from other language families, such as Sino-Tibetan. Example (5) shows an extract from a Chinese messaging interaction between two friends who are discussing their afternoon plans. After Mengjia asks Tingting whether they are going to go out together or not (see #1), Tingting answers in the negative. The EP consisting of six dots, which separate her response from the interjection "AH" (see #2), serve to weaken the negative reply and to indicate that she carefully considered her decision:

(5) Chinese (WeChat database)[3]

	Mengjia:	我们还出去嘛不出去我就下午再洗澡了🤣	**#1 09:44**
	□□□	We still go out question particle not go out I thus afternoon then shower LE[4]	
	~	'Are we going out? If not, I'll wait until this afternoon to take a shower'	
	Tingting:	诶……我猜，可能，不出去	**#2 11:32**
	□□□	Particle……I guess, maybe, not go out LE	
	~	'Ah……I guess, maybe, we won't go out anymore'	

Unlike the examples of Indo-European languages discussed above – German, Polish, French, and Russian, which are synthetic/fusional languages – Chinese is an isolating language with a unique writing system (see Section 3.2). However, since ellipsis points in Chinese were adopted from Western languages (see Guo 2006: 140), the question arises whether there is empirical evidence that the previously described practices are also common in languages from other language families. Thus, we aim to explore how EP are used in Chinese. The research questions and methods will be detailed in Section 4.

3 Examples from Chinese CMC are presented with a morpheme-by-morpheme translation (□□□) as well as a rough translation (~).

4 LE marks the change of an action or a state.

2 Related work

In the past years there has been increasing research interest in the pragmatics of CMC (see e.g. Herring, Stein and Virtanen 2013; Meier-Vieracker et al. 2023) with a special focus on practices of adapting the resources of the writing system to the requirements of sequential interaction (see e.g. Beißwenger 2016; Beißwenger 2020; Androutsopoulos and Busch 2020). Furthermore, the recently published German handbook on language and digital communication (Androutsopoulos and Vogel 2024) covers a range of articles that summarize the research on the pragmatics of CMC.

In this research context, EP – as an element of the contemporary orthographic standard with a history that traces back to practices of adapting the writing system for the mimetic representation of spoken language – can be considered a resource that is downright predestined for the requirements of written interactional discourse (see Section 3.1).

Androutsopoulos (2020) gives a detailed overview and critical appraisal of the international state of research on the use of EP in CMC. In our own work, we build on the examination of EP presented in Androutsopoulos's paper. The author expands on the functional typology of EP suggested by Meibauer (2007). While Meibauer's typology is neither empirically based nor considers written practices in CMC (but only the use of ellipses in "traditional" text genres), Androutsopoulos analyzes 353 Facebook posts by Greek high schoolers and shows that the function of ellipses to indicate omissions (see Meibauer 2007) is of no significance in this type of CMC at all (see Androutsopoulos 2020: 154). Instead, EP in message-final position are used to convey a certain overtone or for implying (see, for instance, Example 1) and those used within posts are a means of text segmentation (see Androutsopoulos 2020: 150; Meibauer refers to this function as *connection;* Example 4). In this sense, they take on syntactic functions similar to other punctuation marks. However, ellipses are more salient, which is why Androutsopoulos (2020: 155) terms them "eine Art Allzweck-Segmentierer" – an "all-purpose remedy" (or universal tool) for segmentation.

In his study on register variation of German middle and high school students, Busch (2021) analyzes WhatsApp chats and shows that ellipses are also used to mitigate face threats, as a means of cohesion, and as a technique for sequential organization/other-selection, i.e. to directly address and elicit input from other interlocutors (see Busch 2021: 391). Busch points out that EP can take on several functions at once (see Busch 2021: 405).

In summary, both Androutsopoulos (2020) and Busch (2021) show that EP serve many different purposes – except for the one purpose that is codified in the official rules of German orthography (see Section 3.1): to signal the omission of words or text components. Building on the work of Androutsopoulos and Busch, Beißwenger and Steinsiek (2023) derived a typology of EP functions from a study on German WhatsApp chats. This study and the resulting typology are addressed in Sections 4 and 5 of this chapter. Furthermore, the cross-linguistic relevance of the EP functions we describe is examined in Section 6, where we analyze a sample from a corpus of Chinese WeChat interactions.

3 Ellipses in written standard language: the case of German and Chinese

Ellipses are a very interesting research topic as they provide insight into how devices of (standard) written language are adapted for the use in written interactional discourse. They are genuinely a feature of written language: there is no equivalent in spoken language and they cannot be verbalized, only paraphrased, for example as "dot, dot, dot".

3.1 Ellipses in the German writing system

The functions and use of EP in the German writing system are well-researched. The official standard of German orthography[5] provides a codified norm for their use:

> § 99 Mit drei Punkten (Auslassungspunkten) zeigt man an, dass in einem Wort, Satz oder Text Teile ausgelassen worden sind. [Ellipsis points are to be used to indicate that elements of words, sentences or texts have been omitted.] (STANDARD-DE 2018: 100, § 99)

The use of EP according to this rule is common in academic papers to denote omissions within quotations, that is to indicate that e.g. sentences or clauses that are irrelevant to the point being made have been left out.

However, in the official rules of standard German orthography there are also examples such as the following (STANDARD-DE 2018: 101):

(a) Du bist ein E...! Scher dich zum ...! [You're an a...! Go to ...!]
(b) „... ihm nicht weitersagen", hörte er ihn gerade noch sagen. ["... don't tell him", he just heard him say.]

5 The German orthography is regulated by the Rat für deutsche Rechtschreibung (Council for German Orthography, https://www.rechtschreibrat.com/, last accessed 14 February 2025).

From a pragmatic perspective, an analysis of the EP in these two fictional examples as omissions is too simplistic as it neglects the writer's intentions. Even though we are lacking further context, we are able to interpret the writer's intentions based on our world knowledge. In Example (a) the omission most likely serves as a means of politeness since taboo phrasemes are alluded to rather than written out. However, addressees should be able to complete what is missing based on the co-text. At the same time, the addressee is made responsible for the interpretation of the utterance rather than the producer. In Example (b) the EP indicate that something that was said by one fictional character before was inaudible to the other. Unlike Example (a), where the EP signal that single letters or words have been omitted, the omission in Example (b) does not specify how many words, clauses or sentences are missing. Thus, readers cannot complete the utterance represented in direct speech. Instead, the EP either highlight the missing or the represented speech and thereby build suspense.

Therefore, it can be noted that ellipses are also often used rather stylistically in standard written language. Besides indicating omissions, EP also take on pragmatic functions. In direct speech, for instance in literary texts, EP have been used even before the standardization of written language. They can serve as a linguistic device to instruct the reader to imagine the respective written text parts as utterances spoken by a literary figure:

> However, the written medium had become so independent of that of the spoken medium having its own complex conventions, that the expectation that one could represent spoken discourse in a work of fiction was itself an illusion. ...[6] The novelist was obliged to impose on readers the responsibility of reconstructing speech, requiring them to contribute their own experience of actual conversation to foster that illusion, and to accept what they found in the text as a record of dialogue. To induce this reaction novelists developed special conventions involving choice of vocabulary and syntactical features, but they also imposed new conventions of layout and punctuation upon the printer to make it as clear to the reader as possible that the representation of spoken language was intended. (Parkes 1992: 93)

The new conventions of punctuation developed by 18th-century English authors that Parkes is referring to are, for instance, dashes and iterated dots. It is important to note that Parkes points to the involvement of the reader – an aspect that Bredel (2011) also highlights. Bredel (2011: 47) considers the involvement of the reader an essential feature of how EP support the cooperation of writers and readers in text communication. She states that EP usages instruct readers to activate their own

6 *Sic!* This ellipsis (used by the authors of this paper) is a prototypical example of a standard-compliant use according to § 99 of the official rules of German orthography.

knowledge (of the co-text and/or context) and fill in missing information on a lexical, syntactic or even pragmatic level (see Bredel 2011: 47).

Both dashes and ellipsis points help readers to scan written texts (see Bredel 2011: 25). As *fillers*, which can stand alone, they take up more space compared to clitics, that are attached to other characters (see Bredel 2011: 20). In standard written language, EP are space-separated and therefore visually salient, which is why Bredel (2011: 25) labels EP as elements of *text cartography*.

The exchange processes between writers and readers are central to Bredel's analysis of the punctuation system. Bredel (2011: 29) describes a relationship of give-and-take, that is writing/encoding and reading/decoding (*actional dimension*). In this relationship the knowledge required for the attainment of meaning and understanding is distributed in a specific manner (*epistemic dimension*). It is assumed by default that the writer has all the knowledge; however, they can also present themselves as the one lacking knowledge and the reader as the one having the knowledge (see Bredel 2011: 29) so that the reader, who needs to activate their knowledge resources, becomes the giver in terms of text comprehension. Thus, the *actional dimension*, that is the understanding of the writer's and reader's role in the interaction with texts,[7] changes. This is especially evident in the case of EP, which can only be interpreted by readers when they activate specific and diverse knowledge resources depending on the context and functions.

In her analysis of EP functions, Bredel does not solely focus on the functions described in the official rules of German orthography, but – in reference to the EP functions described by Meibauer (2007) – also on EP usages in texts that are not subject to the official regulations. Although the examples presented by Meibauer are fictional, they can be backed up with empirical evidence from authentic texts and linguistic corpora. Meibauer distinguishes four function types: *omission*, *continuation*, *connection* and *indication*. Bredel clusters these four function types according to the kind of knowledge resource that has to be activated by the reader in order to reconstruct the intended meaning of an ellipsis within a certain context. She differentiates between the activation of knowledge that is not presented in the text (omission and indication) and the re-activation of knowledge that is presented in the text (continuation and connection) (Bredel 2011: 47).

Following Parkes (1992) and Bredel (2011), EP are punctuation devices that originate from practices of the mimetic representation of spoken language in the written medium (see Bredel 2011: 13). Examples (6) and (7) illustrate the use of these practices in contemporary literature. Some of the EP usages found in the CMC

7 Following Ehlich's (1984) text concept, texts are typically designed for communication that is supposed to "travel through time and space".

examples presented in the introduction and below in Sections 5 and 6 resemble the practices that can be observed in standard written literature. It is therefore important to bear in mind these practices when it comes to the analysis of EP in CMC.

In Example (6), the EP usage serves as an imitation of nonverbal signs: It underlines the struggle of Too Much Coffee Man, a cartoon character, to get out of bed in that it creates the impression that it is arduous to do so. In Example (7), which is taken from a novel, the EP serve to establish conditional relevance.

(6) EP in a comic book (*Too Much Coffee Man saves the universe*, 1997, p. 1)

(7) EP in a novel (Stan Jones: *Village of the Ghost Bears*, 2009, p. 38)

“We’ve got to get that guy out of One-Way Lake,“ Active told the pilot. “If you could just....“

“Sorry, man, it’ll have to wait till tomorrow,“ Cowboy said. “He’s not going anywhere, right?“

Active frowned. “I still don’t like leaving him up there. This time of year, everything’s on the move and hungry. Bears, wolves, foxes, ravens. Wolverines too.“

Cowboy gave him a what-can-I-do? shrug. “One more day won’t hurt.“

3.2 Ellipses in the Chinese writing system

In Chinese writing, the use of punctuation marks is codified in the "General rules for punctuation" (STANDARD-CN 2011), regulated by the "National standards of People's Republic of China" (GB/T 15834–2011). According to these rules,

> [e]llipsis points "……" are six small dots close to the bottom of a line. They are mainly used to indicate omissions from listed items or a quoted text or speech. … If the omitted part is a whole line or a paragraph, the number of dots can be increased to twelve. (Huang and Shi 2016: 587)

The fact that dots are used to indicate ellipses is due to influences from Western languages (see Guo 2006: 140). In Chinese CMC, EP occur in different variants, for example as dots (see Example 5) or small circles[8] (see Example 8, examples of other variants are given in Section 6):

(8) Small-circle EP in WeChat

Tianhao:	应该就是饭卡上的号吧。。	**#2 14:13**
▫▫▫	Maybe thus be canteen card DE number particle。。	
~	'Maybe it's the number on the canteen card。。'	

Huang and Shi (2016: 587) note that "[a]lthough six- or twelve-dot ellipsis points are prescribed, in actual use speakers often use as few as three and sometime even an arbitrary number of dots. It is very rare, however, to see more than thirteen dots." However, there are no examples of EP usages that contain more than six dots in our random sample of WeChat interactions.

4 Research questions, data and method

In Section 5 and 6 we will present results from two studies on ellipses and their functions in German and Chinese text messaging guided by the following research questions:

- To what extent do practices of EP usage found in German text messaging interactions originate from traditions of writing (e. g., mimetic representation of

8 It is important to note that in Chinese standard writing, a period is represented by the symbol "。" (see STANDARD-CN 2011: 2), a small circle placed in the bottom left corner.

spoken language, other-selection, implying as described in Section 3.1)? Can practices of EP usage be described as distinct functional categories?
- Is the typology from study 1 also suitable for the analysis of a random sample of Chinese WeChat messages?

The aim, scope and datasets of the two studies can be described as follows:

Study I: Analysis of ellipses and their functions in German WhatsApp interactions: Beißwenger and Steinsiek (2023) investigated the usage of ellipses in WhatsApp interactions by analyzing two random samples of WhatsApp messages from the *Mobile Communication Database* (*MoCoDa2*), a crowdsourced corpus of German WhatsApp chats (Beißwenger et al. 2019; König et al. 2023). The corpus, which comprises 1,033 chats with 318,212 tokens in 39,035 text messages (as of March 6, 2025), is freely available online for research and teaching purposes under the following link: https://db.mocoda2.de/. Beißwenger and Steinsiek (2023) used the regular expression \.{2,} to search for EP instances with two or more dots in the MoCoDa2 corpus.[9] The first sample of 100 WhatsApp messages containing EP tokens was drawn in 2021 and served to develop the first draft of a typology describing the pragmatic functions of ellipses in messaging interactions. In addition to the analysis of examples of interaction-oriented writing (see Storrer 2018), Beißwenger and Steinsiek (2023) also took different examples and genres of text-oriented writing (see Storrer 2018), such as literary and academic texts, into account. For validation purposes, the typology was subsequently tested on a second sample drawn in 2022. After randomizing the corpus query result (1,196 hits in total) and removing false positives[10] from the sample of 100 WhatsApp messages containing 110 EP tokens, a dataset of 108 EP usages in 98 text messages (Table 1) formed the basis for the quantitative and qualitative analysis in Beißwenger and Steinsiek (2023).

9 Uses of the Unicode character U+2026, which occur only scarcely in the database, have not been included into the dataset because their encoding seems to be a result of autocorrection.

10 One false positive is a doublet (an EP token in a text message which is part of a chat interaction that was mistakenly uploaded to MoCoDa2 twice, cf. MoCoDa2 #BU7E6 and #9q7X7). The other is presumably an instance of incorrect anonymization where a street name was not replaced by an alternative street name but an ellipsis: "Um 16:35 an der ...Str." [16:35 at ...St."] (MoCoDa2, #veczv). Although replacing an element by an ellipsis can be considered a source-related omission, in this case the omission was most likely not done by the author of the text message but by the donor of the chat interaction.

Table 1: Random sample of WhatsApp messages (MoCoDa2) containing EP usages (tokens).

Text messages:		**Hits and true positives:**	
Texts containing EP tokens:	100	Hits (EP tokens):	110
Texts containing false positives:	2	False positives:	2
Texts containing true positives:	**98**	**True positives:**	**108**

Study II: Comparative analysis of ellipses and their functions in German WhatsApp and Chinese WeChat interactions: Building on the results of study I, which are summarized in Section 5, we adopt our functional typology derived from the analysis of German messaging interactions to investigate the usage of ellipses in Chinese messaging interactions. The dataset for our study on WeChat is derived from a WeChat database stored at Xi'an International Studies University (XISU), China. This *corpus in a wider sense* (see Beißwenger and Lüngen 2022: 433) was created in a project carried out by the Department of German Studies at the University of Münster, Germany, and the Department of German Studies at XISU in an Institutional Partnership (GIP)[11] funded by the German Academic Exchange Service (DAAD). The goal of the GIP project was to support and promote research and teaching in German studies abroad. The WeChat database contains 413 crowd-sourced interactions containing 8,200+ messages from XISU German studies students. The data are solely available as screenshots and transcripts on a hard drive at XISU, which means that they are not publicly accessible and cannot be browsed online, which is why the database was searched manually for instances of ellipsis points. A total of 154 WeChat messages containing ellipses in 79 interactions was then randomized. The random sample of 100 messages containing 107 ellipses (Table 2) forms the basis for analyzing ellipsis points in Chinese messaging interactions in comparison with German messaging interactions.

Table 2: Random sample of WeChat messages (XISU WeChat database) containing EP usages (tokens).

Text messages:		**Hits and true positives:**	
Texts containing EP tokens:	100	Hits (EP tokens):	107
Texts containing false positives:	0	False positives:	0
Texts containing true positives:	**100**	**True positives:**	**107**

11 German Language, Literature and Culture: Institutional Partnerships (GIP).

Method:
Both datasets were coded in a hermeneutic procedure. In the first study on ellipses in German WhatsApp interactions, Beißwenger and Steinsiek (2023: 295) progressively revised and refined the first draft of their typology by discussing their categorizations in data sessions. In this paper, we utilize this typology for the analysis of EP usages in Chinese WeChat interactions. We discursively coded the Chinese messaging interactions after they were translated literally (morpheme by morpheme) and freely into English by Yinglei Zang (a native speaker of Chinese).

5 Study I: Ellipses and their functions in the German WhatsApp dataset

In an exploratory study on ellipses in WhatsApp interactions, Beißwenger and Steinsiek (2023) identified four main function types: 1) omission, 2) implying, 3) sequential organization, and 4) segmentation as a basic function that results from the visual quality and salience of ellipsis points. In all of these function types, the EP usage involves a request directed at the reader of a message to activate a certain kind of knowledge in order to be able to interpret the EP usage as intended by the sender. Thus, the following descriptions of the function types as well as paraphrases of the underlying requests directed at the recipient, which are presented in italics, take on the perspective of the producer (for a more detailed description of differences between our function types and Meibauer's (2007) categories see Beißwenger and Steinsiek 2023: 298–299). In Section 6, we provide more detailed qualitative analyses of Chinese WeChat interactions.

TYPE 1: Omission: *Please interpret the ellipsis as a placeholder for missing elements.*
In this function type, the reader has to (or potentially can) fill in parts that have been left out by the author of the text message.
Beißwenger and Steinsiek (2023) differentiate four subtypes of omissions with different involved requests:

- Source-related: *Activate your knowledge of citation guidelines that determine how to indicate omissions within quotes.*

  This subtype is common in academic texts and is often used to shorten longer quotations by leaving out parts that are irrelevant for the point being made.

(9) EP in academic writing (Parkes 1992: 93)

However, the written medium had become so independent of that of the spoken medium having its own complex conventions, that the expectation that one could represent spoken discourse in a work of fiction was itself an illusion. ... The novelist was obliged to impose on readers the responsibility of reconstructing speech, requiring them to contribute their own experience of actual conversation to foster that illusion, and to accept what they found in the text as a record of dialogue. To induce this reaction novelists developed special conventions involving choice of vocabulary and syntactical features, but they also imposed new conventions of layout and punctuation upon the printer to make it as clear to the reader as possible that the representation of spoken language was intended.

– Word-related: *Based on your vocabulary knowledge and from the available context, infer the missing words or word parts.*

Word-related omissions may serve to allude to rather than write out taboo or swear words. Examples: "You're an a...", "Oh, go to ...!". The following example of a word-related omission in a WhatsApp interaction is not documented in our random sample but taken from the MoCoDa2 corpus:

(10) Trip to Belgium 2018 (MoCoDa2, #ewD82)

Heike:	SCH.....😊	**#18 10:22**
translation	'SH.....😊'	

– Context-related omission: *Continue the iteration of words based on the context.*

(11) Meibauer (2007: 34)
„Tack, tack, tack, ... So ging das die ganze Nacht."
'Tick, tick, tick, ... all night long.'

– Frame-related: *From your world knowledge and practical knowledge, infer which elements could be added to an incomplete list.*

In the following example taken from our random sample of WhatsApp interactions, Lea's enumeration of things needed for a sleepover at a friend's house can easily be complemented by other overnight supplies:

(12) A couple planning an upcoming extended weekend (MoCoDa2, #RnbM9)

Lea:	Ich hab die Matratze für uns beide:)	**#25 10:38**
translation	'I have an air mattress for the both of us:)'	
Markus:	Alles klar, muss ich noch was mitbringen?:)	**#26 10:38**
translation	'Okay, should I bring anything else?:)'	
Lea:	Kannst du evt [eventuell] mit deinem großen Rucksack kommen? Ich schlepp den auch, aber dann kann ich da echt alles rein tun:)	**#27 10:38**
translation	'Can you mb [maybe] bring your big backpack? I can carry it, but that one really fits everything we need:)'	
Lea:	Also die Matratze, die Pumpe...	**#28 10:38**
translation	'Like the air mattress, the air pump...'	

TYPE 2: Implying: *Please infer what I am implying based on common knowledge or from assumptions you make about me and my opinions.*

Implying on the other hand is not about leaving something out that is supposed to be filled in, but rather about avoiding concretization. The author chooses not to be too specific, instead, the reader is made "responsible" for inferring what is implied. The main difference between *omission* and *implying* is that omitted parts can actually be realized and reconstructed as concrete linguistic signs. In the following example from our WhatsApp sample, Maja asks her friend Johanna, who is waiting at the train station, if the train has arrived yet. Johanna informs Maja that the train is delayed and quotes a train announcement that is well known to most people who have ever made the experience of "traveling with Deutsche Bahn":

(13) Conversation on the way home (MoCoDa2, #GDIx6)

Maja:	Ist der Zug mittlerweile in Sicht?	**#52 20:16**
translation	'Is the train within sight yet?'	
Johanna:	Nö, hat aber jetzt noch mehr Verspätung 🤦‍♀️😂	**#53 20:17**
translation	'Nope, but it's even more delayed now 🤦‍♀️😂'	

Maja:	Ob shit	**#54 20:17**
Maja:	Oh*	**#55 20:17**
Johanna:	Grund dafür ist eine Verspätung eines voraus-fahrenden Zuges... 😑	**#56 20:18**
translation	'This train is delayed because of train traffic ahead of us... 😑'	
Maja:	Ja na klar wie immer 🙄	**#57 20:18**
translation	'Yeah sure as usual 🙄'	

TYPE 3: Sequential organization: *Activate your knowledge of sequential organization and conditional relevance in spoken conversations and interpret the ellipsis as an imitation of "next speaker selection".*
In this function type, the ellipsis is intended to be interpreted based on common knowledge of sequential organization and conditional relevance in spoken conversations. Beißwenger and Steinsiek (2023) distinguish between *other-selection* and *self-selection*. Both other- and self-selection help to establish interactional coherence (Herring 1999) under the conditions of CMC.

TYPE 3.1: Other-selection (more or less explicit, depending on the context): The recipient is supposed to take on the role of the author and reply to the current text or infer that the current author has nothing (more) to contribute.

– More explicit: *Please take on the role of the author and reply to my message.*

Example (14) from our MoCoDa2 sample displays more explicit other-selection. After Marius lists all the names of the group members coming along on a day trip (#698) and Markus objects that Bernd is planning to join the group a little later (#699), Marius directly addresses Bernd in message #701 in order to establish conditional relevance and elicit a response from Bernd himself:

(14) Group chat among men planning a day trip together (MoCoDa2, #fhLyA)

Marius:	Marvin kommt auch mit.... Und fährt auch 👍🏻 Also dann: JMGJanusBernd FabiMarvinMarius	**#698 13:10**

translation ‘Marvin is coming too....
And he’ll drive too 👍
So then it’s:
JMGJanusBernd
FabiMarvinMarius’

Markus: Bernd doch erst später oder, **#699 13:11**
translation ‘Isn’t Bernd coming along later,’

Janus: Whoooop whoooop **#700 13:11**

Marius: Das ist jetzt die Frage @bernd .... **#701 13:21**
translation ‘That’s the question now @bernd ....’

– Less explicit: *Please infer that I have nothing (more) to contribute at this point of the ongoing conversation.*

Text messages that solely contain a (short) response to previous texts on the other hand can be interpreted as less explicit other-selection.

TYPE 3.2: Self-selection (imitation of floor keeping strategies): *Based on previous messages by an author, (1) project that they plan an expansion by using ellipsis points in final position or (2) interpret an ellipsis in initial position as a cohesive device.*

In this function, EP are typically realized in message-final position and are used as a projective strategy, which means that they create the expectation that the author intends to post another message. In initial position, they mark the extension of a text message and hereby serve as a means of cohesion, as the following example of an interaction among friends from our MoCoDa2 sample illustrates:

(15) Friends planning a dinner together (MoCoDa2, #OGoME)

Luisa: Ach Quatsch stört mich nie :) **#21 16:31**
translation ‘Oh that [if your place is a mess] doesn’t bother me at all :)’

Luisa: ... bei anderen :D in meiner wg treibt mich das zur Weißglut aber das ist ein anderes Thema 😜 **#22 16:31**
translation ‘... as long as it’s not my place :D the mess in my dorm drives me crazy but that’s a different issue 😜’

TYPE 4: Segmentation: *Construct segment boundaries and utilize them to process what you have read.*
Beißwenger and Steinsiek (2023) differentiate two types of segmentation: *Visual* segmentation and *transmodal* segmentation.

TYPE 4.1: Visual segmentation: *Construct segment boundaries and separately process the segments on the left and on the right side of the boundary.*

Visual segmentation can be considered the basic function of ellipsis points within text messages. The ellipsis serves as a marker of boundaries between sentences, syntactic components or communicative units and supports the reading (scanning) process of the recipient, as the following example from our MoCoDa2 sample demonstrates:

(16) Two fellow students chatting (MoCoDa2, #Aqkwk)

Norbert:	Gruess dich! Jetzt hast du auch meine nummer ... lg, norbert	**#2 18:32**
translation	'Hi there! Now you have my number too ... br, norbert'[12]	

TYPE 4.2: Transmodal segmentation: *Activate your knowledge on the multimodality of spoken language and interpret the EP als an imitation of a meaningful nonverbal signal.*

Transmodal segmentation is a means of "fictional orality": In transmodal segmentation, an ellipsis can be interpreted as a simulation of meaningful nonverbal signs in spoken language, like gaps or changes in the way of speaking, for instance to focus on or stress something (see Androutsopoulos 2020: 135) like a punch line or a negative evaluation ("typographic silence" in Busch 2021: 386–387), as the following (shortened) example from our MoCoDa2 sample shows:

(17) Birthday party invitation (MoCoDa2, #6pvIP)

Viktor:	Bitte jeder einen Schlafsack, Luftmatraze und Handtuch mitbringen. Ich habe leider nicht genug Zeug für 15 Leute da. 😅 Wir werden nicht alle (Luftmatrazen) brauchen, weil ich für 5–7 Schlafplätze habe. Aber besseres sind zuviele davon da als... naja.. Holzboden für jemanden.	**#26 23:45**

12 The German acronym "lg" stands for "Liebe Grüße" [br/best regards].

translation 'Everyone please bring a sleeping bag, an air mattress and a towel. I don't have enough stuff for 15 people. 😅 We won't need all of them (air mattresses) because I have sleeping places for 5–7 people. But too many is better than... well.. the wooden floor for anybody.'

6 Study II: Comparative analysis of ellipses and their functions in the German and Chinese dataset

The application of the typology derived from the analysis of the German WhatsApp dataset to the classification of the EP occurrences found in the Chinese WeChat dataset was rather straightforward. Neither an extension of the typology nor an adaptation of the definitions of the types was necessary in order to be able to create informative descriptions of the Chinese EP instances. As result of the analysis of the Chinese dataset, the distribution and frequency of function types for both languages is as follows (see Table 3):

In both German WhatsApp and Chinese WeChat interactions, ellipses are very seldom used to indicate omissions. It must also be noted that the four source-related omissions in the Chinese data were produced by the same person in a single text message (see Example 21). In both samples, the most commonly used functions are implying, sequential organization, and segmentation. However, implying seems to be the main function in the Chinese data as it constitutes nearly half of the EP usages. Another interesting finding is that visual segmentation is much more frequent in the German than in the Chinese data, which might be linked to the fact that EP often occur after sentence boundaries, for instance between main and subordinate clauses, and "that Chinese *juzi* (sentence) is semantically and textually conceptualized rather than syntactically defined and Chinese readers use discourse information to help identify sentence boundaries and perceive meaning completeness" (Sun 2021: 234).

Table 3: Distribution and frequency of function types in both samples.

Function type		**No. of EP tokens**		**%**	
		WA	WE	WA	WE
Omission		*1*	*5*	*0,93*	*4,67*
	| source-related	0	4	0	3,7
	| word-related	0	0	0	0
	| context-related	0	0	0	0
	| frame-related	1	1	0,93	0,9
Implying		28	51	25,93	47,7
Sequential organization		*20*	*29*	*18,52*	*27,1*
	| other-selection	13	14	12,04	13,1
	| self-selection	7	15	6,48	14
Segmentation		*57*	*22*	*52,78*	*20,56*
	| visual	41	12	37,96	11,2
	| transmodal	16	10	14,81	9,3
Ambiguous interpretation[13]		2	0	1,85	0
Total		108	107	100,00	100,00

In the following, we present examples from the WeChat sample that show that the functions EP take on in Chinese messenger interactions are similar to those described for German chats.

In Example (18), two students who like the Harry Potter novels discuss which Hogwarts houses they like best and what kinds of fan merchandise they want to order online together. Ruijie, who is a Gryffindor fan, notes that she dislikes the current Gryffindor attire: “But this time the Gryffindor clothes are......emmmmm”. The EP token comprised of six “regular” dots serves to imply what Ruijie leaves out in her statement: Weilan is supposed to fill in the missing information that Ruijie dislikes the Gryffindor clothes based on her awareness of the latest merchandise collection (see #1). Simultaneously, the EP token serves as a means of transmodal segmentation in that it can be interpreted as an imitation of a gap in spoken language.

13 In order to avoid speculative categorization, we chose not to classify two EP usages in WhatsApp messages that were open to ambiguous interpretation.

(18) Implying

Ruijie:	你喜欢的是四学院那种风格的？	**#1 21:29**
□□□	You like DE[14] be four faculties which style DE?	
~	'Which style of the four houses do you like the most?'[15]	
Weilan:	蛇院！	**#2 21:29**
□□□	Snake faculty!	
~	'Slytherin!'	
Ruijie:	原来！	**#3 21:29**
□□□	Turn out!	
~	'Oh!'	
Ruijie:	如此！	**#4 21:29**
□□□	So!	
~	'I see!'	
Ruijie:	我是狮院粉	**#5 21:30**
□□□	I be lion faculty fan	
~	'I am a Gryffindor fan'	
Weilan:	欸嘿嘿	**#6 21:30**
□□□	Laugh particle laugh particle laugh particle	
~	'Hihihi'	
Weilan:	可以再问问XX [a friend's name]	**#7 21:30**
□□□	Can again ask XX [a friend's name]	
~	'We can ask XX' [a friend's name]	
Ruijie:	但是这次的狮院……emmmmm	**#8 21:30**
□□□	But this time DE lion faculty……emmmmm	
~	'But this time the Gryffindor clothes are…… emmmmm'	

14 DE serves the semantic function of marking a description.

15 Examples from Chinese CMC are presented with a morpheme-by-morpheme translation (□□□) as well as a rough translation (~).

Example 19 displays an example of sequential organization. Keli and Tianhao, who are fellow students, are talking about a teacher at their university who Keli currently assists, what Tianhao formerly did (see #3). After Keli mentions that the teacher probably "doesn't even know he has an employee number" (see #1), Tianhao points out that the employee number might be "the number on the canteen card" (see #2). The EP usage, two small circles, serves as an imitation of floor keeping strategies: In the following text message (see #3), Tianhao "selects himself as the next speaker" and explains why he knows that the employee number is the same as the number on the canteen card.

(19) Sequential organization | self-selection

Keli:	我怕他都不知道自己有工号🤣	**#1 14:13**
□□□	I afraid he even not know self have employee number🤣	
~	'I'm afraid he doesn't even know he has an employee number'🤣	
Tianhao:	应该就是饭卡上的号吧。。	**#2 14:13**
□□□	Maybe thus be canteen card DE number particle。。	
~	'Maybe it's the number on the canteen card。。'	
Tianhao:	我之前给XX [a teacher's name] 老师操作过这个系统	**#3 14:13**
□□□	I previously for XX [a teacher's name] teacher handle GUO[16] this system	
~	'I used to handle this system for XX [a teacher's name]'	
Keli:	嗷嗷	**#4 14:13**
□□□	particle particle	
~	'okay'	
Tianhao:	账号密码都是他工号	**#5 14:13**
□□□	Account password all be his employee number	
~	'Account number and pin are his employee number'	

16 GUO marks the aspect of an action, i.e. that something has been finished.

Example (20) on the other hand shows how an EP token (six dots) is used as a means of other-selection. Chaohui asks Aijia why she needs to download a game called CrossFire if she wants to play the computer game Minecraft (see #1). Aijia responds that Minecraft “is included in cf”. However, Chaohui does not understand the abbreviation Aijia used and thus asks “cf is……?”. The EP token in combination with the question mark establishes conditional relevance and can be interpreted as a more explicit other-selection: Aijia, who sends a text containing more information on the game CrossFire (see #4), presumably at the same time as Chaohui posts her question, subsequently responds that the abbreviation “cf” stands for CrossFire (see #6).

(20) Sequential organization | other-selection

Chaohui:	不是叫绝地求生吗，为什么又要穿越火线	**#1 21:18**
□□□	Not be call desperate place pursue survival, why again need across fire line	
~	‘Isn’t the game called Minecraft, why am I supposed to download CrossFire’	
Aijia:	就是cf里面的，	**#2 21:18**
□□□	thus be cf in DE,	
~	The game is included in cf	
Chaohui:	cf是……?	**#3 21:18**
□□□	cf be……?	
~	‘cf is……?’	
Aijia:	穿越火线很早的游戏了	**#4 21:18**
□□□	Across fire line very old DE game LE[17]	
~	CrossFire is an old game	
Chaohui:		**#5 21:18**
Aijia:	cf就是穿越火线	**#6 21:18**
□□□	Cf thus be across fire line	
~	‘Cf is CrossFire’	

17 LE marks the change of an action or a state.

Chaohui: 哦哦哦 **#7 21:19**
□□□ particle particle particle
~ oh oh oh

In Example (21), Caolin sends her fellow student Mingming feedback on a translation task the two of them are working on together. The two students are supposed to review a translation done by another student, their "academic sister" (a term of address between Chinese students to refer to students in lower or higher grades). The four EP usages (six dots) serve to indicate source-related omissions: In two sentences, Caolin leaves out the direct object in order to emphasize and also visually highlight the wrong translation "to" and the corrected version "with": "I think change ……to……is not translated correctly. So I translated this into change…… with……" (see #1). The missing elements can be reconstructed by Mingming by referring to the source of omission, the translated text that Caolin is commenting on. The fact that Mingming responds that she has "also corrected these two passages" (see #2) demonstrates that she is able to identify which part of the translation Caolin is referring to.

(21) Omission | source-related

Caolin: Mingming～我看完啦 主要就是学姐翻译的将……替换为……那几句我觉得很别扭 所以我改成了以……替换…… 还有一个就是与名词保持一致 我改成了随名词性数变化 具体的咱俩今晚上或者明天再讨论啊 😳 **#1 13:26**

□□□ Mingming~ I read finish particle mainly thus be academic sister translate DE make ……replace to …… those sentences I find very award so I change to LE with …… replace……still one CL[18] thus be with noun keep consistent I change to LE with noun grammatical gender numerous concrete DE we today evening or tomorrow then discuss ah😳

~ 'Mingming~ I have finished the reading. I only have two comments. In the translation done by our academic sister, I think change ……to……is not translated correctly. So I translated this into change……with……Another one is, I corrected

18 CL serves the semantic function of marking noun classes.

the keep identical to noun to gender-numerous-correspondence. We can talk about the details today evening or tomorrow😳'

Mingming: 我也改的是这些～ **#2 13:39**
□□□ I also correct DE be these~
~ 'I have also corrected these two passages~'
那咱俩晚上讨论～ **#3 13:39**
□□□ Then we evening discuss~
~ 'Then let's talk about it tomorrow evening~'

In Example (22), the omission is not source-related, but frame-related. Kangkang, who is planning a trip to Chengdu, asks her friend Liurui, who has traveled there before, "for some recommendations on food and tourist attractions" (see #1). Liurui shares two screenshots (see #2, #3) of pictures she previously posted on WeChat[19] that show food she strongly recommends (see #4) and adds "Then there is Jinli street, there you can find glutinous rice balls, Kongming pie, one-pot chicken……" (see #5). The EP usage (six dots) serves to indicate that the list goes on: Based on knowledge on Chinese cuisine, Liurui assumes that Kangkang is able to imagine several other dishes to find on Jinli street.

(22) Omission | frame-related
Kangkang: Liurui！你有时间不，想请教你一下去成都玩有什么一定要吃和玩的嘛，记得你好像去玩过 **#1 10:55**
□□□ Liurui! You have time not, want request you a while go to Chengdu (a city in China) travel have what must eat and play DE question particle, remember you probably go travelling GUO
~ 'Liurui! Are you available right now? I want to ask you for some recommendations on food and tourist attractions in Chengdu. I remember you've been there'

Liurui: [screenshot] **#2 10:59**

19 Similar to a feature on Instagram, WeChat enables users to post pictures and share posts with their contacts.

Liurui:	[screenshot]	**#3 10:59**
Liurui:	这两个全力推荐！	**#4 10:59**
□□□	These two totally recommend!	
~	'I totally recommend these two here!'	
Liurui:	然后就是锦里小吃街，里面的三大炮，军屯锅盔，钵钵鸡……	**#5 11:00**
□□□	Then thus be Jinli snack street, in DE three big cannon, Kongming pie, pot chicken……	
~	'Then there is Jinli street, there you can find glutinous rice balls, Kongming pie, one-pot chicken……'	

7 Conclusion and outlook

Our analyses show that 1) practices of EP usage in messenger interactions are not completely novel, but originate from traditions of writing. Furthermore, both in German and Chinese CMC, EP are seldom used to indicate omissions – which is their ascribed main function according to official regulations (STANDARD-DE 2018 and STANDARD-CN 2011). Moreover, it has become evident that 2) the EP functions described for German text messaging can also be adopted for the analysis of Chinese WeChat interactions. Ellipses seem to take on similar functions in German and Chinese CMC, which could be linked to the fact that punctuation marks in Chinese were adopted from Western languages. These findings indicate that practices of EP usage that originate from traditions of writing might have also found their way into Chinese CMC. However, we identified differences in the allographic variants. In our German WhatsApp sample, the majority of EP usages contain three (57%) or two (32%) dots. The greater part of ellipses in the Chinese WeChat sample (61%) are the norm-conforming "six small dots" (Huang and Shi 2016: 587), although a considerable number of EP usages contain three (24%) or two (12%) dots or small circles, which are also used for periods in standard Chinese writing (see STANDARD-CN 2011: 2).

Furthermore, we analyzed the frequency of the identified function types in relation to the positions of EP tokens in both samples (see Table 4):

Table 4: Frequency of function types in relation to the positions of EP tokens.

Function type	Single-token message		Message-initial		Message-medial		Message-final	
	WA	WE	WA	WE	WA	WE	WA	WE
Omission | source-related	0	0	0	0	0	4	0	0
Omission | frame-related	0	0	0	0	0	0	1	1
Implying	0	13	1	2	3	2	24	34
Sequential organization | other-selection	0	1	0	0	0	0	13	13
Sequential organization | self-selection	0	1	1	2	0	0	6	12
Segmentation | visual	0	0	0	0	41	12	0	0
Segmentation | transmodal	0	0	0	0	16	10	0	0
Total	0	15	2	4	60	28	44	60

In Chinese text messaging, EP that are used for implying are typically realized in final position or as single-token messages, whereas they are predominantly positioned at the end of German text messages. EP as a means of sequential organization are almost exclusively realized in text-final position in both languages. This seems rather plausible since most instances are examples of other-selection, which serves to elicit responses by the addressee. Both visual and transmodal segmentation only occur in text-medial position in both languages, which can also be explained by the function type itself.

In order to be able to make (statistically) reliable statements, the affinity of function types for EP position should be explored in future research based on larger data sets. Moreover, comparative analyses of other languages with German and Chinese could be very insightful since ellipses – provided that there is a sign for this purpose – are not bound to a single language. Therefore, ellipses are an interesting example of a non-linguistic sign that takes on similar functions in sequential organization, the ensuring of mutual understanding and cooperation in written digital interactions across different languages and cultures.

References

Androutsopoulos, Jannis. 2020. Auslassungspunkte in der schriftbasierten Interaktion. Sequenziell-topologische Analysen an Daten von griechischen Jugendlichen. In Jannis Androutsopoulos & Florian Busch (eds.), *Register des Graphischen. Variation, Interaktion und Reflexion in der digitalen Schriftlichkeit*, 133–158. Berlin & Boston: De Gruyter. https://doi.org/10.1515/9783110673241-006.

Androutsopoulos, Jannis & Florian Busch (eds.), 2020. *Register des Graphischen. Variation, Interaktion und Reflexion in der digitalen Schriftlichkeit*. Berlin & Boston: De Gruyter. https://doi.org/10.1515/9783110673241.

Androutsopoulos, Jannis & Friedemann Vogel (eds.), 2024. *Handbuch Sprache und digitale Kommunikation*. Berlin & Boston: De Gruyter.

Beißwenger, Michael. 2016. Praktiken in der internetbasierten Kommunikation. In Arnulf Deppermann, Feilke Helmuth & Angelika Linke (eds.), *Sprachliche und kommunikative Praktiken*, 279–310. Berlin & Boston: De Gruyter. https://doi.org/10.1515/9783110451542-012.

Beißwenger, Michael. 2020. Internetbasierte Kommunikation als Textformen-basierte Interaktion: ein neuer Vorschlag zu einem alten Problem. In Henning Lobin, Konstanze Marx & Axel Schmidt (eds.), *Deutsch in sozialen Medien: interaktiv, multimodal, vielfältig. Jahrbuch des Instituts für Deutsche Sprache 2019*, 291–318. Berlin & Boston: De Gruyter. https://doi.org/10.1515/9783110679885-015.

Beißwenger, Michael & Sarah Steinsiek. 2023. Interpunktion als interaktionale Ressource. Eine korpusgestützte Untersuchung zur Funktion von Auslassungspunkten in der internetbasierten Kommunikation. In Michael Beißwenger, Eva Gredel, Lothar Lemnitzer & Roman Schneider (eds.), *Korpusgestützte Sprachanalyse. Grundlagen, Anwendungen und Analysen*. Studien zur Deutschen Sprache 88, 287–310. Tübingen: Narr. https://doi.org/10.24053/9783823396109.

Beißwenger, Michael, Wolfgang Imo, Marcel Fladrich & Evelyn Ziegler. 2019. https://www.mocoda2.de: A database and web-based editing environment for collecting and refining a corpus of mobile messaging interactions. *European Journal of Applied Linguistics* 7 (2). 333–344. https://doi.org/10.1515/eujal-2019-0004.

Beißwenger, Michael & Harald Lüngen. 2022. Korpora internetbasierter Kommunikation. In Michael Beißwenger, Lothar Lemnitzer & Carolin Müller-Spitzer (eds.), *Forschen in der Linguistik. Eine Methodeneinführung für das Germanistik-Studium*. UTB 5711, 431–448. Paderborn: Brill Fink. (accessed 17 May 2024).

Bredel, Ursula. 2011. *Interpunktion*. Heidelberg: Winter.

Brown, Penelope & Stephen C. Levinson. 2007. Gesichtsbedrohende Akte. In Steffen Kitty Herrmann, Sybille Krämer & Hannes Kuch (eds.), *Verletzende Worte. Die Grammatik sprachlicher Missachtung*, 59–88. Bielefeld: Transcript Verlag. https://doi.org/10.1515/9783839405659-003.

Busch, Florian. 2021. *Digitale Schreibregister. Kontexte, Formen und metapragmatische Reflexionen*. Berlin & Boston: De Gruyter. https://doi.org/10.1515/9783110728835.

Ehlich, Konrad. 1984. Zum Textbegriff. In: Annely Rothkegel & Barbara Sandig (eds.): *Text – Textsorten – Semantik. Linguistische Modelle und maschinelle Verfahren*, 531–550. Hamburg: Buske.

Guo, Pan. 2006. 二十世纪以来汉语标点符号研究 [Research on Chinese punctuation marks since the 20th century]. Central China Normal University.

Herring, Susan C. 1999. Interactional Coherence in CMC. *Journal of Computer-Mediated Communication* 4 (4). https://doi.org/10.1111/j.1083-6101.1999.tb00106.x.

Herring, Susan C., Dieter Stein & Tuija Virtanen (eds.), 2013. *Pragmatics of Computer-Mediated Communication*. Berlin & Boston: De Gruyter Mouton. Handbooks of Pragmatics 9. https://doi.org/10.1515/9783110214468.

Huang, Chu-Ren & Dingxu Shi (eds.), 2016. *A reference grammar of Chinese*. Cambridge: Cambridge University Press.

König, Katharina, Sarah Steinsiek, Michael Beißwenger & Marcel Fladrich. 2023. Forschendes Lernen mit der Mobile Communication Database (MoCoDa 2). Didaktische Potenziale und Anregungen für den Unterricht Deutsch als Fremdsprache. *Korpora Deutsch als Fremdsprache (KorDaF)*. 61–89. https://doi.org/10.48694/kordaf.3851.

Meibauer, Jörg. 2007. Syngrapheme als pragmatische Indikatoren: Anführung und Auslassung. In Sandra Döring & Jochen Geilfuß-Wolfgang (eds.), *Von der Pragmatik zur Grammatik*, 21–37. Leipzig: Universitätsverlag.

Meier-Vieracker, Simon, Lars Bülow, Konstanze Marx & Robert Mroczynski (eds.), 2023. *Digitale Pragmatik*. Digitale Linguistik 1. Heidelberg: Metzler.

Parkes, Malcolm B. 1992. *Pause and effect. An introduction to the history of punctuation in the West*. Aldershot: Scolar Press.

[STANDARD-CN 2011] Zhonghua renmin gongheguo guojia zhiliang jiandu jianyan jianyi zongju (30 December 2011), 中华人民共和国国家标准 GB/T 15834–2011：标点符号用法 [National Standard of the People's Republic of China GB/T 15834–2011: General Rules for Punctuation]. https://web.archive.org/web/20161109233830/http://www.moe.edu.cn/ewebeditor/uploadfile/2012/06/01/20120601102833791.pdf (last accessed 25 May 2024)

[STANDARD-DE 2018] Deutsche Rechtschreibung. Regeln und Wörterverzeichnis. Aktualisierte Fassung des amtlichen Regelwerks entsprechend den Empfehlungen des Rats für deutsche Rechtschreibung 2016. Mannheim. https://www.rechtschreibrat.com/DOX/rfdr_Regeln_2016_redigiert_2018.pdf (last accessed 17 May 2024).

Storrer, Angelika. 2018. Interaktionsorientiertes Schreiben im Internet. In Arnulf Deppermann & Reineke Silke (eds.), *Sprache im kommunikativen, interaktiven und kulturellen Kontext*, 219–244. Berlin & Boston: De Gruyter. https://doi.org/10.1515/9783110538601-010.

Sun, Kun. 2021. An investigation of the factors influencing Chinese readers' perception of sentence boundaries in Mandarin. In Paul Rössler, Peter Besl & Anna Saller (eds.), *Vergleichende Interpunktion – Comparative Punctuation*, 215–236. Berlin & Boston: De Gruyter. https://doi.org/10.1515/9783110756319-010.

Florian Frenken

A multivariate register perspective on Reddit: Exploring lexicogrammatical variation in online communities

Abstract: Even though social media has become a growing topic of linguistic research in recent years, the internal variation associated with emergent register contexts engendered by its various forms remains largely unknown. To address this gap, the present study evaluates a geometric multivariate approach for the domain of online interactions by investigating patterns in visualisations of forty-two lexicogrammatical features derived from systemic functional theory for individual texts from thirty-three communities on Reddit. Their analysis reveals that these so-called subreddits form overlapping clusters in multidimensional feature space that align with their contextual and thus functional (dis)similarities. It therefore becomes possible to interpret them as subregisters with continuous variation inside a hypothesised macro-register of the website at large. As such, this study argues that Reddit's communities reflect the wider internet landscape on a smaller scale, being an online microcosm of sorts that provides convenient descriptive labels for aggregated content hubs that would otherwise be distributed and hard to find. Subreddits generally fulfil varied purposes, often showing similar features to offline registers on top of more general indicators of user interaction. This attests to their status as independent hybrid registers. At the same time, computer-assisted content moderation emerged as a potentially significant factor in shaping the social context of community interaction – an issue whose linguistic implications demand further attention. Overall, investigating text-level rather than averaged feature correlation patterns appears well-suited for multidimensional analyses of subregisters in general and the web specifically as the sensitivity of the geometric approach helps to operationalise linguistic variation at lower levels of instantiation. This contribution therefore hopes to incentivise further research on platform-internal register differences, potentially with even greater granularity, not least for its practical implications in context-informed automatic classifications of web documents.

Keywords: systemic functional linguistics, (sub)register variation, internet language, online communication, geometric multivariate analysis, social media, reddit

Florian Frenken, RWTH Aachen University, e-mail: florian.frenken@ifaar.rwth-aachen.de

https://doi.org/10.1515/9783111434018-005

1 Introduction

The internet has undoubtedly fundamentally changed everyday communication, seeing as how a significant portion of human-human interactions now occur via computer-mediated means. As users learn to navigate this new environment, they face unique communicative contexts to which they must adapt, socially and linguistically. Online forums, for instance, show certain “transient” characteristics of spoken face-to-face conversations in that responses can be edited and deleted or lost to attention despite being expressed in writing (Berber Sardinha 2018: 131). Naturally then, Biber and Conrad (2009: 177) contend, “anyone interested in register variation will wonder how language is used in these new registers.” Interestingly, however, knowledge about the linguistic characteristics associated with these innovative forms is rather limited as of yet despite technological advancements that would permit accounting for the wealth of data available (Titak and Roberson 2013: 236).

Surely one of the most prominent new variants of computer-mediated communication (CMC) is social media. As with established “offline” registers like research articles and newspapers, which are not native to the internet, Facebook and Twitter represent the salient “online” registers of today “whose labels are instantly recognized” (Berber Sardinha 2018: 126). By mere exposure, these platforms play a disproportionately high role as communicative contexts, so their relevance should not be understated (cf. Biber and Egbert 2018: 3). This becomes especially pertinent considering that such “registers continue to emerge and evolve quickly, illustrating the dynamic nature of language development online” (Titak and Roberson 2013: 236). As the medium matures and the broader register landscape settles, these innovations often arise not only from new platforms but as more subtle variations of already existing forms. One of the most productive examples of this phenomenon is Reddit. It principally differs from other social media in that it seems to foreground not individual users but the specialised communities they form and the content they produce. The website realises this concept through its organisation into subreddits, which show a complex interplay of explicit self-imposed community-specific rules and implicit communicative norms.

In light of these rules governing each subreddit, enforced by self-appointed moderators who can ban users and remove contributions deemed inappropriate, this study argues that Reddit’s communities represent unique contextual variants of the website at large that may engender characteristic linguistic variation. It therefore explores whether subreddits, as user-curated categorisations of web content, are linguistically meaningful, i.e., sufficiently contextually and therefore functionally different that they constitute subregisters of Reddit, as identifiable by systematic clusters in the distribution of lexicogrammatical features like pronoun use or mood choice. This study therefore treads new ground by investigating platform-internal register variation rather than comparing overt differences across conventionally recognised groups of web documents. This perspective can not only improve the current understanding of linguistic differences at lower levels of instantiation but also further ongoing efforts of "anatomizing" (Kilgarriff and Grefenstette 2003: 345) the web since Reddit demonstrates the benefits of functional categorisation at a smaller scale, allowing users to find communities and types of content matching their interests. For information retrieval purposes, then, it may become possible to filter web searches not only semantically by content, but according to exceedingly specific functional purposes and contexts.

The next section will first provide the necessary background information on how Reddit works as a website to justify the assumption that it inherently promotes the emergence of new and diverse situational contexts. This then leads into the motivation for using a multidimensional approach grounded in systemic functional register theory against the background of previous research on online registers. Afterwards, the preprocessing steps and method at the heart of this investigation, namely Geometric Multivariate Analysis (GMA), will be described. This includes the operationalisation of text as threads used in this study as well as the selection criteria for subreddits and lexicogrammatical features. The results section then analyses a sample of ten (out of thirty-three) subreddits and relates their contextual descriptions to textual patterns in a two-dimensional scatterplot visualisation of the linguistic feature space provided by the GMA. This is accompanied by examples from concrete texts illustrating salient register characteristics based on their clustering in this plot. Lastly, the discussion reflects on these results with respect to implications for the status of subreddits as (sub)registers proper and calls attention to the impact of content moderation (especially by bots) and Reddit's social systems (especially voting) as promising avenues for future register research.

2 Background

Reddit is a social news aggregation website where registered users, or redditors, can submit and rate content posted in discussion forums they create. Unlike most other social media, which typically foreground the social networks of its users, Reddit is therefore, by design, not a monolithic platform, but consists of millions of smaller communities specialised for certain topics and purposes. Moreover, Reddit's content policy – platform-wide guidelines establishing a basic code of conduct for everyone – is actually situated "[b]elow the rules governing each community"

(Reddit Inc. 2022). These rules, displayed openly on the respective subreddit's sidebar, are enforced by moderators appointed from the community by the existing team of moderators (and initially its creator) who have the power to ban users, remove contributions in case of rule violations, and close threads if they no longer deem them conducive to the ongoing discourse. In other words, the "culture of each community is shaped explicitly, by the community rules ..., and implicitly, by the upvotes, downvotes, and discussions of its community members" (Reddit Inc. 2022), which naturally filter out contributions that do not follow the subreddit's conventions by reducing their visibility.

What also factors into Reddit's system of self-governance is the so-called Reddiquette. This portmanteau of Reddit and etiquette describes "an informal expression of the values of many redditors, as written by redditors themselves" (Reddit Help 2021), which is endorsed by the administrators, employees of the company Reddit, Inc. who maintain the website and monitor its content. In doing so, they lay the groundwork for respectful interactions, for example by moving against harassment and spam, but generally only involve themselves with specific communities if their rules violate these basic terms. Besides reiterating general communication guidelines, the Reddiquette also recommends more concrete behaviours with implications for the nature of Reddit's content. Most importantly, the users seem to strive for high integrity and thus set an unusually high linguistic standard for themselves. Among other things, they encourage using "proper" grammar and spelling (even encouraging corrections, though no specific standard or guidelines are given) as well as proof-reading submissions, remaining factual, referencing original sources, avoiding redundancy, and providing constructive criticism where appropriate.

In practice, however, subreddits seem to differ in terms of the extent to which they adhere to these ideals. While communities with stricter rule enforcement do exist (e.g., r/AskHistorians, which requires all answers be comprehensive and well-sourced), most subreddits, especially those in the spirit of more casual discussion forums, simply do not provide a reasonable context for such demands. As such, Reddit still offers ample opportunity for variation, not least because its community-driven design encourages users to create subreddits with their own rules if the available options do not agree with them. This freedom will hence engender distinct communicative contexts that cater to the specific needs of groups of people that have not yet found "their community" elsewhere. In combination with Reddit's voting system and the claim to "[m]oderate based on quality, not opinion" (Reddit Help 2021), then, it seems likely that moderation rather reinforces what these communities consider (contextually, i.e., for the respective community) appropriate language use instead of determining standards a priori. The existence of a karma system (named after the religious concept), i.e., points earned by receiving upvotes and paid awards, further amplifies this effect.

Against this background, it should become apparent that Reddit encourages the continuous creation of situationally and hence functionally distinct contexts of language production. In view of this dynamicity, Titak and Roberson (2013: 236) argue convincingly that internet linguistics is in desperate need of a theoretical model that "provides focus for linguistic research across web texts" such that rigorous comparisons of the interplay between sociocultural factors and their linguistic consequences in CMC contexts become possible. One concept that has been repeatedly employed in hopes of fulfilling this purpose is register, a cover term for any "variety associated with a particular situation of use" (Biber and Conrad 2009: 6). Previous research on internet registers has so far largely followed the multidimensional approach (MDA) by Biber (1988), identifying significant linguistic overlaps with offline counterparts (see e.g., Titak and Roberson 2013; Berber Sardinha 2014). Notably, the most prominent dimension of variation online also seems to be the distinction between involved vs. informational production, which contrasts pronoun-heavy personal involvement with content-focused nominal features. However, these studies tend to keep the crucial step from variable contexts to such systematic differences in language use rather vague, selecting features indiscriminately with little theoretical motivation for the registers at hand.

In this context, Biber and Egbert (2018: 26) further criticise that many corpus-based studies of register variation identify registers of interest based on perceptual salience, evaluating texts against the face validity of labels assigned to them. However, their framework, which relies on human coders to categorise texts based on predefined situational characteristics is not decidedly different from relying on perceptual salience as it likewise artificially restricts the types of text deemed linguistically meaningful. Indeed, the fact that raters often disagreed at the lowest granularity due to the seemingly inherent hybridity of web texts, which often combine features from different registers, advocates for an approach that focuses solely on characterising documents by their contextual parameters and connecting them to concrete linguistic correlates (i.e., textual features). Such an approach should form the basis of analysis because "linguistic differences among registers can be derived from situational differences", but "patterns of behaviour cannot be derived from any linguistic phenomena" (Biber and Conrad 2009: 9). As such, though these studies may provide convincing evidence for the existence of variation, they fall short in terms of systematically describing this crucial underlying relationship, which hinders comparable generalisations, especially online.

The present work argues that this gap can be best addressed by conceptualising online registers the same way as offline ones by connecting both perspectives through the concept of instantiation in systemic functional theory (Halliday 1978; see Halliday and Matthiessen 2014 for an introduction). Instantiation describes the gradual process of realisation whereby language users collapse the overall meaning potential of the language system (i.e., all available linguistic choices) into concrete instances (i.e., texts with specific features) according to the particular "scenario ... from which the things which are said derive their meaning" (Halliday 1978: 28). Naturally, this context of situation frequently recurs probabilistically in particular configurations that can be defined in terms of the continuous variables field, tenor and mode of discourse, which broadly correspond to topic/purpose, participant relationships like social distance, and aspects of text construction such as medium or preparedness. Together, these three dimensions enable consistent groupings of web documents because they resonate with the basic metafunctions of language and therefore have immediate functional correspondences (Halliday and Matthiessen 2014: 34). For example, on a subreddit for providing expert answers to historical questions like r/AskHistorians, texts will likely have a high lexical density to provide information and use verb phrases in past tense.

On the so-called cline of instantiation, registers occupy the mid region between the two outer system and instance poles because they exist at "varying degrees of specificity" (Halliday 1978: 111) so that the differences between them can be interpreted as a multidimensional "continuum of variation" (Biber and Conrad 2009: 33). As such, linguistic variation according to context of use should be observed both top-down, i.e., from above at the system pole, as registers defined by situational aspects, and bottom-up, i.e., from below at the instance pole, as text types defined linguistically, since these perspectives provide complementary information, like Biber and Egbert (2018: 213) also conclude. By the same token, register analyses typically focus on different ends of this continuum to foreground one area within the "range from a macro-register to the micro-registers that it consists of" (Matthiessen 2019: 20). Transferred to the present work, Reddit can be theorised as one example of a macro register, comprised of more specific instantiations in the form of specialised communities; after all, the notion of a hierarchy is already implied in its organisation into subreddits. Assuming such a structured perspective on categorisation largely obviates the need for subjective judgements and therefore ensures meaningful comparisons even as the register landscape changes.

For Reddit, Liimatta (2019) found evidence of systematic groupings by community along linguistic dimensions comparable to other internet registers (despite a noticeable personal bias in the corpus design), yet the comparatively low variance explained nicely demonstrates that comparing average frequency scores hides more nuanced differences between these presumably more specific texts (see Matthiessen 2019: 20). To combat this shortcoming, Diwersy et al. (2014) developed GMA, a pipeline for visualising linguistic differences between individual texts in multivariate register space. To do so, GMA uses Principal Component Analysis

(PCA) to identify latent dimensions of variation in the data that combine as much of the features' shared variance as possible. The resulting smaller subspace is chosen such that distances between data points remain meaningful with respect to the linguistic (dis)similarities of the original feature vectors, thereby revealing more delicate distribution patterns than aggregated group centroids or broad feature correlations patterns could (Neumann and Evert 2021: 146). Compared to Biber's (1988) MDA, GMA encourages exploring visualisations based on theoretical considerations, which is particularly helpful in online contexts where the significant functional and linguistic variables may not always be intuitively obvious (see Biber and Egbert 2018).

3 Method

The corpus for this study was compiled as a subset of the ConvoKit (Chang et al. 2020) datasets based on the r/ListOfSubreddits (2018) wiki, which contains a user-sourced list of communities grouped by categories such as discussion, education, or entertainment. Of course, one community is not representative of the entire user-base of Reddit; still, this list naturally emerged as a community effort and was not elicited according to a predefined schema (cf. Biber and Egbert 2018). The categories can therefore be considered authentic, albeit removed from linguistic theory, which is, in fact, desirable for the purposes of this study because it becomes possible to test whether these groupings are not only socially but also linguistically "real" from a register standpoint. To enable comparability, the subreddits were functionally characterised in terms of the field, tenor, and mode parameters above, and selected to cover a wide range of contextual variation. Where multiple options were feasible, the largest one deemed most representative of its category took precedence, assuming a lower specificity of features that is more amenable to this first exploration of linguistic distinctiveness (see Matthiessen 2019: 30). For each one, only the first 5000 threads before May 4th, 2018, were analysed because they had been archived and could therefore be considered complete texts that are fully realised linguistically. To reduce noise in the visualisation, this paper reports on only ten of the thirty-three selected subreddits as illustrative examples (see Table 1).

Table 1: Summary of selected subreddits with descriptions.

Subreddit	Description
AskHistorians	answers to questions about history
DIY	talking about homemade projects
GifRecipes	recipes in short video format
history	general discussions about history
recipes	sharing different kinds of recipes
science	discussing new scientific research
talesfromtechsupport	stories about working in tech support
techsupport	troubleshooting technical issues
UnsentLetters	sharing unsent personal letters
WritingPrompts	prompts for creative writing

Since GMA regards each text individually, sampling issues do not run as high a risk of under-representing registers with more internal variation, like Berber Sardinha (2014: 86) cautions for MDA. At the same time, this means defining what exactly constitutes one text is a crucial theoretical consideration. On Reddit, posts are best viewed as initial turns in a conversation continued by recursive comments from other users, leading to a hierarchical tree-like structure. The present study considers each of these emergent threads as one text for two main reasons. Firstly, the immediate context of situation pertains to the entire thread, so regarding comments separately, like Titak and Roberson (2013: 242) do for blogs, seems arbitrary here since they are not merely about a text but actively co-create it and must therefore be considered a component part that usually cannot stand alone. In a similar vein, the producer-user distinction proposed by Berber Sardinha (2014: 83) appears unfounded, considering that any user actively participating in a thread, by definition, simultaneously produces and consumes it. Additionally, there's the more practical consideration of statistical validity, which demands a certain minimum text length to achieve meaningful quantitative results. For GMA, this threshold lies around 100 words, or 10 sentences (Neumann and Evert 2021: 149), which even threads often fail to reach, so using shorter individual contributions would be unfeasible. Ultimately, this approach resulted in a sample of 74,960 texts.

All texts were normalised in terms of formatting and tokens tagged for their part of speech using the CLAWS C7 tagset (Garside and Smith 1997) whose granularity allows querying more complex lexicogrammatical features. Though not specifically trained on "dirty" web data (Kilgarriff and Grefenstette 2003: 342), a cursory inspection of the results showed no systematic errors that would disproportionately affect certain communities in the statistical analysis, not least because Reddit appears unusually concerned with correctness, as previously discussed. The selected subcorpora were transformed into a verticalised format (one token per line) and indexed for automatic feature extraction with the CWB platform (Evert and Hardie 2011). The query script by Neumann and Evert (2021) was used as the starting point for linguistic operationalisation of their contextual differences. As intended for GMA, the feature catalogue was adapted to count usernames as proper nouns. Additionally, titles were disregarded in favour of contractions and hyperlinks as characteristic features online. Three other features measuring emojis, edits, and forms of address, intended to replace salutations, ended up being too sparse to include. Due to high correlations, which may exaggerate effect sizes by measuring the same underlying structures, aggregate adjective counts were also removed. The input table therefore consisted of 42 features (see Table 2), all normalised as relative frequencies with respect to sensible units of measurement (see Neumann and Evert 2021: 150).

PCA relies on correlations between these features to project them onto new axes, which are chosen such that their combined variance is maximised. Compared to the rather opaque semantic relationships modelled by embeddings, its deterministic visualisation enables systematic interpretations grounded in register theory at the cost of being sensitive to scaling differences. The raw feature scores showed extreme variation and outliers, so log-transformed z-scores are used to deskew the distributions (see Neumann and Evert 2021: 151). Since higher-dimensional visualisations become increasingly harder to grasp and each Principal Component (PC) explains significantly less variance, only the first four components were analysed. Together, they already account for 42.9% of the original data, comparable to Biber and Egbert (2018) and a significant improvement over 17%, achieved by Liimatta (2019) using MDA. Here, only the first two, still accounting for over 30% variance, are described. Due to its overly optimistic group-awareness, a complementary Linear Discriminant Analysis (LDA), which can be used to reveal more subtle variation (Neumann and Evert 2021: 46), hides pronounced differences that emerge quite clearly in the PCA, so this step was omitted for the purposes of this study. All calculations and visualisations were performed in the statistical programming language R (R Core Team 2021) using the GMA utilities provided by Neumann and Evert (2021).[1]

1 The compilation and analysis scripts for the full corpus are available at https://osf.io/a7m9d/ (last accessed 14 February 2025).

Table 2: Summary of selected features with descriptions.

Feature	Description
adv_initial_S	sentence-initial adverbs per sentence
atadj_W	attributive adjectives per word
contr_W	contractions per word
coordination_F	coordinating conjunctions per finite
disc_initial_S	sentence-initial discourse markers per word
finite_S	finites per sentence
imperative_S	imperatives per sentence
infinitive_F	to-infinitives per finite
interrogative_S	interrogatives per sentence
it_P	it-pronouns per pronoun
lexical_density	lexical density (proportion of content words)
modal_verb_V	modal verbs per verb
neoclass_W	neoclassical compounds per word
nn_W	common nouns per word
nom_initial_S	sentence-initial nominal elements per sentence
nominal_W	nominalisations per word
nonfin_initial_S	sentence-initial infinitive clauses per sentence
np_W	proper nouns per word
p1_perspron_P	1st person personal pronouns per pronoun
p2_perspron_P	2nd person personal pronoun per pronoun
p3_perspron_P	3rd person personal pronouns per pronoun
passive_F	passives per finite
past_tense_F	past tense verbs per finite
place_adv_W	adverbs of place per word
pospers1_W	1st person pronouns per word
pospers2_W	2nd person pronouns per word
pospers3_W	3rd person pronouns per word
poss_pronoun_W	possessive pronouns per word

Feature	Description
predadj_W	predicative adjectives per word
prep_initial_S	sentence-initial prepositional phrases per sentence
prep_W	prepositions per word
pronoun_all_W	all pronouns per word
subord_initial_S	sentence-initial subordinate clauses per sentence
subordination_F	subordinating conjunctions per finite
text_initial_S	sentence-initial discourse markers per sentence
time_adv_W	adverbs of time per word
url_W	hyperlinks per word
verb_initial_S	sentence-initial verbal elements per sentence
verb_W	verbs per word
wh_initial_S	sentence-initial wh-elements per sentence
will_F	will futures per finite
word_S	words per sentence

4 Results

Figure 1 shows a grouped scatter plot of the first two PCs for the ten exemplary subreddits analysed in this study, with PC1 on the y-axis and PC2 on the x-axis. The scatter plot is split into two faceting groups for better readability. All axes are scaled equally so as to be understood as different perspectives on the same underlying space comprised by the first four PCA dimensions. Within this space, each dot, colour-coded for subreddit, represents one text whose position is determined by its score for the respective PCs such that their potential clustering can be analysed based on a dumbbell plot of the loadings for PC1 and PC2 (Figure 2). These loadings indicate the relative prominence of each linguistic indicator after reducing the dimensions of the original data vectors by capturing their combined variance as linear combinations of the input features. In other words, the score (and thus the position) of each text on a given PC depends on how strongly its most frequent features are represented by that dimension. The quantitative focus of the results is enriched with selected qualitative analyses to help ground abstract feature frequencies in their functional expression within concrete texts. To protect the pseudonymity of users, examples reference the unique ID of the post they belong to, which enables replicability but hopefully hinders immediate user identification.

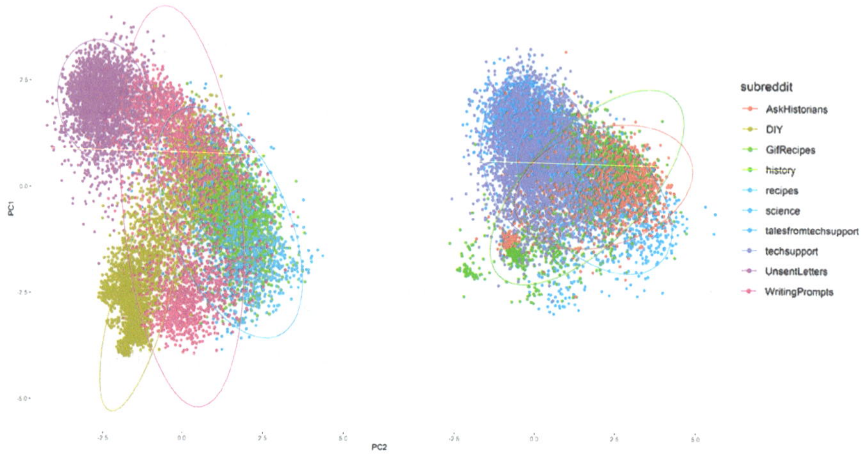

Figure 1: Scatter plot of text scores for PC1 and PC2.

Regarding the loadings of PC1, imperatives, hyperlinks, common nouns, and second person personal pronouns have the strongest negative contributions, being slightly below -0.2. Both imperatives and pronouns point towards an instructional goal orientation and interpersonal albeit authoritative involvement with an addressee for the tenor of discourse. This is also supported by the significant contributions of discourse markers in theme position and, to a lesser extent, initial verbal elements. At the same time, common nouns and, relatedly, lexical density indicate a rather informational character in terms of purpose. That hyperlinks load as strongly as imperatives suggests that language takes on an ancillary role in texts on this part of the first dimension, accompanying content outside of the thread. The positive side of PC1 loadings, on the other hand, is dominated by features typical of a spoken medium with narrative purpose, as evidenced by five out of the seven strongest indicators relating to the use of first- and third-person personal pronouns, which presumably also explains the weights above +0.2 for initial nominal elements. The loading just under +0.2 for past tense in combination with contractions indicate rather informal narration, presumably in the form of personal stories.

For the second PC, the strongest indicators on the negative side resemble the positive side of PC1 in that they largely pertain to pronoun use; however, instead of the third person, second-person pronouns have the highest value, even surpassing said indicator with a value of under -0.3. Since five out of six strong features are again pronoun-related, this is closely followed by a general indicator for all pronouns as well as possessive pronouns slightly below -0.3. Rather than narration, this dimension therefore seems to capture interpersonal involvement more generally, positing conversation as a communicative purpose in itself. The apparent correlation with a high frequency of verbs, which are typical of spoken discourse, supports this notion. On the opposite end, attributive adjectives, which are generally associated with more informational writing, have the highest loading score. Appropriate indicators of nominal style also make considerable contributions to the positive side of PC2, especially lexical density coming in fourth but also common and proper nouns with loadings around +0.2. This is complemented by third person personal pronouns and the pronoun *it*, both above +0.2, which hint at an expository goal orientation. The rest of this section will now relate patterns in the distribution of texts from different subreddits to these feature combinations.

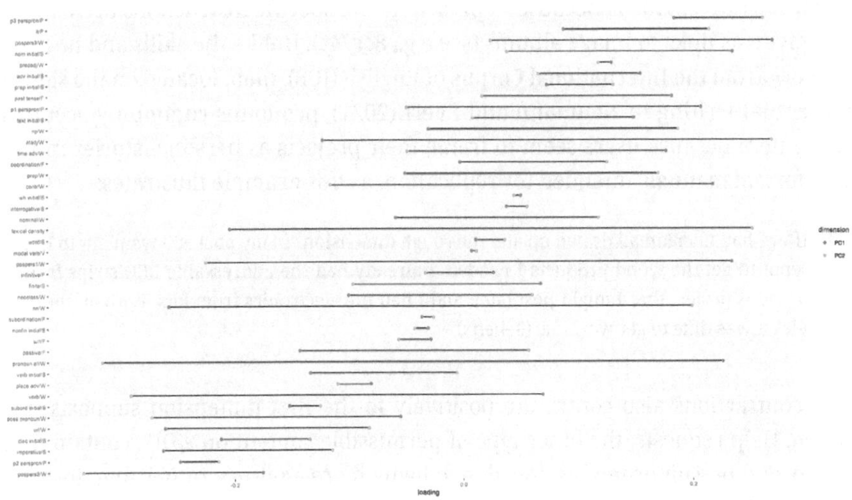

Figure 2: Dumbbell plot of feature loadings for PC1 and PC2.

r/GifRecipes is a media-sharing community, so its texts would be prototypically expected to contain features of ancillary language use, such as hyperlinks and imperatives. Indeed, they strongly favour negative scores on PC1, which is associated with these indicators. Looking at concrete examples reveals that this results from posters including written versions of the recipes shown, which link to the source video and use imperatives to provide step-by-step instructions like "Pat dry the duck breasts with a paper towel." (7jwqig). The list of ingredients, then, also explains the apparent prominence of common nouns, engendering a high lexical density that moves the texts towards positive PC2 scores. Consequently, they often show strong similarities to their printed counterparts in terms of form and content, as seen in Biber and Egbert (2018: 138). Perhaps unsurprisingly, the functionally similar but less specific r/recipes also tends towards negative scores on PC1 and the positive side of PC2 but shows more variation overall, suggesting that one encompasses the other. Outliers are readily explained by posts that only link to a recipe (see e.g., 7s1xcv), or questions (see e.g., 7sir6i). In both cases, personal deixis from the comment section will start to dominate, pushing texts towards the lower right quadrant of higher interpersonal involvement.

In line with formal expectations, r/DIY should likewise be characterised by imperatives and, accordingly, verbs in sentence-initial position since the subreddit requires submissions to include detailed instructions. However, given that the positive indicators for PC1, where these texts primarily cluster, strongly weigh personal pronouns, this subreddit does not seem to be prototypically instructional but rather narrative. This is because, if present at all, specific instructions are usually only given as links to image albums (see e.g., 8cr74f). Unlike the skills and hobbies category from the International Corpus of English (ICE), then, located on the side of conceptual writing in Neumann and Evert (2021), pronouns commonly occur as theme here because users seem to frame their projects as personal stories rather than formal manuals intended for replication, as this example illustrates:

> After I had my plan all drawn up and the rough dimensions in my pocket, I went out to Home Depot to get the wood products I needed. I already had the addressable LED strips from a previous project that I might post later, and I had the electronics from kits. With all the supplies it was time to get working. (8ebeqx)

That contractions also contribute positively to the first dimension supports this notion. Help requests, the other type of permissible content on r/DIY, contain first and second person pronouns, too, due to being more advisory rather than instructional, again indicating that users employ a more involved style (cf. Biber and Egbert 2018: 57).

In contrast, r/WritingPrompts generally favours pronoun usage across PCs where they attest a narrative goal orientation, which is consistent with Neumann and Evert's (2021: 11) findings for the creative writing category in the ICE (cf. Biber and Egbert 2018: 102). For PC2, there are texts that demonstrate indicators more in line with the literate-nominal dimension from Biber and Egbert (2018) as well, however. In the following excerpt, a prompt about Canada dropping an atomic bomb in the First World War was addressed with a historical speech, for instance: "1917, the year everything changed. On April 6 the US declared war on the Allied Powers after an American ship was accidentally sunk by British torpedoes and a French message to Mexico was intercepted by the Germans." (8eg6zf). It seems, therefore, that this variation is attributable to differences in the register targeted by the prompt and its realisation, which may be predictable from the position in the feature space. Still, neither of these functional characterisations explain the joint clustering of r/DIY and r/WritingPrompts at the negative end of the first PC. Taking a closer look at the text with the lowest score on PC1, located at -4, reveals the following comment:

> Your submission has been removed for one or more of the following reason(s): Your question might be answered with a few minutes of basic research of this subject. ... Please read our guidelines before resubmitting. If you believe this was a mistake, please message the moderators. (r/DIY: 8gmgnw)

This response was sent by a moderator of r/DIY because they deemed the poster failed to do their own research before asking a question as is required by the subreddit's guidelines. Since the original submission was removed due to this rule violation, the thread consists solely of the above cited comment. This, then, explains the feature combination that seems to predominantly characterise the negative side of PC1. Across the text, there are several exophoric references in the form of hyperlinks to helpful resources, using imperatives with the discourse marker *please* as theme to point out aspects of their submission (hence also the comparatively high frequency of second person possessive pronouns) and instruct them how to avoid having their posts deleted in the future. Additionally, moderation messages are presumably not produced spontaneously but prepared beforehand and constantly refined, striving for conciseness and intelligibility, which would explain the somewhat nominal style evident in the feature loadings. While these messages could have been removed to bring out the characteristics of user contributions more, the apparent linguistic impact and curating function warrant their inclusion as a prominent register feature, at least for an explorative study such as this.

To provide another example, a nearby text from r/WritingPrompts (8efxuk) has no responses because the user deleted their post and only contains an automated message by a bot that reads: "Off-Topic Discussion: All top-level comments must be a story or poem. Reply here for other comments." Once again, the comment contains imperatives and hyperlinks, but because it is a more general message not directed to a specific user, it lacks second person personal pronouns, so the text is more centred on the second PC. For the sake of thread organisation, every post on r/WritingPrompts automatically receives such a notification. Given this central function, they must likewise be considered part of this community's register despite (or rather because of) their impact on the feature distribution. As texts move towards the positive end of PC1, these kinds of messages become less prominent linguistically. The difference between the lower and upper cluster of texts, then, lies in the prevalence of responses to the prompt. In that case, the distinctive features of moderation will be gradually overshadowed by narrative indicators, which are characteristic of the subreddit. In other words, the higher the proportion of text produced by actual users, the further the data points are pushed along PC1. The writing prompt with the highest positive score (8h2wyr), for example, received only one story, but due to its length, the bot comment becomes negligible in comparison.

Looking at other selected texts in the bottom cluster of the first PC reveals that this phenomenon roughly occurs below scores of -2 and remains consistent across subreddits, so PC1 seems to separate user comments from moderation messages quite well. The respective subgroupings can be traced back to different kinds of rule violations and comparatively minor variation in the posts' titles, which suggests that the underlying causes for moderation action could be reliably derived from linguistic indicators alone. The prominent group of r/DIY texts around -3, for instance, predominantly seem to have been moderated because they consisted of only a single image (see e.g., 8ajadx). This, then, also explains why only a few hundred texts from r/DIY were too short to include in the analysis compared to over half for most others. Instead of potentially indicating the type of content found in a community, or even specific rules (providing detailed instructions for a project presumably requires a certain number of words, after all), text length may therefore hint at how actively the community is moderated. In any case, the presence of such messages adds another layer to the already somewhat opaque social relationships online as interactions need not occur exclusively between humans.

Moving on from r/WritingPrompts to another narrative subreddit, r/talesfromtechsupport expresses the same goal orientation predominantly via first and third person pronouns. The texts also show similarities to phone calls in this respect, as investigated by Neumann and Evert (2021: 10), because they tend to originate in help desk situations and therefore heavily feature quotes of participants. The subreddit seems to be a lot more homogeneous as a result and therefore appears quite concentrated around moderately positive scores on PC1 in the visualisation, similar to creative writing. The following excerpt is a typical example illustrating this overlap:

> I get an email from a user ... to say that they can't send email via our SMTP server. ... I look at the logs and I can see he's having problems authenticating so my guess is that ... he's fiddled with his settings. I phone him up and ask. "No", he says "I've not changed my settings at all". (76068s)

Interestingly, no moderation subgroup pattern emerges for this subreddit despite its rather strict rules because inappropriate posts are filtered, viz. removed, before submission. r/techsupport provides an interesting contrast to r/talesfromtechsupport because it is essentially a more general version of this community without the narrative focus; that its cluster in Figure 1 appears overall less focused, comparable to the difference between r/GifRecipes and r/recipes, aligns with this observation. Even so, for a subreddit about asking for help, the contribution of interrogatives to their position are surprisingly negligible. Looking more closely at individual texts reveals that this is because users often formulate their concerns as statements, such as "Computer will not shutdown" (8ff8qw).

Regarding the more explicit question-answering subreddits, r/AskHistorians is marked for the same nominal features (positive PC2) as r/science (see e.g., 88c69h) and r/history (see e.g., 8852wy, also a question), especially attributive adjectives, lexical density, and common nouns. This, then, means that the Q&A aspect of these subreddits is not dominantly reflected in frequent use of interrogatives either since questions would typically only occur in the post itself. On r/AskHistorians, in particular, comments are expected to be quite detailed and supported by credible sources, leading to a content focus evidenced by its general position in the scatter plot. For instance, one user's explanation for why Italy did not join the Central Powers during WWI starts as follows:

> With the exception of a few people in the Italian High Command no one considered the possibility of Italy joining the side of the Central Empires as a serious eventuality. And that included the Germans and Austrians who had clear understanding of the situation of the Triple Alliance. (8agen9)

In the upper groupings, the cline of experiential specificity from science to history seems to emerge as greater variation in the more general r/science. This is particularly evident on PC2 where outliers are attributable to copies of abstracts (see e.g., 89cpuh) or paraphrases of journal articles (see e.g., 89dxqi), explaining their position on the nominal as opposed to the more characteristically spoken negative end of the dimension. Conversely, the cluster of r/history is overall more focused around moderately positive values for PC2 because all posts are first reviewed by human moderators. In contrast to other moderation messages, the outliers for r/history and r/AskHistorians are therefore considerably less marked for PC1 and rather favour negative PC2 scores because they try to achieve a more personable, conversational tone, as the following examples both illustrate:

> Your submission has been automatically removed because it triggered some filters since you are fairly new. This is nothing to worry about, if your post follows the r/history rules we can approve it for you once you message us. (r/history: 8g1ptc)

> Hi there - unfortunately we have had to remove your question, because /r/AskHistorians isn't here to do your homework for you. (r/AskHistorians: 8ga21p)

Lastly, the userbase of r/ListOfSubreddits (2018) categorises r/UnsentLetters as a support community, but the subreddit's rules expressly forbid unsolicited opinions or advice. Accordingly, its texts lack the typical indicators of problem-solving present in other advice documents, being characterised by first and third rather than second person pronouns (cf. Biber and Egbert 2018: 128). Outliers on the negative end of PC1 and the positive end of PC2 seem to be primarily letters in other languages (see e.g., 8b1vmy). The premise of personal letters that users were too afraid to send explains this linguistic overlap with social letters in Neumann and Evert (2021: 151). At the same time, users frequently narratively reflect on past events in an informal manner, leading to even stronger PC1 loadings due to contractions, verbs in the past tense, and time adverbs. For example, in the letter with the highest positive score, the poster laments, "I wish I didn't love him anymore. I wish I didn't care about him anymore. I wish I didn't need him" (8h2hxj). Presumably due to the aforementioned rule, comments seem to be rare on this subreddit, so the features of such posts become more pronounced (or rather less blurred), which explains why its texts have such a prominent position, even in the full feature space.

5 Discussion

The results reveal that subreddits systematically cluster in terms of their linguistic features, suggesting that they can indeed be considered subregisters of Reddit. Indeed, conceptually related communities generally cover similar areas, attesting to a continuous space of variation in this yet tentative macro register (see Neumann and Evert 2021: 152), perhaps brought out further by their hybrid functions. Specifically, it seems that the majority of subreddits display features of involvement alongside those specific to the respective subreddit, which is expected of a social media site for discussing specialised interests. The analysis has also demonstrated striking overlaps with offline registers, which valorises these communities as registers proper. Based on those salient similarities, one could argue, as Biber and Egbert (2018: 42) do for blogs, that Reddit represents a kind of microcosm of the web, viz. the web at large is reflected on a smaller scale within its communities. In a way, subreddits are dense accumulations of web content that also exists elsewhere, which attract interested users with easily understandable and searchable labels that would otherwise be hard to find. By demonstrating that they can be differentiated linguistically via computational means, these findings pave the way toward automated functional web categorisation, for example for the purpose of informational retrieval.

A significant variable that becomes quite salient on the internet, and particularly public discussion forums, but has so far been ignored in register variation research is moderation. It shapes the context of online communication not only socially but also linguistically since moderators represent the de facto authority over the kind of language permissible in a given community. This has become abundantly clear by the separation of multiple subreddits into moderated and unmoderated texts on the first, most significant PCA dimension. A comparative investigation into the extent to which moderation solely occurs based on violations of conventionalised social norms and formal properties of contributions or if such measures also have a linguistic basis could prove valuable. The fact that certain subreddits evaluate submissions based on goal orientations with well-defined linguistic indicators (e.g., whether they entail a narrative element) certainly suggests so. This is especially relevant considering that many subreddits off-load moderation work to bots, a trend that has become increasingly relevant on the internet in recent years. In general, the issue of bots has likewise not yet received due attention in the field of internet linguistics despite important implications for the representativeness of register corpora and opportunities for variation studies.

Another relevant aspect of Reddit not touched upon in this study was the potential impact that votes and awards (purchased with real money) may have on a communities' language use because they can be used to affect the visibility of contributions. Depending on the chosen sorting strategy, posts with a high score have a chance to land on the website's front page and the respective subreddit's feed, whereas popular comments appear earlier in the thread. Notably, unlike other social media, users are discouraged from downvoting posts based on opinion; rather than emotional reactions, votes are thus supposed to reflect whether a post is "contributing to the community dialogue" (Reddit Help 2021). A post's score, then, is, at least in theory, not as much a stamp of approval as it is a sign of quality. In other words, from a linguistic perspective, one could argue that these ratings may not only indicate a more general value-judgement but also how well a given post fits the userbase's implicit notion of that subreddit's register. Future studies may therefore want to explore the extent to which selecting threads with negative scores would affect the positioning of texts in the visualisation and how this is reflected in terms of changes in the most prominent linguistic features.

A detailed investigation of lexicogrammatical differences for selected subreddits is required to gain more systematic insights into the patterns of linguistic features engendered by community-specific rules revealed in this explorative study. Introducing additional information into the analysis via a weakly supervised LDA could prove fruitful in this context. In particular, LDA may be used to reduce the impact that moderation messages have on the feature space by foregrounding community-specific variation without removing them entirely. Moreover, choosing the thread as the unit of analysis under the assumption that each of them constitutes a single, homogeneous conversation and, by extension, one text, has had significant implications not only in terms of methodological possibilities but potentially also the results overall. Due to the tree-like structure of threads, it seems that contextual parameters often operate at lower levels of instantiation, either in local branches or perhaps even at the level of individual contributions. This was reflected in the fact that the tenor-related effects of user interactions could not be properly accounted for. Any future investigation of the sociolinguistic dynamics on the internet in systemic functional terms therefore presupposes an extensive adaptation of the framework and its operationalisations by considering the characteristic features of CMC. At the heart of this endeavour lies a follow-up study that uses GMA to investigate texts at some level below the thread.

References

Berber Sardinha, Tony. 2014. 25 years later: Comparing internet and pre-internet registers. In Tony Berber Sardinha & Marcia Veirano Pinto (eds.), *Multi-dimensional analysis, 25 years on: A tribute to Douglas Biber*, 81–105. Amsterdam: Benjamins.

Berber Sardinha, Tony. 2018. Dimensions of variation across internet registers. *International Journal of Corpus Linguistics* 23 (2). 125–157.

Biber, Douglas. 1988. *Variation across speech and writing*. New York: Cambridge University Press.

Biber, Douglas & Susan Conrad. 2009. *Register, genre, and style*. New York: Cambridge University Press.

Biber, Douglas & Jesse Egbert. 2018. *Register variation online*. New York: Cambridge University Press.

Chang, Jonathan P., Caleb Chiam, Liye Fu, Andrew Wang, Justine Zhang, & Cristian Danescu-Niculescu-Mizil. 2020. *ConvoKit:* A toolkit for the analysis of conversations. In *Proceedings of the 21th Annual Meeting of the Special Interest Group on Discourse and Dialogue*, 57–60.

Diwersy, Sascha, Stefan Evert & Stella Neumann. 2014. A weakly supervised multivariate approach to the study of language variation. In Benedikt Szmrecsanyi & Bernhard Wälchli (eds.), *Aggregating dialectology, typology, and register analysis: Linguistic variation in text and speech*, 174–204. Berlin & Bosten: De Gruyter.

Evert, Stefan & Andrew Hardie. 2011. Twenty-first century corpus workbench: Updating a query architecture for the new millennium. In: *Proceedings of the Corpus Linguistics Conference 2011*, 1–21.

Garside, Roger & Nicholas Smith. 1997. A hybrid grammatical tagger: CLAWS4. In Roger Garside, Geoffrey Leech & Anthony McEnery (eds.), *Corpus annotation: Linguistic information from computer text corpora*, 102–121. London: Longman.

Halliday, Michael Alexander Kirkwood. 1978. *Language as social semiotic: The social interpretation of language and meaning*. London: Arnold.

Halliday, Michael Alexander Kirkwood & Christian Matthias Ingemar Martin Matthiessen. 2014. *Introduction to functional grammar*, 4th edition. New York: Routledge.

Kilgarriff, Adam. & Gregory Grefenstette. 2003. Introduction to the special issue on the web as corpus. *Computational Linguistics* 29 (3). 333–347.
Liimatta, Aatu. 2019. Exploring register variation on reddit: A multi-dimensional study of language use on a social media website. *Register Studies* 1 (2). 269–295.
Matthiessen, Christian Matthias Ingemar Martin. 2019. Register in systemic functional linguistics. *Register Studies* 1 (1). 10–41.
Neumann, Stella & Stefan Evert. 2021. A register variation perspective on varieties of English. In Elena Seoane & Douglas Biber (eds.), *Corpus based approaches to register variation*, 143–178. Amsterdam: Benjamins.
R Core Team. 2021. *R: A language and environment for statistical computing*. Vienna: R Foundation for Statistical Computing.
Reddit Help. 2021. Reddiquette. https://www.reddithelp.com/hc/en-us/articles/205926439 (last accessed 15 May 2023).
Reddit Inc. 2022. Content policy. https://www.redditinc.com/policies/content-policy (last accessed 15 May 2023).
r/ListOfSubreddits. 2018. List of subreddits. https://www.reddit.com/r/ListOfSubreddits/wiki/listofsubreddits (last modified 14 October 2018).
Titak, Ashley & Audrey Roberson. 2013. Dimensions of web registers: An exploratory multi-dimensional comparison. *Corpora* 8 (2). 235–260.

Louis Cotgrove

Novel methods of intensification in young people's digitally-mediated communication

Abstract: The following chapter proposes a typology of intensification in German digitally-mediated communication (DMC). Intensification has been conventionally understood as a lexicogrammatical process modifying the quality of an element in a sentence – either amplifying or diminishing it – through the use of another element known as an intensifier. However, developments within DMC have seen intensification strategies progress beyond a traditional understanding of the concept and even beyond grammatical categorisation. Using authentic data from the *NottDeuYTSch* corpus of YouTube comments, the chapter classifies intensification in five categories: morphological, syntactic, expressive, graphemic, and typographical, and explores elements containing multiple aspects of intensification. The typology of intensification presented in this chapter showcases the creative usage of digital resources and how this can influence our understanding of traditional linguistic concepts.

Keywords: intensification, semiotics, digitally-mediated communication, youth language, corpus linguistics, pragmatics, interaction

1 Introduction

Written digitally-mediated communication (DMC) has, since its inception in the late 1970s, been characterised by novel and creative writing strategies, such as the use of repeated graphemes to represent prosody (Carey 1980). As DMC has become ubiquitous in much of the world, the strategies have also evolved and matured, moving from simple emulation of features of spoken language (see Runkehl, Schlobinski, and Siever 1998; Storrer 2001) to a sophisticated and often conventionalised system of signs (Androutsopoulos 2018: 742). These conventions include the use of informal language and graphemes for 'expressivity', i.e., writing strategies to convey certain pragmatic functions, such as the use of capital letters (e.g., 'shouting capitals', Crystal 2004), emoji or intensifiers. It is this third group of features, inten-

Louis Cotgrove, Leibniz-Institut für Deutsche Sprache, e-mail: cotgrove@ids-mannheim.de

https://doi.org/10.1515/9783111434018-006

sifiers, that will be the focus of this chapter, in particular the intensification strategies used by young German speakers in DMC.

Intensification has traditionally been defined as a lexicogrammatical process that refers to the modification (both enhancement and reduction) of the quality of an element (usually an adjective) in a sentence by another element (an intensifier) (Bolinger 1972; Quirk et al. 1985). For example, the adverb *sehr* ('very') in Example 1 modifies the adjective *geil* ('awesome') to increase its quality, or the prefix *semi* in Example 2 reduces the quality of the adjective to which it is attached.

(1) *NottDeuYTSch Corpus NDY/264/013889*
das video war **sehr geil**
[the video was **very awesome**][1]

(2) *NottDeuYTSch Corpus NDY/165/002098*
Also den Humor an sich find ich ja eher so **semigeil**
[Well I find the humour itself sort of **semi-awesome**]

Since the 2010s, however, the definition of an intensifier and the analysis of intensification have moved away from a focus on lexemes and morphemes, which this chapter develops further through the analysis of strategies that occur in DMC, specifically DMC written by young people in YouTube comments as part of the *NottDeuYTSch* corpus (Cotgrove 2018).[2]

One of the commonly described features of young people's language overlaps with DMC, namely the tendency towards expressiveness in writing, particularly the use of intensifiers (see Tagliamonte 2016b: 81). Intensifiers have been characterised by Tagliamonte (2016b: 92) as important markers of youth identity and are prone to frequent change, as overuse leads to a loss in effectiveness. Similarly, Hilte, Vandekerckhove, and Daelemans (2019: 295), in a study of youth language online, noted the high use of 'expressive markers', including intensifiers, by Flemish teenagers. Therefore, the data from the *NottDeuYTSch* corpus are likely to contain diverse and emergent intensification strategies, justifying the rationale for selecting the corpus to develop a typology of intensifiers.

---

1 I have taken quite a free approach to translating the intensified expressions, but I have tried to stay consistent with the translations of the same lexical item.

2 The *NottDeuYTSch* corpus contains over 33 million words from YouTube comments written under German-language videos published between 2008 and 2018, constructed to be representative of the language used by young people under mainstream YouTube videos. See Section 3 for more details.

The chapter is divided into four parts: Section 2 first defines the concept of intensification used in this chapter, with reference to previous definitions, before discussing the mainly English and German-language literature on intensification, including competing terms for similar functions and intensification strategies used in youth language or DMC contexts. Section 3 outlines the corpus data used for the analysis, before presenting the typology of intensification in youth DMC, analysing each mode and type in turn with examples from the *NottDeuYTSch* corpus, and identifying novel strategies of intensification. The chapter concludes with a discussion of possible extensions to the typology as DMC evolves, and suggestions for further research.

2 Approaches to intensification

2.1 Discussion of term

There are both competing definitions of intensification and competing terms in the English and German language research traditions, which can lead to either a broad or narrow interpretation of the concept. Both Breindl (2009: 397) and Stratton (2020: 187–188) provided lists of competing terms used in previous research to refer to this function, and, while they will not be listed here in their entirety, tend to share various attributes. The terms often contain "degree", "intensity" or "augmentation", i.e., they follow the definition provided by Bolinger (1972: 17) that an intensifier "scales a quality, whether up or down or somewhere between the two" (see also "amplifiers" and "downtoners" in Quirk et al. 1985: 589–590). However, the competing terms diverge with regard to the elements that are classified as intensifiers, for example, they are variously referred to as "adverbs", "particles" or "modifiers". The terms 'adverb' and 'particle' (e.g., "Intensitäts-Adverbien" or 'adverbs of intensity' in Weinrich et al. 2005: 593) limits the examination of intensification to elements within the grammatical system, but this is perhaps too restrictive for varieties of written language, such as DMC, which tend to creatively use semiotic resources beyond the traditional toolbox of lexicogrammar for meaning-making, as covered later in this section. For a framework that can attempt to account for the semiotic creativity in DMC, this chapter requires a flexible term that can operate outside of grammatical terminology. For this reason, the term 'intensifier', i.e., an element that intensifies, is most appropriate to the data used for this analysis, as it is not tied to a word class, instead it simply describes its function, although this must also be defined.

After discussing the competing terms for intensification, the next step is to find an acceptable definition. Apart from the definition provided by Bolinger (1972: 17) above, van Os (1989: 2) defined intensification as a "functional semantic category of strengthening and weakening", and Ghesquière (2017: 34) defined it as the "modification or measuring of the degree of gradable notions". However, for these definitions to be of use, we must establish which elements can be intensified and how they can be intensified.

Traditionally, only adjectives and adverbs have been considered as "intensifiable entities", but Salzmann (2017: 235–236) showed that nouns and verbs can also be intensified, providing examples from German and Italian, as shown in Examples 3 and 4.

(3) *Adapted from Salzmann (2017: 236): intensified noun*
Er ist **einsame** Spitzenklasse
[He is simply the best]

(4) *Adapted from Salzmann (2017: 236): intensified verb*
corri corri
[run run]

However, lexical choice is not considered intensification in this investigation, e.g., the difference between *dog* and *cur*, as shown in Example 5, where *cur* can be interpreted as amplifying the negative traits associated with a dog.

(5) *Adapted and translated from Frege (1983 [1897]: 152)*
This **dog** howled the whole night.
This **cur** howled the whole night.

The exclusion avoids issues related to the indexicality of the lexical choice, i.e., the socio-culturally constructed and interpreted semantics of a word and its contexts (see Silverstein 2003). For example, it is subjective to several social factors such as age, geographical upbringing, or class, whether a reader would perceive *sick* as an intensified form of *cool* (to paraphrase Tagliamonte 2016a). Therefore, there is no restriction on word class for intensifiable elements in this investigation. However, the intensifiable element must have a quality that is scalable, without replacing the element itself.

Within previous research, it has not always been made clear how scalability or modification in intensification should be distinguished from conceptually related concepts. The following list outlines a selection of such concepts and provides an example from the *NottDeuYTSch* corpus where it is difficult to conclusively differentiate between the related concept and intensification (and a single element fulfilling multiple functions cannot be ruled out):

Focusing (see Ghesquière 2017: 48), i.e., the use of devices, such as modal particles, that "do not change the element or quality they scope over but rather single it out in relation to alternative values, typically countering expectations and presuppositions in the discourse context". In Example 6, the use of the modal particle *ja* (translated here as 'indeed') can be interpreted as expressing mild surprise that the use of emojis could be considered *geil* (awesome), and therefore act as a focus marker.

(6) *NottDeuYTSch Corpus NDY/266/051291*
Das ist ja geil mit den Emojis 😂😂😂
[That's indeed awesome with the emojis 😂😂😂]

Expressivity (see Gutzmann 2019), i.e., "utterances that express, rather than describe, the emotions and attitudes of the speaker". Example 7 contains *geil* prefixed by the onomatopoeic representation of laughter (*HAHAHAHA*, see Thurlow 2003: 7; Tagliamonte and Denis 2008: 11), which can be interpreted as reinforcing the positive sentiment of the message without necessarily directly intensifying *geil* in this case, or highlighting the semantic salience of the message (see McAteer 1992: 350). However, the use of uppercase letters is a common technique in DMC to represent increased volume in speech (i.e., "shouting capitals" Crystal 2006: 37), which is used to phonologically intensify an element (see Section 3.2).

(7) *NottDeuYTSch Corpus NDY/193/019733*
Alter. Ich HEULE HAHAHAHA GEIL
[hahaha awesome]

Illocutionary force (see Searle 1976: 2–3), i.e., the strength of an implication in a message. In Example 8, while the use of *so* functions as an intensifier for *geil*, the use of the 'crying face' and 'red heart' emoji provide extra metacommunicative context to the comment that can be interpreted as an expression of sadness that the project is finished. However, it is debatable as to whether this also scales the quality of *geil*, rather than relating to the wider proposition. This would imply that the emoji cluster functions as an intensifier, in this case scaling *geil* "somewhere between" up or down, following Bolinger (1972: 17). Indeed, Salzmann (2017: 238) argued that illocutionary force can be considered as intensification.

(8) *NottDeuYTSch Corpus NDY/122/009047*
Ich fande [das Projekt] so geil 😢🖤
[I found the project so awesome 😢🖤]

2.1.1 Defining intensification

While it is important to "define [...] and distinguish" intensification from other phenomena to prevent it from becoming a "catch-all" term (Ghesquière 2017: 48), the examples above have shown that this is often difficult, especially when intensification strategies in DMC occur outside of traditional grammatical functions, as will be covered in more detail Section 3. The analysis presented in this chapter takes a pragmatic approach to the analysis of intensification, defining it as the modification of the scalable quality of a lexical item by any semiotic resource, i.e., an intensifier or intensifiers. Section 2.2 now discusses the linguistic and semiotic features of intensification that have been identified in previous studies.

2.2 Previous studies on intensification

Initial research on intensifiers in the German language identified two grammatical sources of intensifiers: syntactic intensifiers, e.g., adjectives as demonstrated in Example 1, and morphological intensifiers, e.g., affixation in Example 2 (see Kirschbaum 2002: 6–7), although English overwhelmingly focused on syntactic intensifiers (referred to as "lexical" intensifiers, see Bolinger 1972).

Syntactic intensifiers, most prominently adjectives and adverbs, have received significant attention in all areas of research, such as the edited collection on adverbial and adjectival intensification by Oebel (2012), and other edited collections, e.g., Napoli and Ravetto (2017a). However, other types of lexical item have also been analysed such as multi-word expressions (e.g., wie Sau, 'as heck [lit. sow]', for Romansh see Liver 2012; for German and Italian Albert 2017; for Dutch Wouden and Foolen 2017), and interrogatives (e.g., *how wonderful*, Siemund 2017). Syntactic intensification has also been the focus in youth language research, such as in Tagliamonte (2008: 363), who highlighted the (micro-)diachronic tendency of syntactic intensifiers to rapidly change, as each subsequent generation of young people seek to "signal in-group membership" (see also Reichelt and Durham 2017). Similarly, Jindrová (2017: 19) and Ito and Tagliamonte (2003: 274) discussed regional and social differences between the preferred choice of syntactic intensifier in their studies of British Englishes, e.g., the use of "right", "well", and "pure" as augmentative intensifiers in Jindrová (2017: 46–47) (for more on "pure" in Glasgow adolescent context, see Macaulay 2006).

Research on morphological intensifiers in German has mostly investigated prefixes, most commonly the prefixation of adjectives, e.g., *arschkalt* (arse-cold) or *ultracool*, but the prefixation of nouns is also well-documented, e.g., *Höllenkrach* (hell-noise) or *Affengeschwindigkeit* (monkey-speed) (Kirschbaum 2002: 6). Calpestrati (2017: 308) also listed hyphenated compounds, such *Hammer-Mega-Obercool* (Hammer-Mega-Uppercool), under morphological intensification, and a similar categorisation for Dutch was proposed by Liebrecht (2015: 149). The *NottDeuYTSch* corpus contains numerous examples where the boundaries between morphological and syntactic intensification is not clear cut, which is further discussed in Section 3. Research on Italian also demonstrated intensification through suffixation, e.g., the augmentative *-issima* in *grassissima* (see Salzmann 2017: 237; Costa 2017), and intensification through infixation has been shown in English, such as *-fucking-* in *abso-fucking-lutely* (Adams 1999).[3]

More recently, additional ways of intensification have been integrated into mainstream research on the topic. Napoli and Ravetto (2017b: 2) argued that linguistic elements that are "involved in the expression of degree" can occur on a "phonological, semantic, grammatical, lexical, pragmatic, cognitive, and textual" level and Salzmann (2017: 235) listed several categories and features that could be used for intensification, including "prosodic devices", "graphics", reduplication, morphology, multi-word expressions, and syntax, although both papers do not go into detail on all of the listed ways to intensify. The inclusion of "graphics" and "textual" as categories of intensification indicates that grapheme-based intensification, popularised by research using DMC texts, rather than just written formal language or spoken language as the basis for the data for analysis, has become legitimised and analysed alongside other forms of intensification, although the formal integration of these strategies within intensification has until now only rarely occurred (see Liebrecht 2015: 150).

The three most popular phenomena within previous DMC studies that are associated with intensification stretch back to the beginning of the field. They are the repetition of individual letters or punctuation (also referred to as 'flooding', see Hentschel 1998; Androutsopoulos 2000; De Decker and Vandekerckhove 2017; 'reduplication', see Herring 2012, although this can refer to the repetition of groups of multiple characters; or as an "Emotionalisierungsstrategie", 'emotionalisation

3 The *-fucking-* infix also entered the German consciousness in 2012 as part of the neologism *unfuckingfassbar* (un-fucking-believable) expressed by Rea Garvey on the *Voice of Germany* TV show.

strategy' Frick 2020), as demonstrated in Example 9, and the use of capital letters (Carey 1980; Bader 2002; Lee 2016), as shown in Example 10.

(9) *NottDeuYTSch Corpus NDY/292/006154*
Ihr seid **sooooooo geeeiiilll** !!!
[You are **sooooooo aaaawwwwesoooommmme** !!!]

(10) *NottDeuYTSch Corpus NDY/193/051547*
WTF?! DAS IST **MEGA**
[WTF?! THAT IS **MEGA**]

However, these features have often not been analysed within the frame of intensification, instead they are highlighted as examples of DMC-typical practices, alongside features such as emoji and other graphicons (e.g.,, emoticons, kaomoji, see Beißwenger and Pappert 2019). The use of graphicons to modify the illocutionary force of a message has been the focus of previous research (see Dresner and Herring 2010), rather than their potential as intensifiers of a specific lexical item within that message. Graphicons have also been treated instead as intensifiable elements that can themselves be intensified through repetition, akin to expressive intensification (see Hougaard and Rathje 2018: 795; Cotgrove 2024). Furthermore, punctuation marks, such as exclamation marks, ellipsis, question marks (as well as combinations, e.g., !?) might not strictly act as intensifiers, instead, similar to graphicons, they modify the illocutionary force of the whole sentence, not just a single lexical item, although they can themselves be intensified.

A further form of intensification that has been remarked in previous research, although not as extensively analysed, is the repetition of a lexical item, referred to as "expressive repetition" (see Quirk et al. 1985: 981; van Os 1989: 106; Aitchison 1994: 19–20), as demonstrated in English in Example 11, and in German in Example 12 (and Italian in Example 4 above). Repetition is commonly seen as a rhetorical device in poetry and has multiple functions, such as anaphora and epistrophe, such as to create rhythm and movement in the text, or to link ideas, but it can also be used to intensify emotions or feelings (Attridge 1994; Engelberg 2022).

(11) *Macbeth 2.3.73, adapted from Aitchison (1994: 20)*
O horror, horror, horror

(12) *NottDeuYTSch Corpus NDY/107/004061*
geil geil geil geil geil geil geil
[awesome awesome [...] awesome]

While the case for the expressive repetition of adjectives is well established, Ghomeshi et al. (2004) argued that the repetition of other lexical elements can also intensify, referring to it as "contrastive reduplication", and later Frankowsky (2022) provided an in-depth examination of this phenomenon in German nouns, calling these structures "identical constituent compounds" (ICCs). Example 13 shows a compound containing the repetition of *Oma* ('grandma'), which, according to Frankowsky, invokes the archetypal characteristics of the lexical item, one of which, in this case, is a tendency to (over-)feed dinner guests. This phenomenon is similar to the use of *real* + *NOUN*, e.g., a real grandma (see Freywald 2015), although this would be categorised under syntactic intensification, not as expressive repetition. The use of repetition to highlight archetypal characteristics is however not limited to nouns, Frankowsky (2022) also provided examples of adjectives (*neu-neu*, 'new new', i.e., really new) and verbs (*schlafen-schlafen*, 'sleep-sleep', i.e., really sleep).

(13) *Adapted from Frankowsky (2022: 13)*
das ist so ne richtige **Oma-Oma**, die auch immer noch nachfragt und immer nochmal nochwas aufn Teller.
[she's a real **grandma-grandma** who always asks and always puts more on your plate.]

Although Quirk et al. (1985) and Aitchison (1994) discuss the two phenomena together, I would argue that expressive repetition and contrastive reduplication, as per Examples 11 to 13, should be treated as their own separate category, iterative intensifcation, from the repetition of existing intensifiers, as shown by the repetition of *very* in Example 14. As an illustration, the repetition of *geil* in Example 12 induces the intensification, but in Example 14, intensification has already been induced by *very*, and the repetition here changes the quality of intensification, but does not change whether or not the intensification has occurred.

(14) *Adapted from Quirk (1985: 981)*
very, very, very good

The use of multiple (syntactic) intensifiers in the same phrase is referred to as "stacking" by Scheffler, Richter, and Van Hout (2023), in an investigation that argued that the intensity of syntactic intensifiers increased from left to right in German. Furthermore, they reported that multiple intensification strategies, e.g., grapheme repetition and syntactic intensifiers, predominantly occur in shorter intensifiers like *so* or *echt*, as in Example 15 (Scheffler, Richter, and Van Hout 2023: 10–11). However, the phenomenon has not received other significant attention in previous literature on intensification; only DMC research has discussed how multiple intensification strategies used in synthesis are a feature of digital writing (see Runkehl, Schlobinski, and Siever 1998; Frick 2020), as demonstrated by the modification of *mega* in Example 16 by the combination of capital letters, graphemic repetition and syntactic intensification, which further increase the intensity. The use of multiple intensification strategies is discussed in more detail in Section 3.3.

(15) *Adapted from Scheffler et al. (2023: 5)*
so echt total hübsch
[**so really totally** pretty]

(16) *NottDeuYTSch Corpus NDY/255/024535*
MEEEGAAA COOLES VIDEO!
[MEGA COOL VIDEO!]

Overall, four kinds of intensification have featured prominently in previous research: morphological, syntactic, iterative, and graphemic, as well as the possibility to combine these strategies together to further increase the intensification of a lexical item. Section 3 discusses how the data in the *NottDeuYTSch* corpus of YouTube comments contain new forms of intensification that expand our understanding of the above-mentioned categories, but also contain forms of intensification that require their own category, namely typographical intensification.

3 Intensification in youth DMC

The following section presents a typology of intensification used in written youth DMC, based on data examined in the *NottDeuYTSch* corpus (Cotgrove 2018). The *NottDeuYTSch* corpus was constructed in 2018 and comprises over 33 million words, taken from roughly 3 million YouTube comments published between 2008 and 2018, written by a young, German-speaking demographic. The comments have been extracted from popular German-language YouTube channels aimed at young people, covering a wide range of topics, such as Social Media Entertainment (e.g., vlogs, gameplay, beauty, Cunningham and Craig 2017: 71–72), films, science, sports, news, and animals. The *NottDeuYTSch* corpus, therefore, provides an authentic and representative linguistic snapshot of young German speakers for this time period, and offers significant opportunities for in-depth research in several linguistic fields and using a variety of methodologies. Potential sites of study include lexis, morphology, syntax, orthography, multilingualism, and conversational and discursive analysis, as well as genre analyses, longitudinal studies, and both qualitative and quantitative approaches. For an in-depth overview of the methodology behind the construction of the corpus, see Cotgrove (2023).

An analysis of the YouTube comments in the *NottDeuYTSch* corpus shows that intensification in youth DMC includes methods of intensification that have not been covered in existing research in this area. These include new ways of intensifying that would fit into existing categories, as well as ways of intensifying that require an additional category. Intensification in youth DMC can be divided into two modes: lexical and graphical. Lexical intensification contains three types: morphological, syntactic and expressive strategies, as these operate through the use of lexical items to modify the scaleable quality of another lexical item. These types of intensification are the most common. Graphical intensification includes strategies that modify the spatio-visual interpretation of a lexical item, e.g., through graphemic strategies, such as altering the spelling (graphemic intensification), or other modifications of appearance, shape or position, such as changing the font, weight or size (typographical intensification). An additional category not considered in this chapter is phonological intensification, which would include all strategies that use phonological modification, such as volume, prosody, or tone (see Cosentino 2017). However, as multimodality within DMC expands, such as the integration of additional audio or video features in messaging applications or the dynamic rendering of graphic-based intensification by screen readers and other accessibility devices, the typology will need to be expanded.

3.1 Lexical

Lexical intensification contains the morphological, syntactic, and iterative intensification, as they all use lexical items, including words and parts of words to intensify. Morphological and syntactic intensification have often been treated as separate in German due to the productivity of compounding, but the two concepts are not as distinct in other languages. Additionally, iterative intensification, i.e., intensification through the repetition of a single lexical item, is classified here as a subcategory of lexical intensification.

3.1.1 Iterative intensification

Iterative intensification, i.e., the repetition of a lexical item to modify the quality of the same lexical item, is ubiquitous in DMC, and is attested in a variety of word classes, such as the repetition of *haben* in Example 17, where *haben* is a clipping of *ich will es haben* ('I want it'), popular in children's speech. Here the desire of the commenter for the item is intensified through repetition.

(17) *NottDeuYTSch Corpus NDY/056/006405*
Supiiiiiiii haben haben haben ;D
[Suuuuuuuper I wannit wannit wannit ;D]

Pragmatically, there is perhaps not so much difference between the use of a particular kind of intensifier if the lexical item is identical, as demonstrated in Examples 18 and 19 with *mega* and *hammer*, functioning as both a morphological and syntactic intensifier. There might be phonological differences if the comments were spoken aloud (see Cosentino 2017), but YouTube comments are (at time of writing) a written medium. The distinction between the two is further blurred in DMC due to the orthographic creativity and flexibility within that medium of communication, or if the commenter has deliberately or accidentally inserted or deleted spaces between *mega*, *hammer*, and *geil*.

(18) *NottDeuYTSch Corpus NDY/178/000946*
Megahammergeil bitte mehr davon
[Mega-hammer-awesome more of the same please]

(19) *NottDeuYTSch Corpus NDY/076/005657*
geil geil super mega hammer geil
[awesome awesome super mega hammer awesome]

3.1.2 Morphological intensification

While research on German intensification focused on the use of prefixes for intensification, intensification through suffixation is also present in German (and other languages), as demonstrated by *-omatico* in Example 20 (also see Mroczynski 2018: 334). Morphological intensification is also communicated through derivation, i.e., changing the word class of a lexical item, such as *-heit* in Example 21, which changes an adjective into a noun, in this case *geil* to *geilheit* ('awesome' to 'awesomeness'). The effect is similar to ICCs, as mentioned in Section 2.2, as derivation to a noun here increases the archetypical qualities of the adjective.

(20) *NottDeuYTSch Corpus NDY/173/026800*
Dass du so oft geklickt wurdest ist doch gar kein Wunder. Du bist einfach **geilomatico**!!!!!
[It is no wonder at all that you get so many views. You are simply **awesomatic**!!!!!]

(21) *NottDeuYTSch Corpus NDY/023/003693*
einfach nur **Geilheit**
[just simply **awesomeness**]

These processes have not been considered within the existing definition of morphological intensification. However, in youth DMC, such constructions are relatively common and productive, for example we find *geilo*, *geili*, and *geilonachtsman* in the *NottDeuYTSch* corpus (as well as graphemic variations, e.g., *geilooo*). Additionally, stacking of multiple affixes is commonplace (Example 22), alongside reduplication (Example 23, also see Kentner 2023). Expanding on Scheffler, Richter, and Van Hout (2023), we can interpret that not just the number of affixes, but also the length of an affix can strengthen the intensification. This is further discussed alongside other aspects of combining intensification strategies in Section 3.3.

(22) *NottDeuYTSch Corpus NDY/182/004386*
weil du einfach **oberhammermegaaffentittengeil** bist
[because you're simply **above-hammer-mega-monkey-tits-awesome**]

(23) *NottDeuYTSch Corpus NDY/181/014866*
Meeeega **geilomaticofabricatio** 🖤🖤🖤😍😍😍😍😍🔝🔝🔝🔝🔝🔝.
[Meeeega **awesomatic-systematic-hydromatic** *(lit. factory-atio)* 🖤🖤🖤😍😍😍😍😍🔝🔝🔝🔝🔝🔝.]

While morphological intensification most commonly occurs with lexical items, the *NottDeuYTSch* corpus contains rare cases where graphicons function as morphological intensifiers. These seem to be restricted to the mimetic replacement of a lexical item, e.g., 🔨 for *Hammer* in Example 24. It is not clear if the 'smiling face with heart-eyes' emoji belongs to the compound or the previous sentence.

(24) *NottDeuYTSch Corpus NDY/228/014455*
Ju du bist einfach der Hammer! 😍🔨**Geil**, einfach geil! Mehr kann man nicht sagen!😍
[Woo you are simply the best! 😍🔨**-awesome**, simply awesome! You can't say more than that!!😍]

The examples from the *NottDeuYTSch* corpus demonstrate that the previous definition of morphological intensification needs to be expanded to account for the novel and creative strategies used in DMC to intensify lexical items, and raises questions if emoji and other graphicons can be considered either as elements that can intensify, be intensified themselves, or be interpreted as lexical items altogether. Therefore, we can expand the definition of morphological intensification to encompass all affixation or alteration of word class through semiotic resources where the scalable quality of the lexical item is increased.

3.1.3 Syntactic intensification

Similarly to morphological intensification, the *NottDeuYTSch* corpus contains examples of syntactic intensification analysed in research to date, e.g.,, adjectives and adverbs such as *so* in Example 25, and multi-word expressions and phrases, such as *wie sau* later in the same example. Additionally, intensification using particles (e.g., *aber* in Example 26), and indefinite pronouns (e.g *etwas* in Example 27) are also attested in the corpus, alongside the use of interrogatives (e.g., *wie* in Example 28). Syntactic intensification is defined therefore as the use of lexical items to modify another, separate lexical item. Frick (2020: 172) stated that keyboard mashing, the seemingly random pressing of letters, e.g., *shahskhhskhsa*, could also be considered as intensification, although I would argue this instead would be classified as expressivity or modifying the illocutionary force of a message, similar to representations of laughter (indeed, keyboard mashing is used to represent laughter in some languages and youth cultures, such as Turkish, where it is called *random atmak/gülmek*, 'random throwing/laughing', Urhan Torun 2018: 629). Keyboard mashing can itself be intensified through other strategies, such as the number of characters and letter case, but this is covered in Section 3.2.

(25) *NottDeuYTSch Corpus NDY/292/020504*
so so geil **wie sau** XD
[**so so** awesome **as hell** XD]

(26) *NottDeuYTSch Corpus NDY/001/004090*
[PERSON] tanzt bei Party Rock **aber** geil o.o
[[PERSON] dances to Party Rock **surprisingly** awesomely o.o]

(27) *NottDeuYTSch Corpus NDY/211/010276*
Haha, ja, die Augenbrauen waren **etwas** strange.
[Haha, yes, the eyebrows were **somewhat** strange.]

(28) *NottDeuYTSch Corpus NDY/122/019058*
Alter **wie** geil!!! :D
[Man **how** awesome!!! :D]

Example 28 also contains the use of the interjection, *Alter* (man), which, alongside other interjections that precede an intensifiable lexical item, such as *omg, jaaa, wow*, could additionally be considered as intensifiers, but it is more likely that they modify the illocutionary force at sentence level, rather than directly modify the scalable quality of the lexical item. The quality conveyed by interjections can, however, be intensified through other means, such as the repetition of the grapheme *a* in *jaaa*, which is covered in the following section.

3.2 Graphical

As mentioned in Section 2.2, intensification using strategies that modify the scalable quality of a lexical item by changing its spatio-visual interpretation has not been fully incorporated into mainstream research on the subject. Previous work on such phenomena initially focused on how graphemes and other characters represented "conceptual orality" (Koch and Österreicher 2007), i.e., the compensation for the lack of spoken features in written communication. Although research on the pragmatics of "digitale Schriftlichkeit" ('digital writing', e.g., Androutsopoulos and Busch 2020) is increasing, graphemic intensification has not frequently been the primary subject of analysis (e.g., Liebrecht 2015). However, the data in the *NottDeuYTSch* corpus contain a wealth of examples demonstrating creative intensification using grapheme and other character-based strategies that not only expand our understanding of intensification, but also our general understanding of the features of digital writing. For example, there is considerable creative use of letter case for intensification that is not just restricted to capital letters, as demonstrated by the alternating letter case of *best* in Example 29. Alternating letter case has since 2017 been used in DMC to symbolise irony or to represent alternate 'voicing' (see Cotgrove 2024: 133; Androutsopoulos 2024), and in some cases, this can be interpreted within the framework of intensification, as it modifies the scalable quality of the lexical item.

(29) *NottDeuYTSch Corpus NDY/002/001732*
hater is the **BeSt**!!!

3.2.1 Graphemic intensification

The repetition of graphemes and punctuation marks is still ever-present in the corpus, as demonstrated by the exclamation marks in Example 29, although the use of exclamation marks here modifies the illocutionary force of the message, albeit intensified through repetition. In Example 30, the repetition of full stops can be interpreted as an awed silence and the capital letters and exclamation marks represent the excitement of the commenter, rather than intensify any one particular lexical item. However, the use of stylised arrows to bracket *FRESH* are a form of intensification using graphemic deixis (analogous to intensification through "speaker signals" in spoken language, see Salzmann 2017: 238), as do the Backhand Index Pointing Left and Right emoji in Example 31, which intensify the negative quality communicated by the Thumbs Down emoji.[4]

(30) *NottDeuYTSch Corpus NDY/109/001687*
DIGGA.....DU HAST DIE PUNCHLINES GEFLOWT!!!!!!!!!! DAS WAR —>FRESH<—
[BRO.....YOU FLOWED THE PUNCHLINES!!!!!!!!!! THAT WAS —>FRESH<—]

(31) *NottDeuYTSch Corpus NDY/263/014338*
😡👉👎👈

Another strategy used in the corpus, but which has not received much attention in previous research on intensification, is the use of spacing to modify lexical items, most commonly whitespace characters, such as spaces, tabs and line breaks, as demonstrated by the spacing between the letters of *MÜLL* in Example 32. Theoretically, altering the letter spacing of the font of a lexical item would also be included, but this is rarely an option in DMC platforms. Within research on visual design, the use of spacing alters the "spatio-visual demarcation" of the lexical item and so alters how it is interpreted (Wyss and Hug 2016), but this aspect has not been incorporated into research on intensification, although it has been discussed in early DMC research (e.g., Werry 1996). Based on previous research and the examples in the corpus, we can define graphemic intensification as the use of characters to modify the spatio-visual interpretation and scalable quality of a lexical item.

(32) *NottDeuYTSch Corpus NDY/017/001228*
Das Video is M Ü L L
[The video is R U B B I S H]

---

4 Outside of intensification, deictic gestures can also have a focusing function to highlight a particular element within a text (see Cotgrove 2024: 155).

3.2.2 Typographical intensification

Alongside graphemic strategies, the data in the *NottDeuYTSch* corpus contain examples of the use of typographical intensification, i.e.,, modifying type face, weight, size, style, colour, and other visual aspects of a lexical item so that it differs from the surrounding text (these techniques are referred to as emphasis in the field of typography, see Bringhurst 2012). While YouTube only offers basic alterations to the text, such as italic or bold, as in Examples 33 (*geil*) and 34 (*legendär*) respectively, this is likely to change as bandwidth, processing power, and multimodal communication increase, as such, we can expect typographical intensification to become more commonplace over the next few years, for example changing the position, orientation, shape, and size of words within a coordinate plane (see Rude 2016: 107). Typographical intensification follows the typographical design credo by McAteer (1992: 347–348) that "the physical salience of a word signals its informational salience", and can be defined as the use of typographical methods to modify the scalable quality of a lexical item. It is up for debate whether the use of spacing should be classified as typographical, rather than graphemic intensification, but it is undoubtedly a strategy of graphic intensification.

(33) *NottDeuYTSch Corpus NDY/266/027155*
[...] Omg und dann auch noch 50 übertrieben Geile Verlosungen😍 *geil* einfach nur *geil*😍😍🖤🖤🖤🖤🖤🖤
[[...] Omg and then also 50 brilliantly Awesome giveaways 😍 *awesome* simply *awesome* 😍😍🖤🖤🖤🖤🖤🖤]

(34) *NottDeuYTSch Corpus NDY/002/000026*
LEGENDÄR...
[LEGENDARY...]

3.3 Multiple intensification strategies

Within DMC, the use of multiple strategies to intensify a single lexical item is commonplace, although research with the field of intensification on such combined strategies has been limited. Example 35 demonstrates the use of syntactic intensification (*so*), combined with the repetition of graphemes and the use of capital letters in both the syntactic intensifier and intensified element, as well as the intensification of the illocutionary force imparted by the use of exclamation marks. Stacking, as per the original definition of Scheffler, Richter, and Van Hout (2023) to mean the use of multiple intensifiers in series to intensify a single lexical item, is also classified under multiple intensification, and is demonstrated by the use of multiple prefixes for morphological intensification in Example 36.

(35) *NottDeuYTSch Corpus NDY/114/011335*
DANKE [...] SOOOOO GEEEIIIILLLLLL!!!!!!!!!!
[THANKS [...] SOOOOO AWWEEEESSOOOMMMMEEE!!!!!!!!!!]

(36) *NottDeuYTSch Corpus NDY/203/012046*
Einhornpupsiglitzerstickerdonutgeiles 🦄 video [...]
[Unicorn-fart-glitter-sticker-donut- awesome 🦄 video [...]]

The *NottDeuYTSch* corpus contains examples that demonstrate that any intensification strategy can be combined with another. **Megagigaatomfacepalmdestotes** in Example 37 illustrates the use of typographical intensification through bold font style combined with stacking several prefixes for morphological intensification, as well as a suffix (***destotes,*** 'of death'). Example 38 shows how both kinds of graphical intensification: graphemic and typographical, are used together, as well as with lexical intensification. The use of bold font style and upper case letters are combined with the lexical intensifier *mega* to intensify the lexical item *cool*, which itself is further intensified by the repetition of the grapheme *o* and upper case (graphemic intensification). The corpus also shows that different kinds of lexical intensification can be combined, as in Example 39, which contains the repetition of syntactic intensification (*ganz*), combined with the stacking of prefixes for morphological intensification, two of which are reduplicated for further intensification (*superduper* and *hyperdyper*).

(37) *NottDeuYTSch Corpus NDY/176/004002*
Echt...xD an alle Leute die das glauben **Megagigaatomfacepalmdestotes**
[Really...xD for all those who believe that
mega-giga-atom-facepalm-of-death]

(38) *NottDeuYTSch Corpus NDY/228/008986*
MEGA COOOOOOOOL

(39) *NottDeuYTSch Corpus NDY/002/002426*
Mal n ganz ganz superdupergeilelhyperdyper[v]ollabgekrasstes Video . Das war keine Beleidigung sondern ein Kompliment .
[Quite a totally totally superduper-awesome-el-hyperdyper-fully-sicked-up video . That was not an insult but a compliment .]

We can make the tentative assumption, following Scheffler, Richter, and Van Hout (2023), that the more intensification strategies used concurrently (i.e., the more effort), or the more space a set of intensifiers occupies (such as repeated graphemes, see Mroczynski 2018: 339), the more intensified a lexical item becomes. However, as an intensification set occupies increasingly more space, the intensification of the lexical item becomes increasingly less effective, and instead the intensifiers can be interpreted as ludic embellishments, in line with the informal and playful nature of DMC (Androutsopoulos 2011: 155). Example 40 is from a comment containing *geil* repeated 101 times, but it is not clear how much more intensified *geil* is compared to Example 12, which only contained seven repetitions of *geil*. If we analyse the regular re-occurence of *geilgeil* in Example 40, we can infer that the commenter typed *geil* out 14 times and then repeatedly copied and pasted the phrase, which takes far less effort. Instead of using the number of repetitions of *geil*, in this instance, it is perhaps better to use how much space the comment takes up on a reader's screen as an indicator of intensification. This method can also be applied to graphical intensification strategies that break out of the confines of linear text production, e.g., in Figure 1 with the use of an ASCII illustration of a person dancing to intensify the word *fabulous* (as well as the combination of graphemic intensification of the syntactic intensifier *so*).

(40) *NottDeuYTSch Corpus NDY/002/002426*
geil geil geil geil geil geil geil geil geil geil geil geil geil geilgeil geil geil geil geil geil geil geil geil geil geil geil geil geilgeil geil geil geil geil geil geil geil geil geil geil geil geil geilgeil geil geil geil
[awesome awesome [...] awesome awesome]

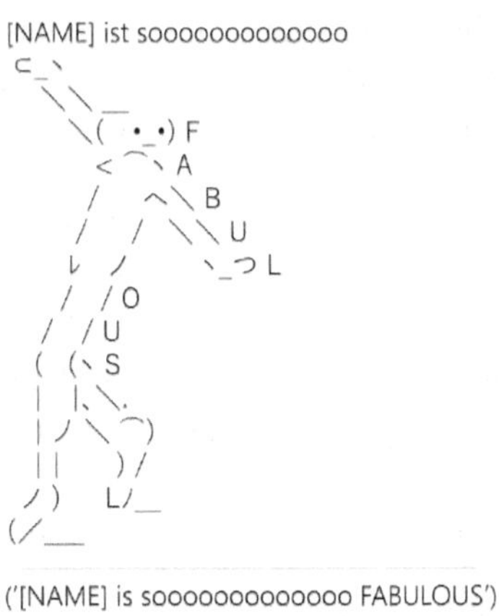

Figure 1: NottDeuYTSch Corpus NDY/193/011190: Comment containing ASCII art to intensify.

4 Conclusion and future research

The examination of YouTube comments in the *NottDeuYTSch* corpus has demonstrated the wide variety of intensification strategies in DMC, which expands our current understanding of intensification. The examples from the corpus exhibit considerable innovation and creativity using the semiotic resources available in DMC to intensify, which justifies the overhaul of the typology and definition of intensification provided in this chapter, i.e.,:

1. The definition of intensification needed to be refined to delineate it from similar concepts, such as focusing, expressivity and illocutionary force.
2. The definitions of existing types of intensification needed to be expanded to account for emergent strategies. For example, I have shown that morphological intensification can occur using not just prefixes, but all kinds of affixes, derivation and the combination of multiple affixes.
3. Additional types of intensification needed to be added to account for the increase in the diversity of semiotic resources used in DMC. For example, graphical intensification strategies, such as the manipulation of the spatio-visual interpretation, alternating letter case, or graphemic deixis have not traditionally been considered within the scope of intensification.
4. The relationship between the types of intensification needed to be reorganised to demonstrate and differentiate the various strategies. This also aids analyses of the use of multiple intensification strategies for the same lexical element.

Figure 2 presents a simplified diagram showing the modes and types of intensification and their relationships. Further developments of the typology would be aided by including more data from other languages, especially those written with logograms or syllabaries, to examine the distribution of intensification types. More work is also needed to analyse how different types of intensification interact with each other (or cannot interact with each other) and with other intensification strategies of the same mode or type, building on the preliminary analyses of Scheffler, Richter, and Van Hout (2023), as well as quantitative analyses of how often these categories of intensification occur in the data. As multimodality in DMC increases, the typology should be extended to include phonological and physical (i.e., body language) intensification strategies, perhaps phonological differences between the perception of syntactic and morphological intensification, and other interactions between emergent combinations of intensification strategies, as well as non-type-based writing such as handwriting (see Rude 2016) and sign languages.

With the typology of intensification presented in this chapter, researchers can take a holistic and pragmatic approach to intensification outside of traditional grammatical categories to more fully understand the creativity, interaction, and dynamic nature of language use within DMC contexts.

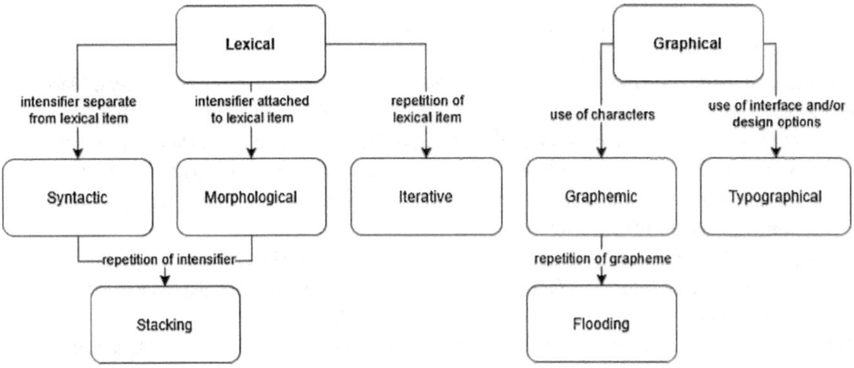

Figure 2: Diagram of intensification categories and types.

References

Adams, Michael. 1999. Another effing euphemism, *American Speech* 74.1, 110–112. https://doi.org/10.1215/00031283-79-1-110.

Aitchison, Jean. 1994. "Say, say it again, Sam": The treatment of repetition in linguistics, *SPELL: Swiss Papers in English Language and Literature*. 15–34. https://doi.org/10.5169/seals-99896.

Albert, Marino Foschi. 2017. The coordination of identical conjuncts as a means of strengthening expressions. In Maria Napoli & Miriam Ravetto (eds.), *Exploring intensification: Synchronic, diachronic and cross-lInguistic perspectives*, 265–287. Amsterdam: John Benjamins.

Androutsopoulos, Jannis. 2000. Non-standard spellings in media texts: The case of German fanzines, *Journal of Sociolinguistics* 4. 514–533. https://doi.org/10.1111/1467-9481.00128.

Androutsopoulos, Jannis. 2011. Language change and digital media: A review of conceptions and evidence. In Tore Kristiansen & Nikolas Coupland (eds.), *Standard languages and language standards in a changing Europe*, Standard Language Ideology in Contemporary Europe, 145–161. Oslo: Novus Press.

Androutsopoulos, Jannis. 2018. Digitale Interpunktion: Stilistische Ressourcen und soziolinguistischer Wandel in der informellen digitalen Schriftlichkeit von Jugendlichen. In Arne Ziegler (ed.) *Jugendsprachen: Aktuelle Perspektiven Internationaler Forschung*, 721–748. Berlin & Boston: De Gruyter.

Androutsopoulos, Jannis. 2024. Graphic cues and heterographic practices in digital discourse. Hamburg: University of Hamburg. https://lecture2go.uni-hamburg.de/en/l2go/-/get/l/6829 (last accessed 5 February 2025).

Androutsopoulos, Jannis, & Florian Busch (eds.), 2020. *Register des Graphischen: Variation, Interaktion und Reflexion in der digitalen Schriftlichkeit.* Berlin & Boston: De Gruyter.

Attridge, Derek. 1994. The movement of meaning : Phrasing and repetition in English Poetry. *SPELL: Swiss Papers in English Language and Literature*. 61–83. https://doi.org/10.5169/SEALS-99899.

Bader, Jennifer. 2002. Schriftlichkeit und Mündlichkeit in der Chat-Kommunikation. *NetWorx* 29.
Beißwenger, Michael, & Steffen Pappert. 2019. *Handeln mit Emojis: Grundriss einer Linguistik kleiner Bildzeichen in der WhatsApp-Kommunikation*. Duisburg: Universitätsverlag Rhein-Ruhr.
Bolinger, Dwight. 1972. *Degree words*. The Hague: Mouton. https://www.degruyter.com/document/doi/10.1515/9783110877786/html (last accessed 14 February 2025).
Breindl, Eva. 2009. Intensitätspartikeln. In Ludger Hoffmann (ed.), *Handbuch der deutschen Wortarten*, 397–422. Berlin & New York: De Gruyter.
Bringhurst, Robert. 2012. *The elements of typographic style*, 4th edition. Vancouver: Hartley & Marks.
Calpestrati, Nicolò. 2017. Intensification strategies in German and Italian written language: The case of Prefissi Intensivi or Fremdpräfixe. A corpus-based study. In Maria Napoli & Miriam Ravetto (eds.), *Exploring intensification: Synchronic, diachronic and cross-linguistic perspectives*, Studies in Language Companion Series, 305–326. Amsterdam & Philadelphia: John Benjamins. https://doi.org/10.1075/slcs.189.16cal.
Carey, John. 1980. Paralanguage in Computer Mediated Communication. In *Proceedings of the 18th Annual Meeting on Association for Computational Linguistics*, 67. Philadelphia: Association for Computational Linguistics. https://doi.org/10.3115/981436.981458.
Cosentino, Gianluca. 2017. Stress and tones as intensifying operators in German. In Maria Napoli & Miriam Ravetto (eds.), *Exploring intensification: Synchronic, diachronic and cross-linguistic perspectives*, Studies in Language Companion Series, 193–206. Amsterdam & Philadelphia: John Benjamins. https://doi.org/10.1075/slcs.189.10cos.
Costa, Marcella. 2017. Augmentatives in Italian and German: From Contrastive Analysis to Translation. In Maria Napoli & Miriam Ravetto (eds.), *Exploring intensification: Synchronic, diachronic and cross-llnguistic perspectives*, 353–370. Amsterdam & Philadelphia: John Benjamins. https://doi.org/10.1075/slcs.189.18cos.
Cotgrove, Louis Alexander. 2018. Das Nottinghamer Korpus Deutscher YouTube-Sprache (the NottDeuYTSch Corpus) (LINDAT/CLARIAH-CZ). http://hdl.handle.net/11372/LRT-4806 (last accessed 5 February 2025).
Cotgrove, Louis Alexander. 2023. New opportunities for researching digital youth language: The NottDeuYTSch Corpus. In Marc Kupietz & Thomas Schmidt (eds.), *Neue Entwicklungen in Der Korpuslandschaft Der Germanistik*, 101–114. Tübingen: Narr.
Cotgrove, Louis Alexander. 2024. *Abogeil! The language of German teens on YouTube*. amades 63. Mannheim: IDS-Verlag.
Cunningham, Stuart, & David Craig. 2017. Being 'really real' on YouTube: Authenticity, community and brand culture in social media entertainment. *Media International Australia* 164 (1), 71–81. https://doi.org/10.1177/1329878X17709098.
Crystal, David. 2004. *A glossary of netspeak and textspeak*. Edinburgh: Edinburgh University Press.
Crystal, David. 2006. *Language and the internet*, 2nd edition. Cambridge: Cambridge University Press.
De Decker, Benny, & Reinhild Vandekerckhove. 2017. *Global features of online communication in local Flemish: Social and medium-related determinants.* Folia Linguistica, 51.1, 253–281: Berlin: De Gruyter Mouton. https://doi.org/10.1515/flin-2017-0007.
Dresner, Eli, & Susan C Herring. 2010. Functions of the nonverbal in CMC: Emoticons and illocutionary force. *Communication Theory*, 20.3, 249–268. https://doi.org/10.1111/j.1468-2885.2010.01362.x.
Engelberg, Stefan. 2022. *Wir sind, wir sind zur Stelle – Die Syntax, Semantik und Pragmatik rhetorischer Wiederholungsfiguren: Anadiplose und Geminatio in Gedichten. Mannheim:* IDS-Verlag. https://doi.org/10.21248/idsopen.4.2022.7.
Frankowsky, Maximilian. 2022. N+N-Komposita mit identischen Konstituenten im Deutschen Theorie und Empirie zu reduplikativer Komposition. Leipzig: Universität Leipzig.

Freywald, Ulrike. 2015. Total reduplication as a productive process in German. *Studies in Language* 39, 4, 905–945. Amsterdam: John Benjamins. https://doi.org/10.1075/sl.39.4.06fre.

Frick, Karina. 2020. Graphische Variation im Rahmen emotionaler Online-Praktiken. In Jannis Androutsopoulos & Florian Busch (eds.), *Register des Graphischen*, 159–182. Berlin & Boston: De Gruyter. https://doi.org/10.1515/9783110673241-007.

Ghesquière, Lobke. 2017. Intensification and focusing. In Maria Napoli & Miriam Ravetto (eds.), *Exploring intensification: Synchronic, diachronic and cross-linguistic perspectives*, Studies in Language Companion Series, 33–53. Amsterdam & Philadelphia: John Benjamins.

Ghomeshi, Jila et al. 2004. Contrastive focus reduplication in English (the salad-salad paper). *Natural Language & Linguistic Theory* 22, 307–357. https://doi.org/10.1023/B:NALA.0000015789.98638.f9.

Gutzmann, Daniel. 2019. *The grammar of expressivity. Oxford:* Oxford University Press.

Hentschel, Elke. 1998. Communication on IRC. *Linguistik Online*. https://doi.org/10.13092/lo.1.1084.

Herring, Susan C. 2012. Grammar and electronic communication. In Carol A Chapelle (ed.), *The encyclopedia of applied linguistics*, Oxford: Blackwell, p. wbeal0466. https://doi.org/10.1002/9781405198431.wbeal0466.

Hilte, Lisa, Reinhild Vandekerckhove, & Walter Daelemans. 2019. Expressive markers in online teenage talk. *Nederlandse Taalkunde* 23 3, 293–323. https://doi.org/10.5117/NEDTAA2018.3.003.HILT.

Hougaard, Tina Thode, & Marianne Rathje. 2018. Emojis in the digital writings of young danes. In Arne Ziegler (ed.), *Jugendsprachen: Aktuelle Perspektiven internationaler Forschung*, 773–806. Berlin: De Gruyter.

Ito, Rika, & Sali Tagliamonte. 2003. *Well* weird, *right* dodgy, *very* strange, *really* cool: Layering and recycling in English intensifiers. *Language in Society* 32, 2, 257–279. https://doi.org/10.1017/S0047404503322055.

Jindrová, Pavlína. 2017. Adverbial intensifiers of adjectives in today's British English. Unpublished Doctoral Thesis, Prague: University of Prague.

Kentner, Gerrit. 2023. Reduplication as expressive morphology in German. In Jeffrey P. Williams (ed.), *Expressivity in European languages*, 103–120. Cambridge: Cambridge University Press. https://doi.org/10.1017/9781108989084.007.

Kirschbaum, Ilja. 2002. *Schrecklich nett und voll verrückt: Muster der Adjektiv-Intensivierung im Deutschen.* Düsseldorf: Heinrich-Heine-Universität Düsseldorf.

Koch, Peter, & Wulf Österreicher. 2007. Schriftlichkeit und kommunikative Distanz. *Zeitschrift für germanistische Linguistik* 35, 346–375. https://doi.org/10.1515/zgl.2007.024.

Lee, Carmen. 2016. Multilingual resources and practices. In Alexandra Georgakopoulou & Tereza Spilioti (eds.), *The Routledge handbook of language and digital communication*, Routledge Handbooks in Applied Linguistics. Abingdon: Routledge, 118–132.

Liebrecht, Christina Cornelia. 2015.'Intens krachtig. Stilistische intensiveerders in evaluatieve teksten. Radboud: Radboud University. https://hdl.handle.net/2066/141116 (last accessed 2 August 2024).

Liver, Richarda. 2012. Phraseologie im Bündnerromanischen. In Guido Oebel (ed.), *Intensivierungskonzepte bei Adjektiven und Adverben im Sprachenvergleich: erster Ergänzungsband mit sprachenübergreifenden ('crosslinguistic') Beiträgen im Nachgang zum Doppelband 'Wörterbuch der Volkssuperlative (Verlag Dr. Kovač, 2011). Crosslinguistic comparison of intensified adjectives and adverbs*. Schriften zur vergleichenden Sprachwissenschaft 8, 171–182. Hamburg: Kovač.

Macaulay, Ronald. 2006. Pure grammaticalization: The development of a teenage intensifier. *Language Variation and Change* 18.03. https://doi.org/10.1017/S0954394506060133.

McAteer, Erica. 1992. Typeface emphasis and information focus in written language. *Applied Cognitive Psychology* 6, 4, 345–359. https://doi.org/10.1002/acp.2350060406.

Mroczynski, Robert. 2018. Geil oder doch porno? Zum Gebrauch und Wandel von emphatisch-evaluativen Ausdrücken in der Jugendsprache. In Arne Ziegler (ed.), *Jugendsprachen: Aktuelle Perspektiven Internationaler Forschung*, 325–342. Berlin & Boston: De Gruyter.

Napoli, Maria, & Miriam Ravetto (eds.), 2017a. *Exploring intensification: Synchronic, diachronic and cross-llnguistic perspectives*. Amsterdam: John Benjamins. https://benjamins.com/catalog/slcs.189 (last accessed 5 February 2025).

Napoli, Maria, & Miriam Ravetto. 2017b. New insights on intensification and intensifiers. In Maria Napoli & Miriam Ravetto (eds.), *Exploring intensification: Synchronic, diachronic and cross-llnguistic perspectives*, 1–12. Amsterdam: John Benjamins. https://benjamins.com/catalog/slcs.189 (last accessed 5 February 2025).

Oebel, Guido (ed.). 2012. *Intensivierungskonzepte bei Adjektiven und Adverben im Sprachenvergleich*. Hamburg: Kovač.

Quirk, Randolph et al. 1985. *A comprehensive grammar Of the English language. London:* Longman.

Reichelt, Susan, & Mercedes Durham. 2017. Adjective intensification as a means of characterization: Portraying in-group membership and Britishness in *Buffy the Vampire Slayer*. *Journal of English Linguistics* 45, 1, 60–87. https://doi.org/10.1177/0075424216669747.

Rude, Markus. 2016. Prosodic writing shows L2 learners intonation by 3D letter shapes: State, results, and attempts to increase 3D perception. *Studies in Language and Culture* 37, 2, 103–20 https://doi.org/10.18999/stulc.37.2.103.

Runkehl, Jens, Peter Schlobinski, & Torsten Siever. 1998. Sprache und Kommunikation im Internet. *Muttersprache* 108, 97–109.

Salzmann, Katharina. 2017. A pragmatic view on intensification. In Maria Napoli & Miriam Ravetto (eds.), *Exploring intensification: Synchronic, diachronic and cross-llnguistic perspectives*, 231–250. Amsterdam: John Benjamins.

Scheffler, Tatjana, Michael Richter, & Roeland Van Hout. 2023. Tracing and classifying German intensifiers via Information Theory. *Language Sciences* 96, 101535. https://doi.org/10.1016/j.langsci.2022.101535.

Searle, John R. 1976. A classification of illocutionary acts. *Language in Society* 1–23. https://doi.org/10.1017/S0047404500006837.

Siemund, Peter. 2017. English exclamative clauses and interrogative degree modification. In Maria Napoli & Miriam Ravetto (eds.), *Exploring intensification: Synchronic, diachronic and cross-linguistic perspectives*, Studies in Language Companion Series, 207–228. Amsterdam & Philadelphia: John Benjamins.

Silverstein, Michael. 2003. Indexical order and the dialectics of sociolinguistic life. *Language & Communication* 23, 3–4, 193–229. https://doi.org/10.1016/S0271-5309(03)00013-2.

Storrer, Angelika. 2001. Getippte Gespräche oder dialogische Texte? Zur kommunikationstheoretischen Einordnung der Chat-Kommunikation. In Andrea Lehr et al. (ed.), *Sprache im Alltag*, 439–465. Berlin & New York: De Gruyter.

Stratton, James M. 2020. Adjective intensifiers in German. *Journal of Germanic Linguistics* 32, 2, 183–215. https://doi.org/10.1017/S1470542719000163.

Tagliamonte, Sali A. 2008. So different and prettycCool! Recycling intensifiers in Toronto, Canada. *English Language and Linguistics* 12, 361–394. https://doi.org/10.1017/S1360674308002669.

Tagliamonte, Sali A. 2016a. So sick or so cool? The language of youth on the internet. *Language in Society* 45, 1–32. https://doi.org/10.1017/S0047404515000780.

Tagliamonte, Sali A. 2016b. *Teen talk: The language of adolescents.* Cambridge: Cambridge University Press.

Tagliamonte, Sali A., & Derek Denis. 2008. Linguistic ruin? LOL! Instant messaging and teen language. *American Speech* 83, 1, 3–34. https://doi.org/10.1215/00031283-2008-001.
Thurlow, Crispin. 2003. Generation Txt? The sociolinguistics of young people's text-messaging. *Discourse Analysis Online* 1, 1, 1–27. http://www.shu.ac.uk/daol/articles/v1/n1/a3/thurlow2002003-paper.html (last accessed 8 March 2024).
Urhan Torun, Bahar. 2018. Z *Kuşağının Akıllı Telefonlar Üzerinden Yazılı İletişimde Emoji Kullanma Eğilimlerine Yönelik Bir Araştırma* 18.
van Os, Charles. 1989. *Aspekte der Intensivierung im Deutschen*. Tübingen: Narr.
Weinrich, Harald et al. 2005. *Textgrammatik der deutschen Sprache*, 3rd edition. Hildesheim: G. Olms.
Werry, Christopher C. 1996. Linguistic and interactional features of Internet Relay Chat. In Susan C. Herring (ed.), *Computer-Mediated Communication: Linguistic, social, and cross-cultural perspectives*, 47–63. Philadelphia: John Benjamins.
Wouden, van der T., & A. P. Foolen. 2017. A most serious and extraordinary problem. Intensification of adjectives in Dutch, German, and English. *Leuvense Bijdragen – Leuven Contributions in Linguistics and Philology* 82–100. https://repository.ubn.ru.nl/bitstream/handle/2066/167628/167628pos.pdf (last accessed 26 March 2024).
Wyss, Eva L., & Barbara Hug. 2016. WhatsApp-Chats. Neue Formen der Turn-Koordination bei räumlich-visueller Begrenzung. In Carmen Spiegel & Daniel Gysin (eds.), *Jugendsprache in Schule, Medien und Alltag*, 259–274. Frankfurt am Main: Peter Lang, https://doi.org/10.3726/978-3-653-04950-3.

Ilia Moshnikov and Eugenia Rykova

Collecting minority language data from Twitter (X): A case study of Karelian

Abstract: The visibility of an endangered language online plays a crucial role in language revitalisation. The internet offers a new domain for using minority languages, especially for speakers living outside the language communities. This article investigates Karelian language visibility on X, formerly known as Twitter, and describes the first corresponding data collection using language-related keywords and hashtags. In total, 2,625 entries written fully or partially in Livvi, South and Viena Karelian were scraped with Postman API. The visibility of Karelian on Twitter (X) has been increasing considerably in the past few years, with Livvi-Karelian being the most prominent dialect. Automatic language detection was tested on such data for Karelian for the first time, and allows the identification of Livvi-Karelian (or a mix of dialects that include Livvi-Karelian) with 99.7% sensitivity, and South Karelian and Viena Karelian as Livvi-Karelian with 90% and 73.8% sensitivity, respectively. The entries were also analysed thematically, and 10 major topics were identified. Since the data was collected using keywords and hashtags related to the Karelian language itself, most of the entries are related to the language and vocabulary in sense of translation or language learning. Language status and policy is another important topic identified in the data. Although language-related topics are the most popular, there are a substantial number of entries on eight further topics. Excluding citations from religious texts and media headlines, 751 Twitter (X) entries could be used for linguistic and sociological research. Further data collection considerations are also discussed.

Keywords: automatic language recognition, data scraping, Karelian, language policy, language revitalisation, language status, minority languages, X (Twitter)

Ilia Moshnikov*, Karelian Institute, University of Eastern Finland, Joensuu, Finland, e-mail: ilia.moshnikov@uef.fi
Eugenia Rykova*, University of Eastern Finland, Joensuu, Finland; Technical University of Applied Sciences TH Wildau, Wildau, Germany; and Catholic University of Eichstätt-Ingolstadt, Eichstätt, Germany, e-mail: eugenryk@uef.fi

* The two authors have contributed equally to the present paper.

https://doi.org/10.1515/9783111434018-007

1 Introduction

The use of the internet and social media has developed rapidly in recent years. Access to the internet offers enormous opportunities not only for majority languages, and minority languages have also found their place online. The internet has become a new domain for the use of minority languages, which supports language revitalisation initiatives. In addition to traditional websites, minority languages have begun to be used in social media and private communication, providing a rich ground for research.

The present article aims to investigate the Karelian language use on X, formerly known as Twitter. X is a leading microblog platform which can serve for data collection on various research questions (Grillenberger 2021), including the use and visibility of minority languages. Languages other than English have been receiving more attention in the last decade. However, studies focusing on minority languages are still scarce (Cunliffe 2019; Valijärvi and Khan 2023). Thus, the Karelian language is not even separately discussed in the X (Twitter) linguistic repertoire of Finland (Hiippala et al. 2020). A lack of corresponding automatic language processing tools further hinders the process.

This article describes an approach to investigate Karelian language visibility on X (Twitter) and collect the corresponding data, and considerations for further data collection are discussed. The following questions are addressed:
- How to collect data in Karelian from X (Twitter)?
- How present has Karelian been on X (Twitter) throughout the years?
- What dialects of Karelian are the most visible on X (Twitter)?
- What are the main topics of tweets published in Karelian?

2 Research background

2.1 The Karelian language and its usage online

Karelian is a minority, critically endangered Finnic language mainly spoken in Russia and Finland (see Figure 1). Currently, the total number of Karelian speakers ranges from 5,000 to 10,000 speakers in Finland and about 15,000 in Russia (Sarhimaa 2017: 115; Federal State Statistics Service 2021).

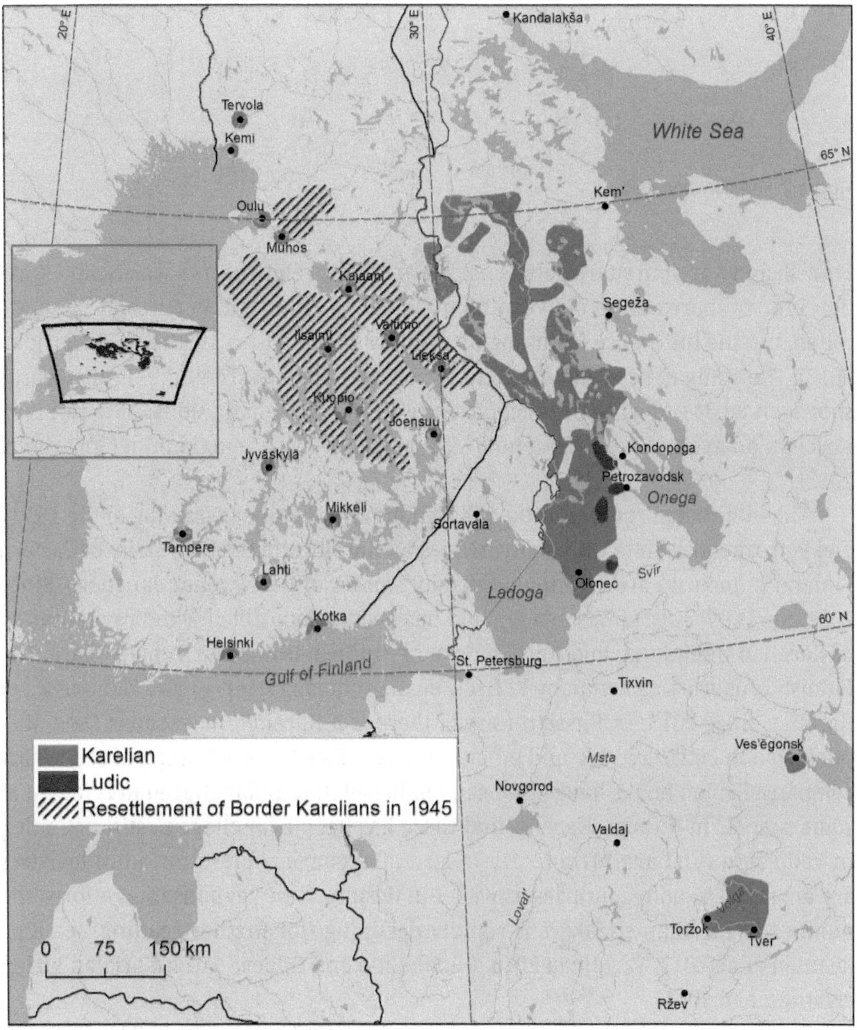

Figure 1: Karelian-speaking territories in the 2020s (Uralic Language Atlas 2024, see Roose et al. 2021).

Linguistically, the Karelian language is divided into two main dialects: Olonets (or Livvi) Karelian, and Proper Karelian. The latter consists of Viena (North) Karelian and South Karelian (Koivisto 2018). Since 1989, several written standards of Karelian based on Latin script were created. In Finland it is common to use the three written standards based on the main dialects mentioned above, while in the Republic of Karelia in Russia only two are used – Livvi and Viena. In 2007, a unified alphabet of the Karelian language was approved (Figure 2).

Aa	Bb	Cc	Čč	Dd	Ee	Ff	Gg	Hh
Jj	Kk	Ll	Mm	Nn	Oo	Pp	Rr	Ss
Šš	Zz	Žž	Tt	Uu	Vv	Yy	Ää	Öö

Figure 2: Karelian alphabet.

Finnish and Karelian share between 2,700 and 2,950 relatively old words, and Karelian Proper shares more old vocabulary with the Finnish dialects than Livvi-Karelian, but the difference is not highly significant (Häkkinen 1990: 216; Söderholm 2012). The study of proximity level based on the 800 most frequent Finnish words shows an 83.34% degree of recognition in Proper Karelian and 66.38% in Livvi-Karelian on average, and 88% and 81.5%, respectively, as a maximum (Söderholm 2012).

The intentional revitalisation of Karelian started at the beginning of the 1990s. The Petrozavodsk State University in Russian Karelia and the University of Eastern Finland in Joensuu are offering university studies of the Karelian language. Since 2021, the University of Eastern Finland has been responsible for the revitalisation of Karelian in Finland, and Karelian can be studied as a minor subject there. The Finnish broadcasting company YLE has been producing internet and radio news in Karelian since 2015. In Russian Karelia there is a Karelian newspaper *Oma Mua* published in Petrozavodsk, and other media produced by the Karelia broadcasting company. Fiction books have also been published in Karelian. Karelian is taught at some schools in Russian Karelia, and there has been a language nest functioning in Vedlozero (Vieljärvi) from 2017 to 2022. Language courses for adult learners are arranged in both countries as well. But despite these revitalisation efforts, the number of Karelian speakers is rapidly declining (for further reading, see Karjalainen et al. 2013; Sarhimaa 2016; Riionheimo and Giloeva 2022; Karjalan kielen elvyttäminen 2024).

The first signs of Karelian being used online date from the late 1990s. The first websites in Karelian were launched in the early 2000s. From the 2010s, the use of Karelian on social media started to grow significantly. Salonen (2017) studied the use of the language in internet services and software, as well as the visibility of the language on social and digital media. According to the research, Karelian speakers show a higher passive use of the language online, which could be explained by the higher average age of the speakers, but also by some psychological factors such as a perceived lack of writing skills in the language, and fear of being teased or provoked (Moshnikov 2022a; Soria 2022). Moshnikov (2016, 2022b) studied the use of Karelian as a language of websites from the virtual linguistic landscape and the theory of language ideologies, as well as the use of the language online focusing on the social media platforms, and the motivation, benefits and challenges of using Karelian online by speakers (Moshnikov 2022a). While Facebook is the most popular social media platform for consuming and creating content in Karelian, the use of Karelian on other social media platforms, including X (Twitter) and Instagram, has increased. As a new domain, the language use on social media reveals ongoing trends and changes in the language itself, and also reflects certain sociocultural processes. Importantly, it has been noted that language use in different domains and its responsiveness to new domains and media are keystones in language survival and vitality (Drude and Intangible Cultural Heritage Unit's Ad Hoc Expert Group 2003).

2.2 X (Twitter)

X (formerly Twitter[1]) is a social media micro-blogging platform, where users can publish short messages (tweets), of a maximum of 280 characters (140 characters until November 2017) and receive feedback from other users (Fausto and Aventurier 2016). The platform was established in 2006 and sold to billionaire Elon Musk in late 2022, after which Twitter underwent significant changes, up to and including an official name change from Twitter to X in July 2023. As social media interaction in general, X is a multilingual source of data that corresponds to the Big Data definition: it has volume, velocity, and variety (Kitchin 2013). Unlike Facebook, Twitter had long allowed researchers to collect data via Twitter API free of charge. In February 2023, Twitter announced the elimination of free API access, which would make further data collection more difficult (Willingham 2023).

At the same time, the changes sparked a wave of protest that led users to leave X (Twitter) and look for alternatives. Several new platforms have recently emerged, such as Threads and Bluesky (Hurst 2023; Mehta 2023; Silberling, Stringer, and Corrall 2024). But as one door closes, another one opens: following ongoing changes on X allows us to see how Karelian speakers adapt to the new conditions, and whether they stay on X or move to another platform. However, building a new community from scratch might take some time, especially for smaller communities using an endangered minority language.

1 In this article we use the names Twitter and X equally, as well as the forms 'tweet' and 'to tweet' as already established concepts that denote a Twitter post or a verb which refers to writing a Twitter post.

2.3 Minority languages and the internet

The use and visibility of a minority and/or endangered language online shows that it can be used in modern environments and new media, which increases the value of the language (Cunliffe 2019). The relationship between minority languages and technology can be described from three dimensions: availability, usability and how technology is developed for minority languages (Soria 2022). *Availability* includes the range of resources available in a given language, such as media, services, interfaces, and applications. While majority languages tend to have a wide range of resources available, minority languages have far fewer options, ranging from a lack of advanced technologies such as speech recognition to the unavailability of a keyboard. *Usability* of resources simply means which resources are used by speakers of a minority language. Minority language speakers easily switch to their dominant language when using language-based digital technologies, either because the technology is inherently better or because the range of services available is much wider. The third dimension describes how well the development of technology meets the *needs* of the language community. Companies often offer ready-made solutions without taking into account the real needs, desires, and expectations of minority language speakers. The context of each community is unique, and while some may value access to e.g., Wikipedia, others may simply value the opportunity to use the language.

Furthermore, minority languages are often overshadowed by major languages in the use and development of language technology tools, which makes minority languages vulnerable in digital environments as well. A minority language can be endangered not only linguistically, but also digitally (Soria 2016), and many minority language speakers are not well connected, or due to their age, do not have the ability or willingness to use the internet or social media, which can lead to a lack of digital competence (Cunliffe 2019).

Multilingual internet users are often faced with the choice of which language to use online, and how the online community will react to the use of a particular language or another, and whether other users will understand the post or comment (Mentrau Iaith Cymru 2014: 18). A minority language speaker constantly makes choices, which of the languages of their linguistic repertoire to use (Cunliffe 2019). In addition, speakers also evaluate their personal language skills, including the mistakes they are making, especially in public situations. Karelian speakers have expressed similar concerns, especially about their language skills and language purism (Moshnikov 2022a). Research further shows that the language choices of other users and the language use of public figures influence the language choices of minority language speakers (Mentrau Iaith Cymru 2014: 3–4).

It is very common for the community of speakers of a minority language to be dispersed. Karelian is no exception. Even if a minority lives compactly in one area, this does not guarantee that the members of the community have close contact with each other. A non-territorial minority language is in a weaker position in this respect, as its speakers are even more dispersed throughout the country or countries.

At the grassroots level, local communities adapt social media platforms for their purposes and interests using specific hashtags. Speakers of a particular language create their own hashtag systems, which makes it easier to find tweets or other posts based on a concrete topic, place, or language (Cocq 2015; Outakoski, Cocq, and Steggo 2018; McMonagle et al. 2019). Communities of speakers also create networks to support and encourage language use and learning. The minority language can be the only connecting thing between users of social media platform, and in small communities, the role of an individual active user could be crucial.

The Indigenous Tweets portal (2024) provides the following data: the total number of tweets in certain minority languages and their distribution among the users. Apparently, the fewer tweets written in a particular language, the fewer unique users produce these tweets. Thus, from 19,936 tweets in Udmurt, 88.6% are written by top 15 users; and from 5,698,636 in Welsh, only 10% are written by top 15 users. The Māori language is in the middle: from 346,434 tweets, 35% are written by top 15 users. As noted by Keegan, Mato, and Ruru (2015), the statistics for the latter (and some other languages) is skewed by individual users: as for 2014, top three users, which might be the same person/organisation, were responsible for 68.4% of all the tweets in Māori. These tweets contained exclusively translated Bible passages.

3 Research data and methods

3.1 Data scraping

Postman API software (2022) was selected to collect data from Twitter using Academic Research access, due to its convenient way of modifying the search parameters and stating the necessary information sections to be retrieved (see Rykova et al. 2023). Unlike other language-specific Twitter data collections (e.g., AbdelHamid 2022; Rykova et al. 2023), Karelian data cannot be collected via specifying the language in the query as Karelian is not among those languages whose identification is supported by Twitter API, nor is it built-in to other software libraries for

Twitter data collection. Post-hoc language identification of Karelian (cf. Ljubešić, Fišer, and Erjavec 2014; Nguyen, Trieschnigg, and Cornips 2015) is also difficult due to a scarcity of corresponding resources and dialect variability. Thus, the applicability of the HeLI-OTS 1.4 language identifier (Jauhiainen, Jauhiainen, and Lindén 2022) to Twitter entries is firstly examined in the current paper.

First, a full-archive search was performed with the help of keywords and hashtags (case and special characters can be ignored), which can be seen in Figure 3. It was assumed that the users would use these hashtags to highlight the use of the language as the speakers of other minority languages often do (Cocq 2015; McMonagle et al. 2019), and keep Karelian apart from the Finnish language. The hashtag #karjala ('Karelia' as a territory or 'Karelian' as a language) was not included in the search because it might be used in irrelevant posts about the Karjala beer produced by the Hartwall brewery or be part of discussions related to the loss of a significant part of Finnish Karelia after the Second World War. The forms of the nominative, genitive, and partitive have been chosen according to their frequency and usage in the closely related Finnish language (Hakulinen et al. 2004, §1228).

Figure 3: Full-archive search query in Postman.

Since Karelian cannot be detected via Twitter API, but is recognised as Finnish, the search query contained the parameter of Finnish as the language of the entry. Additionally, tweets had to be organic, and not an advertisement. The data was retrieved starting from 2007.

After the initial search, additional searches for the parent tweets of the retrieved comments (multiple tweets query) and user information (user lookup query) were performed. Thus, the data included entries, information on public metrics, location (if given), the author, and their 'about' information. For the comments, entries that allowed tracing the conversation back (references) to the parent tweet were included.

3.2 Data reduction

As of March 14, 2023, the collected data consisted of 15,428 entries. Removing retweets – sharing someone's tweets – reduced the number of entries to 8,463. Removing duplicates – tweets with the same content from the same or different users which were not marked as retweet and could be copying the same links or self-repetitions resulted in the final number of 8,224 multilingual entries, which were subject to manual language labelling.

3.3 Data labelling

The text of entries was subject to automatic language detection with the help of HeLI-OTS 1.4 (Jauhiainen, Jauhiainen, and Lindén 2022). This language identifier includes two dialects of Karelian: Livvi-Karelian (*olo*) and Ludic Karelian (*lud*), although nowadays Ludic is generally considered as an independent language (Pahomov 2017: 286). HeLI-OTS is based on scoring the frequency of each word (or a shorter chunk of the word if necessary) in the analysed text against the language models, which is then measured with a negative logarithm of the relative frequency of the word in each language. The final decision corresponds to the average of the scores of the words (named relative frequency score below). The algorithm can output the detected language together with the confidence score or the indicated number of best suiting languages with respective relative frequency scores. The confidence score is the absolute difference between the relative frequency scores of the detected language and the second-best one. An example of the outputs can be seen in Figure 4: the language of the text is detected as Livvi-Karelian (*olo*) with the confidence score 1.98, while the best five suiting languages are Livvi-Karelian (*olo*) with the relative frequency score of 4.11; Finnish (*fin*) with the relative frequency score of 6.09; Ludic Karelian (*lud*) with the relative frequency score of 6.1; Scottish Gaelic (*gla*) with the relative frequency score of 6.38; and Welsh (*cym*) with the relative frequency score of 6.47.

For our dataset, we stored the detected language, information on the algorithm confidence score, the second probable language, and the relative frequency scores for both. As the data was not normally distributed, statistical comparisons were performed with a Mann-Whitney U test with the help of Python scipy.stats library (Virtanen et al. 2020). Splitting the multilingual entries into sentences was performed with sent_tokenize tokenizer from Python nltk library (Bird, Klein, and Loper 2009).

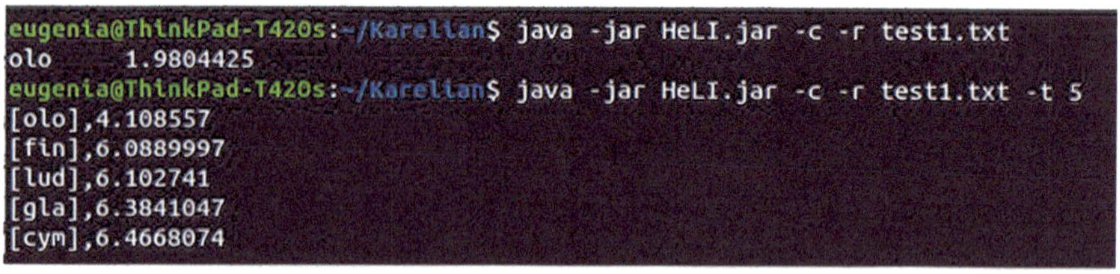

Figure 4: Example outputs of HeLI-OTS 1.4.

The language was also labelled manually by the first author of the present study, who is a native Livvi-Karelian speaker. Manual labels included more specific information on Karelian dialects: in column 'language' generally marked as *olo* or *krl*, and the latter further specified in a separate column 'dialect' (South or Viena Karelian). If an entry contained several sentences written in up to five different languages, the languages were listed in order of appearance. Non-text entries, ones with languages mixed within a sentence, or separate sentences written in more than five languages were labelled as "other".

Manual labelling also included assigning topics to entries written fully or partially in one of the Karelian dialects. The selection of topic was data-driven, and relevant groups were identified and refined during the labelling process.

4 Results

4.1 General results

There are 2,625 entries (2,201 tweets and 424 comments) written either fully or partially in one of the Karelian dialects in the final dataset, which constitutes 32% of the cleaned data. The distribution of these entries by year and dialect is shown in Figure 5. Year 2023 is not included in the graph because the data were not collected for the entire year due to the changes in Twitter policies. If an entry contains more than one dialect, it is counted for each of them. Thus, the total number of entries in the graph is higher than the actual number of entries in the database. In the whole dataset, there are 2,394 entries that include Livvi-Karelian, from which 2,038 are written in this dialect only; 231 entries that include South Karelian, from which 149 are written in this dialect only; and 112 entries that include Viena Karelian, from which 41 are written in this dialect only.

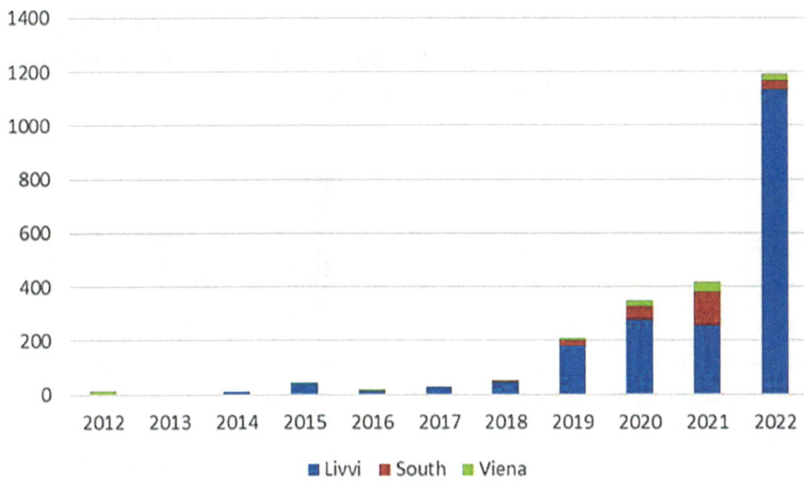

Figure 5: Entries in Karelian per year.

From the hashtags used in the search, the hashtag #karjalakse ('in Karelian', a translative case form for the word 'Karelian' in Livvi-Karelian) is present in 1,529 entries, #karjalankieli ('the Karelian language') in 155 entries, and #karjalaksi ('in Karelian', translative case form for the word 'Karelian' in Finnish, and South and Viena Karelian) in 3 entries only. However, with the help of #karjalankieli in the search, 1,180 entries were found with the hashtag #KarjalanKieliEläy (with orthographic variations meaning 'The Karelian language lives'). One more variation of #karjalankieli is present in 90 entries, and contains an underscore: #karjalan_kieli.

4.2 Language detection

The confusion matrix for automatic and manual language labelling can be seen in Figure 6. It must be noted that this matrix is not a classic confusion matrix as its true and predicted labels are asymmetric. Manual labelling allows more than one language to be included: for example, *krl + eng/fin* means South or Viena Karelian followed by either English or Finnish, *3+ (olo)* means three and more languages, including Livvi-Karelian. The automatic detection algorithm outputs only one language and has (erroneously) output languages that are not present in the original data. The language marked as Indonesian (*ind*) has such a label based on the location of the entries author. However, this variety of Malay is not included separately in the languages detected by HeLI-OTS 1.4, which makes the Malay macrolanguage (*msa*) the closest possible label for the absent *ind.* Sami languages are manually marked as a group (*sami*), without further distinction.

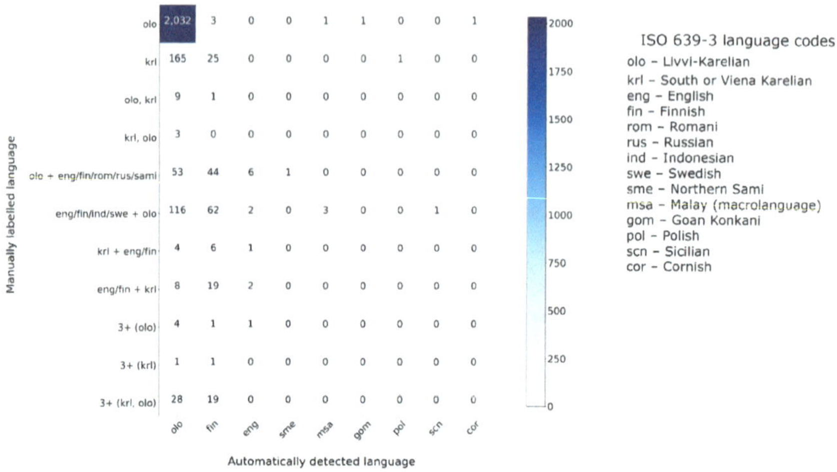

Figure 6: Confusion matrix of manually and automatically identified languages.

Livvi-Karelian is recognised as such in 99.7% of the cases, and as Finnish in 0.15% of the cases. The mean confidence score of the algorithm in cases when Livvi-Karelian is recognised as such, is 1.58±0.43 (standard deviation). The mean relative frequency score in such cases is 4.22±0.5. If Livvi-Karelian is recognised as Finnish, the mean confidence score is 0.7±0.91, and the mean relative frequency score is 5.06±0.9 (there are only 3 data points, which causes such a dispersity of data). When Karelian dialects are not recognised as Livvi-Karelian or Finnish, the mean confidence score is 0.31±0.24, and the mean relative frequency score is 5.15±0.78.

A mix of Karelian dialects is recognised as Livvi-Karelian with a mean confidence score of 1.31±0.52. The mean relative frequency score is 4.17±0.85. These results do not statistically significantly differ from the results for Livvi-Karelian alone according to the Mann-Whitney U rank test ($p > 0.05$). When a mix of dialects was recognised as Finnish, the confidence score is 0.25, and the relative frequency score is 5.31.

If an entry is written in South Karelian, its language is detected as Livvi-Karelian in 90% of the cases and as Finnish – in 9.3% of the cases. The mean confidence score of the algorithm in cases when South Karelian is recognised as Livvi-Karelian is 0.98±0.6, and the mean relative frequency score in such cases is 4.67±0.68. If

South Karelian is recognised as Finnish, the mean confidence score is 0.28±0.21, and the mean relative frequency score is 5.37±0.54. The differences in confidence scores and relative frequency scores between two recognition patterns are statistically significant according to the Mann-Whitney U rank test ($p < 0.01$).

From entries written in Viena Karelian, the detected language is Livvi-Karelian in 73.8% of the cases, and Finnish otherwise (26.2%). The mean confidence score of the algorithm in cases when Viena Karelian is recognised as Livvi-Karelian is 0.79±0.56. The mean relative frequency score in such cases is 4.5±0.67. If Viena Karelian is recognised as Finnish, the mean confidence score is 0.33±0.28, and the mean relative frequency score is 4.68±0.55. According to the Mann-Whitney U rank test, the difference in confidence scores between two recognition patterns is statistically significant ($p = 0.008$), but the difference in relative frequency is not ($p = 0.85$).

For multilingual entries (two or more languages): when the recognised language is one of the entry languages (*olo* is considered as language for *krl*), the mean confidence score is 0.54±0.44 and the mean relative frequency score is 4.87±0.58. From 383 multilingual entries, in 214 (56%), the language was detected as *olo*. From the remaining 169 entries, after automatic sentence split, the language was detected as *olo* for at least one sentence of the entry in 108 cases. It must be noted, however, that automatic sentence splitting does not always perform as ideally desired due to its internal flaws or the nature of data (especially where phrases in different languages do not constitute separate sentences).

In 73% of all cases, when any of the Karelian dialects or their mix is not recognised as Livvi-Karelian (for cases when the language is recognised as Finnish, this is 79%), the latter is still the second language in the language probabilities list. Incorporating thresholds based on discovered mean confidence and relative frequency scores should help to detect entries in Karelian even if their language is erroneously recognised. For example, taking the second option *olo* instead of the detected language, when the confidence score of the algorithm is below 0.3 or the relative frequency score for the detected language is higher than 4.8, this allows a retrieval of 17 entries – 59% for which the detected language is Finnish.

4.3 Users

In total, there were 161 usernames in the final dataset. Information on the 15 users with the greatest amounts of tweets is presented in Table 1. It must be noted that "Tweets in Karelian" means only those that were scraped with the proposed method. As we can see from the table, 89.4% of the collected entries (n=2,347) in Karelian are produced by the top 15 users. Also, it is more common to use one dialect of Karelian among individual users, while organisations or media are posting multidialectal content (e.g., Karelian Youth Organisation, Karelian Cultural Society).

Table 1: Top-15 users posting tweets in Karelian (data as of March 14, 2023).

Description of the user	N of entries in Karelian	Author location (if defined)	N of followers	following	N of tweets	Dialects used
Music teacher, religion activist	1,476	Oulu, Finland	666	1,184	14,622	olo
Professor of linguistics	220	Joensuu, Finland	1,452	1,170	7,487	south, viena, olo
Language activist, account not active anymore	158		722	74	9,809	olo, south, viena
Linguistic researcher, language activist	93	Joensuu, Finland	465	503	332	olo
Researcher, language activist	69	Tampere, Finland	9,044	1,709	32,990	olo
Musician, teacher, language activist	66	Jyväskylä, Finland	82	121	126	south
Karelian Youth Organisation	56	Suomi, Finland	1,167	104	870	olo, south, viena
Language activist, account not active anymore	50	Helsinki, Finland	218	971	1,233	olo, south, viena
Language activist	39		441	952	26,060	viena, south olo
Language activist, account not active anymore	29		888	656	7,769	south, olo
Karelian Cultural Society	24	Helsinki, Finland	249	134	221	viena, olo
Language activist	23		441	494	134,177	viena, south, olo
Language activist	16		344	196	1,880	south
Music band	16	Suomi, Finland	312	282	261	olo, viena, south = olo
Karelian News Portal	12		52	377	29	viena, olo

4.4 Topics

Ten topics identified during the manual labelling procedure are presented in Table 2, including the corresponding number of entries and an example. It must be noted that 98% of the largest topic Religion (n=1,483) comprises extracts from the Bible or other (Christian) religious texts, posted by the same user, starting in February 2021 (see Table 1). Only 28 tweets are posted by other users, and these are mainly related to the greetings on church holidays. The second largest group of tweets labelled Personal (n=327) represent personal opinions and experiences. This material is particularly interesting for studying how Karelian speakers themselves use Karelian online. Topics Vocabulary (n=313), Research (n=54), and Language learning (n=44) are respectively related to the vocabulary, research and learning of the Karelian language in a broad context. Users can use Vocabulary tweets to learn new words, Language learning – to get information about the courses available, and Research – to review or even participate in scientific studies. Tweets on these topics are published not only by educational institutions and organisations, but also by researchers and native speakers themselves.

Most of the entries in the topic Media (n=106) are links to news sources, accompanied by the title (and sometimes subtitle) of the corresponding news article. Usually, these tweets do not contain any personal information or opinions. The purpose is to share the latest news in the Karelian community. From a research perspective, the message of the posts or links is notable as well as the reactions (likes, re-tweets, quotes) and possible discussion based on these tweets. News headlines are also modifying the visibility of the Karelian language online.

There are 217 tweets related to language status and language policy. Despite the growing visibility of the Karelian language on the internet and in the media in general, there are still regular discussions about the status of the Karelian language, the status of Karelian as a language (pro dialect), language policy, and the revitalisation process in general. The mixing of the Karelian language with the Karelian dialects of Finnish, as well as the internal naming of Karelian dialects and their status, are also discussed in these tweets.

Culture (n=41) and Politics (n=12) have a significantly smaller number of tweets in the data. Tweets related to this topic include posts about Karelian music and literature, as well as events related to Karelian culture. Often, such tweets can be interpreted in a variety of ways, from personal to language policy. Political tweets are clearly related to politics, including political parties and elections. Usually, such tweets appear in the run-up to an election to attract voters. Tweets related to language status and policy are included in their own group.

The last group of Other tweets (n=29) includes some randomly written tweets related to different topics often overlapping with other topics. In the most cases, it is simply difficult to label them as belonging to just one topic.

Table 2: Topics identified in the collected data.

Topic	Description	N of entries	Example
Religion	Tweets related to religious holidays or the Bible.	1,455+28	*Hyviä äijänpäivän pruazniekkua! Kristoz voskres! Hristos nouzi kuollielois! #äijänpäivy #äijypäivy #karjalakse* 'Happy Easter holidays! Christ has resurrected! Christ has risen from the dead!'
Personal	Tweets identified as an opinion or experience.	326	*Tänäpiänä lähen otpuskah, ga loma vuottau dačalla! Hyviä heinäkuudu #karjalakse #tiedäjättiijetäh* 'I'm going on holiday today, but the iron scrap is waiting for me at the cottage! Have a good July'
Vocabulary	Tweets related to the learning of the language from the perspective of the vocabulary (e.g., translations and presenting variants from the different dialects of Karelian).	313	*Tänäpäi aijankohtaine sanaine karjalakse on huračču = vasenkätinen. Huraččuloin päiviä pietäh 13. elokuudu jo vuvves 1976. #sanainekarjalakse* 'A relevant word in Karelian today is 'huračču' – left-handed. Left Handers Day has been celebrated on 13 August since 1976.'
Language status and policy	Tweets related to the language status, policy, and revitalisation process in a broad understanding.	217	*Karjalan kieli on oma kieli, ei suomen kielen murreh.* 'Karelian is a proper language, not a dialect of Finnish.'
Media	Tweets of news or other mass-media sources.	106	*Yle Uudizet karjalakse: Päivännouzu-Suomen yliopisto tahtou jatkua karjalan kielen elvytändiä da kehitändiä* 'Yle News in Karelian: The University of Eastern Finland would like to continue its work on the revitalisation and development of the Karelian language.'
Research	Research related topics.	54	*Hyvä karjalan kielen maltai! Vastua kyzelyh karjalan kielen käyttöh näh! #karjalakse #karjalankieli* 'Dear Karelian speaker! Answer the questionnaire on the use of the Karelian language!'

Topic	Description	N of entries	Example
Language learning	Education related topics including university studies and other language courses.	44	*Zavodimma egläin Karjalan Liiton karjalan kursan. Mie opastan varzinkarjalua / suvikarjalua. Opastujat ollah kaikin puolin Suomie, 20 rištikanzuo. Keski-igä ozapuilleh 27,5 vuotta.* 'Yesterday, together with the Karelian Union, we started a Karelian language course. I am teaching Karelian Proper/South Karelian. The students are from all over Finland, 20 people. Average age of the participants is 27.5 years old.'
Culture	Culture related topics.	41	*Elbyygö karjalan kieli? Tulgua terveh Lieksan 11. kul'ttuuraseminuarah piätinččänä 4. muarienkuuda. Väl'l'ä piäzy!* 'Will the Karelian language be revived? Welcome to the 11th Lieksa Cultural Seminar on Friday, 4 March. Free entry!'
Politics	Tweets related to elections or political parties.	12	*Minule mugon! Iänestä minuu Jovensuun kunduvalličuksis 2021!* 'For me it's like this. Vote for me in the Joensuu Municipal Election 2021!'
Other	Other topics not related to other groups mentioned here.	29	*Hyviä puolistusvoimien flagupruazniekkua! #karjalan #kieli #puolistusvoimat #flagu #pruazniekku #Suomi* 'Happy Flag Day of the Finnish Defence Forces!'

5 Discussion

5.1 Karelian presence on Twitter (X)

The method of using language-related keywords and hashtags has proven to be successful to collect X (Twitter) entries in Karelian. From the data available from Twitter until March 2023, 2,625 original entries in three Karelian dialects were collected. The predominant dialect is Livvi-Karelian, which is in line with other research (Moshnikov 2022a). There are no official statistics about the number of speakers of each Karelian dialect, but there might be slightly more speakers of Livvi Karelian than speakers of other dialects. Some other factors, such a Wikipedia and Yle news in Livvi Karelian also increase a visibility of Livvi Karelian dialect on X (Twitter).

Despite the use of such specific hashtags, language-related topics were not the only ones identified in the data. The research data shows that certain events and holidays increase the activity of users. For example, the launch of Yle News in Karelian (Yle Uudizet karjalakse) in 2015 or the establishment of the Association of Young Karelians in Finland (Karjalazet Nuoret Suomes, KNŠ) in November 2019 clearly increased activity in Karelian on Twitter. Some spikes in the use of Karelian on Twitter can also be observed on specific dates, for example, Karelian Language Day, 27th of November (cf. Keegan, Mato, and Ruru 2015). The use of Karelian on Twitter (X) seems to have grown in the last five years. However, this tendency can be affected by "technical" reasons: some user accounts get deleted or become private, so that their entries are no longer available for data scraping.

5.2 Automatic language detection

Automatic detection of language with the help of HeLI-OTS 1.4 (Jauhiainen, Jauhiainen, and Lindén 2022) allows the identification of Livvi-Karelian (or a mix of dialects that include Livvi-Karelian) with 99.7% sensitivity. Two other Karelian dialects, namely South Karelian and Viena Karelian, are identified as Livvi-Karelian with 90% and 73.8% sensitivity, respectively, while the mean confidence of the algorithm becomes lower, and the score based on a negative logarithm of the relative word frequency becomes higher. Each of the three dialects can be confused with Finnish: Livvi-Karelian the least (0.15%), followed by South Karelian (9.3%), and Viena Karelian the most (26.2%). South Karelian is recognised as Finnish with a lower mean confidence score and higher (negative) relative frequency score than Viena Karelian. In fact, for the latter, the (negative) relative frequency score is not different between cases when the text language is recognised as Livvi-Karelian or Finnish. Such results are in line with the knowledge on Karelian dialects' lexicon proximity to Finnish (Söderholm 2012), and suggest that the automatic language detection tool could be of use for language and dialects proximity research. The information on confidence and (negative) relative frequency scores could also provide information on the possible dialect.

Furthermore, when Karelian dialects are erroneously recognised as Finnish, Livvi-Karelian is the second language in the language probabilities list in most of the cases, which with a lower percentage also holds true for other erroneous outputs. In this case, incorporating thresholds or more elaborated statistical models based on confidence and (negative) relative frequency scores seems to be promising for not missing relevant texts in Karelian. Corresponding modelling and testing with data in Finnish itself are left for further research.

Entries with separate phrases or sentences in different languages which include any of the Karelian dialects are usually identified with one of the languages present in the entry. Livvi-Karelian is detected as the language of 56% of such multilingual entries. When automatic sentence splitting is used, the percentage of entries for which Karelian is detected as the language for at least one sentence (or the whole entry) rises to 84%, despite the imperfections of the splitting algorithm. Since the Karelian alphabet contains specific characters (see Figure 2) and the HeLI-OTS 1.4 scoring is based on words, it might be useful to include automatic splitting into words and consider the entry to be at least partially written in Karelian if it contains a certain number of words identified as belonging to Livvi-Karelian.

Summarising the above points, the proposed language detection algorithm can be used for scraping data in Karelian from social media. For better recognition results, in particular avoiding false negatives, automatic splitting into sentences or words and certain mechanisms based on confidence scores, (negative) relative frequency scores, and a language probabilities list should be applied.

5.3 Twitter (X) users posting in Karelian

Certain authors (both individuals and organisations) who regularly write in Karelian on Twitter have been identified. The top 15 users published 89.4% of tweets in Karelian, which is similar to the rate for Udmurt language (Indigenous Tweets portal 2024) and supports the idea of higher concentration of tweets per user for less represented minority languages on Twitter (X). Individuals are posting mostly by using one of the dialects and written standards of Karelian, but organisations are usually posting multidialectal entries. Further data collections could focus on these particular authors and their interactions with other Twitter users (cf. Ljubešić, Fišer, and Erjavec 2014; Nguyen, Trieschnigg, and Cornips 2015).

5.4 Topics of Karelian Twitter (X)

During the manual labelling of the entries, 10 topics were identified in the data. However, the topic of Religion, comprising the largest number of entries, mainly consists of direct citations of (Christian) religious texts, comparable to the case of Māori (Keegan, Mato, and Ruru 2015). While it is relevant to the general visibility of Karelian online, these collected texts cannot be considered as representing personal voices on social media. The same holds true for the majority of entries in the topic Media, because they only copy the titles and subtitles of the news articles and provide corresponding links. The topic Vocabulary predominantly contains word or phrase lists translated into one or more of the Karelian dialects. While such posts are also relevant for visibility and could be used as a language learning resource, their applicability to other research fields is questionable. That reduces our dataset to 751 Twitter entries written fully or partially in one or more Karelian dialect, that could be used for deeper linguistic and sociological analysis. The data can be analysed in the context of language or dialect contacts, lexical and morphological variation, and from the perspective of translation studies and discourse analysis. Tweets and discussions related to the status of the Karelian language are interesting from the perspective of language revitalisation and policy. The modern use of Karelian online has also an important symbolic meaning for the Karelian-speaking community. The collected corpus becomes even more important in the current context of changes in Twitter API access.

6 Conclusion

To the best of authors' knowledge, this paper describes the first corpus of X (Twitter) entries in Karelian. Using language-related keywords and hashtags, 2,625 original entries corresponding to 10 different topics were collected. 29% of the material can be seen as useful for further linguistic and sociological analysis.

The recent changes on X (Twitter) made the new data collection challenging. Regarding the accessibility of the resources mentioned above (Soria 2022), it should be noted that access to Twitter in Russia has been restricted since 1 March 2022. Facebook and Instagram are also blocked. The use of X itself is constantly changing, and the future will show whether the Karelian language will retain its position on X, or whether speakers will move to another platform. Nevertheless, minority languages, including Karelian, have found their place in the online space. Accordingly, it is important to support the use of endangered languages online on a personal and institutional level, and this will support the vitality and revitalisation of the language.

References

AbdelHamid, Medyan, Assef Jafar & Yasser Rahal. 2022. Levantine hate speech detection in Twitter. *Social Network Analysis and Mining* 12. 121. https://doi.org/10.1007/s13278-022-00950-4.

Bird, Steven, Ewan Klein & Edward Loper. 2009. *Natural language processing with Python: Analyzing text with the natural language toolkit.* O'Reilly Media, Inc. https://www.nltk.org/book/ (last accessed 11 March 2024).

Cocq, Coppélie. 2015. Indigenous voices on the web: Folksonomies and endangered languages. *Journal of American Folklore* 128 (509). 273–285. https://www.jstor.org/stable/10.5406/jamerfolk.128.509.0273 (last accessed 11 March 2024).

Cunliffe, Daniel. 2019. Minority languages and social media. In Gabrielle Hogan-Brun & Bernadette O'Rourke (eds.), *The Palgrave handbook of minority languages and communities*, 451–480. London: Palgrave Macmillan.

Drude, Sebastian and Intangible Cultural Heritage Unit's Ad Hoc Expert Group. 2003. *Language vitality and endangerment.* https://unesdoc.unesco.org/ark:/48223/pf0000183699 (last accessed 11 March 2024).

Fausto, Sibele & Pascal Aventurier. 2016. Scientific literature on Twitter as a subject research: Findings based on bibliometric analysis. In Clement Levallois, Morgane Marchand, Tiago Mata, & André Panisson (eds.), *Twitter for Research Handbook* 2015–2016, 1–14. Lyon: EMLYON Press.

Federal State Statistics Service. 2021. *Vserossijskaja perepis' naselenija 2020 [Russian Census 2020].* https://rosstat.gov.ru/vpn/2020 (last accessed 11 March 2024).

Grillenberger, Andreas. 2021. Twitterdaten analysieren mithilfe der blockbasierten Programmiersprache SNAP! [Analyse Twitter data using the block-based programming language SNAP!]. *LOG IN* 41. 54–60. https://dl.gi.de/items/01f69d2c-a8a4-4934-b1ee-40ef56870f1a (last accessed 11 March 2024).

Hakulinen, Auli, Maria Vilkuna, Riitta Korhonen, Vesa Koivisto, Tarja Riitta Heinonen & Irja Alho (eds.), 2004. *Iso suomen kielioppi [Descriptive grammar of Finnish].* Online version. Helsinki: Finnish Literature Society. http://scripta.kotus.fi/visk (last accessed 11 March 2024).

Hiippala, Tuomo, Tuomas Väisänen, Tuuli Toivonen & Olle Järv. 2020. Mapping the languages of Twitter in Finland: Richness and diversity in space and time. *Neuphilologische Mitteilungen* 121 (1), 12–44. https://doi.org/10.51814/nm.99996.

Hurst, Luke. 2023. With Twitter gone and users unsure about X, is Bluesky the future? We try it out. *Euronews*. https://www.euronews.com/next/2023/08/15/with-twitter-gone-and-users-unsure-about-x-is-bluesky-the-future-we-try-it-out (last accessed 11 March 2024).

Häkkinen, Kaisa. 1990. *Mistä sanat tulevat. Suomalaista etymologiaa* [Where do words come from: Finnish etymology]. Tietolipas 117. Helsinki: Suomalaisen Kirjallisuuden Seura.

Jauhiainen, Tommi, Heidi Jauhiainen & Krister Lindén. 2022. HeLI-OTS, Off-the-shelf language identifier for text. *Proceedings of the Thirteenth Language Resources and Evaluation Conference.* 3912–3922. Marseille, France. European Language Resources Association. https://aclanthology.org/2022.lrec-1.416/ (last accessed 11 March 2024).

Karjalainen, Heini, Ulriikka Puura, Riho Grünthal & Svetlana Kovaleva. 2013. Karelian in Russia: ELDIA casespecific report. *Studies in European Language Diversity* 26. Mainz: Research consortium ELDIA https://phaidra.univie.ac.at/detail/o:314612 (last accessed 11 March 2024).

Karjalan kielen elvyttäminen. 2024. *The revitalisation of the Karelian language.* University of Eastern Finland. https://blogs.uef.fi/karjalanelvytys/ (last accessed 11 March 2024).

Keegan, Te Taka, Paora Mato & Stacey Ruru. 2015. Using Twitter in an indigenous language: An analysis of te reo Māori tweets. *AlterNative: An International Journal of Indigenous Peoples* 11:1. 59–75. https://doi.org/10.1177/117718011501100105.

Kitchin, Rob. 2013. Big data and human geography: Opportunities, challenges, and risks. *Dialogues in Human Geography* 3 (3). 262–267. https://doi.org/10.1177/2043820613513388.

Koivisto, Vesa. 2018. Border Karelian dialects – a diffuse variety of Karelian. In Marjatta Palander, Helka Riionheimo & Vesa Koivisto (eds.), *On the border of language and dialect*, 56–84. Studia Fennica Linguistica 21. Helsinki: Finnish Literature Society.

Ljubešić, Nikola, Darja Fišer & Tomaž Erjavec. 2014. TweetCaT: A tool for building Twitter corpora of smaller languages. In *Proceedings of the Ninth International Conference on Language Resources and Evaluation (LREC'14)*. 2279–2283. Reykjavik, Iceland. European Language Resources Association (ELRA). https://aclanthology.org/L14-1642/ (last accessed 11 March 2024).

McMonagle, Sarah, Daniel Cunliffe, Lysbeth Jongbloed-Faber & Paul Jarvis. 2019. What can hashtags tell us about minority languages on Twitter? A comparison of #cymraeg, #frysk, and #gaeilge. *Journal of Multilingual and Multicultural Development* 40 (1). 32–49. https://doi.org/10.1080/01434632.2018.1465429.

Mehta, Ivan. 2023. What is Instagram's Threads app? All your questions answered. *TechCrunch online magazine*. https://tcrn.ch/44d3hB3 (last accessed 11 March 2024).

Mentrau Iaith Cymru. 2014. *The Welsh language and social networks*. Llanrwst: Mentrau Iaith Cymru.

Moshnikov, Ilia. 2016. Karjalankieliset verkkosivut virtuaalisena kielimaisemana [Developing websites in the Karelian language as part of virtual linguistic landscape]. *Lähivõrdlusi. Lähivertailuja* 26. 282–310. http://dx.doi.org/10.5128/LV26.09.

Moshnikov, Ilia. 2022a. The use of the Karelian language online: Current trends and challenges. Eesti ja Soome-Ugri Keeleteaduse Ajakiri. *Journal of Estonian and Finno-Ugric Linguistics* 13 (2). 275–305. https://doi.org/10.12697/jeful.2022.13.2.09.

Moshnikov, Ilia. 2022b. The use of the Karelian language online: websites in Karelian. In Tanja Seppälä, Sirkku Lesonen, Päivi Iikkanen & Sigurd D'hondt (eds.), *Kieli, muutos, yhteiskunta - Language, change, society*. AFinLA Yearbook 2022, 192–216. https://doi.org/10.30661/afinlavk.113920.

Nguyen, Dong, Dolf Trieschnigg & Leonie Cornips. 2015. Audience and the use of minority languages on Twitter. *Proceedings of the ninth international AAAI conference on web and social media*, 9 (1). 666–669. https://ojs.aaai.org/index.php/ICWSM/article/view/14648/14497 (last accessed 11 March 2024).

Outakoski, Hanna, Coppélie Cocq & Peter Steggo. 2018. Strengthening indigenous languages in the digital age: Social media–supported learning in Sápmi. *Media International Australia* 169 (1). 21–31. https://doi.org/10.1177/1329878X18803700.

Pahomov, Miikul. 2017. *Lyydiläiskysymys: Kansa vai heimo, kieli vai murre?* [The Ludian Question: Nation or tribe, language or dialect?]. Helsinki: University of Helsinki & Lyydiläinen Seura.

Postman. 2023. *Postman API Tool*. https://www.postman.com/ (last accessed 11 March 2024).

Riionheimo, Helka & Natalia Giloeva. 2022. Karjalankielinen yliopisto-opetus – vastavirtaan soutamista? [University education in Karelian - rowing against the stream?]. *Kieli, koulutus ja yhteiskunta* 13/5. https://www.kieliverkosto.fi/fi/journals/kieli-koulutus-ja-yhteiskunta-lokakuu-2022/karjalankielinen-yliopisto-opetus-vastavirtaan-soutamista (last accessed 11 March 2024).

Roose, Meeli, Tua Nylén, Harri Tolvanen & Outi Vesakoski. 2021. User-centered design of multidisciplinary spatial data platforms for human-history research. *SPRS International Journal of Geo -Information* 10/7, 467. https://doi.org/10.3390/ijgi10070467.

Rykova, Eugenia, Christine Stieben, Olga Dostovalova & Horst Wieker. 2023. Connected driving in German-speaking social media. *Social Sciences* 12 (1): 46. https://doi.org/10.3390/socsci12010046.

Salonen, Tuomo. 2017. Karelian – a digital language? In Claudia Soria, Irene Russo & Valeria Quochi (eds.), *Reports on digital language diversity in Europe*. https://www.dldp.eu/sites/default/files/documents/DLDP_Karelian-Report.pdf (last accessed 11 March 2024).

Sarhimaa, Anneli. 2016. Karelian in Finland. ELDIA case-specific report. *Studies in European Language Diversity* 27. Mainz: Research consortium ELDIA. https://fedora.phaidra.univie.ac.at/fedora/get/o:471733/bdef:Content/get (last accessed 11 March 2024).
Sarhimaa, Anneli. 2017. *Vaietut ja vaiennetut. Karjalankieliset karjalaiset Suomessa* [Silent and being forced to be silent: Karelian-speaking Karelians in Finland]. *Tietolipas* 256. Helsinki: Finnish Literature Society.
Silberling, Amanda, Alyssa Stringer & Cody Corrall. 2024. What is Bluesky? Everything to know about the app trying to replace Twitter. *TechCrunch online magazine*. https://tcrn.ch/3HDTvi7 (last accessed 11 March 2024).
Soria, Claudia. 2016. What is digital language diversity and why should we care? In Josep Cru (ed.), *Digital media and language revitalisation. Els mitjans digitals i la revitalitzacio lingüística. Linguapax Review* 13–28. https://www.linguapax.org/wp-content/uploads/2015/03/LinguapaxReview2016web.pdf (last accessed 11 March 2024).
Soria, Claudia. 2022. *Decolonizing Minority Language Technology.* https://internetlanguages.org/en/stories/decolonizing-minority-language/ (last accessed 11 March 2024).
The Indigenous Tweets portal. 2024. http://indigenoustweets.com/ (last accessed 18 July 2024).
Twitter Developers. 2023. *Announcing new access tiers for the Twitter API. Twitter.* https://twittercommunity.com/t/announcing-new-access-tiers-for-the-twitter-api/188728 (last accessed 11 March 2024).
Valijärvi, Riitta-Liisa & Lily Kahn. 2023. The role of new media in minority- and endangered-language communities. In Eda Derhemi and Christopher Moseley (eds.), *Endangered languages in the 21st century*, 139–157. Abingdon, Oxfordshire, UK: Routledge. https://www.taylorfrancis.com/chapters/oa-edit/10.4324/9781003260288-12/role-new-media-minority-endangered-language-communities-riitta-liisa-valij%C3%A4rvi-lily-kahn (last accessed 11 March 2024).
Virtanen, Pauli, Ralf Gommers, Travis E. Oliphant, Matt Haberland, Tyler Reddy, David Cournapeau, Evgeni Burovski, Pearu Peterson, Warren Weckesser, Jonathan Bright, Stéfan J. van der Walt, Matthew Brett, Joshua Wilson, K. Jarrod Millman, Nikolay Mayorov, Andrew R. J. Nelson, Eric Jones, Robert Kern, Eric Larson, CJ Carey, İlhan Polat, Yu Feng, Eric W. Moore, Jake VanderPlas, Denis Laxalde, Josef Perktold, Robert Cimrman, Ian Henriksen, E.A. Quintero, Charles R. Harris, Anne M. Archibald, Antônio H. Ribeiro, Fabian Pedregosa, Paul van Mulbregt & SciPy 1.0 Contributors. 2020. SciPy 1.0: Fundamental algorithms for scientific computing in Python. *Nature Methods* 17 (3), 261–272. https://doi.org/10.1038/s41592-019-0686-2.
Willingham, AJ. 2023. *Why Twitter users are upset about the platform's latest change.* CNN. https://edition.cnn.com/2023/02/03/tech/twitter-api-what-is-pricing-change-cec/index.html (last accessed 11 March 2024).

Aris Xanthos, Lliana Doudot, and Prakhar Gupta

What's New, Switzerland? Collecting and sharing half a million WhatsApp messages in French

Abstract: Instant messaging (IM) applications, especially WhatsApp, have become ubiquitous in contemporary computer-mediated communication (CMC) practices. Owing to their similarities with face-to-face conversations, IM data have the potential to constitute a rich source of research material for corpus linguistics and cultural analytics. Their private nature makes them particularly relevant for studies focusing on the communication of socio-emotional content; it also explains why, even though several successful projects have been devoted to the collection of IM datasets in recent years, such corpora remain scarce resources at the time of writing. In this work, we outline the creation process of the *What's New, Switzerland?* corpus, a large, curated dataset of messages exchanged between French-speaking WhatsApp users in Switzerland. The paper covers the protocols used for collecting these messages, de-identifying them and publishing them in a structured format. It provides a high-level quantitative account of the resulting dataset in terms of user, chat, and message properties. The de-identified chats are made available in TEI-XML and plain text formats, in the perspective of fostering research on this specific type of CMC data.

Keywords: WhatsApp, chats, instant messaging, IM, data collection, de-identification, corpus, French

Aris Xanthos, University of Lausanne, Faculty of Arts, Anthropole building, CH-1015 Lausanne, aris.xanthos@unil.ch
Lliana Doudot, Independent researcher, lliana.doudot@gmail.com
Prakhar Gupta, Independent researcher, gupta.prkhr@gmail.com

https://doi.org/10.1515/9783111434018-008

1 Introduction

Colossal amounts of messages are being exchanged daily by users of instant messaging[1] (IM) applications such as WhatsApp (Singh 2020) or Facebook Messenger. These data are of particular interest to language and communication research thanks to features which make them relatively more similar to face-to-face conversations than several other forms of text-based computer-mediated communication (CMC) data (Ueberwasser and Stark 2017). Due to their private nature, IM exchanges are also likely to offer a privileged viewpoint for studies focusing on the communication of socio-emotional content. However, the necessity of de-identifying such data raises considerable challenges. This explains why, despite their many advantages, IM corpora remain vastly underrepresented among datasets available for research on CMC, in particular when compared to data documenting mass communication practices and retrieved from social media such as Twitter or from the web (notably discussion forums, blog posts, and comments). As an illustration of this claim, out of thirty-two corpora listed on the CMC Corpora section of the CLARIN website[2] at the time of writing, only two comprise material which qualifies as IM data as defined above, although others comprise chat room or SMS data, such as the *SMS2Science* (Durscheid and Stark 2011) and *SoNaR* (Sanders 2012) projects.

The work by Decker and Vandekerckhove (2017) is an early example of a large-scale attempt to collect IM data, along with other types of CMC data. The IM part of the corpus, which was produced between 2007 and 2013 by Flemish youth aged 13–20 on the MSN and Facebook messenger platforms, comprises about 1.3M words. Arguably, the largest such project to this date is *What's up, Switzerland?* (Ueberwasser and Stark 2017), which collected more than 600 WhatsApp chats dating from 2010–2014 in a variety of languages spoken in Switzerland (mostly Swiss-German, German, French, Italian and Romansh). This corresponds to about 750K messages and more than 5.5M tokens which have been made publicly available after de-identification. At a smaller scale, Verheijen and Stoop (2016) collected 215 WhatsApp conversations (about 330K words) in Dutch, in the perspective of complementing the *SoNaR* corpus with IM data; in the same language, the *WhatsApp corpus Berntzen* (Spooren et al. 2018) contains 60 WhatsApp chat sessions (about

1 Instant messaging is understood as a private, quasi-synchronous, and mainly text-based form of CMC, typically occurring between two or a relatively limited number of users through such platforms as WhatsApp and Facebook Messenger; in particular, it is distinct from SMS exchange from the point of view of synchronicity, and from chat room communication from the point of view of privacy.

2 https://www.clarin.eu/resource-families/cmc-corpora (last accessed 16 July 2024)

347K words). Dorantes et al. (2018) report on the collection of WhatsApp chats in Spanish gathered in Mexico City in 2017, which resulted in a set of 835 chats with more than 1,300 informants and a total of about 750K tokens available for linguistic research.

All the collections reviewed above comprise IM data produced between 2008 and 2017, and as such they do not document the most recent practices in IM, and particularly WhatsApp messaging, which are constantly changing notably in relation to the evolution of the platforms themselves, or to important societal events such as the COVID pandemics (Seufert et al. 2022). A major exception to this is the *Mobile Communication Database 2* (*MoCoDa2*), an ongoing project active since 2018, which collects WhatsApp messages in German language (Beißwenger et al. 2019). At the time of writing, *MoCoDa2* contains 1,005 chats and 313K tokens from 3,496 participants.[3] The *MMWAH* (*Multilingual / Multimodal WhatsApp discussions at Hanken*) project is another recent initiative that aims to collect WhatsApp discussions from young Swedish-speaking adults in Finland (Mäkinen 2023). Finally, it should be noted that while other works have sought to gather and analyze sometimes very large amounts of IM data (e.g., Schwind & Seufert 2018), most of them did not have an explicit goal of sharing the contents of messages with the research community, contrary to the works cited above.

The present paper reports on the results of a recent effort to collect a large amount of WhatsApp messages exchanged by Switzerland-based users and preprocess them in the perspective of building a shared resource for the scientific community and fostering research on this specific type of CMC data. The remainder of the paper is organized as follows. In section 2 we present the methodology adopted for building our corpus, with special emphasis on data collection and de-identification, including the evaluation of the latter step; a discussion of the formats (TEI-XML and plain text) in which the data are published is also included. In section 3 we give a high-level quantitative overview of the resulting dataset in terms of chat and user metadata as well as message content and properties. Section 4 concludes the paper by discussing the main features that characterize this project and the resulting dataset, and outlining future work directions.

3 https://db.mocoda2.de/c/home (last accessed 17 July 2024)

2 Corpus building

2.1 Data collection

We created a website[4] for registering the consent of donors and other chat members. This platform was made available in the four Swiss national languages (German, French, Italian, and Romansh) as well as English. The platform was also used to collect information pertaining to the donated chats as well as personal information of users. The overall chat collection workflow drew inspiration from the *What's up, Switzerland?* protocol (Ueberwasser and Stark 2017), with the additional requirement that prospective chat donors should register their email-ID on the platform as a preliminary step; in doing so, they committed to donating chats only after having obtained all other chat members' consent for the donation. After this step, they were able to send any number of chats using the email-ID they previously registered.

Donors had to export each donated chat in plain text format from within WhatsApp (excluding media), then send it to one of the five different email-IDs we used to accommodate the different languages supported on the platform. Then they received an automated email reply redirecting them to a form on the website, where they should declare their consent for donating this specific chat under the project's terms and conditions, as well as enter the email address of each other chat member. Another automated email was then sent to the latter, asking them to formally register their consent in a similar way. Optionally, chat participants could indicate a list of sensitive words that they wanted to be redacted in the chat as well as answer a few basic questions about their profile (gender, age class, education level, language skills and use of IM apps). Chat donors also had the option to fill in important details about the chat such as the language(s) of the chat and relationship(s) between the participants.

Each chat member can revoke their consent at any time. We also went further than *What's up, Switzerland?* in terms of the consent scheme we implemented, to the extent that each chat member can unilaterally request that the chat be deleted from the platform and our storage. Moreover, chats for which one or more users did not register their consent after several reminders were scheduled for deletion in this way at the end of corpus constitution.

The chat collection campaign ran from August to October 2022. It was promoted by various means, including a press campaign, social media posts, and by

4 https://whatsnew-switzerland.ch/en (last accessed 16 July 2024)

word of mouth within the researchers' professional and private networks. To incentivize the donation of chats, gift cards with values ranging from 50 to 200 Swiss francs were awarded to a few of the participants selected via a lottery system. By the end of the collection period, we collected a total of 97 chats. Out of these donations, 90 received the consent of all chat members, which amounts to 93% of donated chats with full consent. In comparison, the *What's up, Switzerland?* project collected about 600 chats, but only 40% of donated chats had full consent (Ueberwasser and Stark 2017). We believe that the addition of a preliminary registration step for donors, whereby they committed to obtaining consent of all chat members prior to donation, played a key role in the simultaneous decrease of total donation count and increase of full consent rate.

Among chats with full consent, 73 were in French while 17 were in Swiss German, Italian and English (or multiple languages). Due to the relatively low number of chats in these languages, as well as the considerable workload required for setting up a de-identification workflow for additional languages, we chose to focus our de-identification efforts on French.

2.2 De-identification workflow

We used a combination of automated processes and manual examination steps to detect and process message fragments that were liable to disclose sensitive or identifying information about the users – a crucial endeavor in the perspective of sharing the data with the scientific community. Similarly to the methodology used by Lüngen et al. (2017) among others, these words and phrases were then *categorized*, i.e., replaced with abstract placeholders, except for first names: following the practice adopted in the *What's up, Switzerland?* project (Ueberwasser and Stark 2017), first names were rather *pseudonymized*, i.e., randomly replaced with other first names, in order to preserve data readability.

The following subsections describe the automated processes by which we attempted to capture different sensitive information categories as well as the subsequent manual examination steps which we used to improve the de-identification precision and recall. Finally, we present the method used to evaluate our de-identification workflow and the results we obtained.

2.2.1 Automated de-identification processes

We used two NER (Named Entity Recognition)-based detection models to detect first names and last names in messages: a multilingual model (Tedeschi et al. 2021) and a French NER model fine-tuned on the CamemBERT model (Martin et al. 2020). All entities tagged as *PER* (person) were then matched with a list of last names of the permanent resident population of Switzerland as well as first names of the Swiss population by gender with frequency 10 or more.[5] We also included a list of the 200 most popular baby names in the United States from 2000 to 2021[6] to introduce more diversity in the set of first names. Based on the matching, words were either assigned as last names or as first names (also accounting for middle names).

Last names were replaced with the *_LAST_NAME_* placeholder. First names were replaced with another name of the same gender (male, female, or unisex) and beginning with a similar (vocalic or consonantic) initial letter in the entire chat. Using similar initial letters was important, because in French a few words such as *de* 'of' are realized in a different way when preceding a vowel-initial word, e.g., *de Paul* 'of Paul' vs. *d'Olivia* 'of Olivia'. The system was implemented in such fashion that it could recognize variant spellings of names resulting from letter repetition, e.g., *Jooooohn*; in such cases, a specific marker was appended to the replacement name, e.g., *Marco_REPETITION_*. Replacement first names also preserved the original case information of the replaced token whenever possible.

Names of Swiss towns with less than 30K inhabitants as well as Swiss street addresses were replaced with *_TOWN_NAME_* and *_STREET_ADDR_* placeholders respectively.[7] Most remaining types of sensitive information were captured using regular expressions. Any word containing more than 3 digits was thus replaced by the *_NUMBER_* placeholder, leaving strings indicating date and time untouched wherever possible. URLs, whether partial or complete, and email-IDs were similarly replaced with *_URL_* and *_EMAIL_* placeholders. Moreover, all WhatsApp mentions of chat members using the @ symbol were replaced with the *_MENTION_* placeholder.

As mentioned in section 2.1, users could indicate a list of words and phrases which they deemed sensitive and wanted to be redacted, e.g., nicknames, colloquial ways of naming towns, organization names, etc. Such words and phrases were replaced with the generic *_MASKED_TEXT_* placeholder – unless they had pre-

5 Both lists were retrieved from the Swiss Federal Statistical Office: https://www.bfs.admin.ch/bfs/en/home/statistics/population/births-deaths/names-switzerland.assetdetail.23264628.html (last accessed 17 July 2024) and https://www.bfs.admin.ch/bfs/en/home/statistics/population/births-deaths/names-switzerland.assetdetail.23045212.html (last accessed 17 July 2024).

6 https://github.com/aruljohn/popular-baby-names (last accessed 17 July 2024)

7 Town names along with corresponding population counts were retrieved from the Swiss Federal Statistical Office: https://www.bfs.admin.ch/bfs/en/home/statistics/regional-statistics/regional-portraits-key-figures/communes.html (accessed 17 July 2024). Street addresses were downloaded from the Swiss Official directory of building addresses: https://www.swisstopo.admin.ch/en/official-directory-of-building-addresses (last accessed 17 July 2024).

viously been replaced or redacted by one of the aforementioned, more specific processes.

Finally, all system messages along with references to missing media and documents (which we explicitly asked donors not to export) were replaced with placeholders documenting the nature of the interaction. For example, when one of the chat members is made an admin, the system message was replaced with *__ADMIN_RIGHTS_MESSAGE__* or when an image was shared, the message was replaced with *_IMAGE_OMITTED_*.

2.2.2 Manual de-identification steps

For each chat, the set of replacements identified by the automated steps described in the previous subsection was then manually reviewed to improve the resulting precision and recall. The main error types targeted at this point were the following:

- false positives, e.g., common nouns incorrectly identified as names; this category also includes names of celebrities, historical figures or fictional characters, which do not leak any sensitive information about the users but may contribute to the readability of the data;
- classification errors, e.g., first names or part of street addresses tagged as last names;
- granularity errors, such as first names which are hypocoristic variants of another first name in the chat, like *Ben* and *Benjamin* for example (in this case, the string *_HYPOCOR_* would be appended to the replacement first name);
- context-dependent errors, which concern the relatively rare occurrence of strings whose status as a piece of sensitive information varies from one token to another (e.g., *Max* as a first name or as short for *maximum*).

In addition to these errors, we also attempted to identify false negatives, i.e., items that the automated processes failed to identify altogether – a problem which is both particularly challenging and crucial for privacy protection. To that effect, we mainly used the following two heuristic methods:

- out of those words which had not been marked for redaction, we manually reviewed any word beginning with a capital letter and/or not listed in a large machine-readable French lexicon (New et al. 2004);
- every word which differed from a redacted word by exactly one letter was manually reviewed, which enabled us to capture a few instances of sensitive data which automated processes had missed because of typos or non-standard spellings.

Four human experts were involved in these steps, the result of which was a final set of context-independent replacements for 72 chats with full consent – one large chat between a group of friends could unfortunately not be processed in this way due to the extremely high number of local, international, or fictional soccer player names or nicknames it contained and was therefore excluded from the collection. After these replacements had been automatically performed, the last step in the de-identification process was to deal manually with the few cases which could not be handled in a context-independent way.

2.2.3 Evaluation of de-identification

To gauge the accuracy of our de-identification workflow, we built a sample of 3,000 snippets randomly drawn from the 72 chats in French with full consent in the collection. It is worth noting that this sample is also meant to be used for emotion annotation in the future; therefore, the criteria used for building it were based on two distinct and sometimes conflicting goals: evaluating data de-identification and supporting emotion annotation. To compensate for differences between chats (see section 3.2) and to ensure that smaller ones are represented in the sample, the probability of selecting a given chat was set proportionally to the cube root of the number of messages in the chat. Several additional constraints pertaining to the emotion annotation goal were used to further restrict the random selection of snippets, notably the minimum number of users (2), minimum and maximum number of messages (2–5) and tokens (15–60), maximum proportion of redacted tokens (25%), and maximum duration of exchange (2 hours).

The final set of 3,000 chat snippets randomly drawn based on these criteria contained 9,994 messages, which corresponds to about 2% of the entire collection. These were manually reviewed by three human experts (one per snippet) to determine the expected de-identification output (*gold standard*) for each message. The gold standard was then compared with the actual output of the automated and manual processing outlined in the previous subsections.

1,180 messages of our sample contained sensitive information according to the gold standard (11.8% of all messages in sample). Out of these, 1,080 (91.5%) were de-identified correctly using our protocol. In 39 among the remaining 100, sensitive information was redacted but with wrong replacements/placeholders. In the remaining 61 messages (5.2% of messages with sensitive information), at least part of the sensitive information was not redacted completely. Precision and recall scores for each category can be found in Table 1.[8] We also report the redaction rate for each category, i.e., the proportion of words/phrases in this category that were redacted or replaced with a placeholder either from that category or from some other category, thus preventing the leakage of sensitive information in any case.

The lowest recall and redaction rates are reported for the street address category. A close examination of these false negatives shows that most of them did not concern formal street addresses (which are generally well recognized), but names of public places (restaurants, bars, buildings, etc.), which can be readily mapped to street addresses and have therefore been treated as such in the gold standard. However, leaking the information that an anonymous chat member was present in such a place at some point in time appears as relatively benign when compared to leaking their home address for instance. Aside from this case, all categories had a redaction rate superior to 90%, and even close to 100% for the frequent categories of first names and town names.[9]

Table 1: De-identification evaluation metrics for different word/phrase categories.

Word / phrase category	Count	Precision	Recall	Redaction rate
First names	738	97.4%	98.4%	98.6%
Last names	46	89.5%	83.7%	90.2%
URLs	62	100%	100%	100%
Email-IDs	9	100%	100%	100%
Numbers	73	100%	100%	100%
Town names	207	97.1%	96.8%	98.3%
Street addresses	157	93.8%	76.8%	82.2%
Other	126	95.7%	88.9%	90.5%
Total	1,418	96.9%	94.6%	95.9%

8 For a given category, precision is defined as the proportion of tokens actually belonging to this category (according to gold standard) among all tokens assigned to this category by our algorithm. Recall is defined as the proportion of tokens correctly assigned to this category by our algorithm among all tokens belonging to this category (according to gold standard). We treat each token independently except for multi-word street addresses and town names (e.g., *Av. de la Paix 14* or *St. Sulpice*), which are treated as single entities. For such items, partial matches (i.e., when only part of the tokens of a multi-word address or town name are recognized) are counted as complete mismatches.

9 The 100% precision reported for numbers is due to the fact that we never counted them as false positives. Indeed, we adopted a strict policy which said that sequences of three or more digits should be systematically de-identified, regardless of whether they consisted of personal information or not.

2.4 Data format and availability

De-identified chats have been encoded in XML-TEI format following the proposals of the TEI-CMC special interest group[10] as described by Beißwenger and Lüngen (2020). Each individual message is enclosed in a *post* element with *modality, generatedBy, who,* and *xml.id* attributes as in example (1).

(1) *<post modality="written" generatedBy="human" who="#wns.user.008" xml:id="wns.chat.13.28"><time>2021-09-16 20:05</time>Coucou alors j'ai demandé à une pote pour demain soir mais elle a un anniversaire... toi il y a des gens qui sont chaud ? 🤗</post>*
'Hey there so I asked a friend about tomorrow night but she has a birthday party... HOW about you, any folks up for it? 🤗'

Metadata for each user are stored in a *person* element under the *profileDesc* element of the document header, using TEI markup whenever possible and the generic *note* element otherwise, as shown in example (2). Posts are linked to user metadata by means of their *who* attribute, the value of which is a reference to the corresponding *person* element's *xml:id* attribute value.

(2) *<person role="participant" xml:id="wns.user.008" gender="female" age="18-24">*
<persName type="nickname">_WNS_USER_008_</persName>
<residence>Located in French-speaking area of Switzerland; has been living in Switzerland for 1-4 years.</residence>
<education>University (Master)</education>
<note>
<p>Spoken language(s): French
Language(s) used in text messages: French
Application(s) used for messaging: Instagram, Snapchat, WhatsApp
Smartphone system used: iOS</p>
</note>
</person>

Similarly, chat-level metadata are stored in the *textDesc* element when there exist standardized TEI elements for them (e.g., *channel, preparedness,* etc.) and otherwise in a *xenoData* element using an ad hoc namespace and elements, as in example (3).

10 https://tei-c.org/Activities/SIG/CMC/ (last accessed 17 July 2024)

(3) *<xenoData xmlns:wns="https://whatsnew-switzerland.ch/ns/1.0">*
<wns:metadata>
<wns:num_participants>2</wns:num_participants>
<wns:relation>friends</wns:relation>
<wns:usage>fun/entertainment (fun pictures, fun stories, etc.), general communication/contact, organization (event, gift, meeting, etc.)</wns:usage>
<wns:meeting_frequency>once a week</wns:meeting_frequency>
</wns:metadata>
</xenoData>

A plain text version of each de-identified chat is also provided, in WhatsApp's original export format, i.e., with each message preceded by its timestamp and the (de-identified) name of the user, as in example (4), which corresponds to the same message as example (1).

(4) *2021-09-16 20:05 _WNS_USER_008_: Coucou alors j'ai demandé à une pote pour demain soir mais elle a un anniversaire... toi il y a des gens qui sont chaud ?* 🤗

To complement plain text versions of chats, user and chat metadata are also included in two csv (comma-separated value) files.

The entire dataset is available on demand for research purposes, under a restricted license contract, from the SWISSUbase institutional repository[11] (Xanthos et al. 2024).

3 Quantitative overview of the dataset

In this section, we give a quantitative overview of the dataset resulting from the corpus building process described in the previous section, focusing on user, chat, and message properties.

11 https://www.swissubase.ch/en/catalogue/studies/20713/19924/overview (last accessed 17 July 2024)

3.1 Users

The dataset comprises data from 118 unique users. The vast majority (86%) of them are members of a single chat in the collection, 8% are members of 2 chats, 5% are members of 3–6 chats, and a single user contributed as many as 20 chats (see Table 2).

Table 2: Distribution of chat membership.

Chat membership	Number of users	Percentage of users
1	101	86%
2	10	8%
3	1	1%
4	3	3%
6	2	2%
20	1	1%

As shown on Figure 1 (left), the gender distribution is strongly skewed in favor of female users (62.7%); only 1 user selected *Other* as their gender and 4 did not answer this question. The distribution of age ranges (Figure 1, right) forms a bell-shape around the mode (*25–34 years old*), with 84% of users aged between 18 and 49 at the time of data collection; 4 users indicated an age above 65 years old and only 1 indicated an age below 18 years old (4 did not answer this question).

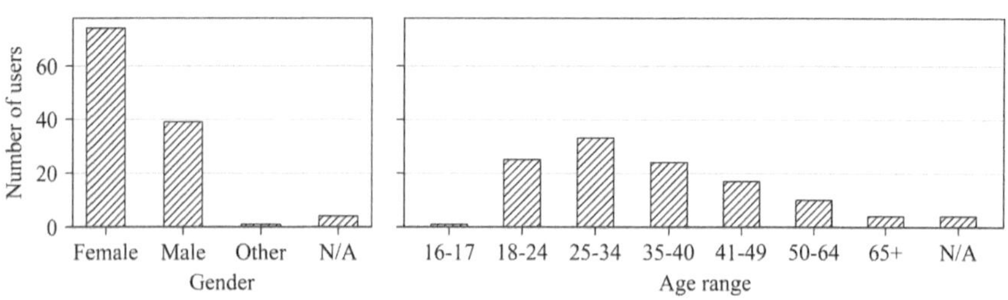

Figure 1: Distribution of user gender (left) and age range (right).

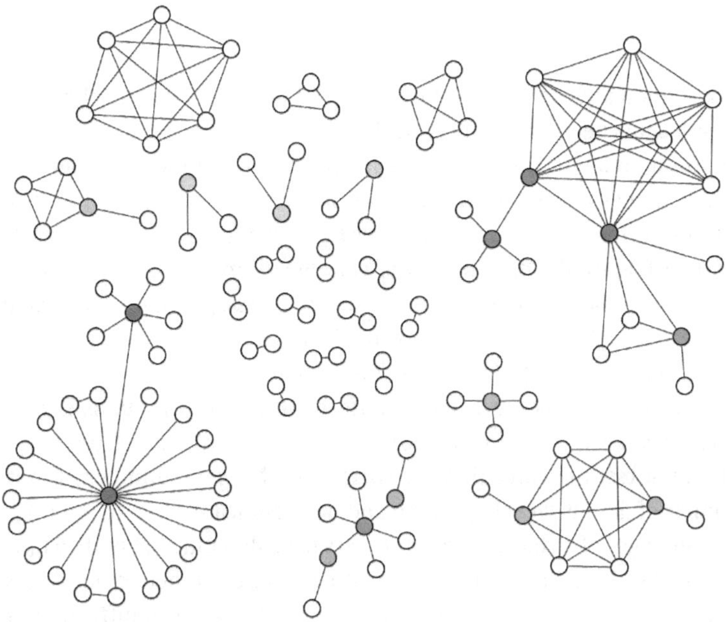

Figure 2: User network: connections represent joint membership in chats and degree of darkness represents betweenness centrality.

Figure 2 shows the interrelations between users in the form of a network. In this figure, each node represents a user and connections between pairs of nodes represent their joint membership in at least one chat. The degree of darkness of each node is proportional to the logarithm of its *betweenness centrality* (Brandes 2001), i.e., their propensity to be located on shortest paths between other nodes. This visualization reveals that while most users are members of a single chat, several of them are indirectly related by virtue of the pivotal role of a small number of users or user clusters.

Table 3: Distribution of number of participants.

Number of participants	Number of chats	Percentage of chats
2	62	86%
3	4	6%
4	3	4%
6	2	3%
8	1	1%

3.2 Chats

Among the 72 chats which constitute the corpus, 62 (86%) are dyadic chats; the number of group chats decreases rapidly as the number of participants increases, with a single group involving 8 users (Table 3). The number of messages per chat varies drastically across the collection, with the smallest chat containing 17 messages and the largest chat containing 177,628 messages (median 1,052 messages). As shown in Figure 3 (right), the distribution of chat length in messages is strongly skewed, with 63 chats (88%) containing less than 10K messages and only 2 chats containing more than 50K messages. Interestingly, Figure 3 (left) shows that the distribution of chat length in days (defined as the total number of days between the first and last day of a chat) is much more uniform, although it remains slightly skewed towards lower values (min. 58, max. 4,062, median 1,100.5). A two-tailed Pearson correlation test indicates that the correlation between number of messages and number of days is weakly positive and not significant ($r = 0.18$, $p = 0.13$). It appears that the "age" of a chat did not stop users from donating it, but they have usually refrained from donating chats containing a very large number of messages, possibly because reviewing them before donation would have been difficult, if at all possible.

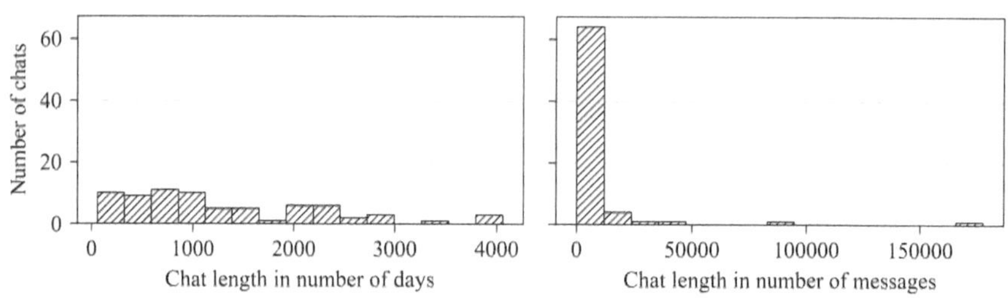

Figure 3: Distribution of chat length in number of days (left) and messages (right).

Finally, Figure 4 shows the number of chats that have been labeled by donors as corresponding to various relation types. Multiple choices were allowed, which was a necessity for group chats, but even in dyadic chats and a given point in time, two chat members may be related to one another in multiple ways. Friendship, which applies to 52 (72%) chats, is by far the most common relation type. Family applies to 15 chats and other relation types are less represented as they concern between 1 and 8 chats.

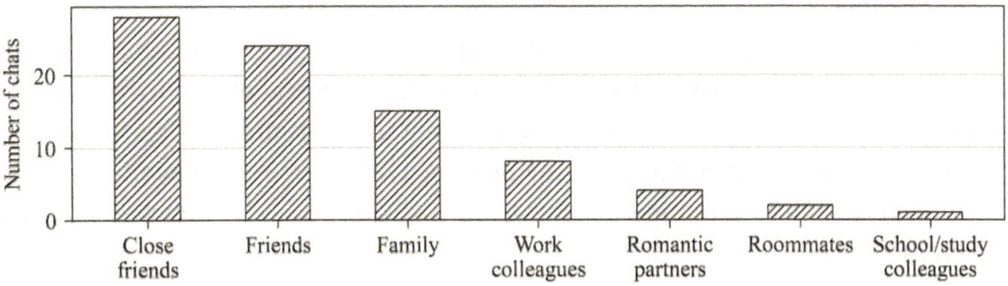

Figure 4: Distribution of relation types.

3.3 Messages

The corpus contains 503,471 messages, out of which 469,098 (93%) consist of user-generated, de-identified, text content. The remaining 7% include 34,205 messages originally consisting of some kind of media (pictures, video, audio, etc.), which are replaced by such codes as _STICKER_OMITTED_ or _GIF_OMITTED_, and a few system messages. Defining formally the possible categories of tokens as alphanumeric sequences, punctuation sequences, emoji and emoticons[12], we evaluate that user-generated text-based messages comprise more than 3.5M tokens (Table 4), yielding an average message length of 7.6 tokens. Most tokens are alphanumeric sequences, although they include a non-negligible proportion of punctuation sequences (5.2%) and individual emoji (3.4%).

Table 4: Categorized token and type counts with most frequent types (on average in chats).[13]

Category	Token count	Type count	Types with highest average frequency
Alphanumeric sequences	3,266,377	63,021	*de* 'of', *je* 'I', *est* 'is', *à* 'in, at, to', *et* 'and'
Punctuation sequences	186,676	220	, ? ! . :
Emoji	122,839	1,386	😂😘😉❤️😊
Emoticon	4,945	28	:) ;) :(:/ :-)
Total	3,580,837	64,655	

12 The latter two categories have been retrieved using the *emoji* and *emot* Python packages.
13 Type count for alphanumeric sequences is calculated in a case-insensitive fashion.

Figure 5 displays the number of messages per day over the entire period covered by the dataset. Data cover a bit more than a decade, although they are sparse in the first few years of the period (2011–2014) and at the very end of it, during data collection (from August 2022 on). There is considerable variation in the number of messages on a day-to-day basis, but the moving average in a window of 30 days is consistently above 10 messages per day from 2015 on, and above 100 messages per day from 2017 on.

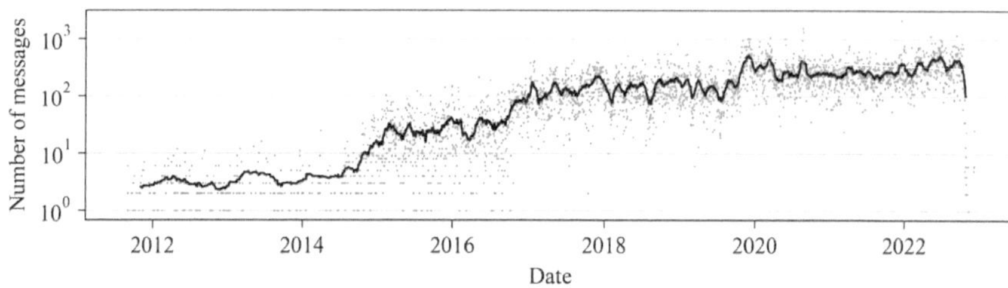

Figure 5: Number of messages per day (solid line represents 30-days moving average).

4 Discussion and conclusion

In this paper, we have reported on our work to build a large corpus of WhatsApp chats for sharing them with the scientific community. The degree of privacy of such data makes them both particularly interesting for CMC research and particularly challenging to collect and properly de-identify, hence the emphasis on these aspects of corpus building in this paper.

Slightly modifying the *What's up, Switzerland?* data collection protocol (Ueberwasser and Stark 2017), we were able to obtain the consent of all members for a very high proportion of collected chats (93%). While the likely cost of this achievement is a decrease in overall number of donations, we believe that this is a favorable trade-off. On the one hand, for many analytic purposes, the usability of chats with only partial content is limited. On the other hand, releasing the partial content raises the question of the exact nature of property, and therefore privacy, in the context of instant messaging (IM) data analysis; regarding this issue, we have adopted the perspective that a chat is the shared property of all its members, so that all of them should explicitly consent to its use.

Based on our evaluation, the partly automated and partly manual de-identification workflow used in this project has enabled us to reach a high estimated rate of redacted items (96%), in most cases with the correct categorization, thus striking a good balance between the sometimes conflicting goals of protecting participants' privacy and making the data as useful as possible for scientific purposes. However, the recall of our method is not perfect: roughly one piece of sensitive information out of twenty is being missed and thus left untouched, with an impact that varies according to the category of information in question. It was clear from the outset of the project that such risks could not be entirely eliminated, even though we were committed to de-identifying the data as diligently as possible and using the most advanced technologies at our disposal, therefore we made them explicit in the privacy policy that users were requested to read as part of the consent process. These risks are mitigated by the fact that the data are not made publicly available, but only shared on demand with people affiliated to research institutions, who are requested to comply with strict license terms such as using the data solely for scientific purposes, avoiding any disclosure of personal data, not sharing the data with third parties, etc.

In several regards, the resulting dataset is a valuable or even unique resource for research on instant messaging (IM) practices. From the point of view of language, the only existing dataset available in French is the *What's up, Switzerland?* corpus, which contains 110K messages (750K tokens) produced between 2010 and 2014; with more than four times this amount of data, the *What's New, Switzerland?* corpus usefully complements the earlier collection, notably for the period 2015–2022. In fact, to the best of our knowledge, the only other resource currently available that documents IM practices in the 2018–2022 period, including the COVID-19 pandemics, is the *MoCoDa2* database (Beißwenger et al. 2019).

The number of chats and participants in our dataset (72 and 118) is relatively lower than several other projects of this kind – the most spectacular counterexample being *Mocoda2*, which currently contains 1,005 chats between 3,496 participants. Conversely, the token count of our corpus is particularly high: it contains more than 3.2M tokens (using only alphanumeric sequences as a conservative estimate) while *MoCoDa2* currently reports 313K tokens. On average, a participant in *MoCoDa2* is thus represented by about 90 tokens, while a participant in our dataset is represented by more than 27K tokens. The latter value is biased, due to the presence of a small number of very large chats in our corpus and a small number of users participating in multiple chats, but half of our chats contain more than one thousand messages, and several thousand tokens per user. To that extent, what the corpus loses in diversity across users, it gains in representativity at the level of individual users.

Another remarkable property of our dataset is its suitability for longitudinal research. Half of the chats in the corpus cover a period of at least three entire years and the longest ones cover as many as eleven years. This is enough to monitor the evolution of several aspects of their participants' communicative practices, as well as the effects of technological changes such as the introduction of new emoji sets or the introduction of reactions (featured in WhatsApp since May 2022). Such possibilities are central requirements in the framework of the larger research consortium in which this project was developed and which is dedicated to the study of language evolution.[14]

Finally, while many topics discussed in the chats are relatively mundane (e.g., day-to-day work or home organization), we were impressed by the personal nature of some discussions we encountered. Participants share intimate thoughts and feelings about their sexual orientation, their experience of parenthood, professional success and failure, the death of loved ones, and many more subjects involving a high emotional load. It would most likely be extremely difficult, if at all possible, to obtain such a wealth of authentic data about the communication of socio-emotional content in any kind of elicited fashion. This is the fundamental reason why donating a chat to science is a gesture that involves a high degree of personal commitment – arguably higher than donating blood, for instance – and necessitates the establishment of a solid trust relationship, in particular regarding the diligent de-identification of the data.

The future of research about IM practices is likely to be more and more dependent on the ability to accurately and efficiently de-identify not only text but an increasing quantity and variety of media. We believe that investigating the possibility of having at least part of these tasks performed by donors themselves, using dedicated apps on their smartphones prior to donation, has the potential of being very beneficial in the long run for research in this area. The fast rate of progress in machine learning technology is sure to be a crucial factor in these developments. In the meantime, the resource presented in this paper is at the disposal of researchers and we hope it will enable them to explore various aspects of IM communicative practices.

Acknowledgements

This research received funding and support from the NCCR Evolving Language, Swiss National Science Foundation Agreement #51NF40_180888. The authors thank Leyla Benkais, Andrea Grütter, Romain Loup, and Kyoko Sugisaki for their collaboration, Elisabeth Stark, Simone Ueberwasser and the *What's up, Switzerland?* team

14 https://evolvinglanguage.ch/ (last accessed 17 July 2024)

for the experience and resources they shared with us, two anonymous reviewers for constructive comments about an earlier version of this paper, and all the participants who generously consented to donating their chats to our project.

References

Beißwenger, Michael, Wolfgang Imo, Marcel Fladrich & Evelyn Ziegler. 2019. https://www.mocoda2.de: a database and web-based editing environment for collecting and refining a corpus of mobile messaging interactions. *European Journal of Applied Linguistics* 7 (2). 333–344.

Beißwenger, Michael & Harald Lüngen. 2020. CMC-core: a schema for the representation of CMC corpora in TEI. *Corpus* 20. https://doi.org/10.4000/corpus.4553.

Brandes, Ulrik. 2001. A faster algorithm for betweenness centrality. *Journal of Mathematical Sociology* 25 (2). 163–177.

de Decker, Benny & Reinhild Vandekerckhove. 2017. Global features of online communication in local flemish: Social and medium-related determinants. *Folia Linguistica* 51 (1). 253–281.

Dorantes, Alejandro, Gerardo Sierra, Tlauhlia Yamín Donohue Pérez, Gemma Bel-Enguix & Mónica Jasso Rosales. 2018. Sociolinguistic Corpus of WhatsApp Chats in Spanish among College Students. In Lun-Wei Ku & Cheng-Te Li (eds.), *Proceedings of the Sixth International Workshop on Natural Language Processing for Social Media*, 1–6. Association for Computational Linguistics. https://aclanthology.org/W18-3501 (last accessed 26 March 2024).

Dürscheid, Christa & Elisabeth Stark. 2011. SMS4science: An international corpus-based texting project and the specific challenges for multilingual Switzerland. In Crispin Thurlow & Kristine Mroczek (eds.), *Digital discourse: Language in the new media*, 299–320. Oxford: Oxford University Press.

Lüngen, Harald, Michael Beißwenger, Laura Herzberg & Cathrin Pichler. 2017. Anonymisation of the Dortmund chat corpus 2.1. In Egon W. Stemle & Ciara R. Wigham (eds.), *Proceedings of the 5th Conference on CMC and Social Media Corpora for the Humanities (CMC-corpora 17)*, 21–24. Bolzano: Eurac Research. https://cmc-corpora2017.eurac.edu/proceedings/cmccorpora17-proceedings.pdf (last accessed 14 March 2024).

Mäkinen, Martti. 2023. MMWAH! Compiling a corpus of multilingual / multimodal WhatsApp discussions by Swedish-speaking young adults in Finland. In Louis Cotgrove, Laura Herzberg, Harald Lüngen & Ines Pisetta (eds.), *Proceedings of the 10th International Conference on CMC and Social Media Corpora for the Humanities*, 136–139. Mannheim: Leibniz-Institut für Deutsche Sprache. https://doi.org/10.14618/1z5k-pb25.

Martin, Louis, Benjamin Muller, Pedro Javier Ortiz Suárez, Yoann Dupont, Laurent Romary, Éric de la Clergerie, Djamé Seddah & Benoît Sagot. 2020. CamemBERT: A tasty French language model. In Dan Jurafsky, Joyce Chai, Natalie Schluter & Joel Tetreault (eds.), *Proceedings of the 58th Annual Meeting of the Association for Computational Linguistics*, 7203–7219. Association for Computational Linguistics. https://aclanthology.org/2020.acl-main.645 (last accessed 26 March 2024).

New, Boris, Christophe Pallier, Marc Brysbaert & Ludovic Ferrand. 2004. Lexique 2: A new French lexical database. *Behavior Research Methods, Instruments, Computers* 36. 516–524.

Sanders, Eric. 2012. Collecting and analysing chats and tweets in SoNaR. In Nicoletta Calzolari et al. (eds), *Proceedings of the Eighth International Conference on Language Resources and Evaluation (LREC'12)*, 2253–2256. European Language Resources Association. http://www.lrec-conf.org/proceedings/lrec2012/pdf/416_Paper.pdf (last accessed 26 March 2024).

Schwind, Anika & Michael Seufert. 2018. WhatsAnalyzer: A tool for collecting and analyzing WhatsApp mobile messaging communication data. In Eitan Altman, Giuseppe Bianchi and Thomas Zinner (eds.), *Proceedings of the 30th International Teletraffic Congress (ITC 30)*, 85–88. https://doi.org/10.1109/ITC3043689.2018.

Seufert, Anika, Fabian Poignée, Tobias Hossfeld & Michael Seufert. 2022. Pandemic in the digital age: analyzing WhatsApp communication behavior before, during, and after the COVID-19 lockdown. *Humanities and Social Sciences Communications* 140 (9). https://doi.org/10.1057/s41599-022-01161-0.

Singh, Manish. (2020, October 30). *WhatsApp is now delivering roughly 100 billion messages a day.* https://techcrunch.com/2020/10/29/whatsapp-is-now-delivering-roughly-100-billion-messages-a-day/ (last accessed 26 March 2025).

Spooren, Wilbert, Manon Berntzen, Micha Hulsbosch, Erwin Komen, Henk van den Heuvel. 2018. *WhatsApp corpus Berntzen* [Data set]. DANS Data Station Social Sciences and Humanities. https://doi.org/10.17026/dans-xzz-ugtw.

Tedeschi, Simone, Valentino Maiorca, Niccolò Campolungo, Francesco Cecconi & Roberto Navigli. 2021. WikiNEuRal: Combined neural and knowledge-based silver data creation for multilingual NER. In Marie-Francine Moens, Xuanjing Huang, Lucia Specia & Scott Wen-tau Yih (eds.), *Findings of the Association for Computational Linguistics: EMNLP 2021*, 2521–2533. Association for Computational Linguistics. https://aclanthology.org/2021.findings-emnlp.215 (last accessed 26 March 2024).

Ueberwasser, Simone & Elisabeth Stark. 2017. What's up, Switzerland? A corpus-based research project in a multilingual country. *Linguistik online* 84 (5). 105–126. https://doi.org/10.13092/lo.84.3849.

Verheijen, Lieke & Wessel Stoop. 2016. Collecting Facebook posts and WhatsApp chats. In Petr Sojka, Aleš Horák, Ivan Kopeček & Karel Pala (eds.), *Text, Speech, and Dialogue*, 249–258. Cham: Springer International Publishing.

Xanthos, Aris, Prakhar Gupta, Leila Benkais, Lliana Doudot & Andrea Grütter. (2024). *What's New, Switzerland? Corpus (Version 1.0.0)* [Data set]. LaRS – Language Repository of Switzerland. https://doi.org/10.48656/pa3t-xh52.

Anne Ferger, André Frank Krause, and Karola Pitsch

A workflow for creating, harmonizing and analyzing structured corpora of multimodal interaction

Abstract: Creating structured and consistent corpus resources for the analysis of multimodal interaction, computer-mediated communication, and socio-technical settings is generally a time-consuming and meticulous task. It involves dealing with various media formats (e.g., audiovisual, eye-tracking, log files), time alignment, and modelling multimodal aspects of communication, including many manual changes to these formats. Based on our work creating a structured corpus of human-robot interaction, we present a workflow focussing on automation, standard formats, and a sustainable approach to research data management. This workflow leverages recent developments in spoken language corpora and takes them beyond mere text and speech. It includes automated procedures to enrich data (e.g., part-of-speech tagging) to achieve higher data consistency and to convert data into a set of standard formats (e.g., TEI XML, dataFrame) from which calculations, visualizations, etc. can be generated for further analysis. Automating this workflow using git for version control and a GitLab Continuous Integration functionality, these procedures are reapplied whenever changes are made to the source data, so that amendments to transcripts, for example, can be reintroduced into the original transcript file. We show how higher data quality can be reached in these corpora and how the proposed workflow can be applied on corpora modelled following the CMC-core TEI schema. By exploring different analyses (including gaze, part-of-speech tagging, and time alignment) on the base of TEI XML documents originating from this workflow, we show how the resulting corpora offer more finely grained possibilities of analysis.

Keywords: multimodal interaction, socio-technical settings, corpus analysis, corpus workflow, TEI format

Anne Ferger, University of Duisburg-Essen, e-mail: anne.ferger@uni-due.de
André Frank Krause, Rhine-Waal University of Applied Sciences,
e-mail: andrefrank.krause@hochschule-rhein-waal.de
Karola Pitsch, University of Duisburg-Essen, e-mail: karola.pitsch@uni-due.de

https://doi.org/10.1515/9783111434018-009

1 Introduction

Different research communities develop resources for qualitative and quantitative analyses of multimodal interaction and socio-technical settings, including computer-mediated communication. For all of them, it is essential to generate multimodal corpora with high data quality and which can be analyzed from various disciplinary perspectives and with different research methods. In this vein, in the fields of interactional linguistics and conversation analysis, including the German *Gesprächsforschung*, approaches that link qualitative and quantitative methods have become more frequent as well (e.g., Pitsch et al. 2014; Stivers 2015; Kendrick and Holler 2017; Rühlemann 2018; Mundwiler et al. 2019; Luginbühl et al. 2021). They benefit from creating structured corpora (in the sense of Schmidt 2016) of interactional situations that are tailored both to human readability and technical means of analysis and thus enable the combination of qualitative and quantitative analyses in a dynamic way. Other applications to leverage these resources can be corpus queries in corpus linguistics (Schmidt 2016) and using the resources for second language teaching (Fandrych 2022).

Against this background, we address the following questions:

a) How can we best structure corpora of multimodal interaction which include novel types of time series data (e.g., robot log files, sensor output), which are human- and machine-readable, and model them using a standard format (e.g., TEI)?
b) How can we assure and enhance the quality of the corpus data with regard to inconsistencies, missing information, and enrichment?
c) How can these measures be applied continuously and automatically, and how can the workflows be reused on other (especially CMC) resources?
d) How can we prepare the corpus so that it allows for different export formats catering for different forms of storage and analyses?
e) How can the created structured corpora facilitate comprehensive analyses?

To address these questions, we suggest that it is beneficial to link tools and methods developed creating spoken language corpora (Schmidt 2016; Schmidt 2018; Hedeland and Ferger 2020; Arkhangelskiy, Hedeland, and Riaposov 2020; Ferger and Jettka 2021; Hirschmann and Schmidt 2022) with a research data management perspective (Hermann, Pietsch, and Cimiano 2021). In recent years within the field of research data management, a prominent focus has been given to the standardization and sustainability of research data formats. This is exemplified by projects like the German National Research Data Infrastructure in Germany (Kraft et al. 2021), for example. These developments are also essential for creating and processing structured corpora, as they lead to standardized corpus resources that are suitable for long-term archiving and are reusable in different contexts, as well as standardized methods, tools, and workflows that minimize efforts in future projects and increase the scientific reproducibility of analyses and their results.

In what follows, we present a semi-automatic workflow based on our experience working with multimodal and multisensorial data of human-robot interaction which includes – beyond common audiovisual data – log files from the robot's speech recognition and voice output in real time and sensor data from motion capture devices (e.g., Kinect). All data are synchronized via the timeline and share central features with chat exports of social media tools (e.g., from WhatsApp chats with time-synchronized text messages, audio recordings, or images).

2 Background: Workflows and tools for creating a structured corpus

For creating structured corpora of oral communication, ISO standard 24624:2016 "Language resource management – Transcription of spoken language" (Hedeland and Schmidt 2022) has been defined. It uses the framework format for encoding recommended by the Text Encoding Initiative (TEI Consortium 2023; the recommended format is abbreviated as TEI in the following). The TEI format is an XML-based format. Also, for the so-called task of "corpus compilation" (Schmidt 2016: 119), extensive workflows and tools exist. These were created when developing the FOLK corpus for spoken German language (Schmidt 2023), for example. Since the editor used to compile the FOLK corpus – called "FOLKER" (Schmidt and Schütte 2010) – is a timeline- and XML-based tool, procedures can be adapted for other data which are organized in timeline and XML format, such as data prepared with editors like EXMARaLDA (Schmidt and Wörner 2014) or ELAN (Sloetjes 2014), which are interoperable with regard to their data format. The TEI standard allows one to import data into the ZuMult tools (Fandrych et al. 2022) for analysis and querying of verbal data, but it does not include modelling of multimodal annotations or robot log files.

Some of these workflows and tools include methods for part of speech (POS) and lemma tagging (Westpfahl and Schmidt 2013; Westpfahl et al. 2017) using Tree-Tagger (Schmid 1995) (see chapter 4.3) and the use of the TEI format following ISO standard 24624:2016. In our workflow, we specifically adapted methods for converting ELAN files into TEI files. These methods included tokenizing verbal utterances based on methods used in the EXMARaLDA code and handling special cases such as robot log files and annotations of bodily conduct (see chapter 4.3). We also adapted and created new consistency checks (see chapter 4.2) and automated them using GitLab CI (see chapter 4.1).

In research on multimodal interaction and pragmatics, there are comprehensive works on corpus linguistics by Rühlemann, among others (Rühlemann 2017, 2018; Rühlemann and Gee 2017; Rühlemann and Ptak 2023). While these works propose XML formats for these corpora (e.g., Rühlemann 2017; Rühlemann and Gee 2017), the TEI format and its ISO standard for spoken language are not used in these cases, which creates barriers for sustainable, long-term archiving, machine readability, and reuse in other contexts. Parisse et al. (2017) propose the TEI format for oral and multimodal language corpora, pointing to ISO standard 24624:2016 as well as preconsiderations for the CMC-core schema, which has been proposed for corpora on computer-mediated communication (Luginbühl et al. 2021). Luginbühl et al. (2021: 2) specify CMC corpora interoperability for combined analysis on various CMC corpora, combining corpora of different types, and integrating CMC corpora into existing infrastructure, for example, as reasons to create and apply a TEI CMC schema.

These advantages (i.e., using a standard format and creating a sustainable workflow for higher corpus consistency) are also relevant concerning the FAIR principles (findable, accessible, interoperable, reusable; Wilkinson et al. 2016), which play an important role in research data management. While the principles of findability and accessibility depend mostly on the respective repositories in which the data are published, standardized metadata, which can be integrated in the TEI XML format in the designated metadata header, can help increase findability. Interoperability and reusability are improved by using standard data formats, such as TEI and ISO standard 24624:2016, and by higher consistency of the research data, which makes our proposed workflow a contribution to FAIRer corpus data.

3 MuMoCorp project: Additional requirements and lessons learned when realizing the corpus creation workflow

The workflow presented in this paper has been developed and tested on human-robot interaction data in the MuMoCorp project. The MuMoCorp project – Data Reuse of Multimodal and Multisensorial Corpora within the Dilthey Fellowship "Interaction & Space. From Conversation Analysis to Dynamic Interaction Models for Human-Robot Interaction" – prepares existing research data (see Pitsch 2016, 2020, 2023; Pitsch et al. 2016; Gehle et al. 2017) for long-term storage and further use as partly open data within the framework of an institutional repository. The rich data material is particularly interesting with respect to human-robot interaction and the multi-dimensionality of the interaction, and it includes different data formats such as videos, XML-based transcriptions, and robot log files. MuMoCorp's challenge is to organize and curate a large amount of data that has been collected, transcribed, and annotated over a period of roughly 10 years. Seven studies have been conducted exploring specific interactional features and procedures, and they have been stored as seven distinct but related subcorpora.

When curating this data and preparing it for reuse by other researchers, we encountered the following additional tasks, which constitute a prerequisite for doing so:

- Collecting and renaming the different files into a new, coherent data structure following a predefined specification
- Anonymizing the audiovisual recordings (see Krause, Ferger and Pitsch 2023a, 2023b)
- Collecting and structuring existing pieces of information about the participants, study details, and recordings as systematic metadata

We identified additional requirements for the corpus creation while using the workflow in practice. These may be specific to the particular project but might also be relevant for other projects and data:

- We wanted to keep the established workflows for transcribing and annotating the data, such as annotation tools (e.g., ELAN) and transcription/annotation conventions, unchanged.
- We wanted a version control for the data which, ideally, would not create any additional workload for researchers. Using Git/GitLab presented as a suitable solution for this task.
- A range of inconsistencies in the data can only be corrected manually. They should be corrected in the source files using the established tools (here: ELAN).
- A range of inconsistencies in the data can be checked automatically. These checks should be automated in a way that check results and where corrections are accessible continuously.

The data in MuMoCorp – stemming from a project on multimodal interaction and socio-technical situations – shares a range of features with computer-mediated communication, such as including various media types and system log files that can be similar to social media log files. Yet, there are also essential differences: In the MuMoCorp settings, the museum guide robot aims to act as an autonomous technical co-participant. The communication between the robot and the participants is not text-centred or internet-based. It occurs in real time and involves text-to-speech output, automatic speech recognition, head and arm movements for the robot, and verbal utterances and other modalities for the human participants. Therefore, the concept of *computer mediatedness* requires rethinking to appropriately grasp such constellations (for a start, see Arminen, Licoppe, and Spagnolli 2016).

4 A workflow to create machine-readable corpora for multimodal and computer-mediated resources

The workflow we propose for creating human- and machine-readable corpora can be applied both when starting a new project beginning with transcription/annotation or when processing an existing dataset for archiving, publication, or further analysis. It serves as our solution to the questions posed in chapter 1.

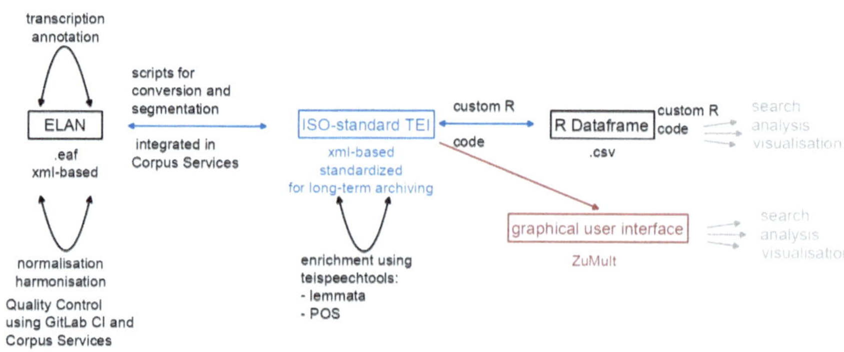

Figure 1: Workflow overview.

The workflow (see Figure 1) starts with (existing) transcription/annotation files which have been created with the ELAN editor (Sloetjes 2014; Max Planck Institute for Psycholinguistics 2020). These files could also be other XML-based source formats, such as EXMARaLDA files or TEI files that are manually generated or exported. To these source files we apply automated scripts for harmonization and normalization, as well as quality checks that require manual work for the harmonization (see chapter 4.2). From this source data, we export the data in the standard format ISO TEI. On the basis of the data available in the standard format, enrichments are added (e.g., lemmatization and part-of-speech tagging of verbal transcriptions), which can be continuously reapplied whenever changes are made to the data (see chapter 4.3). In a next step and as a basis for further analysis, the data – which has so far been normalized, harmonized, quality controlled, and enriched – can be automatically exported from the TEI files to various output formats (see chapter 4.4). The corpus data which is not available in text-based format (video files, etc.) are not altered by this workflow. These steps of harmonizing, checking, and converting the data are continuously reapplied using a dedicated system for version control (see chapter 4.1). This setup allows for dynamic analyses and visualizations to be performed continuously during the corpus creation process, which can help in the iterative development of annotation categories (see chapter 5), for example.

4.1 Automation using git, Continuous Integration, and GitLab

Answering our initial question (C) on how to ensure an automated, continuous control of the data consistency with our workflow, we used methods from software development for automated deployment that go beyond existing methods in continuous quality control (as in Hedeland and Ferger 2020; Ferger and Jettka 2021), namely Git version control and GitLab Continuous Integration (CI). Git version control[1] is the underlying version control system which allows for tracking and managing changes to data. GitLab[2] offers a platform and graphical user interface for the tracked changes and, with the CI functionality, allows automatically running scripts (e.g., validation techniques like schemas or specified consistency checks) on the tracked data without any user interaction. While git and GitLab are widely used, especially in research data management, other tools offer similar functionality, such as Apache Subversion or Gitea. Git versioning for text-based source data offers other benefits, such as the ability to revert to earlier stages of the files and the ability to track all changes to the files. Git for research data also makes research more reproducible and can be seen as best practice for research data management (see Hermann, Pietsch, and Cimiano 2021; Cyra, Politze, and Timm 2022; Erjavec, Kopp, and Meden 2023). Using the GitLab CI setup shown in Ferger, Krause, and Pitsch (2023), scripts are continuously applied when the data under version control is changed. This allows quality checks, correction, and data exports to be automatically reapplied whenever the source data is changed. The results of these checks are used for manually fixing these inconsistencies, but found inconsistencies do not prevent the corpus being used or changed further.

1 https://git-scm.com/ (last accessed 14 February 2025).
2 https://gitlab.com (last accessed 14 February 2025).

4.2 Data consistency

The initial question (B) concerns data consistency, or data quality as defined in Hedeland (2020), which calls for checking data for coherence and consistency. As can be seen in Figure 1, we aim to perform checks and automatic correction of inconsistencies on the XML-based source data, which in our case are ELAN files. An advantage of this approach is that further transcription, annotation, or manual harmonization of the files can be realized using the original tools and workflows. Since transcriptions and annotations are mostly carried out manually (and will continue to be for some time into the future, e.g., for multi-participant discussions and in dialects or less resourced languages), some inconsistencies can also only be resolved in a manual way.

To realize this approach, we used the Corpus Services Framework (Ferger et al. 2020; Hedeland and Ferger 2020) with additional extensions, including those for ELAN files (Arkhangelskiy, Hedeland, and Riaposov 2020), and adapted them to find and fix inconsistencies in the source files.[3] The generated list of identified inconsistencies including file names and locations of the inconsistencies can be used to facilitate manual correction of the files. Checks that have been applied include ELANTranscriptionChecker, which checks the adherence of verbal transcriptions to standardized conventions (here: GAT 2 [Selting et al. 2009]), ELANValidatorChecker, which checks if the ELAN XML file is valid according to ELAN specifications, ELAN-FileReferenceChecker, which checks if the linked media files exist, and ELAN-AnnotationChecker, which checks whether the annotation tiers adhere to annotation conventions – which is especially important for our coded interactional annotations.

4.3 Modelling multimodal interaction using TEI as a standard and base format

The long-existing TEI guidelines, developed by the Text Encoding Initiative (TEI Consortium 2023),[4] are a standard for various text-based research fields. They are also adapted to spoken language, for example, with ISO standard 24624:2016 (hereafter referred to as ISO/TEI standard) "Language resource management – Transcription of spoken language" (Schmidt 2011; Hedeland and Schmidt 2022), which

3 Our adapted version of the Corpus Services Framework is available at https://git.uni-due.de/mumocorp-open-access/corpus-services/ (last accessed 14 February 2025).
4 For the history of the TEI see https://tei-c.org/about/history/ (last accessed 14 February 2025).

we see as an answer to our initial question (A). Similarly, the CMC-core schema for TEI (Beißwenger and Lüngen 2020) streamlines efforts in the CMC community to represent and structure corpora in a standardized way. While the TEI format is not yet widely used in conversation analysis and multimodal interaction research, there are exceptions such as Liégeois et al. (2015) and Parisse et al. (2017). One obstacle has been the amount of manual work required to generate it from multimodal interaction resources. To address this challenge in our proposed semi-automatic corpus creation workflow, we export the source data into TEI format and make the conversion accessible and reusable by including our export script in the Corpus Services Framework (see above). The script is based on exports adapted from the EXMARaLDA software suite (Schmidt and Wörner 2014). The TEI export includes a segmentation following the respective transcription conventions (here: GAT 2 [Selting et al. 2009]).

```
<incident end="ts15" start="ts14" type="act" who="SPK_robmus_2015_01_001_W" xml:id="inc17">
   <desc xml:id="des8">prep-G</desc>
</incident>
<incident end="ts17" start="ts16" type="act" who="SPK_robmus_2015_01_001_W" xml:id="inc18">
   <desc xml:id="des9">peak-G</desc>
</incident>
<incident end="ts19" start="ts17" type="act" who="SPK_robmus_2015_01_001_W" xml:id="inc19">
   <desc xml:id="des10">retr-G</desc>
</incident>
<incident end="ts22" start="ts20" type="smile" who="SPK_robmus_2015_01_001_W" xml:id="inc10">
   <desc xml:id="des11">~</desc>
</incident>
<annotationBlock end="ts25" start="ts23" who="SPK_robmus_2015_01_001_W" xml:id="au1">
   <u xml:id="u1">
      <w lemma="ja" pos="ADV" xml:id="w1">ja</w>
      <anchor synch="ts25"/>
   </u>
</annotationBlock>
<incident end="ts26" start="ts24" type="smile" who="SPK_robmus_2015_01_001_W" xml:id="inc11">
   <desc xml:id="des12">@</desc>
</incident>
<incident end="ts28" start="ts26" type="smile" who="SPK_robmus_2015_01_001_W" xml:id="inc12">
   <desc xml:id="des13">~</desc>
</incident>
```

Figure 2: TEI modelling example.

To model the data in our MuMoCorp project, we drew from modelling of spoken and computer-mediated resources in TEI format. We focused on the ISO/TEI standard for several reasons. This standard is recommended for long-term archiving by the Archive for Spoken German.[5] It is also used as an import format for the ZuMult corpus infrastructure (Frick and Schmidt 2020; Fandrych et al. 2022), which offers

5 https://agd.ids-mannheim.de/uebernahme.shtml (last accessed 14 February 2025).

a graphical user interface to access corpus data, as well as in other tools such as WebLicht and WebMAUS (see Schmidt, Hedeland, and Frick 2021). For the verbal utterances of human participants in our data, no adjustments were needed. However, to use this standard for modelling multimodal aspects of the existing corpus data from human-robot interaction including novel data types, we needed to make some adaptations. These were carried out with the overarching idea of respecting the TEI standard such as to remain compatible with existing models, tools, and workflows. In particular, we used the following data model:

(a) Human utterances are represented by the <u> element, consisting of <w> for words with <pos> and <lemma> attributes, following the existing standard.
(b) To include multimodal annotations, such as bodily conduct and facial expressions, we used and adapted the TEI element <incident> (see Figure 2). According to TEI guidelines, this element "marks any phenomenon or occurrence, not necessarily vocalized or communicative, for example incidental noises or other events affecting communication" (TEI Consortium 2023). "Incident" is typically used to transcribe audible laughter in verbal transcription. We use the "type" attribute to refer to the level of (multimodal) annotation, such as "smile" or "nod", enabling analysis of the same phenomenon in different settings.
(c) The verbal utterances of the robot, which were generated via text-to-speech, were modelled similarly to multimodal annotations and not human verbal utterances because they do not share all the characteristics of human spoken language, such as interjections and prosodic aspects.

In comparison, the CMC-core defines its four basic units as spoken utterances, bodily activity, onscreen activities, and written utterances (Beißwenger and Lüngen 2020). Spoken or multimodal utterances in CMC-core are also represented using the <u> element; bodily activity is modelled using <kinesic>, and onscreen activities are modelled with <incident>. To improve the modelling of multimodal resources and its compatibility across settings and disciplines, it may be worth discussing if there was a benefit to instead use <kinesic> for bodily conduct and facial expressions. Here, further reflection, also in the light of other corpus data, might be helpful for future work.

We applied the Stuttgart-Tübingen Tagset (STTS) extension trained on spoken German on the FOLK corpus (Westpfahl and Schmidt 2013; Westpfahl et al. 2017) to the generated ISO-standard TEI files for participants' verbal utterances (and not the robots' text-to-speech output, which are not modelled as verbal utterances), using the teispeechtools library (Fisseni and Schmidt 2020), which employs TreeTagger (Schmid 1995). For internet-based resources, there are guidelines and a tagset for POS tagging presented in Beißwenger et al. (2015), which are relevant for internet-based CMC resources but which could not be applied in our context, such as emoticons or hashtags (which are not present in our type of resources). Since the tagset is also based on the STTS, the way of applying it can be identical.

4.4 DataFrame to facilitate analysis

Using the ISO-standard TEI as a source format allows various exports into different output formats, which answers our initial question (D). One goal was to generate a simple output with reduced complexity but that still accurately contains the relevant information of the source files, to facilitate analysis and visualizations in R. DataFrames for analyses in R are common for interactional linguistics, as in the tools ACT (Ehmer 2021, 2023) and EXMARaLDAR (Schürmann 2021) or for visualizations and statistics (Rühlemann 2020; Rühlemann and Ptak 2023). The existing tools did not satisfy our need to include all multimodal and sensor-based information in the dataFrame and its generation from a TEI file, so we developed a custom R script for this purpose, generating a dataFrame with columns inspired by those approaches, as seen in Figure 3. To allow for other programming languages and use cases, this dataFrame is additionally written into a csv table file.

X	id	annotation	lemma	pos	type	starttime_ms	endtime_ms	duration	participant_id	utterance_id	file
2393	inc66	zgestezubild2	N/A	N/A	movementTier-it	202631	207154	4523	SPK_	inc66	rob
2394	inc67	standardPose	N/A	N/A	movementTier-it	207197	209579	2382	SPK_	inc67	rob
2395	inc15	repairBild: Leichter Repair	N/A	N/A	Attention-it	209617	212182	2565	SPK_	inc15	rob
2396	inc44	[lookRight] [standardPose] Hier auf Bild 2 sieht man...	N/A	N/A	Say-it	212186	217528	5342	SPK_	inc44	rob
2397	inc68	lookRight	N/A	N/A	movementTier-it	212255	213673	1418	SPK_	inc68	rob
2398	inc69	standardPose	N/A	N/A	movementTier-it	213881	216811	2930	SPK_	inc69	rob
2399	inc16	repairBild: Weiter	N/A	N/A	Attention-it	217694	219826	2132	SPK_	inc16	rob
2400	inc45	Wenn du noch mehr ueber das Mittelalter in Bie le f...	N/A	N/A	Say-it	219871	234325	14454	SPK_	inc45	rob
2401	inc70	bow	N/A	N/A	movementTier-it	228960	232098	3138	SPK_	inc70	rob
2402	inc71	standardPose	N/A	N/A	movementTier-it	232239	234455	2216	SPK_	inc71	rob
2403	w1	ja	ja	NGIRR	verbal	22400	23700	1300	SPK_robmus_2015_01_001_W	u1	rob
2404	w2	eins	eins	CARD	verbal	48709	49316	607	SPK_robmus_2015_01_001_W	u2	rob
2405	w3	ähm	ähm	NGHES	verbal	84688	85942	1254	SPK_robmus_2015_01_001_W	u3	rob
2406	w4	sorry	sorry	NGIRR	verbal	87727	89913	2186	SPK_robmus_2015_01_001_W	u4	rob
2407	w5	kannst	können	VMFIN	verbal	87727	89913	2186	SPK_robmus_2015_01_001_W	u4	rob
2408	w6	du	du	PPER	verbal	87727	89913	2186	SPK_robmus_2015_01_001_W	u4	rob

Figure 3: DataFrame example.

The content in this dataFrame is exported directly from the TEI files and not normalized or changed, since we wanted to keep the harmonization in the source files. This is also important for dealing with the "Killer-Kriterium" (Schütte 2007: 71), a criterium for tools on how they deal with transcriptions during analysis. Many analysis tools process transcriptions in a way that they cannot be exported back into their source format after changes are made to them during analysis, which would make the transcriptions static and not dynamic. Non-dynamic transcripts would mean that after the analysis step, the transcriptions cannot be changed further, and findings in the analysis cannot be integrated easily into the source data, which is something we do want to utilize in our workflow. The continuous creation of this dataFrame helps with keeping the transcripts dynamic by delivering a dataFrame for up-to-date transcripts. Keeping the IDs as exact locations of certain elements in the source files allows for going back to the ELAN editor, for example, and changing things or automatically changing things in the source files based on the dataFrame. As the information of all transcripts comprising the corpus is grouped together in the dataFrame, more complex queries and analysis are made possible. Annotations and transcription in different ELAN files relating to the same video can thus be queried for simultaneity. Information on different levels of information can also be correlated, for example robot log files and verbal utterances of participants.

5 Application to other (CMC) resources

Answering question (C) and in terms of FAIR research data management, we have made the workflow available for reuse.[6] While we have discussed essential differences between the MuMoCorp resources and those of computer-mediated communication, many features of our workflow can be adapted to the specifics of CMC corpus data. In particular, the export of a dataFrame from CMC-core TEI files could be used for easier and more extensive analysis, as will be shown below.

6 Analysis of created corpora

To answer question (E) from our initial questions, the structured corpus facilitates more complex analyses than traditional corpus analysis constricted to verbal utterances for example. In what follows, this will be illustrated by an example analysis inspired by and adapted from Rühlemann (2018) and Rühlemann and Ptak (2023). To utilize aspects of human-robot interaction and sensor data as well as conversational analytic exploration, the example queries for actions of the robot and human reactions. An example for this is analyzing a movement of the robot along with non-verbal reactions of the participant in a study (e.g., the robot pointing to something in the room, and the participant nodding as a reaction; for detailed analysis

6 The workflow and other resources are available at https://git.uni-due.de/mumocorp-open-access/ (last accessed 14 February 2025).

see Pitsch et al. 2016; Pitsch 2023). The first step is to formalize this phenomenon to allow for automatically finding all instances of it in the corpus. The phenomenon of robot movement could be formalized by querying the internal log file instructions of the robot, where movement is annotated as [pointLeftUp] or [pointRightUp]. The reaction of the participant can be formalized by manual annotations of the bodily conduct and facial expressions, such as "nod" or "smile", or transcribed verbal utterances. So, one starting point of the analysis is an overview of all nodding annotations following in a temporal sequence of robot movement annotations. From there on, these instances can be classified using automated preliminary codes, which can be used for further formalizing (such as counting positive or negative reactions) or iterating manual annotation in order to find other instances of the phenomenon that were not technically identified. This iteration of manual or automatic annotation and analysis leads to dynamic transcriptions, since they are not frozen in one state after the analysis.

7 Conclusion

We have addressed the initial questions of this paper by presenting our reusable corpus creation workflow. By harmonizing inconsistencies directly in the source files and modelling data according to a TEI schema or standard, FAIRer and more sustainable research data can be created without too much additional work. Exporting a dataFrame to serve as the basis for complex analyses and visualizations facilitates the reuse of these analyses and visualizations as well. Using Git and GitLab CI capabilities not only allows for the measures for data quality to be applied continuously but also facilitates their reuse across resources. As any workflow is only as good as its output, we have shown that the machine-readable structured corpora generated can be queried by formalizing conversational analytic phenomena. Another benefit of using common standard formats is that the output of the workflow can be used for traditional corpus queries in corpus linguistics (Schmidt 2016) and as resources for second language teaching (Fandrych 2022). The advantages specified by Luginbühl et al. (2021: 2) for the TEI-based CMC core schema (interoperability for combined analysis on various corpora, combination of corpora of different types, and integrating corpora into existing infrastructure) can finally be seen as advantages of our workflow resulting in standardized outputs as well.

Acknowledgements

This project was financed by the Volkswagenstiftung (grant number 90886, PI: Karola Pitsch) and the Ministry of Culture and Science of the State of North Rhine-Westphalia (grant number PB22-076D).

References

Arkhangelskiy, Timofey, Hanna Hedeland & Aleksandr Riaposov. 2020. Evaluating and assuring research data quality for audiovisual annotated language data. In *Proceedings of CLARIN Annual Conference 2020*, Online Edition, 131–135.

Arminen, Ilkka, Christian Licoppe & Anna Spagnolli. 2016. Respecifying mediated interaction. *Research on Language and Social Interaction* 49 (4). 290–309.

Beißwenger, Michael, Thomas Bartz, Angelika Storrer & Swantje Westpfahl. 2015. Tagset und Richtlinie für das PoS- Tagging von Sprachdaten aus Genres internetbasierter Kommunikation. *Guideline document from the Empirikom shared task on automatic linguistic annotation of internet-based communication* (EmpiriST 2015).

Beißwenger, Michael & Harald Lüngen. 2020. CMC-core: A schema for the representation of CMC corpora in TEI. *Corpus. Bases, corpus et langage* – UMR 6039 (20). https://doi.org/10.4000/corpus.4553.

Cyra, Magdalene Alice, Marius Politze & Henning Timm. 2022. A push for better RDM: Erfahrungsbericht aus dem Einsatz von git für Forschungsdaten. *Bausteine Forschungsdatenmanagement* 2. 1–17.

Ehmer, Oliver. 2021. act: Aligned Corpus Toolkit. R package version 1.2.2. https://cran.r-project.org/package=act (last accessed 14 February 2025).

Ehmer, Oliver. 2023. Arbeiten mit zeitalignierten multimodalen Korpora in R. Vorstellung des Aligned Corpus Toolkit (act). *Gesprächsforschung-Online-Zeitschrift zur verbalen Interaktion 24*. 67–126.

Erjavec, Tomaž, Matyáš Kopp & Katja Meden. 2023. TEI and Git in ParlaMint: Collaborative development of language resources. In *Selected papers from the CLARIN Annual Conference 2022*, 44–56.

Fandrych, Christian, Elena Frick, Julia Kaiser, Cordula Meißner, Annette Portmann, Thomas Schmidt, Matthias Schwendemann, Franziska Wallner & Kai Wörner. 2022. ZuMult: Neue Zugangswege zu Korpora gesprochener Sprache. In Heidrun Kämper & Albrecht Plewnia (eds.), *Perspektiven und Zugänge*, 305–312. Berlin & Boston: De Gruyter. https://doi.org/doi:10.1515/9783110774306-018.

Ferger, Anne, Hanna Hedeland, Daniel Jettka & Tommi Pirinen. 2020. Corpus Services. [Computer software]. Zenodo. https://doi.org/10.5281/zenodo.4725655.

Ferger, Anne & Daniel Jettka. 2021. Seamless integration of continuous quality control and research data management for indigenous language resources. In Monachini, Monica, Maria Eskevich (eds.), *Proceedings of CLARIN Annual Conference 2021*, Virtual Edition, 95–99.

Ferger, Anne, André Frank Krause & Karola Pitsch. 2023. A continous integration (CI) workflow for quality assurance checks for corpora of multimodal interaction. In Krister Lindén, Jyrki Niemi & Thalassia Kontino (eds.), *CLARIN Annual Conference Proceedings 2023*, 106–110. Leuven, Belgium.

Fisseni, Bernhard & Thomas Schmidt. 2020. CLARIN web services for TEI-annotated transcripts of spoken language. In Kiril Simov& Maria Eskevich (eds.), *Selected Papers from the CLARIN Annual Conference 2019*. Leipzig, 12–22.

Frick, Elena & Thomas Schmidt. 2020. Using full text indices for querying spoken language data. In Piotr Bański, Adrien Barbaresi, Simon Clematide, Marc Kupietz, Harald Lüngen & Ines Pisetta (eds.), *Proceedings of the 8th Workshop on Challenges in the Management of Large Corpora*, 40–46. Paris: European Language Resources Association. https://nbn-resolving.org/urn:nbn:de:bsz:mh39-98143 (last accessed 14 February 2025).

Gehle, Raphaela, Karola Pitsch, Timo Dankert & Sebastian Wrede. 2017. How to open an interaction between robot and museum visitor? Strategies to establish a focused encounter in HRI. In *Proceedings of the 2017 ACM/IEEE International Conference on Human-Robot Interaction* (HRI '17), 187–195. New York, NY, USA: Association for Computing Machinery. https://doi.org/10.1145/2909824.3020219.

Hedeland, Hanna. 2020. Towards comprehensive definitions of data quality for audiovisual annotated language resources. In Costanza Navarretta & Maria Eskevich (eds.), *Selected Papers from the CLARIN Annual Conference 2020*, 93–103.

Hedeland, Hanna & Anne Ferger. 2020. Towards continuous quality control for spoken language corpora. *International Journal of Digital Curation* 15 (1). 1–13.

Hedeland, Hanna & Thomas Schmidt. 2022. The TEI-based ISO standard 'Transcription of Spoken Language' as an exchange format within CLARIN and beyond. In *CLARIN Annual Conference*, 34–45.

Hermann, Fabian, Christian Pietsch & Philipp Cimiano. 2021. Conquaire infrastructure for continuous quality control. *Studies in Analytical Reproducibility: The Conquaire Project*. https://pub.uni-bielefeld.de/record/2951757 (last accessed 7 June 2021).

Hirschmann, Hagen & Thomas Schmidt. 2022. Gesprochene Lernerkorpora: Methodisch-technische Aspekte der Erhebung, Erschließung und Nutzung. *Zeitschrift für germanistische Linguistik* 50 (1). 36–81. https://doi.org/doi:10.1515/zgl-2022-2048.

Kendrick, Kobin H & Judith Holler. 2017. Gaze direction signals response preference in conversation. *Research on Language and Social Interaction* 50 (1). 12–32.

Kraft, Sophie, Angela Schmalen, Hendrik Seitz-Moskaliuk, York Sure-Vetter, Jennifer Knebes, Eva Lübke & Elena Wössner. 2021. Nationale Forschungsdateninfrastruktur (NFDI) e. V.: Aufbau und Ziele. *Bausteine Forschungsdatenmanagement* 2. 1–9.

Krause, André Frank, Anne Ferger & Karola Pitsch. 2023a. Detecting and tracking persons in video recordings of authentic social interaction: Analysis and anonymization. https://www.liri.uzh.ch/dam/jcr:f104d12e-416e-4246-8bca-dd16bd9808aa/CAMVA_2023_paper_1632.docx (last accessed 14 February 2025).

Krause, André Frank, Anne Ferger & Karola Pitsch. 2023b. Automatic anonymization of human faces in images of authentic social interaction: A web application. In Krister Lindén, Jyrki Niemi & Thalassia Kontino (eds.), *CLARIN Annual Conference Proceedings 2023*, 90–94.

Liégeois, Loïc, Carole Etienne, Christophe Benzitoun, Christophe Parisse & Christian Chanard. 2015. Using the TEI as a pivot format for oral and multimodal language corpora. *Text Encoding Initiative Conference and Member's meeting* 2015, Lyon, France.

Luginbühl, Martin, Vera Mundwiler, Judith Kreuz, Daniel Müller-Feldmeth & Stefan Hauser. 2021. Quantitative and qualitative approaches in conversation analysis: Methodological reflections on a study of argumentative group discussions. *Gesprächsforschung-Online-Zeitschrift zur verbalen Interaktion* 22. 179–236.

Max Planck Institute for Psycholinguistics, Nijmegen, The Language Archive. 2020. ELAN (Version 6.4) [Computer software]. https://archive.mpi.nl/tla/elan (last accessed 14 February 2025)

Mundwiler, Vera, Judith Kreuz, Daniel Müller-Feldmeth, Martin Luginbühl & Stefan Hauser. 2019. Quantitative und qualitative Zugänge in der Gesprächsforschung. Methodologische Betrachtungen am Beispiel einer Studie zu argumentativen Gruppendiskussionen. *Gesprächsforschung–Online-Zeitschrift zur verbalen Interaktion* 20. 323–383.

Parisse, Christophe, Céline Poudat, Ciara R Wigham, Michel Jacobson & Loïc Liégeois. 2017. CORLI: A linguistic consortium for corpus, language, and interaction. In Maciej Piasecki (ed.), *Selected papers from the CLARIN Annual Conference 2017*, Budapest, 15–24.

Pitsch, Karola. 2016. Limits and opportunities for mathematizing communicational conduct for social robotics in the real world? Toward enabling a robot to make use of the human's competences. *AI & SOCIETY* 31 (4). 587–593. https://doi.org/10.1007/s00146-015-0629-0.

Pitsch, Karola. 2020. Answering a robot's questions: Participation dynamics of adult-child-groups in encounters with a museum guide robot. *Réseaux* 220-221 (2-3), 113-150, https://doi.org/10.3917/res.220.0113.

Pitsch, Karola. 2023. Mensch-Roboter-Interaktion als Forschungsinstrument der Interaktionalen Linguistik. In Matthias Meiler & Martin Siefkes (eds.), *Linguistische Methodenreflexion im Aufbruch*, 119–152. Berlin & Boston: De Gruyter. https://doi.org/10.1515/9783111043616-005.

Pitsch, Karola, Timo Dankert, Raphaela Gehle & Sebastian Wrede. 2016. Referential practices. Effects of a museum guide robot suggesting a deictic 'repair' action to visitors attempting to orient to an exhibit. In *2016 25th IEEE International Symposium on Robot and Human Interactive Communication (RO-MAN)*, 225–231. https://doi.org/10.1109/ROMAN.2016.7745135.

Pitsch, Karola, Anna-Lisa Vollmer, Katharina J. Rohlfing, Jannik Fritsch & Britta Wrede. 2014. Tutoring in adult-child interaction: On the loop of the tutor's action modification and the recipient's gaze. *Interaction studies. Social behaviour and communication in Biological and artificial systems* 15 (1). 55–98. https://doi.org/10.1075/is.15.1.03pit.

Rühlemann, Christoph. 2017. Integrating corpus-linguistic and conversation-analytic transcription in XML: The case of backchannels and overlap in storytelling interaction. *Corpus Pragmatics* 1 (3). 201–232. https://doi.org/10.1007/s41701-017-0018-7.

Rühlemann, Christoph. 2018. *Corpus Linguistics for Pragmatics: A guide for research* (1st edition). London & New York: Routledge. https://doi.org/10.4324/9780429451072.

Rühlemann, Christoph. 2020. *Visual linguistics with R: A practical introduction to quantitative Interactional Linguistics*. Amsterdam: John Benjamins. https://doi.org/10.1075/z.228.

Rühlemann, Christoph & Matt Gee. 2017. Conversation analysis and the XML method. *Gesprächsforschung – Online-Zeitschrift zur verbalen Interaktion* 18. 274–296.

Rühlemann, Christoph & Alexander Ptak. 2023. Reaching beneath the tip of the iceberg: A guide to the Freiburg Multimodal Interaction Corpus. *Open Linguistics* 9 (1). 20220245. https://doi.org/doi:10.1515/opli-2022-0245.

Schmid, Helmut. 1995. Improvements in part-of-speech tagging with an application to German. In *Proceedings of the ACL SIGDAT-Workshop*. Dublin, Ireland. https://www.cis.uni-muenchen.de/~schmid/tools/TreeTagger/data/tree-tagger2.pdf (last accessed 28 March 2024).

Schmidt, Thomas. 2011. A TEI-based approach to standardising spoken language transcription. *Journal of the Text Encoding Initiative*. Text Encoding Initiative Consortium (1). https://doi.org/10.4000/jtei.142.

Schmidt, Thomas. 2016. Construction and dissemination of a corpus of spoken interaction–tools and workflows in the FOLK project. *Journal for Language Technology and Computational Linguistics* 31 (1). 105–132.

Schmidt, Thomas. 2018. Gesprächskorpora. In Thomas Schmidt & Marc Kupietz (eds.), *Korpuslinguistik*, 209–230. Berlin & Boston: De Gruyter. https://www.jstor.org/stable/j.ctvbj7k7n.13 (last accessed 6 April 2023).

Schmidt, Thomas. 2023. FOLK – Das Forschungs- und Lehrkorpus für Gesprochenes Deutsch. *Korpora Deutsch als Fremdsprache* 3(1), 166–169. https://doi.org/10.48694/KORDAF.3737.

Schmidt, Thomas, Hanna Hedeland & Elena Frick. 2021. Ein Standard in der Praxis: ISO 24624:2016. Transcription of spoken language. FORGE 2021: Forschungsdaten in den Geisteswissenschaften – Mapping the Landscape – Geisteswissenschaftliches Forschungsdatenmanagement zwischen lokalen und globalen, generischen und spezifischen Lösungen (FORGE2021), Cologne. https://doi.org/10.5281/zenodo.5379639.

Schmidt, Thomas & Wilfried Schütte. 2010. FOLKER: An annotation tool for efficient transcription of natural, multi-party interaction. In Nicoletta Calzolari, Khalid Choukri, Bente Maegaard, Joseph Mariani, Jan Odjik, Stelios Piperidis, Mike Rosner & Daniel Tapias (eds.), *Proceedings of the Seventh Conference on International Language Resources and Evaluation (LREC'10)*. European Language Resources Association (ELRA). http://www.exmaralda.org/files/LREC_Folker.pdf (last accessed 14 February 2025).

Schmidt, Thomas & Kai Wörner. 2014. EXMARaLDA. In Jacques Durand, Ulrike Gut & Gjert Kristoffersen (eds.), *Handbook on corpus phonology*, 402–419. Oxford. Oxford University Press. http://ukcatalogue.oup.com/product/9780199571932.do (last accessed 14 February 2025).

Schürmann, Timo. 2021. ExmaraldaR. https://github.com/TimoSchuer/ExmaraldaR (last accessed 14 February 2025).

Schütte, Wilfried. 2007. ATLAS.ti 5 – ein Werkzeug zur qualitativen Datenanalyse. *Gesprächsforschung – Online-Zeitschrift zur verbalen Interaktion* 8. 57–72.

Selting, Margret, Peter Auer, Dagmar Barth-Weingarten, Jörg R Bergmann, Pia Bergmann, Karin Birkner, Elizabeth Couper-Kuhlen, Arnulf Deppermann, Peter Gilles, Susanne Günthner, Martin Hartung, Friederike Kern, Christine Mertzlufft, Christian Meyer, Miriam Morek, Frank Oberzaucher, Jörg Peters, Uta Quasthoff, Wilfried Schütte, Anja Stukenbrock, Susanne Uhmann. 2009. Gesprächsanalytisches Transkriptionssystem 2 (GAT 2). *Gesprächsforschung – Online-Zeitschrift zur verbalen Interaktion* 10 353–402.

Sloetjes, Han. 2014. ELAN: Multimedia annotation application. In Jacques Durand, Ulrike Gut & Gjert Kristoffersen (eds.), *Handbook on corpus phonology*, 305–320. Oxford. Oxford University Press.

Stivers, Tanya. 2015. Coding social interaction: A heretical approach in conversation analysis? *Research on Language and Social Interaction* 48 (1). 1–19. https://doi.org/10.1080/08351813.2015.993837.

TEI Consortium (ed.). 2023. *TEI P5: Guidelines for Electronic Text Encoding and Interchange. P5 Version 4.7.0. Last updated on 16th November 2023.* http://www.tei-c.org/Guidelines/P5/ (last accessed 14 February 2025).

Westpfahl, Swantje & Thomas Schmidt. 2013. POS für(s) FOLK – Part of Speech Tagging des Forschungs- und Lehrkorpus Gesprochenes Deutsch. *Journal for Language Technology and Computational Linguistics* 28 (1), 139–153.

Westpfahl, Swantje, Thomas Schmidt, Jasmin Jonietz & Anton Borlinghaus. 2017. *STTS 2.0. Guidelines für die Annotation von POS -Tags für Transkripte gesprochener Sprache in Anlehnung an das Stuttgart Tübingen Tagset (STTS)*. Working Paper. Version 1.1, März 2017. https://nbn-resolving.org/urn:nbn:de:bsz:mh39-60634 (last accessed 14 February 2025).

Wilkinson, Mark D., Michel Dumontier, IJsbrand Jan Aalbersberg, Gabrielle Appleton, Myles Axton, Arie Baak, Niklas Blomberg, Jan-Willem Boiten, Luiz Bonino da Silva Santos, Philip E. Bourne, Jildau Bouwman, Anthony J. Brookes, Tim Clark, Mercè Crosas, Ingrid Dillo, Olivier Dumon, Scott Edmunds, Chris T. Evelo, Richard Finkers, Alejandra Gonzalez-Beltran, Alasdair J.G. Gray, Paul Groth, Carole Goble, Jeffrey S. Grethe, Jaap Heringa, Peter A.C 't Hoen, Rob Hooft, Tobias Kuhn, Ruben Kok, Joost Kok, Scott J. Lusher, Maryann E. Martone, Albert Mons, Abel L. Packer, Bengt Persson, Philippe Rocca-Serra, Marco Roos, Rene van Schaik, Susanna-Assunta Sansone, Erik Schultes, Thierry Sengstag, Ted Slater, George Strawn, Morris A. Swertz, Mark Thompson, Johan van der Lei, Erik van Mulligen, Jan Velterop, Andra Waagmeester, Peter Wittenburg, Katherine Wolstencroft, Jun Zhao & Barend Mons 2016. The FAIR Guiding Principles for scientific data management and stewardship. *Scientific Data* 3 (1). 160018. https://doi.org/10.1038/sdata.2016.18.

Dimitra Niaouri, Bruno Machado Carneiro, Michele Linardi, and Julien Longhi

Machine Learning is heading to the SUD (Socially Unacceptable Discourse) analysis: From Shallow Learning to Large Language Models to the rescue, where do we stand?

Abstract: The rapid proliferation of social media platforms has led to a significant increase in online Socially Unacceptable Discourse (SUD). SUD, characterized by offensive language, controversial narratives, and distinct grammatical patterns, poses a substantial challenge for online platforms. Effective detection of SUD necessitates robust Machine Learning (ML) models capable of generalizing across diverse contexts and performing well in binary and multi-class classification. The absence of standardized annotation guidelines and the variability of annotation modalities in existing corpora impede the development of such models in a large-scale scenario typically found in multiple online scenarios (e.g., social media platforms).

This research introduces a comprehensive corpus of manually annotated texts from various online sources to facilitate a thorough benchmarking of state-of-the-art SUD classifiers across twelve distinct discourse categories. We provide a novel comparative analysis of three model families: Shallow Learning Models (SLMs), Masked Language Models (MLMs), and Causal Language Models (CLMs), including models such as Support Vector Machines (SVM), Multinomial Logistic Regression (MLR), BERT, and BERT variants (ALBERT, RoBERTa, ELECTRA), Llama 2, and Mistral among others. We assess the performance of these models in binary and multi-class large classification scenarios, moving beyond the standard binary and limited-class frameworks existing in the literature. We further extend our analyses through various experimental scenarios, including the impact of class imbalances, and enhance model explainability. By applying visualization techniques to the text representations generated by the top-performing model, we observe class overlap and evaluate the model's generalizability.

Dimitra Niaouri, AGORA, CY Cergy Paris Université, e-mail: dimitra.niaouri@cyu.fr ETIS UMR-8051
Bruno Machado Carneiro, ENSEA Engineering School, e-mail: bruno.machadocarneiro@ensea.fr
Michele Linardi, CY Cergy Paris Université, e-mail: michele.linardi@cyu.fr ETIS UMR-8051
Julien Longhi, AGORA, CY Cergy Paris Université, e-mail: julien.longhi@cyu.fr

https://doi.org/10.1515/9783111434018-010

Our findings reveal limitations in current Deep Learning (DL) models for SUD classification due to class imbalances and inconsistent annotation guidelines. While binary SUD classification demonstrates promise, sensitivity to class imbalance in multi-class scenarios underscores the need for improved discriminatory power. Our analysis highlights the trade-off between bidirectional contextual awareness (favoring MLMs) and sequential dependency modeling (advantageous for CLMs), with MLMs emerging as the superior choice due to their bidirectional training approach. Finally, we emphasize the importance of consistent efforts within the ML community and the broader implications for linguistics, discourse analysis, and semantics, advocating for developing formal guidelines.

Keywords: Socially Unacceptable Discourse Analysis, Machine Learning, Deep Learning, Multi-source learning, corpus, Masked Language Models, Causal Language Models

1 Introduction

During these last two decades, the massive popularisation of social media has been changing the way people communicate, interact, and collect worldwide news. The dissemination speed rate and the possibility to quickly reach a large audience are some clear advantages of modern social network platforms. By contrast, the potential anonymity and sense of impunity can bring out the worst in people and make them share ideas that would not be socially acceptable otherwise. As a result, accurate detection and characterization of harmful ideas is crucial for effective social media moderation (Badjatiya et al. 2017; MacAvaney et al. 2019; Röttger et al. 2021; Alkomah and Ma 2022) as it enables targeted interventions, uncovers underlying issues such as prejudice, and supports the development of legal frameworks.

Although Machine Learning (ML) shows potential for automating content detection, there are substantial challenges that limit its effectiveness. Analysts encounter numerous overarching issues when using current ML solutions to detect Socially Unacceptable Discourse (Sulc and Pahor De Maiti 2020) (SUD), which often manifests in different forms and data modalities (Gandhi et al. 2024). A common form of SUD is the use of offensive and abusive language. However, it is important to note that controversial narratives, while not inherently bad or immoral, often have a close connection to radicalization and extremist ideologies. This relationship has become particularly evident in recent historical contexts such as the Covid-19 crisis and the Russian invasion of Ukraine, during which we have witnessed several cases of public debate radicalization, especially favored by the circulation of distorted information (De Giorgio et al. 2022). Another particular trait of SUD is the presence of distinctive grammatical characteristics. To accurately model these features, it is essential to identify specific grammatical substructures, including residual representations, pronoun usage, and future tense (Ascone and Longhi 2018; Pahor De Maiti et al. 2020). Despite this, current publicly annotated corpora used in ML lack standardized guidelines for SUD annotation (Fišer, Erjavec and Ljubešić 2017). While similar terminology or tags are employed, different definitions of SUD may share overlapping characteristics, or a single category may encompass text instances with divergent features depending on the context. Moreover, annotator bias, as highlighted in previous studies (Badjatiya, Gupta and Varma 2019; Yuan et al. 2023; Davidson, Bhattacharya and Weber 2019), can significantly affect the consistency and accuracy of SUD annotations. As Yu et al. 2024 suggest, the primary data quality issues impacting model performance are noisy annotations, class imbalance, and data homogeneity.

Other complex forms of socially unacceptable discourse have recently started to receive attention. One example is the concept of extremist narrative, which identifies online discourses related to multiple social processes like radicalization, populism, demagogy, and other manifestations that endanger democracy. The ARENAS European project aims to significantly advance the extremist narrative analysis (Postigo-Fuentes et al. 2024). One of the main objectives consists of developing strategies for identifying, analyzing, and countering extremist rhetoric, seeking to advance beyond traditional methods by exploring the complex relationship between language and ideology in extremist content.

In this novel context, it is crucial to propose and assess ML solutions that support practical strategies for the accurate classification of multiple kinds of discourse, whose characterization depends on the social phenomenon, political scenario, and legal framework but also on the context, speaker, and intent of the speech itself. In this scenario, it is reasonable to expect a poor generalization capability of ML SUD classifiers trained in a specific context (Yuan and Rizoiu 2022). To that extent, we study and evaluate the capability of current state-of-the-art (SOTA) ML models to characterize SUD within a large-scale, multi-class framework that better reflects real-world scenarios, where naturally multiple distributions exist. The rationale behind this approach is that the diverse range of discourse and topics in such a framework pose challenges to models to adapt, highlighting limitations in automatic detection and paving the way for improvements. Such effort will permit us to define research directions and open challenges to better address imminent requirements in SUD and extremist narrative analysis.

Given the limited availability of high-quality data for SUD detection, we note that transfer learning provides a well-established solution that leverages models trained on datasets from related domains. Such an approach significantly reduces the requirement for extensive labeled examples in the specific target domain (Neyshabur, Sedghi and Zhang 2020).

In our evaluation, rather than considering cross-domain transfer learning, which consists of training a model on a single distribution and testing on another one from a different domain (e.g., Karan and Šnajder 2018; Swamy, Jamatia and Gambäck 2019), we implement a methodology that evaluates the capacity of SOTA models to generalize to SUD classes that naturally occur in multiple distributions (different contexts). Beyond the standard evaluation of models through intra-dataset classification, we also use an inter-dataset classification method. Our approach considers a large dataset resulting from the union of multiple datasets encompassing 12 classes. This methodology allows us to propose interpretable insights into the semantics of SUD and enables the evaluation of pattern learning across different annotation guidelines.

In the intra-dataset classification task, we maintain the same data split (training/test/validation) used in the performance assessment of each single dataset.

Our contributions can be summarized as follows:

1. We construct a unified corpus (G^{SUD}) from 13 publicly available datasets to fine-tune and evaluate pre-trained LLMs for general tasks and Shallow learning models at an intra- and inter-dataset level where the main focus is the generalization over classes rather than datasets.
2. We perform an extensive empirical evaluation of 12 SOTA models in the large-scale (~500K samples) multi-class scenario in G^{SUD}, moving beyond the standard binary and limited-class frameworks existing in the literature that typically involve fewer samples and narrower coverage of the intricate aspects of SUD.
3. We provide a unique comparative analysis of three model families: Shallow Learning Models (SLMs), Masked Language Models (MLMs), and Causal Language Models (CLMs) under a wide range of experimental conditions, including class imbalances, after tweaking the G^{SUD} dataset.
4. We enhance model explainability by employing visualization techniques on the text representations generated by the best-performing model, allowing us to observe class overlap and assess the model's generalizability over different SUD categories.

2 Related Work

Most prior research in cross-dataset and cross-domain generalization has focused on evaluating models trained on one dataset and tested on another, often within binary or limited-class scenarios.

Gröndahl et al. (2018) have explored cross-dataset generalization by replicating seven Machine Learning (ML) and Deep Learning (DL) models, including Logistic Regression (LR), Multi-layer Perceptron (MLP), Convolutional Neural Network (CNN), and Long Short-Term Memory (LSTM). The proposed benchmark considers four datasets from Wikipedia and Twitter in a binary classification setup. The study concludes that transferring knowledge between datasets results in poorer performance than training and testing on the same dataset. Additionally, simpler architectures performed comparably to more complex ones.

Similarly, Karan and Šnajder (2018) investigated generalizability across nine different datasets, including sources such as newspapers, Fox News, Twitter, and Wikipedia, comparing various SVM classifiers under a binary class setup. Their study reaffirms the challenges of cross-domain generalization, noting that models consistently performed better on in-domain test sets than on out-domain ones.

Swamy, Jamatia and Gambäck (2019) also contributed to the discourse by examining cross-dataset generalization using several ML and DL models, including LR, RNN, LSTM, ELMo, and BERT, across four different datasets in a positive vs negative class configuration. Their findings aligned with previous studies, highlighting that BERT was the best-performing model. They also observed that datasets with more positive samples generalized better and noted a significant drop in performance when transitioning from large training datasets to smaller test sets.

Pamungkas and Patti (2019) extended the exploration of generalization to cross-domain and cross-linguistic contexts, using ten publicly available datasets, which they binarized. They hypothesized that training on a dataset with broader coverage and testing on a narrower one would yield better results. Despite the out-domain scenario leading to worse performance, this work demonstrates that broader datasets enhance generalization compared to narrower ones. Salminen et al. (2020) further addressed the lack of cross-platform model development and testing, creating a cross-platform online hate classifier. They employed several ML algorithms (e.g., LR, Naive Bayes (NB), Support Vector Machine (SVM), XGBoost, Feed-Forward Neural Network (FFNN)) in a binary setup using an aggregated dataset from multiple platforms. XGBoost outperformed other models, with BERT-based features yielding the best results. Markov and Daelemans (2021) focused on reducing false positives in hate speech detection, evaluating various ML and DL models, including Bag-of-Words (BOW), CNN, LSTM, SVM, BERT, and RoBERTa. Under a binary setup, BERT and RoBERTa outperformed baselines and SVM in in-domain conditions, though performance dropped in out-domain conditions, with BERT and RoBERTa still leading.

Similarly, to previous studies, Fortuna, Soler-Company and Wanner (2021) conducted experiments with several ML and DL models, including BERT, ALBERT, SVM, and fastText, standardizing dataset labels for intra- and cross-dataset setups. They advanced beyond typical single-dataset studies by examining nine datasets, focusing on those providing the highest generalization. Their results suggested that BERT and ALBERT outperformed the other two models under an intra-dataset classification scenario, while at the same time, they generalize better under an inter-dataset classification one. Yin and Zubiaga (2021) have focused on discovering the factors constraining model generalizability across datasets, highlighting challenges such as differing topics, label definitions, and data source platforms. They found that broader labels facilitated higher generalizability, with models like BERT and ALBERT performing relatively well. Toraman, Şahinuç and Yılmaz (2022) moved towards more complex classifications by creating large-scale tweet datasets in English and Turkish, covering five domains, to analyze the performance of various models for hate speech detection. They used a three-class setup (hate, offensive, normal) and evaluated traditional algorithms (LR), neural networks (CNN, LSTM), and transformers (BERT). As expected, the Transformer architecture outperformed simpler models, although the latter remained competitive.

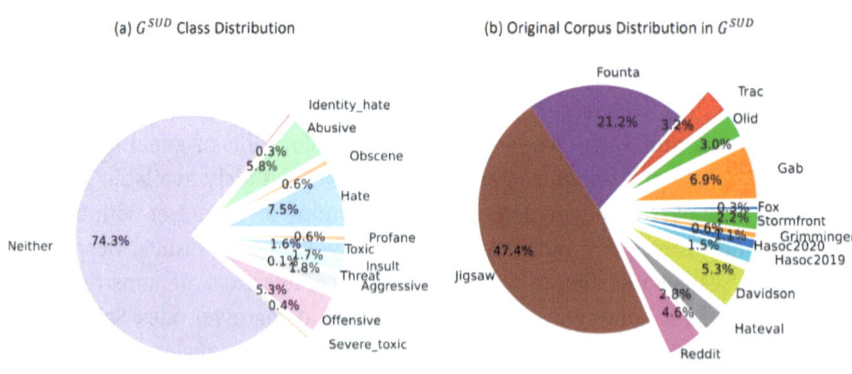

Figure 1: (a) G^{SUD} Class distribution, (b) Corpus distribution in G^{SUD}.

Antypas and Camacho-Collados (2023) took a significant step by examining generalizability across 13 hate speech-related social media datasets, using binary (hate vs. not hate) and multi-class (seven classes including racism, sexism, etc.) settings. They fine-tuned SVM, BERT, RoBERTa, TimeLMs-21, and BERTweet models on individual and unified datasets. Their findings showed that, under the binary and multi-class setup, Transformer models achieve higher performances when trained on the combined dataset rather than on individual test sets different from their training sets. Gandhi et al. (2024) have recently made a step towards exploring multi-class classification. In their study, they consider a dataset of approximately 20,000 samples encompassing various classes, including hate speech, abusive language, individual and group hate, religious hate, and race-based hate, among others. Despite the broad range of classes, the benchmark tested a limited number of models, namely logistic regression and LSTM. Additionally, the research did not address cross-dataset and cross-domain generalization challenges. Finally, Yigezu et al. 2023 focused on multi-class and multi-label hate speech detection against the Mexican Spanish-speaking LGBTQ+ population using BERT and RoBERTa models. They used three classes (LGBTQ+ phobic, not LGBTQ+ phobic, NA) for multi-class and distinguished between various phobias (e.g., lesbophobia, gayphobia) for multi-label. BERT excelled in multi-label tasks, while RoBERTa was superior for multi-class tasks.

In contrast to these studies, our work overcomes previous research limitations by focusing on a multi-class scenario using a consistently larger scenario than the ones considered until now. We employ a unified dataset to develop general models subsequently tested on individual and smaller test sets. Such a choice enables us to capture the real-world complexities of SUD detection and to understand model generalization limitations in a multi-class context, offering novel insights compared to previous studies. In the following sections, we will delve into the datasets utilized and the specificities of our methodology, providing a detailed account of how our approach advances the field.

3 SUD corpora

Many works have proposed annotated datasets for hate speech analysis (e.g., Davidson et al. 2017; Founta et al. 2018; Qian et al. 2019; Grimminger and Klinger 2021). Among the most recognized resources is "hatespeechdata",[1] which compiles various dataset publications and their links. Poletto et al. (2020) conducted a comprehensive survey of available corpora, highlighting key benchmark datasets for evaluating abusive language. More recently, Piot, Martín-Rodilla and Parapar (2024) compiled an updated collection of over 60 datasets, named MetaHate, focusing on detecting harmful online content, including hate speech and cyberbullying, and analyzing text across social media platforms.

1 https://hatespeechdata.com/ (last accessed 14 February 2025).

In Table 1, we report the corpora we consider in our study. We use data from various sources recently adopted to assess the performance of SOTA ML solutions for SUD detection (e.g., hate speech detection, sentiment, toxicity, radicalization, and ideology analysis). We selected 13 publicly available datasets containing 470,768 samples distributed over 12 classes to advance beyond the binary classifications and limited class scopes of earlier research which generally involve fewer samples and less comprehensive coverage of hate speech scenarios. Our dataset choices are based on their comprehensive coverage of various aspects of SUD and their availability in English. By concatenating these 13 datasets, we create a unique English text corpus, which we have labeled G^{SUD}. Note that the datasets we concatenate in G^{SUD} share multiple overlapping SUD labels, which identify the same SUD category. We consider the presence of bias and ambiguities as physiological, and identifying and analyzing the concerned instances is under the lens of our research. In Figure 1(a), we report the instances distribution over SUD classes. Note that the *neither* class subsumes all texts that do not fall in any SUD categorizations proposed by the annotators. As expected, SUD classes have a sensitive lower support compared to the *neither* class denoting the typical class imbalance setting of the SUD detection problem.

2.1 Datasets

Here, we provide the details of each dataset we join in G^{SUD}. Davidson (Davidson et al. 2017) contains around 25,000 tweets labelled as being hateful, offensive or neither of those randomly sampled from a set of 85.40 million tweets produced by 33,458 different users. Each sample was labelled by at least three different annotators. Founta (Founta et al. 2018) contains about 100,000 tweets, labeled with four categories: abusive, hateful, normal, and spam. In this dataset, a variable number of users (between five and ten) have annotated each sample. Fox (Gao and Huang 2018) contains 1528 comments posted on ten different popular threads on the Fox News website. In these data, two native English speakers have produced labels to differentiate hateful from normal content following the same annotation guidelines. Gab (Qian et al. 2019) contains 34,000 samples extracted form Gab, a social media, where users commonly share far right ideologies (Jasser et al. 2021), annotated in the Amazon Mechanical Turk[2] platform, where at least 3 annotators provided a label for each sample.

2 https://www.mturk.com/ (last accessed 14 February 2025).

Table 1: Best performing SUD classification model on each dataset.

Dataset	Sample type	# Samples	Topic	Best performing SUD classifier	F1 Macro (%)
Davidson (Grimminger and Klinger 2021)	Tweets	25,000	Generic	BERT	93
Founta (Swamy et al. 2019)	Tweets	100,000	Generic	BERT	69.60
Fox (Yuan and Rizoiu 2022)	Threads	1,528	Fox News Posts	BERT	65
Gab (Qian et al. 2019)	Posts	34,000	Generic	CNN	89.60
Grimminger (Grimminger and Klinger 2021)	Tweets	3,000	US Presidential Election	BERT	74
HASOC2019 (Wang et al. 2019)	Facebook, Twitter posts	12,000	Generic	LSTM + Attention	78.80
HASOC2020 (Roy et al. 2021)	Facebook posts	12,000	Generic	XLM-RoBERTa	90.30
Hateval (MacAvaney et al. 2019)	Tweets	13,000	Misogynist and Racist content	mSVM/BERT	75.40
Jigsaw (van Aken et al. 2018)	Wikipedia talk pages	220,000	Generic	Bi-GRU + Attention	78.30
Olid (Zampieri et al. 2019)	Tweets	14,000	Generic	CNN	80
Reddit (Yuan and Rizoiu 2022)	Posts	22000	Toxic subjects	BERT	85
Stormfront (MacAvaney et al. 2019)	Threads	10,500	White Supremacy Forum	BERT	80.30
Trac (Aroyehun and Gelbukh 2018)	Facebook posts	15,000	Generic	LSTM	64

Grimminger (Grimminger and Klinger 2021) contains 3,000 tweets in 2020 presidential election topic in the United States. The samples were labelled as hate speech or not by three undergraduate students, who discussed the annotation guidelines during the labelling process. HASOC2019 (Modha et al. 2019) and HASOC2020 (Mandl et al. 2020) are datasets proposed in the Indo-European Languages (HASOC) challenge, which contain 12,000 English text samples extracted from Twitter and Facebook labeled as hateful, offensive, profane or neither of those. Hateval (Basile et al. 2019) gathers around 13,000 tweets containing hateful and normal speech.

The hateful content originates from accounts of potential victims of misogynism and racism. Jigsaw[3] (van Aken et al. 2018) is a dataset provided in the Toxic Comment Classification Challenge. It contains about 220,000 samples extracted from Wikipedia talk pages differentiated into seven classes: toxic, severe toxic, obscene, threat, insult, identity hate, and neither of the previous. Olid (Zampieri et al. 2019) contains 14, 000 tweets annotated using the Figure Eight Data Labelling platform.[4] In this context, tweet selection is executed by keyword filtering and human annotation. Reddit (Qian et al. 2019) has 22,000 samples extracted from Reddit, labeled for hate speech detection by Amazon Mechanical Turk users. Before the labeling task, the text got selected according to a list of toxic subjects on the Reddit platform. Stormfront (De Gibert et al. 2018) contains 10,500 samples taken from a white supremacy forum called Stormfront and divided into four classes: hate, no hate, related, and skip. The related class contains statements that cannot be considered hateful without considering their context. Text belonging to the skip class does not contain enough information to determine if it can be classified as hateful. Trac (Kumar et al. 2018) dataset gathers 15,000 Facebook posts and comments classified into aggressive and non-aggressive language.

4 SUD models

In this section, we examine SOTA models used for SUD detection. In section 3.1, we present the SOTA DL models adopted for the SUD detection task in previous works, and in section 3.2, we introduce the models we fine-tuned for this paper.

4.1 SOTA Deep Learning models

In Table 1, we show the best performer in each corpus. Here, we report the Macro F1 score used to evaluate the performance of our models. It is calculated by averaging the sum of the F1 score of each class. Recall that the F1 score reports the harmonic mean of precision and recall of a classification model. For a particular input class, we compute the precision (P) of a SUD classifier as follows: $P = \frac{TP}{TP + FP}$ and recall (R) as: $R = \frac{TP}{TP + FN}$, where TP denotes the number of correctly classified

3 https://www.kaggle.com/c/jigsaw-toxic-comment-classification-challenge (accessed 14 March 2025).
4 https://f8federal.com/ (last accessed 14 February 2025).

instances of the input class (true positive), FP denotes the number of occurrences that are wrongly assigned with the input class label (false positive), and FN represents the number of the input class samples that are erroneously classified (false negative). Hence, we have that $F1 = 2 \times \frac{P \times R}{P + R}$. From Table 1, we observe that BERT (Bidirectional Encoder Representations from Transformers (Devlin et al. 2019)) is the best performing model in the majority of the datasets. BERT adopts a DL architecture released by the Google AI Language team in early 2019, which is pre-trained by masked language model (MLM) and next sentence prediction (NSP) tasks over a large corpus of English data containing more than 3B words (Devlin et al. 2019). MLM consists of training the model to predict masked tokens in the corpus sentences, whereas the NSP training aims to predict if two sentences form a sequence in the original text. XLM-RoBERTa (Conneau et al. 2020) is a multilingual variant of the original BERT model. BERT has clearly shown its superiority over other types of DL models previously adopted in SUD classification, such as Convolutional Neural Networks (CNN) (Qian et al. 2019) and Long-short term memory networks (LSTM) (Wang et al. 2019). The attention mechanism used by BERT represents a robust solution avoiding the limitation of LSTM networks, which assumes that each token depends only on previous ones. By contrast, BERT learns relationships considering all the tokens in a sentence simultaneously.

Table 2: Overview of the fine-tuned models.

Category	Models	Citation
SLM (Shallow Learning Models)	Gradient Boosting (GB)	Friedman (2001)
	Multinomial Logistic Regression (MLR)	Wright (1995)
	Multinomial Naive Bayes (MNB)	Kibriya et al. (2004)
	Random Forest (RF)	Breiman (2001)
	Support Vector Machines (SVM)	Hearst et al. (1998)
MLM (Masked Language Models)	$BERT_{BASE}$	Devlin et al. (2019)
	$ALBERT_{BASE}$	Lan et al. (2019)
	$RoBERTa_{BASE}$	Liu et al. (2019)
	$ELECTRA_{BASE}$	Clark et al. (2020)
CLM (Causal Language Models)	Llama-2-7b	Touvron et al. (2023)
	Mistral-7B-v0.1	Jiang et al. (2023)
	mpt-7b	MosaicML NLP Team (2023)

4.2 Fine-tuned models

In our study, we empirically evaluate the SUD classification performance of three different model families: Shallow Learning Models (SLMs), Masked Language Models (MLMs), and Causal Language Models (CLMs). An illustrative summary of the fine-tuned models can be found in Table 2. In the next sections, we elaborate on the specific characteristics of each category.

4.2.1 Shallow Learning Models

Shallow learning models represent a category encompassing conventional ML algorithms proposed prior to 2006 (Xu et al. 2021). This involves simple models with a few layers or processing units. They are suitable for tasks with straightforward data patterns, but their simplicity may limit their ability to capture complex relationships and adapt to new data. Hencc, the performances of such models are closely tied to the effectiveness of the feature extraction process (Janiesch, Zschech and Heinrich). Within this overarching categorization, we specifically investigate Gradient Boosting (GB), Multinomial Logistic Regression (MLR), Multinomial Naive Bayes (MNB), Random Forest (RF), and Support Vector Machines (SVM).

4.2.2 Masked Language Models

Masked Language Models (MLMs), as explained in (Devlin et al. 2019), are DL models trained to reconstruct the original words of masked tokens based on the surrounding context. The significant advantage of those models lies in their bidirectional context, considering both preceding and subsequent tokens during the prediction process.

Within this category we evaluate $\text{BERT}_{\text{BASE}}$ (Devlin et al. 2019; Yuan and Rizoiu 2022) and some of the architectural variants introduced to enhance overall performance and reduce computational complexity. The BERT variants considered are the following:

1. $\text{ALBERT}_{\text{BASE}}$, which implements two parameter reduction techniques, namely Cross-layer parameter sharing and Factorized Embedding Parameterization. This results in a significantly smaller model compared to BERT (Lan et al. 2019). Moreover, ALBERT diverges from BERT's training approach by incorporating Sentence-Order Prediction (SOP) instead of Next Sentence Prediction (NSP).

2. RoBERTa$_{BASE}$, an optimized BERT pre-training approach, introduces several key modifications, including dynamic token masking for varying epochs, larger byte-level Byte-Pair Encoding (BPE), elimination of the NSP task, and an expanded corpus with increased training steps (Liu et al. 2019).
3. ELECTRA$_{BASE}$, another BERT variant, replaces the MLM training task with a replaced token detection task. This approach introduces binary classification to distinguish between original and replaced tokens, while omitting the NSP, aligning with the trends observed in ALBERT and RoBERTa (Clark et al. 2020). Despite its unique architecture that includes a replaced token detection task instead of a MLM one, ELECTRA is still categorized within our framework under the MLM family for ease of classification given its shared characteristics with BERT and other variants.

4.2.3 Causal Language Models

As introduced, MLMs are bidirectional models trained to consider context from both directions. Conversely, CLMs are unidirectional, considering only the previous context when making predictions. Specifically, they are trained to predict the next token in a sequence based on previous tokens, making them particularly efficient in text generation tasks. The CLM models fine-tuned and evaluated in this study are:

4. Llama 2 is a series of generative text models with varying parameters, ranging from 7 billion to 70 billion. Developed by Meta on an optimized transformer architecture (Touvron et al. 2023), these models are pre-trained and fine-tuned for language generation tasks. Notable innovations include pre-normalization using Root Mean Square Layer Normalization (RMS Norm), the use of Swigglue activation function, self-attention with KV Cache, and Rotary Positional Embedding (ROPE). For this study, we consider Llama 2 of size 7B parameter (Llama-2-7b-hf) fine-tuned on our datasets.
5. Mistral is a series of pre-trained generative text models developed by the Mistral AI team (Jiang et al. 2023). The model's innovation compared to Llama 2, as summarized in their paper, lies in its use of Sliding Window Attention (SWA), Rolling Buffer Cache, and Pre-fill and Chunking. Again, the size of the model is of 7B parameters (Mistral-7B-v0.1).
6. MPT, proposed by the MosaicML NLP team (2023) and released in various sizes and fine-tuned variations, constitutes another series of Large Language Models (LLMs). Adopting a GPT-style architecture with a decoder-only transformer, MPT features refinements such as performance-optimized layer implementations and architectural modifications for enhanced training stability among others. The 7B parameter sized model (mpt-7b) is tested in this study.

Table 3: Optimal performing SLM per class and dataset.

	Macro F1 Score												
	Abusive	**Agressive**	**Hate**	**Identity Hate**	**Insult**	**Neither**	**Obscene**	**Offensive**	**Profane**	**Severe Toxic**	**Threat**	**Toxic**	**Best model**
G^{SUD}	0.77	0.52	0.61	0.11	0.35	0.93	0.11	0.69	0.24	0.30	0.40	0.11	**SVM**
Davidson	–	–	0.31	–	–	0.86	–	0.95	–	–	–	–	GB
Founta	0.89	–	0.37	–	–	0.95	–	–	–	–	–	–	MLR
Fox	–	–	0.54	–	–	0.86	–	–	–	–	–	–	MLR
Gab	–	–	0.89	–	–	0.91	–	–	–	–	–	–	GB
Grimminger	–	–	0.29	–	–	0.96	–	–	–	–	–	–	GB
HASOC2019	–	–	0.24	–	–	0.79	–	0.16	0.40	–	–	–	MLR
HASOC2020	–	–	0.08	–	–	0.89	–	0.36	0.82	–	–	–	SVM
Hateval	–	–	0.63	–	–	0.78	–	–	–	–	–	–	RF
	–	–	0.66	–	–	0.76	–	–	–	–	–	–	MNB
	–	–	0.64	–	–	0.77	–	–	–	–	–	–	MLR
	–	–	0.62	–	–	0.79	–	–	–	–	–	–	GB
Jigsaw	–	–	–	0.32	0.50	0.97	0.26	–	–	0.28	0.53	0.19	SVM
Olid	–	–	–	–	–	0.82	–	0.62	–	–	–	–	SVM
	–	–	–	–	–	0.83	–	0.61	–	–	–	–	MLR
Reddit	–	–	0.76	–	–	0.92	–	–	–	–	–	–	GB
Stormfront	–	–	0.42	–	–	0.95	–	–	–	–	–	–	MLR
Trac	–	0.78	–	–	–	0.61	–	–	–	–	–	–	MNB

5 Experiments

In the following sections, we present the results of our empirical evaluation for the three model families we examined. Throughout all our experiments, we split the datasets, allocating 80% for training, 10% for validation, and 10% for testing purposes. For the sake of reproducibility, we provide the code, and the data used in the experiments along with the respective instructions in an online repository (Niaouri et al. 2024). The repository includes details on the hyperparameters that differ across the models employed in this study, including learning rate, batch size, number of epochs, and the number of layers, among others. For reproducibility purposes, we can provide the saved models, which are substantial in size.

5.1 Shallow Learning Models

We implement our framework employing Natural Language Toolkit (nltk) functions for preprocessing textual data, including tokenization, stop-word removal, lemmatization, and stemming. We then transform processed text data into numerical features using the TextVectorization layer of TensorFlow. In Table 3, we report the performance of the best performing model for each dataset on individual SUD classes.

We observe that MLR consistently emerges as a strong performer across multiple datasets, showcasing its robustness in handling diverse SUD classes. Similarly, GB demonstrates competitive performance, often ranking as the best model on several datasets, while SVM exhibits varying success, with notable achievements in the G^{SUD}, HASOC2020, Jigsaw, and Olid. Consequently, a definitive consensus concerning the best-performing model is lacking in this framework.

The performance variations highlight the algorithm's sensitivity to the characteristics of specific datasets. It is important to note that in a large-scale context, namely in the G^{SUD} dataset, the generalization performance of the models falls short of expectations. The shallow model's ability to discriminate the classes worsens compared to the performance observed on individual datasets.

Table 4: Optimal performing MLM per class and dataset.

	Macro F1 Score												
	Abusive	Agressive	Hate	Identity Hate	Insult	Neither	Obscene	Offensive	Profane	Severe Toxic	Threat	Toxic	Best model
G^{SUD}	0.79	0.64	0.66	0.36	0.50	0.94	0.25	0.75	0.31	0.40	0.43	0.18	**BERT**
	0.80	0.64	0.66	0.38	0.51	0.94	0.34	0.75	0.33	0.42	0.46	0.20	**ELECTRA**
	0.80	0.67	0.68	0.42	0.50	0.94	0.25	0.75	0.37	0.42	0.46	0.17	**RoBERTa**
Davidson	–	–	0.46	–	–	0.90	–	0.94	–	–	–	–	ELECTRA
Founta	0.88	–	0.41	–	–	0.95	–	–	–	–	–	–	BERT
	0.88	–	0.42	–	–	0.95	–	–	–	–	–	–	ALBERT
	0.89	–	0.41	–	–	0.96	–	–	–	–	–	–	RoBERTa
Fox	–	–	0.60	–	–	0.79	–	–	–	–	–	–	RoBERTa
Gab	–	–	0.88	–	–	0.91	–	–	–	–	–	–	ALBERT
	–	–	0.89	–	–	0.91	–	–	–	–	–	–	RoBERTa
Grimminger	–	–	0.58	–	–	0.95	–	–	–	–	–	–	ELECTRA
HASOC2019	–	–	0.29	–	–	0.80	–	0.36	0.57	–	–	–	ELECTRA
HASOC2020	–	–	0.22	–	–	0.91	–	0.30	0.83	–	–	–	ELECTRA
Hateval	–	–	0.75	–	–	0.79	–	–	–	–	–	–	ELECTRA
	–	–	0.75	–	–	0.80	–	–	–	–	–	–	RoBERTa
Jigsaw	–	–	–	0.46	0.57	0.98	0.38	–	–	0.40	0.56	0.30	ELECTRA
Olid	–	–	–	–	–	0.85	–	0.67	–	–	–	–	BERT
	–	–	–	–	–	0.84	–	0.68	–	–	–	–	ELECTRA
Reddit	–	–	0.76	–	–	0.92	–	–	–	–	–	–	ALBERT
	–	–	0.76	–	–	0.92	–	–	–	–	–		RoBERTa
Stormfront	–	–	0.60	–	–	0.96	–	–	–	–	–	–	RoBERTa
Trac	–	0.81	–	–	–	0.71	–	–	–	–	–	–	BERT

5.2 Masked Language Models

We conduct an experimental evaluation of MLM models using $BERT_{BASE}$ (Devlin et al. 2019; Yuan and Rizoiu 2022), pre-trained on text tokenized with the WordPiece algorithm (Wu et al. 2016), and its variants: $ALBERT_{BASE}$ (Lan et al. 2019), $RoBERTa_{BASE}$ (Liu et al. 2019) and $ELECTRA_{BASE}$ (Clark et al. 2020). To perform SUD classification, we connect BERT's pooled output layers to a Multi-Layer Perceptron (MLP) architecture that contains 12 output neurons (one per class). We have fine-tuned the MLP layer of the proposed model on the G^{SUD} corpus, adopting a stratified sampling technique to keep the same class distribution throughout the three splits.

Table 4 reports the optimal performing model for each dataset. ELECTRA is shown to be the best performer in most of the corpora as it exhibits the highest Macro F1 score in eight datasets, including G^{SUD}. When comparing the performance of the BERT variants with that of the original BERT model, the results suggest a slightly higher ability of ELECTRA and RoBERTa to discriminate the SUD classes.

5.3 Causal Language Models

Following the methodological steps outlined in the previous section, we conducted fine-tuning on the pre-trained models Llama-2-7b (Touvron et al. 2023), Mistral-7B-v0.1 (Jiang et al. 2023), and mpt-7b (MosaicML NLP team 2023) using our datasets. The fine-tuning procedure employed the Parameter-Efficient Fine-Tuning (PEFT) method, where specific hyperparameters such as learning rates, batch sizes, and adapter weights were configured. Notably, we utilized the SFTTrainer class from the TRL library, designed for training LLMs. Additionally, we created custom prompts to input the categorization of text into the respective classes. For details on the hyperparameters and prompts used see our online repository (Niaouri et al. 2024).

In Table 5, we report the best-performing model for each dataset. The results indicate a notable advantage of the Mistral at a single dataset scale. The second-best performing model, Llama 2, showcases similar results but holds a significant advantage with an F1 score of 41% on the G^{SUD} dataset compared to Mistral's 26% showing that Llama 2 performs better on a larger scale.

Here, the results exhibit similar patterns to the ones observed for the previous models, where we obtain shaky classification results in the hate and offensive classes (majority classes) and low performances in the underrepresented SUD types (i.e., *severe toxic*, *threat*, and *toxic*).

Table 5: Optimal performing CLM per class and dataset.

	Macro F1 Score												
	Abusive	**Agressive**	**Hate**	**Identity Hate**	**Insult**	**Neither**	**Obscene**	**Offensive**	**Profane**	**Severe Toxic**	**Threat**	**Toxic**	**Best model**
G^{SUD}	0.76	0.63	0.30	0	0.48	0.84	0.13	0.32	0.13	0.32	0.36	0.23	**Llama-2-7**
Davidson	–	–	0.45	–	–	0.87	–	0.94	–	–	–	–	Mistral-7B-v0.1
Founta	0.89	–	0.42	–	–	0.91	–	–	–	–	–	–	Mistral-7B-v0.1
Fox	–	–	0.67	–	–	0.82	–	–	–	–	–	–	Mistral-7B-v0.1
Gab	–	–	0.88	–	–	0.89	–	–	–	–	–	–	Llama-2-7b
	–	–	0.89	–	–	0.90	–	–	–	–	–	–	Mistral-7B-v0.1
Grimminger	–	–	0.37	–	–	0.76	–	–	–	–	–	–	Mistral-7B-v0.1
HASOC2019	–	–	0.16	–	–	0.80	–	0.19	0.54	–	–	–	Llama-2-7b
HASOC2020	–	–	0.08	–	–	0.82	–	0.11	0.74	–	–	–	Llama-2-7b
Hateval	–	–	0.76	–	–	0.78	–	–	–	–	–	–	Mistral-7B-v0.1
Jigsaw	–	–	–	0.41	0.53	0.97	0.28	–	–	0.18	0.38	0.10	Llama-2-7b
Olid	–	–	–	–	–	0.85	–	0.64	–	–	–	–	Llama-2-7b
	–	–	–	–	–	0.83	–	0.66	–	–	–	–	mpt-7b
Reddit	–	–	0.77	–	–	0.92	–	–	–	–	–	–	Llama-2-7b
	–	–	0.78	–	–	0.93	–	–	–	–	–	–	Mistral-7B-v0.1
Stormfront	–	–	0.58	–	–	0.95	–	–	–	–	–	–	Llama-2-7b
	–	–	0.61	–	–	0.93	–	–	–	–	–	–	Mistral-7B-v0.1
Trac	–	0.84	–	–	–	0.71	–	–	–	–	–	–	Mistral-7B-v0.1

6 Model comparison and further analyses

In this section, we present the findings from our supplementary evaluations conducted on the optimal model within each model family for the G^{SUD} dataset. We conducted these new experiments in a more controlled environment that allowed us to empirically test our hypothesis on the causes behind the poor generalization performance we observed. We selected ELECTRA for the MLM family due to its superior performance not only on G^{SUD} but also across other datasets, alongside BERT and RoBERTa. For the CLMs, our choice was Llama 2, as it demonstrated a notably higher performance compared to Mistral on the G^{SUD} dataset. Regarding the SLMs, despite the higher performance of SVM on G^{SUD}, MLR was preferred due to enhanced scalability.

Table 6 contains the results for each of the different experimental setups, where we report the Macro F1 score of the SUD classification. Considering that G^{SUD} contains highly unbalanced classes, we repeated classification tasks after training our model on a balanced dataset. Given the dominance of *neither* class, we examined a setting with undersampled non-SUD text (neither class). Hence, we selected 10% of the non-SUD samples in a stratified way, maintaining the same proportion of the *neither* class samples in every dataset. We note that undersampling the *neither* class has a sensitive effect on the model prediction capability as the Macro F1 score increases in two out of three model families, with the most noteworthy improvement attested in the SLMs and a significant drop of performance for the CLMs.

Furthermore, we tested the binary classification scenario where models had to differentiate between SUD and non-SUD content, providing a balanced binary setup. To that extent, we performed random oversampling of minority classes as suggested by several works (Yuan and Rizoiu 2022; Swamy, Jamatia and Gambäck 2019; MacAvaney et al. 2019). In this scenario, we achieved a relatively high Macro F1 score (86%, 89%, and 88% for SLMs, MLMs and CLMs respectively) and a tiny improvement when classes were balanced (88%, 90%, and 90%). These outcomes underscore the model's capability to effectively distinguish the *neither* class from generic SUD in the broader contextual framework we built.

A substantial improvement is evident when exclusively assessing the model's performance in a dataset containing only the following classes: *hate*, *offensive*, *toxic*, and *neither*, whose instances are about 90% of the total G^{SUD}. Discriminating over such classes is challenging as they appear in multiple datasets with different annotation schemas.

By removing the *neither* class, and focusing solely on the three specified categories – hate, offensive, and toxic – we aimed to sharpen the analysis of the models' discriminatory power specifically within the SUD classes. This choice was made to assess whether the models could more effectively differentiate between the nuanced forms of harmful content. The results demonstrated a noteworthy enhancement, reaching a Macro F1 score of 81%, 85%, and 59%, respectively. This rise in performance for the SLMs and MLMs implies that the models can generalize better when the neutral category is absent. Such a scenario indicates a sensitive decrease in false dismissals on the positive SUD classes due to the absence of the neutral class. Conversely, this pattern is not observed within the CLM family, suggesting that the efficacy of Llama 2 is contingent upon the prevalence of the neither class in substantial proportions, as also shown in cases where neither was undersampled.

7 Multi-source learning

In this part, we present the result of our test around the models' capability to learn knowledge from different sources whose labels belong to different annotation schemas. We recall that our main research questions are: Which is the SOTA model generalization capability in a global context, where the models are trained on a general dataset and tested on individual datasets that share some of its classes? What are the main challenges hampering the SUD modeling effectiveness, and how do the different model families perform in a multi-class vs a binary setup? We present the results of our evaluation hereafter.

Table 6: Comparison between all experiments.

	F1 Score		
	SLMs - MLR	**MLMs ELECTRA**	**CLMs Llama-2-7**
Training set	Macro	Macro	Macro
G^{SUD}	0.41	**0.54**	0.41
G^{SUD} with Neither Undersampled	**0.76**	0.60	0.23
G^{SUD} (Binary classification)	0.86	**0.89**	0.88
G^{SUD} balanced (Binary classification)	0.88	**0.90**	**0.90**
G^{SUD} (*hate, offensive, toxic, neither*)	0.63	**0.69**	0.63
G^{SUD} (*hate, offensive, toxic*)	0.81	**0.85**	0.59

Table 7: Multi-class SUD classification results (F1 score) with the model trained on GSUD vs on each individual dataset.

	Macro F1 Score (%)					
	Multi-class SUD Classification					
	SLMs - MLR		MLMs - ELECTRA		CLMs - Llama-2-7	
Dataset	**Classified in G^{SUD}**	**Individual**	**Classified in G^{SUD}**	**Individual**	**Classified in G^{SUD}**	**Individual**
G^{SUD}	0.41	–	0.53	–	0.41	–
Davidson	0.07	0.70	**0.79**	0.77	0.50	0.73
Founta	0.43	0.74	**0.79**	0.73	0.55	0.74
Fox	0.35	0.70	**0.59**	0.56	0.55	0.65
Gab	0.08	0.89	**0.92**	0.89	0.72	0.89
Grimminger	0.44	0.50	0.72	0.76	**0.57**	0.52
HASOC2019	0.24	0.40	0.45	0.51	**0.44**	0.42
HASOC2020	0.28	0.53	0.54	0.57	0.37	0.44
Hateval	0.51	0.71	0.75	0.78	0.60	0.75
Jigsaw	0.02	0.41	**0.57**	0.52	0.29	0.41
Olid	0.23	0.72	0.74	0.76	0.44	0.75
Reddit	0.09	0.83	**0.85**	0.82	0.71	0.85
Stormfront	0.47	0.68	**0.87**	0.75	0.60	0.77
Trac	0.26	0.69	**0.86**	0.75	0.57	0.76

7.1 Multi-source learning in multi-class SUD classification

In Table 7, we depict the classification results obtained for each dataset by models trained on the (large-scale) G^{SUD} corpus compared to the models trained in each dataset.

We note that, almost exclusively in the MLM family and in ~50% of the cases (highlighted in bold), the model trained on G^{SUD} is slightly better than the special-ized counterpart. This outcome allows us to conclude that leveraging more knowl-edge from multiple domains has several advantages despite different dataset incongruences observed in the previous experiments.

Table 8: Binary SUD classification with the models trained in GSUD.

	Macro F1 Score (%)		
	Binary SUD Classification – Classified in G^{SUD}		
Dataset	**SLMs-LR**	**MLMs - ELECTRA**	**CLMs - Llama-2-7**
G^{SUD}	0.86	**0.89**	0.88
Davidson	0.06	**0.96**	0.79
Founta	0.15	**0.95**	0.86
Fox	0.51	**0.79**	0.49
Gab	0.15	**0.89**	0.78
Grimminger	0.60	**0.85**	0.58
HASOC2019	0.58	**0.82**	0.53
HASOC2020	0.82	**0.95**	0.78
Hateval	0.66	**0.79**	0.59
Jigsaw	0.06	**0.93**	0.74
Olid	0.22	**0.87**	0.62
Reddit	0.19	**0.81**	0.74
Stormfront	0.67	**0.86**	0.64
Trac	0.35	**0.88**	0.38

7.2 Multi-source learning in binary SUD classification

For each of the experiments reported in this section, we have also tested the capability of the models to discriminate SUD and non-SUD text in G^{SUD} (depicted in Table 8).

Here, we obtain a relatively high Macro F1 score (~90%) under the G^{SUD} condition, noticing that the models discriminate well the *neither* class from the generic SUD in the global context we built. Such results confirm the current trend observed in the ML literature so far (e.g., Swamy et al. 2019; Antypas and Camacho-Collados 2023). Concerning the generalization capabilities of the models, the MLM family seems to be the best-performing one, followed by the CLMs. However, the generalization capability of the SLM models is low, as seen from the performances attested for each of the individual datasets.

8 Model explainability

Here, we focus on the most effective model family, namely the MLMs. We aim to explain several aspects regarding the performance of ELECTRA, examining the relationship between the model's capability to distinguish SUD classes and the impact of balanced datasets on classification performance. To clarify the discriminative capacity of the adopted model across SUD classes, we employ a visualization technique on the generated text representation, specifically on ELECTRA's pooled output layer. We reduce the output dimensionality (2 dimensions) using t-distributed Stochastic Neighbor Embedding (t-SNE). The resulting plot, as shown in Figure 2, illustrates the outcomes of the test set under two distinct training scenarios: (a) the model trained on the complete G^{SUD} corpus, and (b) the model trained on the G^{SUD} with the *neither* class being undersampled.

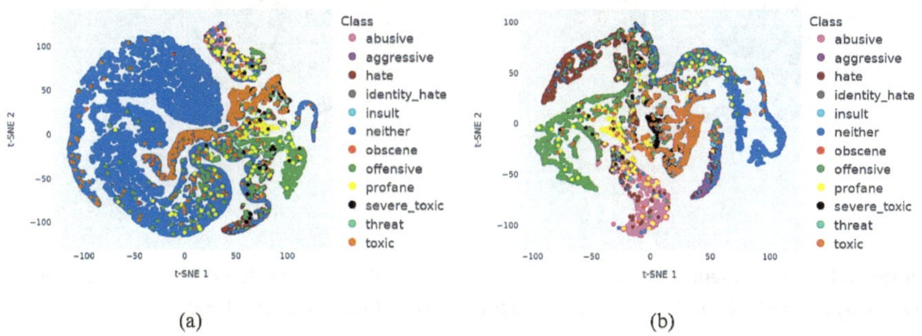

Figure 2: Two dimensional t-SNE visualization of sample embedding produced by ELECTRA's pooled output layer: (a) G^{SUD} (b) G^{SUD} with neither undersampled.

Observations from Figure 2(a) reveal that certain classes, such as *abusive* (top-right) and toxic (center-right), form distinct clusters, indicating a clear separation in the data. This behavior reflects the exclusive occurrence of these classes in the individual datasets, as evidenced in Table 4. Conversely, classes like *profane*, *obscene*, *threat*, and *severe toxic*, are distributed throughout the plot and are not easily distinguishable. Overall, we note that low performances are observed not only in classes with minimal training samples but also in those sharing samples from multiple corpora, indicating the presence of heterogeneous intraclass samples. The *hate* class represents a notable example, encompassing samples from ten datasets (out of thirteen).

In Figure 2(b), where *neither* class is undersampled, we observe a notable enhancement in clustering quality. This is evidenced by the improved performance in F1 score, as illustrated in Table 6, highlighting the model's more accurate classification under balanced conditions. Notably, the clusters representing the *abusive* and *aggressive* classes are easily distinguishable, further confirming that the model can more accurately classify classes originating from a single dataset. Next, we observe that the classes for *hate*, *offensive*, and *toxic* content also form distinct clusters, although some outliers are still present. Finally, the categories of *profane*, *severe toxic*, *threat*, *insult*, and *obscene* content remain more scattered.

In Figure 3, we visualize the embeddings produced by models trained on (a) G^{SUD} with *hate*, *offensive*, *toxic*, and *neither* classes and (b) G^{SUD} with *hate*, *offensive*, and *toxic* classes excluding the *neither* class.

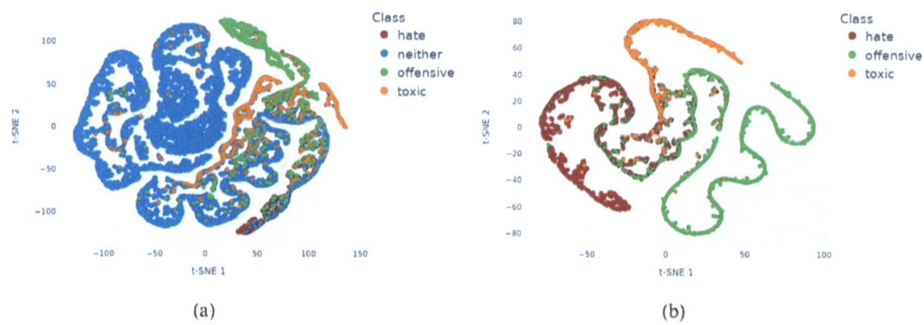

Figure 3: Two components t-SNE visualization of samples embedding produced by ELECTRA's pooled output layer: (a) G^{SUD} (hate, offensive, toxic, neither), (b) G^{SUD} (hate, offensive, toxic).

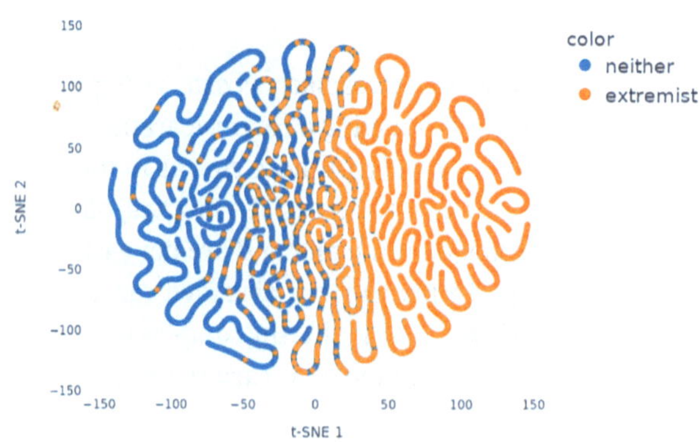

Figure 4: Two components t-SNE visualization of samples embedding produced by ELECTRA's pooled output layer: Binary Classification.

Figure 3(a) validates the hypothesis that a less overlapping annotation schema yields more promising results and better-defined clusters. Figure 3(b) demonstrates the model's ability to differentiate SUD classes even when *neither* class is absent, confirming its crucial (negative) role in the multi-class model fine-tuning.

Finally, in Figure 4, we present the binary classification case, emphasizing the high discriminative power of ELECTRA, which in this problem setting (simpler than multi-class) can separate the search space with high accuracy.

9 Discussion

Our study delves into assessing the effectiveness of three distinct categories of language models, namely Shallow Learning Models (SLMs), Masked Language Models (MLMs), and Causal Language Models (CLMs), in classifying SUD. Within the SLMs, MLR consistently demonstrated the best performance. Among the MLMs, ELECTRA exhibited superior efficacy, while within the CLM family, Mistral showed its superiority in individual datasets but fell short in the G^{SUD} dataset. Balanced dataset configurations and binary classification scenarios enhanced model performance, underscoring the significance of clearly defined class boundaries and balanced training data. This result is expected, given that various studies have highlighted the advantages of balanced datasets in hate speech classification (Qureshi and Sabih 2021) and the improved performance of models in binary rather than multi-class settings (Bouazizi et al. 2016). Our findings further suggest that inadequate training samples and intraclass variability – where a class encompasses a diverse range of samples from multiple sources – can negatively impact model performance. Current SOTA models for SUD classification require consistent dataset annotations and homogeneous samples to optimize classification performance.

Another significant finding from our study, which focused on large-scale multi-source learning, is that MLMs displayed superior generalization capabilities compared to the other two model families followed by the CLMs that demonstrated comparable performances yet exhibited difficulties in the experimental conditions where the *neither* class was either undersampled or absent.

The superiority of MLMs in SUD classification stems from their bidirectional context awareness, as at the training stage, they consider both preceding and following tokens. This characteristic has consistently led to better performance in comparison to Shallow Learning approaches, as demonstrated by models like BERT, RoBERTa, and ALBERT (Swamy, Jamatia and Gambäck 2019; Markov and Daelemans 2021; Fortuna, Soler-Company and Wanner 2021). Notably, ELECTRA stands out in G^{SUD} and individual datasets due to its distinctive architecture, which involves training a generator whose task is to replace sentence tokens and a discriminator that learns to identify the replaced token. Several studies have highlighted ELECTRA's efficacy in various classification and sentiment analysis tasks, and its performances often remain closely aligned with other BERT variants (Guven 2021; Pedersen et al. 2022; Kowsher 2023). While ELECTRA offers certain advantages, the overall effectiveness of MLMs is robust across different architectures. Another advantage of the MLM model family is the significantly faster learning task concerning CLMs. In our case, on the G^{SUD} dataset, CLMs required up to a week to complete tasks, whereas the slower MLM learning process took less than 24 hours. We observe a similar trend in smaller datasets, where MLMs completed tasks in a few hours, while CLMs took several days. Among all model families, SLMs generally exhibited the fastest running time, except for the SVM model.

10 Conclusion and future work

In this work, we present an empirical evaluation of automatic SUD detection using a variety of models constructing a comprehensive framework of SOTA solutions for SUD classification. To test generalization capability, we considered a large and heterogeneous context in which we obtained varying results, not always in line with the expected performance of the model trained at the local level, i.e., on every individual corpus. In this sense, we argue that to build more general and reliable models, the ML community should consider formal guidelines provided by language experts (mostly neglected so far), which can sensibly reduce local bias (e.g., annotation policy, context, etc.).

For future work, we plan to closely analyze the inter-domain mismatches we observe at the class sample level. Such effort would be beneficial to understand how to improve textual feature learning and to communicate requirements and expectations from the annotation task. We additionally highlight the significant potential of our findings for researchers in linguistics, discourse analysis, and semantics as they show, from a knowledge base constituted by the main works on SUD corpora, the semantic links and conceptual relationships between several labels or tags. In fact, over and above terminology, it is crucial to clearly state and understand the specific features of hate speech, offensive speech, or extremist speech. These initial results are necessary to foster several research discussions in the Horizon Europe ARENAS project into which this work integrates. Finally, the explicability of these categories and the classification provided by Artificial Intelligence is central to future research. Making transparent outcomes will enable us to propose valuable results for all those involved in hate speech and extremism analysis. In the context of a multidisciplinary project like ARENAS, which brings together scientists with different backgrounds (i.e., linguists, political scientists, etc.) and targets a heterogeneous audience, such as lawyers and journalists, the clarity of descriptors and their ability to be understood by different stakeholders, is an essential element.

Acknowledgments

The work presented in this paper is part of the ARENAS project. This project has received funding from the European Union's Horizon Europe research and innovation programme under grant agreement No:101094731.

This work was granted access to the HPC resources of IDRIS under the allocation 2024-AD010615085R1 made by GENCI.

References

Antypas, Dimosthenis & Jose Camacho-Collados. 2023. Robust hate speech detection in social media: A cross-dataset empirical evaluation. *The 7th Workshop on Online Abuse and Harms (WOAH).* Association for Computational Linguistics. https://doi.org/10.18653/v1/2023.woah-1.25.

Alkomah, Fatimah & Xiaogang Ma. 2022. A literature review of textual hate speech detection methods and datasets. *Information* 13 (6). 273. https://doi.org/10.3390/info13060273.

Aroyehun, Segun Taofeek, & Alexander Gelbukh. 2018. Aggression detection in social media: Using deep neural networks, data augmentation, and pseudo labeling. *TRAC@COLING 2018*. https://aclanthology.org/W18-4411 (last accessed 14 February 2025).

Ascone, Laura, & Julien Longhi. 2018. The expression of threat in jihadist propaganda. *Fragmentum* 50. 85. https://doi.org/10.5902/2179219428823.

Badjatiya, Pinkesh, Manish Gupta & Vasudeva Varma. 2019. Stereotypical bias removal for hate Speech detection task using knowledge-based generalizations. *The World Wide Web Conference*. https://doi.org/10.1145/3308558.3313504.

Badjatiya, Pinkesh, Shashank Gupta, Manish Gupta & Vasudeva Varma. 2017. Deep learning for hate speech detection in Tweets. *Proceedings of the 26th International Conference on World Wide Web Companion*. https://doi.org/10.1145/3041021.3054223.

Basile, Valerio, Cristina Bosco, Elisabetta Fersini, Debora Nozza, Viviana Patti, Francisco Manuel Rangel Pardo, Paolo Rosso & Manuela Sanguinetti. 2019. SemEval-2019 Task 5: Multilingual detection of hate pseech against immigrants and women in Twitter. *International Workshop on Semantic Evaluation*. https://doi.org/10.18653/v1/s19-2007.

Bouazizi, Mondher & Tomoaki Ohtsuki. 2016. Sentiment analysis: From binary to multi-class classification: A pattern-based approach for multi-class sentiment analysis in Twitter. *2016 IEEE International Conference on Communications (ICC)*. https://doi.org/10.1109/icc.2016.7511392.

Breiman, Leo. 2001. Random forests. *Machine Learning* 45 (1). 5–32. https://doi.org/10.1023/a:1010933404324.

Clark, Kevin, Minh-Thang Luong, Quoc Le V & Christopher D. Manning. 2020. ELECTRA: Pre-training text encoders as discriminators rather than generators. *arXiv (Cornell University)*. https://doi.org/10.48550/arxiv.2003.10555.

Conneau, Alexis, Kartikay Khandelwal, Naman Goyal, Vishrav Chaudhary, Guillaume Wenzek, Francisco Guzmán, Edouard Grave, Myle Ott, Luke Zettlemoyer & Veselin Stoyanov. 2020. Unsupervised cross-lingual representation learning at scale. *Annual Meeting of the Association for Computational Linguistics*. https://doi.org/10.18653/v1/2020.acl-main.747.

Davidson, Thomas, Dana Warmsley, Michael Macy & Ingmar Weber. 2017. Automated hate speech detection and the problem of offensive language. *Proceedings of the International AAAI Conference on Web and Social Media* 11 (1). 512–515. https://doi.org/10.1609/icwsm.v11i1.14955.

Davidson, Thomas, Debasmita Bhattacharya & Ingmar Weber. 2019. Racial bias in hate speech and abusive language detection datasets. *Proceedings of the Third Workshop on Abusive Language Online*. https://doi.org/10.18653/v1/w19-3504.

De Giorgio, Andrea, Goran Kuvačić, Dražen Maleš, Ignazio Vecchio, Cristina Tornali, Wadih Ishac, Tiziana Ramaci, Massimiliano Barattucci & Boris Milavić. 2022. Willingness to receive COVID-19 booster vaccine: Associations between green-pass, social media information, anti-vax beliefs, and emotional bBalance. *Vaccines* 10 (3). 481. https://doi.org/10.3390/vaccines10030481.

De Gibert, Ona, Naiara Perez, Aitor García-Pablos & Montse Cuadros. 2018. Hate speech dataset from a white supremacy forum. *ArXiv, Abs/1809.04444*. https://doi.org/10.18653/v1/w18-5102.

Devlin, Jacob, Ming-Wei Chang, Kenton Lee & Kristina Toutanova. 2019. BERT: Pre-training of deep bidirectional transformers for language understanding. *North American Chapter of the Association for Computational Linguistics*. https://doi.org/10.18653/v1/n19-1423.

Fišer, Darja, Tomaž Erjavec & Nikola Ljubešić. 2017. Legal framework, dataset and annotation schema for socially unacceptable online discourse practices in Slovene. *ALW@ACL*. https://doi.org/10.18653/v1/w17-3007.

Fortuna, Paula, Juan Soler-Company & Leo Wanner. 2021. How well do hate speech, toxicity, abusive and offensive language classification models generalize across datasets? *Information Processing & Management* 58 (3). 102524. https://doi.org/10.1016/j.ipm.2021.102524.

Founta, Antigoni, Constantinos Djouvas, Despoina Chatzakou, Ilias Leontiadis, Jeremy Blackburn, Gianluca Stringhini, Athena Vakali, Michael Sirivianos & Nicolas Kourtellis. 2018. Large scale crowdsourcing and characterization of Twitter abusive behavior. *Proceedings of the International AAAI Conference on Web and Social Media* 12 (1). https://doi.org/10.1609/icwsm.v12i1.14991.

Friedman, Jerome H. 2001. Greedy function approximation: A gradient boosting machine. *The Annals of Statistics* 29 (5). https://doi.org/10.1214/aos/1013203451.

Gandhi, Ankita, Param Ahir, Kinjal Adhvaryu, Pooja Shah, Ritika Lohiya, Erik Cambria, Soujanya Poria & Amir Hussain. 2024. Hate speech detection: A comprehensive review of recent works. *Expert Systems* 41 (8). https://doi.org/10.1111/exsy.13562.

Gao, Lei & Ruihong Huang. 2017. Detecting online hate speech using context aware models. *ArXiv, Abs/1710.07395*. https://doi.org/10.26615/978-954-452-049-6_036.

Grimminger, Lara & Roman Klinger. 2021. Hate towards the political opponent: A Twitter Corpus study of the 2020 US elections on the basis of offensive speech and stance Detection. *arXiv (Cornell University)*. https://doi.org/10.48550/arxiv.2103.01664.

Gröndahl, Tommi, Luca Pajola, Mika Juuti, Mauro Conti & N. Asokan. 2018. All you need is "love." *Proceedings of the 11th ACM Workshop on Artificial Intelligence and Security*. https://doi.org/10.1145/3270101.3270103.

Guven, Zekeriya Anil. 2021. The effect of BERT, ELECTRA and ALBERT language models on sentiment analysis for Turkish product reviews. *2021 6th International Conference on Computer Science and Engineering (UBMK)*. https://doi.org/10.1109/ubmk52708.2021.9559007.
Hearst, M.A., S.T. Dumais, E. Osuna, J. Platt & B. Scholkopf. 1998. Support vector machines. *IEEE Intelligent Systems and Their Applications* 13 (4). 18–28. https://doi.org/10.1109/5254.708428.
Janiesch, Christian, Patrick Zschech & Kai Heinrich. 2021. Machine learning and deep learning. *Electronic Markets* 31 (3). 685–695. https://doi.org/10.1007/s12525-021-00475-2.
Jasser, Greta, Jordan McSwiney, Ed Pertwee & Savvas Zannettou. 2021. 'Welcome to #GabFam': Far-right virtual community on Gab. *New Media & Society* 25 (7). 1728–1745. https://doi.org/10.1177/14614448211024546.
Jiang, Albert Q., Alexandre Sablayrolles, Arthur Mensch, Chris Bamford, Devendra Singh Chaplot, Diego De Las Casas, Florian Bressand, et al. 2023. Mistral 7B. *arXiv (Cornell University)*. https://doi.org/10.48550/arxiv.2310.06825.
Karan, Mladen & Jan Šnajder. 2018. Cross-Domain Detection of Abusive Language Online. *Workshop on Abusive Language Online*. https://doi.org/10.18653/v1/w18-5117.
Kibriya, Ashraf M., Eibe Frank, Bernhard Pfahringer & Geoffrey Holmes. 2004. Multinomial naive bayes for text categorization revisited. *In Lecture notes in computer science* 488–499. https://doi.org/10.1007/978-3-540-30549-1_43.
Kowsher, Md. 2023. Analyzing the impact of transfer learning from pretrained transformers on text classification: A cross-model study. *ResearchGate*. https://doi.org/10.13140/RG.2.2.29289.26729/1.
Kumar, Ritesh, Aishwarya N. Reganti, Akshit Bhatia & Tushar Maheshwari. 2018. Aggression-annotated corpus of Hindi-English code-mixed data. *ACL Anthology*. https://aclanthology.org/L18-1226/ (last accessed 14 February 2025).
Lan, Zhenzhong, Mingda Chen, Sebastian Goodman, Kevin Gimpel, Piyush Sharma & Radu Soricut. 2019. ALBERT: A lite BERT for self-supervised learning of language representations. *arXiv.org*. http://www.arxiv.org/abs/1909.11942 (last accessed 14 February 2025).
Liu, Yinhan, Myle Ott, Naman Goyal, Jingfei Du, Mandar Joshi, Danqi Chen, Omer Levy, Mike Lewis, Luke Zettlemoyer & Veselin Stoyanov. 2019. ROBERTA: A robustly optimized BERT pretraining approach. *arXiv (Cornell University)*. https://doi.org/10.48550/arxiv.1907.11692.
MacAvaney, Sean, Hao-Ren Yao, Eugene Yang, Katina Russell, Nazli Goharian & Ophir Frieder. 2019. Hate speech detection: Challenges and solutions. *PLoS ONE* 14 (8). e0221152. https://doi.org/10.1371/journal.pone.0221152.
Mandl, Thomas, Sandip Modha, Anand Kumar M & Bharathi Raja Chakravarthi. 2020. Overview of the HASOC track at FIRE 2020: Hate speech and offensive language identification in Tamil, Malayalam, Hindi, English and German. *Forum for Information Retrieval Evaluation*. https://doi.org/10.1145/3441501.3441517.
Markov, Ilia & Walter Daelemans. 2021. Improving cross-domain hate speech detection by reducing the false positive rate. *Proceedings of the Fourth Workshop on NLP for Internet Freedom: Censorship, Disinformation, and Propaganda*. https://doi.org/10.18653/v1/2021.nlp4if-1.3.
Modha, Sandip, Thomas Mandl, Prasenjit Majumder, Daksh Patel. 2019. Overview of the HASOC track at FIRE 2019: Hate Speech and Offensive Content Identification in Indo-European Languages. *Conference-proceeding*. https://ceur-ws.org/Vol-2517/T3-1.pdf (last accessed 14 February 2025).
MosaicML NLP Team. 2023. Introducing MPT-7B: A new standard for open-source, commercially usable LLMs. *Databricks*. https://www.databricks.com/blog/mpt-7b.
Neyshabur, Behnam, Hanie Sedghi & Chiyuan Zhang. 2020. What is being transferred in transfer learning? *arXiv (Cornell University)*. https://doi.org/10.48550/arxiv.2008.11687.

Niaouri Dimitra, Bruno Machado Carneiro, Michele Linardi, and Julien Longhi (2024). Machine _ learning_heading_to_SUD. https://github.com/diniaouri/Machine_Learning_heading_to_SUD (last accessed 14 February 2025).

Pamungkas, Endang Wahyu & Viviana Patti. 2019. Cross-domain and cross-lingual abusive language detection: A hybrid approach with deep learning and a multilingual lexicon. *Annual Meeting of the Association for Computational Linguistics*. https://doi.org/10.18653/v1/p19-2051.

Pahor De Maiti, Kristina, Darja Fišer, Nikola Ljubešić, Tomaž Erjavec. 2020. Grammatical footprint of socially unacceptable Facebook comments. Journal-article. *FRENK Corpus*. http://nl.ijs.si/jtdh20/pdf/JT-DH_2020_PahordeMaiti-et-al_Grammatical-Footprint-of-Socially-Unacceptable-Facebook-Comments.pdf (last accessed 14 February 2025).

Pedersen, Jannik S., Martin S. Laursen, Cristina Soguero-Ruiz, Thiusius R. Savarimuthu, Rasmus Sogaard Hansen & Pernille J. Vinholt. 2022. Domain over size: Clinical ELECTRA surpasses general BERT for bleeding site classification in the free text of electronic health records. *2022 IEEE-EMBS International Conference on Biomedical and Health Informatics (BHI)*. https://doi.org/10.1109/bhi56158.2022.9926955.

Piot, Paloma, Patricia Martín-Rodilla & Javier Parapar. 2024. MetaHate: A dataset for unifying efforts on hate speech detection. *arXiv (Cornell University)*. https://doi.org/10.48550/arxiv.2401.06526.

Poletto, Fabio, Valerio Basile, Manuela Sanguinetti, Cristina Bosco & Viviana Patti. 2020. Resources and benchmark corpora for hate speech detection: A systematic review. *Language Resources and Evaluation* 55 (2). 477–523. https://doi.org/10.1007/s10579-020-09502-8.

Postigo-Fuentes, Ana Yara, Rolf Kailuweit, Alexander Ziem, Stefan Hartmann. 2024. Defining extremist narratives: A review of the current state of the art. In *HORIZON – CL2-2022-DEMOCRACY -01-05* [Report]. Momentum Consulting. https://arenasproject.eu/download/1545/?tmstv=1721660114 (last accessed 14 February 2025).

Qian, Jing, Anna Bethke, Yinyin Liu, Elizabeth Belding & William Yang Wang. 2019. A benchmark dataset for learning to intervene in online hate speech. *Conference on Empirical Methods in Natural Language Processing*. https://doi.org/10.18653/v1/d19-1482.

Qureshi, Khubaib Ahmed & Muhammad Sabih. 2021. Un-compromised credibility: Social media based multi-class hate speech classification for text. *IEEE Access* 9. 109465–109477. https://doi.org/10.1109/access.2021.3101977.

Röttger, Paul, Bertie Vidgen, Dong Nguyen, Zeerak Waseem, Helen Margetts & Janet Pierrehumbert. 2021. HateCheck: Functional tests for hate speech detection models. *arXiv Preprint arXiv:2012.15606*. https://doi.org/10.18653/v1/2021.acl-long.4.

Roy, Sayar Ghosh, Ujwal Narayan, Tathagata Raha, Zubair Abid & Vasudeva Varma. 2021. Leveraging multilingual transformers for hate speech detection. *arXiv (Cornell University)*. https://doi.org/10.48550/arxiv.2101.03207.

Salminen, Joni, Maximilian Hopf, Shammur A. Chowdhury, Soon-Gyo Jung, Hind Almerekhi & Bernard J. Jansen. 2020. Developing an online hate classifier for multiple social media platforms. *Human-centric Computing and Information Sciences* 10 (1). https://doi.org/10.1186/s13673-019-0205-6.

Sulc, Ajda & Kristina Pahor De Maiti. 2020. No room for hate: What research about hate speech taught us about collaboration? https://www.semanticscholar.org/paper/No-room-for-hate%3A-What-research-about-hate-speech-Sulc-Maiti/b04049a663c7c91dc87a16d4a179073861978798 (last accessed 14 February 2025).

Swamy, Steve Durairaj, Anupam Jamatia & Björn Gambäck. 2019. Studying generalisability across abusive language detection datasets. *Proceedings of the 23rd Conference on Computational Natural Language Learning (CoNLL)*. https://doi.org/10.18653/v1/k19-1088.

Toraman, Cagri, Furkan Şahinuç & Eyup Halit Yılmaz. 2022. Large-scale hate speech detection with cross-domain transfer. *arXiv (Cornell University).* https://doi.org/10.48550/arxiv.2203.01111.

Touvron, Hugo, Thibaut Lavril, Gautier Izacard, Xavier Martinet, Marie-Anne Lachaux, Timothée Lacroix, Baptiste Rozière, et al. 2023. LLAMA: Open and efficient foundation language models. *arXiv (Cornell University).* https://doi.org/10.48550/arxiv.2302.13971.

Van Aken, Betty, Julian Risch, Ralf Krestel & Alexander Löser. 2018. Challenges for toxic comment classification: An in-depth error analysis. *ArXiv, Abs/1809.07572.* https://doi.org/10.18653/v1/w18-5105.

Wang, Bin, Yunxia Ding, Shengyan Liu & Xiaobing Zhou. 2019. YNU_Wb at HASOC 2019: Ordered neurons LSTM with attention for identifying hate speech and offensive language. https://www.semanticscholar.org/paper/YNU_Wb-at-HASOC-2019%3A-Ordered-Neurons-LSTM-with-for-Wang-Ding/421b9e3f18202b757f0de42ca4a1d2de7dbe29ba (last accessed 14 February 2025).

Wright, Raymond E. 1995. Logistic regression. In L. G. Grimm & P. R. Yarnold (eds.), Reading and understanding multivariate statistics. 217–244. *American Psychological Association.* https://www.scirp.org/reference/referencespapers?referenceid=3007390 (last accessed 14 February 2025).

Wu, Yonghui, Mike Schuster, Zhifeng Chen, Quoc V. Le, Mohammad Norouzi, Wolfgang Macherey, Maxim Krikun, et al. 2016. Google's neural machine translation system: Bridging the gap between human and machine translation. *arXiv (Cornell University).* https://doi.org/10.48550/arxiv.1609.08144.

Xu, Yayin, Ying Zhou, Przemyslaw Sekula & Lieyun Ding. 2021. Machine learning in construction: From shallow to deep learning. *Developments in the Built Environment* 6. 100045. https://doi.org/10.1016/j.dibe.2021.100045.

Yigezu, M., O. Kolesnikova, G. Sidorov & A. Gelbukh. 2023. Transformer-Based hate speech detection for multi-class and multi-label classification. *IberLEF@SEPLN.* https://www.semanticscholar.org/paper/Transformer-Based-Hate-Speech-Detection-for-and-Yigezu-Kolesnikova/165e336c9c6780fad66a68b7be938593b4221149 (last accessed 14 February 2025).

Yin, Wenjie & Arkaitz Zubiaga. 2021. Towards generalisable hate speech detection: A review on obstacles and solutions. *PeerJ Computer Science* 7. e598. https://doi.org/10.7717/peerj-cs.598.

Yu, Zehui, Indira Sen, Dennis Assenmacher, Mattia Samory, Leon Fröhling, Christina Dahn, Debora Nozza & Claudia Wagner. 2024. The unseen targets of hate: A systematic review of hateful communication datasets. *Social Science Computer Review.* https://doi.org/10.1177/08944393241258771.

Yuan, Lanqin & Marian-Andrei Rizoiu. 2022. Detect hate speech in unseen domains using multi-task learning: A case study of political public figures. *arXiv (Cornell University).* https://doi.org/10.48550/arxiv.2208.10598.

Yuan, Lanqin, Tianyu Wang, Gabriela Ferraro, Hanna Suominen & Marian-Andrei Rizoiu. 2023. Transfer learning for hate speech detection in social media. *Journal of Computational Social Science* 6 (2). 1081–1101. https://doi.org/10.1007/s42001-023-00224-9.

Zampieri, Marcos, Shervin Malmasi, Preslav Nakov, Sara Rosenthal, Noura Farra & Ritesh Kumar. 2019. Predicting the type and target of offensive posts in social media. *North American Chapter of the Association for Computational Linguistics.* https://doi.org/10.18653/v1/n19-1144.

Steven Coats

An automatic pipeline for processing streamed content: New horizons for corpus linguistics and phonetics

Abstract: Large volumes of audio and video data are accessible through video sharing sites, streaming services, and social media platforms, but until recently, relatively little of this content has been utilized as research data for large-scale studies of grammatical or phonetic variation. This chapter discusses a notebook-based pipeline designed to analyze phonetic data from online video content, made possible by recent advances in language technology such as improvements in automatic speech recognition and forced alignment. It provides an overview of open-source frameworks for working with speech data, noting that while several tools have been developed to handle some or all of these tasks, their installation and setup may be complex and incompatibility issues may arise. Notebook-based pipelines, increasingly used in all fields of data science, offer the advantages of flexibility and adaptability. In this chapter, we introduce the Video Phonetics Pipeline (ViPP) for the extraction and analysis of audio and transcript data from video and streaming sites such as YouTube, 𝕏, TikTok, and many others, a pipeline which leverages functions from the open-source Python library yt-dlp to retrieve data, then utilizes the Montreal Forced Aligner to align audio with text. Formants are measured with Praat-Parselmouth, and packages from Python's standard library can be used for statistical analysis and visualization. The script pipeline, available as a notebook at GitHub and in a Google Colab environment, is customizable. The utility of the pipeline is demonstrated with an example: a consideration of diphthong trajectories in contemporary North American English, based on data from the Corpus of North American Spoken English (CoNASE).

Keywords: Corpus linguistics, phonetics, vowels, formants, YouTube, DASH, CoNASE, forced alignment, World Englishes

Steven Coats, University of Oulu, Finland, e-mail: steven.coats@oulu.fi

https://doi.org/10.1515/9783111434018-011

1 Introduction

The creation of speech corpora has traditionally required significant expenditure in terms of person-hours and resources, comprising collection of audio data in the form of targeted individual recordings, often in different locations, and time-consuming manual transcription of those recordings. In the past 15 years, however, it has become increasingly feasible to collect high-quality naturalistic speech data from online sources, and advances in automatic speech recognition (ASR) algorithms have greatly facilitated the preparation of orthographic transcripts, developments which are ongoing and are expected to contribute to the burgeoning field of corpus phonetics (Liberman 2019).[1]

These new perspectives make it possible to analyze linguistic variation by using automated scripting pipelines which collect, transcribe, process, and analyze speech produced in different locations, interaction contexts, or by different social groups. Compared to traditional speech corpora, much larger volumes of data can be collected, potentially enabling analysis of constructions that are rare in spoken language. Online collection and processing of speech data via pipelines is also facilitated by changes in the way people communicate: In the past 15 years, there has been an explosion in the online availability of video content, a shift which reflects the increased use of video sharing and streaming in computer-mediated communication (CMC) environments and on social media platforms. While traditional CMC formats such as mailing lists, discussion forums, and chat rooms still exist, they now typically also can include multimedia content such as embedded videos or sound files. These changes in online communication behavior are concomitant with and ultimately result from advances in the underlying communication technologies: increases in bandwidth availability and data transmission capabilities, increases in processing speed and memory which allow large files such as videos to be efficiently processed, larger storage capacities on servers, standardization of audio and video codecs, and standardization of technical protocols for video streaming under variable bandwidth conditions. Multimedia content, or simultaneous use of text, speech, and video, is the default communicative setting for CMC on popular platforms such as YouTube, Facebook, Twitch, or TikTok, whether as live streams or as recorded videos.

As of early 2024, much video content is shared using one of two transmission protocols: DASH (Dynamic Adaptive Streaming over HTTP; Sodagar 2011) and HLS (HTTP Live Streaming). These standards serve content as sequentially ordered data chunks via automatically generated URLs; the chunks are consumed by the

1 This chapter is a revised and expanded version of Coats (2023c).

end-user's browser and processed as they arrive. Depending on bandwidth availability, the protocol will serve lower-quality (i.e., requiring less data) or higher-quality (i.e., requiring more data) video and audio to the browser. Textual content such as concurrent chat interaction or comments require less bandwidth; these are also served to the end user via DASH and HLS.

From the perspective of linguistic research, the standardization of these protocols and their widespread use mean that the data is available for harvesting and analysis for anyone with an internet connection. Depending on the configuration of the processing pipeline and the individual components that are included, the researcher has access not only to audio data for phonetic analysis, but also to various ASR or manually generated transcripts, as well as to video content.[2] Transcripts can be analyzed in terms of lexis, grammar, syntax, and discourse content, for example for sociolinguistic or geolinguistic/dialectological studies, and acoustic properties of the audio can be analyzed for vowel quality and quantity, pitch, prominence, or other phonetic and prosodic phenomena. The automated analysis of video-recorded nonverbal concomitants of spoken interaction such as facial expression, gesture, kinesics, or proxemics is still in its infancy, but the relatively new field, related to *social signal processing* (Vinciarelli et al. 2009), is likely to develop rapidly in coming years.

In this chapter, existing tools and approaches for working with data of this type are briefly reviewed. Although a variety of open-source tools for the management and analysis of phonetic corpora exist, a pipeline-based approach can be well suited for collection, annotation, and analysis of online speech. The Video Phonetics Pipeline (ViPP)[3] is a Python-based set of scripts that can be implemented quickly, without lengthy setup, in a Jupyter Notebook or a cloud computing environment such as Google's Colaboratory. The pipeline is designed specifically to access YouTube content, but with minor modifications can also retrieve content from other platforms by implementing widely used open-source tools and code libraries or packages. For content download of audio, video, transcript, comment, or chat data, the pipeline makes use of yt-dlp,[4] as of early 2024 the most popular Python library for harvesting YouTube content. The Montreal Forced Aligner[5] (MFA; McAuliffe et al. 2017a) is used to align transcript content with the audio signal in the down-

2 The legal contexts pertaining to copyright, fair use, and GDPR legislation are not discussed in this chapter. For a discussion of some of these issues for data collected from YouTube, please see Coats (2023b).

3 https://github.com/stcoats/phonetics_pipeline (last accessed 14 February 2025).

4 https://github.com/yt-dlp/yt-dlp (last accessed 14 February 2025).

5 https://montreal-forced-aligner.readthedocs.io (last accessed 14 February 2025).

loaded video/audio files. For the extraction of phonetic features, Python bindings for functions from the widely used Praat software (Boersma and Weenink 2023) are implemented from the Parselmouth-Praat package (Jadoul et al. 2018).[6]

The modular nature of ViPP makes it suitable for adaptation and modification for a variety of data collection and analysis tasks. For example, the script can target YouTube's own ASR captions, or manually uploaded captions. Content from platforms other than YouTube, such as videos uploaded to Twitter, Twitch, or national broadcasters such as ARD or the BBC can be retrieved. If transcripts are unavailable, the pipeline can be modified to incorporate an ASR module such as Whisper (Radford et al. 2022) or WhisperX (Bain et al. 2023). The Montreal Forced Aligner can utilize specific acoustic models, grapheme-to-phoneme models, and language models, depending on the needs of the project at hand. For phonetic analysis, Parselmouth-Praat allows virtually all of the functions in Praat to be applied. Visualization can be undertaken using widely employed packages such as Matplotlib (Hunter 2007) or Seaborn (Waskom 2021).

The remainder of the paper is organized as follows: The second section reviews some tools, architectures, and pipelines used for ASR, forced alignment, and acoustic analysis. The third section discusses the architecture of ViPP, as well as alternative implementations for specific tasks that incorporate different components. Section 4 describes a short exploratory analysis that illustrates the utility of the pipeline: the trajectory of F1 and F2 formants for the /eɪ/ diphthong is plotted for videos indexed in the *Corpus of North American Spoken English* (Coats 2023a). In the fifth section, an overview and a summary are provided and the outlook for future developments for ViPP and for similar pipelines is discussed.

2 Previous work

2.1 Software frameworks and tools

Several comprehensive free or open-source software packages for acoustic and phonetic analysis have been developed. Most tools and software for forced alignment are built on one of two frameworks: the Hidden Markov Model Toolkit (HTK, Young 1993)[7] and Kaldi (Povey et al. 2011).[8] The Penn Forced Aligner, P2FA (Yuan

6 https://github.com/YannickJadoul/Parselmouth (last accessed 14 February 2025).
7 https://htk.eng.cam.ac.uk (last accessed 14 February 2025).
8 http://kaldi-asr.org (last accessed 14 February 2025).

and Liebermann 2008), is based on HTK. It serves as the basis for forced alignment tools that have been widely used in phonetics in the last 15 years, including FAVE (Forced Alignment and Vowel Extraction, Rosenfelder et al. 2014), a Python package that, in addition to calling P2FA, can also extract vowel formant values. MAUS, or the Munich Automatic Segmentation tool (Schiel 1999), uses P2FA to align audio and text files; the web implementation WebMAUS (Kisler et al. 2017) can handle different languages and dialects of German or English by employing different underlying acoustic and grapheme-to-phoneme models. The output of MAUS and WebMAUS can be rendered as Praat TextGrid files or in other formats such as EXMARaLDA's .exb or .flk, ELAN's .eaf, .json, .xml, or .csv files.

Somewhat similar to WebMAUS, the DARLA (Dartmouth Linguistic Annotation, Reddy and Stanford 2015) framework is a website that can automatically align audio files that have been uploaded together with orthographic transcript files. The system sends user-uploaded files to the Montreal Forced Aligner for alignment and then to FAVE for vowel extraction and formant measurement; normalization and visualization (for example of vowel locations in F1/F2 formant space) are handled by the R package *vowels* (Kendall and Thomas 2010). In addition, DARLA can generate ASR transcripts from audio files by using Deepgram, a paid service.

An additional framework used for speech recognition and alignment is Julius (Lee et al. 2001; Lee and Kawahara 2009), which provides the basic underlying signal processing and acoustic modeling framework for the SPPAS software suite (Speech Phonetization Alignment and Syllabification, Bigi 2015). SPPAS can be used for alignment, annotation, and other tasks. Several other aligners are noted by Pettarin (2022).

The Language, Brain and Behaviour Corpus Analysis Tool (LaBB-CAT, Fromont and Hay 2012; Fromont 2019), developed for the Origins of New Zealand English Corpus, is a browser-based environment, implemented in Java, that powers an Apache Tomcat server and a MySQL database on a local installation. The system handles management, analysis, and visualization of audio files, transcripts, and annotations. Forced alignment can be undertaken in LaBB-CAT using a local installation of HTK and the CELEX dictionary for pronunciations (Baayen et al. 1996), as well as other pronunciation dictionaries. LaBB-CAT provides extensive search and visualization functionality, and Praat scripts can be used to analyze transcripts and audio data. Additional linguistic annotation tasks can be implemented with scripts that call third-party tools.

The Emu speech corpus database system (Cassidy and Harrington 1996) was developed to organize and provide query functionality to recorded speech data with multiple levels of annotation. Emu has been refined and developed over the years, resulting in an R-based tool suite comprising several libraries (Winkelmann et al. 2017) as well as a web application for visualization, annotation, and analysis, the EMU-WebApp;[9] collectively, these comprise the EMU-SDMS (Speech Database Management System). While EMU-SDMS is suitable for a range of visualization and analyzation tasks, it is not designed for retrieval of online video or audio content, ASR, or forced alignment.

The PolyglotDB system (McAuliffe et al. 2017b) is a database for corpus-phonetic management, written mostly in Python, which enables a variety of analysis tasks from data with various input formats. The related Integrated Speech Corpus Analysis (ISCAN) platform (McAuliffe et al. 2019), similar in some ways to EMU-SDMS, provides extensive functionality for visualization and phonetic analysis. ISCAN, available in a dockerized container from source files hosted on GitHub, creates a browser-based interface in which queries and functions from PolyglotDB are automated for ease of use.[10] PolyglotDB and ISCAN notably include functions for formant extraction which automatically discard formant tracking errors, as described in Mielke et al. (2019). While PolyglotDB and ISCAN provide extensive functionality, setup may be complicated due to many possible dependency and installation issues that can arise, and the tools are not designed for the purposes of online content harvesting, ASR, or forced alignment.

Additional tool suites that allow organization, transcription, search functionality, visualization, and analysis of speech corpora include EXMaRALDA (Schmidt and Wörner 2014) and ELAN (Wittenburg et al. 2006), developed specifically for annotation and analysis of video data. *Visible Vowels* (Heeringa and Van de Velde 2018) is a site built using Shiny in R that can perform various types of analysis and visualization of vowels for files containing speaker, vowel, timing, duration, and formant information that have been uploaded in Excel format.[11]

For high-quality audio, accurate transcripts, and well-resourced languages, HTK- and Kaldi-based aligners can produce alignments that are generally comparable in quality to those produced by human annotators. DARLA, which uses MFA for alignment, and FAVE, which uses P2FA, both generate accurate alignments for regional British English speech (MacKenzie and Turton 2020), despite the acoustic models and phonemic representation dictionaries not having been trained on those specific varieties. Similarly, MFA can generate accurate alignments of Australian English speech, even when using the default American English language models and phoneme-grapheme dictionaries (Gonzalez et al. 2020).

9 https://ips-lmu.github.io/EMU-webApp (last accessed 14 February 2025).

10 As of early 2024, the dockerfile and requirements.txt files for ISCAN need manual editing in order to be launchable and the resulting docker environment may generate errors due to package inconsistencies.

11 https://www.visiblevowels.org/ (last accessed 14 February 2025).

2.2 Pipeline approaches

Convergence of tools has resulted in the development of similar approaches, often making use of core functionalities of HTK- or Kaldi-based aligners and Praat (Boersma and Weenink 2023) for acoustic analysis. Specifically for YouTube, the PEASYV tool (Phonetic Extraction and Alignment of Subtitled YouTube Videos; Méli and Ballier 2023; Méli et al. 2023)[12] utilizes yt-dlp-based data collection, then alignment with P2FA and SPPAS; acoustic analysis is conducted with Praat scripts. Ahn et al. (2023) used a pipeline comprising Praat and Python scripts to identify outlier values in vowel formant measurements values for several speech corpora. A number of projects have developed and documented automated pipeline approaches for the acoustic analysis of World Englishes (e.g., Fuchs 2023; Meer 2020; Meer et al. 2021).

Recent approaches have also incorporated the general-purpose speech recognition model Whisper (Radford et al. 2022) into speech processing pipelines for linguistic analysis. Whisper can generate high-quality ASR transcripts in multiple languages, for example on the multilingual Fleurs dataset (Conneau et al. 2022). As of early 2024, transcriptions generated by Whisper contain timestamps indicating the start and end of utterance chunks of variable length, ranging from one to twenty or more words; word timestamps can also be generated. Although the transcription accuracy of Whisper ASR is high, especially for the large models, the word timing information can be inaccurate and is not immediately suitable for further phonetic processing tasks such as forced alignment. WhisperX (Bain et al. 2023) is a set of tools and a Python package that generates word-level alignment and speaker diarization from Whisper output. The package harnesses other open-source models and repositories such as Wav2Vec2 (Baevski et al. 2020) for word and phone alignment and Pyannote.audio for speaker diarization (Bredin 2023; Plaquet and Bredin 2023). Likewise, these packages build upon algorithms, models, and training data sets that have been made available to the research community at large, such as the AVA-AVD dataset (Xu et al. 2022). Pipelines for automatic analysis of pause and lexical stress have also been developed, incorporating Whisper, WhisperX, Pyannote, MFA, and other tools (e.g., Coulange et al. 2023).[13] As of 2024, the use of WhisperX in phonetics research is ongoing in several projects. WhisperX can easily be integrated into notebook-based pipelines such as ViPP.

The possibilities offered by new tools and models have been embraced by researchers, but audio from online sources such as videos may be vulnerable to

---

12 https://adrienmeli.xyz/peasyv.html (last accessed 14 February 2025).

13 https://gricad-gitlab.univ-grenoble-alpes.fr/lidilem/plspp (last accessed 14 February 2025).

measurement errors. Formant frequencies can be affected by the acoustic properties of the recording space, and algorithms may have difficulties reliably detecting formants at low and high frequencies (Aalto et al. 2018). The suitability of audio data collected under highly variable recording conditions has been investigated in several recent studies. Freeman and de Decker (2021a) compared the audio quality of vowels and nasals from recordings made on smartphones, tablet devices, and laptops with recordings made on professional equipment in a studio environment. Recordings from personal devices were mostly able to recapitulate the major divisions of the vowel space "relatively faithfully". Similarly, in Freeman and de Decker (2021b), audio from video conferencing platforms was found to be mostly suitable for sociophonetic analysis, albeit with the caveat that measurement points for low back vowels exhibited considerable variability. Conklin (2023) compared vowel reduction in lossless recordings undertaken in a controlled studio environment with lossless recordings from smartphones and lossy recordings from laptops made via a website interface. She found that the different recording setups and audio compression settings result in values that are generally reliable for coarse comparisons but are not suitable for fine comparisons requiring precision.

Overall, a wide variety of tools for the collection, processing, alignment, and analysis of speech have been developed, and continued advancements in the application of neural networks and large acoustic and language models have resulted in new possibilities for phonetic research. Still, in some cases, existing tools are difficult to install and setup due to dependency incompatibilities, or are not well suited for collection of online data. The next section describes a notebook-based pipeline that can be used out-of-the-box.

3 ViPP Notebook

The Video Phonetics Pipeline (ViPP) was developed as a Jupyter Notebook that offers the analyst a fast means of retrieving, accessing and analyzing audio from online video without requiring extensive installation of software or tools. The pipeline is hosted on GitHub and designed to run on Google's Colab service or comparable cloud computing environments. Its main functionality comprises use of the open-source Python libraries yt-dlp and Praat-Parselmouth (Jadoul et al. 2018); alignment is achieved with a temporary local installation of the Montreal Forced Aligner in a Miniconda environment.

ViPP retrieves YouTube ASR transcripts and audio with functions from yt-dlp, a fork of the popular YouTube-DL library in Python. The pipeline's default settings retrieve, for a given video, the highest-quality audio available and convert it to .wav format, if necessary, using ffmpeg. Transcripts are converted from .vtt files to one of two formats: a string representing the orthographic transcription, or a string in which each word token has attached timing information, which can be used if the pipeline is modified to target utterances or sequences. By specifying the language of transcripts to be targeted, the script can be used with videos in languages for which YouTube provides ASR captions: as of early 2024, English, Dutch, French, German, Italian, Japanese, Korean, Portuguese, Russian, and Spanish. If desired, part-of-speech annotation can be implemented using models from SpaCy.[14]

The pipeline scripts install the Montreal Forced Aligner in a local Miniconda environment and retrieve a pronunciation dictionary and an acoustic model for English.[15] Calling the aligner will analyze and align the converted ASR transcript with the .wav file, outputting files in Praat's .TextGrid format.

Textgrid files, together with the corresponding .wav files, can then be used to examine acoustic properties of speech segments by using functions from Praat-Parselmouth. The default code in ViPP measures F1 and F2 formant values, but other acoustic properties can also be measured with minor changes to the code. ViPP's formant extraction approach uses the default Praat parameter values to retrieve F1 and F2 at a monophthong's durational midpoint, as determined by the Montreal Forced Aligner. Formant values can then be plotted in F1/F2 space for a single or for multiple videos using Mahalanobis distance to exclude outliers. For analyses of format trajectories, multiple measurement points can be used.

4 Example: Diphthong trajectory in F1/F2 space

Recent studies have sought to characterize vowel quality in terms of dynamic trajectories, rather than as single measurement points for monophthongs or onset/target measurement points for diphthongs (see, e.g., Fox and Jacewicz 2009; Sóskuthy et al. 2019; Renwick and Stanley 2020). The Video Phonetics Pipeline can be used to quickly assemble data for comparison from YouTube videos, then visualize and assess diphthong trajectories for locations or social groups.

As an example, Figure 1 shows the trajectories of 92 tokens of /eɪ/ extracted from YouTube videos uploaded to the channel of the city of California City, California. These tokens, which were filtered on the basis of having at least 5 measure-

14 For example, the en_core_web_sm model (https://spacy.io/usage/models, last accessed 14 February 2025).

15 Available models are described and can be downloaded from https://mfa-models.readthedocs.io/en/latest/ (last accessed 14 February 2025).

ment points as well as monotonic decreases in F1 values and increases in F2 values, are represented by dashed lines, with circles showing the values at individual measurement points, which are evenly distributed throughout the duration of the phone. The black line shows the mean diphthong trajectory for the 92 tokens. The exploratory visualization implies a bimodal distribution for the values which may correspond to the sex of the speakers in the sampled videos. Such analyses can serve as the starting point for comparisons of diphthong trajectories for different social groups or in different locations.

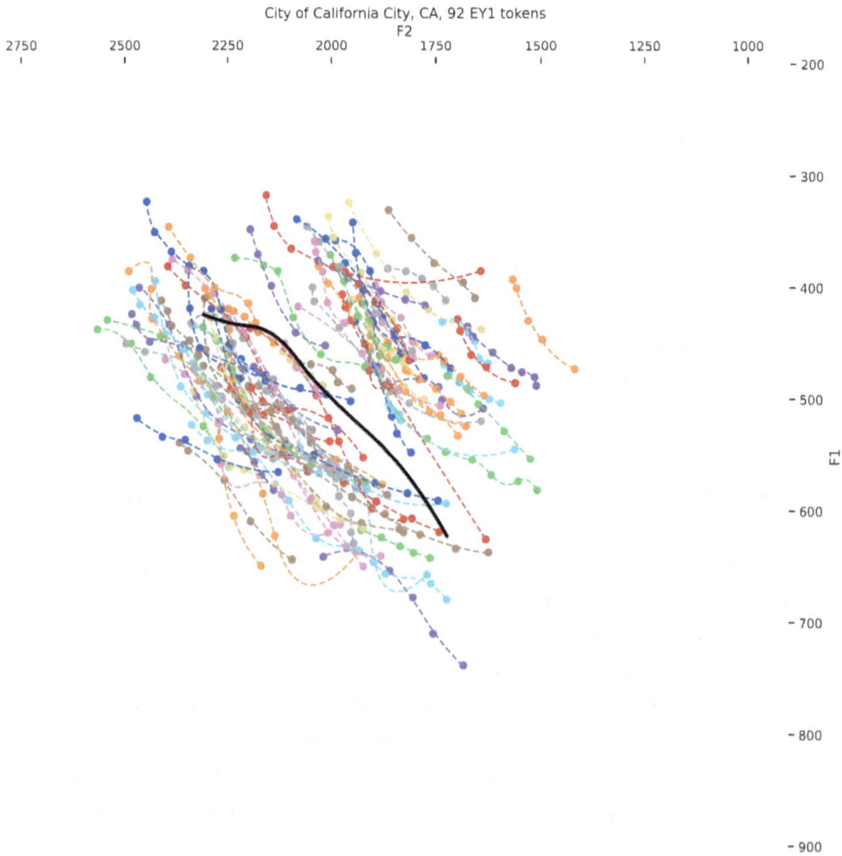

Figure 1: /eɪ/ trajectories from the YouTube channel of California City, California.

With minor modifications and the use of functions from interactive visualization libraries in Python such as Bokeh (Bokeh Development Team 2024), the ViPP can also render interactive visualizations that play the audio for a token upon a mouse click or rollover.[16]

The pipeline can be used to extract formants from large numbers of videos in order to (for example) gauge regional variation in vowel quality. Figure 2 shows the values of a spatial autocorrelation statistic, the Getis-Ord G_i^* (Getis and Ord 1992; Ord and Getis 1995), for F2 values of the onset of the /eɪ/ diphthong, based on millions of vowel tokens from videos uploaded by American local government YouTube channels (see Coats 2023a). Each point on the map represents a location in which at least 100 tokens were sampled; a 20-nearest-neighbors binary spatial weights matrix was used to calculate the statistic on the basis of the mean formant value at each location. As can be seen in Figure 2, /eɪ/ onsets are more back in the American Southeast, and more front in the upper Midwest, Canada, and Southern California, a pattern which corresponds to intuitions about American dialects as well as quantitative findings (e.g., Labov et al. 2006: 94; Grieve et al. 2013: 49).

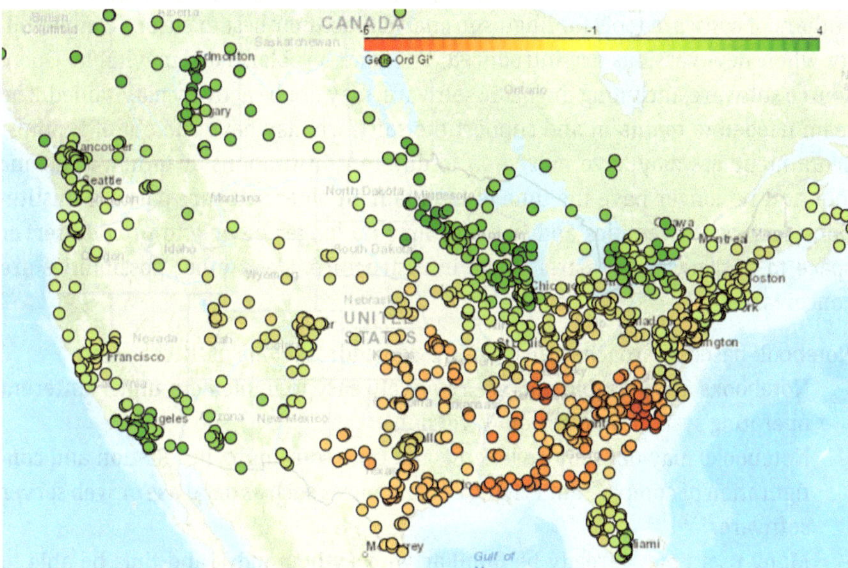

Figure 2: Getis-Ord Gi* values for F2, onset of /eɪ/ diphthong (8,788,999 tokens).

16 An example, from the YouTube channel of a town in Tennessee, can be found at https://cc.oulu.fi/~scoats/example_Gallatin_all.html (last accessed 14 February 2025).

5 Discussion

Many open-source libraries, frameworks, and tools have been developed to facilitate corpus creation and phonetic analysis, but the tools themselves, as well as internet data transmission protocols, programming languages, and operating systems, are in a constant state of flux. Not all tools and frameworks are robust to changes in underlying operating system architecture or package dependencies. Open-source software may stop working for any number of reasons, but common causes include incompatible dependencies (i.e., the software requires a newer or older version of a package than what is installed), syntax changes in the underlying programming language that may introduce conflicts (e.g., Python 3.11 instead of 3.4, or Python 3 instead of 2), non-portability of code to different operating systems, or incompatibility of code in different OS environments of the same OS due to different availability of packages (for example, Ubuntu vs. Red Hat Linux). Developers of operating systems, programming languages, and libraries/packages, as well as authors of software tools for linguistic analysis, do their best to ensure compatibility when new versions are introduced, but some problems are inevitable. Open-source software, including linguistic software, may not be actively maintained. The team needed to maintain and support the software may have run out of funding. Team members may have moved on to different institutions or to non-academic jobs and no longer have the time to maintain an older software package. Institutions such as universities and libraries may no longer be able to provide server space to host necessary parts of the infrastructure. Many other possibilities are conceivable.

Notebook-based approaches such as ViPP can address some of these issues:

- Notebooks are portable and are relatively easy to implement under different operating systems and Python/R versions.
- Notebooks may not require lengthy and time-consuming installation and configuration of complex underlying dependencies such as database or web server software.
- Many users may already be familiar with Python and R and thus be able to follow and modify code cells.
- Data collection and analysis tasks which are divided into modular code blocks, implemented as notebook cells, are easier to customize and modify in the case of problems, compared to stand-alone programs run from the command line or in a custom interface.
- Notebooks designed to run in cloud-based environments may be less subject to dependency or incompatibility issues, compared to more static scripts and tools. A notebook can be designed to install and use software packages and library

versions which are mutually compatible in the local operating environment, for example. Colab automatically uses a recent, stable version of Linux and a recent Python kernel, and the most widely used packages are automatically installed in the environment.
- Using a notebook in a cloud-based environment generally does not require administrator knowledge (or system privileges), and data collection, analysis, and visualization can be done almost immediately.

The use of notebooks is not without its own set of problems, which may include missing documentation for code in cells, lack of modularity for scripts, or unclear/incompatible dependency declarations, among others (Pimentel et al. 2021). In addition, notebook setups may offer only limited functionality compared to dedicated software platforms. ViPP, for example, does not implement syllabification of input data. Depending on the local settings, a notebook may not be suitable for long-running tasks or for processing large amounts of data. Google's default access to the Colab service has limitations on runtime, processor, and memory availability. In addition, the processing of data on commercial platforms such as Colab may introduce privacy and copyright issues that need to be carefully considered before research is undertaken.

Nevertheless, despite these limitations, notebook-based data collection, processing, and analysis approaches may offer an expedient means to quickly retrieve and analyze linguistic data. Especially for YouTube content, ViPP provides a framework which can be implemented immediately, allowing the analyst to focus on linguistic phenomena, rather than troubleshooting the installation of open-source phonetic analysis software.

6 Summary and outlook

Software and tools for linguistic and phonetic analysis change and evolve rapidly. For some data collection and analysis tasks, a notebook-based approach may be suitable. The Video Phonetic Pipeline is a Python notebook that incorporates functionality from yt-dlp, the Montreal Forced Aligner, and Parselmouth-Praat to harvest transcript and audio data from YouTube videos. With minor modifications, the pipeline can be adapted to collect data from other platforms. ViPP can be used for creation of small, specialized corpora from YouTube content as well as for larger corpora of YouTube transcripts and audio (Coats 2023c, 2024). The pipeline, and the notebook-based approach in general, represent a framework for the creation, processing, and analysis of online data for a diverse range of content types which is compatible with the general trend towards use of cloud-based services and tools for data analysis, rather than processing with software installations on local machines.

As notebooks are by design customizable, recent AI models such as Whisper or WhisperX for automated ASR transcript generation and diarization can be incorporated into the pipeline. Additional tools for specific speech processing tasks can be included, for example with models from Hugging Face. From the perspective of linguistic analysis, research involving the correlation of speech content or acoustic quality with automatically annotated facial expression, gestures, proxemics, or kinesics remain a relatively under-researched domain. Because data harvested from video platforms is fundamentally open, and considering the "generalizability of the body activity cues across datasets" (Beyan et al. 2023: 16), one future perspective may be to modify ViPP to incorporate sophisticated large models for tasks such as automated analysis of video content, including movement, gesture, or facial expression.

While these perspectives are expected to materialize in the future, the capabilities of ViPP, and the versatility of notebook approaches in general, offer practical utility for linguistic data collection and analysis tasks such as creation of transcript corpora and phonetic analysis of vowel space. In this context, ViPP shows potential for researchers aiming to quickly access interesting, new, or notable linguistic phenomena in the ever-growing universe of online content.

References

Ahn, Emily P., Gina-Anne Levow, Richard A. Wright & Eleanor Chodroff. 2023. An outlier analysis of vowel formants from a corpus phonetics pipeline. In *Proceedings of Interspeech 2023*.

Aalto, Daniel, Jarmo Malinen & Matti T. Vainio. 2018. Formants. In *Oxford research encyclopedia of linguistics*. Oxford: Oxford University Press. https://doi.org/10.1093/acrefore/9780199384655.013.419.

Baayen, R. Harald, Richard Piepenbrock & Leon Gulikers. 1996. *The CELEX lexical database* (cd-rom).

Baevski, Alexei, Henry Zhou, Abdelrahman Mohamed & Michael Auli. 2020. wav2vec 2.0: A Framework for Self-Supervised Learning of Speech Representations. *arXiv*:2006.11477 [cs.CL]. https://doi.org/10.48550/arXiv.2006.11477.

Bain, Max, Jaesung Huh, Tengda Han & Andrew Zisserman. 2023. WhisperX: Time-Accurate Speech Transcription of Long-Form Audio. In *Proceedings of Interspeech 2023*, 4489–4493. https://doi.org/10.21437/Interspeech.2023-78.

Beyan, Cigdem, Alessandro Vinciarelli & Alessio Del Bue. 2023. Co-located human-human interaction analysis using nonverbal cues: A survey. *ACM Computing Surveys* 56 (5). 1–41.

Bigi, Brigitte. 2015. SPPAS – Multi-lingual approaches to the automatic annotation of speech. *The Phonetician – International Society of Phonetic Sciences* 111. 54–69.

Boersma, Paul & David Weenink. 2023. *Praat: doing phonetics by computer* [Computer program]. Version 6.3.09. http://www.praat.org (last accessed 14 February 2025).

Bokeh Development Team. 2024. *Bokeh: Python library for interactive visualization*. http://bokeh.org (last accessed 14 February 2025).

Bredin, Hervé. 2023. Pyannote.audio 2.1 speaker diarization pipeline: Principle, benchmark and recipe. In *Proceedings of Interspeech 2023*, 1983–1987. https://doi.org/10.21437/Interspeech.2023-105.

Cassidy, Steve & Jonathan Harrington. 1996. Emu: An enhanced hierarchical speech data management system. In *Proceedings of the Sixth Australian International Conference on Speech Science and Technology*, 361–366.

Coats, Steven. 2023a. Dialect corpora from YouTube. In Beatrix Busse, Nina Dumrukcic & Ingo Kleiber (eds.), *Language and linguistics in a complex world*, 79–102. Berlin: De Gruyter. https://doi.org/10.1515/9783111017433-005.

Coats, Steven. 2023b. A new corpus of geolocated ASR transcripts from Germany. *Language Resources and Evaluation*. https://doi.org/10.1007/s10579-023-09686-9.

Coats, Steven. 2023c. A pipeline for the large-scale acoustic analysis of streamed content. In Louis Cotgrove, Laura Herzberg, Harald Lüngen, and Ines Pisetta (eds.), *Proceedings of the 10th International Conference on CMC and Social Media Corpora for the Humanities (CMC-Corpora 2023)*, 51–54. Mannheim: Leibniz-Institut für Deutsche Sprache. https://doi.org/10.14618/1z5k-pb25.

Coats, Steven. 2024. CoANZSE Audio: Creation of an online corpus for linguistic and phonetic analysis of Australian and New Zealand Englishes. In Nicoletta Calzolari, Min-Yen Kan, Veronique Hoste, Alessandro Lenci, Sakriani Sakti & Nianwen Xue (eds.), *Proceedings of the 2024 Joint International Conference on Computational Linguistics, Language Resources and Evaluation (LREC-COLING 2024)*, 3407–3412.

Conklin, Jenna. 2023. Examining recording quality from two methods of remote data collection in a study of vowel reduction. *Laboratory Phonology* 14 (1). https://doi.org/10.16995/labphon.10544.

Conneau, Alexis, Min Ma, Simran Khanuja, Yu Zhang, Vera Axelrod, Siddharth Dalmia, Jason Riesa, Clara Rivera & Ankur Bapna. 2022. FLEURS: Few-shot Learning Evaluation of Universal Representations of Speech. *arXiv*:2205.12446 [cs.CL]. https://doi.org/10.48550/arXiv.2205.12446.

Coulange, Sylvain, Tsuneo Kato, Solange Rossato & Monica Masperi. 2023. *Comprehensibility diagnosis of spontaneous L2 English: Automated analysis of pausing and lexical stress patterns*. Paper presented at the workshop Tools in L2 research, November 2023, Zurich, Switzerland. http://i3l.univ-grenoble-alpes.fr/~coulangs/languages2023/CoulangeAl2023_Zurich.pdf (last accessed 14 February 2025).

Fox, Robert Allen & Ewa Jacewicz. 2009. Cross-dialectal variation in formant dynamics of American English vowels. *Journal of the Acoustical Society of America* 126 (5). 2603–2618.

Freeman, Valerie & Paul de Decker. 2021a. Remote sociophonetic data collection: Vowels and nasalization from self-recordings on personal devices. *Language and Linguistics Compass* 15. https://doi.org/10.1111/lnc3.12435.

Freeman, Valerie & Paul de Decker. 2021b. Remote sociophonetic data collection: Vowels and nasalization over video conferencing apps. *The Journal of the Acoustical Society of America* 149 (2). 1211–1223. https://doi.org/10.1121/10.0003529.

Fromont, Robert. 2019. Forced alignment of different language varieties using LaBB-CAT. In *Proceedings of the 19th International Congress of Phonetic Sciences (ICPhS)*, 1327–1331.

Fromont, Robert A., & Jennifer Hay. 2012. LaBB-CAT: An annotation store. In *Proceedings of the Australasian Language Technology Association Workshop 2012*, 113–117.

Fuchs, Robert. 2023. Analysing the speech rhythm of New Englishes: A guide to researchers and a case study on Pakistani, Philippine, Nigerian and British English. In Guyanne Wilson & Michael Westphal (eds.), *New Englishes, New Methods*, 132–155. Amsterdam: Benjamins.

Getis, Arthur and Ord, J. Keith. 1992. The analysis of spatial association by use of distance statistics, *Geographical Analysis* 24 (7). 189–206.

Gonzalez, Simon, James Grama & Catherine E. Travis. 2020. Comparing the performance of forced aligners used in sociophonetic research. *Linguistics Vanguard* 5. https://doi.org/10.1515/lingvan-2019-0058.

Grieve, Jack, Dirk Speelman & Dirk Geeraerts. 2013. A multivariate spatial analysis of vowel formants in American English. *Journal of Linguistic Geography* 1. 31–51. https://doi.org/10.1017/jlg.2013.3.

Heeringa, Wilbert & Hans Van de Velde. 2018. Visible Vowels: A tool for the visualization of vowel variation. In *Proceedings of the CLARIN Annual Conference 2018, 8 - 10 October, Pisa, Italy*, 120–123. CLARIN ERIC.

Hunter, John D. 2007. Matplotlib: A 2D graphics environment. *Computing in Science & Engineering* 9 (3). 90–95.

Jadoul, Yannick, Bill Thompson & Bart de Boer. 2018. Introducing Parselmouth: A Python interface to Praat. *Journal of Phonetics* 71. 1–15. https://doi.org/10.1016/j.wocn.2018.07.001.

Kendall, Tyler & Erik R. Thomas. 2010. *Vowels: Vowel manipulation, normalization, and plotting in R.* R package. https://cran.r-project.org/web/packages/vowels/index.html (last accessed 14 February 2025).

Kisler, Thomas, Uwe Reichel & Florian Schiel. 2017. Multilingual processing of speech via web services. *Computer Speech & Language* 45. 326–347.

Labov, William, Sharon Ash & Charles Boberg. 2006. *The atlas of North American English.* Berlin: Mouton de Gruyter.

Lee, Akinobu, Tatsuya Kawahara & Kiyohiro Shikano. 2001. Julius—an open source real-time large vocabulary recognition engine. In *Proceedings of the European Conference on Speech Communication and Technology (EUROSPEECH)*, 1691–1694.

Lee, Akinobu & Tatsuya Kawahara. 2009. Recent development of open-source speech recognition engine Julius. In *Proceedings of APSIPA ASC 2009*, 131–137.

Liberman, Mark Y. 2019. Corpus phonetics. *Annual Review of Linguistics* 5. 91–107. https://doi.org/10.1146/annurev-linguistics-011516-033830.

MacKenzie, Laurel & Danielle Turton. 2020. Assessing the accuracy of existing forced alignment software on varieties of British English. *Linguistics Vanguard* 6. https://doi.org/10.1515/lingvan-2018-0061.

McAuliffe, Michael, Michaela Socolof, Sarah Mihuc, Michael Wagner & Morgan Sonderegger. 2017a. Montreal Forced Aligner: Trainable text-speech alignment using Kaldi. In *Proceedings of the 18th Conference of the International Speech Communication Association*.

McAuliffe, Michael, Elias Stengel-Eskin, Michaela Socolof & Morgan Sonderegger. 2017b. Polyglot and speech corpus tools: A system for representing, integrating, and querying speech corpora. In *Proceedings of Interspeech 2017*, 3887–3891.

McAuliffe, Michael, Arlie Coles, Michael Goodale, Sarah Mihuc, Michael Wagner, Jane Stuart-Smith & Morgan Sonderegger. 2019. ISCAN: A system for integrated phonetic analyses across speech corpora. In *Proceedings of Interspeech 2019*, 1322–1326.

Meer, Philipp. 2020. Automatic alignment for New Englishes: Applying state-of-the-art aligners to Trinidadian English. *The Journal of the Acoustical Society of America* 147 (4). 2283–2294. https://doi.org/10.1121/10.0001069.

Meer, Philipp, Thorsten Brato & José A. Matute Flores. 2021. Extending automatic vowel formant extraction to New Englishes: A comparison of different methods. *English World-Wide* 42 (1). 54–84. https://doi.org/10.1075/eww.00060.mee.

Méli, Adrien & Nicolas Ballier. 2023. PEASYV: A procedure to obtain phonetic data from subtitled videos. In *Proceedings of the International Congress of Phonetic Sciences 2023*, 3211–3215.

Méli, Adrien, Steven Coats & Nicolas Ballier. 2023. Methods for phonetic scraping of Youtube videos. In *Proceedings of the 6th International Conference on Natural Language and Speech Processing (ICNLSP 2023)*, 244–249.

Mielke, Jeff, Erik R. Thomas, Josef Fruehwald, Michael McAuliffe, Morgan Sonderegger, Jane Stuart-Smith & Robin Dodsworth. 2019. Age vectors vs. axes of intraspeaker variation in vowel formants measured automatically from several English speech corpora. In *Proceedings of the International Congress of Phonetic Sciences 2019*, 1258–1262.

Ord, J. Keith & Arthur Getis. 1995. Local spatial autocorrelation statistics: Distributional issues and application. *Geographical Analysis* 27 (4). 286–306.

Pettarin, Alberto. 2022. *Forced-alignment-tools*. https://github.com/pettarin/forced-alignment-tools (last accessed 14 February 2025).

Pimentel, João Felipe, Leonardo Murta, Vanessa Braganholo & Juliana Freire. 2021. Understanding and improving the quality and reproducibility of Jupyter notebooks. *Empirical Software Engineering* 26. https://doi.org/10.1007/s10664-021-09961-9.

Plaquet, Alexis & Hervé Bredin. 2023. Powerset multi-class cross entropy loss for neural speaker diarization. In *Proceedings of Interspeech 2023*, 3222–3226. https://doi.org/10.21437/Interspeech.2023-205.

Povey, Daniel, Arnab Ghoshal, Gilles Boulianne, Lukas Burget, Ondrej Glembek, Nagendra Goel, Mirko Hannemann, Petr Motlicek, Yanmin Qian, Petr Schwarz, Jan Silovsky, Georg Stemmer & Karel Vesely. 2011. The Kaldi speech recognition toolkit. In *Proceedings of the IEEE 2011 Workshop on Automatic Speech Recognition and Understanding*. IEEE Signal Processing Society.

Radford, Alec, Jong Wook Kim, Tao Xu, Greg Brockman, Christine McLeavey & Ilya Sutskever. 2022. Robust speech recognition via large-scale weak supervision. *arXiv*:2212.04356 [eess.AS]. https://doi.org/10.48550/arXiv.2212.04356.

Reddy, Sravana & James Stanford. 2015. A web application for automated dialect analysis. In *Proceedings of NAACL-HLT 2015.*

Renwick, Margaret E. L. & Joseph A. Stanley. 2020. Modeling dynamic trajectories of front vowels in the American South. *The Journal of the Acoustical Society of America* 147 (1). 579–595. https://doi.org/10.1121/10.0000549.

Rosenfelder, Ingrid Josef Fruehwald, Keelan Evanini, Scott Seyfarth, Kyle Gorman, Hilary Prichard & Jiahong Yuan. 2014. *FAVE (Forced Alignment and Vowel Extraction) Program Suite v1.2.2* https://doi.org/10.5281/zenodo.22281.

Schiel, Florian. 1999. Automatic phonetic transcription of non-prompted speech. In *Proceedings of the 14th International Congress of Phonetic Sciences (ICPhS)*, 607–610.

Schmidt, Thomas & Kai Wörner. 2014. EXMARaLDA. In Jacques Durand, Ulrike Gut & Gjert Kristoffersen (eds.), *The Oxford handbook of corpus phonology*, 402–419. Oxford: Oxford University Press.

Sodagar, Iraj. 2011. The mpeg-dash standard for multimedia streaming over the internet. *IEEE multimedia* 18 (4). 62–67.

Sóskuthy, Márton, Jennifer Hay & James Brand. 2019. Horizontal diphthong shift in New Zealand English. In *Proceedings of the 19th International Congress of Phonetic Sciences*, 597–601.

Vinciarelli, Alessandro, Maja Pantic & Hervé Bourlard. 2009. Social signal processing: Survey of an emerging domain. *Image and Vision Computing* 27 (12). 1743–1759.

Waskom, Michael L. 2021. Seaborn: Statistical data visualization. *Journal of Open Source Software* 6, 60, 3021. https://doi.org/10.21105/joss.03021.

Wittenburg, Peter, Hennie Brugman, Albert Russel, Alex Klassmann & Han Sloetjes. 2006. ELAN: A professional framework for multimodality research. In *Proceedings of the 5th International Conference on Language Resources and Evaluation (LREC 2006)*, 1556–1559.

Xu, Eric Zhongcong, Zeyang Song, Satoshi Tsutsui, Chao Feng, Mang Ye & Mike Zheng Shou. 2022. AVA-AVD: Audio-visual speaker diarization in the wild. In *Proceedings of the 30th ACM International Conference on Multimedia (MM '22)*, 3838–3847. New York: Association for Computing Machinery. https://doi.org/10.1145/3503161.3548027.

Young, Steve J. 1993. *The HTK hidden Markov model toolkit: Design and philosophy*. Cambridge: Cambridge University.

Yuan, Jiahong & Mark Liberman. 2008. Speaker identification on the SCOTUS corpus. *Journal of the Acoustical Society of America* 123 (5). 3878.

Selenia Anastasi, Tim Fischer, Florian Schneider, and Chris Biemann

IDA – Incel Data Archive

A multimodal comparable corpus for exploring extremist dynamics in online interaction

Abstract: Extremist online communities connected to the male supremacist ecosystem are rapidly growing worldwide in insular groups outside the mainstream social network sites, which is a concerning phenomenon on a global scale. To understand the dynamics of these groups, we introduce IDA, the Incel Data Archive. While existing research largely focuses on English-language forums dominated by North American Incels (and to a lesser extent, European), our work addresses this gap by creating a multilingual and multimodal corpus from the Italian and English Incel forums. The Incelosphere, comprising forums, blogs, and websites, serves as a cross-cultural case study of male supremacist communities. Our contribution lies in offering an original cross-cultural perspective on incels and discussing challenges in constructing a multimodal and multilingual corpus, which preserves the linear and conversational structure of the forum. To achieve this, we employ a mixed-method approach to Computer Mediated Communication. In order to shed light on important differences between the two communities, we conducted an exploratory analysis using a novel topic modeling technique based on Transformer architectures. Results reveal differences in discussion topics and in the targets of hate between Anglophone and Italian communities. The Anglophone incel community displays frequent marks of anti-Semitic and racist discourses, associating Incel identity with perceived social issues among non-white users. Conversely, the Italian forum exhibits less emphasis on such trends, with stereotypes and discrimination focusing on regional distinctions (so called *antimeridionalism*) rather than immigration. This disparity represents a point of divergence between the two communities and may offer valuable insights for future analyses aimed at deepening the cultural context of the user base and their radical expressions.

Selenia Anastasi, University of Genoa, Language Technology Group (Hamburg University), e-mail: selenia.anastasi@edu.unige.it
Tim Fischer, Language Technology Group (Hamburg University), e-mail: tim.fischer@uni-hamburg.de
Florian Schneider, Language Technology Group (Hamburg University), e-mail: florian.schneider-1@uni-hamburg.de
Chris Biemann, Language Technology Group (Hamburg University), e-mail: biemann@informatik.uni-hamburg.de

https://doi.org/10.1515/9783111434018-012

Keywords: Computer Mediated Communication, cross-cultural analysis, Incels, online extremism, topic modeling, multimodal corpora, comparable corpora

1 Introduction

In this chapter we describe the steps that led to the creation and exploratory analysis of *IDA – Incel Data Archive*, a multimodal comparable corpus of forum-based interactions of the incel community in English and Italian. For the composition of the comparable corpus, data were collected from two of the most populated incel fora in both languages: *incels.is* and *Il Forum Dei Brutti* (*Forum of the ugly people*, from now on abbreviated in FDB). As we will detail below, our contribution is twofold. Primarily, we aim to contribute to a deeper understanding of Incel communities from a cross-cultural perspective. Secondly, from a methodological standpoint, our objective is to present a framework for the construction of a corpus designed to study forum-based communities, drawing on insights from the field of Computer-Mediated Communication, Social Sciences and Corpus Linguistics. We argue that this interdisciplinary approach holds particular value within the domain of Digital Linguistics, as digital environments constitute a multifaceted nexus of technological affordances and communicative practices. Furthermore, for researchers engaged in the analysis of online discourse, it is crucial to situate linguistic performances within the broader socio-political context.

After spreading within Reddit, Incel communities gradually aggregated outside mainstream social networks, creating an independent ecosystem of forum-based communities. Recently, several studies (Gillett and Suzor 2022; Trujillo and Cresci 2022) supported the hypothesis that moderation and quarantine practices adopted by mainstream social media, such as Facebook and Instagram, may foster the growth of hateful insular peripheral communities akin to echo chambers. The creation of the dataset presented in this work was motivated by the need to draw upon spontaneous examples of digitally mediated communication that exhibited similar ideological content from various perspectives, framing the phenomenon of *toxic technoculture* (Massanari 2017) in different languages and contexts. Furthermore, even though the discourse of the Incelosphere is characterised by hate speech primarily targeting women (Heritage and Koller 2020; Sugiura 2021; O'Malley et al. 2022), we argue that a corpus consisting of data from the Incelosphere is not only of interest to those studying misogynistic discourse. Indeed, it can contribute to the research community engaged in the study of digitally mediated communication more broadly by providing real examples of spontaneous conversations for the study of asynchronous interactions between users in fora strictly connected to instances of white supremacy and to new form of populist far-right (Nagle 2017; Mamié et al. 2021).

Beyond these wider aspects, this article specifically aims to respond to recent calls for the need to contextualise violent online behaviour also in non-English speaking communities (Dwyer 2017; Schoenebeck et al. 2023). The research questions that prompted the development of the IDA corpus can thus be summarised as follows:

1. Is it possible to compare the discourses of Anglophone and non-Anglophone incel communities, and from what perspective?
2. How do such communities articulate their beliefs and aggregation purposes?

Indubitably, contextual understanding of violence, coupled with a multifaceted approach that includes political, social and interactional dimensions, can assist in developing effective forms of resistance and counteraction, highlighting the role of background culture in determining how individuals may disseminate online violence and articulate their extremist narratives. Moreover, it is crucial to investigate extremist phenomena from a perspective that is both geographically and linguistically situated. As recently stressed by Vessey (2024), "the meanings that can emerge from a multilingual perspective are generally non-obvious, and perhaps as a result they tend to be overlooked" (ibid.: 7). Therefore, this work provides a resource that allows for a more nuanced and complex understanding of the spread of such ideologies and their manifestations within different cultural domains.

Finally, it is worth noting that the discursive boundaries of online spaces are permeable, allowing content from certain web niches to infiltrate more controlled and secure spaces, such as those offered by mainstream social media. The result is that instances of violence generated by subcultures on the Internet are becoming accessible to the vast majority of people who are exposed to them. Thus, digital linguistics studies can provide a useful point of view for overcoming the limitations of the media's often incomplete and inaccurate representation of online subcultures (Heritage 2023).

2 The Incelosphere so far: a transnational ecosystem

Anglophone Incel communities have been studied from a wide variety of perspectives, ranging from psychology to sociology and discourse analysis. Many of these studies were focused on Reddit groups, such as *r/ForeverAlone* and *r/Incels subred-*

dits, which are archived in datasets and can be easily used as corpora. Therefore, given the availability of resources in the English language, our current understanding of this community primarily revolves around the Anglophone context, and particularly that of the United States. In the North American context, the academic scholarship has produced a multitude of studies related to the broader concept of the Manosphere. Here, the Manosphere is defined as an umbrella-term used by scholars to delineate a vast range of realities that share the same vision of heterosexual hegemonic masculinity (Lilly 2016; Ribeiro et al 2021), of which the Incelosphera is the most extreme of the groups. To a lesser extent, other Manosphere groups have also received attention from the academic community studying online misogyny, such as PUAs (Pick Up Artists), MRAs (Men's Right Activists) and MGTOWs (Men Going Their Own Way). The scholarly attention towards the Incels arises from the urgent need to comprehend and contextualize instances of real-world violence perpetrated by members of the community, such as the 2014 Isla Vista massacre and the 2018 Toronto Van Attack. This focus reflects a significant effort to understand the social and psychological dynamics within these groups and their impacts on society.

In Sociology, studies focused on the discursive practices, rhetoric and argumentation style, symbolism, and sexual imagery of Incel communities (Massanari 2017; Wasniewska 2020; Tranchese and Sugiura 2021; Aiston 2023; Prazmo 2022), in-group and out-group identity construction (Ging 2019; Chang 2022; Thorburn et al. 2023; Scotto di Carlo 2022), target of the hateful content (Pelzer et al. 2021), thematic and rhetorical connections to far-right oriented groups (Nagle 2017), anti-feminism, values, normative orders, and group beliefs (Sugiura 2021; O'Malley 2022; Heritage and Koller 2020). Empirical analyses and terrorism studies have sought to trace, also through dynamic cross-platform approaches, the spreading of violent extremism in the main Anglophone Incel communities (Ribeiro et al. 2021; Baele et al. 2021, 2023; Heritage 2023), as well as their misogynistic stances (Lilly 2016; Farrell et al. 2019).

For Baele and colleagues, "incel discourse demonstrates typical markers of extremist language: an essentialist categorization of society into sharply delineated ingroups and outgroups where the latter are linguistically dehumanized, and a conspiratorial narrative presenting the ingroup as the victim of an all-powerful structure of oppression" (Baele et al. 2023: 383–384). Moreover, although incels construct clear boundaries to define ingroups and outgroups within their discourses in relation to different social actors, "the language used towards different groups is more complex than 'in-group evaluation is good; out-group evaluation is bad'. Incels do often represent some out-group members in positive ways, and also do construct in-group members as undesirable" (Heritage 2023: 201).

The interest of academic research in understanding how incels represent social actors is not trivial and reflects a more general interest in the discursive aspects underlying the formation of groups aggregated on the basis of extremist ideologies with transnational boundaries. Indeed, this kind of research can even reveal deep cultural continuities and fractures in how incel ideology is framed, perceived, and promoted by users. Such differences are found not only where cultural discrepancies are most evident, between the Global East and West and Global North and South, but also between countries that are considered homogeneous because they are generally associated with the industrialized West.

In terms of incel identity formation, the link between the construction of masculinity and femininity is also largely determined by the culture to which the subject belongs. This was made very clear in studies of gender and racial identity construction by Heritage (2023), who recognizes a link between the continuous and frequent intertextual references made by users and U.S. culture. Indeed, according to the author, although the Incels Wiki[1] points to the existence of several incel and related fora in France, Italy, Germany, Japan, Taiwan, Turkey, Russia, and Poland, the majority of users within the English-speaking community can be identified as coming from North America and are often associated with related white supremacist ideologies.

Looking more closely at the European landscape outside of the Anglophone context, however, we see a thriving ecosystem that is highly diversified on both a linguistic and ideological basis. Indeed, the Incels Wiki notes that many of these international communities maintain beliefs and terminologies that differ from those found within the Anglophone Incelosphere. In this regard, some studies have already begun to analyse local aspects of Incel slang and identity construction in relation to users' nationality of origin. For example, Voroshilova and Pesterev (2021) analyse the Russian community by highlighting some key differences between Russian and Western spaces, which were found to be less hostile and more welcoming to women than other English-speaking Incel spaces. The same conclusions were reached for Italian spaces, which have not been extensively studied. The few studies on Italian incels have shown that the community often revolves around pop icons like Joker (Capalbi 2021), but also figures from the Italian literary canon like poet Giacomo Leopardi. De Gasperis's (2021) study, for example, emphasizes the connection between the collective imagination of Italian literature and the processes of masculine identity definition within the most popular Italian forum. Anastasi (2022) showed that Italian and European communities in general, in contrast to Anglophone and U.S. communities, are open to welcoming individuals who identify as women. However, the latter are welcomed as actual members of the communities when they are judged to be functional in perpetuating and reinforcing sexist

1 https://incels.wiki/w/Main_Page (last accessed 14 February 2025).

and heteronormative discourses. In Germany, users of the main forum define themselves as *absolute beginners* (AB), after a song by David Bowie. In the main German community, the acronym "AB" is used to describe people who are involuntarily single, or who were deprived of sexual activity and romantic experiences until adulthood. The main forum is also free of explicitly misogynistic content, and its netiquette advises tolerant behaviour and peaceful discussion. According to Brzuszkiewicz (2020), who analysed a Francophone incel forum, French users also exhibit the same characteristics. Finally, to the best of our knowledge, few studies have investigated visual and multimodal aspects of communication within Incels' communities, such as the creation and circulation of images, videos and Internet memes (Aulia and Rosida 2022).

Despite the apparent pluralism and inclusiveness of the European Incelosphere, in our view it would be a mistake to underestimate the potential for violence within these communities. The use of language, strategies for communicating hateful content, acceptance of essentialist instances, underlying prejudice and stereotyping that contribute to discriminatory and violent attitudes, can vary based on the cultural roots of the social actors involved. In agreement with Czerwinsky's (2023) critical review, we believe that it is necessary to investigate these differences more thoroughly. This requires the development of appropriate resources for studying country-specific, non-English-speaking groups. The construction of comparable, multilingual, and accessible language resources such as IDA is therefore a fundamental first step in this direction.

3 Online discussion fora and CMC

The Computer-Mediated Communication (CMC) approach traditionally concerns the study interactions where communication occurs through computers or mobile devices (Herring and Androutsopoulos 2015). While much of the research has focused on texts, recent attempts have been made to incorporate multimodality, as well as stylistic, stylometric and pragmatic elements that could provide useful insights into the process of meaning-making at the level below the utterance. Additionally, this approach distinguishes itself from other approaches to the analysis of online discourses by considering the importance of platform-specific affordances and how they can shape interaction, an aspect we aimed to preserve in the development of IDA. Indeed, forum-mediated conversations are not simply digital versions of every-day conversations, but rather represent a distinct genre, with its conditions of production and interpretation. For example, non-synchronous digital interaction promotes the presence of complex sequential organizations, with connections to previous levels and the management of multiple lines of interaction in parallel. This necessitates participants to develop new methods for indexing sequential connections, self-introduction, greetings, and attention calls.

Considering these aspects, the specificity of IDA should not come as a surprise. In recent years, with the advent of numerous novel social networking platforms, such as TikTok and Twitch, there has been a notable expansion in the creation of digital language corpora, designed to examine specific discourse phenomena such as those pertaining to the anti-vaccine movements, fake news, and conspiracy theories (Miani et al. 2021). As for the corpora of computer-mediated communication that are partly or wholly composed of fora, efforts are still limited.[2] They include The Mixed Corpus: New Media in Estonian[3]; the SFNET Corpus (Tuominen et al. 2003) and the Suomi 24 Corpus[4] in Finnish; the LITIS v.1 corpus[5] in Lithuanian, the Janes corpora 1.0 (Fišer et al. 2018) in Slovenian, the CoMeRe repository[6] in French (as listed in Frey et al. 2020).

Due to the lack of systematicity in the literature devoted to fora, Holtz et al.'s (2012) study was a useful starting point for understanding both the specifics of forum-mediated interaction and the reasons why fora are particularly attractive virtual venues for extremist communities. Indeed, "in fora for radical, extremist or other ideologically sensitive communities, users will express their opinions more freely and may be less concerned about social desirability" (Holtz et al. 2012: 4). Moreover, this work has guided us in understanding why, despite the advent of technologically sophisticated mainstream social media, fora are still a useful source of data collection, particularly for building linguistic resources to study online hate speech. Among the most obvious reasons, one is the almost unlimited amount of data from spontaneous conversations, which are not subject to social constraints and/or strict moderation policies. Second, the hierarchical organization into sections that allows for simplified and rapid selection of specific sections related to content of interest. However, the collection of data from discussion fora, as well as the step to create corpora that can be considered comparable, are not without prac-

2 For the mapping of the corpora, I used the repository offered by the CLARIN infrastructure (available at the link: https://www.clarin.eu/resource-families/cmc-corpora, last accessed 14 February 2025). Not in all cases the authors of the corpus are cited, and in some cases the construction of the corpus takes place over time and involves many researchers. For this reason, in some cases I have preferred to provide direct links to the resource rather than citing a scholarly article.

3 https://www.cl.ut.ee/korpused/segakorpus/ (last accessed 14 February 2025).

4 http://urn.fi/urn:nbn:fi:lb-2017021502 (last accessed 14 February 2025).

5 http://hdl.handle.net/20.500.11821/11 (last accessed 14 February 2025).

6 https://repository.ortolang.fr/api/content/comere/v3.3/comere.html (last accessed 14 February 2025).

tical challenges. We discuss this process in the next section, providing description of the criteria used to select the two fora, the corpus design and the data collection criteria.

4 Corpus construction

4.1 Methodology for comparability

Traditionally, the construction of bilingual and multilingual corpora can be distinguished into two sub-categories, depending on the purposes, the characteristics of the texts, and the design methods. A first type of multilingual corpora are *parallel corpora*, mainly used in translation studies, facilitating a variety of interlingual comparisons. A second type of multilingual corpora, to be distinguished from the first, are *comparable corpora*.

We can say a corpus is a comparable corpus if its components or subcorpora are collected using the same sampling frame and similar balance and representativeness (McEnery and Xiao 2007). These are corpora that are not translations of texts in one or more languages, but rather texts of genres belonging to the same domains in the same time range, in different languages. In the case of comparable corpora, their juxtaposition depends on a number of complex factors concerning the frame of reference and the sampling criteria for collecting similar texts. Despite the introduction of statistical measures to determine similarity between corpora of different languages, there is no consensus within the community as to the most accurate statistical method (Sharoff et al. 2013). Moreover, López Arroyo (2020) note that comparability should consider the nature of the purposes for which the comparable corpus is designed. Considering these, McEnery and Xiao (2007) identified three criteria that need to be met to ensure comparability between two or more corpora:

1. Same genre and domain.
2. Same period of time.
3. Same participants or community.

To these criteria, López Arroyo (2020) adds three others:

4. Same format.
5. Same style.
6. Same content or topic.

Considering the last prerequisite, a problem with large comparable corpora is that we cannot always know the content of the texts *a priori*. This problem is particularly acute when trying to collect large comparable corpora from the Web using data mining techniques. To address and overcome this challenge, and to assess the comparability of corpora of unknown composition, one possibility is to apply unsupervised clustering methods such as topic modelling. (Sharoff 2013). Thus, topic modelling was applied on both datasets to attest the effective comparability of the two fora in terms of content. This is mainly because, if for *incels.is* the ideological commitment is openly declared, starting from its name, for the *FDB* forum the assessment of the adherence to the incel ideology required some further steps. In addition to the application of topic modelling, a netnographic analysis (Kozinets 2015) was conducted on the site affordances and community practices.

Finally, it is perhaps useful to specify that the choice of FDB as a source of data for the Italian language depended mainly on the size of its user base, which at the time of collection was the largest in the Italian Incelosphere.

4.2 Methodology for the analysis of the affordances

Here, *affordances* are defined as the relationship between user and technology in terms of how this relationship is constrained by the features of a site that can influence and shape user behaviours (Evans et al. 2017). In a recent study, Diaz-Fernandez and Garcia-Mingo (2023) explored the concept of *affordances* in relation to an extensive nethnographic investigation of Forocoches, a prominent Spanish forum associated with the Manosphere. The authors posited the necessity of examining online communities as digital spaces where boundaries are delineated by specific digital practices and particular performances of digital masculinity. In this study, the same methodology is employed to examine the affordances of the incels.is forum and the Italian FDB in four dimensions of analysis:

1. Criteria for forum membership.
2. Access protocols.
3. Privacy control.
4. Normative tightness.

The first dimension concerns the criteria established by the moderators for granting access to a user wishing to join the forum, while the second concerns access protocols and describes the hierarchical approach implemented to access certain types of information. The third dimension consists of managing the users' personal information. Finally, analysing the fourth dimension, there might be a wide range of rules concerning what is considered as appropriate behaviour by the users.

These codes of conduct not only relate to permissible content to share but can also define the appropriate modality of communication. This last remark has a direct impact on the pragmatic as well as the sociolinguistic aspects of communication within the digital places analysed.

4.2.1 Structure of *incels.is*

The site *incels.is* is reported by the IncelWiki[7] to be the largest incel forum in the Anglophone Incelosphere and so far, together with redpill[8]-related subreddits, represents the preferred source of knowledge about the incel culture for scholars engaged in the study of this community (Heritage and Koller 2020; Heritage 2023; Chang 2022; Ging 2019; Bogetić et al. 2023; Sugiura 2021). Established in 2017 after the r/incels subreddit has been shut down, it now has more than 25,000 members and hundreds of external visitors per day.

In terms of content organization, each section may contain more than one thread about roughly one topic. Each thread can contain a minimum of one post, and conversations can proceed asynchronously, from top to bottom of the page, and on multiple pages (the hierarchical structure of the forum is summarised in Figure 1).

Threads can also be resumed several years later. This aspect can pose a challenge for forum-mediated communication analysis, as the dates of creation of a thread may also be far remote in time from the individual posts within it. Finally, within a post it is possible to invoke another member through the tagging functionality offered by the *@Nickname* and to quote texts from other posts, thus triggering a mechanism of nesting between content.

At the time of writing, the rules of *incels.is* include: an account creation system that allows relative anonymity through the use of nicknames. Only members with formally registered accounts can access private sections and participate in conversations. Over time, access to the Anglophone forum has been restricted to: men aged 18 and over who *want a romantic relationship but are unable to have one.* Women and queer individuals are explicitly excluded.

7 https://incels.wiki/w/Incels.is (last accessed 14 February 2025).

8 The Red Pill is defined as an ideology that opposes feminism. Adherents of this ideology idealise a past in which masculinity was expressed through physical strength, economic and sexual power, and wish for a return to such dynamics (Heritage 2023).

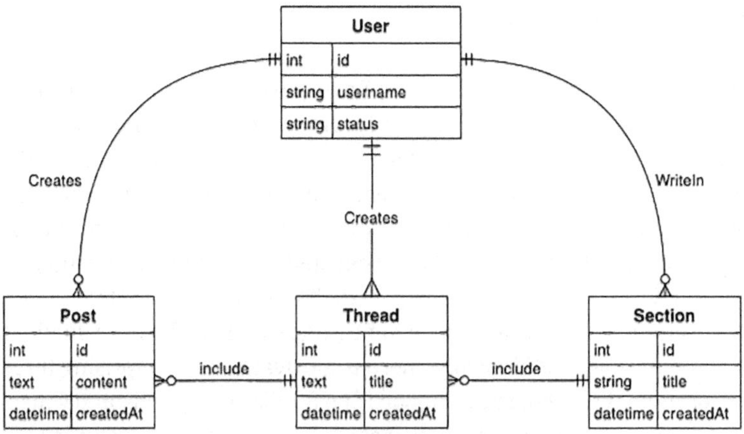

Figure 1: Fora structure diagram and associated users' metadata.

The second dimension of analysis concerns the access protocols. In fact, although most sections are public in the *incels.is* forum, others are likely to be visible and accessible only to registered users and/or users with a high hierarchical status. In addition, newcomers are not allowed to send private messages or vote in polls. These privileges are acquired over time by improving ranking and status. Status (symbolised by colourful stars) can increase on the basis of activities and longevity of the user.

On the third dimension, privacy control, incels.is invites users to take responsibility for their own privacy, for example by not publishing photos and personal information, and by connecting through proxies and VPNs. However, potentially just Admins and moderators can have access to private information about the users.

Finally, analysing the fourth dimension, there are a wide range of rules concerning what is considered appropriate behaviour by users within the sections, such as the prohibition of sharing child pornography or violent and gore-oriented content. Moreover, spamming and advertising, the expression of so-called *bluepilled* positions, sharing content that in any way supports or represents the LGBTQA+ community, posting images or content that show explicit abuse of animals, to name but a few, is prohibited. It should also be noted that it is not possible to post personal images for the purpose of receiving an aesthetic evaluation from other users, a practice which is instead the dominant theme of the community.

4.2.2 Structure of the *Forum dei Brutti*

The *Forum dei Brutti* (a possible translation in English would be Forum of the ugly people, and henceforth FDB) is the largest forum of the Italian Incelosphere, although at the time of writing it is not the only one. An element of continuity between FDB and the *incels.is* forum is represented by the homepage's organisation into sections. These sections include a *shoutbox* where temporary messages can be posted in sequence, as well as a special section devoted only to the introductions of newcomers. A section is dedicated to topics related to the Red Pill, including personal self-disclosure and stories, advice on appearance, and aesthetic evaluations of ingroups and outgroups. Additionally, there is a private area comprising three sections: one for mutual psychological support, one for discussing conspiracy theories, and one for exchanging pornographic material. Finally, a section entitled Off Topic is provided, in which users may discuss television series and other topics not related to the Red Pill ideology. This section generally hosts topics about national and foreign politics.

Considering the first dimension, formally, membership in the Italian community is open to all, regardless of gender or sexual orientation. The criteria for FDB membership are less rigid than that of *incels.is*, and more subject to case-by-case evaluation.

However, in order to participate in the discussion sections of FDB, an access protocol has been developed by moderators. In the first place, to be able to participate in conversations, every newcomer is asked to submit a detailed introduction and provide a rationale for joining the group; second, female users only have to identify themselves by posting personal data (personal picture or a voice message in which specific words are clearly pronounced) in order to verify the offline identity of the person. This is done in a special private section of the forum, accessible only upon authorisation by the admins.

With regard to the third dimension, at the time of data collection, there is a scarce control over users' privacy. For example, in a forum section with no restricted access, members of the group regularly post images of themselves in order to obtain feedback and aesthetic evaluation. The practice of aesthetic evaluation is in fact very much felt within the Italian community, in contrast to incels.is, where moderation explicitly invite users to avoid posting selfies and other sensitive material. Finally, considering the fourth dimension of analysis, the code of conduct comprises the following prohibitions: blasphemy, racism, violence against women or paedophilia; the posting of explicit violent and pornographic visual content is permitted only within the private section of the forum; incitement to suicide or self-harm, the use of demoralising phrases and insulting the moderation is forbidden.

The main affordances of the two fora and the corresponding levels of analysis considered are summarised below.

Table 1: Summary of the affordances of the two fora.

	incels.is	***FDB***
Membership criteria	Only male heterosexual users	Formally open to all gender and sexual orientation
Access protocols	Subscription and status acquisition	Mandatory introduction Off-line identity verification (only for female users)
Privacy control	Privacy control towards in-groups and out-groups Responsibility of the users	No clear rules Privacy control towards out-groups
Normative tightness	Code of conduct	Code of conduct

4.3 Collection and design rationale

For the dataset collection, we considered that both fora are structured hierarchically in sections, threads, and posts. Every section can contain a varied number of threads of different lengths that relate to roughly one topic. Worth noting, we took in consideration only the public sections of the fora. For the Italian forum, we collected data from: 1. the presentation section; 2. the section dedicated to discussion about the incel condition; 3. two sections dedicated to aesthetic evaluations, 4. a section called off topic, where users can discuss topics that are not related to the Incel ideology. For the Anglophone forum, we collected data from 1. Inceldom discussions, 2. gaming, entertaining and lifestyle; 3. two sections related to off topic discussions, such as politics, philosophy and religion. We also chose to collect images, video and other multimodal material embedded in the posts, users' avatars and emoticons. The metadata collected were related to users' *nicknames, posting time, title, permalink, date* and *id* for threads and *speaker, content, permalink, date, id, thread id, title, image urls* and *reply to* for posts. Additionally, we decided to deal with *quotes* and *replies-to* because part of the future goal of this project is to analyze the flow of the asynchronous conversations between users. Thus, we opted to automatically tag these elements in post-processing.

To collect the data, we implemented multiple crawlers, one for each forum, in order to systematically download threads and posts from the very beginning of the platform until March 2023, when we ended the process.

The crawler performs the following steps:
1. Visit each section. Collect URLs to all threads of that section.
2. Visit every thread. Extract metadata of the thread and collect URLs to all its posts.
3. Visit every post. Extract metadata of the post and its content. If available, download linked materials such as image, video, or audio data.

With this procedure, the corpus is organized to capture the hierarchical structure of the fora of sections, threads and posts as well as the conversational flow of the threads and posts of referring, quoting and replying to other users. The entire content of each threads is organized as in a list of python dictionaries that associate each key with a corresponding value, as is exemplified below. For each dictionary, keys are *speaker* of each post in the thread, the *thread id* and the *post id, data and time* of publication, the *text, number of like* of the post, *images, videos* and *external links* (where present).

Visually, the data are organized as follow:

```
[{'speaker': 'speakername',
'thread_id': '39483990',
'content': 'Apro questa discussione ispirandomi
ancora una volta a un topic aperto su GirlPower. [...]',
'reply_to': None,
'created': datetime,
'permalink': 'https://...',
'score': 10,
'images': ['http://...'],
'videos': [],
'post_id': '323680962',
'id': '93f5dcd7-21e7-42bd',
'image_urls': [],
'video_urls': [],
'external_links': ['http://...'],
}]
```

This organisation of data in the key-value structure allows easy retrieval of the information contained within each thread.

The crawlers for data extraction are implemented with Scrapy[9], a Python framework for extracting data from websites. To navigate the for a and to extract metadata, content, or linked materials, it is required to specify CSS and Xpath selectors that point directly to the desired content. These identifiers are specific to every website and forum, which makes the development of such crawlers a complex and time-consuming endeavour.

Table 2: Composition of the Anglophone and Italian datasets.

	incels.is	***FDB***
Forum sections	3	5
Number of threads	369,174	35,624
Number of posts per threads	7,359,727	740,278
Average post per thread	20	21
Average post lengths (in chars)	161.45	281.90
Images (unique)	425,259	20,183
Time span	November 2017 – March 2023	April 2009 – March 2023
Number of users (at the time of collection)	12,584	7,010

As can be observed from Table 2, despite the Italian dataset is older, it is markedly smaller in size than the Anglophone one, comprising approximately 10% of the total.

9 https://www.sbert.net/docs/pretrained_models.html (last accessed 14 February 2025).

5 Methodology for the analysis of textual content

5.1 Transformer-based topic modeling

As Hotlz et al. (2012) points out, Internet fora are often analysed using qualitative methods. Common qualitative methods include content analysis, conversation and discourse analysis, and thematic analysis. However, having to compare two large datasets, as mentioned in section 4.1, the exploration of the content relied on topic modelling and then supporting our interpretation by reading the concordance lines (Baker and Egbert 2016).

Regarding the topic modeling, given the disproportion of the two datasets, we randomly sampled 10% of the threads from the incels.is forum (36,917), balancing the smallest FDB (35,624). Although criticised as being non-scientific method (Brookes and McEnery 2019; McEnery and Brezina 2022), in Social Sciences and Digital Humanities, topic modeling is still a widely used technique for exploring large unlabelled corpora (Jaworska and Nanda 2021). One of the main reasons for this criticism lie in the subjectivity and low intersubjective verifiability in selecting the topics to be studied. In fact, it is usually the analyst who decides how to interpret the list of words associated by the algorithm at the output stage, discarding topics that she considers wrong.

To address these criticisms, in our analysis, we replaced the LDA approach (Blei et al. 2003), based on bag-of-words representations, with a new approach based on a transformer architecture (Vaswani 2017), which allows for the extraction of words not only in relation to their distribution throughout the documents, but also in relation to their context of occurrence. Topic modeling based on BERT embeddings (Grootendorst 2022) proved to be reliable for its high versatility and stability across domains, the possibility to perform analysis on multilingual data, and the ability to automatically extract the appropriate number of topics based on the sample size (Egger and Yu 2022). This allowed us to obtain meaningful word lists and minimized output manipulation, such as the ex-post removal of topics considered uninformative. To perform the transformer-based Topic Modeling, we used the Sentence Transformers model all-mpnet-base-v2[10] (Reimers and Gureyych 2019) to compute vector representations of the threads. Topic modeling allowed us to obtain some preliminary insights on the topic trends, both synchronically and diachronically (see Figure 2 and 3).

10 List of pretrained sentence transformers models: https://www.sbert.net/docs/pretrainedmodels.html (last accessed 14 February 2025).

While the static visualisation of topics allowed us to obtain a general overview of the types of discourses addressed by users in the two fora, as pointed out by Jaworska and Nanda (2021), the visual representation of topics over time is an effective method to clarify the narrative dynamics or changes of topics over time. This approach has made it possible to demonstrate several trends indicative of evolving practices.

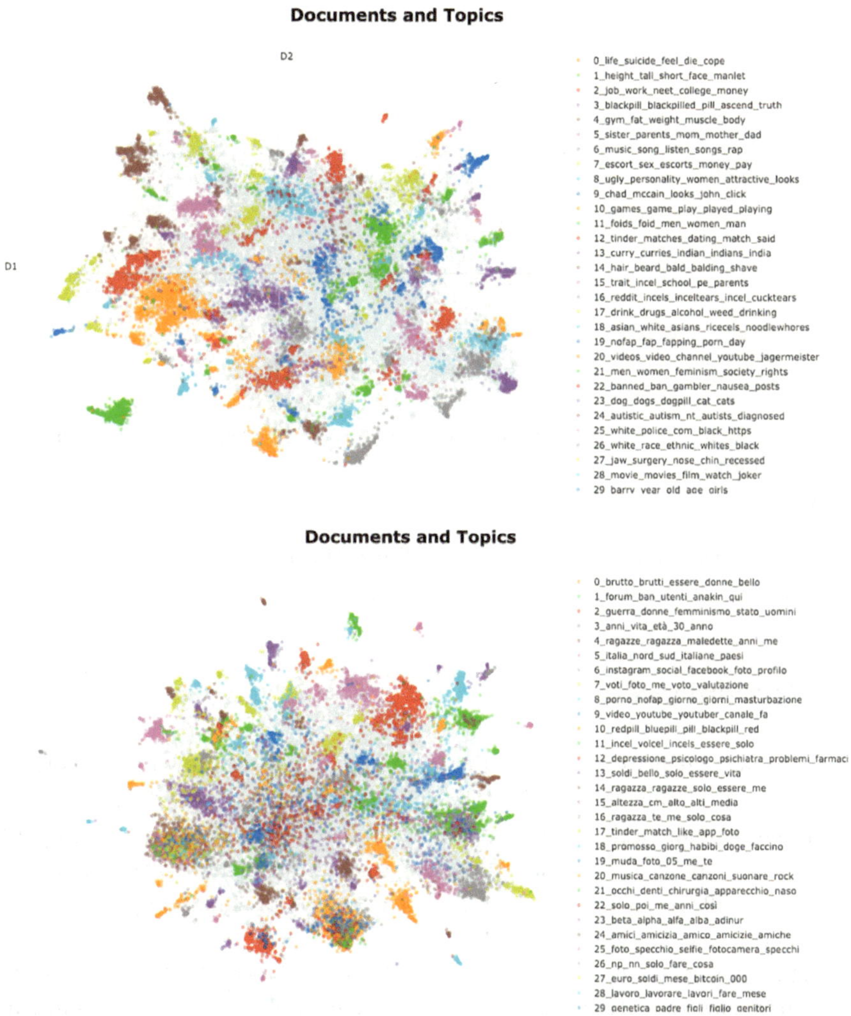

Figure 2: Static topic modelling comparison of the Anglophone (Top) and Italian (Bottom) fora. Best viewed with colour and zoom.

Figure 3: Dynamic topic modelling comparison of the Anglophone (Top) and Italian (Bottom) fora. Best viewed with colour and zoom.

For the purposes of this chapter, we have chosen to report only the first 30 topics generated by the static visualisation for both datasets.

5.2 Concordances

Concordance analysis consists of the in-depth study of words within a corpus, examining the immediate context in which they appear. Concordances can be organised alphabetically or according to grammatical categories, such as nouns or verbs that precede or follow a specific word, to highlight recurring patterns (Tranchese 2023). This method is useful for identifying language patterns that would otherwise be difficult to detect.

Since it is not possible to report all derived concordance lines for a single term in a large corpus, Sinclair (1999) suggests selecting random samples of concordances to identify and confirm patterns. In our case, SketchEngine's *random sample* function was used to select the concordances lines. Concordance analysis is crucial because it integrates quantitative analysis with a qualitative perspective, contextualising the results. This is one of the classical approaches in corpus linguistics, as it allows single terms to be studied in their contexts.

5.3 Overall interpretation and content comparison

So far, we have attested the comparability of the two fora from a qualitative point of view by comparing the main functionalities of the two platforms, their internal organisation, user management and rules. The results of the dynamic topic modelling (see Figure 3) offer preliminary insight into the narrative shift in both fora over the years. In the incels.is community, the top 10 topics remain stable. In particular, Topic 0 related to mental health (*life_suicide_feel_die*) seems to be significantly more discussed in the community compared to others. Furthermore, in the *incels.is* community, the most frequent topics over time are those related to aesthetics (Topic 1, Topic 4 and Topic 8). The Italian forum, on the other hand, shows a noticeable shift in user interest, with 2017 marking a crucial point in this trend. Before 2017, the dominant topic of discussion was the identity traits that characterised the user base and gave the group its name (being ugly, Topic 0). After 2017 (notably, corresponding to the opening of the incels.is forum), the focus of the community seems to have shifted to discussions about maintaining community boundaries and the internal life of the forum, as evidenced by the presence of keywords such as *ban* and *users* (Topic 1). The latter concern was assessed in the light of the development of internal forum netiquette, which saw an increase in the registration of new users as a result of the growing popularity of the Italian forum in the media.

The static clustering of the two datasets shows the top 30 general topics. These are summarised in Table 3 and each topic is associated to a semantic category.

As it can be observed from the summary Table 3, all the semantic categories identified have a counterpart in both languages, with the exception of the category *Animals*. In some cases, such as for the categories Off-line entertainment, Women and Men, and Ethnicity and Nationality, the concentration of topics is much higher in one of the two fora. This might indicate either the centrality and importance of the topic within the fora, or the interconnectedness of the topic with other discussion topics.

Table 3: The most frequent topics in the IDA corpus (summarisation of the static topic modeling).

Semantic category	incels.is topics	FDB topics
Mental health	**Topic 0**: life_suicide_feel_die_cope **Topic 24**: autistic_autism_nt_autists_ diagnosed.	**Topic 12**: depressione_psicologo_ psichiatra_problemi_farmaci
Aesthetics	**Topic 1**: height, tall, short, face, manlet. **Topic 4**: gym, fat, weight, muscle, body. **Topic 8**: ugly, personality, women, attractive, looks. **Topic 14**: hair, beard, bald, balding, shave. **Topic 27**: jaw, surgery, nose, chin, recessed.	**Topic 0**: brutto, brutti, essere, donne, bello. **Topic 7**: voti, foto, me, voto, valutazione. **Topic 15**: altezza, cm, alto, alti, media. **Topic 21**: occhi, denti, chirurgia, apparecchio, naso. **Topic 25**: foto, specchio, selfie, fotocamera, specchi.
Economic status and Employment	**Topic 2**: job, work, neet, college, money.	**Topic 13**: soldi, bello, solo, essere, vita. **Topic 27**: euro, soldi, mese, bitcoin, 000. **Topic 28**: lavoro, lavorare, lavori, fare, mese.
Affective sphere	**Topic 5**: sister, parents, mom, mother, dad.	**Topic 29**: genetica, padre, figli, figlio, genitori. **Topic 24**: amici, amicizia, amico, amicizie, amiche.
Sexuality	**Topic 7**: escort, sex, escorts, money, pay. **Topic 19**: nofap, fap, fapping, porn, day.	**Topic 8**: porno, nofap, giorno, giorni, masturbazione.
Off-line entertainment	**Topic 6**: music, song, listen, songs, rap. **Topic 10**: games, game, play, played, playing. **Topic 28**: movie, movies, film, watch, joker. **Topic 17**: drink, drugs, alcohol, weed, drinking.	**Topic 20**: musica, canzone, canzoni, suonare, rock.

Semantic category	incels.is topics	FDB topics
Social media and web application	**Topic 20**: videos, video, channel, youtube, jegermeister. **Topic 12**: tinder, matches, dating, match, said. **Topic 16**: reddit, incels, inceltears, incel, cucktears.	**Topic 6**: Instagram, social, facebook, foto, profile. **Topic 9**: video, youtube, youtuber, canale, fa. **Topic 17**: tinder, match, like, app, foto.
Forum life	**Topic 22**: banned, ban, gambler, nausea, posts.	**Topic 1**: forum, ban, utenti, Anakin, qui. **Topic 23**: beta, alpha, alfa, alba adinur.
Women and Men	**Topic 21**: men, women, feminism, society, rights. **Topic 11**: foids, foid, men, women, man.	**Topic 2**: Guerra, donne, femminismo, stato, uomini. **Topic 4**: ragazze, ragazza, maledette, anni, me. **Topic 14**: ragazza, ragazze, solo, essere, me. **Topic 16**: ragazza, te, me, solo, cosa. **Topic 26**: np, nn, solo, fare, cosa.
Ethnicity and Nationalities	**Topic 13**: curry, curries, Indian, Indians, india. **Topic 18**: Asian, white, Asians, ricecels, noodlewhores. **Topic 26**: white, race, ethnic, whites, black.	**Topic 5:** Italia, nord, sud, italiane, paesi.
Incel ideology	**Topic 3**: blackpill, blackpilled, pill, ascend, truth.	**Topic 10**: redpill, bluepill, pill, blackpill, red. **Topic 11**: incel, volce, incels, essere, solo.
Age	**Topic 29**: barry, year, old, age, girls.	**Topic 3**: anni, vita, età, 30, anno.
Animals	**Topic 23**: dog, dogs, dogpill, cat, cats.	–
Unclear	**Topic 9**: chad, mccain, looks, john, click. **Topic 15**: trait, incel, school, pe, parents. **Topic 25**: white, police, com, black, https.	**Topic 18**: promosso, giorg, habibi, doge, faccino. **Topic 19**: muda, foto, 05, me, te. **Topic 22**: solo, poi, me, anni, così.

The Aesthetics category was found to contain the highest number of topics in both languages. References to facial features (*occhi*, *denti*, *naso* in Italian, *nose*, *jaw* and *chin* in English) and height (*altezza*, *cm*, *alto* in Italian e *tall*, *short* in English) are prominent. Below are some examples of in-context usage for terms related to aesthetics in both languages:

Concordances related to Aesthetic category in Italian:[11]

1. Cmq 176 al nord mica è **alto** siamo seri, solo al sud sei normale intorno a 175. *[176 in the north is not tall let's be serious, only in the south are you normal around 175.]*
2. Il suo difetto principale è il **naso**, e direi anche gli **occhi** ma questo è per via degli occhiali. *[His main flaw is his nose, and I would say also his eyes, but that's because of the glasses.]*
3. Secondo me con un taglio di capelli diverso e una piccola aggiustatina ai **denti** guadagna qualche punto. *[In my opinion with a different hairstyle and a little adjustment of the teeth he gains a few points.]*

Concordances related to Aesthetic category in English:

4. Just kill everyone **taller** than you.
5. I had an extremely recessed **jawline** and no **chin**.
6. In addition, curries have longer, thinner **noses** which makes their appearance sharper.

This confirms the fundamental tenets of the so-called *LMS* theory, an acronym for Look, Money, and Status. This theory posits that both men and women are regarded as, and perceive themselves to be, "sexual objects to be evaluated and placed in a hierarchical order characterised mainly by aesthetics and economic status" (Dordoni and Magaraggia 2021: 46, *our translation*). For incels, being aesthetically attractive is a value that is attributed to the subject by genetic factors and is judged in an objective way. As such, it can be measured within a numerical range from 1 to 10 (the so-called decile scale),[12] based on certain physical characteristics (i.e. bone structure, height, jaw). In these fora users often lament their physical appearance and being rejected because of it, blaming women for being superficial, materialistic and *hypergamous.*[13] This is particularly true for users of the Italian community, which have made being *brutti veri* (truly uglies) their identity claim.

Other important shared topics concern users' relationship with social media platforms and web applications. In particular, references to dating apps such as Tinder are present in both languages. Recent transdisciplinary studies have highlighted the prominent role of YouTube in disseminating and reinforcing ideologies related to both, the Manosphere and heteronormative and toxic masculinity (Papadamou et al. 2021; Mamié et al. 2021; Champion and Frank 2021, Sugiura

11 Translations from Italian to English are provided by the authors.
12 https://incels.wiki/w/Decile (last accessed 14 February 2025).
13 https://incels.wiki/w/Hypergamy (last accessed 14 February 2025).

2021). Indeed, Tinder appears to play a significant role in both fora in shaping users' affective and sexual imaginaries of the opposite sex.

Concordances related to social media and applications category in Italian:

1. Però da quello che ho capito è che Meetic è un sito per incontri più sobri, mentre **Tinder** è praticamente più a sfondo sessuale. *[As far as I had understood Meetic is a site more akin to serious meetups, while Tinder is basically more sexual]*
2. Piuttosto mi rattrista questa cosa perché io mi ero illuso di trovare una relazione su **Tinder** e alla fine il livello medio di ragazze che si incontrano è questo. *[I am saddened by this because I was convinced that I would find a serious relationship on Tinder, while it turns out that the average level of girls that you meet there is this.]*
3. **Tinder** è per i bellocci da almeno 7 che sanno farsi le foto. *[Tinder is for handsome guys at least a 7 who know how to take pictures.]*

Concordances related to social media and applications category in English:

4. He is the type of guy to get 100% match rate on **Tinder.**
5. I bet the day when she arrives in Europe the first thing she'll do is install **Tinder** and fuck a white Chad.
6. On **Tinder** females can choose whoever the fuck they want.

Pornography, money and female prostitution also play an important role within the category of Sexuality. By analysing the language of the (now closed) incel communities on Reddit, Tranchese and Sugiura (2021) have traced a deep connection between incel discourses and mainstream pornography. Indeed, both discourses share a highly dehumanising vocabulary and metaphorical repertoire, even to the extent of normalising violence and rape. The stereotypical and dehumanising view of women is evident in the lexical preferences of the two communities, which have developed specific slang terms to talk about women. In fact, in the category of Women and Men we find, in addition to conventional terms such as *man, woman, girl*, slang terms such as *foid* (short form of *femoid*) and its Italian counterpart *np* (*non-person*). Analysing the representation of male and female individuals, Heritage (2023) observed that the dehumanising aspect of the use of the word foid is metaphorically derived from the mixture of the terms *female* and *android.* In the Italian community, on the other hand, the dehumanising aspect comes out of metaphor: women simply do not belong to the category of people. Finally, within the categories of Women and Men, in both languages, we find references to feminism. In fact, in both communities it is not only the biological aspect linked to the feminine that is threatened, but also the possible emancipation of women through feminism, which is to blame for the economic and social crises of contemporary society.

Concordances related to the Women and Men category in Italian:
1. Le **np** guardano un brutto con disgusto rabbioso come fossi una minaccia alla loro felicità. *[The np look at an ugly with angry disgust as I were a threat to their happiness]*
2. E io sono fiero di essere misogino, ma non solo odio le **donne**, IO ODIO ANCHE CHI NON LE ODIA MA LE RISPETTA, PERCHÈ LE **NP** DI MERDA NON RISPETTANO NOI COME UMANI. *[And I am proud of being misogynous, I do not only hate women, BUT I ALSO HATE THOSE WHO DO NOT HATE THEM BUT RESPECT THEM, BECAUSE THE SHITTY NPs DO NOT RESPECT US AS HUMANS.]*
3. E piacere ad una **NP (cioè ad un essere subumano)** non è così validante, è come avere una zecca attaccata alle palle, non vedi l'ora di liberartene. *[And to be liked by an NP (meaning a subhuman) is not that validating, it is like having a tick attached to your balls, you cannot wait to have it removed.]*

Concordances related to Women and Men and applications category in English:
4. I hate **foids** and **foids** combined with **feminism** is like pure cancer.
5. The only reason I'd pay a **foid** for is to use up and cum in her holes.
6. **Foids** can't give you this, they just use it as a tool to get stuff out of you. **Beta** for his bucks, **chad** for his semen.

In addition to these themes that emphasise, from various points of view, the centrality of sexuality within the discussions in the two fora, with often openly stereotypical and denigrating meanings, we find themes that are more akin to those of support groups. Topics such as mental health, offline entertainment, work and education, and references to the family unit were also discussed. The latter theme may also provide insight into the demographic composition of both fora, which are predominantly used by young individuals (Botto and Gottzén, 2024).

It is also noteworthy that the category of Ethnicity and Nationalities deserve particular attention. In this category, we find references to ethnic and racial groups, including both commonly used terms such as *Asian*, *white*, and *Indian*, as well as specific slang terms such as *ricecels*, *curries/curries*, and *noodlewhores*.[14]

14 The terms *ricecel* and *curry* are used derogatorily to refer to men of different ethnicities who identify as incel (involuntarily celibate). The term noodlewhore, on the other hand, refers to women of Asian descent perceived as promiscuous.

The prominence of the theme of Nationality and Ethnicity within the Anglophone community is indicated not only by the greater number of topics associated with this category, but also by the linguistic creativity observed. This aspect does not appear to be as prominent within the Italian community. In contrast, within the Italian community, the rhetoric of supremacism addresses the distinction between men and women in southern and northern Italy. This aspect represents a point of partial continuity between the two communities and may provide interesting clues for future analyses aimed at revealing the mutual influence and adaptation of Anglophone incel discourses by peripheral communities such as the Italian one. In particular, the relationship between racist instances and white supremacy is adapted and contextualised in the Italian scenario, which is characterised by a strong north-south economic divide and an extreme stereotyping of southern Italians. This phenomenon has been documented since the beginning of Italian unification and is known as *anti-meridionalism*.

6 Conclusions and future work

In this study, we detail the processes behind the development of IDA – Incel Data Archive, as well as an initial exploration of its content. With this work, we aim to contribute to the field of digital linguistics by demonstrating how an interdisciplinary methodology combining qualitative and quantitative techniques can be used to compare corpora across languages. We also show that the development of comparable corpora requires a deep and nuanced understanding of source texts and their contextual production, emphasising the central role of the researcher's experience. In light of these consideration, we believe that digital linguistics can benefit greatly from interdisciplinary synergies, particularly those studies that integrate the analysis of computer-mediated communication with social science perspectives on the role of media in shaping human interactions. To the best of our knowledge, this represents the first comparable corpus developed from the online forums of the incel community, in multiple languages. A crucial initial step towards a deeper understanding of these transnational communities, and the threat they may pose, involves data collection and the involvement of scholars specialising in digital linguistic research outside the English-speaking world. Expanding the collection to include non-English-speaking incel communities remains a key goal of this project. Furthermore, we intend to incorporate a semantic annotation phase of IDA to capture the unique discursive features of these communities.

Although unsupervised content exploration through topic modelling has only partially revealed the potential of this dataset, we believe that the results presented here already raise important questions about cross-national influences among these groups. The computational analysis of the linguistic and non-linguistic characteristics of these communities not only offers new insights into their discursive and social structure, but also helps to delineate the dynamics of radicalisation and ideological diffusion in globalised contexts. It also suggests the need for coordinated academic and policy efforts to understand and prevent extremist phenomena developing in the shadows of digital networks.

References

Aiston, Jessica Alexandra. 2023. *Argumentation strategies in an online male separatist community*. Ph.D. thesis, Lancaster University (United Kingdom).

Anastasi, Selenia. 2022. 'I am not like all the other girls'. Femcel, pinkpilled and women in the Incel communities. A qualitative analysis of the Italian 'Il Forum dei Brutti'. *28th Lavender Languages and Linguistics International Conference*. Catania, Italy, 23–25 May.

Arroyo, Belén López. 2020. Can comparable corpora be compared? *Ibérica: Revista de la Asociación Europea de Lenguas para Fines Específicos (AELFE)* 39, 43–68.

Aulia, Mahirza Putra & Ida Rosida. 2022. The phenomenon of involuntary celibates (Incels) in internet meme culture: A reflection of masculine domination. *International Journal of Media and Information Literacy* 7 (1), 4–17.

Baele, Stephane, Lewys Brace & Debbie Ging. 2023. A diachronic cross-platforms analysis of violent extremist language in the incel online ecosystem. *Terrorism and Political Violence* 36 (3), 1–24.

Baker, Paul & Jesse Egbert (eds.), 2016. *Triangulating methodological approaches in corpus linguistic research*. London: Routledge.

Baroni, Marco, Silvia Bernardini, Adriano Ferraresi & Eros Zanchetta. 2009. The wacky wide web: a collection of very large linguistically processed web-crawled corpora. *Language Resources and Evaluation* 43, 209–226.

Blei, David, Andrew Ng & Michael Jordan. 2003. Latent dirichlet allocation. *Journal of Machine Learning Research* 3, 993–1022.

Bogetić, Ksenija, Frazer Heritage, Veronika Koller & Mark McGlashan. 2023. Landwhales, femoids and sub-humans: Dehumanising metaphors in incel discourse. *Metaphor and the Social World* 13 (2), 178–196.

Botto, Matteo & Lucas Gottzén. 2024. Swallowing and spitting out the red pill: Young men, vulnerability, and radicalization pathways in the manosphere. *Journal of Gender Studies* 33 (5), 596–608.

Brookes, Gavin & Tony McEnery. 2019. The utility of topic modelling for discourse studies: A critical evaluation. *Discourse Studies* 21 (1), 3–21.

Brzuszkiewicz, Sara. 2020. *Incel radical milieu and external locus of control* 1. International Centre for Counter-Terrorism (ICCT).

Capalbi, Antonella. 2021. Le rappresentazioni audiovisive come strumento di indagine della manosphere. Joker, supereroe per gli Incel italiani? *AG About Gender-International Journal of Gender Studies* 10 (19), 105–130.

Champion, Amanda & Richard Frank. 2021. Exploring the "radicalization pipeline" on YouTube. *Terrorism Risk Assessment Instruments: Contemporary Policy and Law Enforcement Challenges*, 152–359.

Chang, Winnie. 2022. The monstrous-feminine in the incel imagination: investigating the representation of women as "femoids" on r/braincels. *Feminist Media Studies* 22 (2), 254–270.

De Gasperis, Arianna. 2021. "Giacomino uno di noi". Letteratura italiana e pratiche di maschilità nel Forum dei Brutti. *AG About Gender-International Journal of Gender Studies* 10 (19), 68–104.

Díaz-Fernández, Silvia & Elisa García-Mingo 2022. The bar of Forocoches as a masculine online place: Affordances, masculinist digital practices and trolling. *New Media & Society* 26 (9), 5336–5358.

Dordoni, Annalisa & Sveva Magaraggia. 2021. Modelli di mascolinità nei gruppi online incel e red pill: Narrazione vittimistica di s'e, deumanizzazione e violenza contro le donne. *AG About Gender-International Journal of Gender Studies* 10 (19), 35–67.

Egger, Roman & Yu, Joanne. 2022. A topic modeling comparison between LDA, NMF, top2vec, and BERtopic to demystify twitter posts. *Frontiers in sociology* 7.

Evans, Sandra K., Katy E. Pearce, Jessica Vitak & Jeffrey W. Treem. 2017. Explicating affordances: A conceptual framework for understanding affordances in communication research. *Journal of Computer Mediated Communication* 22 (1), 35–52.

Farrell, Tracie, Miriam Fernandez, Jakub Novotny & Harith Alani. 2019. Exploring misogyny across the manosphere in reddit. In *Proceedings of the 10th ACM Conference on Web Science*, 87–96.

Fišer, Darja, Nikola Ljubešić & Tomaž Erjavec. 2018. The Janes project: language resources and tools for Slovene user generated content, *Language Resources and Evaluation* 54 (1), 1–24.

Frey, Jennifer-Carmen, Alexander König, Egon Stemle, Achille Falaise, Darja Fišer & Harald Lüngen. 2020. The FAIR Index of CMC Corpora. In Julien Longhi & Claudia Marinica (eds.), *CMC Corpora through the prism of digital humanities*, 127–144. Paris: L'Harmattan. https://cmc-corpora.org/publications/frey-et-al-2020-fair-index-cmc/ (last accessed 25 October 2024).

Gillett, Rosalie & Nicolas Suzor. 2022. Incels on reddit: A study in social norms and decentralised moderation. *AoIR Selected Papers of Internet Research*. https://doi.org/10.5210/spir.v2021i0.12171.

Ging, Debbie. 2019. Alphas, betas, and incels: Theorizing the masculinities of the manosphere. *Men and Masculinities* 22 (4), 638–657.

Grootendorst, Maarten. 2022. Bertopic: Neural topic modeling with a class-based tf-idf procedure. https://arxiv.org/pdf/2203.05794 (last accessed 25 October 2024).

Heritage, Frazer & Veronika Koller. 2020. Incels, in-groups, and ideologies: The representation of gendered social actors in a sexuality-based online community. *Journal of Language and Sexuality* 9 (2), 152–178.

Heritage, Frazer. 2023. *Incels and ideologies: Exploring how incels use language to construct gender and race*. Cham: Springer Nature.

Herring, Susan C. & Jannis Androutsopoulos. 2015. Computer-mediated discourse 2.0. In Deborah Tannen, Heidi E. Hamilton & Deborah Schiffrin (eds.), *The handbook of discourse analysis*, 127–151. Wiley Blackwell.

Holtz, Peter, Nicole Kronberger & Wolfgang Wagner. 2012. Analyzing internet forums: A Practical Guide. *Journal of Media Psychology* 24 (2), 55–66.

Jaworska, Sylvia & Anupam Nanda. 2018. Doing well by talking good: A topic modelling-assisted discourse study of corporate social responsibility. *Applied Linguistics* 39 (3), 373–399.

Kozinets, Robert. 2015. *Netnography: Redefined*. Los Angeles: Sage.

Lilly, Mary. 2016. *"The world is not a safe place for men": The representational politics of the Manosphere*. Doctoral dissertation, University of Ottawa.

Mamié, Robin, Manoel Horta Ribeiro & Robert West. 2021. Are anti-feminist communities gateways to the far right? Evidence from Reddit and YouTube. In *Proceedings of the 13th ACM Web Science Conference*, 139–147.

Massanari, Adrienne. 2017. #gamergate and the fappening: How reddit as algorithm, governance, and culture support toxic technocultures. *New Media & Society* 19 (3), 329–346.

McEnery, Tony & Richard Xiao. 2007. Parallel and comparable corpora: What is happening. Incorporating corpora. *The Linguist and the Translator* 2 (5), 18–31.

Miani, Alessandro, Thomas Hills & Adrian Bangerter. 2021. LOCO: The 88-million-word language of conspiracy corpus. *Behavior Research Methods*, 1–24.

Nagle, Angela. 2017. *Kill all normies: Online culture wars from 4chan and Tumblr to Trump and the alt-right.* John Hunt Publishing.

O'Malley, Roberta Liggett, Karen Holt & Thomas J. Holt. 2022. An exploration of the involuntary celibate (incel) subculture online. *Journal of Interpersonal Violence* 37, 7–8, 4981–5008.

Papadamou, Kostantinos, Savvas Zannettou, Jeremy Blackburn, Emiliano De Cristofaro, Gianluca Stringhini & Michael Sirivianos. 2021. "How over is it?" Understanding the Incel Community on YouTube. *Proceedings of the ACM on Human-Computer Interaction*, 1–25.

Pelzer, Björn, Lisa Kaati, Katie Cohen & Johan Fernquist. 2021. Toxic language in online incel communities. *SN Social Sciences* 1, 1–22. https://doi.org/10.1007/s43545-021-00220-8.

Prazmo, Ewelina. 2022. In dialogue with non-humans or how women are silenced in incels' discourse. *Language and Dialogue* 12 (3), 383–406.

Reimers, Nils & Iryna Gurevych. 2019. Sentence-BERT: Sentence embeddings using siamese BERT-networks. https://arxiv.org/pdf/1908.10084 (last accessed 25 October 2024).

Ribeiro, Manoel Horta, Jeremy Blackburn, Barry Bradlyn, Emiliano De Cristofaro, Gianluca Stringhini, Summer Long, Stephanie Greenberg & Savvas Zannettou. 2021. The evolution of the manosphere across the web. *In Proceedings of the International AAAI Conference on Web and Social Media* 15, 196–207.

Scotto di Carlo, Giuseppina. 2023. An analysis of self-other representations in the incelosphere: Between online misogyny and self-contempt. *Discourse & Society* 34, 1, 3–21.

Sharoff, Serge, Reinhard Rapp, Pierre Zweigenbaum & Pascale Fung (eds.), 2013. *Building and using comparable corpora*. Berlin & Heidelberg: Springer.

Sharoff, S. 2013. Measuring the distance between comparable corpora between languages. In Serge Sharoff, Reinhard Rapp, Pierre Zweigenbaum & Pascale Fung (eds.), *Building and using comparable corpora*, 113–130. Berlin & Heidelberg: Springer.

Sinclair, John. 1999. A way with common words. In Hilde Hasselgard & Signe Oksefjell (eds.), *Out of corpora: Studies in honour of Stig Johansson*, 157–179. Amsterdam: Rodopi.

Sugiura, Luisa. 2021. *The incel rebellion: The rise of the manosphere and the virtual war against women.* Bingley, UK: Emerald Group Publishing.

Thorburn, Joshua, Anastasia Powell & Peter Chambers. 2023. A world alone: Masculinities, humiliation and aggrieved entitlement on an incel forum. *The British Journal of Criminology* 63, 1, 238–254.

Tognini-Bonelli, Elena. 2007. The corpus-driven approach. In Wolfgang Teubert & Ramesh Krishnamurthy (eds.), *Corpus linguistics: Critical concepts in linguistics*, 74–92. London: Routledge.

Tranchese, Alessia & Luisa Sugiura. 2021. "I don't hate all women, just those stuck-up bitches": How incels and mainstream pornography speak the same extreme language of misogyny. *Violence Against Women* 27, 14, 2709–2734.

Tranchese, Alessia. 2023. *From Fritzl to #metoo*. Cham: Springer International Publishing.

Trujillo, Amaury & Stefano Cresci. S. 2022. Make reddit great again: Assessing community effects of moderation interventions on r/the_donald. In *Proceedings of the ACM on Human Computer Interaction* 6 (CSCW2), 1–28.

Tuominen, Tuuli, Panu Kalliokoski & Antti Arppe. 2003. SFNET Corpus [data set]. Kielipankki. http://urn.fi/urn:nbn:fi:lb-20150126 (last accessed 25 October 2024).

Vessey, Rachelle. 2024. 'From cross-linguistic to intersectional corpus-assisted discourse studies', *Journal of Corpora and Discourse Studies* 7 (1), 7–21.

Voroshilova, Anzhelika I. & Dmitriy O. Pesterev. 2021. Russian incels web community: Thematic and semantic analysis. In *2021 Communication Strategies in Digital Society Seminar* (ComSDS), 185–190.

Vaswani, Ashish, Noam Shazeer, Niki Parmar, Jakob Uszkoreit, Llion Jones, Aidan N. Gomez, Łukasz Kaiser & Illia Polosukhin. 2017. Attention is all you need. *31st Conference on Neural Information Processing Systems (NIPS 2017)*, Long Beach, CA, USA.

Waśniewska, Małgorzata. 2020. The red pill, unicorns and white knights: Cultural symbolism and conceptual metaphor in the slang of online incel communities. In Barbara Lewandowska-Tomaszczyk (ed.), *Cultural conceptualizations in language and communication*, 65–82. Cham: Springer International.

Eva Triebl

Not an expert, but not a fan either. A corpus-based study of negative self-identification in web forum interaction

Abstract: This study examines the linguistic micro-management of identity in and across online contexts, drawing upon corpus-based pragmatic analyses of a structure with a meaning potential to examine wider questions about identity in digitally mediated social life. The structure in focus is negative self-identifiers of the type "I + copula + not + indefinite NP" used in UK web discussion forums. This structure was chosen because it is the most explicit linguistic realization of non-identification with a nominally expressed conceptual category, which serves to contrast the speaker with explicit or presupposed claims and thus indexes how speakers perceive, and discursively create, the context they are writing into. By means of qualitative and quantitative analysis of the forms and functions of 936 instances of the structure in their co-texts, it was found that negative self-identifiers from the fields of expertise and preferences were salient in the examined corpus. They were frequently used to frame co-texts in which speakers linguistically enacted various forms of expertise, pointing to heightened reflexivity regarding the epistemic status and social impact of their utterances and a reconceptualization of expertise as a transient discourse phenomenon rather than a more permanent identity feature.

Keywords: negation, self-identification, corpus pragmatics, expertise, stance management

1 Introduction: Why study what forum users say they are not

Negative self-identifiers of the type "I + copula + not + indefinite NP" (henceforth NSIs) are a pragmatically noteworthy linguistic choice. From a formal semantic viewpoint, negation merely reverses the truth-value of statements. However, accounting for the ontological status of negative statements and their meanings in

Eva Triebl, University of Vienna, e-mail: eva.triebl@univie.ac.at

https://doi.org/10.1515/9783111434018-013

social interaction is considerably more complex[1] (Miestamo 2017: 405; Horn and Wansing 2020). Considered in isolation, negatives[2] are uninformative (Leech 1983: 101); after all, a non-state does not correspond to a reality that could be defined truth-conditionally. Vice versa, it is impossible to set up conditions under which a negative utterance is true, as this would amount to an infinite list of propositions that hold in spite of the asserted state of affairs. From a performance-oriented perspective, the question of what is propositionally expressed by negative utterances is less important than the functions they serve for speakers' identity management in discourse. For example, the 'truth' of the statement *I'm not an expert* depends on what is seen as representing expertise in the particular communicative situation, and it may not (only) serve to provide ideational information about the speaker (except in cases where they are direct responses to questions of the type "Are you an X?"). Negatives of this type are marked linguistic choices that interact with cues to familiar mental models and thereby presuppose and construe irrealis mental spaces, which are defined as background knowledge assumed to be shared among discourse participants. Against this background knowledge, negatives stand out as salient and relevant (Sperber and Wilson 1986; Lewandowska-Tomaszczyk 2006; van Dijk 2008). Thus, they serve to "correct[] the hearer's mistaken beliefs" (Givón 1993: 190), either explicitly asserted or implied to be present in the immediate co-text, the situational context or the wider cultural context of the utterance (Givón 1993: 191; Jordan 1998: 706). As such, they are also socially more delicate, which, coupled with their uninformativeness, probably explains why they have been found to be used less frequently than affirmatives (Martínez 1995: 214).

To study how NSIs manage claims and guide meaning in interaction, they can be effectively approached from an interactional sociolinguistic perspective (Gumperz 1996). In this view, NSIs can be seen as discourse markers, which are defined as meaning potentials that, rather than contributing to the propositional content, reflect users' awareness and co-construction of the interactional context. Thus, they serve procedural functions and index aspects such as speaker identity and

1 The question of what negatives mean becomes even more complex when considering their scope and interaction with other logical operators (Horn 2020). While a detailed discussion of the scope and presupposition of negatives is beyond the scope of this article, it is important to note that negative statements do activate presuppositions. This activation has relevance for this study because the use of negatives indexes orientation toward "mutual contextual beliefs" (Bach and Harnish 1979: 5). These beliefs help make the referent relevant (Sperber and Wilson 1986) and allow us to arrive at the fully fledged, contextually enriched meaning of the indefinite NP.

2 This study is concerned with statements containing *not-* and *no-*negation, but negativity may also be realized through morphological negation (e.g. *possible* vs. *impossible*) and inherent negation (e.g. *lack* as opposite of *have*) (Givón 1993: 202).

stance (Ochs 1996). NSIs relate the speaker to an identifying NP and, due to their negative polarity, activate the noun phrase's conceptual meaning (Aijmer 2015: 89). Unlike typical discourse markers like 'actually,' which have conventionalized meanings (Aijmer 2013: 30), NSIs provide a reflexive comment on the speaker's perception of and stance toward what is being interactionally accomplished. By strategically mobilizing a nominally expressed concept, they provide metadata about the ongoing discourse and function as a multifunctional conversational resource (Ekström and Stevanovic 2023), similarly to a conversational tag (Huang, Hornton, and Ethimiadis 2010).

Because the NSIs examined here are part of the main text of web forum postings, they are neither functionally equivalent to nor searchable like hashtags (Zappavigna 2015). However, they can be studied to see how forum users informally interacting on a shared topic index their non-identification with certain categories in strategic and patterned ways. From a critical talk-in-interaction perspective (Speer 2005; Wilkes and Speer 2021), negative self-identification with nouns and the recurrence of certain nouns across texts are particularly interesting because members' categories may be interactionally significant and ideologically charged (Haugh 2013: 11; Stokoe and Attenborough 2014: 161). Studying the mobilization of referential expressions in web forum discourse can therefore reveal speakers' metapragmatic awareness, i.e., their evaluations of what is pragmatically appropriate or 'sayable', and by whom (Silverstein 2003; Spitzmüller and Warnke 2011), in collapsed online contexts (Marwick and boyd 2011 space missing after). This study thus contributes to research on the performance and conceptualization of the self in contemporary digitally mediated social practices, in which individualization (Giddens 1991; Beck and Beck-Gernsheim 2001) and social affiliation through shared authenticity (Leppänen et al. 2015; Lüders, Dinkelberg, and Quayle 2022) are key paradigms for meaning-making. Social media platforms such as forums are well-suited sites to study the functions of linguistic disalignment, as they bring together users from diverse offline backgrounds around shared interests and are shaped by users' interactions (Androutsopoulos 2014: 63; Tagg et al. 2017: 32). To find how the template "I + copula + not + indefinite NP" is used in authentic interaction on web forums, a corpus of 936 UK web forum discussions in English language was collected based on the occurrence of this structure. The remainder of this article will report and critically discuss the findings of these analyses, which aimed to answer the following research questions:

RQ 1: What nouns and noun phrases do people use to negatively identify themselves on web forums? To which conceptual categories can these be assigned, and how prominently (in terms of frequency and lexical variation) are the identified categories represented in the data?

RQ 2: What are the formal-functional relationships between NSIs and their immediate co-texts? What ideational and pragmatic functions do these co-texts fulfill, and are there patterned relationships between specific conceptual categories of NSIs and certain co-texts?

RQ 3: What are the implications of potentially patterned functions of NSIs for the reflexive performance of identity in informal interactions on web forums?

2 Study design and data

A corpus of NSIs from web forums was compiled to identify the categories of identification linguistically represented and their functions in relation to their immediate and wider co-texts. The aim was for this corpus to represent variants of the formally defined structure "I + copula + not + indefinite NP" within their utterance-internal and sequential co-texts as used in this type of discourse. Corpus compilation was guided by both linguistic and platform-related criteria. For the linguistic criteria, customized Google searches were employed to identify the formal variants of the matrix clause.

- **Tenses**: present simple, present perfect simple (*I'm/am not, I've/have never been*)[3]
- **Contraction**: *I'm not, I am not*
- ***No*-negation**: *I am no, I'm no*
- **Constructions with *never***: *I have never been*[4]
- **Adverbs**: e.g. *I'm not really, I'm definitely not*
- **Indefinite article**: *I'm not a/an*

The data was collected from publicly available English-language UK websites that included the words *forum* or *thread* in their domains.[5] The data was not controlled for topic, purpose, or user characteristics, thus representing a wide variety of con-

3 NSIs were excluded from the corpus if they appeared in instances of active voicing (e.g., *He said, "I'm no liar"*) or in embedded clauses with subjects other than the first-person singular (e.g., *She can't argue that I am not an expert*). This is because referring to someone else's identity ascription is not the same as negatively identifying with a particular NP oneself.

4 Constructions with *never* are considered a distinct variant because they occurred significantly more often in the data compared to present perfect tense NSIs without adverbial modifiers (e.g., *I haven't been a basketball player for two years*).

5 Using these two search terms was intended to systematically gather data from at least two (out of many) possible URL formats that discussion threads may take.

texts in which variants of the formally defined structure appeared. Regarding corpus size and balance, data collection was systematically randomized by retrieving an equal number of instances for each formally defined variant from each page of Google search results until a target of 100 occurrences was reached. In cases where a variant occurred fewer than 100 times, all instances were included.

Sampling the corpus to represent all variants of the target structure (Biber 1993: 244) means that the corpus does not accurately reflect the actual proportions of the frequencies of these formal variants. As a result, the quantitative information about the categories identified in the data and their relationships is not statistically significant. This methodological approach was chosen nonetheless for two main reasons. First, proportional sampling was not feasible with the Google searches used. No single search string could capture all formal variants in proportion. Second, the study's focus is on the functions of NSIs, emphasizing the meaning of the identifying NP over the specific form of the structure. Therefore, unless there is a known patterned relationship between the formal variants of the structure and the meanings of identifying NPs (such as expertise disclaimers and present perfect tense forms), which exploratory analyses have shown does not exist, the overrepresentation of a particular form does not affect the overall insights gained.

To capture a sufficiently large sample of the structure in use and considering the potentially asynchronous nature of forum interactions, the data collection period was set from July to September 2019. The only constraint was that postings needed to be published after 2015. As a result, the corpus represents a snapshot of NSIs as they appeared on web forums during this timeframe, while also reflecting interactions where the structure had been present over a longer period. The focus on adequately representing the form while allowing for contextual variation stems from the study's microlinguistic orientation, which involves examining linguistic details to identify patterns that may indicate longer-term, gradual phenomena.

Regarding the co-text included in the corpus, NSIs were collected with both their utterance-internal and sequential, utterance-external co-text. This means each NSI was gathered along with the posting it appeared in and the postings to which it replied. The resulting corpus consists of 936 instances of formal variants of the matrix clause in their contexts of use, totalling 295,164 tokens. Table 1 shows the number of instances of the pre-defined NSI variants collected from the two different types of web domains.

Table 1: Overview of formal variants searched for, and numbers of NSIs included in the corpus.

Data group	Variants searched for	Corpus examples	URL: forum site: .uk	URL: thread Site: .uk	Total
1	*I'm not a/n*	***I'm*** *not a fan of pizza*	101	100	201
2	*I am not a/n*	*I* ***am*** *not a person who can advise you on the matter*	101	101	202[6]
3	Modified variants of 1 & 2: *I'm/am not * a/n* *I'm/am * not a/n*	*I'm not* ***much*** *of a fan of butly based inhalants*	35	14	49
4	*I'm/I am no*	*I'm* ***no*** *thief!!!*	101	99	200
5	Modified variants of 4: *I'm * no* *I am * no* *I * am no*	*I'm* ***still no*** *expert*	7	4	11
6	*I've/have never been a/n*	***I have never*** *been a perfume buyer*	100	101	201
7	Modified variants of 6: *I've * never been a/n* *I have never * been a/n* *I * have never been a/n* *I have * never been a/n*	*i've* ***just never*** *been a fan of the kit*	6	5	11
8	*I've/I have not/ haven't been a/n*	***I've*** *not been a fan of Gewurtztraminer*	47	12	59
9	Modified variants of 8: *I've * not been a/n* *I've not * been a/n* *I have * not been a/n* *I * have not been a/n*	*I have not* ***always*** *been big fan of Phase scanners*	2	0	2
Total					936

6 During my research, a few instances were deleted as false positives, and additional NSIs were identified. As a result, the size of some data groups changed slightly, and the upper limit of 100 was exceeded in a few cases.

In an iterative process, metadata about textual and contextual aspects was manually added to the data using tags. This metadata included the meaning of the identifying NP, the formal appearance and functions of the immediate and wider co-texts in which the structure appeared, the topic of the thread, and the forum featuring the NSI. Annotation and qualitative analysis began with the conceptually most important and syntactically most narrow level: the semantic meaning of identifying NPs. The analysis then proceeded in structurally ascending steps, involving the formal and functional categorization of the sentence-internal and sentence-external co-texts of NSIs. Frequencies of the identified categories and their relationships were determined using the concordancing function of WordSmith 5.0 (Scott 2008) and Excel's sorting and calculation functions. The corpus-based study was complemented by detailed qualitative analyses of entire post events where NSIs from frequently instantiated conceptual domains were used.

3 The empirical study

3.1 The meanings and co-textual relations of NSIs

The first step in the analysis was to create a conceptual profile of NSIs in the corpus, summarized with examples in Table 2.[7] Conceptual profiling involves retrieving linguistic realizations of a predefined formal paradigm (in this case, identifying NPs) from the corpus in a vertical format and then conducting a qualitative analysis. The goal is to identify and differentiate groups of formally and semantically related linguistic elements, providing an overview of the conceptual structure of the paradigm (Marko 2015). In this analysis, some categories were identified based on specific lexemes, such as the frequent nouns *expert* and *fan*, which appeared with various modifiers and thus defined certain categories. Other categories were established based on the meanings of head nouns and their modifiers. For example, the NP *hater of CGI* was categorized under "preferences" due to the prepositional phrase specifying a phenomenon of (non-)'hate,' whereas the unmodified *hater* was categorized as an evaluative characteristic. The data prominently featured domains of preferences (especially constructions with *fan*) and expertise (especially constructions with *expert*).

7 Due to space limitations, only the most prominently represented conceptual categories and up to three examples per category are included.

Table 2: Overview of the most frequently occurring conceptual categories of identifying NPs.

Preference (+*fan*) (200)

- **General/unspecific (15):** *huge fan*
- **Postmodified (165):**
  - **Products (60):** *ear buds, Hornby decoders, the P20*
  - **Visual features/designs (24):** *magenta, the exhaust tip on the black car, the opacity*
  - **Persons/clubs (20):** *Blake, Cameron, Pitman*
  - **Activities and events (19):** *chasing the dragon, going out, my birthday*
  - **Food/drink/substances (14):** *brown chocolate, garlic, whiskey*
  - **Nature/animals (7):** *gulls, mice, moths*
  - **IT/app-related (7):** *cgv, downloading file, track*
  - **Ideas and ideologies (5):** *ranks, these '5 year plan' type of things, violence for the sake of violence*
  - **Business-related (3):** *guaranteed stops, partnerships, the Scandinavian market*
  - **Entertainment (3):** *Nemesis Sub-Terra, stand-up, "So Broken"*
  - **Body care (3):** *fasting, shaving, the steam method*
- **Head in compounds (16):**
  - **Commodities (8):** *big e21 fan, big Lambo fan, BMW fan*
  - **Persons/clubs (8):** *Chelsea, Heyman, Leicester*
- **Prepositional phrase + referring expression (4):** *of these*

Preference (-*fan*) (44)

- **Products (13):** *avid collector of TP, Dore enthusiast, great believer in tablets*
- **Styles (8):** *big dress person, makeup kind of girl, particularly 'pink' person*
- **Ideas/Ideology (5):** *advocate of couples separating, Labour lover, slavish adherent to their politics*
- **Activity-related (4):** *H/C snob, lover of positions 2/4, lover of the Beagle Point systems*
- **Sexual (3):** *masturbator, thong man, tit man*
- **Medical treatment (3):** *advocate of high doses, lover of taking laxatives, serial doctors apt person*
- **Persons/groups (3):** *Hodgson basher, Radiohead hater, supporter of Jim Price*
- **IT/app-related (2):** *database guy, piping guy*
- **Food (2):** *big chocolate lover, cream lover*
- **Nature:** *dog lover*

Expertise (+*expert*) (192)

- **General/unspecific (105):** *expert*
- **Prepositional phrase + referring expression (18):** *at this*
- **Premodified (5):**
  - **Legal (2):** *legal*
  - **Business/services (2):** *financial, postal*
  - **Medical:** *medical*
- **Postmodified (40):**
  - **Nature (12):** *in fish, in mammals, on bees*
  - **Technical appliances and processes (7):** *on metal detecting, on small horticultural engines, on the various types of gas cylinders*
  - **IT (6):** *at drivers/optimization, in this verification lark, with Meshlab*

  - **Products (5):** *on military uniforms, on shoes, on the dot product*
  - **Arts/sports (4):** *in training techniques, on ski jumping, on the 2 step*
  - **Medical:** *on HRT*
  - **Science:** *at geology*
  - **Business/services:** *on house prices*
  - **Language:** *at pronouncing things*
  - **Leisure:** *at this game*
  - **Ideological:** *on religious matters*
- **Head in compounds (24):**
  - **IT/gaming (8):** *class CPU, Linux server, programming*
  - **Technical (6):** *asbestos, electronics, vehicle electronics*
  - **Nature (5):** *conformation, shark, wood*
  - **Particular products (5):** *Dennis, DICOM, jeans*

Expertise (*-expert*) (56)

- **General/unspecific (13):** *pro, professional, specialist*
- **Noun (1):**
  - **Technical:** *techie*
- **Adjective + noun (16):**
  - **Language (3):** *eloquent wordsmith, great blogger, particularly lyrical guy*
  - **Medical (3):** *medical person (2), medical professional*
  - **Nature (2):** *big grower of mesembs, good birdwatcher*
  - **Sports (2):** *expert runner, tactical guru*
  - **Technical (2):** *expert builder, technological man*
  - **Legal:** *legal eagle*
  - **Housework:** *very good cook*
  - **Science:** *astronomical type*
  - **Other:** *confident driver*
- **Noun + noun (13):**
  - **IT (7):** *advanced IT person, bash guru, computer boff*
  - **Technical (4):** *electronics guru, fire door specialist, tech geek*
  - **Business:** *VAT specialist*
  - **Science:** *math wiz*
- **Noun + prepositional phrase (9):**
  - **Health (4):** *professional on OCD, stranger to how PD affects people, stranger to injecting*
  - **Housework (2):** *great one for composting, natural in the kitchen*
  - **Nature:** *great one for bird song*
  - **Arts:** *authority on paintwork*
  - **IT/Gaming:** *noob to UAE4ALL*
- **Metonymic proper names (4):** *Mo Farah, Nostradamus, Aladdin's genii*

Professions (142)

- **Medical (41):** *doctor, neurologist, pharmacist*
- **IT (21):** *coder, dev, developer*
- **Technical (21):** *chainsaw technician, electrical engineer, mechanic*
- **Arts/Sports (15):** *cheerleader, designer, dj*
- **Science (14):** *chemist, geologist, historian*

- **Business/Finance (11):** *accountant, experienced investor, financial advisor*
- **Education (7):** *du student, pshe teacher, qualified teacher*
- **Legal (6):** *lawyer (5), solicitor*
- **Nature (4):** *botanist, hymenopterist, zoologist*
- **Other (2):** *butler, fieldtester*

Personal Characteristics (136)

- **Evaluative (44):** *bad person, drama queen, hater*
- **Health-related (21):** *addict, alcoholic, bedwetter*
- **Ideological/religious (16):** *agnostic, buddist, communist*
- **Relational/demographic (10):** *parent, schoolboy, youngster*
- **Emotional/psychological (10):** *anxious person, happy bunny, masochist*
- **Physiological/physical (10):** *flexible person, heavy guy, tall or stocky kind of person*
- **Social (9):** *follower, leader, loner*
- **Geographic/residential status (8):** *Aberdonian, EU resident, resident*
- **Linguistic background (5):** *native speaker, native English speaker*
- **Gender-specific (3):** *girly-girl, one of those girls, sir*

The analysis revealed that the nouns *fan* and *expert* not only appear prominently in the corpus overall but also in many compounds and prepositional phrases referring to specific kinds of fandom and expertise. For the category of preferences, the analysis distinguished between constructions with *fan* as the head noun (200 tokens) and other lexemes indicating speakers' relationships with things, people, and activities, such as *avid collector* (44 tokens). Constructions with *fan* can be further divided into several thematic subcategories. The largest subcategory is "products", which includes instances where the focal structure is postmodified by prepositional phrases denoting a wide range of commodities (e.g., *earbuds*, *exercise bikes*, or *the old Astra*) and their design features (e.g., *the yellow*, *it being silver*, or *the Mac-style icon*). Other semantic domains of non-preference include references to people, food, and activities, as well as detailed aspects relating to specific activities, such as *new menus for selecting vehicles in a game*.

In constructions without *fan*, analyzing the semantic heads of noun phrases shows that speakers often negatively identify with affective categories, such as *lovers* or *enthusiasts*, and combine phenomena of non-preference with general head nouns like *guy*, *girl*, or *person*.

The high frequency and specificity of noun phrases in this domain demonstrate that speakers use NSIs to position themselves attitudinally toward a wide range of topics relevant to the immediate interactional context, linguistically expressing their identity through very specific tastes (Liu 2007). One function of emphasizing non-preference is to index expertise, which, as Carr (2010: 20) explains, can be enacted by "establishing a deliberate stance in relation to a set of culturally valued or valuable objects." This is illustrated by Example (1) below. Here, the NSI contrasts the speaker's positive evaluation of *the 5010* with their previously low opinion of Phase scanners. It is followed by a detailed description of the scanner's features, which includes numerous indicators of authority, such as references to prior experience with earlier models and metapragmatic reflections on sincerity (e.g., *I must say*) and truth (e.g., *I think I am correct in saying*) (Bublitz and Hübler 2007). Thus, while the speaker does not explicitly highlight the category of expertise, they showcase their experience with the product category in question. By using *us* to refer to the forum community and representing the producer, *Z+F*, as someone who *demonstrated* their scanner to them, the speaker constructs an in-group of product reviewers to whom novelties are presented. By starting their post with a remark about how some may be aware of their attitude toward Phase scanners, the speaker positions themselves as an established member of the projected community. Their closing statement, *I look forward to seeing more from this scanner*, not only predicts the future of the scanner but also implicitly addresses the producer, who, after presenting their new product to the forum 'jury', may now 'leave the stage'.

(1) As some of you may know **I have not always been a big fan of Phase scanners** but things change. Z+F demonstrated the 5010 to us recently and I must say that I was really, really impressed. Its a lot smaller than previous models but has a large on board screen which is easy to use. The data looked a lot cleaner than I have seen before with phase scans and the fact that it can scan at similar ranges to TOF is impressive. And I think I am correct in saying that it now has a level compensator. I look forward to seeing more from this scanner

Regarding the second semantic category of NSIs frequently instantiated in the data – expertise – three types of nouns were identified: first, NPs with the head noun *expert*; second, other lexical elements denoting (non-)expertise (e.g., *noob*); and third, references to specific professions and job titles (e.g., *accountant*). As shown in Table 2, the high type/token ratio for the expertise category is largely due to the generic use of *expert*. In contrast, the low lexical variation for professions is mainly attributable to the unspecific noun *doctor*. The recurrence of these unspecific terms in NSIs suggests a formulaic and procedural, rather than conceptual, use of expertise disclaimers. Speakers commonly and generically self-identify as experts without specifying their domain of knowledge. This may indicate a tacit understanding among forum participants that lay expertise is being exchanged, with neither the speakers nor their audience needing to know the precise label, if such a label even exists – for someone with expertise in a particular field. As Rueger, Dolfsma and Aalbers (2021) explain, lay expertise can be understood as peer endorsement, representing a form of discourse where accredited experts – such as cardiologists, developers, and chemists – are inherently absent. By contrasting themselves with these perceived authorities on the topic, speakers seem to acknowledge their relevance while light-heartedly connecting over their absence. Example (2) below illustrates how an expertise disclaimer mitigates the speaker's diagnosis of a photo shared on the forum. In contrast to Example (1), this post employs several devices that position the speaker as a layperson. For instance, the term *fur balls* is placed in inverted commas and described as *loose*, while the adverbs *a bit* and *possibly*, along with the caveat that they *may be well off the mark*, reduce epistemic certainty.

(2) Hi [Name]
Looks like fur from a cat! They sometimes bring up what are loosely called 'fur balls' and they can look a bit like this. Or some other animal possibly. **I'm no expert** and may be well off the mark [Name]!

Besides preferences and expertise, the categories of personal characteristics and situational roles and behaviors were also notably present in the data (136 and 83 tokens, respectively). This indicates that the reflexive portrayal of an authentic persona – beyond simply being knowledgeable and opinionated – is crucial for the relationships formed on the examined forums. For instance, NSIs were used to describe speakers in terms of personality traits and social skills (e.g., being a *bad person*), social roles both external and internal to the forum (e.g., a *parent* or a *forum admin*), and characteristics related to gender (e.g., *girlie-girl*), age (e.g., *youngster*), or health (e.g., *sound sleeper*).

To summarize, the semantic profile discussed in this section suggests that negative self-identification is a linguistic strategy allowing speakers to emphasize different aspects of their social persona based on the interactional demands of the conversation. Preference disclaimers position speakers as informed peers by specifying contextually relevant non-preferences. Disclaimers of expertise serve to hedge opinions epistemically, thus highlighting common ground among lay users by emphasizing their shared lack of expert knowledge. A third function of negative self-identifiers (NSIs) identified in the corpus is to reflect speaker individuality by positioning them in relation to locally relevant personality traits and social roles.

3.2 Functionally profiling the co-texts of NSIs

The functions of NSIs, similar to those of discourse markers, depend on their sequential and functional relationships within their immediate co-text and broader co-text (Aijmer 2015: 89). Therefore, the analyses presented in this section examined the forms and functions of NSIs within their textual surroundings at the levels of phrase, clause, and turn. This approach aimed to identify tendencies for NSIs from specific conceptual categories (as discussed in 3.1) to occur within particular types of co-text. The first step involved qualitatively analyzing and annotating the immediate left (1L) and right (1R) co-texts of all instances of NSIs and determining the frequencies of the identified categories. Next, to identify linguistic patterns in the co-text of NSIs, the clauses formally linked to the matrix clause were functionally profiled using the transitivity framework (Halliday and Matthiessen 2014). Frequently occurring co-textual categories were then analyzed more holistically in terms of their pragmatic functions. Finally, the broader co-texts of NSIs – specifically, their preceding co-texts beyond the sentence level that lack formal links to the structure – were pragmatically analyzed as well.

3.2.1 NSIs in their sequential co-text

The first step of the functional analysis was to establish the formal-functional relationships of NSIs with their immediate co-texts and their sequential position in the turns, or postings, in which they appeared. It was found that NSIs were predominantly used in response turns, namely in 593 of 936 instances examined; in 230 cases, they appeared turn-initially, and in 87 cases turn-finally. 458 NSIs were followed by independent sentences, mainly declaratives (378 cases), and 138 were preceded, and 535 were followed, by a conjunction. Thus, in the examined corpus, there is a tendency for NSIs to be employed right at the beginning of turns which are intended to provide, rather than ask for, advice. As can be seen from Table 3, NSIs appear as part of a complex clause in 717 of 936 cases, with 76% of NSIs preceding textual material to which they are formally linked. The most frequent type of relationship between NSIs and clauses with which they are formally linked is contrast and concession (42%). This, coupled with the fixed forms of frequent NSIs, often appearing as variants of the forms "I'm not an expert" and "I'm not a fan", indicates that NSIs serve as framing devices, pre-emptively negating anticipated implications of utterances following them. Judging from these findings, NSIs seem to be utilized to reduce the potential face threat of advice (Goldsmith 2000), thereby ensuring the 'safe landing' of opinions they preface.

Table 3: Relationships between NSIs and their immediate co-texts.

Relationship	Example	1L co-text	1R co-text	No. of NSIs	% of all NSIs in the corpus
Contrast and concession					
Contrast	*I'm not an expert but* [+S]	86	279	365	
NSI = concessional clause	*Whilst I'm not a single traveler*, [S]	7	16	23	
1R/1L = concessional clause	*I am not a forum person myself, although* [+S]	4	5	9	
Total				397	42%
Cause and consequence					
NSI as cause	[S], *since* I am not a technician	41	93	134	
NSI as consequence	*I am not a big fan of fasting, as* [+S]	4	20	24	
Total				158	17%
Addition					
Coordination	*I am not a Dore enthusiast, and* [+S]	24	138	162	
Total				162	17%
Total		**166**	**551**	**717**	**76%**

3.2.2 The meanings of co-texts formally related to NSIs

This analysis employed the transitivity framework to differentiate between ideational meanings in 717 clauses related to NSIs (see Table 2). It found that 443 of these clauses had a first-person participant as thematic subject,[8] often representing speakers' thoughts and ideas through mental or relational processes. Inanimate[9] third-person subjects appeared in 170 clauses, mainly in relational processes of

8 Because thematic roles do not necessarily coincide with grammatical subjects, the study subsumed participants appearing as actors, experiencers, carriers/tokens, sayers, existents and behavers under the label of "Role 1"-participants, and the corresponding thematic objects, i.e. goals, phenomena/inducers, attributes/values and verbiages under "Role 2"-participants.

9 The distinction between animate and inanimate subjects was made in this analysis because it was considered to make a difference for the functions of negative self-identification whether it is used in relation with a claim about someone (another person, or animal) or something (an object or idea of common interest).

attribution and identification, that is, claims about objects and ideas. This shows that NSIs in the examined data frequently occur in co-texts in which speakers state their opinions, either subjectively or impersonally. Notably, in mental process contexts, identifying NPs from the fields of expertise and professionalism were identified in over half the clauses, while preference disclaimers appeared in only 20%. These findings indicate the patterned use of disclaimers of expertise in conjunction with clauses indexing the subjectivity of claims they project, modifying a claim already marked as opinion. Myers (2006) notes that phrases like "in my opinion" signal awareness of the multiple functions and context-specific constraints of opinion statements. Thus, NSIs modifying expressions of opinion highlight aspects of a speaker's identity, particularly expertise, impacting the appropriateness of their claims. This suggests that epistemic hedging is just one function of NSIs, which also play a role in face management. For instance, *I'm not an expert but I believe I have a good grasp of the laws of the game* shows awareness of potential face threats in claiming expertise.[10]

Table 4: Process types represented by co-texts with different formal links to NSIs.

	Role-1 participant: 1st person sg.	
Process Type	**Examples**	**Total**
Mental	***I believe*** *any GAD test over 50 indicates an autoimmune condition*	192
Relational	***I am confidant*** *[confident] the first photo is a common and harmless hover fly*	125
Material	*when something hurts,* ***I change*** *the way that I run to stop it hurting*	84
Verbal	***I suggest*** *Lantus alone might not be the best choice*	42
Total		443
	Role-1 participant: 3rd person sg. & pl. (inanimate)	
Relational	***cocaine is*** *the second most addictive and most harmfull [sic] drug out there*	118
Material	*Wouldn't* ***this bypass*** *AVG [...]?*	33
Other	***There's*** *something weird about a person who can take 200mg of trazadone*	19
Total		170
	Other Role 1 partcipants	**104**
Total		**717**

10 While the modesty indexed by this specific NSI appears genuine – it precedes an advice-giving response to a question –it could also be an exaggerated understatement meant to mock interlocutors who doubt the expertise of a highly knowledgeable speaker. This underscores, once again, that the functions of negatively identifying as an expert cannot be separated from the interactional context.

In the context of presenting speakers' views, it has been noted that preference disclaimers often appear in textual environments that feature linguistic markers of authority. The self-confidence and 'sassy' rhetoric of Example (3) below, which includes a preference disclaimer, is another case in point. Despite framing their assessment as a personal opinion, the speaker conveys certainty through their (mocking) evaluation of the product's appearance (e.g., *like a fat grey lump [which] certainly does not stand out*) and implicitly addresses the designers with suggestions for improvement (e.g., *Perhaps just a little metallic band across it*). Thus, the speaker presents themselves as openly subjective yet situationally authoritative:

(3) Yes, I can see that, it certainly does not stand out. [...] Perhaps just a little metallic band across it, in a similar tone to the fabric. [...] To be totally honest, **I'm not a fan of the Home Max Speaker** for the same reason. It's just lacking something, just an element to stop it looking like a fat grey lump :) All personal opinion of course :)

Based on the results of these analyses, the two prominent phrases, "I'm not an expert" and "I'm not a fan", reflect different notions of expertise relevant to the surrounding post. Specifically, "I'm not an expert" indicates a lay (as opposed to formal) expertise, while "I'm not a fan" suggests preference as a marker of experiential expertise.

3.2.3 The pragmatic functions of co-texts formally related to NSIs

To complement the transitivity-informed analysis presented in Table 4, a subset of co-texts preceding NSIs – specifically, mental, relational, and material process clauses with "I" as the Role-1 participant and formally linked to the matrix clause – were analyzed in terms of their overall interactional accomplishment, considering features such as polarity, tense, and aspect. Thus, for example, I distinguished between emotive verbs with a complement referring to the addressee (e.g., *I highly appreciate your reply*), verbs of perception with a complement referring to a contextually relevant object or question (e.g., *I can see small teeth at the front of the lower jaw*), and verbs of perception in the past tense that refer to experiences rather than immediate impressions (e.g., *I have not experienced many changes in medication*).

The results of this analysis, presented in Table 5 below, show that NSIs were characteristically used in textual environments representing speakers' beliefs and opinions (93 instances), reflexive comments on their knowledge (62 instances), and their experiences (62 instances). In these co-texts, NSIs from the conceptual domain of expertise were frequent linguistic choices, meaning that speakers often stated they were not experts of various kinds just before or after presenting or reflecting on their knowledge and experience with the subject matter. This further supports findings from previous analyses, which indicated that disclaimers of expertise tend to modify speakers' claims or references to different kinds of knowledge.

Table 5: Functional profile of clauses formally related to NSIs.

Functional profile of clauses formally related to NSIs					
Functional category	**Examples**	**Mental**	**Relational**	**Material**	**Total**
Representation of knowledge/Opinion	*I'm pretty sure you can get the original Grange*	72	20	1	93 [61 expertise NSIs]
Reference to knowledge/ understanding	*I probably had sufficient experience*	31	26	5	62 [29 expertise NSIs]
Experience	*[O]ver the last 5 years or so I have seen a lot of things said and written about "bioidentical/compounded" hormones.*	18	22	22	62 [54 expertise NSIs]
Preferences/Habits/ Principles	*[I] usually prefer the OEM option*	24	10	19	53 [31 preference NSIs]
Others[11]		47	47	37	131
Total		**192**	**125**	**84**	**401**

Qualitative examination of posts from these categories revealed that disclaimers of expertise not only serve to justify potential limitations in expertise but also project epistemic self-confidence. They indicate that speakers, despite not identifying as experts, are well aware of their knowledge and skills. For example, the following expertise disclaimer serves to position the speaker as layperson and highlights

11 For reasons of space, categories with fewer than 30 instances assigned to them were not included in this table.

potential flaws in their map, whilst also setting the stage for describing how they autodidactically acquired the skills to create the map in question:

(4) **I am not an expert in Normandy maps,** so I based on GJS Close Combat Maps and books I've read about the battle.

Indeed, the rest of their posting suggests that they take pride in what they have created:

> To this I add that the battle in BA be attractive and entertaining for both sides. I tried to simulate the map as I know... and can.

3.2.4 Beyond the clause: Moves preceding NSIs

The final analysis aimed to explore the relationships between NSIs and their immediately preceding co-texts beyond the sentence level. It examined the 376 declarative sentences that preceded NSIs, as well as the functional discourse units they were part of. This means that the sentence in the L1 position preceding the NSI was included, and, if it was part of a larger discourse move, the entire move was analyzed. For this study, moves were defined as "contiguous units that are characterized by coherent communicative purposes" (Egbert et al. 2021: 715) and a hypertheme (Forey and Sampson 2017: 134). For example, a product experience story – the most frequent category identified – serves the purpose of narrating a speaker's experience with a particular item they purchased, thereby constituting the overall theme of that stretch of text.[12]

The functions of these co-texts were cross-categorized with conceptual categories of NSIs. The three most prominent categories identified were: (1) discourse units representing users' experiences with products (67 instances), (2) representations of and reflections on knowledge and information (38 instances), and (3) advice (34 instances). Product experience stories were most frequently followed by preference disclaimers (26 out of 67 instances). Factual claims and reflections on speak-

12 However, it should be noted that while categorization and quantification may give the appearance of systematicity and empirical soundness – and are intended to make the analysis as transparent as possible – functional categorization inherently involves some degree of subjectivity. Thus, the categories identified are somewhat fuzzy, with frequencies indicating tendencies rather than providing definitive accounts of the data.

ers' understanding, as well as instances of advice, predominantly preceded disclaimers of expertise (27 out of 38 and 23 out of 34 instances, respectively).

The product experience story in (5) below – classified as such because of its title, "just a few thoughts from a couple of hundred mixed-use miles" – is a case in point. Incidentally, it features two NSIs from the two most frequent semantic domains, viz. expertise/professionalism and preference. The first NSI positions the speaker as a layperson in motoring journalism, indicating that they do not possess the expertise to write authoritatively about engines. This is coordinated with a contrasting clause that frames their account as subjective (*a few thoughts*). The second NSI, a preference disclaimer, follows their experience story and serves to specify their engine preferences. Again, the posting overall is marked by a high degree of linguistically enacted expertise, featuring technical terms and numbers as well as unmitigated claims (*can't fault*). Thus, it positions the speaker as an opinionated car expert, though not a professional one, as would be the case with a motoring journalist.

(5) Big thanks again to elmsDirect for the loan of the big 7 over the Gaydon weekend. **I'm no motoring journalist**, but here's a few thoughts from a couple of hundred mixed-use miles....I've never driven the logical competition (Merc S class, Lexus LS, Jag XJ etc) and assuming this niche of car is aimed at big mileage, (mainly) motorway use, the 7 hits the mark. **I'm no fan of diesels**, but can't fault over 300 bhp, loads of torque and still an average of 28 mpg overall and approaching 40 on the motorway

To sum up, this analysis provided additional support for the patterned use of disclaimers of expertise in contexts where knowledge is shared and negotiated. It also revealed a tendency for preference disclaimers to be used in the context of reporting experiences, suggesting that highlighting non-preferences is an effective way to signal awareness of specific choices in peer endorsement contexts.

4 Summary and concluding remarks

This study explored the discursive functions of negative assertions of the type "I + copula + not + indefinite NP" in disembodied social encounters in online contexts defined by topics of shared interest. It examined a corpus of 936 instances of NSIs used in UK web forum discussions to learn what categories speakers contrasted themselves with, in which co-texts NSIs appeared, what they pragmatically accomplished, and the implications for identity work in contemporary digitally mediated interaction.

It was found that two paradigms of identification stand out in the data: expertise and preference. Both types of NSIs serve tightly intertwined epistemic and social functions. The salience of disclaimers of expertise in contexts of exchanging knowledge on areas where expertise is perceived to matter may reflect struggles with certainty and credibility in anonymous lay communities. The formulaic phrase "I'm not an expert" was found to be routinely used to meta-pragmatically frame subjective opinions as non-absolute, allowing speakers to perform their individually accrued expertise while formally canceling the power differential implied by metadiscursive processes of explaining, rationalizing, and assessing information (Silverstein 2003). As Au and Eyal (2022: 34–35) put it, "presenting oneself as 'not an expert' is a useful strategy to bypass the crisis of expertise that would shut down lines of communication when the contested identity of the credentialed expert is invoked". This seems to be the case in Example (6). Here, an NSI follows an otherwise unmitigated piece of advice but precedes an invitation for others to voice their views, illustrating the tension between enacting and disclaiming expertise.

(6) Whatever oil you use change it at the recommended times and keep the air filter clean. I repeat that **I am not an expert** and welcome other opinions.

Conversely, the second most frequent conceptual category of NSIs, preference disclaimers, was used to represent speakers in terms of subjective but refined tastes by making reference to inherently perspectival identification categories – those of *fans*, *lovers*, and *enthusiasts*.. Given the high risk of emotional disagreement and the importance of appreciation in online contexts (Langlotz and Locher 2012; Petroni 2019), expressing preferences (rather than knowledge) may serve as a socially advantageous, non-confrontational way of enacting expertise. As Page (2019: 191) puts it, this can be seen as an "interactionally 'safe' option".

What counts as expertise and how speakers use NSIs to position themselves in relation to it appear to depend on the speech situation; that is, drawing upon pragmatically appropriate registers is what construes credibility online (Mey 2001: 220). This supports the view of identity as a transient phenomenon (Hoffmann and Bublitz 2017: 17) and suggests that, in the context of forum interaction, where being appreciated or sanctioned depends on successful facework, expertise is an interactional accomplishment rather than something that is permanently 'held' by individuals. In this light, NSIs can be seen as part of an array of linguistic strategies by which speakers emphasize commonalities to construct an in-group of peers and create distance from implicitly absent out-groups associated with formal authority.

To conclude, the findings of this study underscore that authority is interactionally accomplished on web forums and hinges on users' ability to mediate relevant information about a situationally relevant cultural good (Carr 2010: 18) in ways that encourage open debate and promote social affiliation. In the local context of web forums – where users are connected through highly specific domains of knowledge and interest – disalignment with expertise and negative identification with particular preferences were found to be interactionally favorable strategies for constructing stance. Considering that small social actions reflect broader systemic trends (Blommaert, Smits, and Yacoubi 2020: 56), the use of NSIs to frame opinions expressed online through the prism of taste, rather than expertise, may relate to the wider context of amplified epistemic uncertainty and distrust. To better understand the semiotic strategies that legitimize certain (post-)expert identities and the realities they endorse, meticulous linguistic analysis of mundane interaction serves as a fruitful starting point.

References

Aijmer, Karin. 2013. *Understanding pragmatic markers: A variational pragmatic approach*. Edinburgh: Edinburgh University Press.

Aijmer, Karin. 2015. Analysing discourse markers in spoken corpora: *Actually* as a case study. In Paul Baker & Tony McEnery (eds.), *Corpora and discourse studies*, 88–109. London: Palgrave Macmillan. https://doi.org/10.1057/9781137431738_5.

Androutsopoulos, Jannis. 2014. Languaging when contexts collapse: Audience design in social networking. *Discourse, Context & Media* 4–5. 62–73. https://doi.org/10.1016/j.dcm.2014.08.006.

Au, Larry & Gil Eyal. 2022. Whose advice is credible? Claiming lay expertise in a COVID-19 online community. *Qualitative Sociology* 45 (1). 31–61. https://doi.org/10.1007/s11133-021-09492-1.

Bach, Kent & Robert M. Harnish. 1979. *Linguistic communication and speech acts*. Cambridge, MA: MIT Press.

Beck, Ulrich & Elisabeth Beck-Gernsheim. 2001. *Individualization: Institutionalized individualism and its social and political consequences*. London: SAGE.

Benwell, Bethan & Elizabeth Stokoe. 2019. *Discourse and identity*. Edinburgh: Edinburgh University Press.

Biber, Douglas. 1993. Representativeness in corpus design. *Literary and Linguistic Computing* 8 (4). 243–257. https://doi.org/10.1093/llc/8.4.243.

Blommaert, Jan, Laura Smits & Noura Yacoubi. 2020. Context and its complications. In Anna De Fina & Alexandra Georgakopoulo (eds.), *The Cambridge Handbook of Discourse Studies*, 52–69. Cambridge: Cambridge University Press. https://doi.org/10.1017/9781108348195.004.

Blommaert, Jan, Laura Smits & Noura Yacoubi. 2018. Context and its complications. *Tilburg Papers in Culture Studies* 208. 1–21.

Bublitz, Wolfram & Axel Hübler. 2007. *Metapragmatics in use*. Amsterdam & Philadelphia: John Benjamins.

Caluya, Gilbert. 2010. The post-panoptic society? Reassessing Foucault in surveillance studies. *Social Identities* 16 (5). 621–633. https://doi.org/10.1080/13504630.2010.509565.

Carr, E. Summerson. 2010. Enactments of expertise. *Annual Review of Anthropology* 39. 17–32. https://doi.org/10.1146/annurev.anthro.012809.104948.

Egbert, Jesse, Stacey Wizner, Daniel Keller, Douglas Biber, Tony McEnery & Paul Baker. 2021. Identifying and describing functional discourse units in the BNC Spoken 2014. *Text & Talk* 41 (5–6). 715–737. https://doi.org/10.1515/text-2020-0053.

Ekström, Mats & Melisa Stevanovic. 2023. Conversation analysis and power: Examining the descendants and antecedents of social action. *Frontiers in Sociology* 8. Article 1196672. https://doi.org/10.3389/fsoc.2023.1196672.

Forey, Gail & Nicholas Sampson. 2017. Textual metafunction and theme: What's 'it' about? In Tom Bartlett & Gerard O'Grady (eds.), *The Routledge Handbook of Systemic Functional Linguistics*, 131–145. London & New York: Routledge.

Giddens, Anthony. 1991. *Modernity and self-identity: Self and society in the late modern age*. Cambridge: Polity Press.

Givón, Talmy. 1993. *English grammar: A function-based introduction*. Amsterdam: John Benjamins.

Goldsmith, Deana J. 2000. Soliciting advice: The role of sequential placement in mitigating face threat. *Communication Monographs* 67 (1). 1–19. https://doi.org/10.1080/03637750009376492.

Gumperz, John J. 1996. The linguistic and cultural relativity of inference. In John J. Gumperz & Steven Levinson (eds.), *Rethinking linguistic relativity*, 374–407. Cambridge: Cambridge University Press.

Halliday, M.A.K. & Christian Matthiessen. 2014. *Halliday's introduction to functional grammar*, 4th edn., Revised by Christian Matthiessen. Oxford & New York: Routledge.

Haugh, Michael. 2013. Speaker meaning and accountability in interaction. *Journal of Pragmatics* 48. 41–56. https://doi.org/10.1016/j.pragma.2012.11.009.

Hoffmann, Christian R. & Wolfram Bublitz. 2017. *Pragmatics of social media*. Berlin & Boston: De Gruyter Mouton.

Horn, Laurence R. & Heinrich Wansing. 2022. Negation. In Edward N. Zalta & Uri Nodelman (eds.), *The Stanford encyclopedia of philosophy*. https://plato.stanford.edu/archives/win2022/entries/negation/ (last accessed 14 April 2024).

Huang, Jeff, Katherine Thornton & Efthimis Efthimiadis. 2010. Conversational tagging in Twitter. In *Proceedings of the 21st conference on hypertext and hypermedia (HT)*, 173–178. https://doi.org/10.1145/1810617.1810647.

Jordan, Michael P. 1998. The power of negation in English: Text, context and relevance. *Journal of Pragmatics* 29. 705–752.

Kuna, Ágnes & Ágnes Hámori. 2023. Metapragmatics and reflections in support of knowledge transfer and common ground in doctor-patient interaction. In Sarah Bigi & Maria G. Rossi (eds.), *A Pragmatic agenda for healthcare: Fostering inclusion and active participation through shared understanding*, 200–226. Amsterdam: John Benjamins.

Langlotz, Andreas & Miriam A. Locher. 2012. Ways of communicating emotional stance in online disagreements. *Journal of Pragmatics* 44. 1591–1606. https://doi.org/10.1016/j.pragma.2012.04.002.

Leech, Geoffrey N. 1983. *Principles of pragmatics*. London & New York: Longman.

Leppänen, Sirpa, Janus Møller, Rune Sørensen, Thomas Nørreby, Andreas Stæhr & Samu Kytölä. 2015. Authenticity, normativity and social media. *Discourse, Context & Media* 8. 1–5. https://doi.org/10.1016/j.dcm.2015.05.008.

Lewandowska-Tomaszczyk, Barbara. 2006. A cognitive-interactional model of direct and indirect negation. In Stéphanie Bonnefille & Sébastien Salbayre (eds.), *La négation*, 379–402. Tours: Presses universitaires François-Rabelais. https://doi.org/10.4000/books.pufr.4856.

Liu, Hugo. 2007. Social network profiles as taste performances. *Journal of Computer-Mediated Communication* 13 (1). 252–275. https://doi.org/10.1111/j.1083-6101.2007.00395.x.
Lüders, Adrian, Alejandro Dinkelberg & Michael Quayle. 2022. Becoming "us" in digital spaces: How online users creatively and strategically exploit social media affordances to build up social identity. *Acta Psychologica* 228. 103643. https://doi.org/10.1016/j.actpsy.2022.103643.
Marko, Georg. 2015. Making informed healthy lifestyle choices: Analysing aspects of patient-centred and doctor-centred healthcare in self-help books on cardiovascular diseases. In Jesús Romero-Trillo (ed.), *Yearbook of corpus linguistics and pragmatics 2015: Current approaches to discourse and translation studies*, 65–88. Cham: Springer.
Martínez, Ignacio. 1995. Notes on the use and meaning of negation in contemporary written English. *Atlantis: Revista de la Asociación Española de Estudios Anglo-Norteamericanos* 17 (1–2). 207–227. https://www.researchgate.net/publication/28049808_Notes_on_the_use_and_meaning_of_negation_in_contemporary_written_English (last accessed 14 April 2024).
Marwick, Alice E. & danah boyd. 2011. 'I tweet honestly, I tweet passionately': Twitter users, context collapse, and the imagined audience. *New Media & Society* 13 (1). 114–133. https://doi.org/10.1177/1461444810365313.
Mey, Jacob L. 2001 [1993]. *Pragmatics: An introduction*, 2nd edition. Oxford: Blackwell.
Miestamo, Matti. 2017. Negation. In Alexandra Aikhenvald & R. M. W. Dixon (eds.), *The Cambridge handbook of linguistic typology*, 405–439. Cambridge: Cambridge University Press.
Myers, Geoff. 2006. 'In my opinion': The place of personal views in undergraduate essays. In Martin Hewings (ed.), *Academic writing in contexts: implications and applications*, 63–78. London & New York: Continuum.
Ochs, Elinor. 1996. Linguistic resources for socializing humanity. In John J. Gumperz & Steven Levinson (eds.), *Rethinking linguistic relativity*, 407–437. Cambridge: Cambridge University Press.
Page, Ruth. 2019. Self-denigration and the mixed messages of 'ugly' selfies on Instagram. *Internet Pragmatics* 2 (2). 173–205. https://doi.org/10.1075/ip.00035.pag.
Petroni, Sandra. 2019. How social media shape identities and discourses in professional digital settings: Self-communication or self-branding? In Patricia Bou-Franch Blitvich & Pilar Garcés-Conejos (eds.), *Analyzing digital discourse: New insights and future directions*, 251–281. Cham: Springer.
Rueger, Jasmina, Wilfred Dolfsma & Rick Aalbers. 2021. Perception of peer advice in online health communities: Access to lay expertise. *Social Science & Medicine* 277. 113117. https://doi.org/10.1016/j.socscimed.2020.113117.
Scott, Mike. 2008. *WordSmith Tools Version 5*. Liverpool: Lexical Analysis Software.
Silverstein, Michael. 2003. Indexical order and the dialectics of sociolinguistic life. *Language & Communication* 2 (3–4). 193–229. https://doi.org/10.1016/S0271-5309(03)00013-2.
Speer, Susan A. 2005. *Gender talk: Feminism, discourse and conversation analysis*. London: Routledge.
Sperber, Dan & Deidre Wilson. 1986. *Relevance: Communication and cognition*. Oxford: Blackwell.
Spitzmüller, Jürgen & Ingo Warnke. 2011. *Diskurslinguistik: eine Einführung in Theorien und Methoden der transtextuellen Sprachanalyse*. Berlin & Boston: De Gruyter. https://doi.org/10.1515/9783110229967.
Stokoe, Elizabeth & Frederick Attenborough. 2014. Gender and categorial systematics. In Susan Ehrlich, Miriam Meyerhoff & Janet Holmes (eds.), *The handbook of language, gender, and sexuality*, 2nd edition., 161–199. John Wiley & Sons, Ltd.
Tagg, Caroline, Philip Seargeant & Amy A. Brown. 2017. *Taking offence on social media: Conviviality and communication on Facebook*. Cham: Palgrave Macmillan.
Upton, Timothy A. & Martin A. Cohen. 2009. An approach to corpus-based discourse analysis: The move analysis as example. *Discourse Studies* 11 (5). 585–605. https://doi.org/10.1177/1461445609341006.

Van Dijk, Teun A. 2008. *Discourse and context: a socio-cognitive approach*. Cambridge: Cambridge University Press.

Wilkes, Julie & Susan A. Speer. 2021. 'Child's time': Kinship carers' use of time reference to construct parental identities. *Journal of Pragmatics* 175. 14–26. https://doi.org/10.1016/j.pragma.2021.01.001.

Zappavigna, Michele. 2015. Searchable talk: The linguistic functions of hashtags. *Social Semiotics* 25. 1–18. https://doi.org/10.1080/10350330.2014.996948.

Tatjana Scheffler

Social media corpora for analyzing linguistic variation

Abstract: Computer mediated communication (CMC) has become a popular source of data for analyses in linguistics and social science, aided by convenient access to large-scale ad-hoc corpora. While the medium has been in focus as an influencing factor on linguistic expression in CMC for a long while, I argue that other factors have similarly significant effects on individual linguistic variation in online texts. In the paper, I address the interplay of variation by topic, register, and individual user with the medium of social media communication. I develop best practices for constructing CMC corpora that allow research into intra-author variation, by controlling for other factors that may confound results based merely on the comparison of different pre-existing corpora.

I then present one case study for the construction of a CMC corpus that demonstrates linguistic variation across two social media within the same group of authors. In particular, there is considerable inter- and intraindividual variation in linguistic features of informal, spontaneous and situated communication such as the use of emojis. Large CMC corpora with open research licenses, rich metadata and linguistic annotations thus make it possible to tease apart the particular effect of the factors medium, register, topic, and individual author on linguistic phenomena.

Keywords: CMC, corpora, individual variation, medium, sociolinguistics, emojis

1 Introduction

Individual language users show distinct individual patterns in their linguistic expressions. These individual patterns may align with the patterns shown by others sharing certain demographic properties (e.g., gender, age, community, etc.), or may be idiosyncratic. The field of sociolinguistics has its central focus on this kind of individual linguistic variation. Sociolinguistics and corpus linguistics as applied to corpora of computer mediated communication (CMC) share a common goal, the collection and study of 'the language used by ordinary people in their everyday

Tatjana Scheffler, Ruhr-University Bochum, e-mail: tatjana.scheffler@rub.de

https://doi.org/10.1515/9783111434018-014

affairs' (Labov 1972: 69). Where traditionally, variational sociolinguists have been primarily interested in elicited and everyday spoken language, studied in-depth for individual speakers, CMC corpus researchers study spontaneous (i.e., not elicited) language use in the written mode, often produced by a large number of different users. The intersection between these two interests, investigating the effects of social properties on linguistic expression and the study of naturally occurring spontaneous written data in CMC corpora, has been an active area of interest as well (c.f. Androutsopoulos 2000; Tagliamonte and Denis 2008; Androutsopoulos 2006, 2011; Herring, Stein and Virtanen 2013; Bock, Busch and Truan 2023, and many others).

The methodologies of these two subdisciplines differ: The primary method in classical sociolinguistics is the sociolinguistic interview as well as additional in-depth observations of the linguistic behavior of individuals, for example their conversations at work or in their friend group (discussed in detail in Meyerhoff 2016, where she also distinguishes sociolinguistic and corpus linguistic approaches). In contrast, social media corpus research mainly assembles language data from many individuals on one platform and analyses this data in an aggregated way. The disadvantage of such pure corpus research based on one source is that it can be difficult to draw conclusions about the linguistic system used by each speaker. Even when comparing several such corpora, two corpora may differ for many reasons, including language and speaker external ones such as the medium or topic of conversation. In addition, two separately collected corpora contain data from distinct sets of language users, and in the case of CMC corpora, these language users often belong to distinct communities, based on their age, place in society, or their interests.

A very much simplified view of the matter may therefore be that on the one hand, the sociolinguistic method permits the study of individual linguistic variation and enables us to draw conclusions about the underlying linguistic systems, but does not typically have access to the large data sets of CMC. On the other hand, CMC corpus linguistics studies spontaneous, natural linguistic expressions in social media corpora, but so far shows limited potential for investigating individual linguistic variability due to excessive aggregation, which permits only group-level comparisons. In the following, I will propose an approach for analyzing individual linguistic behavior on social media. I will develop some best practice recommendations for collecting social media corpora that support this kind of research.

2 Causes of linguistic variability in computer mediated communication

It is a well-known and well-studied fact about language that linguistic expressions depend on the communicative situations they are uttered in. For example, it is immediately obvious that (1) was originally a spoken utterance while (2) surely originated from a written source (both examples have been translated from their German originals from the parallel blog and podcast corpus PARADISE; see Seemann et al. 2023). We can understand this immediately, even though both samples are quite short and presented outside of their original context in written form.

(1) So a lot of practical policy has been made here
A lot of language policy been made
Specialist terminology developed
For example, also, soccer terminology comes from this
Take a look at French, they say 'penalty', a real anglicism
We say 'Strafstoß'
They say 'futbol', we say 'Fußball', etc. These were all fairly welldeveloped core German words at the time that were invented and developed
[FG007_Transkript]

(2) Time and again we read and hear of displeasure about the state of the German language: new spelling rules have been introduced - and then immediately withdrawn. German is losing its international significance. English words are flooding everyday language usage. In short, the selfimage of our language seems to have developed unsightly cracks. Peter Eisenberg, however, takes a relaxed view of linguistic developments and is not afraid of anglicisms.
[FG007_Blog]

But spoken vs. written presentation mode is not the only axis of variation for linguistic expressions. Koch and Oesterreicher (1985) argue that while the distinction between speech and writing is a categorical, binary one, individual media of communication differ more gradually between prototypically, 'conceptually' oral language (such as a spoken conversation between friends) and prototypically, conceptually written language (such as a legal text). According to Koch and Oesterreicher (1985), the pole of conceptual orality is characterized by communicative conditions typical for the 'language of closeness': spontaneity, dialog, expressivity, co-presence, etc. In contrast, the pole of conceptual writing is characterized by the 'language of distance': prior planning, monologue, separation of place and time, detachment, objectivity, etc. These different conditions for utterances are reflected in the linguistic phenomena that we can observe in them, for example, first and second person pronouns in conceptual orality and almost exclusively third person pronouns in conceptually written material (Yates 1996; Tagliamonte and Denis 2008). It is proposed that communicative settings (telephone call with a friend, diary entry, job interview, scientific talk, academic paper) can be arranged along the conceptual orality dimension, as they correspond to varying degree to one of the two poles in both conditions of communication and means of linguistic expressions.

This multi-faceted view of communicative setting and corresponding linguistic phenomena carries over to social media as well, which typically use written mode,[1] but can vary a lot wrt. their communicative conditions and the linguistic phenomena they exhibit. To investigate both the communicative conditions of specific media platforms, as well as the linguistic phenomena which occur based on the affordances the specific media offer to their users, a whole range of CMC corpora have been collected and linguistic research using these corpora has been documented, not least in the CMC Corpora conference series (Hendrickx, Verheijen and van de Wijngaert 2021, and previous editions).

Linguistic variation can be observed between social media, but also within individual media, due to the fact that communicative situations differ starkly even within a medium (Koch and Oesterreicher 1985; Dürscheid 2003): a text message chat with a friend will exhibit linguistic features that cannot be observed in a chat with a prospective new landlord when applying for an apartment, maybe starting with the frequency of emojis. Thus, comparing two CMC corpora is likely to lead to systematic changes in some linguistic variables if their communicative situations do not match. The point that register affects linguistic variables has also been empirically demonstrated within a given social medium, which may be used to interact in different registers, such as narrative, informative, or persuasive. Scheffler, Kern and Seemann (2022) show that the use of German modal particles and intensifying particles varies along these register dimensions, even within a given CMC medium (blog posts or tweets).

Since other factors influence linguistic expression in CMC, comparing linguistic data across different corpora invites the intrusion of confounds. We can not always be sure that the differences that are necessarily found between two corpora, since no two sets of text can be identical, can be linked back to the medium distinctions.

1 Social media can be implemented in a variety of modalities, including written text (blogs, Facebook, forums), speech (podcasts, voice messages), images (Instagram, Facebook, Pinterest, chat programs), video (Youtube, TikTok, Instagram reels), or combinations of all of them. In this paper, I focus on written social media corpora for practical reasons.

Even within a single medium, significant differences are found between subcorpora, and the dimensions of variation are not limited to communicative situation and register. For example, Schler et al. (2006) investigated gender and age effects on blog texts and found clear differences between blogs written by female and male authors. However, the most noticeable differences on the level of word frequencies they found are at most indirectly related to gender, since they mainly reflect topic differences (tech related words like *linux*, *programming* lean heavily male, while words such as *shopping*, *mom* predict a female author). In authorship analysis or profiling, which aims at identifying linguistic variation based on individual preferences or linked to demographic properties of the individual author, content words are often ignored for this reason, as they may reflect the topic of a text more than properties of its author. We can thus note topic as an additional cause of variation in CMC texts.

As an interim summary, we can note that linguistic expressions may be affected by many aspects that characterize a given text, such as mode, text type, register, topic, demographic (age, gender) or group properties of the author (hobbies, subculture), or individual idiosyncrasies. In order to tease apart which part of the linguistic variability observed in a corpus is due to the underlying mechanisms of the linguistic system, and which part is affected by these to some extent language-external factors, it is important to try to control for these effects when comparing data in corpus linguistics. I will therefore aim to construct a CMC corpus which exhibits individual variability but is matched for mode, register, topic, as well as author properties.

3 Constructing CMC corpora for individual linguistic variation

To investigate naturalistic language use in CMC, corpora of CMC have to be constructed and studied. The availability of such naturally occurring language in everyday use from CMC is simultaneously affected both positively and negatively: On the one hand, linguistic production by users on various digital media is constantly increasing in quantity. On the other hand, recent tendencies in restricting the open web make it harder for researchers to access and ethically source that data. However, it is necessary for academic research not only in linguistics to continue to strive for broad access to a representative sample of CMC, since restricting ourselves to only the most accessible, abundant data sources would lead to a very biased view of language (as well as of the topics and contents represented in online media).

3.1 Principles of CMC corpus construction

Principles of open datasets (such as the FAIR principles, Wilkinson et al. 2016) apply with particular urgency to the construction of CMC corpora, since only openly available and reusable data can be *sustainable* in two senses of the word: (i) CMC corpora must be sustainable as in cost-effective, since it is often complex and expensive to construct them, much less to pre-process and annotate the data for linguistic analysis. Only by making our data available to other researchers can we get our "money's worth" and speed up scientific progress. (ii) Results of CMC corpora should be long-lasting and verifiable even after a project's end. The case of the demise of Twitter and subsequent closure of its APIs has shown that corpora that are not openly shared in the research community can be rendered worthless in a minute. Not only reviewers, but also other researchers must be able to verify and build on previous research results.

In the case of CMC corpora, though, the data is typically produced by a large number of private persons who are using language for their idiosyncratic, private communication needs. A third consideration in constructing CMC corpora is therefore the ethics of data collection and redistribution:[2] (iii) CMC corpora for studying individual linguistic behavior must necessarily contain data produced for personal purposes by many individuals, who may also reveal potentially identifying information. Ethical (as well as legal) concerns dictate that personal data collected should be as minimal as possible, and that if possible, data authors should be consulted or at least informed.

Luth, Marx and Pentzold (2022) develop best practice guidelines for ethically and legally responsible CMC data collection for research which they instantiate in several case studies, from the researchers' perspective. Fiesler et al. (2024) conducted a meta analysis of studies using Reddit data and conclude with ethical guidelines for such research. As a main takeaway, they co-opted Reddit's first user clause, "Remember the human". In order to preserve the linguistic features under investigation, the expressions often cannot be transformed enough to fully conceal authorship to a dedicated observer. Thus, fully anonymized corpora are not possible, and

2 I will not really touch on legal issues here. While important, they underlie dynamic processes and furthermore in this domain are often subsumed by ethical obligations scientists have wrt. the individuals they are studying as well as the society that benefits from their research. What I mean is that ethical constraints on data collection and use are often much more restrictive than legal constraints; in addition, the consequences of the violation of ethical constraints in my view weigh more heavily. For a detailed discussion of legal considerations see e.g. Beißwenger et al. (2017).

linguistic researchers, as well, should "remember the human" behind the data they collect and analyze.

3.2 How not to construct CMC corpora for investigating individual variation

There are several non-ideal ways in which individual variation in social media could be investigated, which I will briefly sketch here to contrast them with the approach proposed below. One may try to work exclusively with existing corpora and compare them to find systematic linguistic effects. As discussed above, this will not reliably lead to the observation of inter- or intra-individual variation, as external factors and the selection criteria of corpora may carry too much weight. For example, many social media corpora have been collected using specific keywords (e.g., "Corona, COVID") which by necessity limits the kinds of linguistic expressions found based upon such a search. In addition, many existing corpora contain only very few contributions or even single posts from each individual author, and/or do not contain sufficient metadata to link authors between posts. In such corpora, intra-individual variability cannot be observed.

In order to study linguistic variability, a larger set of CMC posts is needed for any given author – similar to the in-depth sociolinguistic interviews and observations across various situation used by sociolinguists studying the oral mode. If the dataset doesn't contain clear identifying information, computational linguists have tried to reconstruct demographic information about the authors, either by using human crowd workers, for example to manually annotate profile pictures for gender (Ciot, Sonderegger and Ruths 2013), by using the available textual data (Nguyen et al. 2016, 2021), or by using network effects such as homophily (Li, Ritter and Hovy 2014). All methods share several drawbacks. First, they exhibit significant error rates; second, inducing demographic properties from the data in order to then use it in comparing the linguistic behavior of demographic subgroups may lead to circular reasoning that serves to confirm pre-existing biases; and third, it is not clear that users consent to or are even aware of the possibility of tracking their long-term behavior on social media and their personal identity information (such as age, gender, occupational status, ethnicity, etc.).

In the past, certain platforms have tried to aggregate information on social media profiles across other platforms for a given user, which enables linking different profiles. The most usable version of this was Google+, which provided an API for reading the profiles and made it possible to scrape individualized corpora across various CMC platforms. However, the interface was closed in early 2019 and similar tools have not become available. In a more limited fashion, users sometimes self-identify alternative accounts on other platforms by linking to them in their profiles. In the next section, I will use this selflinking to create a cross-media corpus of individual CMC communication.

3.3 How to construct CMC corpora for investigating individual variation: Principles of best practice

It has been noted, for example via surveys, that authors interacting on social media, even public ones, are often not aware of the possibility that their data may be scraped and used by companies or researchers (Fiesler and Proferes 2018).[3] If they are asked about the use of their text for research, authors generally state that they would like to be asked or at least informed.

Legal as well as ethical considerations further require that the personal information of authors should be protected. Thus, private information cannot be ethically collected by researchers, unless the authors explicitly agree to this use, via donation,[4] or if users are active in a platform specifically meant for research use.[5] Private information that is not publicly shared should also not be reconstructed automatically or with the help of crowd workers, as authors may not intend to share this personal information.

Finally, the case of Twitter's demise (only the most impactful in a long string of CMC platforms that have disappeared or changed ownership) has demonstrated that relying on software interfaces provided by technology platforms puts researchers at constant risk for losing their data or losing access to published corpora and losing the ability to reproduce research results. Even large data platforms such as GitHub are just one sale or strategic decision away from making years of research disappear. Thus, it is important to develop methodologies that use free and open tools and simple techniques of the internet (web scraping) as much as possible to collect data. Further, data should be shared as widely and comprehensively as possible in order to ensure both the reproducibility of existing results as well as the reuse of precious resources.

Based on these observations I propose the following best practice principles for sustainable CMC corpus research for linguistic variation.

---

3 Breuer et al. (2024) showed that virtually none of the servers on the decentralized platform Mastodon discuss whether or not their data can or should be used for scientific research.

4 One example is the MoCoDa2 chat database https://db.mocoda2.de (last accessed 14 February 2025).

5 E.g. the platform used in (Beißwenger and Pappert 2019), if users were informed about the text collection

3.3.1 Data collection

Consent. Gather consent prior to data collection if possible (opt-in), or at minimum inform authors of the data collection and give them the option to have their data deleted (opt-out).

Prior consent is possible in the case of clearly delineated author groups such as in more typical sociolinguistic studies, or when linguistic research is carried out within and benefits a specific community. At least a minimum effort should be made to post-hoc inform authors of data collection if prior consent is not feasible. For example, it is often possible to inform a community via their platform moderators and to provide contact options for opting out of datasets.

Use public data. Gather only public data; private data, e.g. from chat systems, should be collected only via donations or with explicit consent prior to the production of the data. In general, private data that requires a login is not freely viewable and underlies specific restrictions.

Web scraping. Collect textual data via the web, making use of legal permissions for text and data mining for research (e.g., the German §60d UrhG).

Web scraping operates by simulating a web browser interface and the clicks a human user would make, while collecting the data presented to a human user viewing the platform's content. As long as it considers public data, this interface should always be open and available for data collection, for example by using JavaScript tools. However, additional effort may be required, particularly for creating scraping tools and data representations that can capture this content. Also, such tools must often be adapted when an interface changes.

Limit metadata. Collect only self-identified user metadata. Do not attempt to reconstruct personal information such as gender or sexual orientation (and many more) beyond the information explicitly shared by the authors themselves.

Metadata is often very valuable for (socio-)linguistic research. Self-provided metadata is easy to collect when it is presented to the public on a platform, and much more reliable than automatically inferred metadata which may be prone to enhance biases.

Anonymization. Anonymize or pseudonymize the data thoroughly in order to avoid harm, if necessary manually. Remove personal information from own records.

This requires a significant effort on the researchers' behalf but can be mitigated by sharing resources and corpora. Some semi-automatic tools can help, but typically a corpus must be anonymized manually if there is a danger of exposing personal information, for example when a platform uses real-world user names.

3.3.2 Research and distribution

After data collection, ensuring the sustainability of the data is in the researchers' hands:

- Archive everything.
- Annotate full datasets ensuring high data quality and save annotations in a reusable format, independently of tools via which the data can be used (e.g., XML, tabular text formats such as CSV).
- Share all (anonymized) data, including annotations, with reviewers and other researchers on request via private links, or if possible openly on the web.
- Extract the informative or relevant linguistic data from CMC posts to share freely and separately from any personal information (e.g., see the data set of extracted English it-clefts in Bevacqua and Scheffler 2020).
- Develop derived text formats that can be freely shared with anyone via repositories and the web (Schöch et al. 2020).

4 A corpus for linguistic variation in CMC

In the following I will describe an approach for collecting a cross-media corpus aimed at investigating individual linguistic variation. The best practices described in the previous section have been developed in part by drawing upon the experiences in constructing this corpus, as well as others. They are therefore not yet all followed to the fullest in this effort.

Given the observations in Section 2, the central goal for the corpus consisted of the following criteria: It should contain naturalistic CMC data from a selection of people. It should cover at least two different media in order to enable cross-media comparison. To investigate intra-speaker adaptation to the medium, the identical users should be represented in the subcorpus for each medium, and we should be able to identify authors across the two (or more) media. The topics and registers should match as much as possible across the social media, in order to minimize the influence of topic and register on the linguistic expressions. This would mean that any remaining variation could be traced either to the medium or to the individual behavior of users. The texts itself should be spontaneous and not too restricted (e.g., public speeches or newspaper articles adhere to many externally imposed norms and rules and only partially reflect "everyday language" used for free communicative goals).

The corpus was constructed by collecting tweets and blog posts from users belonging to the German parenting blogger community. It draws centrally on a human curated list of "parenting bloggers" on Twitter from 2017, called the "Elternbloggerkarte".[6] The list aggregated Twitter accounts around a single topic or community, parenting, and already imposed the filter that the users included are active both on the platform Twitter (their accounts were listed) as well as operated a blog (inclusion criterion for the list). The focus on this community has the advantage that it is not too specialized: Tweets and blog posts by users from this community generally relate to family life and daily events.

Constructing the corpus consisted of several steps:
1. The Twitter list was read out using Python and the Twitter API, and included 195 members. Three additional prolific parenting bloggers and tweeters were manually added to the list.
2. All available tweets (in cases of very active users, the most recent 3200 tweets) were collected for each profile using tweepy.
3. Each Twitter profile was crawled using the tweepy package and the Twitter API, to collect the URL linked in there. In the parenting blogger community, this URL in most cases links to a personal blog.
4. The URL was manually cleaned and links to Facebook and other non-blog websites were removed. For the remaining URLs, the Python package feedreader was used to automatically scrape the RSS feed, if available, and retrieve the most recent available blog posts (usually, 5–10 posts).
5. Blog posts were cleaned from boilerplate via BeautifulSoup.

The collection process used the APIs available at the time. More recently, those programmatic interfaces to the Twitter platform's content have been closed and the new instantiation, X, does not provide this kind of access in the same way. A possible alternative to the use of APIs is web scraping.[7] Scraping has the advantage that it exploits the public interface of a platform, which is always available via a web browser for a public social media platform. A possible disadvantage is the limited availability of metadata (such as user networks and other internal information that

6 *Elternbloggerkarte* ('parenting blogger map') is a project to log the physical locations of bloggers active in the parenting community, starting from Germany. The map is still available here: https://familiert.de/elternbloggerkarte/ (last accessed 14 February 2025).

7 Luca Hammer regularly makes scraping tools available: https://github.com/lucahammer (last accessed 14 February 2025).

is not openly displayed to viewers). However, a lot of the data interesting for linguistic research is still available on the web, albeit with more effort than before.

In addition, it must be noted that it is not always possible to link authors' accounts on different platforms to each other in order to capture cross-platform linguistic adaptation. There are two ways in which this can be achieved: First, via self-tagging by users as in this case. On many CMC platforms, user profiles include links to other providers. For example, this is the case for many Fediverse platforms such as Mastodon, on platforms such as Wikipedia, GitHub, or on personal blogs. Users are often happy to identify their alternative activities elsewhere on the web. For some communities, dedicated personal identifiers have even been created to uniquely identify each individual (such as with OrcID for scientists). Second, in studies based on data donation, users can be asked to provide textual data from not only one platform but several, such that the linguistic output can be linked.

The data collection for the parenting corpus was carried out in Spring 2017; tweets were acquired between February 14–16, blog posts on February 20, 2017. Both tweets and blog posts were obtained for 62 users, after some quality checks (for example, users who primarily posted in a language other than German were removed). While the data collection for research purposes follows §60d of the German *Urheberrechtsgesetz* (copyright law), we nevertheless retroactively informed the users and obtained their consent prior to analysis and distribution of the corpus. All blogs were consulted in 2020 to retrieve contact information for their operators.[8] All users were contacted and asked to explicitly respond if they do not want their data included in the corpus (opt-out). Out of 50 users who could be contacted (some blogs had become inactive), three asked for their data to be removed, six explicitly agreed after some additional questions to be included in the corpus, and the remainder quietly acquiesced to inclusion. Indeed several people even responded positively by actively agreeing to being part of the corpus and showing an interest in the results. All data from users that could not be contacted or asked to be removed was deleted, yielding a final corpus of 44 users for whom both tweets and blog posts in sufficient quantity could be collected. The corpus data is summarized in Table 1, the corpus is available as the "TWItter and BLOgs COrpus: Parenting" (TwiBloCoP),[9] in raw text format or TEI-XML.

8 Contact information is a legal requirement for public or commercial web sites in Germany.
9 https://staff.germanistik.rub.de/digitale-forensische-linguistik/forschung/textkorpus-sprachliche-variation-in-sozialen-medien/ (last accessed 14 February 2025).

Table 1: Size of the TwiBloCoP corpus.

	blog posts	tweets
users	44	44
posts	468	81,440
tokens	~360,000	~1,200,000

In the following, several data preprocessing steps were carried out, including anonymization of all data, sentence splitting and tokenization, as well as part of speech tagging. Anonymization was applied manually by replacing all personal names, blog names, emails, places, @usernames, urls, and phone numbers with placeholders in brackets such as [NAME], [PLACE] etc. The users were assigned random 4-digit ID numbers to link tweets to their corresponding blog posts that share the same author. The sentences and tokens were then automatically split using the Python package SoMaJo,[10] and part of speech tagged with SoMeWeTa.[11]

Topic-wise, the corpus is quite homogeneous: Both blog posts and tweets are concerned with family life and parenting, see examples (3)–(4).[12] Any remaining linguistic variability can then be traced to individual variability (by observing authors across their different texts) or cross-medium variability (by showing tendencies across different authors within a medium).

(3) Children are our mirrors. If you want to change your child, change YOUR behavior, not the child's. My son has these tantrums all the time. Regularly. Then it is very difficult to get him out of it. And that is exactly what I would like to do. [...] Hm. At some point I asked myself why these fits upset me so much.
[blog-4421-10]

(4) Alarm rang every 5 minutes since 6 am. Got up right before 8. Great. Worked like a charm 🙈
[tweets-7291]

Looking specifically at intensifying and modal particles, Scheffler et al. (2022) have shown that in addition to the medium and the individual author, register still remains as an additional source of variability in the corpus. They show that within

10 https://github.com/tsproisl/SoMaJo (last accessed 14 February 2025).
11 https://github.com/tsproisl/someweta (last accessed 14 February 2025).
12 All examples have been translated from German.

the general parenting topic, individual texts and text parts differ wrt. whether they are intended to convey information in a relatively neutral fashion, whether they are meant to convince or argue, or whether they are mainly meant to tell a narrative story about the author's personal life. The corpus has been completely manually annotated for register, so that this dimension can also be taken into account in studies of variability.

5 Individual variation in social media

A corpus with texts from the same authors in two social media makes it possible to study both how individuals differ from each other when communicating about the same topics in the same media, as well as how authors adapt to the medium while communicating similar content. In the aggregate, simple complexity measures such as type-token ratio (computed over the first 1000 tokens of each text, tweets are aggregated by user) and average word length show that the blog posts and tweets are of medium linguistic complexity, right in between spoken conversations and newspaper texts (see Figure 1).

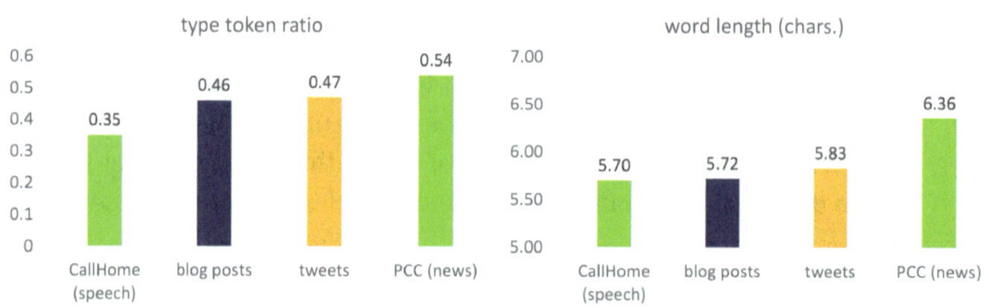

Figure 1: Type-token ratio (left) and average word length (right) for German tweets and blog posts from the TwiBloCoP corpus, compared to telephone conversations (CallHome) and newspaper commentaries (PCC).

While the blog posts and tweets are quite similar to each other in complexity (interestingly and maybe unexpectedly, the tweets are slightly more complex than the blog posts according to these measures), they show stark differences wrt. the frequency of non-standard spelling such as word lengthening by letter reduplication (*niiiiiice*), across-the-board capitalization (*AWESOME*), or socalled inflectives marked with asterisks (**yawn**), and particularly the presence of emojis (Figure 2).

These phenomena are virtually nonexistent in standard monological written media such as newspaper texts.

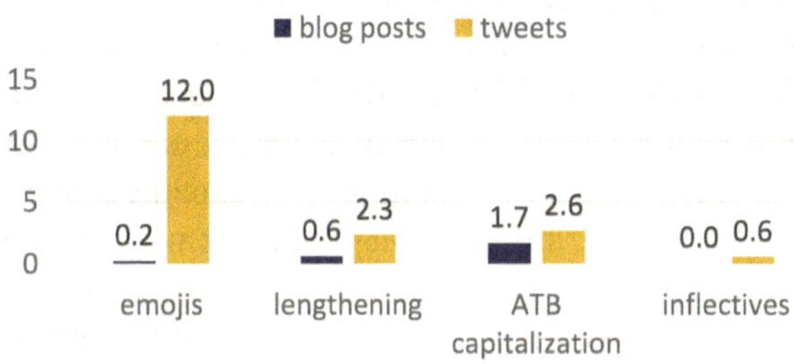

Figure 2: Frequency of non-standard items in blog posts and tweets, per 1000 tokens.

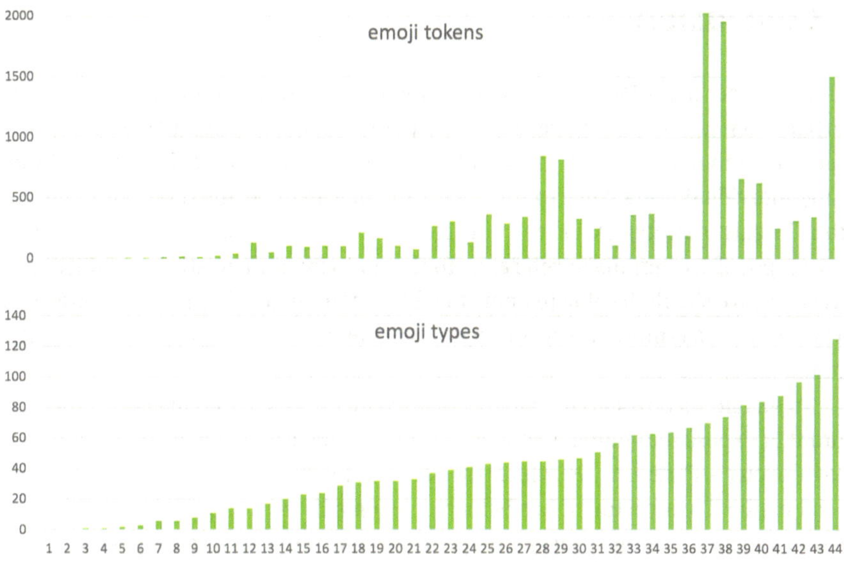

Figure 3: Individual variation in emoji usage frequency among authors in TwiBloCoP; each bar in the top graph represents the same author as in the corresponding bar in the bottom graph.

It is interesting to have a closer look at these differences between the two CMC subcorpora, because both media contain the same users writing about very similar topics. However, while they use almost exclusively standard graphematic tools in their blog posts, the same users are much more likely to use non-standard writing phenomena in their tweets. Looking specifically at the emojis (as the most frequent phenomenon), we can observe significant individual variation in their use. For example, the 77 emojis that occur in blog posts are used by only 13 of the 44 authors, and only 3 of them use emojis more than 5 times in their blog (the large majority of these emojis are red hearts). In Twitter, the distribution of emojis is also not uniform among authors. 14 authors use fewer than 100 emojis in total in their tweets, while the overall high frequency of emojis is mostly due to three power users, see Figure 3. In addition, authors also show diverse amounts of internal emoji variation: most use fewer than 50 different emojis, while some pick from a much larger variety. The individual style of emoji use can be compared between these three authors by observing the "emoji clouds" generated from their subcorpora (Figure 4).

6 Conclusion

While the fact that CMC as a domain of linguistic research shows great variety is perhaps well-known, this paper made the point that even individual media or text types of computer mediated communication are not monolithic. In each medium, many individual users congregate to express their own personalities and idiosyncratic linguistic strategies. We can only characterize the linguistic system employed in a corpus if we can make reference to this individual linguistic variability. And adversely, we should be able to know to what extent linguistic variability observed in large corpora is due to the medium, register, topic, or individual properties of the author.

To enable such research, I have presented an approach for collecting CMC corpora that expose individual linguistic variability. One case study is the Twitter and Blog Corpus – Parenting, in which the same authors are represented across two social media. Constructing it has helped develop a list of best practices for the collection and distribution of social media corpora for research into the everyday language use in the digital domain.

Acknowledgements

I would like to thank the reviewers of this volume for their helpful comments and the editors for their patience. I am grateful to the audience at the CMC Corpora conference in Mannheim for their questions.

Figure 4: Emojis used by the three authors with the most emoji tokens.

Hannah Seemann has contributed significantly to the creation and development of the TwiBloCoP corpus, many thanks to her and to Lesley-Ann Kern for their work on the corpus and to our student annotators for their contributions. All remaining errors are my own.

This work was partially supported by the Deutsche Forschungsgemeinschaft (DFG, German Research Foundation) – Project ID 317633480 – SFB 1287.

References

Androutsopoulos, Jannis. 2006. Introduction: Sociolinguistics and computermediated communication. *Journal of Sociolinguistics* 10 (4). 419–438.

Androutsopoulos, Jannis. 2011. From variation to heteroglossia in the study of computer-mediated discourse. In Crispin Thurlow & Christine Mroczek (eds.), *Digital discourse: Language in the new media*, 277–298. Oxford University Press.

Androutsopoulos, Jannis K. 2000. Non-standard spellings in media texts: The case of German fanzines. *Journal of Sociolinguistics* 4 (4). 514–533. doi: 10.1111/1467-9481.00128. http://doi.wiley.com/10.1111/1467-9481.00128.

Beißwenger, Michael, Harald Lüngen, Jan Schallaböck, John H. Weitzmann, Axel Herold, Pawel Kamocki, Angelika Storrer & Julia Wildgans. 2017. Rechtliche Bedingungen für die Bereitstellung eines Chat-

Korpus in CLARIN-D: Ergebnisse eines Rechtsgutachtens. In Michael Beißwenger (ed.), *Empirische Erforschung internetbasierter Kommunikation*, 7–46. Berlin & Boston: De Gruyter.

Beißwenger, Michael & Steffen Pappert. 2019. How to be polite with emojis: a pragmatic analysis of face work strategies in an online learning environment. *European Journal of Applied Linguistics* 7 (2). 225–254. https://doi.org/10.1515/eujal-2019-0003. https://www.degruyter.com/view/journals/eujal/7/ 2/article-p225.xml (last accessed 14 February 2025).

Bevacqua, Luca & Tatjana Scheffler. 2020. Form variation of pronominal itclefts in written English: A corpus study in Twitter and iWeb. *Linguistics Vanguard* 6 (1). 20190066. https://doi.org/10.1515/lingvan-2019-0066. Bock, Cornelia F, Florian Busch & Naomi Truan. 2023. Introduction: The sociolinguistics of exclusion–indexing (non) belonging in mobile communities. *Language & Communication* 93. 192–195.

Breuer, Johannes, Marco Wähner, Annika Deubel & Katrin Weller. 2024. Collecting and archiving Mastodon data: Ethical enquiries on decentralized networks. Talk presented at the DNB conference "After Twitter". https://wiki.dnb.de/pages/viewpage.action?pageId=337119232 (last accessed 14 February 2025).

Ciot, Morgane, Morgan Sonderegger & Derek Ruths. 2013. Gender inference of Twitter users in non-English contexts. In David Yarowsky, Timothy Baldwin, Anna Korhonen, Karen Livescu & Steven Bethard (eds.), *Proceedings of the 2013 Conference on Empirical Methods in Natural Language Processing*, 1136–1145. Seattle, Washington, USA: Association for Computational Linguistics. https://aclanthology.org/D13-1114 (last accessed 14 February 2025).

Dürscheid, Christa. 2003. Medienkommunikation im Kontinuum von Mündlichkeit und Schriftlichkeit: Theoretische und empirische Probleme. *Zeitschrift für Angewandte Linguistik* 38. 37–56.

Fiesler, Casey & Nicholas Proferes. 2018. "Participant" perceptions of Twitter research ethics. *Social Media + Society* 4 (1). https://doi.org/10.1177/2056305118763366.

Fiesler, Casey, Michael Zimmer, Nicholas Proferes, Sarah Gilbert & Naiyan Jones. 2024. Remember the Human: A Systematic Review of Ethical Considerations in Reddit Research. *Proceedings of the ACM on Human Computer Interaction* 8 (GROUP). 5:1–5:33. https://doi.org/10.1145/3633070. https: //dl.acm.org/doi/10.1145/3633070 (last accessed 14 February 2025).

Hendrickx, Iris, Lieke Verheijen & Lidwien van de Wijngaert (eds.), 2021. *Proceedings of the 8th Conference on Computer-mediated Communication CMC and Social Media Corpora (CMC-Corpora 2021)*. Nijmegen, NL: Radboud University. https://surfdrive.surf.nl/files/index.php/s/Lcgx6d3EwGMjugR (last accessed 14 February 2025).

Herring, Susan C., Dieter Stein & Tuija Virtanen. 2013. Introduction to the pragmatics of computer-mediated communication. In Susan C. Herring, Dieter Stein & Tuija Virtanen (eds.), *Pragmatics of computer-mediated communication*, 3–31. Berlin & Boston: De Gruyter.

Koch, Peter & Wulf Oesterreicher. 1985. Sprache der Nähe – Sprache der Distanz. Mündlichkeit und Schriftlichkeit im Spannungsfeld von Sprachtheorie und Sprachgeschichte. *Romanistisches Jahrbuch* 36. 15–43.

Labov, William. 1972. *Language in the inner city: Studies in the Black English vernacular* 3. Philadelphia: University of Pennsylvania Press.

Li, Jiwei, Alan Ritter & Eduard Hovy. 2014. Weakly supervised user profile extraction from Twitter. In Kristina Toutanova & Hua Wu (eds.), *Proceedings of the 52nd Annual Meeting of the Association for Computational Linguistics (volume 1: Long papers)*, 165–174. Baltimore, MD: Association for Computational Linguistics. https://doi.org/10.3115/v1/P14-1016. https: //aclanthology.org/P14-1016 (last accessed 14 February 2025).

Luth, Janine, Konstanze Marx & Christian Pentzold. 2022. Ethische und rechtliche Aspekte der Analyse von digitalen Diskursen. In Eva Gredel (ed.), *Diskurse digital: Theorien, Methoden, Anwendungen*, 99–134. Berlin & Boston: De Gruyter. https://doi.org/10.1515/9783110721447-006.

Meyerhoff, Miriam. 2016. Methods, innovations and extensions: Reflections on half a century of methodology in social dialectology. *Journal of Sociolinguistics* 20 (4). 431–452. https://doi.org/10.1111/josl.12195.

Nguyen, Dong, A. Seza Doğruöz, Carolyn P. Rosé & Franciska de Jong. 2016. Computational sociolinguistics: A Survey. *Computational Linguistics* 42 (3). 537–593. https://doi.org/10.1162/COLI_a_00258. https://aclanthology. org/J16-3007 (last accessed 14 February 2025).

Nguyen, Dong, Rilana Gravel, Dolf Trieschnigg & Theo Meder. 2021. "How old do you think I am?" A study of language and age in Twitter. *Proceedings of the International AAAI Conference on Web and Social Media* 7 (1). 439–448. https://doi.org/10.1609/icwsm.v7i1.14381. https://ojs.aaai.org/index.php/ICWSM/ article/view/14381 (last accessed 14 February 2025).

Scheffler, Tatjana, Lesley-Ann Kern & Hannah Seemann. 2022. The medium is not the message: Individual level register variation in blogs vs. tweets. *Register Studies* 4 (2). 171–201. https://doi.org/10.1075/rs.22009.sch.

Schler, Jonathan, Moshe Koppel, Shlomo Argamon & James W. Pennebaker. 2006. Effects of age and gender on blogging. In *Aaai spring symposium: Computational approaches to analyzing weblogs, vol. 6*, 199–205.

Schöch, Christof, Frédéric Döhl, Achim Rettinger, Evelyn Gius, Peer Trilcke, Peter Leinen, Fotis Jannidis, Maria Hinzmann & Jörg Röpke. 2020. Abgeleitete Textformate: Text und Data Mining mit urheberrechtlich geschützten Textbeständen. *Zeitschrift für digitale Geisteswissenschaften*. https://doi.org/10.17175/ 2020_006. https://zfdg.de/2020_006 (last accessed 14 February 2025).

Seemann, Hannah, Sara Shahmohammadi, Manfred Stede & Tatjana Scheffler. 2023. PARADISE: A German PARAllel DIScoursE annotated multi-media corpus. https://doi.org/10.17605/OSF.IO/59ACQ. https://doi.org/10.17605/OSF. IO/59ACQ.

Tagliamonte, Sali A & Derek Denis. 2008. Linguistic ruin? LOL! Instant messaging and teen language. *American Speech* 83 (1). 3–34.

Wilkinson, Mark D., Michel Dumontier, IJsbrand Jan Aalbersberg, Gabrielle Appleton, Myles Axton, Arie Baak, Niklas Blomberg, Jan-Willem Boiten, Luiz Bonino da Silva Santos, Philip E. Bourne, Jildau Bouwman, Anthony J. Brookes, Tim Clark, Mercè Crosas, Ingrid Dillo, Olivier Dumon, Scott Edmunds, Chris T. Evelo, Richard Finkers, Alejandra Gonzalez-Beltran, Alasdair J. G. Gray, Paul Groth, Carole Goble, Jeffrey S. Grethe, Jaap Heringa, Peter A. C. 't Hoen, Rob Hooft, Tobias Kuhn, Ruben Kok, Joost Kok, Scott J. Lusher, Maryann E. Martone, Albert Mons, Abel L. Packer, Bengt Persson, Philippe Rocca-Serra, Marco Roos, Rene van Schaik, Susanna-Assunta Sansone, Erik Schultes, Thierry Sengstag, Ted Slater, George Strawn, Morris A. Swertz, Mark Thompson, Johan van der Lei, Erik van Mulligen, Jan Velterop, Andra Waagmeester, Peter Wittenburg, Katherine Wolstencroft, Jun Zhao & Barend Mons. 2016. The FAIR Guiding Principles for scientific data management and stewardship. *Scientific Data* 3 (1). 160018. https://doi.org/10.1038/sdata.2016.18. https://www.nature.com/articles/sdata201618 (last accessed 14 February 2025). Publisher: Nature Publishing Group.

Yates, Simeon J. 1996. Oral and written aspects of computer conferencing: A corpus based study. In Susan C. Herring (ed.), *Computer-mediated communication: Linguistic, social and cross-cultural perspectives*, 29–46. Amsterdam: Benjamins.

Annamária Fábián and Igor Trost

Computer-Mediated Communication to facilitate inclusion: Digital corpus analysis on disability diversity on social media

Abstract: Whereas there is a wealth of studies on computer-mediated communication (CMC), publications (e.g., Oussalah et al. 2016; Beißwenger 2016; Scheffler et al. 2019; Brookes and McEnrey 2020; Clausen and Scheffler 2020; Heritage and Baker 2022; Grieve and Woodfield 2023) specifically addressing diversity and inclusion in both, CMC and Digital Linguistics, are underrepresented. At the same time, many linguistic studies make use of data from digital media, itself an increasingly popular field of study in linguistics (Crystal 2006; Zappavigna 2012; De Decker and Vandekerckhove 2017; Bubenhofer 2017; Abel et al. 2020; Marx and Weidacher 2020; Wright 2020), but none of them focuses on disability-related diversity and inclusion. Simultaneously, inclusion has become significant in digital societies and has attracted raising awareness by the participation of people with a disability via communication on social media. This study on CMC therefore examines digital language use concerning disability and inclusion – contributed by people with and without a disability – on social media, which is in times of digital participation of diverse groups highly relevant to empowerment and inclusion in digital societies. A Twitter corpus comprising 2,559 tweets of 61,249 tokens is therefore used for this representative analysis. The corpus consists of German tweets published on *#Behinderung* ('disability') and *#Inklusion* ('inclusion') between 1st of December – 31st of December 2020. This linguistic study provides valuable first insights into the lexicon concerning disability and inclusion on social media as well as the co-occurrences of the lexical units.

Keywords: disability discourse, discourse of inclusion, sentiment analysis, Computer-Mediated Communication, Digital Linguistics

Annamária Fábián, University of Bayreuth, e-mail: Annamaria.Fabian-Trost@uni-bayreuth.de
Igor Trost, University of Passau, e-mail: Igor.Trost@uni-passau.de

https://doi.org/10.1515/9783111434018-015

1 Brief overview of the research in linguistics on Social Media discourses concerning social diversity

Whereas there is a wealth of studies on the language of discrimination, particularly within discourse studies, studies specifically addressing the linguistic practices of inclusion of diverse individuals and collectives are comparatively rare. At the same time, many linguistic studies make use of data from digital media, itself an increasingly popular field of study in linguistics (Crystal 2006; Zappavigna 2012; De Decker and Vandekerckhove 2017; Bubenhofer 2017; Abel et al. 2020; Marx and Weidacher 2020; Wright 2020). The communication of inclusion and exclusion of diverse individuals and collectives has been the focus of numerous studies within the social sciences, and discourse analysis is becoming increasingly prevalent. In recent years, linguistic studies have focused on discourses pertaining to refugees and migrants (e.g., Viola and Musolff 2019), as well as on gender-related issues (e.g., Paknahad and Baker 2016; Gnau and Wyss 2019), disability (e.g., Sties 2013; Grue 2014) and on mental health issues (e.g., Harvey 2012) in various countries and contexts. Many of these studies make use of data from digital media (e.g., Marx and Weidacher 2020; Wright 2020; Knuchel and Bubenhofer 2023). These important studies have raised awareness regarding the importance of analyzing issues related to diversity, including diverse individuals and diverse collectives from the point of view of Corpus Linguistics and Discourse Analysis. In CMC, as well as in human-centered data science, research on an inclusive digital transformation is underrepresented. Herrera (2022) argues that social media analytics tools need to be designed to support inclusive public services for all, including those with disabilities. Sinclair (2011) emphasizes the importance of paying attention to social barriers that inhibit inclusion, rather than simply technological barriers. Zelena (2020) explores, how new media platforms become the platform of communal loss for users of different ages, genders, social statuses, and diverse internet usage habits and socialization. Finally, Pan et al. (2014) examine the role of community diversity in influencing perceived inclusion of newcomers in the online community and the influence of such perception on newcomers' engagement intention. This wide range of the corpus linguistic research on language on social media as well as on, in general, inclusion in digital societies indicates not only the lack of interest in studies in terms of disability-related diversity in CMC but also in interdisciplinary studies on an inclusive digital transformation via CMC for diversity visibility.

In keeping with the scientific tradition of Corpus Linguistics, CMC (e.g., Oussalah et al. 2016; Beißwenger 2016; Scheffler et al. 2019; Brookes and McEnrey 2020; Clausen and Scheffler 2020; Heritage and Baker 2022; Grieve and Woodfield 2023) and Computational Social Science (e.g., Brantner and Pfeffer 2018; Ralev and Pfeffer 2022; Strathern et al. 2022), this study focuses on the digital communication of disability diversity and inclusion in one month (December 2020) selected for this quantitative lexical analysis from a corpus of 14 years between 2009–2023 as well as on methodological considerations for processing with digital corpora for CMC and human-centered data science.

2 Lexical study and sentiment analysis of the language use regarding inclusion and disability on social media as a key research objective

CMC encompasses various forms of communication, which take place by way of digital devices and networks. The language used in CMC can vary depending on the platform, context, and participants involved. According to Barbaresi (2019: 29-30), “specialized corpora of the language of CMC and social media are increasingly vital for the analysis of diversity in terms of speakers and settings in digital contexts”. As it is important to notice that people with a disability face ableism in education internationally and have consequently limited access to academia, this study wants to contribute to speakers’ and platform diversity in CMC by listening to the perspectives of disabled persons. Minorities (including individuals with a disability) contribute to the visibility of social diversity, and with this, to inclusion by raising awareness to different diversity dimensions, their own personal situation and their perspectives on inclusion, discrimination, and exclusion as well as on everyday life. Furthermore, the digital communication of individuals with a disability evoke digital conversations between people with and without a disability essential to inclusion. This significant digital activism of disabled individuals often leads to a social transformation through the shift of perspectives in society via CMC. Moreover, individuals with a disability, have been successfully engaged on social media for inclusion through visibility for more than 10 years. For a study on significant voices and perspectives on disability and inclusion as a result of the communicative co-construction of both, diversity and inclusion, on German Twitter, we set up a corpus along *#Behinderung* (‘disability’) and *#Inklusion* (‘inclusion’), mainly but not exclusively written by individuals with a disability and their representatives. The corpus underlying this research consists of 2,559 German tweets, together with 61,249 tokens, as part of a large corpus made up of 14,926 tweets in total with 5,663,504 tokens. The large corpus however includes mainly German tweets published 2009–2023 under the hashtags ‘inclusion’ and ‘disability’, while the small corpus was published in a time period of one month, from the 1st to the 31st of December 2020 UTC. This paper therefore provides an analysis of the communication of disability diversity on social media. For the analysis, we chose to examine the data for a single month, in order to gain first insights into the lexicon and the sentiment of the entire corpus. The outcome of this corpus-driven study contributes to decision-making on data processing for further qualitative and quantitative CMC-related studies and facilitates effective navigation of large-scale data by introducing a methodological design combining the user friendly tools AntConc and SentiStrength for the initial evaluation of digital discourses and corpora.

Before processing with the quantitative examination of the corpus on *#Behinderung* ('disability') and *#Inklusion* ('inclusion') on Twitter, we would like to introduce our decision for processing with Twitter (rebranded to X in July 2023) data. Before Twitter's acquisition by Elon Musk, the platform with several members of the German former and current government, journalists, and other significant public figures was broadly used for disability agenda setting by individuals with a disability in Germany as well as in other countries.[1] The selection of the corpus from December 2020 is based on the progress of the German words 'Behinderung' and 'Inklusion' in the corpus of 14 years as those words show a particularly high frequency in this one month compared to the time due to and after 2020. The reason of this comparatively high frequency is associated with COVID19 as a serious threat to human life, in particular to those with health impairments, which has clearly resulted in this heightened interest in disability and inclusion. Similar to other digital social movements, (e.g., Dang-Anh 2013; Fábián 2020), language and computer-mediated-communication are verified essential keys for activism concerning inclusion in digital societies. As this corpus consequently is of high significance to people with health impairments, also including many individuals with a disability, we conduct a computer-driven lexical examination of relevant parts of the German discourse on disability and inclusion. This quantitative CMC-study was prepared to gain insights into the sentiment of self-representation of people with disabilities as well as of inclusion on social media based on the investigation into the language and communication used when discussing disability and inclusion on Twitter under the participation of people with a disability.

1 As Elon Musk has refused the free use of the API to scientists since the end of April 2023, the data gathered prior to this time is also historically relevant to German society as well as to people with a disability in Germany.

For this examination, we therefore undertake a combined software-based lexical and sentiment analysis with AntConc and SentiStrength,[2] in particular of the nouns *Inklusion* ('inclusion') and *Behinderung* ('disability') and associated lexical entities, which is prevalent for a CMC-based linguistic study of minority languages reporting on issues and agenda of individuals with a disability, but not exclusively of those with a disability. Our research is guided by the hypothesis that the German discourse on *#Inklusion* ('inclusion') and *#Behinderung* ('disability') can be lexically classified and characterized on social media, and that the discourse is highly positive from the point of view of the discourse participants, which we will demonstrate on the corpus. First, corpus linguistic insights from an excerpt of a digital discourse on disability and inclusion on social media is essential as Fábián et al. (2024: 24) demonstrate the participation of individuals with a disability on Social Media based on the German Twitter (X) example and their community organization by using the hashtags 'disability' and 'inclusion'. This kind of human-centered studies contribute to gathering information on self-empowerment of diverse individuals and collectives often facing discrimination in society, essential for inclusion. Although our first CMC study (Fábián et al. 2024) provides the first information on disability participation in a digital society via computer-mediated communication, the semantic evaluation of digital discourses on disability and inclusion has not been covered, neither in CMC nor in human-centered data science, making this study unique, and simultaneously essential for first insights into data on disability self-empowerment and public disability visibility for an inclusive transformation in society. A semantic classification of tweets into the categories negative, neutral and positive with SentiStrength as part of a Sentiment Analysis will supplement this investigation (e.g., Kiritchenko et al. 2014; Dai et al. 2017; Palomino et al. 2020) on the lexicon by AntConc. AntConc was developed by Anthony Lawrence (Waseda University/Japan), SentiStrength by Mike Thelwall (University of Wolverhampton/UK). Both of them are at no cost available for non-profit goals and can also be easily used by students, early-career scientists as well as by scientists without knowledge of Computational Linguistics engaged in qualitative studies on corpora, which convinced us to use these tools. Our research design includes quantitative research methods, while pursuing the following goals:

1. We observe the lexicon (incl. collocations) in the Twitter discourse on disability and inclusion in order to arrive at a first impression on the semantic and emo-

2 SentiStrength was only developed for the "sentiment strength detection for short informal text" but not for large corpora.

tional aspects of communication in digital discourse concerning disability and inclusion.
2. We provide a lexical analysis including the analysis of collocations (Corpus-driven lexical Analysis) on disability and inclusion in our Twitter corpus.
3. We classify the tweets as part of our digital corpus in negative, neutral and positive (Sentiment Analysis).

In addition, the project aims to gain insights into effective digital linguistic methods (tools, software etc.) adaptable for the communicative analysis of data on social media. Dai et al. (2017) propose a word embedding-based clustering method for tweet classification that achieves good accuracy without requiring labeled training data. Lui and Baldwin (2014) but also Heaton et al. (2023) evaluate off-the-shelf language identification systems for tweets and their usability for linguistic analysis. Lui and Baldwin (2014) find that simple voting over three specific systems consistently outperforms any specific system. Yang and Srinivasan (2014) propose a methodology for translating surveys into social media surveillance, which achieves better precision and recall than standard methods using lexicons or classifiers. While Yurchenko and Ugolnikova (2021) focus on linguistic methods in social media marketing, the paper highlights the relevance of simple linguistic methods for a short overview of corpora before processing with further and more detailed analysis of communication in corpora. We decided to combine therefore AntConc often used for a quick analysis of the lexicon and the collocations, and SentiStrength, which is far less widespread among corpus linguists making this paper useful for a corpus linguistic sentiment analysis. According to Palomino et al. (2020: 8), SentiStrength has the methodological advantage of simple application for the identification of "the polarity of tweets as positive, negative or neutral, though SentiStrength can also work as a binary classification tool – positive or negative.", which is the main reason for using this specific tool for a semantic evaluation of the analyzed digital corpus.

3 A Data-Driven Semantic Study of 'disability' and 'inclusion' in a Digital Corpus on Twitter

3.1 Conducting a Data-Driven Semantic-Analysis with SentiStrength and AntConc – methodological Considerations for corpus linguists

As highlighted in chapter 3, the quantitative background of this digital linguistic study is twofold:

1. First, we conduct a lexical analysis of the corpus on *#Behinderung* ('disability') and *#Inklusion* ('inclusion')[3] by using AntConc, a tool often used by digital linguists. We chose AntConc as a tool as the adaptability of AntConc is useful for capturing and visualizing the lexical units and their collocates.
2. Second, we carry out a sentiment analysis with SentiStrength. SentiStrength is a sentiment classification tool which does not need proficiency in Machine Learning and can also be easily used by digital linguists without a background in Computational Linguistics.

Before processing with our corpus linguistic study with SentiStrength, it was necessary to prepare the corpus for processing with SentiStrength as SentiStrength was developed to analyse shorter texts line by line especially for business purposes. First, it was necessary to eliminate all line breaks in the corpus on the hashtags *Inklusion* ('inclusion') and *Behinderung* ('disability') for an overall analysis at sentence level. In addition, SentiStrength does not output the results in a separate file but puts them to a txt-UTF-8 corpus file, which slightly doubles in size as a result. While these framework conditions imply that the program cannot analyse large corpora and is therefore not useful for studies on large-scale data, SentiStrength enables first insights into the sentiment along lexical items in selected parts of a large-scale corpus. The outcome of this kind of first analysis supports scientists involved in studies on CMC with navigating through large-scale corpora and making decisions on how to process with the data for further examinations of communication as part of a research project. This triggered our decision to reduce our corpus for this paper and provide a Sentiment analysis on the communication of one month. For the analysis, however, we chose December 2020, which was in the midst of the Covid lockdown in German-speaking countries, exposing many indi-

3 We developed a register with keywords for the data collection. Our main keywords for the collection were *#Behinderung* ('disability') and *#Inklusion* ('inclusion').

viduals, particularly with those with health impairments and/or a disability, at a high risk. This international health emergency prompted our choice to process with the data for this time period. This part of our large corpus consists of 2,559 tweets, 950 full sentences,[4] 61,249 tokens and 11,251 types. Our corpus choice consequently has an impact on the Sentiment Analysis in the corpus as 'COVID' is quite frequent.[5]

The German sentiment strength dictionary file, *EmotionLookupTable_v5_fullforms*, for the program SentiStrength was provided by SentiStrength (http://sentistrength.wlv.ac.uk, last accessed 14 February 2025) and Hannes Pirker, Interaction Technologies Group at the Austrian Research Institute for Artificial Intelligence (OFAI) with additions from Elias Kyewski of the University of Duisburg-Essen.

SentiStrength performs the sentiment analysis using a sentiment strength dictionary, in which lexemes are assigned a sentiment rating. Positive sentiment ratings are marked with a scale of 1 to 5, negative ones with a scale -1 to -5. Each lexeme is rated with a maximum of 4 or -4, only repeated occurrences can result in a rating of 5 or -5 for a phrase. A neutral sentiment of a lexeme is marked with 0. In this paper, the positive numbers are always marked with a plus sign, i.e., the positive scale is +1 to +5.

Pertaining to sentences, the rating is always made up of a negative and a positive rating, e.g., -2/+3. These two ratings of a sentence are the results of the addition of the positive ratings and the addition of negative ratings. The sum is capped at +5 or -5. When the overall sentiment rating of a sentence is calculated, the maximum values which can result are +4 (=+5-1) or -4 (=+1-5).

While using SentiStrength, our first considerations were that this dictionary file *EmotionLookupTable_v5_fullforms* is very extensive for negative words such as insults. We also considered that the negative ratings are occasionally inconsequent as serious verbal insults such as *Scheiße* ('shit', 'fuck' or 'fucking') are rated at -3, but *leider* ('unfortunately') at -4. In light of this consideration, we decided to implement the necessary corrections: In our new sentiment strength dictionary file, *EmotionLookupTable_v6_fullforms*, *Scheiße* ('shit', 'fuck' or 'fucking') is rated at -4, and *leider* ('unfortunately') at -3. Another observation on SentiStrength was that the sentiment strength dictionary v5 contains only few positive words. Positive foreign words and positive word formations (very frequent in German morphology) are highly underrepresented in the lexicon of SentiStrength. Particularly in the Ger-

4 Not every tweet contains a full sentence.

5 Individuals with health impairment and/or disability often used 'COVID' as a lexeme, also combined with a hashtag, for protection by governmental regulations.

man-speaking countries, non-partisan recognized political words which express a high level of positivity ('Hochwertwörter') such as *gerecht* ('just') or *sozial* ('social') – also often occurring in corpora on social issues such as disability, and inclusion – are missing and, as a consequence, classified by SentiStrength as neutral (0). In this respect, the sentiment strength dictionary v5 had to be significantly revised for a sentiment analysis of public communication in the social and political sphere. In addition, we realized that strongly discourse-relevant keywords for our study, which are associated with a positive semantic, have not been included in the old sentiment strength dictionary file v5. Keywords in our study with a positive semantic include words such as *Inklusion* ('inclusion'), *Teilhabe* ('participation'), and *Barrierefreiheit* ('accessibility'), and the adjective *barrierefrei* ('accessible'). After recognizing the inadequately trained vocabulary of SentiStrength in German, we developed a register essential to our corpus linguistic analysis and finalized the list with – from the point of view of our CMC study on disability and inclusion – words not registered in the SentiStrength vocabulary. We therefore conducted a corpus-linguistic analysis of the lexicon key to the discourse on disability and inclusion along the hashtags #Inklusion ('inclusion') and #Behinderung ('disability'), which built the basis for detecting the key words in the corpus. Consequently, we developed a core register for the Sentiment Analysis with SentiStrength only after detecting the vocabulary by using AntConc. In this way, we augmented our register with the most important lexemes highly relevant to the discourse on disability and inclusion.

3.2 Findings of the corpus-driven analysis with AntConc and SentiStrength

A log-likelihood[6] analysis with the corpus linguistic tool AntConc of the collocates of the #-words *Inklusion* ('inclusion') / *inklusiv* ('inclusive') and *Behinderung* ('disability')/*behindert* ('disabled') illustrates the lexicon mostly significant and consequently highly-frequent in the discourse:

6 Standard settings: threshold $p<0.05$ (3.84 with Bonferroni), effect measure size: MI, search window span from five words left to five words right.

Table 1: Collocates of *inklusi**.

Collocates of *inklusi**	FreqLR	FreqL	FreqR	Likelihood
Inklusion (inclusion)	335	172	163	369.051
Hilfe (help, aid, assistance)[7]	347	11	336	247.531
Deutschland (germany)	366	21	345	238.594
News[8]	358	25	333	215.490
Berlin	322	37	285	169.196
Teilhabe (participation)	223	97	126	111.421
mit (with)[9]	301	164	137	80.026
Barrierefreiheit (accessibility)	149	77	72	68.312
Menschen (humans)	192	93	99	56.250
SARS	18	13	5	38.405
barrierefrei (accessible)	74	47	27	35.526
CoV	20	14	6	34.365
Behinderung (disability)	624	476	148	33.453
Pflege (care)	79	17	62	26.221
Menschenrecht (human right)	29	6	23	20.427

7 The lexeme *Hilfe* ('help') is mainly used by one of the mostly 'visible' actors around disability and inclusion, which is a professional organization. The productivity of this organization in terms of the production of tweets has an impact on the evaluation of the entire corpus. Other frequently posting users – especially individuals with disabilities without institutional background – however do not use 'help' very often.

8 see comment above

9 This frequency is related to the frequent usage of the inclusive reference *Menschen mit Behinderung* ('people with disability').

Table 2: Collocate of *behinder**.

Collocate of *behinder**	FreqLR	FreqL	FreqR	Likelihood
Menschen (humans)	732	669	63	781.086
mit (with)	865	797	68	610.112
Deutschland (Germany)	375	23	352	436.349
Hilfe (help)	333	13	320	377.870
News	316	16	300	279.251
Tag[10] (day)	188	165	23	198.911
Berlin	261	27	234	178.352
Behinderung (disability)	144	61	83	162.125
internationalen[11] (international)	65	58	7	83.670
der[12]	478	340	138	61.514
internationaler[13] (international)	42	36	6	60.523
internationale[14] (international)	39	35	4	51.498
Welttag (World Day)	35	30	5	48.299
von (of)	210	159	51	40.894
es (it, e.g., in *es braucht = it is necessary*, also there: *es gibt = there is*)	48	12	36	38.631
vielen (many)	5	2	3	35.567
Gesundheit (health)	31	19	12	35.339
Inklusion (inclusion)	701	171	530	31.376

10 The noun *Tag* occurs in the corpus as part of the phrase Internationaler *Tag der Menschen mit Behinderung* (International Day of People with Disability, the 3rd of December) very often.
11 The lexeme *international* occurs in our corpus in many different forms as the German grammar system has a complex flexion system with many different endings. This leads, however, to frequent appearance of the same word with different endings which are recognized as different findings by programs for processing with language data.
12 *der* can be understood as a definite article in German (masculinum), for instance in the collocation ***der*** *internationale Tag* ('the international day'), but also the pluralform with genitive, for instance in the collocation *der internationale Tag* **der** *Menschen mit Behinderung* ('The International Day of People with Disability')
13 See Footnote 11
14 See Footnote 11

Collocate of *behinder**	FreqLR	FreqL	FreqR	Likelihood
ich (I)	36	5	31	31.161
Corona (COVID 19)	116	68	48	29.127
SARS	12	7	5	28.751
CoV	14	9	5	24.455
das	80	22	58	23.811
Beschäftigung (employment)	21	19	2	23.027
veröffentlicht (published)	4	4	0	20.749
Teilhabe (participation)	113	63	50	19.797
Erinnerungen (memories)	8	6	2	19.710

Our quantitative lexical analysis shows the highest frequency of *Behinderung* ('disability') in a collocation with *inklusi** (FreqLR) and the highest significance (log-likelihood) of *Inklusion* ('inclusion') in a collocation with *inklusi**. Although *Hilfe* ('help') and *News* occur with high frequency in the corpus and are significant for *inklusi**, both tokens are mainly used only by one of the mostly 'visible' actors around disability and inclusion, which is a professional organization. The productivity of this organization in terms of the production of tweets has an impact on the evaluation of the entire corpus. Other frequently posting users – especially individuals with disabilities without institutional background – however do not use 'help' very often. Also, the toponyms *Deutschland* ('Germany') as well as *Berlin* occur in the collocation with *inklusi** quite frequent in the corpus, which depends on the use of these tokens on the one hand for setting the local context of disability- and inclusion-related topics referred to in the digital discourse, on the other hand as part of a metonym [*Berlin*] for the German government. This frequent use is in the context of policies necessary for more inclusion. While *Teilhabe* ('participation') and *Barrierefreiheit* ('accessibility')/*barrierefrei* ('accessible') show medium frequency and significance in the corpus, *Menschenrecht* ('human right') occurs infrequently in the time period of one month. This gives rise to the hypothesis that individuals with a disability focus more on inclusion and accessibility and their practical transformation in everyday life.

The second table includes the highest collocations (FreqLR) and mostly significance (log-likelihood) with *behinder** ('disabled'). *Menschen* ('humans') and the preposition *mit* ('with') were the most frequently used tokens examined. This frequent use of both tokens is associated with the self-reference of people with disabilities (*Menschen mit Behinderung*/'people with disability'). The reference is often used for agenda setting by people with a disability and civil society fostering inclusion in German society. Although *Inklusion* ('inclusion') is particularly frequent in the collocation profile, the log-likelihood ratio of this token is comparatively low, because *Inklusion* is to be expected in the discourse and therefore idiomatic. The token *der* occurs often in the collocation ***der** internationale Tag **der** Menschen mit Behinderung* ('the International Day of People with Disability') or in *Welttag **der** Menschen mit Behinderung* ('World Day of People with a Disability'). While *Barrierefreiheit* ('accessibility')/*barrierefrei* ('accessible') occurred frequently in a collocation with *inklusi**, they remained statistically insignificant with *behinder**. This finding depends on the propensity that people with a disability seek *inclusion*. In a second step, as a consequence of the demand for *inclusion*, individuals with a disability and their representative organizations seek *accessibility*, which is reflected in the corpus. This is why *accessibility/accessible* appears as a collocate of *inclusion/ inclusive* and not of *disability/disabled*.

The corpus-linguistic AntConc analysis has shown that the collocates of the lexemes *Inklusion* ('inclusion') and *Behinderung* ('disability') in the German discourse on inclusion occur in the corpus with positively framed words (*Hochwertwörter*) for instance *Hilfe* ('help', 'aid', 'assistance'), *Menschenrecht* ('human right'), *Teilhabe* ('participation'), and *Welttag* ('World Day'). In addition, they are associated with individuals (*Menschen* 'humans'), places (for instance *Berlin* as a metonym for the German federal government), professional lexicon (for instance social: *Beschäftigung* 'employment' or medical *Corona*) and function words (for instance *mit* 'with').

The quantitative lexical analysis and its findings facilitated in conducting the sentiment analysis as the evaluation of SentiStrength's register is based on the outcome of the quantitative analysis. While the lexical analysis confirmed that the collocates *Inklusion* 'inclusion', *Teilhabe* 'participation', *Barrierefreiheit* 'accessibility', *barrierefrei* 'accessible' (in bold in the Tables 1 and 2) are keywords of the discourse, we discovered that these tokens are not included in the original register of SentiStrength. We therefore added these words to our register to make the SentiStrength program more sensitive to our discourse study on disability and inclusion. In terms of these lexical findings, we would like to point out that the corpus-linguistic program AntConc recognizes all German morphological forms as separate types. Due to the variety of forms of the German adjective inflection with up to 17 endings (including the Ø-ending and the combinations with the endings of comparative forms), the log-likelihood analysis for adjectives by AntConc is often incorrect as AntConc does not recognize the morphological relations. The adjective *inklusiv* ('inclusive') has 87 tokens with eight morphological forms in the corpus and therefore AntConc rated *inklusiv* falsely as non-significant. This prompted our decision to add it to our extended register. Further proof checks on SentiStrength's register revealed that not only the lexemes with positive ranking such as *Inklusion* ('inclusion')/ *inklusiv* ('inclusive') and *Behinderung* ('disability')/ *behindert* ('disabled') were not recognized by the program, but also the most frequent words with a negative sentiment rating in the corpus such as *Exklusion* ('exclusion'), *exklusiv* ('exclusive'), *Diskriminierung* ('discrimination'), and *diskriminierend* ('discriminatory').

As a result, we trained SentiStrength by adding the above vocabulary to the evaluation list of the sentiment strength dictionary: We rated the positive words *Inklusion* ('inclusion')/ *inklusiv* ('inclusive')/ *Teilhabe* ('participation')/ *Barrierefreiheit* ('accessibility'), and *barrierefrei* ('accessible') with +4 and the negative words *Exklusion*/ ('exclusion'), *exklusiv* ('exclusive'), *Diskriminierung* ('discrimination'), and *diskriminierend* ('discriminatory') with -4. These rating values were concluded from the point of view of the discourse participants – mainly individuals with disabilities – as inclusion is essential for users with a disability, while discrimination and exclusion have an enormous negative impact on the lives of many people with a disability. In its default settings, the program SentiStrength will rate these lexemes with +4 or -4 for single occurrences and with the maximum rate +5 or -5 for multiple occurrences within a sentence. These rating values also help to provide us

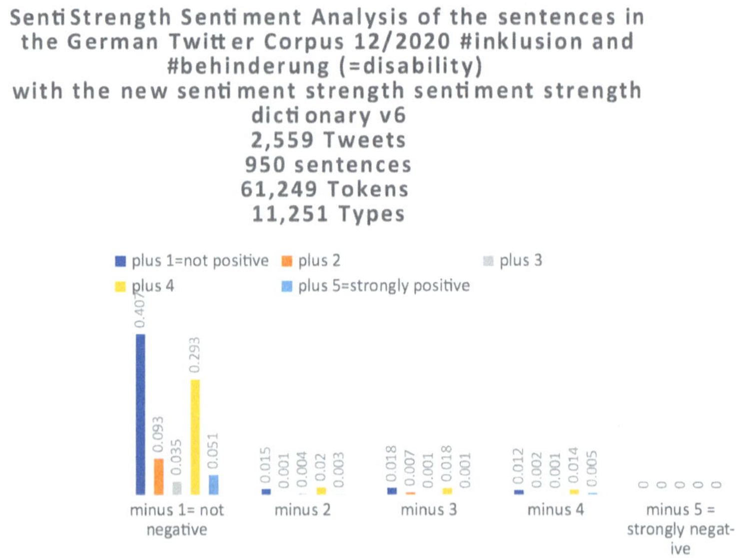

	minus 1= not negative	minus 2	minus 3	minus 4	minus 5 = strongly negative
plus 1=not positive	0.407	0.015	0.018	0.012	0
plus 2	0.093	0.001	0.007	0.002	0
plus 3	0.035	0.004	0.001	0.001	0
plus 4	0.293	0.02	0.018	0.014	0
plus 5=strongly positive	0.051	0.003	0.001	0.005	0

Diagram 1: Results of the SentiStrength Sentiment Analysis

with an insight into the polarized positions on inclusion, discrimination and exclusion in the analysed discourse.

The chart (see diagram 1) illustrates the results of the sentiment analysis with the corrected sentiment strength dictionary file *EmotionLookupTable_v6_fullforms* and the corpus without the # characters.

The overall sentiment rating of a sentence is calculated from the positive and the negative sentiment rating. Overall, a neutral or a positive sentiment rating of the discourse on inclusion can be seen:

- **40.7 %** of all 950 sentences are somewhat **neutral (+1-1=0)**, they have a neutral positive (+1) and a neutral negative (-1) sentiment rating.
- **47.2 %** of all 950 sentences have a **positive sentiment without negative sentiments,** i.e., they primarily consist of positive words:
- 29.3 % of all 950 sentences are **very positive (+4-1=+3)**, they have a highly positive (+4) and a neutral negative (-1) sentiment rating.
- 9.3 % of all 950 sentences are **slightly positive (+2-1=+1)**, they have a positive (+2) and a neutral negative (-1) sentiment rating.
- 5.1 % of all 950 sentences are **highly positive (+5-1=+4)**, they have a strongly positive (+5) and a neutral negative (-1) sentiment rating.
- 3.5 % of all 950 sentences are **positive (+3-1=+2)**, they have a very positive (+3) and a neutral negative (-1) sentiment rating.

Only 4.5 % of the sentences show a **negative sentiment rating**, i.e., they mainly consist of negative words:

- 1.8 % of all 950 sentences are **negative (+1-3=-2)**, they have a neutral positive (+1) and a very negative (-3) sentiment rating.
- 1.5 % of all 950 sentences are **slightly negative (+1-2=-1)**, they have a neutral positive (+1) and a negative (-2) sentiment rating.
- 1.2 % of all 950 sentences are **very negative (+1-4=-3)**, they have a neutral positive (+1) and a highly negative (-4) sentiment rating.

Some sentences are contradictory regarding their sentiment analysis, e.g.,:

- 1.8 % of all 950 sentences are **confrontational and positive in the result (+4-2=+2)**. These sentences include as well a highly positive (+4) as a negative (-2) sentiment rating, as they contain many positive words but also some negative words.

These contradictory results of positive and negative sentiment ratings in a sentence are partly due to controversies in the discourse, but above all, they are attributed by the program SentiStrength to sentences with negations of positively rated lexemes, e.g., *keine* (=-2) *Inklusion* (=+4) (‘*no inclusion*’).

While the first column indicates an enormous positive evaluation of the German discourse on disability and inclusion on Social Media regarding the example of Twitter (X), the second, third, fourth, and the fifth column illustrate that the corpus is barely associated with a negative sentiment. As the fifth column does not include any result with the lowest and highly negative sentiment (-5) in the corpus, a highly negative evaluation of the discourse can be excluded. In summary, the positive evaluation of the discourse dominates significantly over the negative evaluation. More negative sentiments occur mainly associated with #Barrierefreiheit (accessibility) as people with a disability and their families report on their experience with discrimination and exclusion on social media requiring inclusion and accessibility. Furthermore, the log-likelihood values in the collocation analysis have already provided an indication that the discourse related to inclusion is positive. This outcome is particularly significant as many digital discourses are conducted in a confrontational and polarizing style due to high polarization such as the German discourse (cf. Trost 2023) on COVID19, which also depends on the discourse participants. While the principal participants involved in the discourse on disability and inclusion for inclusion are individuals with a disability, the discourse on COVID19 is often dominated by members and voters of the German Radical-Right-Party "Alternative für Deutschland" (AfD) targeting democratic decisions, government, politicians affiliated with democratic parties, but also diversity and inclusion. From the point of view of human-centered data science and social sciences, this positive sentiment verifies the high level of acceptance of the discourse on disability and inclusion among the digital discourse participants who – according to Fábián et al. (2024) – predominantly are individuals with a disability, their digital community, their allies, and their representatives (representative organizations). In addition, the positive evaluation also reflects the emotional value of this discourse to individuals with disabilities and their allies, which makes it even more emergent to present additional digital data on the digital self-empowerment of individuals with a disability regarding information essential to inclusive agenda setting in society.

Our quantitative analysis based on this integrative research design consisting of AntConc and SentiStrength illustrated that this combined method provides first insights into the lexicon and the sentiment of a particular discourse. This kind of initial corpus linguistic studies on diversity-related discourses can serve CMC as well as HCDS with choosing a particular focus for further research. This combination enables an analysis, which takes both keywords and non-keywords into account as a concise keyword analysis can be carried out with AntConc supplemented by an analysis with SentiStrength adding non-keywords to the results conducted with AntConc. In addition, a sentiment analysis thus enables the validation of log-likelihood values by a detailed analysis of the framing at the level of individual lexemes and sentences. Studies in Digital Linguistics consequentially allow a concise analysis of CMC corpora revealing contents of substantial significance to politics and society, which can contribute to research in Computational Social Science, Social Science, and Political Science essential to society. In addition, methodological considerations from Digital Linguistics can contribute to the development of programs and tools for data-driven language processing. Even though our findings indicate the relevance of our corpus linguistic study for human-centered data science with valuable information on disability participation in digital society, more accurate and, in particular, large-scale studies between Corpus Linguistics, CMC, Human-centered Data Science, and Computational Social Science on disability and inclusion in digital society are necessary for further research. These initial insights demonstrate solely the contribution of data analysis to disability empowerment, which could support communities of individuals with disability, their representative organizations as well as institutions and representatives for anti-discrimination as first indications reveal topics, content and views on the inclusion of individuals with a disability in an online or even offline society.

4 Conclusion

In terms of methodological impact, SentiStrength developed by computational scientists needs to be adapted and sometimes also trained for Corpus Linguistic Studies. This paper highlights that tools and methods of Digital Linguistics and Computational Science, also relevant to Computational Social Science, can be integrated in a research design for the analysis of digital discourses on diversity, disability and inclusion, including discriminatory phenomena such as discrimination, and exclusion. For a more concise study of social and political language use on social media, we would like to advocate for more interdisciplinary collaborations between Corpus Linguistics and Social and Political Science as well as Human-centered Data Science, Computational Social Science and, in general, Computational Science. Our methodological findings indicate that SentiStrength is an important tool with significant potential for Corpus Linguistics. However, its' usability for Corpus Linguistic research studies is extremely limited, which could be improved by interdisciplinary research projects for the development of tools and programs for language-based data-processing between Computational Science, Corpus Linguistics, and Social as well as Political Science including a vocabulary-based training of programs and tools. One of the most valuable methodological findings of this study for Linguistics is, however, that an AntConc analysis combined with an analysis with SentiStrength is useful for gaining valid first insights concerning the semantics of a particular digital discourse. This initiative outcome and underlying methods are useful for further data exploration in a larger corpus. Although there is an abundance of methods such as these, this method enables a quick yet concise examination of the lexicon and the sentiment of digital discourses without requiring specialised knowledge in Computational Linguistics and Computational Science, which makes science more inclusive by reducing methodological complexity. In addition, the methods illustrated in this chapter guided us to the verification of the relevance of the discourse in German on disability and inclusion on Twitter (X) for individuals with a disability and their self-representations. The Sentiment Analysis of the vocabulary demonstrates the significance of computer-mediated communication for an inclusive transformation in a digital society by disability agenda setting, and by vital community organization among individuals with a disability. As there is little knowledge with regards to the communication of individuals with a disability, more language-focused research on disability and inclusion is essential. In summary, research on computer-mediated communication and human-centered data science can be used for gaining insights concerning digital activism for diversity, equity, and inclusion as well as, in general, into digital societies.

References

Abel, Andrea, Aivars Glaznieks, Carolin Müller-Spitzer, Angelika Storrer (eds.), 2020. Themenheft „Textqualität im digitalen Zeitalter". *Deutsche Sprache* 48 (2). https://doi.org/10.37307/j.1868-775X.2020.02.

Anthony, Laurence. 2023. *AntConc (Version 4.2.2).* Tokyo Waseda University. Available from https://www.laurenceanthony.net/software (last accessed 14 February 2025).

Aragon, Cecilia, Shion Guha, Marina Koga, Michael Muller, Gina Neff. 2022. Human-centred data science. An introduction. Cambridge, MA, USA: MIT Press.

Barbaresi, Adrien. 2019. The vast and the focused: On the need for thematic web and blog corpora. In Piotr Bański, Adrien Barbaresi, Hanno Biber, Evelyn Breiteneder, Simon Clematide, Marc Kupietz, Harald Lüngen & Caroline Iliadi (eds.), *Proceedings of the Workshop on Challenges in the Management of Large Corpora (CMLC-7) 2019. Cardiff, 22nd July 2019*, 29–32. Mannheim: Leibniz-Institut für Deutsche Sprache. https://doi.org/10.14618/ids-pub-9025.

Beißwenger, Michael. 2017. *Empirische Erforschung internetbasierter Kommunikation.* Berlin & Boston: De Gruyter. https://doi.org/10.1515/zrs-2018-0027.

Brantner, Cornelia & Jürgen Pfeffer. 2018. Content analysis of Twitter – Big data, big studies. In *The Routledge handbook of developments in digital journalism studies*. 79–92. Abingdon: Taylor & Francis. https://doi.org/10.4324/9781315270449.

Brookes, Gavin & Tony McEnery. 2020. Correlation, collocation and cohesion: A corpus-based scritical analysis of violent jihadist discourse. *Discourse and Society* 31, 4. 351–373. https://doi.org/10.1177/0957926520903528.

Bubenhofer, Noah. 2017. Kollokationen, n-Gramme, Mehrworteinheiten. In Kersten Sven Roth, Martin Wengeler, Alexander Ziem (eds.): *Handbuch Sprache in Politik und Gesellschaft, Sprachwissen*. Berlin & Boston: De Gruyter. 69–93. https://doi.org/10.1515/9783110296310.

Clausen, Yulia & Scheffler, Tatjana. 2020. A corpus-based analysis of meaning variations in German tag questions: Evidence from spoken and written conversational corpora. Corpus Linguistics and Linguistic Theory. *Corpus Linguistics and Linguistic Theory*. 18 (1), 1-31. https://doi.org/10.1515/cllt-2019-0060.

Crystal, David. 2006. *Language and the internet*. Cambridge: Cambridge University Press. https://doi.org/10.1017/CBO9781139164771.

Dai, Xianfeng, Marwan Bikdash & Bradley Meyer. 2017. From social media to public health surveillance: Word embedding based clustering method for twitter classification. In *SoutheastCon 2017*, 1–7. Concord: IEEE. https://doi.org/10.1109/SECON.2017.7925400.

Dang-Anh, Mark, Jessica Einspänner & Caja Thimm. 2013. Mediatisierung und Medialität in Social Media: Das Diskurssystem „Twitter“. In Konstanze Marx & Monika Schwarz-Friesel (eds.): *Sprache und Kommunikation im technischen Zeitalter. Wieviel Internet (v)erträgt unsere Gesellschaft?*, 68–91. Berlin & Boston: De Gruyter. https://doi.org/10.1515/9783110282184.68.

De Decker, Benny & Reinhild Vandekerckhove. 2017. Global features of online communication in local Flemish: Social and medium-related determinants. *Folia Linguistica* 51 (1). 253–281. https://doi.org/10.1515/flin-2017-0007.

Fábián, Annamária. 2020. Verblose Sätze und kommunikative Praktiken in den Sozialen Medien am Beispiel der #MeToo-Bewegung. In Anne-Laure Daux & Anne Larory (eds.): *Kurze Formen in der Sprache / Formes brèves de la langue. Syntaktische, semantische und textuelle Aspekte / aspects syntaxiques, sémantiques et textuels*, 215-227. Tübingen: Stauffenburg.

Fábián, Annamária, Igor Trost, Kevin Altmann & Mara Schwind (2024). The analysis of “inclusion” and “accessibility” in Computer-Mediated-Communication for an inclusive transformation in digital societies. In Céline Poudat, Matilda Guernut. *Proceedings of the 11th Conference on CMC and Social Media Corpora for the Humanities*. 11th Conference on CMC and Social Media Corpora for the Humanities (CMC 2024), CORLI; Université Côte d'Azur, 2024. 20-26. https://shs.hal.science/halshs-04673776 (last accessed 14 February 2025).

Gnau, Birte C. & Eva L. Wyss. 2019. Der #MeToo-Protest. Diskurswandel durch alternative Öffentlichkeit. In Stefan Hauser, Roman Opiłowski & Eva L. Wyss (eds.), *Alternative Öffentlichkeiten. Soziale Medien zwischen Partizipation, Sharing und Vergemeinschaftung*, 131–165. Bielefeld: transcript. https://doi.org/10.14361/9783839436127-006.

Grieve, Jack & Helena Woodfield. 2023. *The language of fake news*. Cambridge: Cambridge University Press. https://doi.org/10.1017/9781009349161.

Grue, Jan. 2014. *Disability and Discourse Analysis*. London: Routledge. https://doi.org/10.4324/9781315577302.

Harvey, Kevin. 2012. Disclosures of depression: Using corpus linguistics methods to interrogate young people's online health concerns. *International Journal of Corpus Linguistics* 17 (3). 349–379. https://doi.org/10.1075/ijcl.17.3.03har.

Heaton, Dan, Jeremie Clos, Elena Nichele & Joel Fischer. 2023. Critical reflections on three popular computational linguistic approaches to examine Twitter discourses. *PeerJ Computer Science* 9: e1211. https://doi.org/10.7717/peerj-cs.1211.

Heritage, Frazer & Paul Baker. 2022. Crime or culture? Representations of chemsex in the British press and magazines aimed at GBTQ+ men. *Critical Discourse Studies* 19 (4). 435–453. https://doi.org/10.1080/17405904.2021.1910052.

Herrera, Lucia Castro & Terje Gjøsæter. 2022. Community segmentation and inclusive social media listening. In Rob Grace & Hossein Baharmand (eds.), *ISCRAM 2022 Conference Proceedings – 19th International Conference on Information Systems for Crisis Response and Management*, 1012–1023. Tarbes, France. https://idl.iscram.org/files/luciacastroherrera/2022/2467_LuciaCastroHerrera+TerjeGjosaeter2022.pdf (last accessed 14 February 2025).

Jaborooty, Maryam Paknahad & Paul Baker. 2016. Resisting silence: Moments of empowerment in Iranian women's blogs. *Gender and Language* 11 (1). 77–99. https://doi.org/10.1558/genl.22212

Kiritchenko, Svetlana, Xiaodan Zhu & Saif M. Mohammad. 2014. Sentiment analysis of short informal texts. *Journal of Artificial Intelligence Research* 50. 723–762. https://doi.org/10.1613/jair.4272.

Knuchel, Daniel & Noah Bubenhofer. 2023. Machine Learning und Korpuspragmatik. Word Embeddings als Beispiel für einen kreativen Umgang mit NLP-Tools. In Simon Meier-Vieracker, Lars Bülow, Konstanze Marx & Robert Mroczynski (eds.), *Digitale Pragmatik.* Digitale Linguistik 1, 213–235. Berlin & Heidelberg: Springer. https://doi.org/10.1007/978-3-662-65373-9_10.

Lui, Marco & Timothy Baldwin. 2014. Accurate language identification of Twitter messages. In *Proceedings of the 5th Workshop on Language Analysis for Social Media (LASM)*, 17–25. Gothenburg, Association for Computational Linguistics. https://doi.org/10.3115/v1/W14-1303.

Marx, Konstanze & Georg Weidacher. 2020. *Internetlinguistik. Ein Lehr - und Arbeitsbuch*, 2nd edition. Tübingen: Narr.

Oussalah, Mourad Chabane, B. Escallier & D. Daher. 2016. An automated system for grammatical analysis of Twitter messages. A learning task application. *Knowledge-Based Systems* 101. 31–47. https://doi.org/10.1016/j.knosys.2016.02.015.

Palomino, Marco A., Aditya Padmanabhan Varma, Gowriprasad Kuruba Bedala & Aidan Connelly. 2020. Investigating the lack of consensus among sentiment analysis tools. In Zygmunt Vetulani, Patrick Paroubek & Marek Kubis (eds.), *Human Language Technology. Challenges for Computer Science and Linguistics. LTC 2017. Lecture Notes in Computer Science 12598*, 58–72. Cham: Springer. https://doi.org/10.1007/978-3-030-66527-2_5.

Pan, Zhao, Yao-bin Lu & Sumeet Gupta. 2014. How heterogeneous community engage newcomers? The effect of community diversity on newcomers' perception of inclusion: An empirical study in social media service. *Computers in Human Behavior* 39. 100–111. https://doi.org/10.1016/j.chb.2014.05.034.

Ralev, Radoslav & Pfeffer, Jürgen. 2022. Hate speech classification in Bulgarian. In *Proceedings of the 5th International Conference on Computational Linguistics in Bulgaria (CLIB 2022)*, 49–58. Sofia, Bulgaria: Department of Computational Linguistics, IBL – BAS. https://dcl.bas.bg/clib/wp-content/uploads/2022/09/CLIB2022_PROCEEDINGS_v1.0.pdf (last accessed 14 February 2025).

Scheffler, Tatjana, Berfin Aktaş, Debopam Das & Manfred Stede. 2019. Annotating shallow discourse relations in Twitter conversations. In *Proceedings of the Workshop on Discourse Relation Parsing and Treebanking 2019*, 50–55. Minneapolis, MN: Association for Computational Linguistics. https://doi.org/10.18653/v1/W19-2707.

Sinclair, Stephen & Bramley, Glen. 2011. Beyond virtual inclusion – communications inclusion and digital divisions. *Social Policy and Society* 10 (1). 1–11. https://doi.org/10.1017/S1474746410000345.

Sties, Norat. 2013. Diskursive Produktion von Behinderung: Die marginalisierende Funktion von Personengruppenbezeichnungen. In Jörg Meibauer (ed.), *Hassrede/Hate Speech. Interdisziplinäre Beiträge zu einer aktuellen Diskussion*, 194–222. Gießen: Gießener Elektronische Bibliothek. http://geb.uni-giessen.de/geb/volltexte/2013/10121/ (last accessed 14 February 2025).

Strathern, Wienke, Raji Ghawi, Mirco Schönfeld, & Pfeffer, Jürgen. 2022. Identifying lexical change in negative word-of-mouth on social media. *Social Network Analysis and Mining* 12: 59. https://doi.org/10.1007/s13278-022-00881-0.

Thelwall, Mike. 2023. *SentiStrength (Version 2.3).* University of Wolverhampton. Available from http://sentistrength.wlv.ac.uk/ (last accessed 14 February 2025).

Trost, Igor. 2023. Corona als Basis sprachlicher Argumentation an die eigene Nation und andere Nationen – vom Impfnationalismus bis hin zur Public Diplomacy. In Aleksandra Salamurović (ed.), *Konzepte der NATION im europäischen Kontext im 21. Jahrhundert*, 311–327. Berlin & Heidelberg: J.B. Metzler. https://doi.org/10.1007/978-3-662-66332-5_15.

Viola, Lorella & Andreas Musolff. 2019. *Migration and media. Discourses about identities in crisis*. Amsterdam & Philadelphia: Benjamins. https://doi.org/10.1075/dapsac.81.
Viola, Lorella. 2023. On the use of sentiment analysis for linguistics research. Observations on sentiment polarity and the use of the progressive in Italian. *Frontiers in Artificial Intelligenc*, 6, 1101364. https://doi.org/10.3389/frai.2023.1101364.
Wright, David. 2020. The discursive construction of resistance to sex in an online community. *Discourse, Context & Media* 36: 100402. https://doi.org/10.1016/j.dcm.2020.100402.
Yang, Chao & Padmini Srinivasan. 2014. Translating surveys to surveillance on social media: Methodological challenges & solutions. In *Proceedings of the 2014 ACM conference on Web Science*, 4–12. New York: Association for Computing Machinery. https://doi.org/10.1145/2615569.2615696.
Yurchenko, Oleno & Nataliia Ugolnikova. 2021. Linguistic methods in social media marketing. In *Proceedings to the "International Conference on Computational Linguistics and Intelligent Systems"*, 12pp. https://ceur-ws.org/Vol-2870/paper55.pdf (last accessed 20 May 2022).
Zappavigna, Michele (2012). *Discourse of Twitter and social media: How we use language to create affiliation on the web*. London: Bloomsbury.
Zelena, András. 2020. The psychology of inclusion on new media platforms and the online communication. *Acta Universitatis Sapientiae, Communicatio* 7 (1). 54–67. https://doi.org/10.2478/auscom-2020-0005.

Laura Gärtner

The representation of the Jew as enemy in French public Telegram channels within an identitarian-conspiratorial milieu

Abstract: In many modern societies, the ambivalent status of the Jew as the ultimate foreigner has made them subject to violence, ghettoization and even extinction (Bauman 1991). However, according to the French CNCDH Report, discourses reminiscent of conspiracy theories have resurfaced during the Covid-19 pandemic (CNCHD 2022), in which the Jew is represented as the omniscient puppet-master that controls everything. The hatred against Jews is partly driven by a milieu that situates itself between conspiracism and identitarianism and prefers to spread its ideas on the Internet and through social networks (Froio 2017). Super-conspiratorial narratives (Soteras 2019), like the Great Reset or transhumanist ideas circulate in these networks that stigmatise a supposedly homogeneous Jewish community. These cognitive representation units of the Jew as enemy are transmitted through recurrent language patterns (Schwarz-Friesel and Reinharz 2013). A corpus of 90,000 messages, produced between January 2018 and May 2022 and drawn from ten Telegram messenger channels, was assembled and studied to detect language patterns used by conspiracists to describe the Jew. The given social media channels are particularly characterised by the homogeneity of its users and the absence of a counter-discourse. We extracted these patterns by calculating co-occurrences and collocations. In addition, multi-modal technographics like memes and GIFs that reflect language patterns were taken into account in this study. The analysis is based on the notion of constructions (Fillmore 1988) and discourse formulae (Krieg-Planque 2003) from the field of CxG and discourse analysis. Up until now, these fields have been developed independently (François and Legallois 2022).

Keywords: Telegram, discourse analysis, formula, construction, conspiracy theories, CMC, corpus linguistics

Laura Gärtner, Heidelberg University, e-mail: laura.bothe@hcts.uni-heidelberg.de

https://doi.org/10.1515/9783111434018-016

1 Introduction

Many modern societies maintain a stereotypical image of the Jew as stranger (Baumann 1991). The ambivalent status of being integrated into society yet remaining *other* has led to violence, ghettoization and obliteration of a community that is often perceived as homogeneous and threatening. During the Covid-19 pandemic, Jews were held responsible for the decline of the French society (Commission nationale consultative des droits de l'homme and Premier Minister 2022). Super conspiracies (Soteras 2019) such as the Great Reset, the Great Replacement or Q-anon were discussed in the public sphere. French protestors attributed vaccination campaigns, restrictions and bans to the manipulation of 'the Jews'. The hatred against this constructed enemy (Eco 2008) was partly driven by a milieu that situates itself between conspiracism and identitarianism.

Although many French identitarian organizations emerged from ultra nationalist groups, such as the *Groupe Union Défense* (GUD), they distanced themselves from racist ideologies in the early 2000s and adopted an ethnopluralist approach (François and Lebourg 2016: 12). Nonetheless, antisemitism and anti-zionism remain today's main instigators in many of its sub-organizations. The complex extremist network is versatile. The so called *cause enracinée* (Eng. cause of the rooted) is supported by ultra-Catholic subgroups and pagans, nationalists and regionalists, fascists, royalists and identitarian anarchists.

Identitarians disseminate their ideas across the Internet and social networks (Froio 2017) while shaping their online presence through two communication strategies. First of all, an information network, manifest in websites like *fdesouche.fr* or *novopress.fr*, delegitimizes the "mainstream media". By aiming to spread interpretations of articles in the "mainstream media" from the perspective of Catholicism, nationalism or regionalism, this *réinfosphère*[1] disperses opinions rather than journalistic information (Blanc 2016). In addition, more informal social media channels foster a counterculture (Bouron 2017) by denouncing the norms and mainstream values while promoting essays, music, novels and events, reflecting the political, religious, cultural and moral interpretations from the *réinfosphère*.

This paper strives to examine language patterns which stage the Jew as an enemy in both fake news and counterculture channels of the identitarian-conspirational movement. To gain insights into such syntagmata and their use, a corpus of

1 The French *réinfosphère* often relates to what in anglophone context is referred to a network of fake news. The term fake news translates into *réinfomation*. This paper uses both terms in their French spelling coined in the article by Charlotte Blanc (2016).

90,000 Telegram messages from ten channels were explored. Notions from discourse analysis and frame semantics will serve as tools to study these structures and contextualize their uses.

2 The corpus

Over 25 Telegram channels linked to different subgroups of the identitarian milieu, such as ultra-Catholic organizations, the conspiratorial sphere and nationalist identitarian groups, were monitored regularly from January 2021 to May 2021. In order to obtain a sufficient and manageable volume of data to study, ten channels were chosen for the construction of the corpus. To represent the diversity of genres within Telegram messenger, three press reviews, two individuals with clear names (one male and one female) and five channels of anonymous administrators were selected and their data was prepared for exploration.

2.1 Telegram as source for linguistic analysis

Since the Covid-19 pandemic, more and more linguists have been interested in analyzing hate speech (Solopova, Scheffler and Popa-Wyatt 2021; Vergani et al. 2022), disinformation networks (Willaert et al. 2022) as well as antisemitism and conspiracy narratives (Steffen et al. 2023) generated on Telegram. The messenger, similarly to WhatsApp, functions through private chats and public channels, some of which allow the users to comment on the post emitted by the administrators of the channel. Due to a lack of of moderation policies in these public channels Telegram appeals to "individuals who feel censored by the stricter moderation policies" (Simon et al. 2023: 3056). Extremist groups see Telegram as a "harbinger for freedom" (Wijermars and Lokot 2022: 126) as it allows for asynchronous and allegedly anonymous conversations. The generally ideologically homogenous Telegram channels typically lack counter-discourse and are frequently unregulated by their often anonymous administrators even when it comes to unlawful statements. Thus, Steffen et al. (2023: 1090) assume that negative attitudes towards Jews become more visible in these publicly available, but mainly unknown spaces, compared to more heterogeneous environments such as Twitter. The Telegram desktop app provides a simple download option for all public posts along with attached pictures and video materials, without the need for an application programming interface (API) or external scrapping methods.

2.2 Key figures of the Telegram corpus

After compiling the data in May 2022, a total of 90,023 Telegram posts were downloaded covering a periode from 2018 to 2022. 77,035 of those messages contained linguistic data. An analysis of videos, images and voice messages was not carried out for this contribution. The corpus comprises of a total of 4,417,995 words. A Python code allowed for the semi-automated cleaning of the data set. Some of the metadata in the JSON source files was deleted and the files were converted to XML. The created XML files contained the preserved metadata (an identification code for each message, the date of the message, the number of views, the number of replies) encoded in tags based on the guidelines of the Text Encoding Initiative (TEI).[2] The TEI guidelines help align linguistic analysis (lexicon, semantics, syntax) with incorporated metadata, like channel information or details about the time and date of the messages. The xml documents were transferred into the corpus software, TXM, developed by ENS Lyon (Heiden, Magué and Pincemin 2010). The tagset itself was based on the TEI format, but included self-named tags. This hybrid approach towards TEI allowed for an easier exploration of the different metadata in TXM. For this work, queries of concordances, calculation of collocations and the computation of a correspondence analysis (c.f. Salem 1982) were performed in TXM.

Three sub-corpora represent the genres of the channels. We differentiate between individuals hosting a channel, anonymous administrators creating content or press reviews aiming for *réinformation*. As of July 2022, the three press reviews selected for this study had a reach of 18,036 subscribers, with the majority subscribed to *Egalité & Réconciliation* (E&R) and *fdesouche*, both of which come from the national-identitarian milieu.[3] *Fdesouche* is also the biggest channel of the corpus in terms of wordcount. The third press review (*media-presse-info, MI*) can be linked to identitarian Catholics, as the channel has close ties to the far right, ultra-catholic *Civitas* organization.[4]

2 TEI Consortium, eds. *TEI P5: Guidelines for Electronic Text Encoding and Interchange.* Version 4.8.0. Last modified on 8th July 2024. TEI Consortium. http://www.tei-c.org/Guidelines/P5/ (last accessed 8 December 2024).

3 E&R was created by Alain Soral whose ideology was already subject to an article of Bernard Bruneteau in n° 62/2 of the *revue d'histoire moderne & contemporaine* in 2015 (https://doi.org/10.3917/rhmc.622.0225.). His discourse was analyzed by Lucy Raymond in n°104 de Quadern (https://doi.org/10.4000/quaderni.2140i.). As for *fdesouche*, its founder declared himself neo-Nazi according to an article of *Le Monde* from 2017 (https://www.lemonde.fr/politique/article/2017/04/14/pierre-sautarel-l-apprenti-droitier_5111064_823448.html, last accessed on 29 August 2024).

4 The Civitas movement was officially dissolved by the French government in October 2023.

The individuals were the least productive of the channel-administrators. The male emitter is believed to have radicalized himself alongside Alain Soral and Dieudonné. He emits nearly 80% of the subcorpus' messages. The female is a former member of the FN and convicted to six months of prison for public provocation to racial hatred. She hosts a small channel where she shares links and videos from other channels rather than emitting her own.

Table 1: Key Figures of the corpus.

Channel	Subcorpus	First posted	Subscribers (as of July 12th 2022)	Comments allowed	Number of posts	with signs	Word-count	Dimensions (%)
Canal Natio	anonymous	26.03.2020	7.797	Non	5.436	4.201	202.379	4,6
Chroniques	anonymous	09.06.2020	1.935	Oui	2.343	1.560	161.945	3,7
kadosh	anonymous	15.08.2021	8.032	Oui	6.493	2.279	188.464	4,3
LVC	anonymous	02.12.2020	8.483	Oui	28.972	23.125	1.274.568	28,8
Trad. catholique	anonymous	13.09.2019	1.905	Non	1.833	1.630	268.135	6,1
Female Individ.	individual	18.08.2021	1.431	Non	512	327	18.322	0,4
Male Individ.	individual	13.03.2020	11.419	Oui	1.769	1.290	152.571	3,5
fdesouche	press review	13.11.2019	9.599	Non	23.999	23.987	1.315.264	29,8
MI	press review	15.01.2021	1.749	Non	3.060	3.036	185.201	4,2
E&R	press review	28.02.2018	6.688	Non	15.615	15.600	651.146	14,7
				Total	**90.032**	**77.035**	**4.417.995**	**100**

A third sub-corpus groups together the anonymous channels. Half of the total messages collected are emitted by these five channels belonging to the counterculture network. As of July 2022, the most popular channels in terms of subscribers are *LVC* and *kadosh*. *LVC* serves a more national-identitarian audience with conspirative tendencies while *kadosh* is to be situated within the ultra-catholic movement. Furthermore, *LVC* is hosted by multiple anonymous administrators, making it by far the most productive channel of the subcorpus.

3 Approaching linguistic representations of the Jew as enemy through recurrencies

In their work on language and hostility towards Jews in the 21st century in Germany, Schwarz-Friesel and Reinharz argue that antisemitic linguistic structures constitute and transmit mental models into the collective communicative memory (2013: 6). According to the authors, the naming of Jews has been subject to negative amalgams for centuries. The collective memory systematically depicts Jews as enemies or outsiders. The authors provide examples of underspecified paraphrases such as die "*Religionsgemeinschaft, die uns am Wickel hat*" (the religious community that has us wrapped around its finger) and "*die Banker an der Ostküste*" (the bankers on the East Coast). These syntagmas have become fixed formulas for referring to American Jews (Schwarz-Friesel and Reinharz 2013: 37). Through the recurrence and disseminated conceptual patterns inherent to these structures, interlocutors are capable of easily identifying the very often negative connotation of such statements.

3.1 Formulaicity in French Discourse Analysis

In the discipline of discourse analysis (DA), patterns that occur recurrently in language can be analyzed through the prism of discursive formulaicity. The French concept of *formule discursive* (e.g. Faye 1972; Krieg-Planque 2003) generally refers to any statement with a fixed structure that fits within a discursive dimension, functions as a social reference, and has a polemical aspect (Krieg-Planque 2009: 63).

Krieg-Planque (2003) analyzes in her work the notion of "ethnic purification" within the context of the Yugoslav wars. She observes the sociolinguistic circumstances of the event in which the examined syntagma emerges and its use in different newspapers and media. For her, the formula is the result of the discursive shaping of a lexical-syntactic association that speakers fashion and take up when positioning themselves and their values (Krieg-Planque 2009: 104).

Once the genesis of the pattern is discovered, the analysis focuses on the mediatic environment. That is to say, the emphasis is put on the stance, which pertains to the structural and lexical changes of the pattern. Thus, the metadiscussions and the interpretation of the structure by the traditional and social media shapes its meaning. Using the syntagma becomes the act of taking a stance. Speakers and writers who use it out of its original context position themselves vis-à-vis a doxastic attitude that is inherent to the syntagma. To investigate stance-taking in more detail, Krieg-Planque proposes to focus on two topics when analyzing the notion *formule discursive*: its denominative function and the different varieties of an expression (2003: 306).

It is not so much the formal aspects, but rather the revealing of the discursive context (Weiland 2020: 85) that plays the major role in this approach. Still, the relative syntactic fixity of the *formule discursive* allows it to be identified through a frequency analysis in public discourse.

A more lexical approach to discursiveness was taken by Marcellesi in 1976. The Discourse Analysis of Lexical Entries (*Analyse de Discours à Entrée Lexical*, A.D.E.L.) includes distributional examinations of lexical units but specifically excludes semantics (Née et Veniard 2012: 16). By adding a semantic perspective to Marcellesi's A.D.E.L, Née et Veniard aim for a more formalized analysis of DA. However, the formalization primarily affects the context. Their examination of the word *crisis*, for instance, is described as follows:

crisis + domain reference [+period [+intensity] [+rupture] [+ what to resolve]

Domain references could be related to medicine, ecology or health. The first three brackets show semantical units encountered with the keyword. The fourth marks a pragmatical component (Née and Vinaird 2012: 22). The process of formalization here, once more, does not revolve around the morpho-syntactical facets of a particular structure. Instead, Née and Viniard do engage in the analysis of primarily lexical features that co-occur. They identify the use of the French indefinite and impersonal pronoun *on* and verbs like resolve (fr. *résoudre*), quit (fr. *sortir*) and manage (fr. *gérer*) as lexical environment of *crisis*.

3.2 Lexical recurrency in pairs of form and function

In addition to the discursive approach, a more formal consideration is made for this study, since a construction grammar approach to formulaicity has made its way into discourse analysis (Filatkina 2018). Idiomatic or formulaic language is described here as words which develop their meaning only in combination with others. For those patterns to be comprehensible "and allow speakers to achieve their communicative goals, they must necessarily be conventionalized" (Filatkina 2018: 4).

The conventionalization of a pair of form and function (Fillmore, Kay and O'Connor 1988; Goldberg 2006; Langacker 2010; Croft 2022) in a construction can, for example, be studied through the lens of frame semantics (Ziem 2008). As claimed by Ziem, frames make "relatively stable, discursively solidified background knowledge cognitively available" (Ziem 2008: 232). According to him, each lexical item evokes a semantic frame. Ziem's statement implies that conventionalized cognitive knowledge is manifested through formulaic language. He argues that meaning, or a "predication", is conventionalized if it is frequently used by a community of speakers (Ziem 2013: 234).

When considering all possible predications, the ones that are most frequently used become *default values*, which the speaker memorizes as implicit knowledge (Ziem 2008: 242). For example, the author discusses the semantic frames of the lexical unit (swimming) pool. By most readers in most contexts, it will be referred to as a rather small area of immobile water. Hence, "water" is seen as an implicit default value of "pool". Through semantic annotation and the use of statistical frequency analysis of the predications, the semantic layers of a lexical unit can be revealed.

We see that recurrencies can be adressed on different levels. On the one hand, the French discourse analytical approach focusses on discoursive recurrencies. It requires a lexically fixed structure that shows little variation in order examine closer the co-text and context in which the syntagma is used. Frame semantics on the other hand, investigate how patterns transmit meanings. By formalizing the patterns, variations of structurly similar but lexically varying syntagmata can be grouped into analyzable frames.

4 The Jew as enemy in identitarian-conspiratorial Telegram channels

Two works served as a first entry point to find lexical entities representing the Jew as enemy. The German study on antisemitic language of Schwarz-Friesel and Reinharz (2013) and the French lexicological monography of Sarfati (1999) on dictionary entries about Jews from the Middle Ages to the 20th century were used to assemble a list of lexical units referring to the Jew. In addition, the lemma *qanon* and the star of David pictogram were incorporated into the analysis. The conspiracy of Qanon gained prominence in France around 2020 (Hughey 2021: 78) so that its popularity falls within the periode of data collection. The star of David was discovered regularly during the monitoring of the Telegram channels to categorize messages containing references to Jewish people, Israel or judaism.

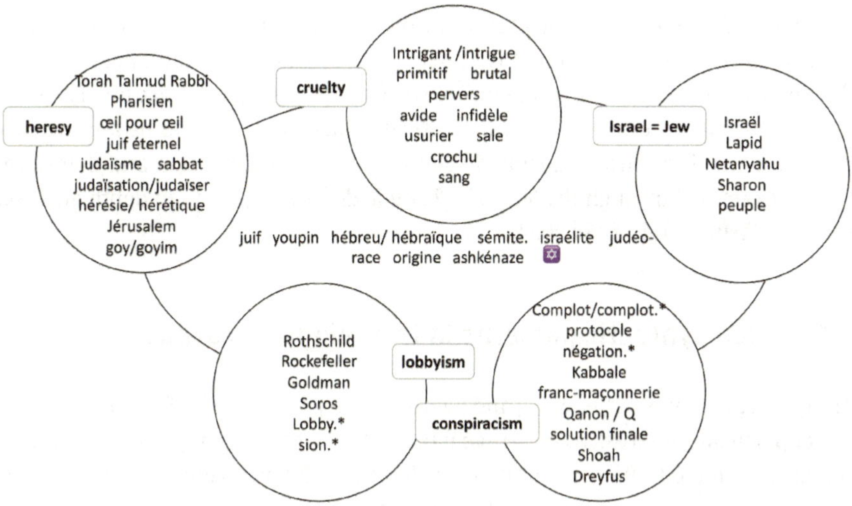

Figure 1: Investigated items and their categories.

For a total of 60 collected lexical items, a query in TXM produced 12.000 results. The most frequent collocations of each item were determined and their concordances semantically annotated. The annotation scheme corresponds to a categorization of the stereotypes underlying each term.[5] Five hierarchically superordinated categories to the searched items were established: heresy, cruelty, conspiracism, lobbyism and a generalization of the type "the state of Israel = all Jews" (cf. Figure 1). The label *heresy* groups utterances with references to the Jew as heretic, thus as enemies towards the Christian religion. *Cruelty* refers to messages containing physical or psycological violence committed by Jews. The label *conspiracy* accounts for utterances with explicite reference to known conspiracy therories (such as the Great Reset, the Great Replacement or Transhumanism) whereas *lobbyism* associates messages referring to a more or less occulte influence of Jewish people and institutions.[6]

5 The classification was done to simplify the analysis and to help synthesize the century-old traditions of anti-Jewish stereotypes that are transmitted through predications. They were made on the basis of the findings of Schwarz-Friesel and Reinharz (2013) and Sarfati (1999). Nevertheless, it is not intended to be universally valid.

6 Most notably, the distinction between lobbyism and conspiracy theories is artificial and the annotation phase showed that they are often inseparable. However, we wanted to stretch the fact that there is a belief of a certain Jewish lobby that is not necessary conspirational according to the pre-

Out of the 103 collocations found in the corpus, three were selected as they provide an excellent basis for this paper's goal of examining the intersection of discourse analysis and frame semantics. The first two syntagmata are described on a more formal level because they are lexically variable. They will be analyzed as constructions. The third syntagma displays a discursive dimension and therefore, will be examined through the lens of a *formule discursive* (for an in depth analysis see also Gärtner and Große 2024).

4.1 Lexico-syntactic patterns in the Telegram corpus

The queries [frlemma = "judéo.*"] and [word="le | la"][frlemma="juif"][frpos="NAM"] are of particular interest, as they reveal the differences in the approaches of frame semantics and DA. Both constructions described below would not have been detected by the DA approach to *formules discursives*.

Due to their high lexical variability, both patterns lack a concrete discursive dimension. They are used in a variety of contexts. This makes it difficult to pin them to a particular discourse. Even though the patterns mentioned describe a certain polemic by their use (*le juif XY*) or by the amalgam they are representing (*judéo-*), they do not show the lexical stability required by a stricter definition of formulaicity in DA.

4.1.1 *Le/la juif/ve* + Anthroponym

The structure *the Jew XY* can be interpreted as a conventionalized form of stigmatization. All occurrences Telegram corpus show explicit or implicit negative stereotypes. In over 80% of the messages containing the construction, the reference to one (or more) negative stereotypes is explicit. From an A.D.E.L. angle, we could formalize the context as stereotypical depiction of a Jew with the pragmatic function to stigmatize or denunciate the referent of the antroponym.

Det. + JUIF + anthroponym [+stereotypical depiction of a Jew]
[+stigmatization, denunciation]

---

vailing threefold definition of nothing happens by accident, nothing is as it seems, and everything is connected (Butter 2018:22).

Collocation analysis shows a high frequency of words that presume a Jewish influence, e.g. to take control (fr. *prendre contrôle*), to direct (fr. *diriger*) or a certain aim, e.g. to target (fr.*viser*) or to want (fr. *vouloir*). Despite the French preference for making an animated agent the subject of a sentence (Haase 2000: 123), *the Jew XY* is often the agent in passive structures, see (1).

(1) *La volonté d'une partie de l'intelligensia occidentale de détruire le monde blanc hétéro et chrétien existe, elle a même été planifiée dans les années 50* ***par le juif Theodor Adorno*** *et son équipe dans le livre Etudes sur la personnalité autoritaire (financé par l'American Jewish Committee)*
The desire of part of the Western intelligentsia to destroy the white, hetero-Christian world exists, it was even planned in the 1950s **by the Jew Theodor Adorno** and his team in the book Studies on the Authoritarian Personality (financed by the American Jewish Committee).
(Telegram post from 10-27-2022)

The proper noun can be dislocated to the right. In the corpus at hand, this variation is only used with personalities of the current political world, such as Jacques Attali and Eric Zemmour. Both are, along with Volodymyr Zelenskyy, only referred to by their last names. Adjectives like *bolshevist*, *free-mason* or *American* are found to determine the noun. With the exception of Christine Lagarde, all occurrences reference male individuals.

Frame semantics allows one to find different semantic layers by annotating the stereotypical depiction. The most frequent implicit or explicit meaning of the syntagma concountered in the Telegram corpus is the reference to a Jewish lobby that influences and respectively controls Western society (41% of the messages). According to the annotation, this is the most conventionalized predication behind the pattern *the Jew XY* in the Telegram corpus. The second most frequently occurring predication is the allegation of heresy (18%), followed by the denunciation of violent and cruel acts by Jews (17%) and the explicit naming of a conspiracy theory such as the *Great Reset* or *QAnon* (12%) (figure 2).

However, classifying those stereotypes has proven to be difficult. Religious and secular stereotypes are intertwined into a conspiracy theory (Soteras 2019) like the Great Replacement or the Great Reset. Sentences referencing those theories inevitably carry semantic traces of all stereotypes combined. Century-old cognitive units underline the utterances (Schwarz-Friesel and Reinharz 2013: 6). Hence, most messages referred to at least two or more classes.

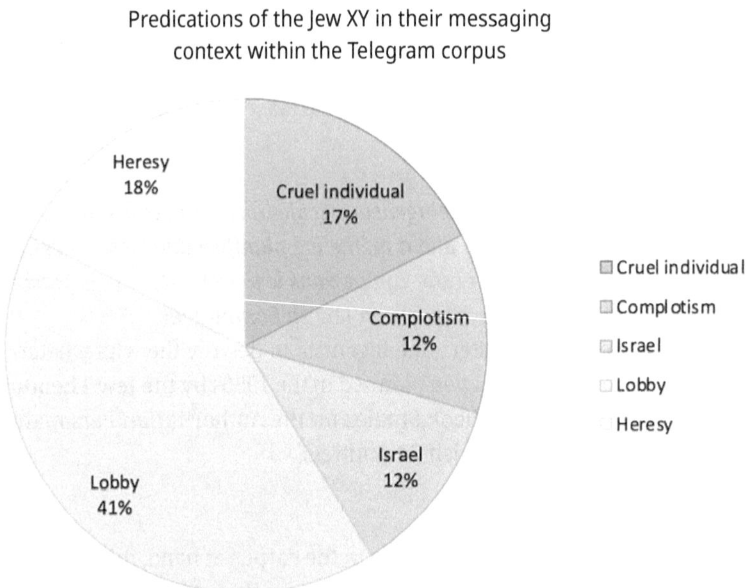

Figure 2: Predications in *determinant - Jew- proper noun* structures in the Telegram corpus.

The annotation scheme used here allows the categorization of only one stereotype.[7] This artificially reduces the complexity of the patterns since they have multiple layers of conventionalized meanings.

The following example, for instance, was originally classified into the category of lobbyism. This decision was made on the implied influence that is accorded to the Jewish population in general. Nevertheless, it also shows signs of heresy, as it is assumed that the Jewish religion aims to change the world into a "better place", see (2).

In accordance with Christensen and Au's (2023) interpretation of *the Great Reset*, it would be pertinent to categorize the latter as an indirect reference to a conspiracy theory. The "new" thread of a globalist leftism corresponds to what was

7 Within the framework of this work only one annotation was made. The difficult cases were discussed in a working group at the Romanisches Seminar in Heidelberg, to which I owe special thanks. Despite the lack of an inter-annotator agreement, the discussion around the annotation and the results underline the complexity of the endeavor of classifying the predications. Nevertheless, a follow up study should be made with at least three annotators in order to confirm the overall impression of the present annotations.

referred to as "New World Order" in cabal conspiracies in the 19th century (Christensen and Au 2023: 2358).

(2) ***Le juif Dennis Prager*** *explique pourquoi les Juifs quittant la religion reste malgré tout religieux en se convertissant à la religion du gauchisme (rendre le monde meilleur mais sans Dieu).*
The Jew Dennis Prager explains why Jews who leave religion still remain religious by converting to the religion of leftism (making the world a better place, but without God).
(Telegram post from 01-05-2022)

A factorial correspondence analysis was calculated on a lexical table of the most frequent adjectives of the overall Telegram corpus. It confirms the link between lobbyism and conspiracy theories that we see within the use of *determinant - Jew-proper noun.* Adjectives such as *globalist* (fr. *mondialiste*), *masonic* (fr. *maçonnique*), *vaccinal* or *scientific* (fr. *scientifique*) correlate with *Jewish (*fr. *juif)* and resonate well with the narratives of the Great Reset, which came up during the pandemic, particularly in the two anonymous channels *kadosh* and *lvc* (figure 3).

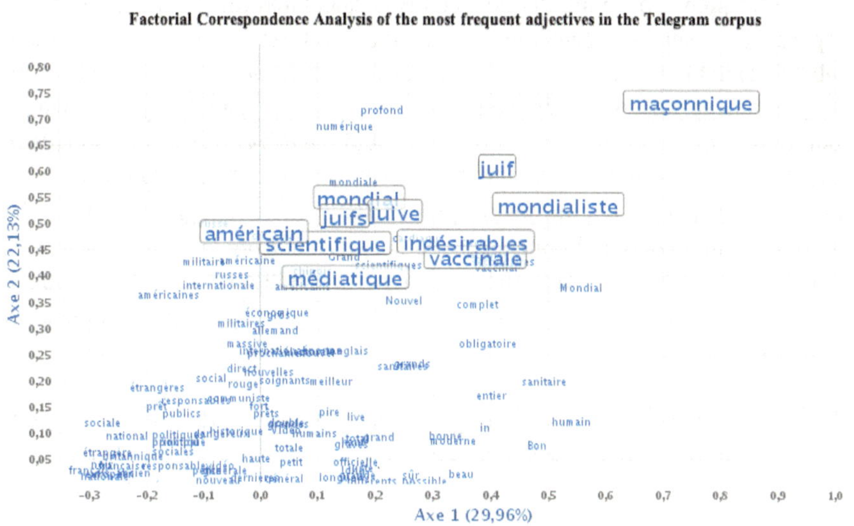

Figure 3: CA of the most frequent adjectives in the Telegram corpus.

Despite the syntagmas lack of stability, the analysis of the explicit and implicit content of the formal pattern in Telegram provided information about the predications prevailing the identitarian-conspiratorial discourse about the Jew as enemy. A lexical analysis (cf. A.D.E.L.) helped to formalize the context of the occurrences and complemented the formal approach. Both approaches reveal recurent cognitive patterns in the structure *le juif XY*.

4.1.2 The qualifier judéo-

The qualifier *judéo-* finds itself connected to many adjectives in the corpus at hand. It appears in ideologically opposed variants (*judéo-bolchévique* vs. *judéo-nazi*), as well as in religiously (*judéo-chrétien*), ethnically (*judéo-arabe*) and conspirationally motivated (*judéo-maçonnique, judéo-mondialiste*) pairs. Other lexical units that occur in the corpus are built on the prototype *ethnicity/religion/nation+o* to form a qualifier (e.g. *islamo-*, *arabo-*, *africano-*, *indo-*, *anglo-*, and *americano-*). None of the listed terms are as diversely used as the qualifier *judéo-*. While *judéo-maçon* is mostly employed with the subject *conspiracy* (fr. *complot judéo-maçon*), *judéo-chrétien* appears within the context of the lexical units *culture* and *history*. *Judéo-bolchévique*, in contrast, is used following the nouns *tribunal, invention* and *revolutionary*.

The frequency per million tokens (f) was calculated for the qualifier in two corpora, the assembled Telegram corpus and a reference corpus. The French-Web20[8] available on SketchEngine was chosen as reference for this analysis. In the Telegram corpus, the morpheme presents itself as being more productive (f= 5.66) than in the reference corpus (f=2.28).[9] While *judéo-chrétien* corresponds to about half of the occurrences in the FrenchWeb2020 (f=1.08), it only represents a third of the *judéo-* results in the Telegram corpus. Even though it is only to be found in the anonymous channels, the lemma *judéo-maçonnique* amounts to 30% of the total of the *judéo-* results and a frequency per million of 2.94. After a single post in 2019, the qualifier gains prominence in the anonymous channels in autumn 2021, see (3).

(3) *un début de réponse à cela est que les musulmans sont des suppôts du* ***complot judéo-maçonnique*** *par exemple actuellement lorsqu'ils viennent en*

8 The reference corpus was chosen for two reasons. Firstly it consists of computer mediated data (websites in that case) and secondly it was the most recent large-scale corpus available at the moment of research.

9 CQL-Query in both corpora: [lemma = "judéo.*"]

France c'est pour contribuer au projet républicain de vivre-ensemble et d'égalité des religions
one first answer to this is that Muslims are henchmen of the **Judeo-Masonic conspiracy**. For example, when they come to France now, it's to contribute to the republican project of living together and the equality of religions
(Telegram post from 09-15-2021)

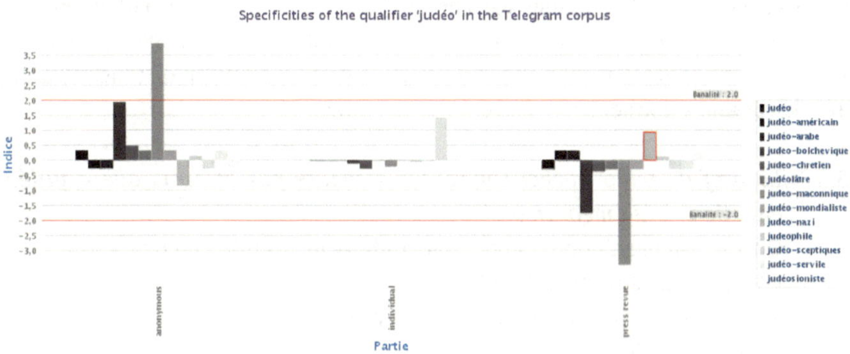

Figure 4: Repartition of the qualifier *judéo-* in the subcorpora of the Telegram corpus.

The individuals use the qualifier *judéo-* few (figure 4). "*Judéosceptique*" is the only term that appears within their channels. Figure 4 also suggests that press reviews show a low interest in this particular lexeme. E&R represents one press review that does use it, creating the amalgam *judéo-nazi*, a term that appears for the first time in Mai 2022 to designate Ukrainian individuals after the Russian invasion, see (4a) and (4b).

(4a) *Chutzpah : **le judéo-nazi Zelensky** dénonce le nazisme hitlérien*
Chutzpah: **Judeo-Nazi Zelensky** denounces Hitler's Nazism
(Telegram post from 05-08-2022)

(4b) *Arrestation du **judéo-nazi Mikhail Kavun** (financeur de Pravy Sector) en Russie*
Judeo-Nazi Mikhail Kavun (Pravy Sector financer) arrested in Russia
(Telegram post from 05-15-2022)

The context and uses of the qualifier are so diverse that it is difficult to implement a formalized context analysis using the model of A.D.E.L. for *judéo-*. However, when interrogating the structure from the perspective of frame semantics, the flexibility of the qualifier *judéo-* could be seen as a sign for high type-frequency (Ziem 2008:

360). The object itself may be cognitively present to the recipient, but there is not one single default value. The qualifier must be specified by adding explicit predications. Each merging lexeme acquires the stigmatization of *judéo-*.

In the Telegram corpus, only *judeo-christian* demonstrates a high rate of explicit predications (85%). The conventionalization of this construction relies on the frequent use of the syntagm in the media and a broader discourse where *judéo-chrétien* normally refers to the common roots of European society (Greene 2021; Jolibert 2014; Teixidor 2008). All messages in the Telegram corpus show a divergent use of the supposed default value. The explicit use of quotation marks, see (5a) and (5b), presents a modalization that elicits a sense of detachement or distance (Siouffi, Steuckardt and Wionnet 2016: 6) from the utterance.

(5a) *Le prof de philo Michel Onfray n'a toujours pas compris que « **judéo-chrétien** » était un oxymore*
Onfray still hasn't understood that **"judeo-christian"** is an oxymoron
(Telegram post from 06-18-2021)

(5b) « L'Europe est de culture **judéo-chrétienne** »
*"Europe is of **Judeo-Christian** origins"*
(Telegram post from 11-05-2020)

Attached to (5b) is a meme that shows two pictures, a nail in the sun titled "*judéo* and a picture of a hand pierced by that nail titled *christian*".

Figure 5: Meme attached to Telegram post from May 11, 2020.

In all messages of the corpus, the qualifier is linked to a supposed predominance of the "Jewish" over the "Christian". This is particularly noteworthy, as the predications for all other instances of the qualifier *judéo-* tend to be implicit. No other structure's meaning is explained to that extent.

4.2 *La communauté que vous connaissez bien*, a discursive formula ?

Taken from an interview broadcasted on television with a former French general, in the summer of 2021, the syntagma *la communauté que vous connaissez bien* made its way through various media platforms and into the streets of France during the protests against the vaccine pass. When asked on air who controls today's media, the general answered, "Well, it's the community you know well", referring to a generalized Jewish community. The French term "community" presents itself as problematic because it evokes a homogenized group of people, without taking into consideration the fluidity and plurality of religiosity and secularity in Jewish environments (Endelstein 2016).

The ideologically homogeneous Telegram corpus is not suitable for mapping a meta-discourse in which the meaning of the formula is negotiated and shaped by the emitters of messages (Krieg-Planque 2009: 63). As far as observed in the present Telegram data, there is no questioning of the semantics and no counter-discourse regarding the observed syntagmata. Consequently, for the examination of the supposed *discourse formula*, a Twitter corpus was created to analyze the meta-discourse of the presumed formula more in depth. 1538 tweets emitted between June 2021 and November 2022 that contain the string "*La communauté que vous connaissez bien*"[10] give an insight into the negociation of the syntagma's meaning (see also Gärtner and Große 2024).

The *communauté que vous connaissez bien* gives the impression that it refers to a universally known, but not specified group. In theory, every group of people that has "something in common" can be designated here (Lecolle 2008: 325). However, in all detected cases in the Telegram corpus and on Twitter, the syntagma is used as a substitute only for the Jewish community. As such, the formula circumvents censorship while stigmatizing Jews as string pullers without naming them directly. It transmits all predications of the lexical unit Jew.

While emphasizing the conspirational notion of a homogenous Jewish community that has control over the media, the context of the interview enters the semantic layers of the syntagma.

---

10 The syntagma was aleady analyzed from a discourse analytical point of view by Gärtner and Große (2024). The present chapter thus only presents a fragmental analysis of the supposed formula *La communauté que vous connaissez bien.*

Using memes and GIFs in this context, speakers show creativity in their desire to adopt ideological stances with regards to *la communauté que vous connaissez bien*. Memes link words to images and combine the utterances' predications with those of (pop)cultural references. Used in the context of *la communauté que vous connaissez bien*, the "For the Better, Right?[11]" meme, for instance, connects the prospect of doing evil to the world to the syntagma (Gärtner and Große 2024: 9–10).

Despite the formula's rare usage in the homogeneous Telegram channels after its peak in June and July 2021, *la communauté que vous connaissez bien* still circulates in computer-mediated communication. Between June 2021 and November 2022, more than 1500 occurrences of this pattern were found on Twitter.

August 2021 marks a phase of counter-discourse on Twitter. On a meta discursive level, users negotiate the meaning of the pattern, see (6a) and (6b). They denounce the anti-Jewish character of the utterance, see (6a), or the supposedly false interpretation of it, see (6b).

(6a) *Ceux qui feignent de ne ps comprendre que le „Qui?" sur la pancarte est une ref à la scène entre @claudeposternak & le Général Delawarde, le 1er demandant „Qui contrôle le Washington Post, le NYT ? Qui?", le 2nd répondant* ***„la communauté...que vs connaissez bien",*** *vous me fatiguez*
Those who pretend not to understand that the "Who?" on the sign is a reference to the scene between @claudeposternak & General Delawarde, the 1st asking "Who controls the Washington Post, the NYT? Who?", the 2nd replying **„the community...that you know well".**
(Tweet from 08-08-21)

(6b) *Et du coup* ***„la communauté que vous connaissez bien"*** *pour vous c'est automatiquement les juifs ? ....ok.*
And so **„the community you know well"** for you automatically means the Jews? ....ok.
(Tweet from 08-09-21)

After the negotiation phase, the syntagma appears as reference to a supposedly homogeneous Jewish community on Twitter too. It gains transcendency and is able to adapt to many different contexts, see figure 6. At the end of 2022, the expression resurfaced around Kanye West's antisemitic comments, see (7c), the ban of the Russian soccer team at the World Champion ships, see (7b), and xenophobic statements directed toward the LGBTQ community, see (7a).

11 https://knowyourmeme.com/memes/for-the-better-right (last accessed on 26 March 2024).

Figure 6: Examples of Tweets in 2022 on *"la communauté que vous connaissez bien"*.

(7a) *What kind of shitty job is this the more time goes by the more our society regresses what's the point of dressing up as a woman when you're a man another strike of* ***the community you know well***
(Figure 6, left-hand side)

(7b) *Why isn't the country of* ***the community you know well*** *excluded?*
(Figure 6, middle)

(7c) ***The community you know so well*** *really has a long arm.*
(Figure 6, right hand side)

On Twitter, the pattern also occurs in variations such as *the community we know well* (fr. *la communauté que nous connaissons bien*), *the community we all know* (fr. *la communauté que nous conaissons* tous) and *a certain community we know well* (fr. *une certaine communauté que nous connaissons bien*). While construction grammarians would tend to see a case for the conventionalization of the pattern (cf. Ziem 2008: 242), the different variations of a *formule discursive* (Krieg-Planque 2003: 222) could also indicate their adaptation to the respective discourse. However, all encountered variations in the data set remain close to the syntagma used by the general Delawarde.

5 Conclusion

The use a corpus, composed primarily of Telegram messages along with some Tweets, allows for insightful conclusions on the particular inner workings of Telegram. The Telegram channels used for this study are publicly accessible. However, to gain access to these channels, users must know of their existence. It is important to note that channels advertise other channels with similar content, which contributes to the network of *réinformation*. This mode of operation enables the interlocutors to feel unobserved, as they are supposedly surrounded by like-minded people and shielded from the so-called mainstream censorship. While channel administrators alert members about algorythms that detect harmful speech, emitters of the messages in the respective corpus tend to express more unconventional opinions that seem less accepted in wider society. In this respect, the Telegram channels showed no signs of a metadiscourse or the negotiation of implict stereotypes. The doxastic attitudes transmitted by the various syntagma appear to be unanimously accpeted. Moreover, within the chosen Telegram channels, structures transmitting representations of the Jew as enemy simply appear in high frequency. That is why, overall, this paper confirms the hypothesis of Steffen et al. (2023: 1090): The depiction of the Jew as *other* is more present in Telegram than in the examined reference corpus.

By tracing a conspirationalist and identitarian discourses on Telegram, we have detected a number of denominational forms that depict the Jew. Methods from frame semantics and discourse analysis both revealed patterns which are providing a deeper understanding of the semantic functions and conceptual cognitive units that underlie the discourse on the Jew as enemy. Since both perspectives derive from different approaches to language, they consequently lead to the discovery of different, implicit layers of the patterns. With the help of frame semantics, we examined the structures' predications in the discourse of the identitarian and conspirationalist milieu. Even when the structure itself lacked discursivity (e.g., *le/la juif/ve* + Anthroponym), the patterns' lexical environment testifies lexical diversity by transmitting the same set of longlasting stereotypes about the Jew as an enemy, most notably the notion of a Jewish lobby or the Jewish thread to Christianity (heresy). The use of the qualifier *judéo-* shows once more the diversity of contexts in which Jews are stigmated as enemies through amalgamation or in multi-modal GIFs and memes.

The evolution of "*la communauté que vous connaissez bien*" and its examination through the lens of discourse analysis also reveals a semantic focus on recurrent and conventionalized cognitive preconceptions, such as the Jew as a string-puller. This image perpetuates the stereotype that Jews not only control the media, but society as a whole (see also Gärtner and Große 2024: 14).

Due to technical limitations of the corpus program used, the present work only partially investigated polygonal chains and hyperlinks (Longhi 2020) for the semantic analysis of the detected patterns. In addition, comments to channel messages in Telegram or threads on Twitter were not included. In future studies, more attention should be placed on technographics (Paveau 2017), such as memes, GIFs or stickers since these play a major role in illustrating and negociating certain structures. Furthermore, they can reveal the status of conventionalized linguistic expressions. The more a structure is conventionalized the more it tends to be utilized for graphical means. Memes and GIFs thus account for the creativity that arises in the rapidly changing world of language patterns undergoing computer-mediated communication (Vásquez and Aslan 2021).

To conclude, the intersection of methods from two linguistic traditions proves to be fruitful and complementary when attempting to tackle the complex and ambivalent concept of enmity (Becke, Jaspert and Kurz 2023). Both formal and lexical patterns provide information about the representation of the Jew as enemy in the present corpus and beyond.

References

Bauman, Zygmunt. 1991. *Modernity and ambivalence*. Cambridge: Polity Press.

Becke, Johannes, Nikolas Jaspert & Joachim Kurz. 2023. Ambivalent enmity: making the case for a transcultural turn in enmity studies. *The Journal of Transcultural Studies* 14 (1–2).

Blanc, Charlotte. 2016. Réseaux traditionalistes catholiques et « réinformation » sur le web : mobilisations contre le « Mariage pour tous » et « pro-vie ». *Tic & société* 9 (1–2).

Bouron, Samuel. 2017. Des « fachos » dans les rues aux « héros » sur le web: La formation des militants identitaires. *Réseaux* 202–203 (2). 187–211.

Butter, Michael. 2018. *„Nichts ist, wie es scheint": über Verschwörungstheorien*. Berlin: Suhrkamp.

Christensen, Michael & Ashli Au. 2023. The Great Reset and the cultural boundaries of conspiracy theory. *International journal of Communication* 17. 2348–2366.

Commission nationale consultative des droits de l'homme & Premier ministre. 2022. *La lutte contre le racisme, l'antisémitisme et la xénophobie: année 2021*. La documentation Française.

Croft, William. 2022. *Morphosyntax: constructions of the world's languages*. Cambridge Textbooks in Linguistics. Cambridge, New York, Port Melbourne, New Delhi & Singapore: Cambridge University Press.

Eco, Umberto & Myriem Bouzaher. 2016. *Construire l'ennemi: et autres écrits occasionnels*. Paris: Le Livre de poche.

Faye, Jean Pierre.1972. *Théorie du récit: introduction aux „Langages totalitaires"; la raison critique de narrative l'économie*. Paris: Hermann.

Filatkina, Natalia. 2018. *Historische formelhafte Sprache*. Berlin & Boston: De Gruyter.

Fillmore, Charles J ., Paul Kay & Mary Catherine O'Connor. 1988. Regularity and idiomaticity in grammatical constructions: the case of let alone. *Language* 64 (3). 501.

François, Jacques & Dominique Legallois. 2022. Discourse traditions and Construction Grammar. In Esme Winter-Froemel & Álvaro S. Octavio De Toledo Y Huerta (eds.), *Manual of discourse traditions in Romance*, 283–296. Berlin & Boston: De Gruyter.
François, Stéphane & Nicolas Lebourg. 2016. *Histoire de la haine identitaire: mutations et diffusions de l'altérophobie*. Valenciennes: Presses universitaires de Valenciennes.
Froio, Caterina. 2017. Nous et les autres: L'altérité sur les sites web des extrêmes droites en France. *Réseaux* 202–203 (2). 39–78.
Gärtner, Laura, & Sybille Große. 2024. La *communauté que vous connaissez bien* et son usage dans des réseaux socionumériques comme dénomination pour un groupe stigmatisé. In SHS Web of Conf. 191, 01022.
Goldberg, Adele E . 2006. *Constructions at work: the nature of generalization in language*. Oxford & New York: Oxford University Press.
Greene, Toby. 2021. Judeo-Christian civilizationism: challenging common European foreign policy in the Israeli-Palestinian arena. *Mediterranean Politics* 26 (4). 430–450.
Haase, Martin. 2000. Das Französische als exotische Sprache. In Bruno Staib (ed.), *Linguistica romanica et indiana : Festschrift für Wolf Dietrich zum 60. Geburtstag*, 117–130. Tübingen: Narr.
Heiden, Serg, Jean-Philippe Magué & Bénédicte Pincemin. 2010. TXM: Une plateforme logicielle open-source pour la textométrie – conception et développement. In *10th International Conference on the Statistical Analysis of Textual Data – JADT 2010*. 1021–1032. Rome.
Hughey, Matthew W. 2021. The who and why of QAnon's rapid rise. *New Labor Forum* 30 (3). 76–87.
Jolibert, Bernard. 2014. Que peut-on entendre par « morale judéo-chrétienne »?: *L'enseignement philosophique* 64 (1). 54–73.
Krieg-Planque, Alice. 2003. *« Purification ethnique »: Une formule et son histoire*. Paris: CNRS Éditions.
Krieg-Planque, Alice. 2009. *La notion de formule en analyse du discours: cadre théorique et méthodologique*. Besançon: Presses universitaires de Franche-Comté.
Langacker, Ronald W . 2010. *Foundations of Cognitive Grammar*. Vol. 1.: Theoretical prerequisites. Berlin & Boston: De Gruyter Mouton.
Lecolle, Michelle. 2008. Identité/altérité et noms collectifs humains: Le cas de communauté. *Questions de communication* 13. 323–342.
Lecolle, Michelle, Marie-Anne Paveau & Sandrine Reboul-Touré. 2009. Les sens des noms propres en discours. *Les carnets du Cediscor* 11. 9–20.
Longhi, Julien. 2020. Les usages stratégiques du commentaitre sur Twitter comme contributions aux processus d'idéologisation. *Repères-Dorif* (22). https://www.dorif.it/reperes/les-usages-strategiques-du-commentaire-sur-twitter-comme-contributions-aux-processus-dideologisation/ (last accessed 26 March 2024).
Née, Émilie & Marie Veniard. 2012. Analyse du Discours à Entrée Lexicale (A.D.E.L.): le renouveau par la sémantique? *Langage et société* 140 (2). 15–28.
Paveau, Marie-Anne. 2017. *L'analyse du discours numérique: dictionnaire des formes et des pratiques*. Paris: Hermann.
Salem, André.1982. Analyse factorielle et lexicométrie : synthèse de quelques expériences. *Mots* 4 (1). 147–168.
Sarfati, Georges-Elia. 1999. *Discours ordinaires et identités juives: la représentation des juifs et du judaïsme dans les dictionnaires et les encyclopédies de langue française, du Moyen Age au XXe siècle*. Paris: Berg.
Schwarz-Friesel, Monika & Jehuda Reinharz. 2013. *Die Sprache der Judenfeindschaft im 21. Jahrhundert*. Berlin & Boston: De Gruyter.

Simon, Mónika, Kasper Welbers, Anne C . Kroon & Damian Trilling. 2023. Linked in the dark: a network approach to understanding information flows within the Dutch Telegramsphere. *Information, Communication & Society* 26, 15. 3054–3078.
Siouffi, Gilles, Agnès Steuckardt & Chantal Wionet. 2016. Les modalisateurs émergents en français contemporain: présentation théorique et études de cas. *Journal of French Language Studies* 26, 1. 1–12.
Solopova, Veronika, Tatjana Scheffler & Mihaela Popa-Wyatt. 2021. A Telegram corpus for hate speech, offensive language, and online harm. *Journal of Open Humanities Data* (7) 8. 1–15.
Soteras, Eva. 2019. Les enjeux politico-religieux du conspirationnisme à l'ère postmoderne: *Sociétés* 142 (4). 7–18.
Steffen, Elisabeth, Helena Mihaljevic, Milena Pustet, Nyco Bischoff, Maria Do Mar Castro Varela, Yener Bayramoglu & Bahar Oghalai. 2023. Codes, patterns and shapes of contemporary online antisemitism and conspiracy narratives – an annotation guide and labeled German-language dataset in the context of COVID-19. In *Proceedings of the International AAAI Conference on Web and Social Media* 17. 1082–1092.
Teixidor, Javier. 2008. Judaïsme et christianisme et non pas « judéo-christianisme ». *Cités* (34). 43–52.
Vásquez, Camilla & Erhan Aslan. 2021. "Cats be outside, how about meow": Multimodal humor and creativity in an internet meme. *Journal of Pragmatics* 171. 101–117.
Vergani, Matteo, Alfonso Martinez Arranz, Ryan Scrivens & Liliana Orellana. 2022. Hate Speech in a Telegram Conspiracy Channel During the First Year of the COVID-19 Pandemic. *Social Media + Society* 8 (4). https://journals.sagepub.com/doi/10.1177/20563051221138758 (accessed 26 March 2024).
Weiland, Verena. 2020. *Sprachwissenschaftliche Zugriffe auf Diskurse: ein korpuslinguistischer Ansatz am Beispiel des Themas „Sicherheit und Überwachung" in Frankreich.* Heidelberg: Universitätsverlag Winter.
Whitehouse, Andrew J. O., Murray T. Maybery & Kevin Durkin. 2006. The development of the picture-superiority effect. *British Journal of Developmental Psychology* 24 (4). 767–773.
Wijermars, Mariëlle & Tetyana Lokot. 2022. Is Telegram a "harbinger of freedom"? The performance, practices, and perception of platforms as political actors in authoritarian states. *Post-Soviet Affairs* 38 (1–2). 125–145.
Willaert, Tom, Stijn Peeters, Jasmin Seijbel & Nathalie Van Raemdonck. 2022. Disinformation networks: A quali-quantitative investigation of antagonistic Dutch-speaking Telegram channels. *First Monday* 27 (5). https://firstmonday.org/ojs/index.php/fm/article/view/12533 (accessed 26 March 2024).
Ziem, Alexander. 2008. *Frames und sprachliches Wissen: kognitive Aspekte der semantischen Kompetenz.* Berlin: De Gruyter.
Ziem, Alexander. 2013. Wozu Kognitive Semantik? In Dietrich Busse & Wolfgang Teubert (eds.), *Linguistische Diskursanalyse: neue Perspektiven*, 217–240. Wiesbaden: Springer Fachmedien.

Rachel McCullough, Daniel Drylie, Mindi Barta, Cass Dykeman, and Daniel Smith

CoDEC-M: The multi-lingual manosphere subcorpus of the Corpus of Digital Extremism and Conspiracies

Abstract: In 2023, the U.S. Surgeon General warned the public of the current "loneliness epidemic" and its potential consequences on physical and mental health. One possible consequence of this epidemic is the growth of a movement defined by loneliness and isolation: the incel ("involuntary celibate") movement. This warning presents a worrying glimpse at the future, as the incel movement, along with other parts of the manosphere, is one that espouses violently misogynist rhetoric which is intrinsically linked to right-wing extremism. While linguistic studies have been conducted on the speech of incels and other constituent movements of the manosphere, few of these studies look at the language of these communities from a cross-cultural and cross-linguistic perspective. To address this gap, we have created CoDEC-M, a subcorpus of the Corpus of Digital Extremism and Conspiracies (CoDEC). CoDEC is an open-source, open-access corpus made up of several subcorpora documenting different online spaces where extremists and conspiracy theorists gather. CoDEC-M is our response to the growing interest in the manosphere and the gap in scientific knowledge on the language used in its non-English speaking communities.

In this paper, we use the text analysis software Sketch Engine to compare the top twenty keywords and bigrams in the English and Russian sections of CoDEC-M ranked by their keyness score. In doing so, we have uncovered evidence of language transfer between these two segments of the manosphere via direct borrowings from English into Russian and thematic overlap between keywords and bigrams that refer to gender, dating, and physical appearance. We have also uncovered and define a number of neologisms unique to each dataset and examine the real-world impact of the manosphere in English- and Russian-speaking

Rachel McCullough, Bolante.NET, e-mail: rechalmccullough@protonmail.com
Daniel Drylie, Old Dominion University, e-mail: ddrylie@odu.edu
Mindi Barta, Oregon State University, e-mail: bartam@oregonstate.edu
Cass Dykeman, Oregon State University, e-mail: cass.dykeman@oregonstate.edu
Daniel Smith, Bolante.NET, e-mail: danielvsmithpsyd@gmail.com

https://doi.org/10.1515/9783111434018-017

countries in support of our argument that non-Anglo portions of the manosphere warrant further analysis.

Keywords: corpus linguistics, multilingual corpora, language and gender, computer mediated discourse, Russian language, sociolinguistics

1 Introduction

As the 2020's unfold, we have witnessed misogynist domestic terrorism emerge as a serious threat to women. Of 32 ideologically-motivated acts of mass violence committed between 2016 and 2020, the perpetrators of four attacks (12.5%) were named by the U.S. Secret Service as being associated with the incel or "involuntary celibate" movement (NTAC 2023). In other words, more than one in ten perpetrators of ideologically-motivated mass violence in the United States are not only motivated by misogyny, but belong to one community in particular: the incel movement. Paired with this statistic is the adoption of language and rhetoric originating from incel communities into popular discourse on social media platforms like Reddit, YouTube and TikTok.[1] Alarming as these two facts are in conjunction, the present study does not intend to examine their relationship. Instead, we are interested in the spread of the incelosphere beyond the English-speaking parts of the web – specifically, how self-identified incels on the Russian-speaking internet communicate, what they have in common with their English-speaking counterparts, and some possible implications of any language transfer we find.

The influence of misogynist rhetoric on popular media of the 2020's has been palpable. According to a 2023 report, over 40% of surveyed men under 30 trust a prominent figure or movement associated with the manosphere (Barker et al. 2023). The list of trustworthy sources referenced includes controversial figures like Andrew Tate and Jordan Peterson, web forums like Reddit's r/TheRedPill, and hate groups like the Proud Boys. Alarmingly, the shared feature among all members of this list is a virulently anti-woman ideology and rhetoric that sometimes correlates with real world violence, as described above.

"Incel" is a compound-clipping of "involuntary celibate," an initially gender-neutral phrase coined in the late 1990's by a woman who also shared her struggles to find a romantic partner on a website she created, *Alana's Involuntary Celi-*

1 For more on the integration of incel rhetoric into mainstream social media apps, see Solea and Sugiura (2023).

bacy Project (Taylor 2018). Decades later, contemporary online spaces that use the "incel" label are typically male-dominated and known for extremely misogynistic attitudes, with some even restricting membership to exclude female incels (known as "femcels"; Incels 2017). Since shifting to its present male-as-norm state, the movement has brought like-minded men experiencing loneliness together to share grievances over sexual and romantic exclusion.

However, this sense of community has not proven beneficial to these men or society at large. Known members of the movement have committed acts of violence against women, like the 2018 Toronto van attack or the mass shooting in a Tallahassee yoga studio in the same year. While these incidents are frequently represented in news headlines, mass violence is not the only form of misogynist action taken by members of these communities. Two terrorists described in *Mass Attacks in Public Spaces: 2016–2020* participated in online misogynist communities and nonconsensually distributed sexual photographs of women to terrorize them before acting out violently (NTAC 2023). Men themselves are also suffering and at risk of harm due to these ideologies. The mental health of young men is at particular risk, as observed by Equimundo, with nearly half of all survey respondents aged 18–30 reporting thoughts of suicide in the previous two weeks (Barker et al. 2023). While concern for misogynist violence is significant, the prevalence of suicide notes posted by self-identified incels indicates another fatal consequence of this movement's growth.[2]

While this cultural context comes from predominantly English-speaking communities, misogyny is a polyglot. Lonely adults from various language communities have shared similar concerns online long before English-speaking incels dominated the headlines, like the German-speaking *Absolute Beginner* community described by Sprenger (2014) or the French-speaking *Virginité-tardive* forum, which hosts threads dating back to 2007. In the last decade, though, self-identified incel spaces outside the online anglosphere have been appearing as the movement has gained notoriety (e.g., the Italian language *Forum Dei Brutti* and the Russian language /incel/ thread on 2ch.hk). These spaces are distinct from the previously mentioned *Absolute Beginners* and *Virginité-tardive* forums in that they identify specifically with the incel movement, borrowing the name of the predominantly English-speaking group for themselves. In light of this development, we ask: How much linguistic overlap is there between the speech of non-English speaking incel communities and the their English-speaking counterparts, and what is this overlap like?

2 For an examination of suicide notes from incel community members, see Daly and Laskovtsov (2021).

This study seeks to address how the speech patterns and ideologies of English-speaking incels have or have not permeated into the language of non-English speaking incel communities. As a case study, we will compare and contrast the language of speakers in both English- and Russian-speaking incel communities, and identify common rhetorical themes, shared beliefs, and lexical borrowings. While we cannot guarantee the national origin or place of residence of the users of either 2ch.hk or incels.is, we will consider these two populations as representative of incels as they exist on the anglophone web (on incels.is) and as they exist on the Russian-speaking web (commonly referred to as "Runet"; on 2ch.hk). Our reason for selecting Russian-speaking incels to compare to English-speaking incels is twofold. First, the availability of data: the ongoing /incel/ thread on 2ch.hk provides a sizable amount of data in Russian from self-identified incels. Second, we are especially interested in Russian speakers in contrast with speakers of the languages of North America and Western Europe because of the popular notion that Russian culture exists separate from "Western" or other European cultures. Does this supposed cultural difference impact the speech and attitudes of lonely, disaffected young men? To what degree do we see evidence of language contact between incel populations that speak different languages?

A comparison of parallel subcultures from two different digital linguistic traditions will demonstrate how the internet age has allowed this specific variety of misogyny to spread to other languages. It will also provide a greater understanding of the factors that contribute to the formation of these communities. While we are only comparing two communities for the present study, the model we propose for comparing keywords and phrases across two subcorpora in different target languages has potential for use in the comparison of other non-English speaking sections of the manosphere (e.g., the *Forum Dei Brutti* or other under-researched communities).

Three research questions were designed for the present study. These were:

1. When compared to mainstream online discourse, what conversational subjects and vocabulary are associated with the speech of the English incelosphere?
2. When compared to mainstream online discourse, what conversational subjects and vocabulary are associated with the speech of the Russian incelosphere?
3. How do the conversational subjects and vocabulary of the English- and Russian-speaking incels compare with one another?

The formation of research questions was guided by existing literature on the English- and Russian-speaking portions of the manosphere. To address these questions, we will compare the top 20 keywords and phrases – specifically bigrams – in data from English- and Russian-speaking incel forums to general web discourse in the target language. We will also compare and contrast how the resultant datasets overlap at the word level and their semantic or thematic overlap.

2 Literature review

To establish the greater context of this study, we will first give a brief explanation of the greater "manosphere" as it exists in the 2020's online anglosphere and its relationship to incels in specific. Second, we will briefly examine the current and past state of gender roles in English- and Russian-speaking communities offline. While we specifically base our data collection and analysis on a target language rather than nationality due to the international nature of line communication, we will limit this examination of gender offline to North America and Russia for the sake of brevity, due to their outsized representation in popular culture and online.

2.1 "The Manosphere" and red pill ideology

The manosphere is a name for a group of overlapping communities centered around men's perspectives and issues. These range from fitness and dating advice, to men's rights, to antifeminist and incel communities. Incels are one of the most visible communities in the manosphere, producing misogynist content that has drawn massive mainstream media attention in the late 2010s and early 2020s – including coverage from the *BBC*, the *New York Times*, and *Al-Jazeera* (Griffin 2021; Chokshi 2018; Cunha 2020). Crucial to the understanding of the ideologies of the manosphere is red pill ideology.

In the context of the manosphere, red pill ideology refers to an awakening among men to the supposed deceit and cultural brainwashing of feminism (further described in Ging 2019). The red pill ideology of the manosphere has spread rapidly across the web from its origins in an eponymous subreddit (r/TheRedPill), a space Debbie Ging describes as "dedicated to antifeminism and the defense of rape culture" (2019: 645). Ging also notes a spread of both red pill ideology and its language into other communities that constitute the manosphere, specifically naming "red pill terminology" as a unifying feature between otherwise disparate male-centric communities that have begun to coalesce in some ways due to a shared sense of identity (645).

2.2 Incels and their speech

Members of the incel movement define themselves by their lack of sexual success with women despite a desire for it. While many manosphere communities espouse red pill ideology, self-identified incels are primarily concerned with the *black pill*, a red pill-derived ideology founded in hopelessness and pessimism. While redpilled members of the manosphere believe that they can partake in the sexual marketplace by manipulating it and working within it, blackpilled incels feel defeated at the hands of supposed systemic misandry (described in Fernquist et al. 2020; Preston et al. 2021).

Not all incels are blackpilled: some of them attempt to "ascend" from inceldom – that is, enter a romantic or sexual relationship. Blackpilled community members, however, will attempt to dissuade this behavior by arguing that one's incel status is genetically predetermined (Quiroz 2022). In fact, to ascend would seem to invalidate their very identity, which they have based on a supposed inability to find companionship. This loss of incel status would almost certainly result in being ousted from the community that had long served as a comfort for these vulnerable young men, as non-incels are explicitly banned from having an account on incels.is (see "Rules and FAQ"). Accordingly, maintaining and promoting the worldview of hopelessness and perpetual victimhood associated with blackpilled incels described by Fernquist et al. (2020) and Preston et al. (2021) can promote continued group membership.

The way incels speak is an important indicator of group membership and in-group status. Incels have developed an insular community of practice with its own subculture and what some refer to as a "cryptolect" enmeshed in their misogynist ideology, which can obfuscate their conversations from newcomers (Gothard 2021: 2–6). This often opaque language both furthers a sense of in-group identity among incels and marks non-group members as outsiders if they fail to conform. Self-identified incels are present in numerous parts of the world, according to self-reported survey data from incels.is.[3] Not all incel communities speak English exclusively, though English-speaking incel communities appear to be the most widely studied, with most of the literature cited in this very paper referring to studies of English-speaking incel communities (e.g., Baele et al. 2023; Daly and Laskovtsov 2021; and Ging 2019, among others). There exist some exceptions – see Voroshilova and Pesterev's (2021) study of Russian-speaking incels and Fernquist et

3 SergeantIncel (2020)'s survey indicated that 42.8% of users were European and 38% were American, with most of the remainder logging on from Central America, South America, and Asia.

al.'s (2020) section on Swedecels, for example – but few of these directly compare the speech of multiple incel communities with different primary languages.

Previous studies on incels identified in-group jargon, including terms shared with other parts of the manosphere – particularly the greater red pill community – and those originating from the incel community (see Gothard 2021; Moonshot 2020). These studies typically focus solely on anglophone communities of the manosphere and their rhetoric. This study, however, focuses on incels specifically and compares the words and phrases most frequently used among Russian-speaking incels to those used by English-speaking incels. Similar cross-linguistic studies of English- and Russian-speaking incels like Voroshilova and Pesterev's (2021) are rare and have not, to the authors' knowledge, covered lexical distribution and difference.

2.3 Misogyny and gender in North America

Part and parcel of the rise of conservatism in North America that began in the 2010's is the normalization of misogyny in mainstream media and politics. Described by DiBranco as a "'gateway drug' for the recruitment of disaffected White men into racist communities," the misogyny exemplified by incel communities has ramifications beyond these spaces (2017: 15). This is especially visible in the United States, where the 2016 U.S. presidential election witnessed red pill communities grow vocal in their support of then-candidate Donald Trump, a figure community members held up as an "alpha male" who, when elected, would combat the feminist agenda in their stead (Dignam and Rohlinger 2019: 603). Dignam and Rohlinger further describe the mobilization of Reddit's red pill communities in support of Trump during the 2016 election, claiming that Trump "caused hypermasculinity, blatant misogyny, and violent tough talk to resurge in popularity on the national stage" (2019: 603). While not directly inciting violent misogynist acts, the continued platforming of such rhetoric by successful politicians and those that follow in their footsteps may serve to legitimize underlying misogyny.

Contemporaneously, several high profile acts of misogynistic terrorism in North America have taken place, including the 2014 Isla Vista shooting and the 2018 Toronto van attack, among others (further described in O'Donnell 2021). As a result of these attacks, the threat of misogynist terrorism has been acknowledged by the U.S. Secret Service and covered extensively in American media via profiles of the manosphere, especially incels (NTAC 2023; Bosman et al. 2019; Townsend 2022). The perpetrators of these incidents have been revered by incels on public web forums and even, in the case of Elliot Rodger, acknowledged in the manifestos of those who go on to commit similar acts of mass violence (Moonshot 2020: 11).

In light of both the political context and recent incidents of misogynist terrorism, it should not be surprising that the speech of English-speaking incels is markedly misogynistic. Pelzer et al. (2021: 211–212) found that the language on incels.is was 20% more toxic than control data.[4] More specifically, attacks on women for their gender identity, race, ability, and sexuality (Czerwinsky 2023) are characteristic of discourse in incel communities.

2.4 Misogyny and gender in Russia

While singular incidents of mass violence against women such as those described in the previous section are not found in Russian headlines, systematic discrimination against women via legislation have made international news. For example, a piece of legislation was signed into law in 2017 that decriminalized domestic violence, so long as it is the accused's first offense (HRW 2017). This type of legislation is aligned with the "traditional family values" agenda pushed by Vladimir Putin, Russia's longtime authoritarian leader with a political persona built on an exaggerated performance of masculinity (described further in Novitskaya 2017).

Russia's misogyny problem does not end with the institutionalization of conservative "family values". Emboldened by this type of legislation and popular media coverage of Putin's domestic policies, the Runet has been slowly developing an "atmosphere of permissiveness for homophobic voices and misogynistic rhetoric" (Lokot 2019: 217). Like North America, Russia is also host to social movements espousing regressive gender norms. Russian misogynist movements have been buoyed by their acceptance in online spaces, reminiscent of their English-speaking counterparts emboldened by Gamergate.

Consider the Male State (*Мужское государство*), an anti-feminist movement whose page on the Russian social network VKontakte had over 150,000 members before being banned in 2020 due to reported calls for violence (Meduza 2020). According to Gaufman (2022), the organization has since been declared an extremist organization and consequently banned from operating in Russia. Members of the Male State have conducted harassment campaigns against and released the personal information of prominent women and feminists (Gaufman 2022). The group's acts of misogyny are not limited to online harassment campaigns and doxxing: in one documented instance, a female blogger was physically attacked by a

4 For the purpose of the cited study, "toxicity" was determined by a BERT model which measured toxic language by targeting insults, fantasies of violence, and bigoted language, among other types of negativity directed toward outsiders, other forum users, and the speakers themselves.

follower of the Male State in 2020 for posting sexual content online (Bellingcat 2021). While some media outlets have described the "supposed fall" of the Male State, the community continues to operate on the privacy-oriented messaging app Telegram after its ban from VKontakte – albeit with a smaller audience.

3 Method

3.1 Design

In this study, we use a set of three corpora to target both word and multi-word unit keyness, specifically of bigrams.[5] All of the processes described in this section (e.g., preprocessing, generating keyness scores) were performed in Sketch Engine, a corpus management system. Word and multi-word keyness factor into the collection of keywords and key phrases, respectively. For the purpose of this study, keywords and phrases are those that appear in the target corpus more frequently than they would in mainstream discourse on the web, represented by a reference corpus. Keywords and phrases can then be used to begin to understand the "contents, style and discourse of a corpus" (further detailed in Moreno-Ortiz 2024). While keywords can certainly provide information about the prevalent topics and the type of discourse found in CoDEC-M, analysis of concordance lines and collocates would provide further nuance to our understanding of these texts from the incelosphere and are a topic of interest for future study.

With respect to the corpora used, this study uses a single study corpus consisting of two parts – the manosphere subcorpus of the Corpus of Digital Extremism and Conspiracies, henceforth CoDEC-M – in conjunction with two reference corpora. To create the first iteration of CoDEC-M, we collected and compared web data consisting of around 2 million tokens in English and around 3.6 million tokens in Russian.[6] The size of these subsections was determined by the space available on our Sketch Engine account, which was limited to a total of 7 million tokens.

The English section of CoDEC-M was collected using the Selenium Python package to scrape the entirety of incels.is. This consisted of far more tokens than our

5 While the full results include multi-word units with more than two words, these have been excluded from our analysis as we chose to target bigrams specifically.

6 The Russian data was collected from 2ch.hk on 25 July 2023, and the English data was collected from incels.is on 23 February 2023. This data is available for download on this project's Github page: https://github.com/ddryl001/codec (last accessed 14 February 2025).

Sketch Engine account would store (46,000 texts), so we randomly selected 5% of these texts to create an extract for analysis. To avoid biasing the dataset toward any period of time or subsection of the website, the 2,300 texts files were selected at random. While the size of these subsections of CoDEC-M are somewhat disproportionate, this will not affect our analysis. Because each subsection of the corpus is relatively large (at least 2 million words) and the algorithm used to determine keyness score is a ratio of relative frequencies, this size discrepancy is negligible.

The Russian section of CoDEC-M was collected using Beautiful Soup to scrape manually retrieved links for the 472 most recent threads from 2ch.hk's ongoing /incel/ thread on the /sex/ board. Recent threads were chosen because they are the most accessible to users, as 2ch.hk does not have a formal archive of all of its threads – the most recent instance of the /incel/ thread simply links back to the previous iteration, and so on. The scraping process for the Russian data could not be automated using Selenium due to a bevy of broken links and nonstandardized archival practices typical of imageboards. Because of this, 2ch.hk links were collected manually and limited such that the resultant body of texts would not take up over 4 million of the 7 million tokens available on the Sketch Engine account.

The Russian subcorpus of CoDEC-M uses ruTenTen17 as a reference corpus, while the English subcorpus uses enTenTen21.[7] The data contained in ruTenTen17 in particular is not as new as we would have preferred for the study of such a nascent community as Russian-speaking incels, with the most recent iteration of ruTenTen scraped in 2017. Additionally, the TenTen corpus family is not restricted to a single genre of texts from the Web, while our target corpora are all from discussion forums, which is suboptimal. This genre problem is also present in enTenTen21. However, ruTenTen17 is the most recent, widely available large corpus of Russian language data from the Web. These factors, along with the availability of the TenTen corpus family on Sketch Engine, led to our ultimate decision to use this corpus family as reference corpora. When analyzing the Russian data, we consulted several resources developed by native speakers to provide English translations for our results.

Once compiled, the target corpora were preprocessed and run through the Wordlist and Keywords tools in Sketch Engine to determine the top keywords and bigrams via relative frequency (RF) and keyness. Preprocessing of both English and

7 These corpora are part of the TenTen Corpus Family, a multi-language family of corpora made up of web data hosted by Sketch Engine.

Russian data included lemmatization[8] of both the English and Russian data[9] and stop word removal, with custom stop words added for the Russian dataset to remove formatting text from 2ch.hk – these can be found in full on this project's page at https://osf.io/ytrsx and include words related to date, time, and post authors that are included with every post on 2ch.hk.

3.2 Data analysis

Only the top 20 keywords and phrases in the English and Russian language datasets are presented in this paper, along with a keyness score and – for the Russian items – English translation. While the remainder of the 1,000 keywords and phrases provided by Sketch Engine warrant study, we only present the top 20 items from each category in this paper for the sake of parsimony. The full results can be found on this project's OSF page.[10] Also found on this project's OSF page are brief explanations of the words and phrases from Tables 1–4 that cannot be found in mainstream dictionaries. These are more words more typically used by internet users and young people (including members of incel communities) that may be unknown to outsiders.

To avoid keyness results being dominated by the appearance of a word in just a few texts, Average Reduced Frequency (ARF) has been factored into these results and has been reported in our full results tables. Using ARF to factor in dispersion, we followed the example set by Venuti and Fruttaldo (2019) and excluded from Tables 1–4 any keywords or multi-word terms with an ARF score less than 2.00. The full results for this study also contain each keyword and phrase's absolute and relative frequency in both the target and reference corpora.

8 A note on lemmatization and CoDEC-M: while it was performed, Sketch Engine's lemmatization function seems to not do well with lexical innovation and slang. This is true for both the English and Russian data; in the full English keyword data, for example, both "incel" and "incels" can be found, and in the full Russian keyword data, we see both *инцел* ('incel') and *инцелы* ('incels').

9 A note on lemmatization of Russian data: while no white paper is available for Sketch Engine's Russian lemmatizer, correspondence with the developers revealed that it holds space for certain inflected forms (e.g., gender lemmas and lemmas of degree), which can be seen in Table 4.

10 The data presented in the spreadsheet of this study's full results includes manual annotation performed during analysis, primarily consisting of color-coding performed during cleaning and translation notes for the Russian data. A key is provided in the full results. This annotation was performed for at least the top 20 items of each category, but additional translation notes are provided for the remaining top 100 keywords and phrases in Russian.

The difference in magnitude between the study and reference corpora was addressed using Kilgarriff's simple maths, a ratio of relative frequencies with a smoothing function (Kilgarriff 2009). This smoothing factor offers a balance between identifying common and rare words with respect to keyness (Kilgarriff 2012). The smoothing factor selected for this study was 1, the default setting in Sketch Engine, because we were interested in terms that are both frequently used and characteristic of the community.

Keyword overlap was measured via the Jaccard Similarity Index. This commonly-used index indicates the number of shared elements $|A \cap B|$ divided by the unique number of elements $|A \cup B|$ (da F. Costa 2021). This results in a score between 0 and 1, where a higher score indicates a higher degree of overlap.

4 Results

4.1 The English data

Table 1 contains the top 20 keywords in order of keyness from the English section of CoDEC-M, followed by their keyness score. No duplicate word stems were present, and no words were omitted from the results presented here. For the results in their entirety, please visit this project's OSF page at https://osf.io/ytrsx.

Table 1: Top 20 English keywords by Simple Maths score (RQ1).

Word	Simple Maths	Word	Simple Maths
foid	252.037	cuck	46.448
incel	249.685	tbh	45.559
normie	112.083	blackpill	39.550
chad	99.381	ugly	39.148
fuck	75.115	cope	34.882
nigger	58.452	mog	33.901
jfl	50.840	iq	32.583
whore	49.448	curry	32.367
shit	47.448	ascend	32.212
subhuman	46.714	fakecel	30.640

Table 2 contains the top 20 bigrams from the English section of CoDEC-M, ordered by keyness score. While they are present in the complete results, five phrases were removed due to being part of boilerplate text; 12 were removed because they were usernames; three were removed due to suspicion of spamming; and one was removed because it was not a bigram.

Table 2: Top 20 English bigrams by Simple Maths score (RQ1).

Word	Simple Maths	Word	Simple Maths
white woman	13.103	black pill	6.357
white man	9.097	average look[12]	5.963
good look[11]	8.636	white girl	5.941
white foid	8.206	white knight	5.784
ugly man	7.153	i dont	5.730
incel forum	7.099	black man	5.623
white guy	7.057	virtue signal	5.551
video game	6.736	asian woman	5.288
average height	6.660	short man	5.209
foid worship	6.609	social circle	5.154

4.2 The Russian data

Table 3 contains the top 20 keywords in the Russian section of CoDEC-M in order of keyness, followed by their English translations and their keyness score. Translations were initially obtained via transliteration and/or machine translation and were further refined by consulting Russian dictionaries and language learning

11 Because lemmatization was performed as a preprocessing step, the bigrams "good-looking" and "average-looking" are rendered "good look" and "average look", respectively.
12 See previous footnote.

resources,[13] Russian speakers, and the *Incels Wiki*'s page on the Russian incelosphere.[14]

Table 3: Top 20 Russian keywords by Simple Maths score (RQ2).

Word	Translation	Simple Maths	Word	Translation	Simple Maths
тян	*chan*; a young woman	935.261	скуфидрон	an unappealing man, often bald or overweight	138.582
инцел	incel*	830.620	опухший	swollen, puffy[15]	130.147
чед	Chad*	390.290	ирл	irl*	129.181
ебало	*(mat)* mouth	233.049	лвл	*lit.* lvl* ("level"); age	127.649
спок	chill, calm down (v.)	231.235	двачую	*lit.* twice; seconded (as in agreement)[16]	123.876
нахуй (cf. хуй)	(*mat*) fuck it	188.297	нормис	normies*	114.207
пиздец (cf. пизда)	*(mat)* fuckload; or, clusterfuck	164.862	блять (cf. блядь)	vulgar exclamation	108.317
ебать	(*mat*) to fuck	157.79	кунов (cf. кун)	*kun*'s (belonging to a young man)	106.935
бетабакс	betabucks*	144.278	максилла	maxilla	105.402
всратый	*lit.* shitted-in; ugly	138.732	подкатывать	hit on; pick up	103.714

13 The dictionaries consulted for the results in Table 3 were Barron's *Dictionary of Russian Slang and Colloquial Expressions* and Terminy.info's *Словарь молодежного сленга,* a community-sourced online dictionary that was able to account for more recent lexical innovations.

14 While the *Incels Wiki* is not a source reviewed or edited by professionals, it is the only community-developed resource known to the authors that describes language used by Russian-speaking incels. Terms are only available in transliteration rather than Cyrillic, but those that overlapped with our results were identified via transliteration.

15 Literally means 'swollen'. This same root can be used figuratively to indicate boredom or tiredness in one sense, and eccentricity in another; see Šljachov and Adler (2006: 185). However, concordance lines from CoDEC-M indicate that this word is primarily used to refer to a swollen face or a person with such a face.

16 Online slang originating on 2ch but now used across Russian language web forums. Used to agree to a prior message, comparable to "^this" as used on English-language forums (*Двачую* n.d.).

Eighteen words were not included in Table 3 due to repeated word stems.[17] Some of these words were inflected (e.g., *инцел*, 'incel'; and *инцелы*, 'incels'), but others were derived from words whose roots are already in the top 20 keywords.[18] One spelling variant (*чэд*, cf. *чед*, or 'Chad') and one abbreviation via clipping (*скуф*, cf. *скуфидрон*, or '*skuf*', cf. '*skufidron*') were also removed. Asterisks in the "Translation" column indicate that the Russian words are direct borrowings from English transliterated into Cyrillic. These consist of the transliterations of *incel, Chad, betabucks, normies, irl,* and *lvl.* We also note in the "Word" column which words are derived from *mat* (Russian profanity).

Table 4 contains the top 20 bigrams in the Russian section of CoDEC-M ordered by keyness, followed by their English translations. These translations were also obtained via machine translation and further refined by consulting the previously-named resources. One phrase was not included in this table because it was identified as spam, and two were not included because they are not bigrams.

Table 4: Top 20 Russian Bigrams by Simple Maths score (RQ2).

Bigram	Translation	Simple Maths	Bigram	Translation	Simple Maths
тёмная триада	dark triad	33.913	линия волос	hairline	15.370
сын шлюхи	son of a whore	27.697	средний рост	average height	14.514
невольное воздержание	involuntary abstinence	27.064	будка чеда	strong jaw[19]	13.533
пониже рост	shorter height	24.627	глазе жертвы	prey eyes[20]	13.376

17 The words excluded from the results presented in Table 3 are as follows: *тянки, тянок, тянка, тянками*, and *тянку* (all derived from *тян*, '*chan*'); *инцелы, инцелов, инцела*, and *инцелом* (all derived from *инцел*, 'incel'); *чеда, чеды*, and *чедов* (all derived from *чед*, 'Chad'); *похуй, хуйня, нихуя*, and *хуй* (all derived from *хуй*; because *нахуй* is the form with the highest keyness score, it was included in the table); *ебаный* (derived from *ебать*); and *скуфынья* (derived from *скуфидрон*).

18 Words inflected with derivational affixes were not included in Table 3 because of our team's lack of a native Russian speaker – without a native speaker, we were unlikely to achieve the level of nuance in translation that these inflected words would warrant.

19 Literally translated as 'chad's booth' or 'chad's box'; refers to a strong, square jawline.

20 Literally translated as 'victim's eye'.

Bigram	Translation	Simple Maths
осознанное воздержание	conscious abstinence	24.191
желание секса	desire for sex	23.411
фаза знакомства	dating phase	19.149
размер хуя	dick size	17.754
наибольший хуй	biggest dick	16.465
линия роста	growth line[21]	16.331

Bigram	Translation	Simple Maths
процентом жира	fat percentage	13.002
зона глаз	eye area	12.818
черта лица	facial feature	12.788
ментальный чед	mental Chad	12.536
основная теория	basic theory	12.374
большинство тян	most girls[22]	12.109

4.3 Overlap

With respect to RQ3, the number of shared elements in Tables 1 and 3 ($|A \cap B| = 4$) divided by the unique number of elements ($|A \cup B| = 36$) produced a Jaccard Similarity Index score of 0.111, which is rather low. However, when we expand our view to the datasets as a whole, we see more overlap. Of the Russian keywords in Table 3, 40% of them (n=8) are found in the full set of English keywords, and in the top English keywords in Table 1, 70% of them (n=14) are found in the full set of Russian keywords.[23] Overlap between bigrams was not possible to calculate in a meaningful way, and was therefore not calculated.

21 Part of the phrase *линия роста волос*, 'hairline'.

22 Literally translated as 'most chans'.

23 Because translating all 1,000 Russian keywords would be too laborious for this pilot study, we elected to seek out the top 20 English words in translation in the greater Russian dataset – because the full Russian dataset is not translated, we are unable to provide a Jaccard Similarity Index score for the full keyword dataset.

5 Discussion

At the outset of this study, we sought to uncover the top 20 keywords and phrases used by English- and Russian-speaking incels and compare these words and phrases. In the following sections, we will look in greater detail at the trends in both the English and Russian language data, as well as compare and contrast the data from Tables 1–4.

It must be noted that the primary limitation of this study has been our team's lack of a native Russian speaker – while a number of Russian speakers and Russian language data sources have been consulted over the course of this project, our analysis and any future analysis of Russian-speaking incels would greatly benefit from the knowledge of a native speaker.

5.1 Trends in the English incelosphere

Looking to the English keywords and phrases shown in Tables 1 and 2, we observed the following: 1) English-speaking incels are responsible for a sizeable amount of lexical innovation; 2) a number of words and phrases indicate that a sense of community and in-group identity has taken shape among English-speaking incels; 3) use of profanity – including slurs – is the norm; and 4) there is a thematic focus on social categories, particularly race and gender.

Other than redefining *incel* to be male-as-default, English-speaking incels were early adopters of lexical innovations like *foid* (woman; pejorative); *mog* (to dominate or outclass); *curry* (South Asian person; pejorative); *ascend* (have sex or enter a romantic relationship); and the prolific use of the *-cel* suffix. In Table 1, we see *fakecel*, a non-incel who claims incel group membership, but the full dataset also includes terms like *volcel*, *ricecel*, and *mentalcel*, among others.

This unique lexicon, while cryptic to outsiders, has been extensively documented by community members on the *Incels Wiki* and is, like the presence of the incels.is forum itself, indicative of a strong group identity. The designation of in-group members (*incel*), outsiders (both *normie* and *Chad*), and wannabes (*fakecel*) helps establish this identity. Additionally, the phrase *incel forum* is found in Table 2, representative of not only the existence of a (digital) space for the community to gather, but also meta-commentary about the existence of such a space.

While the presence of profanity is not as extensive as it is in the Russian data, it is still notable due to the presence of pejoratives: the top 20 English keywords include an anti-Black slur (the 'n-word'), as well as *fuck* and *whore*. The first of these words is especially jarring, as the use of this word is both highly salient and highly taboo in English-speaking communities.[24] Other language that could be considered profane or pejorative is also present in Table 1, including *cuck*, the newly-coined pejoratives *curry* and *foid*, and *jfl* ("just fucking laugh" or "just fucking lol").

The slurs found in the top 20 English keywords are also indicative of the final theme to be discussed with respect to the English data: a focus on society and social categories. Race and gender – as separate issues and in conjunction – are all heavily featured in the results. In addition to the extensive use of the n-word and the pejorative *curry* seen in Table 1, we also see a focus on race within the key phrases in Table 2. For example, seven of the phrases in Table 2 refer to a specific race of women or men (e.g., *black man*, *asian woman*). Gender is also a topic of concern: nine of the key phrases explicitly refer to people by their gender (e.g., *short man*, *ugly man*). Additionally, we observe discussion among English-speaking incels on how women and men treat each other (e.g., *cuck*, *foid worship*, *white knight*) and perceive one another, especially physically (e.g. *ugly*, *good look*, *average look*).

5.2 Trends in the Russian incelosphere

Regarding the Russian keywords and phrases identified in Tables 3 and 4, several trends are apparent. In this discussion, we will focus on the following: an intense focus on physical appearance – often the physical appearance of men – and the prevalence of three types of lexical items: profanity, online jargon, and borrowings from other languages.

The most apparent theme, especially in Table 4, is the scrutiny of physical appearance, particularly that of men: men are concerned with their hairlines (*линия роста*, 'growth line'; *линия волос*, 'hairline'), penis size (*размер хуя*, 'dick size'; *наибольший хуй*, 'biggest dick'), and height (*пониже рост*, 'shorter height'). More generally, we also see discussion of body fat (*процентом жира*, 'fat percentage'), eye shape (*глазе жертвы*, 'prey eyes'; *зона глаз*, 'eye area'), and other facial features (*будка чеда*, 'strong jaw'; *черта лица*, 'facial feature'). Additionally, some of the language used is typical of an academic register, like the phrase *основная теория* ('basic theory') or scientific names for physical features (*максилла*; 'maxilla' or 'jaw'). Additionally, we see a reference to the dark triad ('*тёмная триада*'), which refers to a psychological theory of three negative personality traits some-

24 While we cannot guess the race of those using this word, use of this slur with a "hard R," as seen in Table 1, is highly salient and almost always pejorative, unlike the truncated variant that has been reclaimed by in-group members.

times conflated with sexual and financial success. While noteworthy, academic keywords and phrases are outweighed by profanity and slang associated with youth culture.

The profanity in Table 3 may be understated due to the elimination of duplicate word stems, which are numerous due to the nature of Russian profanity (*mat*). There are four lexical roots from which the bulk of *mat* is derived. These are *хуй* ('dick'), *пизда* ('cunt'), *ебать* ('fuck'), and *блять* ('whore'). While we have provided simple translations for these four words in parentheses, the versatility with which they may be used far exceeds that of English profanity and cannot be overstated. *Mat*, known for its ubiquity among the working class and youth culture (Erofeyev 2003), appears to also be ubiquitous among users on 2ch.hk. Not only are each of the four pillars represented in Tables 1 and 2, but five of the omitted words were derived from one of these four words. Additionally, three of the bigrams in Table 4 (*сын шлюхи*, 'son of a whore'; *размер хуя*, 'dick size'; *наибольший хуй*, 'biggest dick') feature one of these words.

Lexical items from youth and internet culture are also prevalent in our results: several top keywords are more modern than the colloquial Russian covered in traditional dictionaries, including *ирл* ('*irl*; in real life') or *подкатывать* ('hit on'). These words may also come from subcultures based around hobbies closely associated with young people. Examples include *лвл* ('*lvl;* level'), used to refer to age – used by gamers – or the pair of borrowings *тян* ('*chan*; young woman') and *кунов* ('*kun;* young man'), initially used by anime enthusiasts (see *Словарь молодежного сленга*).

Additionally, words originating from online subcultures like incels themselves and 2ch.hk users are also attested in Table 3. Words like *скуфидрон* ('*skufidron*') and *всратый* ('shitted-in') are claimed by *Incels Wiki* users to be "current terminology" in the Russian incelosphere (2022). *Двачую* (*lit.* 'twice'; 'seconded') is an expression of agreement and a play on the imageboard's name (*Двач*), likely representative of users' affiliation with the site where the /incel/ thread is hosted.

Last among the words we see most frequently in Tables 3 and 4 are borrowings from other languages, primarily English. These words typically surfaced as transliterated jargon used by English-speaking incels (e.g., *betabucks*; *normies*), suggesting that Russian-speaking incels are consuming content created by English-speaking incels. These borrowings appear to be used in a similar context to their English counterparts, and some are so integrated in the speech of Russians-speaking incels that they are incorporated into metaphors, as in the bigram *будка чеда*, seen in Table 4. Literally translated, this phrase means 'Chad's booth' or 'Chad's square,' but concordance lines from CoDEC-M show it being used figuratively to refer to a strong or square jawline.

Also present in the data are one Latin borrowing (*максилла*, a transliteration of 'maxilla,' used primarily in the sciences in Russian and English) and two borrowings from Japanese. The Japanese borrowings differ from the English borrowings in that they derive not from lexical words, but from Japanese honorific suffixes for young women and men (*-chan* and *-kun*, respectively). As borrowings, these honorifics are instead used and inflected as nouns by Russian speakers to refer to their corresponding demographic groups, as indicated in Table 3.

5.3 Overlap

Despite the fact that the Jaccard Similarity Index score was quite low, this is not the only means by which we can consider linguistic overlap or even evidence of language contact. This low score is due in part to lexical items without a one-to-one translation, including expressions that are a single word in Russian but translated as a multi-word unit in English (e.g., *нахуй*, 'fuck it'). To examine other dimensions of overlap between these two datasets, we shall first consider any overlap of the previously-discussed themes, followed by a discussion of loanwords.

Looking first at Tables 1 and 3, we see considerable overlap in the words with the three highest keyness scores: a word that refers to women has the highest keyness score (*foid* in English and *тян* in Russian), *incel* has the second highest score (*инцел* in Russian), and a term for an out-group member holds the third highest score (*normie* in English and *чед* in Russian, both populations often contrasted with incels). This thematic overlap indicates similar topics of conversation between English- and Russian-speaking incels, even though the translations may not be exact. The tendency of Russian-speaking incels to borrow words from the English-speaking incel community also indicates that similar ideologies are circulating among both populations (e.g., married men are used by women for their money – exemplified by *betabucks*). Both datasets also indicate similar attitudes toward profanity – i.e., it is the norm in both spaces – and place emphasis on physical appearance. This is particularly true of height, which 48.5% of incels.is (then incels.co) users perceived as a "factor significantly preventing [them] from finding a partner" (SergeantIncel 2020).

While both datasets focus on physical appearance (possibly in relation to either a desire for or lack of romantic success), the Russian data trended toward a focus on specific physical features, while the English data focused mostly on race. While one might instinctively attribute this to the legacy of whiteness and history of institutionalized racism in the United States, only 38% of incels.is members surveyed in 2020 reported that they were from the United States, so this is unlikely to be the case.[25] It is beyond the scope of this study to posit *why* English-speaking incels discuss race more than Russian-speaking incels, but it may be due to the greater prevalence of American culture – including notions of race and whiteness – on the English-speaking internet.

One final similarity between these two datasets is the presence of words that were coined or popularized in the English-speaking manosphere: *foid, incel, normie, Chad, jfl, blackpill, mog, curry, ascend,* and *fakecel* are found in the English data, while transliterations of *incel, Chad, betabucks* (also spelled "betabux") and *normies* are found in the Russian data. Each of these terms is documented in Moonshot's "Incels: A Guide to Symbols and Terminology" as being characteristic of the speech of self-identified incels. It is evident that the English-speaking incels are prolific lexical innovators, with 55% (n=11) of the top 20 keywords represented in Moonshot's *Guide*, but what of the Russian-speaking incels? While 30% of the words in Table 3 are borrowed from English-speaking incels, there are also Russian words in Tables 3 and 4 that could be characteristic of their speech. This particularly true of *будка чеда* ('strong jaw'), *опухший*, ('swollen'), *всратый* ('ugly'), and *скуфидрон* ('*skufidron*'), because they belong to the same semantic domain where much lexical innovation has occurred with English-speaking incels: physical appearance.

Many of the words Moonshot and other researchers associate with incel culture bleed into mainstream English language internet subcultures, especially those unique to imageboards. So, it is reasonable to suggest that some of the Russian keywords may be similarly characteristic of Russian-speaking incels.[26] Consider *лвл* ('lvl'), *двачую* ('seconded'), *тян* ('*chan*'), and *кун* ('*kun*'), all of which are associated with being a user of 2ch.hk (*Словарь молодежного сленга*; Uglova 2020). As a parallel, terms like *kek* and *mang* associated with 4chan users can be found in the full English results, and may have similarly developed an association with English-speaking incels through repeated use.

If these words are all considered part of the Russian incel cryptolect, the keywords in Table 3 would consist of 13 words (65% of keywords) unique to or characteristic of incels, including borrowings. This is a similar ratio of markedly incel-adjacent terms to the English keyword data, and suggests that Russian-speaking incels

25 Incidentally, the majority of users (42.8%) were from Europe, per SergeantIncel, "Survey Results".

26 Additionally, while some uses of *mat* may also be specific to Russian-speaking incels, the complexity of Russian profanity and its diversity of meaning suggests that without an L1 or near L1 Russian speaker immersed in contemporary youth culture, we lack the cultural context to determine whether or not this is the case.

are similarly prolific with respect to lexical innovation, whether it is through borrowing from English, adaptation from other internet subcultures, or other means.

6 Conclusion

While there is not a significant overlap of the top keywords used by English- and Russian-speaking incels at first glance, there is significant thematic overlap between the keywords and phrases collected. These include extensive use of profanity, language associated with mainstream online youth culture, and a fixation on physical appearance – particularly that of men. Additionally, the data from both communities contains lexical items that have become integrated into their respective communities that are comparatively absent from mainstream discourse, suggesting that both incel communities are lexically productive. Generally, the discussion of English-speaking incels seems to skew more toward discussing women, race, and community membership, while the Russian data suggests a more intense focus on physical appearance. Finally, the Russian data also includes a significant number of borrowings from English-speaking incels, indicative of language transfer between English- and Russian-speaking incel communities.

Our cross-linguistic comparison of incel communities illustrates some degree of contact between the English- and Russian- speaking incel communities. This language transfer, exhibited by the numerous borrowings in the Russian data, suggests a shared, toxic ideology between these two groups. The ideologies of both incel communities center around obsession with physical appearance and discontent with society, as demonstrated by the keywords and bigrams. One can also observe overlap between the themes discussed by the English-speaking incel community and rhetoric from the manifestos of prominent violent criminals affiliated with the subculture, particularly with respect to race and women (further discussed in O'Donnell 2021). As events like the 2018 Toronto van attack have shown, this discontent has been directed at out-group members such that it has a death toll.

While large-scale acts of misogynist terrorism like the mass shootings seen in North America are not yet attested in predominantly Russian-speaking areas, we have established that these communities are not bereft of misogynist violence: consider the targeted harassment campaigns of the Russian Male State movement described in Section 2.4. It is not within the scope of this study to gauge the capacity for violence of a group based on its speech, but the noted similarities are certainly worthy of notice as these two groups continue to operate in parallel. Mass media does not seem to reflect the same level of concern about ideologically-motivated violence from incel communities in larger Russian-speaking society compared to the current concern about incels in English-speaking communities – North America, for example. Contrary to this, the current study illustrates that both groups of incels have comparable grievances, hold comparable views about society, and deserve comparable amounts of attention.

More in-depth study of the speech of Russian-speaking incels and their lexis would prove useful to the study of international incel movements; while we have provided a glossary of some salient terms that appeared in the Russian data on this project's OSF page, the full Russian dataset could be further harnessed to put together a wordlist of key lexical items used by Russian-speaking incels. Lastly, we would like to emphasize the importance of further cross-linguistic studies of non-English speaking incels with other non-English speaking communities and with English-speaking incels. Such studies could shed light on patterns across the greater incel subculture: how similar is the rhetoric, what level of lexical overlap can we find, and what themes emerge?

References

Baele, Stephane, Lewys Brace & Debbie Ging. 2023. A Diachronic Cross-Platforms Analysis of Violent Extremist Language in the Incel Online Ecosystem. *Terrorism and Political Violence* 1–24. https://doi.org/10.1080/09546553.2022.2161373.

Barker, Gary, Hayes Caroline, Heilman Brian & Reichert Michael. 2023. *The State of American Men: From crisis and confusion to hope*. Washington, DC: Equimundo.

Bellingcat. 2021. Meet the Male State: Russia's Nastiest Online Hate Group. *Bellingcat*. https://www.bellingcat.com/news/uk-and-europe/2021/10/20/meet-the-male-state-russias-nastiest-online-hate-group/ (last accessed 28 March 2024).

Bosman, Julie, Kate Taylor & Tim Arango. 2019. A Common Trait Among Mass Killers: Hatred TowardWomen.*TheNewYorkTimes*.https://www.nytimes.com/2019/08/10/us/mass-shootings-misogyny-dayton.html (last accessed 28 March 2024).

Chokshi, Niraj. 2018. What Is an Incel? A Term Used by the Toronto Van Attack Suspect, Explained. *New York Times*. https://www.nytimes.com/2018/04/24/world/canada/incel-reddit-meaning-rebellion.html (last accessed 28 March 2024).

Costa, Luciano da F. 2021. Further Generalizations of the Jaccard Index. *arXiv*. https://arxiv.org/abs/2110.09619 (last accessed 28 March 2024).

Cunha, Darlena. 2020. Red pills and dog whistles: It is more than 'just the internet'. *Al Jazeera*. https://www.aljazeera.com/opinions/2020/9/6/red-pills-and-dog-whistles-it-is-more-than-just-the-internet (last accessed 28 March 2024).

Czerwinsky, Allysa. 2023. Misogynist incels gone mainstream: A critical review of the current directions in incel-focused research. *Crime, Media, Culture: An International Journal*. https://doi.org/10.1177/17416590231196125.

Daly, Sarah E. & Albina Laskovtsov. 2021. "Goodbye, My Friendcels": An Analysis of Incel Suicide Posts. *Journal of Qualitative Criminal Justice & Criminology*. https://doi.org/10.21428/88de04a1.b7b8b295.

DiBranco, Alex. 2017. Mobilizing Misogyny. *Political Research Associates*. https://politicalresearch.org/2017/03/08/mobilizing-misogyny (last accessed 28 March 2024).

Dignam, Pierce Alexander & Deana A. Rohlinger. 2019. Misogynistic Men Online: How the Red Pill Helped Elect Trump. *Signs: Journal of Women in Culture and Society* 44(3). 589–612. https://doi.org/10.1086/701155.

Erofeyev, Victor. 2003. Dirty Words. *The New Yorker*. https://www.newyorker.com/magazine/2003/09/15/dirty-words-2 (last accessed 28 March 2024).

Fernquist, Johan, Björn Pelzer, Katie Cohen, Lisa Kaati, & Nazar Akrami. 2020. Hope, cope & rope: Incels i digitala miljöer [Hope, cope & rope. Incels in digital environments]. Memo 7040. Totalförsvarets forskningsinstitut (FOI).

Gaufman, Elizaveta. 2022. It's a male, male world: rise and fall of "the Male State", a far-right misogynistic organization in Russia. *C-REX - Center for Research on Extremism*. https://www.sv.uio.no/c-rex/english/news-and-events/right-now/2022/it%E2%80%99s-a-male-male-word-rise-and-fall-of-%E2%80%9Cthe-male-s.html (last accessed 28 March 2024).

Ging, Debbie. 2019. Alphas, Betas, and Incels: Theorizing the Masculinities of the Manosphere. *Men and Masculinities* 22(4). 638–657. https://doi.org/10.1177/1097184X17706401.

Gothard, Kelly Caroline. 2021. *The incel lexicon: Deciphering the emergent cryptolect of a global misogynistic community*. Burlington, VT: University of Vermont MS Thesis. https://scholarworks.uvm.edu/graddis/1465/ (last accessed 28 March 2024).

Griffin, Jonathan. 2021. Incels: Inside a dark world of online hate. *BBC*. https://www.bbc.com/news/blogs-trending-44053828 (last accessed 28 March 2024).

Human Rights Watch. 2017. Russia: Bill to Decriminalize Domestic Violence. *Human Rights Watch*. https://www.hrw.org/news/2017/01/23/russia-bill-decriminalize-domestic-violence (last accessed 28 March 2024).

Incels. 2017. Rules and FAQ. Forum post. *Incels.is*. archive.ph/PcMw8 (last accessed 14 March 2024).

Incels Wiki. 2022. "Russian incelosphere". https://archive.ph/bsqg3 (last modified 27 April 2023).

Kilgarriff, Adam. 2009. Simple Maths for Keywords. In *Proceedings of Corpus Linguistics Conference CL2009*. University of Liverpool, UK. https://api.semanticscholar.org/CorpusID:124884692 (last accessed 28 March 2024).

Kilgarriff, Adam. 2012. Getting to Know Your Corpus. In Petr Sojka, Aleš Horák, Ivan Kopeček & Karel Pala (eds.), *Text, Speech and Dialogue*. Lecture Notes in Computer Science 7499, 3–15. Berlin, Heidelberg: Springer Berlin Heidelberg. https://doi.org/10.1007/978-3-642-32790-2_1.

Lokot, Tetyana. 2019. Affective Resistance Against Online Misogyny and Homophobia on the RuNet. In Debbie Ging & Eugenia Siapera (eds.), *Gender Hate Online*, 213–232. London: Palgrave Macmillan. https://doi.org/10.1007/978-3-319-96226-9_11.

Meduza. 2020. Паблик «Мужское государство» заблокировали за «призывы к насильственным действиям» [The "Male State" page has been taken down due to "calls for violence"]. *Meduza*. https://meduza.io/news/2020/07/01/pablik-muzhskoe- gosudarstvo-zablokirovali-za-prizyvy-k-nasilstvennym-deystviyam (last accessed 28 March 2024).

Moonshot. 2020. *Incels: A Guide to Symbols and Terminology*. https://moonshotteam.com/resource/incels-a-guide-to-symbols-and-terminology/ (last accessed 28 March 2024).

Moreno-Ortiz, A. 2024. Keywords. In *Making Sense of Large Social Media Corpora: Keywords, Topics, Sentiment, and Hashtags in the Coronavirus Twitter Corpus*, 59–102. Cham, Switzerland: Palgrave Macmillan. https://doi.org/10.1007/978-3-031-52719-7.

National Threat Assessment Center. 2023. *Mass Attacks in Public Spaces: 2016-2020*. U.S. Secret Service. https://www.secretservice.gov/sites/default/files/reports/2023-01/usss-ntac-maps-2016-2020.pdf (last accessed 8 March 2024).

Novitskaya, Alexandra. 2017. Patriotism, sentiment, and male hysteria: Putin's masculinity politics and the persecution of non-heterosexual Russians. *NORMA* 12(3–4). 302–318. https://doi.org/10.1080/18902138.2017.1312957.

O'Donnell, Kelly M. 2021. Incel Mass Murderers: Masculinity, Narrative, and Identity. *Ohio Communication Journal*. Ohio Communication Journal 59. 64–76. https://stanford.idm.oclc.org/login?url=https://search.ebscohost.com/login.aspx?direct=true&site=eds-live&db=ufh&AN=150697570 (last accessed 28 March 2024).

Pelzer, Björn, Lisa Kaati, Katie Cohen & Johan Fernquist. 2021. Toxic language in online incel communities. *SN Social Sciences* 1(8). 213. https://doi.org/10.1007/s43545-021-00220-8.

Preston, Kayla, Michael Halpin & Finlay Maguire. 2021. The Black Pill: New Technology and the Male Supremacy of Involuntarily Celibate Men. *Men and Masculinities* 24(5), 719–909. https://doi.org/10.1177/1097184X211017954.

Quiroz, Joselyne. 2022. *"Life Wasn't Supposed to be This Way": Involuntary Celibacy Among Young Men Online*. Chicago, IL: University of Chicago MA Thesis.

SergeantIncel. 2020. Survey Results - March 2020. Forum post. *Incels.co*. archive.vn/Vde6H (last accessed 14 March 2024).

Sketch Engine. 2018. Keywords and terms – lesson. *Sketch Engine*. https://www.sketchengine.eu/quick-start-guide/keywords-and-terms-lesson/ (last accessed 28 March 2024).

Šljachov, Vladimir I. & Eve Adler. 2006. *Dictionary of Russian slang and colloquial expressions*. 3rd edition. Hauppauge, NY: Barron's.

Solea, Anda Iulia & Lisa Sugiura. 2023. Mainstreaming the Blackpill: Understanding the Incel Community on TikTok. *European Journal on Criminal Policy and Research* 29(3). 311–336. https://doi.org/10.1007/s10610-023-09559-5.

Speckhard, Anne, Molly Ellenberg, Jesse Morton, & Alexander Ash. 2021. Involuntary Celibates' Experiences of and Grievance over Sexual Exclusion and the Potential Threat of Violence Among Those Active in an Online Incel Forum. *Journal of Strategic Security* 14, 2. 89–121. https://doi.org/10.5038/1944-0472.14.2.1910.

Sprenger, Robin. 2014. *Männliche Absolute Beginner: Ein kommunikationswissenschaftlicher Ansatz zur Erklärung von Partnerlosigkeit* [Absolute Beginner Men: a Communication Science Approach to an Explanation for Partnerlessness]. Wiesbaden: Springer Fachmedien Wiesbaden. https://doi.org/10.1007/978-3-658-05924-8.

Taylor, Jim. 2018. The woman who founded the "incel" movement. *BBC*. https://www.bbc.com/news/world-us-canada-45284455 (last accessed 28 March 2024).

Townsend, Mark. 2022. Experts fear rising global 'incel' culture could provoke terrorism. *The Observer*. https://www.theguardian.com/society/2022/oct/30/global-incel-culture-terrorism-misogyny-violent-action-forums (last accessed 28 March 2024).

Uglova, Julia. 2020, May 30. Вы знаете больше языков, чем кажется. Интернет заставил вас выучить их [You know more languages than you think. The internet made you learn them]. *hi-tech* (30 July, 2024).

Venuti, Marco & Antonio Fruttaldo. 2019. Contrasting News Values in Newspaper Articles and Social Media: A Discursive Approach to the US Ruling on Same-Sex Marriage. In Barbara Lewandowska-Tomaszczyk (ed.), *Contacts and Contrasts in Cultures and Languages*. Second Language Learning and Teaching, 147–161. Cham, Switzerland: Springer International Publishing. https://doi.org/10.1007/978-3-030-04981-2_11.

Voroshilova, Anzhelika I. & Dmitriy O. Pesterev. 2021. Russian Incels Web Community: Thematic and Semantic Analysis. In *2021 Communication Strategies in Digital Society Seminar (ComSDS)*, 185–190. St. Petersburg, Russia: IEEE. https://doi.org/10.1109/ComSDS52473.2021.9422872.

Словарь молодежного сленга. Двачую (Dvachuyu). *Словарь молодежного сленга [Dictionary of Youth Slang]*. http://www.terminy.info/jargon/dictionaries-of-teen-slang/dvachuyu (last accessed 28 March 2024).

Словарь молодежного сленга. Кун (Kun). *Словарь молодежного сленга [Dictionary of Youth Slang]*. http://www.terminy.info/jargon/dictionaries-of-teen-slang/kun (last accessed 28 March 2024).

Словарь молодежного сленга. Лвл (Lvl). *Словарь молодежного сленга [Dictionary of Youth Slang]*. http://www.terminy.info/jargon/dictionaries-of-teen-slang/lvl (last accessed 28 March 2024).

Словарь молодежного сленга. Тян тянка (Tyan tyanka). *Словарь молодежного сленга [Dictionary of Youth Slang]*. http://www.terminy.info/jargon/dictionaries-of-teen-slang/tyan-tyanka. (last accessed 28 March 2024).

Carolina Flinz, Eva Gredel, and Laura Herzberg

The negotiation of pronominal address on talk pages of the German, French, and Italian Wikipedia

Abstract: The adequate use of social deixis is highly dependent on the situation and context and has therefore always been at the center of linguistic pragmatics. So far, principles of pronominal address have mainly been modelled with a focus on oral, co-present interaction. The use of pronominal address in computer-mediated communication (CMC) with its translocal and partially anonymous contexts is still a research gap.

This paper asks, from a contrastive perspective, how the appropriate use of address pronouns is negotiated on talk pages of the German, French, and Italian Wikipedia. The talk pages of Wikipedia share features of CMC genres such as a dialogic structure and an informal writing style with non-standard language. There are two types of Wikipedia talk pages, whose data are considered in this study based on the multilingual corpora by the Leibniz Institute for the German Language: article talk pages, where authors negotiate online encyclopedic content, and user talk pages, where the contributions of individual authors are discussed. These two types of talk pages will be analysed for the study.

Based on corpus data, it can be shown that the unidirectionality of this transition from the formal form (in German: *Sie*, in French: *vous*, in Italian: *Lei*) to the informal form (in German: *du*, in French: *tu*, in Italian: *tu*) in CMC is not always given. In both analysed Wikipedia subcorpora, i.e., the Wikipedia article talk pages on the one hand and the article talk pages on the other hand, a greater deal of discussions about addressing styles takes place on the user talk pages, with the informal *you* variant being discussed more frequently than the formal *you* variant. Aspects of pronominal address among speakers of German, French and Italian are characterized by instability and uncertainty – especially in CMC. Moreover, it can be shown that Wikipedia authors discuss, among others, the reasoning behind their preference for a certain form as well as the notion of "distance" in which informal variants show familiarity which is not perceived as desirable by all users.

Carolina Flinz, Università degli Studi di Milano, e-mail: carolina.flinz@unimi.it
Eva Gredel, University of Duisburg-Essen, e-mail: eva.gredel@uni-due.de
Laura Herzberg, Leibniz Institute for the German Language, e-mail: herzberg@ids-mannheim.de

https://doi.org/10.1515/9783111434018-018

Keywords: social deixis, corpus linguistics, crosslingual study, Wikipedia, linguistic pragmatics, computer-mediated communication, pronominal address

1 Introduction

One of the central tasks that interlocutors have to solve in interaction is to make others feel addressed and thus obliged to respond.[1] Hence, "[a]ddress forms are an indispensable part of the communicative process" (De Oliveira 2013: 291). While in face-to-face communication, addressing can be achieved multimodally through various resources (in addition to language, such resources include bodily orientation, facial expressions, gestures as well as gaze), interlocutors in many CMC genres are highly dependent on linguistic means of address. In this context, pronouns are among the most important means by which linguistic addressing can be realized.[2] In many languages, the selection of certain pronouns from a pronominal paradigm allows the speaker or writer to encode social relations or social distance between the interlocutors linguistically. This has been studied since Fillmore (1975: 76) under the label "social deixis".

The appropriate use of socio-deictic signs is highly dependent on the situation and context and has always been at the center of linguistic pragmatics (cf. Nübling et al. 2017: 205). However, principles of pronominal address have so far been mainly modeled with a focus on oral interaction where speakers are co-present (cf. Kretzenbacher 2010). The use of pronominal address in CMC with its translocal and (partially) anonymous contexts poses special challenges for writers and has been considered in only a few initial studies (see Gredel 2023 for German and Rabelos and Strambi 2009 for Italian). This paper aims to fill this research gap by analyzing meta-discourses on pronominal address in the CMC genre of Wikipedia talk pages. With the multilingual Wikipedia corpora of the Leibniz Institute for the German Language, digital language resources are used that allow a contrastive approach to this object of investigation.

The languages German, French, and Italian, which are considered in this paper, each have a binary system of pronominal address comprising a T form (GER: *du*,

1 The three authors have written the paper jointly. Carolina Flinz is responsible for the data and analyses of Italian, Eva Gredel for German, Laura Herzberg for French. Introduction (§1) and Conclusion (§5) were written jointly.

2 Other means of address are lexical forms, such as first names, familiarizers and terms of endearments (cf. Helmbrecht 2006; Formentellii and Hajek 2015).

FR: *tu*, IT: *tu*) and a V form (GER: *Sie*, FR: *vous*, IT: *Lei*).[3] In oral face-to-face interaction, the selection of the appropriate pronoun in each communicative dyad is generally linked to variables such as social status, age, gender, and conversation situation of the interaction partners (cf. Nübling et al. 2017: 205). In CMC, these variables are not always apparent to writers, so the selection of appropriate pronouns must follow other principles. This paper focuses on this aspect through the analysis of meta-discourses in which interlocutors controversially discuss forms of pronominal address in metapragmatic comments on Wikipedia talk pages and thereby adopt certain stances with the aim of positioning themselves and others.

Regarding CMC, it is interesting that different customs or netiquettes for the use of the appropriate address pronouns have developed on various digital platforms (cf. Gredel 2023). On the multilingual platform Wikipedia, there are differences between the netiquettes of the considered language versions. However, there is no consensus on these netiquettes, and they are subject to controversial discussions. Based on the Wikipedia corpora of the Leibniz Institute for the German Language (IDS), in this paper we explore whether and how writers negotiate the use of address pronouns on Wikipedia talk pages. We also analyze which aspects of the use of pronominal address are being discussed on talk pages of the German, French, and Italian Wikipedia. Specifically, we would like to find answers to the following questions:

- Do writers negotiate the use of pronominal address on German, French and Italian Wikipedia talk pages?
- How frequent do writers negotiate the use of pronominal address on German, French, and Italian Wikipedia talk pages?
- Which aspects of the use of pronominal address are discussed on Wikipedia talk pages of the German, French, and Italian language versions?

First, we describe the theoretical background to pronominal address in general and in CMC in particular for the three languages studied (section 2). Then we discuss the data and methods (section 3), followed by the empirical analysis of the corpus data (section 4). Section 5 summarizes the results.

---

3 For the sake of simplicity, we use the abbreviations T and V here in the tradition of Brown and Gilman (1960), because they seem adequate for this case study of German, French and Italian pronominal address. However, we are well aware of the criticism of this approach (Simon 2003: 7) that the reduction to a binary system is not appropriate for all languages and for all stages of a language (In Italian for example in the past there were more forms, but after a process of simplification, some of them are no more used, see among others Formentelli and Hajek 2015).

2 Pronominal address

The following section provides a theoretical outline of studies that examine pronominal forms of address in general for the three languages under investigation: German, French, and Italian (section 2.1). This is followed by a description of the current state of research on pronominal forms of address in CMC (section 2.2). Finally, central concepts of the discussion of pronominal address in sociolinguistics (including 'power', 'solidarity' and 'social distance') are specified and metalinguistic utterances on address are theoretically framed as stancetaking (section 2.3).

2.1 Pronominal address in German, French, and Italian

Many languages in the world make it possible to encode social relationships with interlocutors linguistically by selecting pronouns from a pronominal paradigm (cf. Simon 2003), that is specific to each individual language.[4] Which elements or grammatical forms of the pronominal paradigm are used as honorific pronouns[5] varies from language to language. There are languages that have developed the honorific form of address from the 2nd person plural (e.g., in French *vous*). This can be explained from a cognitive-linguistic and diachronic perspective with the metaphor "plural is power": Whoever is addressed in the plural is attributed power (Nübling et al. 2017: 2008). According to Brown and Levinson (1987: 23), this represents an act of positive politeness and has developed over time from a conversational implicature to a conventional one (Nübling et al. 2017: 2008). Other languages, such as Italian, use the 3rd person singular (e.g., in Italian *Lei*),[6] whereby the indirect address using the 3rd person instead of the 2nd person is intended to mitigate face-threatening acts (FTAs) in the sense of Brown and Levinson (1987). From a typological perspective, German is a special case here: It combines both described strategies for linguistic politeness (i.e., the plural and the 3rd person), as the 3rd person plural is used as honorific pronoun of address (Duden 2016: §361 on the pronoun *Sie*).

4 Depending on the type of language, verbal morphology may play a central role too. For Italian for example subject pronouns are inherent in the verb conjugation: the suffix is pertinent to the grammatical person (cf. Renzi 1995).

5 Honorifics are linguistic forms (e.g., in many languages certain pronouns) that can be used to signal politeness (cf. Brown and Levinson 1987: 102; 185).

6 This applies to modern Italian. There is in fact another V form, i.e., the third person plural (*Loro*), which is considered archaic and limited to very formal and ritual social situations (Rebelos and Strambi 2009).

At the end of the 20th century, the *Grammatik der deutschen Sprache* (GDS) described the prototypical contexts for using the T form (cf. Zifonun et al. 1997: 317) in German, including interactions with relatives, friends, and children as well as with peers, colleagues, and party members. As in many other languages, the choice of the appropriate form of address in German depends on factors such as age, social status, and gender. However, Kretzenbacher points out that both T form contexts and V form contexts have "fuzzy edges", such as the pronominal form of address for parents-in-law of one's own children (Kretzenbacher 2010: 7).

In addition to such "fuzzy edges" regarding pronominal address, the transition from the T form to the V form is also associated with uncertainty among the interlocutors and must be brought about explicitly. The transition from the V form to the T form in German takes place consensually on the initiative of the older, higher-ranking or female interlocutor (Zifonun et al. 1997: 317). The one-time transition from the V form to the T form is also common when a change in the interactants' social relationship has taken place (e.g., a longer acquaintance); this transition is essentially irreversible (Simon 2003: 124). Changing between different pronouns within a communicative dyad is basically not possible (Simon 2003: 124). Moreover, the transition is only common in one direction – namely from the V form to the T form (Zifonun et al. 1997: 317).[7]

In French, the address pronoun system consists of the T forms singular *tu*/plural *vous* and the V forms singular *vous*/plural *vous* (cf. Clyne 2004: 1). The pronominal usage in France, from the late Middle Ages to the early eighteenth century, remained essentially the same. It was based on class status: T forms were used to address inferiors, and V forms to address superiors (cf. Maley 1972: 1002). This pattern of pronoun usage remained dominant in France until the French Revolution, when the Committee for Public Safety ordered everyone to use T forms on all occasions. Nonetheless, V forms did not completely diminish. More so, T forms were applied in areas in which they have not been used previously, for example, husbands and wives are using T forms with each other as well as children when addressing their parents. Further, Maley points out the majority of grammarians from the preceding centuries made few detailed comments on the usages of the T and V forms. This continued to the twentieth century as well (cf. Maley 1972: 1002).

7 The homonymy of the honorific form of address with *Sie* and the form of address of a group in the 3rd person plural (also with *sie*) can lead to ambiguities in German. These ambiguities could lead to misunderstandings in digital interaction, especially if capitalization plays a subordinate role in interaction-oriented writing. However, no such hits were found in our corpus samples, which is why we did not consider this aspect further in the qualitative analysis.

V forms are the default form for neutral interactions but indicate respect or subservience when used in opposition to the T forms that indicate closeness and intimacy (cf. Schoch 1978: 57; Bouissac 2019: 140). Bouissac suggests that the use of titles commands the V form. The use of the first name is compatible with both the T and V forms. The nickname belongs to the realm of the T form (cf. Bouissac 2019: 143). Students of the French language are taught that the forms of the second person singular are *tu*, *te*, and *toi*, but that the plural form *vous* is also used as the proper way of address to address a single interlocutor formally (cf. Bouissac 2019: 140). Helmbrecht also points out the importance of the singular V form *vous* as politeness marker:

> As an honorific pronoun it stands in a paradigmatic opposition to *tu* […]; the driving force for the development of this usage is politeness, i.e., the avoidance of direct reference to the socially superior hearer/addressee (cf. Helmbrecht 2015: 181).

A greater use of T forms correlates with the younger age group with some decline over time as people grow older. In addition, T forms are the norm for relations between people of equal status and who have known each other for a certain length of time, for example, coworkers. Reciprocal V forms have an important place, and are still the pronoun of choice in initial encounters between strangers and between people who want to avoid familiarity (cf. Clyne 2004: 5; Helmbrecht 2006: 428). They are also used between people who know and see each other on a regular basis but want to show respect or deference, or to keep a certain distance one with respect to another, for example, doctors and patients, or parents and their children's teachers (cf. Morford 1997: 12). Additionally, Morford describes the existence of two basic dyadic forms: symmetrical *vous* and asymmetrical *tu*/*vous* or *vous*/*tu* usages. Symmetrical *vous* is in fact still the normal starting point for public interactions between adults who have no prior relation. It is commonly used between strangers or people who see each other rarely. People who otherwise address one another as *tu* may also adopt a symmetrical *vous* to mark the formality of certain circumstances, such as professional evaluations (cf. Morford 1997: 12).

Social deixis can be expressed in Italian by the pronouns of the second person singular *tu*, *ti*, and plural *voi*, *vi*, the pronouns of third person singular *Lei*, *Le* and plural pronoun *Loro* (cf. Da Milano 2015: 70).

Subject pronouns are not always expressed phonetically but are inherent in the verb conjugation (cf. Renzi 1995). They are considered as an optional rule in Italian, so when they are used, they strategically add pragmatic meanings to a speaker's utterance (Davidson 1996), because they are a marked choice in discourse (see among others Duranti 1984; Dal Negro and Pani 2019). Stewart (2003) argues, in fact that, when adding a non-obligatory subject pronoun, speakers flout Grice's "Maxim of Quantity" and, by doing so, they generate pragmatic implicatures.

Italian deploys personal pronouns and related verbal morphology depending on the two parameters of symmetry/asymmetry and familiarity/distance coupled with context formality (Brown and Gilman 1960; Renzi 1995, 2001; Molinelli 2002; Formentelli and Hajek 2015). There is a complexity of norms regulating address pronoun choice. The current standard of address system in Italian is a bipartite T-V-system with the personal pronouns *tu* as the T form and *Lei* as the V form (Maeder and Werner 2019). The binary distinction of address strategies is also codified by lexical forms as honorifics (*signore, signora*), titles (*professore, professoressa*), "titles + last names" as V forms; first names, familiarizers (*bello, bella*), and terms of endearments (*tesoro*) are used instead as T forms (see also Helmbrecht 2006; Formentelli and Hajek 2015). Address pronouns and nominal forms are often found in the same utterance in Italian, where they take on similar pragmatic values (cf. Formentelli and Pavesi 2022).

The reciprocal use is preferred to index familiarity or to signal social distance and/or mutual respect (cf. Formentelli and Hajek 2015: 122). Reciprocal V forms are for example, considered the default option in academic interactions. The non-reciprocal use (*Lei/tu*) occurs to a lesser extent when there is an asymmetrical distribution of power (age, job rank, and social status, see also Renzi 1993). In particular, it is well established in primary and secondary education, with an increase in the use of "tu + first names" by teaching staff (cf. Formentelli and Hajek 2013: 88–90). Also, in the family, there can still be a non-reciprocal use, for example, the interaction with the mother-in-law (the relationship change comes from the superior person and happens through a ritual). It is important to say that this is not unchangeable as roles and identities are continuously negotiated depending on different factors as levels of formality of the setting, degree of familiarity, and individual preferences (cf. Clyne, Norrby, and Warren 2009).

2.2 Pronominal address in German, French, and Italian CMC

Pronominal forms of address in CMC have been mentioned in linguistic publications since the 1990s and early 2000s, which De Oliveira explains as follows:

> Computer-mediated communication (CMC) offers a different investigative milieu in which to study interaction than does face-to-face communication, as both the researcher and the interaction itself are place-independent and, in asynchronous CMC, time-independent, as well. A researcher can gain access to enormous quantities of data that are neither 'contaminated' by her presence [...] nor dependent on it. (De Oliveira 2013: 292)

The first mentions of pronominal address in CMC can be found in Schulze (1999: 80–81), Bader (2002: 52 and 127) and Hess-Lüttich and Wilde (2003: 167), who see the T form as the unmarked and predominant form of address in CMC.

More comprehensive work focusing on pronominal forms of address in CMC has been done for German mainly in the context of the Melbourne Address Project. In an explorative case study based on Usenet data (news groups and Internet Relay Chat) groups, Kretzenbacher takes a differentiated look at the question of the appropriate form of pronominal address in CMC:

> Based on the research we have done with focus groups and Network interviews, we can hypothesize that in the case of the Usenet, we find a parallel to off-line communication in the coexistence of two systems, one tending towards unmarked *du*, the other towards unmarked *Sie*. (Kretzenbacher 2005: 6)

This thesis was examined in the course of the project on the basis of a broader database, which also contains data from German speaking online fora: Kretzenbacher (2011) and Kretzenbacher and Schüpbach (2015) came to the conclusion that the T form is not the exclusive and not always the dominant form of pronominal address in German-speaking CMC genres. When the T form is used, Kretzenbacher (2010: 6) interprets this as a symptom of a shared "perceived commonalities" (in German: *geteilte virtuelle Lebenswelt*).

A more recent study on pronominal forms of address is that of Truan (2022), who analyzed data from the Twitter account of *Deutsche Bahn*. She also comes to the conclusion that pronominal forms of address are a controversial topic in CMC, with both supporters and opponents of the T form. Gredel (2023) is the first study on pronominal forms of address in Wikipedia. She shows that beyond the pure question of the form of address (T form versus V form), aspects such as reciprocity of the pronominal form or irreversibility of the transition from the V form to the T form are also important aspects of the analysis with regard to CMC.

For French and Italian, the analysis of pronominal address in CMC has so far largely been a research gap. Williams and van Compernolle (2007, 2009a) studied pronominal address in French CMC, in particular in IRC (Internet Relay Chat) messages. They pointed out factors that "favor" either using T or V forms such as syntactic frame, discursive effect, transitivity, ambiguity, linguistic conservatism and ease with address (cf. Williams and van Compernolle 2009a: 417). When investigating the chat messages, the authors found an overwhelming preference for *tu* as T form (98.02%) compared to V forms (1.08%). These results confirmed their findings from a study two years prior, in which the authors matched the reported *tu* use as high as 99.02% (Williams and van Compernolle 2007). The authors illustrated that the uttered V forms happened to be produced relatively soon after the participants had entered the room, at the same time when people were still using V forms to address individuals in the room. All made the switch to *tu* as a form of address rather quickly (cf. Williams and van Compernolle 2009a: 420). In addition to chat, Williams and van Compernolle (2009b) analyzed pronominal address in discussion fora. They concluded that two primary factors influence the T and V usage in discussion fora:

> 1) the medium itself (i.e., the technological affordances and constraints of discussion fora)
> 2) each participant's preference to maintain a traditional, off-line paradigm instead of the on-line system of address pronoun use that has emerged in synchronous chat and discussion fora (Williams and van Compernolle 2009b: 364).

The results are similar to the usage of T forms in chat with an overall usage rate of 84.5% when compared to V forms. Similarly, the number of a specific posting plays a role as well. Since the first turn in almost all new threads is a message to anyone and everyone who might happen to read the posting, almost all subject pronouns in Turn 1 were either V forms or a non-second-person pronouns, like *on* (Williams and van Compernolle 2009b: 371).

Lastly, a study on blogs by Douglass (2009) underlines the online preference for T forms. The author compared different genres of blogs: personal blogs, current events blogs, and sports and entertainment blogs. Overall, *tu* was the most frequently used form (68.2%), followed by *vous* (31.8%). Importantly, this result averages all *tu* and *vous* usages across all blog genres. When looking at each of the genres individually, *tu* was overwhelmingly preferred on the personal blogs (93.3%) whereas *vous* was preferred by 71.9% on the current events blogs. Besides the aforementioned factors by Williams and van Compernolle (2007, 2009a), the computer-mediated format has to be taken into consideration as well.

For Italian, Pistolesi (1998), considering the reduced availability of visual and auditory cues, highlights the more egalitarian character of the CMC communication, being age, gender, social, and racial background unavailable; social hierarchy is therefore weakened and simplified. Gastaldi (2002) investigating the linguistic features of chat exchanges between native Italian speakers, finds out a high incidence of the familiar *tu* pronoun between interlocutors. Studies on IRC make vident typical colloquial and informal features (cf. Pistolesi 1997). Rebelos and Strambi (2009), in their study which focuses on the potential role of CMC in promoting learners' understanding of norms regulating address pronoun choice, analyses address pronouns across different forms, asynchronous and synchronous, concluding that in chat rooms participants address each other exclusively with the informal pronouns (*tu*, fewer *voi*). There is a complete absence of a formal address. In discussion boards, there is a higher frequency of explicit forms of address, with a higher incidence of singular informal pronouns. The only formal pronoun used, *Lei*, is observed on three occasions to signal opposition and social distance in conflict. The identified use is considered a formal demonstration of respect but also a way for the interlocutors to signal the superiority of one of them (see also Dewaele 2004: 384). The two authors show that the most common form of address used across all types of CMC is the informal *tu* pronoun, confirming their initial hypothesis that the observed informality of CMC would manifest itself in the data through a prevalent use of informal pronouns. Another interesting point is whether users perceived the exchange as one-to-one or one-to-many. All of the observed interactions took place in a public space accessible by the online community, with the possibility of participants to observe the interaction and join the conversation. Thus the communication can be between an infinite number of interlocutors, and often the plural address pronoun *voi* is used to reflect this. In the case of a direct and public interaction with a well-known figure of high social standing, the perceived formality of the exchange leads to a more frequent use of the formal pronoun *Lei*. It was also found an instance of explicit reference to a discussion of address form: a participant explained his choice of using an informal pronoun in addressing an interlocutor whom he did not know personally. Maeder and Werner (2019) also cite the study of Rebelos and Strambi (2009), highlighting the dominance of T forms, considering vicinity, familiarity and solidarity the norm.

The contrastive analysis for the languages German, French, and Italian is also still a desideratum, which we would like to address in this case study. The Wikipedia data are interesting and adequate for this project because although the Wikipedia talk pages of the three language versions can be assigned to one and the same CMC genre, the institutional dimension of the language versions (e.g., via wikiquettes and other metalinguistic negotiations) has developed relatively differently in the more than 20 years of Wikipedia's existence. The data is therefore particularly suitable for comparing language and culture in the context of pronominal forms of address.

2.3 Further theoretical framing of pronominal address

This paper is interested in what meta-linguistic utterances Wikipedia authors make about the use of pronominal forms of address and the associated social deixis. As such meta-linguistic utterances are used by authors to reveal their position on the use of the T or V form and associated values, they can be linked to the sociolinguistic concepts of 'social positioning' (Deppermann 2015) and 'stancetaking' in the tradition of Ochs (1996) and Du Bois (2007), as Truan (2022) does for pronominal forms of address in Twitter. Du Bois states:

> One of the most important things we do with words is take a stance. Stance has the power to assign value to objects of interest, to position social actors with respect to those objects, to calibrate alignment between stance takers, and to invoke presupposed systems of sociocultural value. (Du Bois 2007: 139)

In the context of the theory of social positioning, linguists are concerned with the fact that identities are not simply "brought into" interactions as stable entities, but must be negotiated again and again in social interaction. In doing so, the interlocutors permanently position themselves and others in the social space (Spitzmüller 2022: 272).

Stancetaking is then specifically about the positioning of subject 1 in relation to an object of evaluation in the interaction with subject 2. In interaction, the viewpoints of subject 1 and subject 2 considering the object are then also compared and a (dis-)alignment takes place (see figure 1). Du Bois (2007) conceptualizes this as a triadic process, which he reduces to the following formula: "I evaluate something, and thereby position myself, and thereby align with you" (Du Bois 2007: 163).

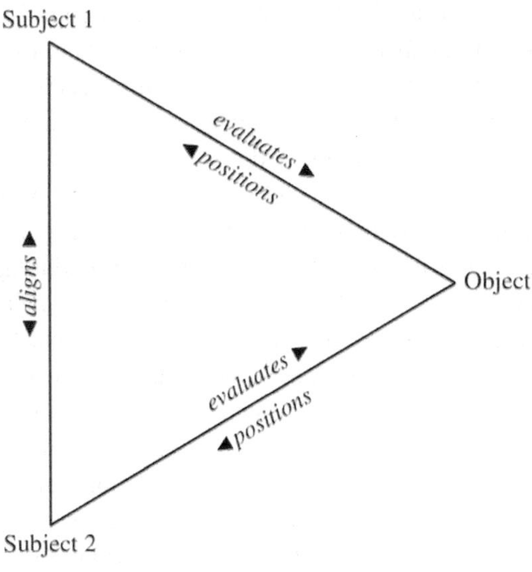

Figure 1: The stance triangle (Du Bois 2007: 164).

Contexts in which the objects of evaluation are linguistic forms, linguistic patterns and language ideologies are particularly interesting for sociolinguistic work (Spitzmüller 2022: 275). It is precisely such explicit meta-linguistic comments that can be found in the corpus data analyzed for this case study. In this context, it is also interesting to note which values and aspects are associated with the use of the T and V form (see section 4). Very often, aspects of power are addressed by the authors (cf. Gredel 2023) because Wikipedia was launched as a project on the social web with egalitarian and grassroots democratic aspirations (Stegbauer 2009). However, the reality of the platform is that, over the years, roles and hierarchies have gradually emerged in the ad hoc meritocracy of the online encyclopedia for the purposes of quality assurance.

A theoretical framework for thinking about hierarchies in the context of addressing in linguistics was provided by Brown and Gilman (1960) in their widely received paper "The pronouns of power and solidarity". In this paper, they introduce the vertical scale of the power dimension and the horizontal scale of the solidarity dimension. The power dimension is concerned with hierarchical structures, which can lead to non-reciprocal forms of address (the higher-ranking interlocutor is addressed with the V form, while the lower-ranking interlocutor only receives the T form). The horizontal dimension of solidarity is about the fact that interlocutors with a higher intimacy or familiarity address each other (i.e., reciprocally) with the T form, whereas the use of the V form indicates a lack of familiarity and intimacy. Later, the two authors use the concept 'distance' instead of the politically connotated concept of 'solidarity' (Kretzenbach 2010: 4). In the meantime, this approach by Brown and Gilman (1960) has been widely criticized. One reason for this is that the use of the abbreviations V and T for all languages suggest a binary system of pronominal address for all languages, although there are systems of pronominal address with more than two elements (Simon 2003: 7). Nevertheless, even today many linguists continue to build on this theoretical background and expand the theory by introducing new categories and concepts or further differentiating the concepts of Brown and Gilman (cf. Leech 1983: 126; Svennevig 1999: 34; Molinelli 2002: 283). Molinelli (2002) for example argues that the dichotomy solidarity (parity of communication; every participant uses the same instruments and there is reciprocity) and power (who has more power determinates the interaction and when there is difference of power there is an asymmetric communication, in which the power uses *tu*, see also Orletti 2000) and their interplay, are not sufficient. Respect and distance have to be added. Respect is in fact different from power, so there can be respect between persons at the same power level. Distance is more changeable than the other parameters; it depends on the culture and is determinant in the culture in which it is socially codified (Molinelli 2002: 294). So all four dimensions, expressed in parameters [± power], [± solidarity], [± distance], [± respect] have to be considered, because they are present in the speaker and in the hearer (codification/decodification), cf. Figure 2:

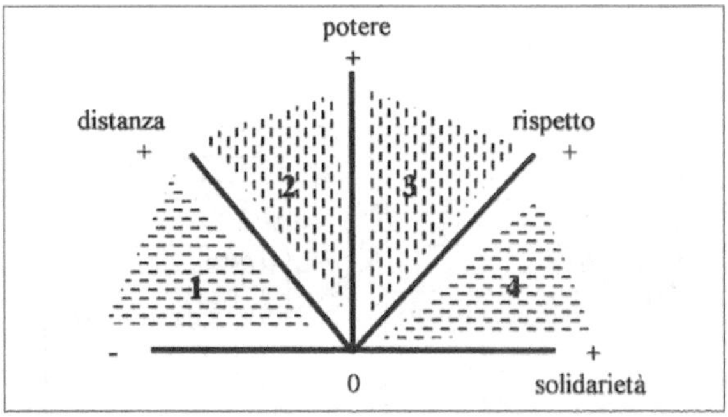

Figure 2: Four address parameters by Molinelli (2002: 296): Distance - Power - Respect - Solidarity.

Molinelli (2002: 296) explains that in the figure, which represents a scheme not necessarily realised in every language and at every stage of a language, each parameter is conceived as a continuum from presence (+) to absence (-) of the trait.

3 Method & data

Wikipedia consists of many structural elements, referred to as namespaces. A namespace is "a virtual container for different types of content on the wiki; namespaces are defined by different prefixes, such as *talk:* or *Wikipedia:* which appear before page names; articles are in the main namespace" (Ayers et al. 2008: 473). Figure 3 presents a schematic overview of the Wikipedia data and namespaces.

In addition to the well-known articles as the core content of Wikipedia, the talk pages also have a central function, because the online encyclopaedic content is negotiated there in digital interaction. It is often a matter of controversy in which terms events or facts are described in Wikipedia. Additionally, the revision history documents in detail the development of articles over the years and allows one to understand the dynamics of the content. Many long-standing authors introduce themselves to the community on user pages and the corresponding user talk pages offer the opportunity to thank or criticize authors. Finally, there are many wiki pages with policies and guidelines as well as links to external sources. From these different areas of Wikipedia, different digital language resources have been compiled in the form of linguistic corpora at the IDS.

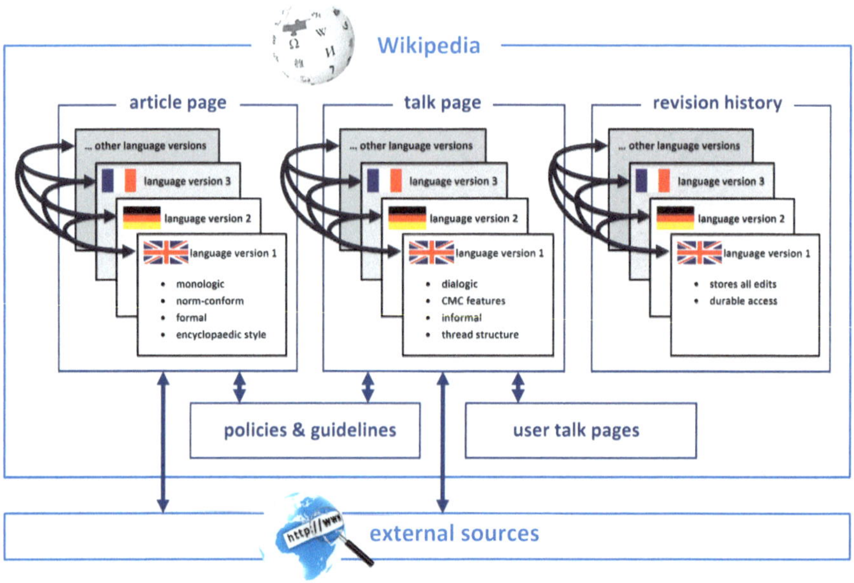

Figure 3: Schema of data and namespaces in Wikipedia (Gredel 2017).

The Wikipedia terms of use permit sharing and reusing of Wikipedia content under free and open licenses, which makes the language data it contains usable for research, IDS has been offering access to Wikipedia data via its corpus infrastructure since 2005. Wikipedia language data is converted into linguistically processed corpora and thus made accessible for research purposes. This is done in a structured way, e.g., by namespace, i.e., there are Wikipedia sub-corpora for article, talk, and user talk pages. In addition to different namespaces, several language versions are also available. Since 2011, corpora of all German-language encyclopedia articles as well as all associated talk pages have been created every two years for this purpose from a Wikipedia dump published by the Wikimedia Foundation. This dump contains a "snapshot" of the database content of an entire single-language Wikipedia at a specific point in time (Beißwenger and Lüngen 2022: 439). The Wikipedia corpora collection is thus constantly being expanded and extended. The Wikipedia data forms an archive of the German Reference Corpus (DeReKo), which is the most comprehensive collection of written contemporary language (cf. Lüngen and Kupietz 2020). The Wikipedia corpora are available via the IDS corpus research systems COSMAS II_{web} and KorAP. COSMAS II_{web} is an operating system-independent WWW application that enables corpus research in a conventional WWW browser. In COSMAS II_{web}, the corpora are managed in three archives, whereby the German and English Wikipedia content is organized in one archive each and a further eight language versions are available in one archive.

The talk pages of Wikipedia share features of CMC genres such as a dialogic structure and an informal writing style with non-standard language (cf. Storrer 2017). As we look at the Wikipedia talk pages, we would like to make one more linguistic differentiation: There is text-oriented writing that can be found on the article pages with monologic structure, standard language and elaboration of conventional textual patterns. On Wikipedia talk pages other different specifics can be identified such as dialogic structure, informal writing style and the tendency for the speed of an answer to outweigh an elaborate wording. This study focuses on the interaction-oriented language on Talk pages. There are two types of Wikipedia talk pages: article talk pages, where authors negotiate online encyclopedic content and user talk pages, where the contributions of individual authors are discussed. The metadata for the corpora used are as follows, cf. Table 1:

Table 1: Size of the corpora in tokens and corpus abbreviations[8] (DeReKo 2022 in COSMAS II$_{web}$ 2024).

Language	Article talk pages	User talk pages
German	373,161,686 (wdd17)	309,390,966 (wud17)
French	138,068,162 (wdf15)	374,390,445 (wuf15)
Italian	52,070,465 (wdi15)	130,067,969 (wui15)

To be able to investigate meta-discourses and thus the negotiation of appropriate address pronouns, we use the following search strings when conducting queries in COSMAS II$_{web}$:

- GER: *&siezen* and *&duzen*
- FR: *vouvoyer* and *tutoyer*[9]
- IT: *dare del Lei* and *dare del tu*[10]

8 The corpus abbreviations read as follows, ***wdd17*** is the **W**ikipedia corpus of German (***d**eutsch*) article talk (***D**iskussion*) pages created from a 2017 Wikipedia dump; *w**u**d17* represents the **u**ser discussion pages.

9 All inflected forms were queried in a rather complex REG# (regular expression) search string: #REG(^tuto(ie(nt|r(a(i(s|(en)?t)|s)?|i?(ez|ons)|ont)?|s)?|y(a(i(s|(en)?t)?|nt|s(s(e(nt|s)?|i(ez|ons)))?)?|â(mes|t(es)?)|é(es?)?|er|èrent|i?(ez|ons)))$) oder #REG(^vouvo(ie(nt|r(a(i(s|(en)?t)|s)?|i?(ez|ons)|ont)?|s)?|y(a(i(s|(en)?t)?|nt|s(s(e(nt|s)?|i(ez|ons)))?)?|â(mes|t(es)?)|é(es?)?|er|èrent|i?(ez|ons)))$).

10 All inflected forms were queried in a rather complex REG# (regular expression) search string: #REG(^d(à(nno)?|a(i|n((d|n)o|te)|r(à|a(i|nno)|e(bbe(ro)?|i|mm?o|st(e|i)|te)?|ò)|t(a|e|i|o)|v(

The German search string uses the base form operator „&-ampersand“, also called *lemmatization operator* or short: *lemmatizer* that allows searching not only for inflectional forms, but also for word formation forms for a base form.[11] The lemmatization of COSMAS II$_{\text{web}}$ is tailored to German. Therefore, the usage of the basic form operator '&' in queries to the foreign language Wikipedia corpora cannot be applied. For English and Italian, a workaround, i.e., placeholder operators, can be used (e.g., search operator *) or the specific forms can be explicitly listed in the search expression. We used the latter option and implemented queries consisting of regular expressions to gain results. A total of 12 queries, four for each language version with two for each Wikipedia subcorpus, i.e., T form and V form on article talk and user talk pages were conducted via the COSMAS II$_{\text{web}}$ interface.[12]

4 Data analysis

In this section, the results of the quantitative analysis as well as the language-specific qualitative analyses are presented. First, the results of the queries that were conducted using the Wikipedia corpora within the COSMAS II$_{\text{web}}$ research interface are described in section 4.1. In section 4.2, examples from the German, French and Italian Wikipedia article talk and user talk pages are used to show the crosslingual similarities and differences when Wikipedia authors make meta-linguistic utterances about the use of pronominal forms of address.

4.1 Quantitative analysis

In the following, it will be quantitatively demonstrated to what extent corpus hits referring to a meta-discourse on social deixis can be found in the three languages under consideration.

a((m|n)o|te|i)?|i|o))?|e(mmo|s(s(e(ro)?|i(mo)?))|st(e|i)|tt(e(ro)?|i))|i(a((m|n)?o|te)?|e(d(e(ro)?|i)))|o|ò)$) /+w1 del /+w1 (tu oder lei oder Lei).

11 A *base form* describes an uninflected word or word formation morpheme.

12 The results of these queries are described in detail in section 4.

Table 2: Results of the search queries in the Wikipedia corpora (DeReKo 2024 in COSMAS II 2024).

Language	Wikipedia namespace	Query	Occurrences	pMW[13]	Texts
German	Talk page	wdd17: V form (*siezen*)	322	0.86	208
		wdd17: T form (*duzen*)	993	2.66	682
	User talk page	wud17: V form (*siezen*)	395	1.21	290
		wud17: T form (*duzen*)	2,052	6.29	1,659
French	Talk page	wdf15: V form (*vouvoyer*)	103	0.75	95
		wdf15: T form (*tutoyer*)	449	3.25	426
	User talk page	wuf15: V form (*vouvoyer*)	200	0.53	181
		wuf15: T form (*tutoyer*)	1,655	4.42	885
Italian	Talk page	wdi15: V form (*dare del L/lei*)	29	0.56	9
		wdi15: T form (*dare del tu*)	61	1.17	61
	User talk page	wui15: V form (*dare del L/lei*)	84	1.61	82
		wui15: T form (*dare del tu*)	372	7.14	308

For the German language version, it can be shown that both corpora (wdd17 and wud17) contain hits for both search strings (V form *siezen* and T form *duzen*), cf. Table 2, with occurrences of *duzen* being more frequent in both name spaces, i.e., the article talk as well as the user talk pages. For the French language version, Table 2 shows that both search strings (V form *vouvoyer* and T form *tutoyer*) yield results which, however, differ in their frequency: For both Wikipedia name spaces, i.e. the article talk pages as well as the user talk pages, inflected forms of the T form *tutoyer* are more frequently discussed than forms of the V form *vouvoyer*. French Wikipedia authors debate the means of addressing with each other; in sum more often on their own talk pages than on the article talk pages. The Italian language version contains hits for both search strings in both corpora, cf. Table 2. In particular the T form *dare del tu* is more discussed than the V form *dare del Lei/lei*.

Across all three investigated languages, meta-linguistic utterances about the use of pronominal forms of address are more frequent on the user talk pages than the article talk pages.

13 The abbreviation *pMW* stands for *occurrences per million words*. It is a measure of relative occurrence frequencies that are also normalized to a common base (one million current word forms). This allows for comparing frequencies in corpora of different sizes. To calculate pMW values, we need to divide the raw frequency by the total number of words in the corpus and multiply the result by one million.

We used a qualitative corpus-based approach in our study. For hit lists with more than 100 hits, random samples of N=100 were drawn, which were then used to deductively test the hypotheses mentioned at the beginning of the paper.[14]

4.2 Qualitative analysis

This section presents the qualitative results of the pronominal address analyses in German (section 4.2.1), French (section 4.2.2) and Italian (section 4.2.3) using language specific examples from the Wikipedia talk pages.

4.2.1 Pronominal address on German Wikipedia talk pages

Wikipedia's policies and guidelines in the German language version contain a detailed Wikiquette. There it says on pronominal address:

> Viele der Umgangsformen der Wikipedia stammen noch aus der Zeit, als sich eine überschaubare Gruppe von Enthusiasten die Aufgabe gestellt hatte, eine Enzyklopädie zu schreiben, und nicht ahnen konnte, welchen gesellschaftlichen Stellenwert die Wikipedia eines Tages einnehmen würde. Aus dieser Zeit stammt auch das hier übliche vertrauliche „Du" im Miteinander der Benutzer.
>
> *Many of Wikipedia's codes of conduct date back to the time when a small group of enthusiasts set themselves the task of writing an encyclopaedia and had no idea of the social status Wikipedia would one day have. The customary confidential "Du" form of address among users also dates from this time* (Wikipedia 2024).

However, this seems to be the view of those Wikipedia authors who have been part of the online community for a long time (= high level of seniority) and came up with this rule in the early Wikipedia. The reason is that these authors have shared "perceived commonalities" (in German: *geteilte virtuelle Lebenswelt*, Kretzenbacher 2006: 10) for many years and are familiar with each other, even if they have never met face-to-face.

This is also shown by the example (1) from 2008. A long-time author demands the *Du* with reference to the Wikiquette: He not only refers linguistically to the Wikiquette (*nachlesbar auch unter WP:DU – also available at WP:DU*), but even

14 Our aim was to conduct a qualitative cross-linguistic study of forms of address. The examples in the following sub sections are taken from these lists and grouped thematically.

adds a corresponding hyperlink to the abbreviation WP:DU. In doing so, he suspends the factors (age and level of education) that are usually decisive in face-to-face communication for the choice of the appropriate pronominal form of address. Another author in (2) states on a talk page that *Sie* – the German V form – is impolite in Wikipedia. In (3) an author characterizes the V form of address as inappropriate (*unangebracht*) in Wikipedia:

(1) Also vielleicht auch zum Einstieg die Information, dass sich in der **WP alle duzen**, unabhängig von Alter und Bildungstand (nachlesbar auch unter WP:DU) (WUD17/K37.41593)
So maybe to start with the information that everyone in the WP uses du, regardless of age and level of education (also available at WP:DU)

(2) Ich habe mit dir nichts zu diskutieren, und **sieze mich** nicht, das ist hier sehr unhöflich.
I have nothing to discuss with you, and don't use Sie, that's very impolite here (WDD17/C81.68097)

(3) Es steht dir selbstverständlich frei zu **Siezen**, es wirkt aber **unangebracht**.
You are of course free to use the pronoun Sie, but it seems inappropriate. (WDD17/B09.74909)

The long-standing Wikipedia authors therefore adopt a pro T form stance and a contra V form stance and propagate the T form as the only correct form of address in Wikipedia: In their view, deserving authors correctly use the familiar T form with the aim to suspend differences due to various educational levels, for example. They thus suggest, at least superficially, an egalitarian claim. The V form, on the other hand, is characterized by them as an index of limited experience with Wikipedia. Through this stancetaking, they position themselves as superior to other interlocutors who use the V form.

Examples (4) to (6) are three examples of authors rejecting this wikiquette and also shared perceived commonalities:

(4) Wir leben nicht mehr in den 90er Jahren. Wie Sie vielleicht festgestellt haben, wird sich mittlerweile auch im Internet auf seriösen, ‚erwachsenen' Seiten **zunehmend gesiezt**. Der Wikipedia würde ein seriöserer Anspruch auch unter seinen Mitarbeitern sicherlich nicht schaden. (WUD17/B72.41245)
We no longer live in the 1990s. As you may have noticed, on serious, 'adult' sites on the Internet authors now increasingly use the V form. Wikipedia

would certainly not be harmed by a more serious standard, even among its contributors.

(5) ich sieze, weil sie mich auch Siezen würden, **stände ich vor Ihnen** – ebenso würde ich Sie siezen. (WDD17/E85.13333)
I use the V form because if I were standing in front of you, you would also use the V form – and vice versa.

(6) Da ich Sie (Herr Hob) nicht kenne und ich Ihnen **das ‚Du' nicht angeboten** habe bitte ich, mich zu Siezen. (WDD17/B60.35170)
Since I don't know you (Mr. Hob) and I haven't offered you the T form, I ask that you address me with the V form.

From the broader context of the examples (4) to (6), it can be concluded that these are authors who have not been contributing to Wikipedia for that long. In (4), the informal form of address is dismissed as a 1990's bad habit. In (5), the comparison is drawn to the face-to-face situation in which strangers would be formally addressed. In (6), the author points out that there was no offer to change from V to T. Thus, he sees no legitimate basis for using the informal form. Authors with a low level of seniority in the ad hoc meritocracy therefore reject the use of the T form by default on the talk pages. Therefore, they adopt a pro V form stance and a contra T form stance.

Interesting insights also arise from corpus hits in which not only pronominal forms of address, but also nominal forms of address and nominal reference play a crucial role, as in examples (7) to (9):

(7) Du/Sie?: Bei Wikipedia duzen wir uns alle – egal, ob 14 oder 140, **Schüler oder Professor** (oder sonst was). (WUD17/B58.97203)
T/V: On Wikipedia, we all use T - no matter if you're 14 or 140, a student or a professor (or whatever).

(8) P.S. Das Duzen stellt tatsächlich in der Wikipedia die Höflichkeitsform dar, Siezen gilt allgemein als Zeichen von Distanzierung bzw. von Unkenntnis **(‚Newbie')** (WUD17/P51.87518)
P.S. Duzen actually represents the polite form in Wikipedia, Siezen is generally considered a sign of distancing or of ignorance (‚newbie')

(9) Letzten Endes möchte ich noch darauf hinweisen, dass man sich in der Wikipedia allgemein duzt. Ich habe Sie bis zu diesem Punkt gesiezt, um Sie als **Wikipedia-Neuling** nicht vor den Kopf zu stossen, gehe zukünftig aber zum ‚Du' über, wie es in der Wikipedia-Etikette Standard ist. (WUD17/K25.79885)

Lastly, I would like to point out that on Wikipedia we generally say Sie. *I have been using* Du *with you up to this point so as not to offend you as a Wikipedia newcomer, but will switch to 'you' in the future, as is standard in Wikipedia etiquette.*

Long-time authors pretend to abolish hierarchies of institutional offline contexts and to suspend professional roles (example 7). They do this with the alleged aim of achieving maximum equality between all authors. At the same time, however, long-time authors introduce a new hierarchy in the ad hoc meritocracy Wikipedia, which focuses on seniority in the online encyclopedic project. New authors are explicitly addressed nominally as *newbie* (8) or Wikipedia newcomer (*Wikipedia-Neuling*, 9) and thus degraded in a certain respect. Via the analysis of metalinguistic comments in the German language version, it thus becomes clear that lines of conflict do not run along classical hierarchies, but along newly created hierarchies that are oriented towards the level of seniority in the Wikipedia project.

4.2.2 Pronominal address on French Wikipedia talk pages

In French, the usage of the V form *vous* form of address is greatly reflected upon. There are for example specific user boxes which can be implemented on a user page that indicate how a user wishes to be addressed. Although some users prefer the informal *tu*, the formal *vous* form of address still plays a rather important role in Wikipedia user addressing.

The following examples show a preference for the formal form of address, i.e., a pro V form and contra T form stance:

(10) Serait-il possible d'éviter les familiarités, **je ne tutoie personne**, merci de faire de même, nous ne sommes pas des amis ou ennemis de Facebook ! (WDF15/A73.66675)
Would it be possible to avoid familiarities, I'm not addressing anyone with „tu", please do the same, we're not Facebook friends or foes!

(11) Merci de **ne me pas me tutoyer**, on n'a pas gardé les cochons ensemble. (WDF15/B68.70940)
Thanks for not addressing me with „tu", "we didn't keep pigs together".

(12) Je vous ai vouvoyé, je **n'accepte donc pas être tutoyée** (WDF15/M14.64419)
I addressed you with the formal „you", I won't accept being addressed with the informal „you"

In (10) the user prefers being addressed with *vous* and makes a clear distinction between Wikipedia and other digital platforms, such as Facebook.

In (11), the French idiom *ne pas avoir garder les cochons ensemble* (*don't get so familiar with me!* or *don't get so pally with me!*) is generally used if somebody expresses an inappropriate or unwanted level of familiarity. The term *familiarity* plays a keyword role in the discussion about pronominal address, as it is also being explicitly mentioned in Example 1.

In example (12), the formal addressing given to the receiver is equally demanded by the sender.

(13) @Guil2027 Le vouvoiement, vois-tu, permet de **maintenir une certaine distance** avec des contributeurs dont on souhaite justement éviter la proximité (WDF15/C18.89546)
You see, being formal allows you to maintain a certain distance from contributors whose proximity you wish to avoid.

(14) Donc **merci** d'éviter de me tutoyer comme si j'étais un copain et **de garder vos distances** ; je garderai les miennes à votre égard comme je l'ai toujours fait (WDF15/M66.99763)
So please don't address me with "tu" as if I were a friend, and keep your distance; I'll keep mine from you as I've always done.

(15) Je ne tutoie pas, c'est **une distance nécessaire** : nous ne sommes pas une bande de copains qui causent au coin d'un comptoir de troquet (WDF15/D18.63069)
I'm not on familiar terms, it's a necessary distance: we're not a bunch of buddies chatting at the corner of a bar.

The notion and importance of 'distance' as another key concept is explicitly addressed in postings. Again, the authors take a pro V form stance by underlining the importance of social distance between each other, as in (13) and (14). In (15) the user draws a clear distinction between work in Wikipedia and, for example, communication to close people, such as friends. Looking at this from another perspective, it could also exemplify a general hesitation in terms of committing to a more informal T form. Once the authors are exchanging terms of familiarity and closeness, it might be difficult to return to the initial situation. Peeters summarizes this accordingly:

> Le tutoiement signale souvent un point de non-retour, un degré d'intimité auquel il est difficile de renoncer, alors que le vouvoiement constitue un comportement moins engagé. (Peeters 2004: 7)

> *Being on familiar terms often signals a point of no return, a degree of intimacy that is difficult to relinquish, whereas being formal is a less committed behavior.*

Lastly, personal preference as a factor, closely related to linguistic conservatism and ease with address, is also mentioned as a reasoning in terms of opting for a T form:

(16) Bonjour, vous **pouvez me tutoyer**, depuis le temps que nous nous croisons sur le projet ! (WDF15/F62.64673)
Hello, you can address me with "tu" for as long as we're working on this project together!

(17) Certes, le **tutoiement est d'usage sur Wikipédia** comme sur beaucoup de sites collaboratifs, mais n'est en rien une obligation. (WDF15/C18.89546).
Of course, as on many collaborative sites, it's customary to use informal forms of address on Wikipedia, but it's by no means compulsory.

(18) Je suis fatigué de faire des listes de personnes à tutoyer ou à vouvoyer: **sur WP le tutoiement est quasi l'usage général** et je tutoie toute personne qui a un compte (pour les IP c'est selon mon humeur...) (WDF15/H09.03179)
I'm tired of making lists of people to be addressed with „vous" or „tu": on WP, „tu" is almost the general rule, and I use „tu" with anyone who has an account (for IPs, it's up to me...)

In (16), the joint project work qualifies for using the informal *tu*. (17) and (18) underline the defacto-standard, or customary usage of informal forms of address on Wikipedia. Moreover, in (18) the user expresses some level of frustration regarding the topic of addressing by stating that they are *tired of making lists of people to be addressed with „vous" or „tu": on WP, „tu" is almost the general rule, and I use „tu" with anyone who has an account* – again, one's own, personal preference is highlighted.

In several user surveys no consensus regarding a standardized form of address in the French Wikipedia could be generated, so both forms of addressing continue to be used depending on a user's preference.[15] Such a preference can be publicly stated on a user page by implementing the respective *Wikipedia:Userbox*.[16] There are boxes dedicated to the preferred form of pronominal address. A userbox stating

15 https://fr.wikipedia.org/wiki/Wikip%C3%A9dia:Le_Bistro/24_novembre_2014#Tutoiement (last accessed 14 February 2025).
16 Note that userboxes are not mandatory therefore their frequency should not be used in terms of generalization.

the preference for a V form is called *Modèle:Utilisateur vouvoiement* and for a T form it is *Modèle:Utilisateur Tutoiement*. It is possible to assess the numbers of each userbox by consulting the respective category pages. A total of 112 users has the userbox *Tu ou vous*[17] shown on their page, indicating they do not mind using V and T forms interchangeably, depending on the preference of their counterpart. On 83 user pages the box *Utilisateur vouvoivement*[18] is placed, showing that these users would like to be addressed with a V form. A total of 411 user pages has the userbox *Utilisateur Tutoiement*[19] implemented, i.e., being in favor of T forms of address.

4.2.3 Pronominal address on Italian Wikipedia talk pages

The shared "perceived commonalities" and the familiarity due to being part of a community, even if they have never met face-to-face, is also a characteristic of the Italian Wikipedia talk pages. The use of ‚tu' is considered a convention (examples 19 and 20) and used so by default. The fact of belonging to a community of Wikipedians and being so among *wikifili* is highlighted in (21), while in (22) the focus is on being part of a group. The use of the deictic „here" is often present to emphasize this use in a specific context: namely Wikipedia. It can be deduced from the examples that new authors tend probably at first to use the V form (19 and 20) (it is an index of limited experience with Wikipedia). Longtime authors are the ones who propose the T form, propagating the T form as the only correct form of address in Wikipedia, enforcing the wikiquette and suspending, superficially, differences (22). Through this stancetaking, they position themselves as superior to other interlocutors who use the V form.

(19) […] qui ci si da del **TU** per **convenzione** […] (WUI15/A28.07711)
[…] *here we adress each other with ‚TU' by convention* […]

(20) […] Per **convenzione**, wikipedia usa "di default" il **tu** […] (WUI15/A06.20577)
[…] *By convention, wikipedia uses 'by default' ‚tu'* […]

(21) Credo che una distinzione più appropriata potrebbe essere fatta sulla committenza e sul pubblico cui l'opera si rivolge: volendo passare al tuo esempio musicale (**ti do del tu**, visto che siamo tra **wikifili**), ti invito a riflettere come

17 https://fr.wikipedia.org/wiki/Cat%C3%A9gorie:Utilisateur_Tu_ou_vous (last accessed February 2025).
18 https://fr.wikipedia.org/wiki/Cat%C3%A9gorie:Utilisateur_vouvoiement (last accessed February 2025).
19 https://fr.wikipedia.org/wiki/Cat%C3%A9gorie:Utilisateur_Tutoiement (last accessed February 2025).

canzoni di musica leggera hanno valore artistico riconosciuto e successo di pubblico (vd. il caso De André). (WDI15/B24.05597)
I think a more appropriate distinction could be made on the patronage and the audience to which the work is addressed: turning to your musical example (I'm adressing you with ,tu', since we are among wikifili), I invite you to reflect on how pop music songs have recognised artistic value and public success (see the De André case).

(22) Caro Alberto. Non ti do del tu perché sono d'origine siciliana o perché sono anch'io un arabista (in realtà sono più storico e islamista, ma con 40 anni di studio dell'arabo, una laurea e un perfezionamento con Francesco Gabrieli e Alessandro Bausani). **Ti do del tu** perché qui **da noi si usa darsi del tu**, a meno che non ci siano particolarissime idiosincrasia in merito. (WUI15/A08.57762)
Dear Alberto. I do not use 'tu' because I am of Sicilian origin or because I too am an Arabist (actually, I am more of a historian and Islamist, but with 40 years of Arabic studies, a degree and further education with Francesco Gabrieli and Alessandro Bausani). I use 'tu' because it is customary to adress each other 'tu' here, unless there is a particular idiosyncrasy about it.

Social status, hierarchies, age are no more a factor in choosing the appropriate form of address pronoun. Factors such as titles in (23), age in (24 and 25) and sympathy (25) are suspended. Other aspects like equality of all Wikipedians are applied (26): there are no differences between administrators and users.

(23) Ciao, meglio essere meno formali, di solito **su wikipedia ci si dà del tu** e **si evita l'uso dei titoli**. (WUI15/A26.79745)
Hi, better to be less formal, usually on wikipedia we adress each other using „tu" and avoid the use of titles.

(24) [...] Un cordiale benvenuto anche da parte mia! (ovviamente sai già che qui **ci si da del TU** [...] **senza tener conto di alcun limite**; io ad es. sono del **1945**) [...] (WUI15/A28.07711)
A warm welcome from me too! (Of course, you already know that we adress us with ,tu' here by convention, regardless of any limits; I, for example, am from 1945) [...]

(25) **Non conta l'età o la simpatia**. Siamo tutti coinvolti in un progetto (**noi wikipediani** amiamo scrivere Progetto, con la maiuscola) [...] (WUI15/A08.57762)

Age or liking does not count. We are all involved in a project (we Wikipedians like to write Project, with a capital)

(26) [...] e anche per un discorso che, su wikipedia, **non ci sono distinzioni di sorta**, cioé un **amministratore è importante tanto quanto un utente** [...] (WUI15/A06.20577)
and also for a discourse that, on Wikipedia, there are no distinctions whatsoever, i.e., an administrator is just as important as a user

Uncertainty can be attributed to new authors, but in the corpus, we can also find examples of rejection to the wikiquette and rejection to the shared virtual reality. In (27) and (28) authors realize that they have been addressing with 'tu' from the start and ask for confirmation (27) or even apologize (28). In (29) the author alternates between ‚Lei' and 'tu', emphasizing that it is a matter of new habits. In (30) there is a mixing of the two forms, with a tone of criticism and muted with irony (the character from a comedy film (Fantozzi) who tended to mix forms in speech is quoted). In (31) and (32) the use of the form is simply an adaptation to the chosen form of the interaction partner.

(27) Grazie (**ti ho dato del tu** fin dal primo momento ... posso, vero?) (WUI15/A04.67431)
Thank you. I've been on familiar terms with you from the first moment ... I can, can't I?

(28) Salve Angelo, perdonami se **ti do del tu** [...] (WUI15, 18.03.2009)
Hello Angelo, forgive me for adrressing you with ‚tu' [...]

(29) **Guardi**, ovvero **guarda** bisogna che mi abitui agli usi correnti dove qui **tutti si danno del TU** (WUI15/A15.97376)
Look, I mean look I have to get used to the current customs where everyone here calls each other TU

(30) LOL, pure la lezione di grammatica. Il problema è che l'hai usato eccome in altre occasioni **il terzo pronome singolare per rivolgerti a me** (stile: «Fantozzi che fa? **Mi dà del tu? No, no batti lei**!» :-PPP). Pace e bene, fratello :-P" (WUI15/A17.53481)
LOL, even the grammar lesson. The problem is that you've used the third singular pronoun to address me on other occasions (like: 'Fantozzi, what are you doing? Are you calling me 'you'? No, no, you're beating me!' :-PPP). Peace and good, brother :-P'

(31) Ciao. Visto che **mi ha dato del Lei**, glielo daro' anch'io." (WUI15/A19.40028)
Hi. Since you addressed me with ,Lei', I'll address you like that too.

(32) Visto che **mi dai del tu** te lo do anche io. (WUI15/A24.27639)
,Since you adress me with ,tu', I'll address you like that too.

The analysis of metalinguistic comments in the Italian language version shows again that lines of conflict do not run along classical hierarchies; there are new hierarchies, in which the level of seniority in the Wikipedia project plays a central role.

5 Conclusion

This paper analyzed pronominal forms of address in the CMC genre of Wikipedia talk pages for three language versions (German, French, and Italian). When comparing all three languages, the frequencies of discussing pronominal address meta-linguistically are significantly different between the German, French, and Italian Wikipedia language versions.[20] In both analysed Wikipedia subcorpora of the three language versions, i.e., the Wikipedia article talk pages on the one hand and the user talk pages on the other hand, a greater deal of discussions about addressing styles takes place on the user talk pages, with the T form being discussed more frequently than the V form.

In German, people who meet for the first time in face-to-face encounters often use the V form (*Sie*) for pronominal address. Only in special cases (e.g., in the case of certain shared leisure activities such as football) do interlocutors switch directly to the T form *(du)*. In the case of the CMC genre of Wikipedia talk pages considered here, the wikiquette explicitly stipulates that interlocutors also address each other directly using the T form – even if they have never met before. This wikiquette was

20 This holds for testing between the three languages, with the chi-square statistic being *87.5197*. The p-value is < *0.00001*. The result is significant at $p < .05$ for comparing together the frequencies of the formal *you* variant as well as the informal *you* variant between the three languages, with the chi-square statistic being *61.361*. The p-value is < *0.00001*. The result is significant at $p < .05$, cf. https://www.socscistatistics.com/tests/chisquare2/default2.aspx. For each language, the differences in frequencies between the two analysed corpus types, i.e., Wikipedia article talk pages and user talk pages, are significant for the formal *you* variant in German and French, e.g., for the formal *you* variant in German, *Sie*, the difference between the name spaces is significant with the chi-square statistic being *27.5725*. The p-value is < *.00001*. The result is significant at $p < .05$; French: The chi-square statistic is *7.6534*. The p-value is *.005667*. The result is significant at $p < .05$.; not for Italian: The chi-square statistic is *0.4735*. The p-value is *.491403*. The result is not significant at $p < .05$.

established by authors with a high level of seniority. This preference of longstanding authors for the T form goes hand in hand with the fact that they explicitly suspend the usual factors and hierarchies that are decisive for the choice of the appropriate pronominal form of address in face-to-face communication (e.g., age, level of education, professional roles) in their utterances on the talk pages. With this strategy, they suggest – at least superficially – that all authors of the Wikipedia online community have egalitarian rights.

However, new Wikipedia authors do not necessarily share this preference for the T form, as they lack the "perceived commonalities". The qualitative analysis also showed that the discussions on the pronominal forms of address on the talk pages are particularly controversial when long-time Wikipedia authors linguistically construct new Wikipedia-specific hierarchies (*newbie)* in order to discredit new authors. Basically, the use and negotiation of pronominal forms of address in Wikipedia is an indication that Wikipedia is not comprehensively a platform with egalitarian aspirations, but that long-standing authors constitute linguistically an ad-hoc-meritocracy.

In French, symmetrical *vous* is in fact still the normal starting point for public interactions between adults who have no prior relation. It is commonly used between strangers or people who rarely interact with each other. In several user surveys no consensus regarding a standardized form of address in the French Wikipedia could be generated, so both forms of addressing continue to be used depending on a user's preference. When investigating Wikipedia talk pages, there are users who prefer the informal *tu*; nonetheless, the formal *vous* form of address plays an important role in Wikipedia user addressing. The authors adopt a pro-V form stance, emphasizing the value of social distance between themselves and others. They make a clear separation between work on Wikipedia and, say, communicating with friends or family. These findings point to a certain degree of reluctance to adopt a less formal T form. Once the writers express terms of familiarity and intimacy, it might be challenging for them to get back to a formal stage of using V forms. In cases where Wikipedia authors are explicitly opting for a T form, personal preference as a factor closely related to one's own overall ease with address are mentioned as reasonings by Wikipedia authors.

Subject pronouns are considered as an optional choice in Italian, because they are inherent to the verbal morphology. So when they are used, sometimes also together with nominal forms, they strategically add pragmatic meanings to a speaker's utterance. Symmetry/asymmetry and familiarity/distance coupled with context formality regulate their use. The reciprocal use is preferred to index familiarity or to signal social distance and/or mutual respect: reciprocal V forms are considered the default option in academic interactions; the non-reciprocal use when there is an asymmetrical distribution of power (age, job rank, and social status). Different factors as levels of formality of the setting, degree of familiarity, and individual preferences play an important role.

The dominance of T forms, considering vicinity, familiarity and solidarity, the norm in CMC communication is confirmed also in Wikipedia, where social hierarchy is weakened and simplified. The shared "perceived commonalities" and the familiarity due to being part of a community, even if they have never met face-to-face, is also a typical characteristic of the Italian Wikipedia. The use of the T form is considered a convention and used by default from longtime authors as the only correct form of address in Wikipedia, enforcing the wikiquette and suspending, superficially, differences. Through this stancetaking, they position themselves as superior to other interlocutors (new authors with limited experience with Wikipedia), who use the V form. The analysis of metalinguistic comments in the Italian language version shows again that lines of conflict run along new hierarchies, in which the level of seniority in the Wikipedia project plays a central role.

Aspects of pronominal address among speakers of German, French, and Italian are characterized by instability and uncertainty. The use of T forms (GER: *du*, FR: *tu*, IT: *tu*) is controversial among Wikipedia authors. They discuss aspects of hierarchies, seniority, levels of proximity and distance, as well as preference. The overall preference for either a V or a T form is highly individual and greatly influenced by notions of social status and familiarity between the users. Pronominal address in this CMC genre is a topic that has received little attention so far, but is very informative for linguistic investigation: This is the case because in CMC with its (partially) anonymous and translocal contexts, pronominal address poses different challenges for interlocutors than in face-to-face communication. In addition, the CMC genre of Wikipedia talk pages is particularly suitable for cross-linguistic comparisons because comparable corpus data is available in large quantities in numerous languages. In further studies, it would certainly also be interesting to examine the difference between pronominal forms of address on the various talk pages in more detail: The central question would then be whether the types of pronominal form of address on user talk pages differ from that on article talk pages.

References

Ayers, Phoebe, Charles Matthews & Ben Yates. 2008. *How Wikipedia works: And how you can be a part of it*. San Francisco: No Starch Press.

Bader, Jennifer. 2002. *Schriftlichkeit und Mündlichkeit in der Chat-Kommunikation*, Networx Nr. 29.

Beißwenger, Michael & Harald Lüngen. 2022. Korpora internetbasierter Kommunikation. In Michael Beißwenger, Lothar Lemnitzer & Carolin Müller-Spitzer (eds.), *Forschen in der Linguistik. Eine Methodeneinführung für das Germanistik-Studium*, 431–448. Paderborn: Fink.

Bouissac, Paul. 2019. Forms and functions of the French personal pronouns in social interactions and literary texts. In *The Social Dynamics of Pronominal Systems*. 133–150, Amsterdam: John Benjamins.
Brown, Penelope & Stephen C. Levinson. 1987. *Politeness: Some universals in language usage*. Cambridge: Cambridge University Press.
Brown, Roger & Albert Gilman. 1960. The pronouns of power and solidarity. In Thomas A. Sebeok (ed.), *Style in Language*, 253–276. Cambridge: MIT Press.
Clyne, Micheal, Heinz L. Kretzenbacher, Catrin Norrby & Jane Warren. 2004. Address in some Western European languages. In Christo Moskovsky (ed.), *Proceedings of the 2003 Conference of the Australian Linguistic Society*.
Clyne, Michael, Catrin Norrby & Jane Warren. 2009. *Language and Human Relations. Styles of Address in Contemporary Language*. Cambridge: Cambridge University Press.
Da Milano, Federica. 2015. Italian. In Konstanze Jungbluth & Federica Da Milano, Federica (eds.), *Manual of Deixis in Romance Languages*, 59–74. Berlin & Boston: De Gruyter.
Dal Negro, Silvia & Giuseppina Pani. 2019. Tu ed io nel discorso: deissi, allocuzione e accordo come problema di ricerca e di didattica. In Elena Nuzzo & Ineke Vedder (eds.), *Lingua in Contesto: La Prospettiva Pragmatica*. Studi AItLA, 9, 47–63.
Davidson, Brad. 1996. 'Pragmatic weight' and Spanish subject pronouns: the pragmatic and discourse uses of 'tú' and 'yo' in spoken Madrid Spanish. *Journal of Pragmatics*. 26, 543–565.
De Oliveira, Sandi Michele. 2013. 12. Address in computer-mediated communication. In Susan Herring, Dieter Stein & Tuija Virtanen (eds.), *Pragmatics of Computer-Mediated Communication*, 291–314. Berlin & Boston: De Gruyter Mouton.
Deppermann, Arnulf. 2015. Positioning. In Anna de Fina & Alexandra Georgakopoulou (eds.), *The Handbook of Narrative Analysis*, 369–387. Oxford: Wiley-Blackwell.
Dewaele, Jean-Marc. 2004. "Vous or tu? Native and non-native speakers of French on a sociolinguistic tightrope". *IRAI* 42, 383–402.
Douglass, Kate. 2009. Second-person pronoun use in French-language blogs: Developing L2 sociopragmatic competence. In Abraham, Lee B. & Lawrence Williams (eds.), *Electronic Discourse in Language Learning and Language Teaching*, 213–240. Amsterdam: John Benjamins.
Du Bois, John W.. 2007. The stance triangle. In Robert Englebretson (ed.), *Stancetaking in Discourse: Subjectivity, Evaluation, Interaction*, 139–182. Amsterdam: John Benjamins.
Duden-Grammatik = Wöllstein, Angelika. 2016. *Die Grammatik.* Duden, Band 4. Berlin: Dudenverlag.
Duranti, Alessandro. 1984. The social meaning of subject pronouns in Italian conversation. *Text* 4, 277–311.
Formentelli, Maicol & John Hajek. 2013. Italian L2 address strategies in an Australian university setting: a comparison with L1 Italian and L1 English practice. In Bert Peeters, Kerry Mullan & Cristine Béal (eds.), *Cross-culturally Speaking, Speaking Cross-culturally*. 77–106. Newcastle: CSP.
Formentelli, Maicol & John Hajek. 2015. Address in Italian academic interactions: the power of distance and (non-)reciprocity. In Catrin Norrby & Camilla Wide (eds.), *Address Practice as Social Action. European Perspectives*, 119–140, Basingstoke: Palgrave Macmillan.
Formentelli, Maicol & Maria Pavesi. 2022. The pragmatic functions of tu and lei in films: Converging patterns of address across translated and original Italian dialogue. *Journal of Pragmatics* 201, 15–31.
Fillmore, Charles. 1975. *Santa Cruz lectures on deixis 1971.* Bloomington: Indiana University Linguistics Club.
Gastaldi, Erika. 2002. Italiano digitato. *Italiano e oltre* 17, 3, 134–138.
Gredel, Eva. 2017. Digital discourse analysis and Wikipedia: Bridging the gap between Foucauldian discourse analysis and digital conversation analysis. *Journal of Pragmatics* 115, 99–114.

Gredel, Eva. 2023. Siezt du noch oder duzt du schon? Korpusstudie zum Gebrauch und zur Aushandlung sozialdeiktischer Zeichen auf digitalen Plattformen. In Simon Meier-Vieracker, Lars Bülow, Konstanze Marx & Robert Mroczynski (eds.), *Digitale Pragmatik*, 39–57. Berlin & Heidelberg: Metzler.

Helmbrecht, Johannes. 2006. Typologie und Diffusion von Höflichkeitspronomina in Europa, *Folia Linguistica* 39, 3–4, 417–452.

Helmbrecht, Johannes. 2015. A typology of non-prototypical uses of personal pronouns: synchrony and diachrony, *Journal of Pragmatics* 88, 176–189.

Hess-Lüttich, Ernest W.B. & Eva Wilde. 2003. Der Chat als Textsorte und/oder als Dialogsorte?, *Linguistik online* 13, 1, 161–180.

Kretzenbacher, Heinz & Doris Schüpbach. 2015. Communities of Addressing Practice? Address in Internet forums Based in German-Speaking Countries. In Catrin Norrby & Camilla Wide (eds.), *Adress Practice As Social Action: European Perspectives*, 33–53. New York: Palgrave.

Kretzenbacher, Heinz & Wulf Segebrecht. 1991. Vom *Sie zum Du – mehr als nur eine Konvention?* Hamburg: Wallstein Verlag.

Kretzenbacher, Heinz. 2010. Man ordnet ja bestimmte Leute irgendwo ein für sich ...". Anrede und soziale Deixis. *Deutsche Sprache* 38, 1, 1–18.

Kretzenbacher, Heinz. 2011. Addressing Policy on the Web: Netiquettes and Emerging Policies of Language Use in German Internet Forums. In Catrin Norrby & John Hajek (eds.), *Uniformity and Diversity in Language Policy: Global Perspectives*, 226–241. Bristol: De Gruyter, Blue Ridge Summit: Multilingual Matters.

Kretzenbacher, Heinz. 2005. *‚hier im großen internetz, wo sich alle dududuzen' Internet discourse politeness and German address*. Paper given at the 3rd International Conference on Language Variation in Europe (ICLaVE).

Leech, Geoffrey. 1983. *Principles of pragmatics*. London & New York: Longman.

Lüngen, Harald & Marc Kupietz. 2020. IBK- und Social Media-Korpora am Leibniz-Institut für Deutsche Sprache. In Konstanze Marx, Henning Lobin & Axel Schmidt (eds.), *Deutsch in Sozialen Medien: Interaktiv – multimodal – vielfältig*, 319–342. Berlin: De Gruyter.

Maeder, Costantino & Romane Werner. 2019. T-V address practices in Italian: diachronic, diatopic, and diastratic analyses. In Paul Bouissac (ed.), *The Social Dynamics of Pronominal Systems: A Comparative Approach*. 99–131, Amsterdam: John Benjamins.

Maley, Catherine. 1972. "Historically Speaking, Tu or Vous?" *The French Review* 45, 5, 999–1006.

Molinelli, Piera. 2002. "Lei non sa chi sono io!": potere, solidarietà, rispetto e distanza nella comunicazione. In *Linguistica e fonologia* 14, 283–302.

Morford, Janet. 1997. Social Indexicality in French Pronominal Address. *Journal of Linguistic Anthropology* 7, 1, 3–37.

Nübling, Damaris, Antje Dammel, Janet Duke & Renata Szczepaniak. 2017. *Historische Sprachwissenschaft des Deutschen. Eine Einführung in die Prinzipien des Sprachwandels*. Tübingen: Narr.

Ochs, Elinor 1996. Linguistic resources for socializing humanity. In John J. Gumperz & Stephen Levinson (eds.), *Rethinking Linguistic Relativity*. 407–437, New York: Cambridge University Press.

Orletti, Franca. 2000. *La conversazione diseguale. Potere e interazione*. Roma: Carocci.

Peeters, Bert. 2004. TU OU VOUS ? *Zeitschrift Für Französische Sprache Und Literatur* 114, 1, 1–17.

Pistolesi, Elena. 1997. "Il visibile parlare di IRC (Internet Relay Chat)". In *Quaderni del Dipartimento di Linguistica* 8, 213–246.

Pistolesi, Elena. 1998. IRC (Internet Chat Relay): Una nuova tecnologia Guida storica, linguistica e tecnica. *Web Italica della RAI*.

Renzi, Lorenzo. 1993. La deissi personale e il suo uso sociale. *Studi digrammatica italiana* 15, 347–390.

Renzi, Lorenzo. 1995. La deissi personale e il suo uso sociale. In Lorenzo Renzi & Anna Cardinaletti (eds.), *Grande grammatica italiana di consultazione*, 350–375, Bologna: il Mulino.
Rebelos, Margareta & Antonella Strambi. 2009. Address Pronouns in Italian CMC Exchanges: A 'Good Example' for L2 Learners?. *Italica* 86, 1, 59–79.
Schoch, Marianne. 1978. Problème sociolinguistique des pronoms d'allocution < tu > et < vous >. Enquête à Lausanne, *La linguistique* 14, 1, 55–73.
Schulze, Markus. 1999. Substitution of paraverbal and nonverbal cues in the written medium of IRC. In Bernd Naumann (ed.) *Dialogue analysis and the mass media*. Proceedings of the international conference in Erlangen, April 2-3, 1998, 65–82, Tübingen: Niemeyer.
Simon, Horst. 2003. *Für eine grammatische Kategorie ›Respekt‹ im Deutschen: Synchronie, Diachronie und Typologie der deutschen Anredepronomina*. Tübingen: Niemeyer.
Spitzmüller, Jürgen. 2022. *Soziolinguistik. Eine Einführung*. Berlin: Springer.
Stegbauer, Christian. 2009. *Wikipedia: Das Rätsel der Kooperation*. Wiesbaden: VS Verlag für Sozialwissenschaften.
Stewart, Miranda. 2003. 'Pragmatic weight' and face: pronominal presence and the case of the Spanish second person singular subject pronoun tú. *Pragmat* 35, 2, 191–206.
Svennevig, Jan. 1999. *Getting acquainted in conversation: A study of initial interactions*. Amsterdam: John Benjamins.
Truan, Naomi. 2022. (When) Can I say *Du* to You? The metapragmatics of forms of address on German-Speaking Twitter. *Journal of Pragmatics* 191, 227–239.
Williams, Lawrence & Rémi A. van Compernolle. 2007. Second-Person Pronoun Use in On-Line French-Language Chat Environments. *The French Review* 80, 4, 804–20.
Williams, Lawrence & Rémi A. van Compernolle. 2009a. On versus tu and vous: Pronouns with indefinite reference in synchronous electronic French discourse, *Language Sciences* 31, 4, 409–427.
Williams, Lawrence & Rémi A. van Compernolle. 2009b. Second-person pronoun use in French language discussion fora. *Journal of French Language Studies* 19, 3, 363–380.
Zifonun, Gisela, Ludger Hoffmann & Bruno Strecker. 1997. *Grammatik der deutschen Sprache*. Berlin & New York: De Gruyter.

Ludovic Tanguy, Céline Poudat, and Lydia-Mai Ho-Dac

Investigating extreme cases in Wikipedia talk pages: Some insights on user behaviours

Abstract: The study presented in this paper is part of a larger project that explores various dimensions of Wikipedia talk pages, in which we propose to examine the dynamics of interaction between Wikipedians. Based on a dataset of 3.4 million threads from the English Wikipedia talk pages, we specifically focus on extreme cases. Our approach targets the general and structural features of these threads (who posts when, and in which order) and not primarily their language content. After a quantitative overview of the main structural characteristics of our dataset, focusing on the general features of the discussions, we select a subset of items for a closer examination. These include the most prolific users, the longest threads (in terms of total duration, number of posts or number of distinct users involved) and the longest monologues (threads with multiple posts by the same single user). In each case we propose a coarse-grain typology and a number of features that relate to the origin of the underlying behaviours. We assume that the analysis of such extreme cases can help to better understand expected and unexpected interactions between Wikipedians. In other words, extreme cases may help us better understand various phenomena in Wikipedia dynamics of interaction, but also in the way individuals interact in writing on the Web. Indeed, some of the observed behaviours are mainly specific to the collaborative editing objective and context of Wikipedia, such as polls, logbooks, diaries, to-do lists etc. But other unusual types of discussion (long-time exchanges, monologues) can be expected to be found in other forms of asynchronous computer-mediated communication.

Keywords: Wikipedia talk pages, Wikipedia discussions, interaction dynamics, thread analysis, user behaviour

Ludovic Tanguy, CLLE: CNRS & University of Toulouse, France, e-mail: ludovic.tanguy@univ-tlse2.fr
Céline Poudat, BCL: CNRS & University of Nice Côte d'Azur, France,
e-mail: celine.poudat@univ-cotedazur.fr
Lydia-Mai Ho-Dac, CLLE: CNRS & University of Toulouse, France,
e-mail: lydia-mai.ho-dac@univ-tlse2.fr

https://doi.org/10.1515/9783111434018-019

1 Introduction

Wikipedia talk pages contain the discussions that take place behind the well-known encyclopaedic articles. They represent a valuable source of computer-mediated communication data which is abundant, multilingual and freely accessible, making them suitable for large-scale studies on generic online interactions (Gómez et al. 2011, Lüngen and Herzberg 2019). They have indeed been extensively studied in the last decades to better understand the dynamics of cooperation and interaction in the collaborative encyclopaedia. Many dimensions of Wikipedia talk pages have already been studied and described, including the topics discussed (Schneider et al. 2010), the dialog acts (Ferschke et al. 2014) or the moves and arguments within the interactions (Kopf 2022). These studies have highlighted some of the main practices in Wikipedia talk pages, providing some insights in the dynamics of interaction between Wikipedians (Laniado et al. 2011).

Our study takes an unprecedented look at the data, concentrating on the marginal, or even extreme phenomena and behaviours in Wikipedia talk pages. Our objective is to observe specific behaviours of the Wikipedia community which can be found in other more inconspicuous contexts. Our methodological approach focuses exclusively on outliers i.e., the items that exhibit unexpected characteristics at the thread or user levels. The characteristics for which we chose to identify the outliers are only structural features that could be computed in every language available in Wikipedia because the same collaborative writing technology is used in every language. As a result, our method could be applied in every version of Wikipedia in order to contrast the extreme behaviours in different languages and cultures.

The extreme behaviours we identified are highly prolific users, excessively long threads (in terms of duration, number of posts or users involved) and monologues. We assume that the analysis of such extreme cases can help to better understand expected and unexpected interactions between Wikipedians. This will also allow us to highlight practices which are generally neglected although they may be found in more typical configurations.

In this chapter, we only present the study of the extreme cases found in the English Wikipedia. After presenting our data and method in section 2, section 3 gives for each extreme behaviour a quantitative and a qualitative analysis in order to take a first step towards a typology of extremes in Wikipedia.

2 Looking for the extremes: Data overview and method

We will present in the following the data used for investigating the user's behaviours, namely a large collection of Wikipedia talk pages. Section 2.1 describes how it has been collected and prepared. We then present (2.2) the behavioural features we have selected and an overview of their statistics, and discuss in 2.3 the methodological approach of focusing on extreme values.

2.1 Dataset: English Wikipedia talk pages

We base our study on the English part of the *EFG_WikiCorpus*, a comparable corpus which consists of talk pages extracted from the August 2019 dumps of the English, French and German Wikipedia. Multilingual links between talk pages are made according to the links between article, portal and category pages (Ho-Dac 2024). In the *EFG_WikiCorpus*, the English part contains 2,025,888 talk pages. We limited the corpus to the generic talk pages directly associated with the articles, including the archives, but discarding discussions that occur in other places of the Wikipedia ecosystem (users' home pages, administrative debates, etc.). The data is available online on the Ortolang repository[1] with a Creative Commons license (https://hdl.handle.net/11403/efg-wikicorpus, last accessed 14 February 2025).

It is worth noting that talk pages on Wikipedia are produced on the same infrastructure as the articles, using *wikicode* formatting. This means that a talk page is fully editable by any user and that its layout and organisation can be freely modified, in spite of strong recommendations from the Wikipedia community. Talk pages typically feature a section-based structure, with each section representing a distinct discussion having its own heading and clear boundaries. Individual messages are organised along a tree structure which follows the example of the more traditional online discussion platforms. However, the wikicode allows freeform editing which may lead to unusual structures in discussion threads, such as the re-sectioning of existing talk pages (used for archival purposes for example), the writing of non-contiguous answers to a previous long message (similar to emails), or postings appearing in a non-chronological order. This situation has direct consequences on the parsing of Wikipedia talk pages, which requires additional efforts to identify the network of interactions.

1 https://www.ortolang.fr/ (last accessed 14 February 2025).

Despite these challenges, we segmented each talk page into sections, with each section representing a thread. Each thread was segmented into posts (or comments or messages) following a heuristic based on signatures and indentations. The whole structure was then converted into XML format following the TEI-CMC guidelines, so that each post is associated with its author's name and date. Finally, threads containing a post written by a bot were discarded. In the end our corpus contains 3,385,583 threads and 8,873,620 messages.

2.2 Central tendencies and typical discussion in Wikipedia talk pages

Here we present the dataset characteristics that we considered relevant for this study. These features are directly related to the users' behaviour (as individuals or as a group), straightforward to interpret, and easy to extract.

All these features are either counts or durations, allowing for a simple overview using central tendency metrics. Table 1 shows the main statistics for each feature: maximum value, median and mean. Minimal values were not indicated as they are trivially equal to 1 for counts and to the precision value for timestamps (1 minute).

Table 1: Overview of the behavioural features taken into account: number of users, number of posts and duration.

Feature	Maximum	Median	Mean
Number of posts per user	25,078	1	20.06
Number of posts per thread	651	1	2.62
Number of users involved	97	1	1.85
Duration of threads with 2 or more posts (N=1,688,939)	16.6 years	5.3 days	260 days
Longest duration between 2 posts in the thread	16.1 years	4.1 days	233 days
Number of posts per single user thread (N=1,812,457)	150	1	1.08

Users author an average of 20 messages in their global participation to the Wikipedia effort discussion. Note that the median value indicates that a majority of users post a single message in all.

A Wikipedia discussion is quite short in average (2–3 messages) and involves 2 users. The duration can be very short, but a thread usually lasts several months (as late replies arrive after this amount of time). The example in Figure 1 illustrates a typical short thread in terms of number of posts (only 2) and duration (15 hours).

oops

Gah, I can't believe I reverted to that wrong version, was by accident, apparently someone did it before me and it messed it up. Sorry. -- Natalinasmpf 00:31, 12 July 2005 (UTC)

Stay cool Natalinasmpf, it has nothing to do with you or this Wikipedia article. It is about the Wikipedia as a whole. Ww ww ww 15:32, 12 July 2005 (UTC)

Figure 1: A typical thread with a 2 users collaborating behind the article about "Wikipedia" https://en.wikipedia.org/wiki/Talk:Wikipedia/Archive_5#oops (last accessed 14 February 2025).

In this thread, a user opens a discussion to report an action (*Natalinasmpf* informed the community of an editing accident she made) and a different user expresses a positive attitude towards her (*Ww ww ww* replied 15 hours later to reassure her). As stated in Ferschke et al. (2012), these two dialog acts are fairly frequent in the English Wikipedia talk pages. Among the 2,729 posts for which their dialog acts' annotation scheme was applicable, 749 posts (27%) concern *Self commitment* (report of past action or commitment to action in the future) and 655 (24%) are *Interpersonal* (positive or negative attitude towards another user). The most frequent dialog act they observed is *Article criticism* with 65% posts. The less frequent category is *Requests* with only 16% posts (as the first post in Figure 6). As a result, according to Ferschke et al. (2014), the most frequent Wikipedia discussion profile is when users criticise the quality of a specific part of the article.

Nevertheless, these findings only cover 45% of the posts that composed their dataset. In fact, Ferschke et al. (2014) plan to annotate 1,864 threads extracted from the April 2011 dump. Among the 4,923 posts composing these threads, only 2,729 posts fall into at least one dialog act label. According to them, this is mainly because their annotation scheme focuses only on dialog acts that are relevant for article quality assessment and improvement activities. But Wikipedia talk pages are also used for other purposes that we propose to discover and examine in our analysis of the extreme cases.

As seen in Table 1, there are large differences between mean and median counts or durations. This suggests highly skewed distributions with numerous high-value outliers for each variable. This is confirmed by the maximum values each of these features can rise to.

Some users can be extremely prolific (25,078 is the equivalent of 5 messages per day over 15 years), which is quite impressive considering that a Wikipedia comment is quite long (average of 78 tokens in our corpus) and addresses complex matters. In other words this number cannot be directly compared to the quantities achieved per user in social networks such as Twitter/X. The discussions themselves can be very long, involve a large number of users and last for years. Finally, a discussion can be very long even without an interlocutor. These specific phenomena are the target of our investigation.

2.3 Focusing on extremes and outliers: Methodological aspects

As explained in the introduction, our methodological approach is atypical as it focuses exclusively on the items at the extremities of the spectrum. This methodological choice calls for justification and background.

The presence of atypical values and items in a collection is a well-known issue, certainly as ancient as statistics themselves. Their identification and the measure of their impact is a concern for any statistical analysis. Osborne and Overbay (2019) give an overview of their potential causes (such as an error in the original data, its sampling or processing), insisting on the fact that outliers can be genuine data items and should therefore be taken into consideration. Of course, the authors provide the most usual methods for identifying them (e.g., z-score thresholds) and discuss their impact on the central tendency measures that generally requires their removal from the dataset. In most cases, extreme cases are ignored and discarded as noise.

Certainly, extreme cases or anomalies are logically the natural target of specific studies that focus on crises (such as anatomical pathology or climate science).

However, a number of authors from very diverse domains have proposed to use these specific items as a focus of their investigation, and have advocated the insights that can be gained from them.

Authors promoting the study of extreme cases can be found in sociology (Chen 2016), history (Ginzburg 2014) or economics (Beamish and Hasse 2022). From a more epistemological point of view, Flyvberg explained the reasons for doing so.

> When the objective is to achieve the greatest possible amount of information on a given problem or phenomenon, a representative case or a random sample may not be the most appropriate strategy. This is because the typical or average case is often not the richest in information. Atypical or extreme cases often reveal more information because they activate more actors and more basic mechanisms in the situation studied. (Flyvbjerg 2011).

We also found that the proponents of extreme cases are more generally advocates of qualitative studies, and they generally regret that these approaches are quite rare and disregarded by scientific editors. Indeed, they insist that focusing on mainstream phenomena cannot lead to substantial advance in the development of theory.

Flyvberg more precisely states that (among other strategies to divert from the simple typical or case) extreme or deviant individuals are specifically useful in order *"[t]o understand the limits of existing theories and to develop new concepts, variables, and theories that are able to account for deviant cases"* Flyvbjerg (2011).

In our case, we considered that previous extensive studies have been able to give a quite complete view of what is the "average" discussion on a Wikipedia talk page, and that further investigation may benefit from such an approach.

Technically, we isolated the users and discussions in our corpus which exhibit the highest values for each selected variable. We then examined the individual items and proposed a coarse-grain typology in order to explain the underlying behaviours. As we will see in the next section, the qualitative analysis of these outliers allows us to identify behaviours that are made possible by the Wikipedia device, and that may even be typical of Wikipedia interactions.

3 Extreme cases

We will examine the extreme cases for each of the dimensions considered. We will begin with the users themselves before examining specific discussions.

3.1 Most prolific message authors

Our first investigation targets Wikipedia users who have produced a significant number of posts on talk pages. In our dataset, we found a total of 499,137 different usernames in the signatures of all talk pages (without including the bots or the unregistered users who are only identified by their IP addresses). As expected, the number of posts per user follows a Zipfian distribution, meaning that while a majority of users have only written a single comment, a few Wikipedians are the authors of a very large number of messages. The user ranking #1 posted 25,078 messages, the user ranking #10 14,281, and the user ranking #100 5,900.

To compare message-posting behaviour with actual Wikipedia editing activity, we gathered data on the number of edits (i.e., the modifications made on any page of the Wikipedia, including posts in any kind of talk page) and the number of posts in the article talk pages for the 1000 most productive Wikipedia editors, as indicated in the official leader board[2] (as of July 2019), shown in Figure 2. We measured

2 https://en.wikipedia.org/w/index.php?title=Wikipedia:WBE (last accessed 14 February 2025).

a weak positive correlation (ρ=0.09) between the number of edits and the number of messages. As an example, the most active editor of the English Wikipedia (Steven Pruitt, who was responsible for more than 3 million edits as of 2019, and over 5 million as of 2023) has never participated in any discussion in an article talk page (although he did post some messages in a few users' personal talk pages, not included in our dataset). Similarly, several of the most prolific authors on the articles talk pages rarely modify the articles themselves, limiting their role to commenting or proofreading the text written by others, or to enforcing Wikipedia policy and rules through discussion. This observation is undoubtedly an interesting parameter to consider for creating user profiles in Wikipedia.

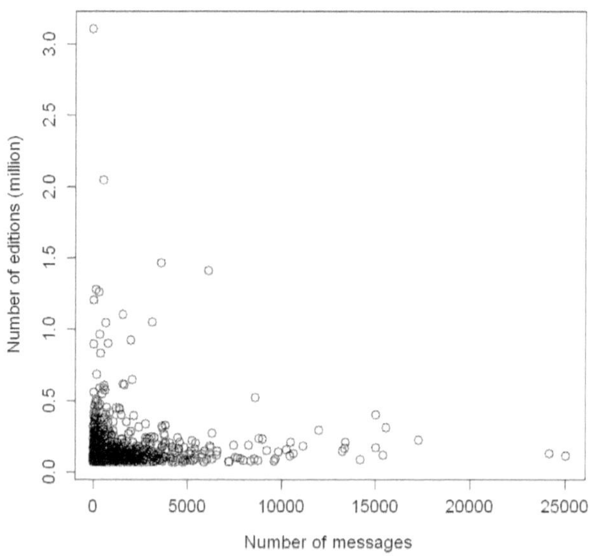

Figure 2: Number of editions versus number of messages for the 1000 most productive Wikipedia editors.

Although it is difficult to outline a precise profile for these most productive posters, it seems that many of them assume a role of referee and intervene on a large number of topics and issues. This role can either be self-attributed or officialised as a Wikipedia administrator. In some cases their interventions are considered as problematic for the community, for example defending political or ethical positions and therefore not following the neutrality principle that is a pillar of the Wikipedia effort. This can lead to their banishment from Wikipedia, as was the case for the most productive user in our dataset.

These first observations would clearly show that taking part in a Wikipedia discussion can to some extent be considered as a specific activity, uncorrelated from article writing, at least for a subset of the Wikipedia users.

3.2 Most active threads (highest numbers of posts/users)

The second phenomenon we investigated is the number of posts per thread. If 53% of the threads consist of a single message, some of them contain several hundred posts.

We examined the 100 longest threads in our dataset (threads with more than 90 posts, up to 651). Surprisingly, these very long threads rarely imply a large number of participants (median of 14 different users) and they may even be written by a single user (this particular category is examined more closely in §3.5).

If we only consider their organisation and structure, these very long threads can be classified as follows:

- 68 of the 100 examined threads can be qualified as *standard discussions*. Indeed, these threads follow the conventional organisation where users exchange their views and arguments, following a tree-like structure where the replies and reactions to previous posts are indicated through cumulative indentations. However, due to the extensive size and depth of the threads, indentation can hinder their readability. To address this, some users (most of the time participants to the discussion) sometimes use the flexibility of the talk pages (based on the same wikicode used for article pages) to organise them into sections. When appropriate, subtopics can be identified and used to start a new nested thread in a subsection, while remaining in the same section and therefore related to the same topic. When not, arbitrary breaks are introduced to reset the indent level when it becomes too deep, as can be seen in Figure 3 below. Although this was not the focus of our inquiry, it appears that, as could be expected, the longest discussions are invariably conflictual in nature (as Denis et al. had already shown in 2012). However, Wikipedia discussions remain globally polite and moderate, especially when compared to other forms of public online communication (Hobman et al. 2002, Poudat and Chandelier 2024).

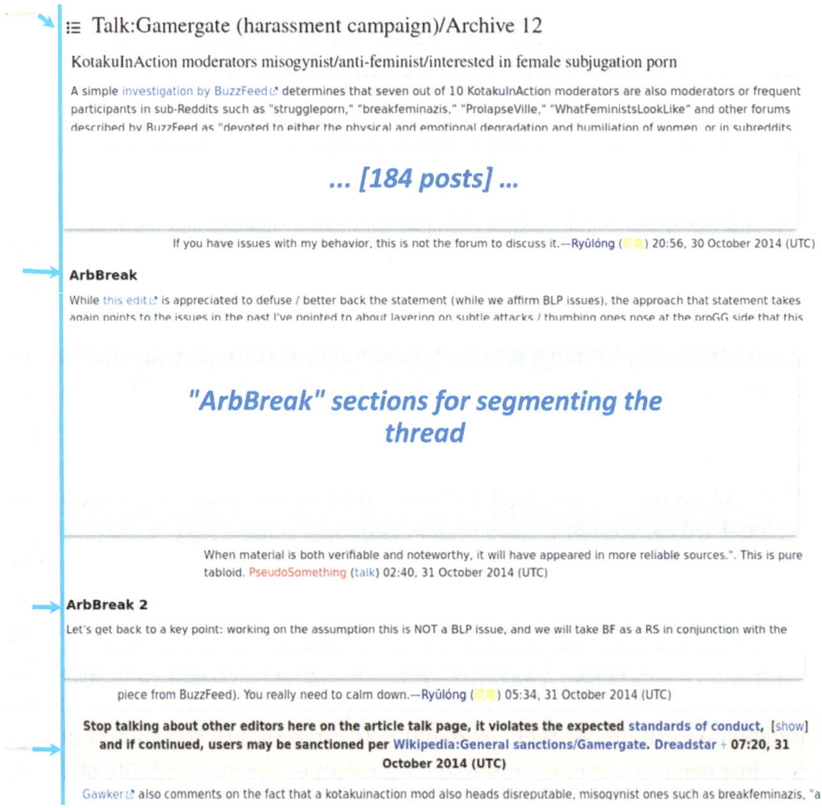

Figure 3: Overview of a long discussion with arbitrary breaks. On the left is a bird's eye view of the thread with indents, from which the arrows indicate specific points. https://en.wikipedia.org/wiki/Talk:Gamergate_(harassment_campaign)/Archive_12#KotakuInAction_moderators_misogynist/anti-feminist/interested_in_female_subjugation_porn (last accessed 14 February 2025).

– 26 of the 100 longest threads are *polls* or *series of polls*. In these threads a user collects the position or opinion of others on specific topics, which is a common practice in Wikipedia talks, as we develop below. As such, every single vote by the polled users counts for a message. The length of these threads can be attributed to the high number of participants (up to 97), multiple related polls grouped together (with the same users posting a message for each subtopic), or one or more nested threads developing inside the poll. The longest thread in our data (651 posts) falls in this category; an extract can be seen in Figure 4.

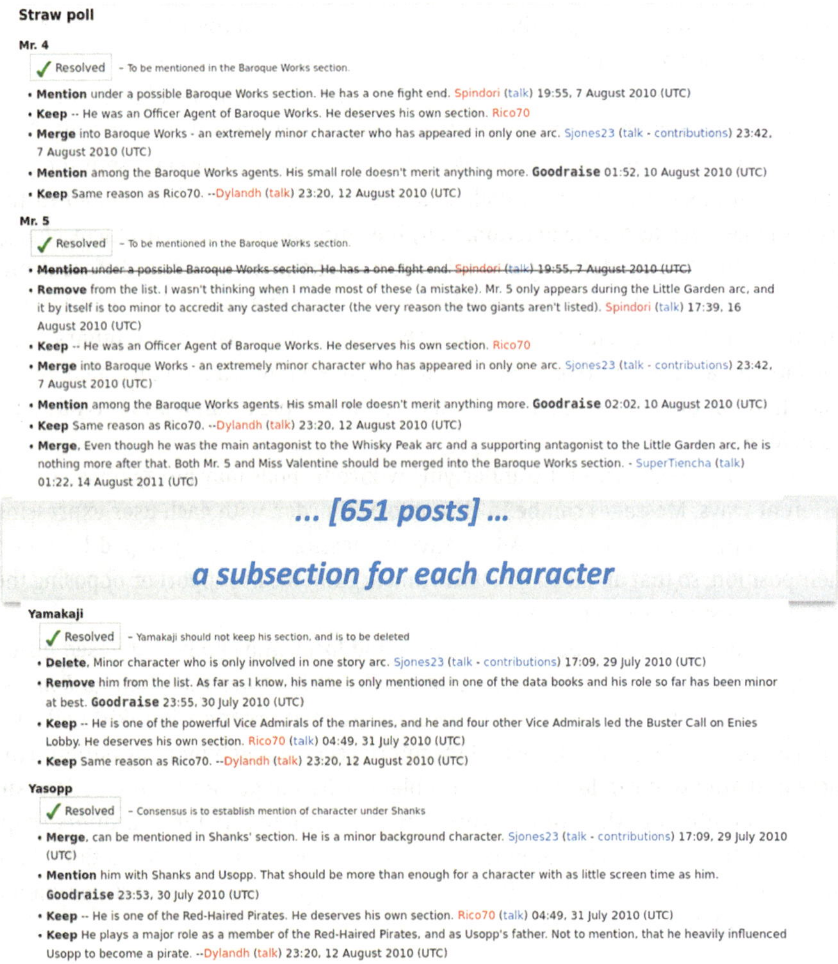

Straw poll

Mr. 4

✓ Resolved – To be mentioned in the Baroque Works section.

- **Mention** under a possible Baroque Works section. He has a one fight end. Spindori (talk) 19:55, 7 August 2010 (UTC)
- **Keep** -- He was an Officer Agent of Baroque Works. He deserves his own section. Rico70
- **Merge** into Baroque Works - an extremely minor character who has appeared in only one arc. Sjones23 (talk - contributions) 23:42, 7 August 2010 (UTC)
- **Mention** among the Baroque Works agents. His small role doesn't merit anything more. **Goodraise** 01:52, 10 August 2010 (UTC)
- **Keep** Same reason as Rico70. --Dylandh (talk) 23:20, 12 August 2010 (UTC)

Mr. 5

✓ Resolved – To be mentioned in the Baroque Works section.

- ~~**Mention** under a possible Baroque Works section. He has a one fight end. Spindori (talk) 19:55, 7 August 2010 (UTC)~~
- **Remove** from the list. I wasn't thinking when I made most of these (a mistake). Mr. 5 only appears during the Little Garden arc, and it by itself is too minor to accredit any casted character (the very reason the two giants aren't listed). Spindori (talk) 17:39, 16 August 2010 (UTC)
- **Keep** -- He was an Officer Agent of Baroque Works. He deserves his own section. Rico70
- **Merge** into Baroque Works - an extremely minor character who has appeared in only one arc. Sjones23 (talk - contributions) 23:42, 7 August 2010 (UTC)
- **Mention** among the Baroque Works agents. His small role doesn't merit anything more. **Goodraise** 02:02, 10 August 2010 (UTC)
- **Keep** Same reason as Rico70. --Dylandh (talk) 23:20, 12 August 2010 (UTC)
- **Merge**. Even though he was the main antagonist to the Whisky Peak arc and a supporting antagonist to the Little Garden arc, he is nothing more after that. Both Mr. 5 and Miss Valentine should be merged into the Baroque Works section. - SuperTiencha (talk) 01:22, 14 August 2011 (UTC)

... [651 posts] ...

a subsection for each character

Yamakaji

✓ Resolved – Yamakaji should not keep his section, and is to be deleted

- **Delete**. Minor character who is only involved in one story arc. Sjones23 (talk - contributions) 17:09, 29 July 2010 (UTC)
- **Remove** him from the list. As far as I know, his name is only mentioned in one of the data books and his role so far has been minor at best. **Goodraise** 23:55, 30 July 2010 (UTC)
- **Keep** -- He is one of the powerful Vice Admirals of the marines, and he and four other Vice Admirals led the Buster Call on Enies Lobby. He deserves his own section. Rico70 (talk) 04:49, 31 July 2010 (UTC)
- **Keep** Same reason as Rico70. --Dylandh (talk) 23:20, 12 August 2010 (UTC)

Yasopp

✓ Resolved – Consensus is to establish mention of character under Shanks

- **Merge**, can be mentioned in Shanks' section. He is a minor background character. Sjones23 (talk - contributions) 17:09, 29 July 2010 (UTC)
- **Mention** him with Shanks and Usopp. That should be more than enough for a character with as little screen time as him. **Goodraise** 23:53, 30 July 2010 (UTC)
- **Keep** -- He is one of the Red-Haired Pirates. He deserves his own section. Rico70 (talk) 04:49, 31 July 2010 (UTC)
- **Keep** He plays a major role as a member of the Red-Haired Pirates, and as Usopp's father. Not to mention, that he heavily influenced Usopp to become a pirate. --Dylandh (talk) 23:20, 12 August 2010 (UTC)

Figure 4: Overview of the longest thread in our dataset: 651 posts forming a series of 153 polls in which 6 users indicate whether each character in the One Piece manga series deserves a dedicated section. https://en.wikipedia.org/wiki/Talk:List_of_One_Piece_characters/Archive_4#Reducing_article_size_(I) (last accessed 14 February 2025).

– 6 of the 100 longest threads are long *lists*, the items of which are expressed as separate messages, and are initially posted by the same user. As these discussions only marginally contain posts by different users we study in more detail this specific type in §3.5.

To summarise, our findings indicate that only two thirds of the 100 longest threads can be classified as discussions, highlighting the diverse uses of talk pages.

If we now consider the 100 most populous threads, with the highest numbers of different participants, we observe that they are all polls or series of polls. Polls are indeed a common practice in Wikipedia talk pages as they represent the pursuit of consensus (Kopf 2022). Polls can cover various decisions related to the article page, such as article deletion, merging with another related article, changing the article's title, deleting a whole section, choosing between different pictures etc. These polls may be created after inconclusive discussions or as a first intent when dealing with a new issue. The questions asked can be binary (support/oppose a suggestion) or open-ended (propose a new title, picture etc.). As we focus here on the number of different users, our sample is limited to threads with a single poll.

Due to the flexibility of the underlying wikicode, polls may be organised in two different ways. Messages can be in chronological order, with each user expressing his/her opinion in sequences. Alternatively, messages can be grouped based on their position, so that all messages, users and arguments in support or opposing the initial proposition are in the same section.[3]

Some of the polls are both spontaneous and local, and can be organised inside a discussion: they are qualified as *straw polls*. Others are qualified as *Request for Comments* (RfC) and follow a more sophisticated organisation. RfC polls are indexed in the Wikipedia space and therefore receive much more attention. This increased attention can lead to some problems when high stakes motivate certain users to manipulate the voting process with additional or fake accounts (*puppetry*), leading to their abandonment.[4] Several of our most massive threads show such cases that are explicitly flagged, but all expressed votes and comments remain available.

3.3 Longest-lasting threads

The temporal dynamics of Wikipedia discussions has been studied in (Kaltbrunner and Laniado 2012) but, as seen in Table 1, some threads can last more than 15 years, nearly the timespan of our dataset. In 2019, the 100 longest-lasting threads covered

---

3 https://en.wikipedia.org/wiki/Talk:Campaign_for_the_neologism_%22santorum%22/Archive_6#Proposal_to_rename,_redirect,_and_merge_content (last accessed 14 February 2025).

4 https://en.wikipedia.org/wiki/Talk:K._P._Yohannan#Keeping_the_controversy_Section_in_this_article (last accessed 14 February 2025).

a duration of over 14.5 years. Eight of the threads we examined are false positives: the prolonged duration is due to the fact that some unrelated messages have been placed in a generic section of the talk page (labelled as "Comments" or similar). Therefore these messages simply do not constitute a genuine discussion; but the 92 other cases are clear instances of communication occurring over an extended period of time.

About 10% of these threads exhibit a continuous spread over a significant period, with regular postings and no extended periods of silence exceeding a couple of years. This is the case of the example presented in Figure 5, which has continued even after our data collection, involving different users over the years but remaining focused on the initial topic.

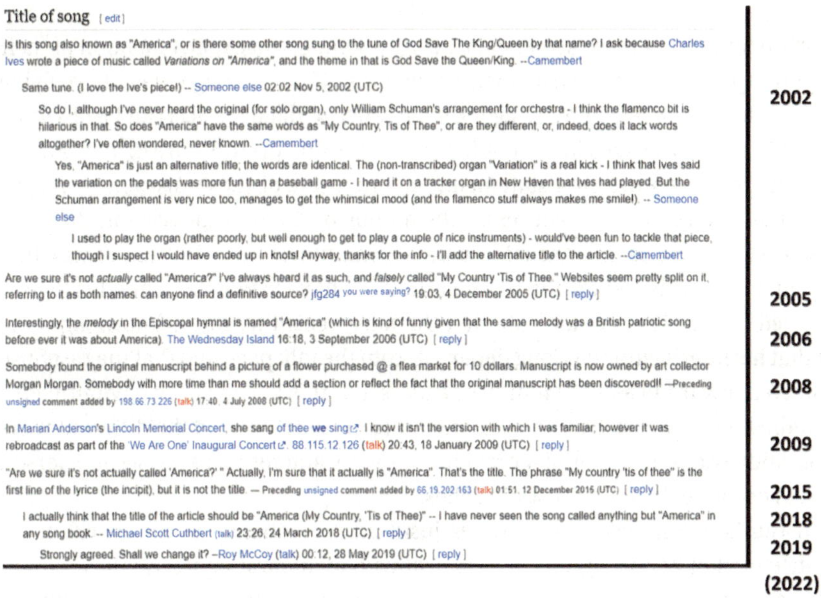

Title of song [edit]

Is this song also known as "America", or is there some other song sung to the tune of God Save The King/Queen by that name? I ask because Charles Ives wrote a piece of music called *Variations on "America"*, and the theme in that is God Save the Queen/King. --Camembert

Same tune. (I love the Ive's piece!) -- Someone else 02:02 Nov 5, 2002 (UTC)

So do I, although I've never heard the original (for solo organ), only William Schuman's arrangement for orchestra - I think the flamenco bit is hilarious in that. So does "America" have the same words as "My Country, Tis of Thee", or are they different, or, indeed, does it lack words altogether? I've often wondered, never known. --Camembert

Yes, "America" is just an alternative title; the words are identical. The (non-transcribed) organ "Variation" is a real kick - I think that Ives said the variation on the pedals was more fun than a baseball game - I heard it on a tracker organ in New Haven that Ives had played. But the Schuman arrangement is very nice too, manages to get the whimsical mood (and the flamenco stuff always makes me smile!). -- Someone else

I used to play the organ (rather poorly, but well enough to get to play a couple of nice instruments) - would've been fun to tackle that piece, though I suspect I would have ended up in knots! Anyway, thanks for the info - I'll add the alternative title to the article. --Camembert

Are we sure it's not *actually* called "America?" I've always heard it as such, and *falsely* called "My Country 'Tis of Thee." Websites seem pretty split on it, referring to it as both names. can anyone find a definitive source? jfg284 you were saying? 19:03, 4 December 2005 (UTC) [reply]

Interestingly, the *melody* in the Episcopal hymnal is named "America" (which is kind of funny given that the same melody was a British patriotic song before ever it was about America). The Wednesday Island 16:18, 3 September 2006 (UTC) [reply]

Somebody found the original manuscript behind a picture of a flower purchased @ a flea market for 10 dollars. Manuscript is now owned by art collector Morgan Morgan. Somebody with more time than me should add a section or reflect the fact that the original manuscript has been discovered!! —Preceding unsigned comment added by 198.66.73.226 (talk) 17:40, 4 July 2008 (UTC) [reply]

In Marian Anderson's Lincoln Memorial Concert, she sang of thee we sing. I know it isn't the version with which I was familiar, however it was rebroadcast as part of the 'We Are One' Inaugural Concert. 88.115.12.126 (talk) 20:43, 18 January 2009 (UTC) [reply]

"Are we sure it's not actually called 'America?' " Actually, I'm sure that it actually is "America". That's the title. The phrase "My country 'tis of thee" is the first line of the lyrice (the incipit), but it is not the title. — Preceding unsigned comment added by 66.19.202.163 (talk) 01:51, 12 December 2015 (UTC) [reply]

I actually think that the title of the article should be "America (My Country, 'Tis of Thee)" -- I have never seen the song called anything but "America" in any song book. -- Michael Scott Cuthbert (talk) 23:26, 24 March 2018 (UTC) [reply]

Strongly agreed. Shall we change it? –Roy McCoy (talk) 00:12, 28 May 2019 (UTC) [reply]

Figure 5: Example of a continuous thread spanning over 17 years (dates have been added to the right). https://en.wikipedia.org/wiki/Talk:My_Country,_%27Tis_of_Thee#Title_of_song (last accessed 14 February 2025).

However, the majority of threads demonstrate a single notable jump across time, with a message being posted in response to a comment made over a decade ago, such as the example in Figure 6.

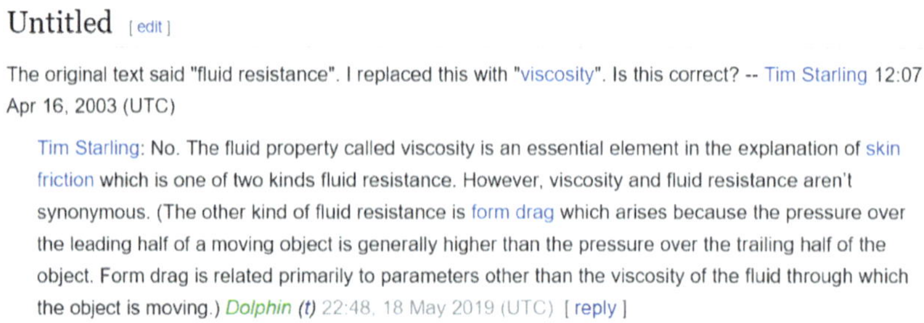
Untitled [edit]

The original text said "fluid resistance". I replaced this with "viscosity". Is this correct? -- Tim Starling 12:07 Apr 16, 2003 (UTC)

Tim Starling: No. The fluid property called viscosity is an essential element in the explanation of skin friction which is one of two kinds fluid resistance. However, viscosity and fluid resistance aren't synonymous. (The other kind of fluid resistance is form drag which arises because the pressure over the leading half of a moving object is generally higher than the pressure over the trailing half of the object. Form drag is related primarily to parameters other than the viscosity of the fluid through which the object is moving.) Dolphin (t) 22:48, 18 May 2019 (UTC) [reply]

Figure 6: sample thread with a question answered after 16 years https://en.wikipedia.org/wiki/Talk:Charles-Augustin_de_Coulomb#Untitled (last accessed 14 February 2025).

Surprisingly, most of these actual dialogues (72) contain no explicit mention of their temporal specificity. Users write their comment as if the message they are replying to was posted just a few minutes ago. A wide range of dialogue acts can be observed in such situations: answering a simple factual question (as in Figure 6), providing a reference, commenting on a statement,[5] etc. In a few of these cases however we found that the respondent addresses the author of the first message in the third person, which may seem unusual in online communications ("Related to why that was put by an earlier editor, the reason is [...]",[6] "I have to wonder what this IP user imagined [...]"). This may indicate that the most recent author acknowledges the fact that his interlocutor has long departed from the talk page and that the response is directed toward present and future readers. But this particular behaviour has to be studied more precisely; Herzberg and Lüngen (2024) studied the different ways a user addresses the author of a previous message, and found that a second person address occurs in less than 30% of replies.

If the late response is sometimes justified by a change in the world or an advancement of knowledge, it can also deal with atemporal topics. All these efforts to provide answers and additional information across time, even in the absence of the original participant, reflects the global dynamics and objective of the Wikipedia project.

In the remaining cases, users also take advantage of the flexibility of Wikipedia talk pages. Some users explicitly modify the timestamp of their message, pre-dating them to several years in the future to prevent their automatic archival. This is a

5 https://en.wikipedia.org/wiki/Talk:T-shirt#Capitalisation (last accessed 14 February 2025).
6 https://en.wikipedia.org/wiki/Talk:Brondesbury#Place (last accessed 14 February 2025).

move similar but somewhat more drastic to "bumping" a thread in online forums (i.e., adding empty messages to an existing thread to keep it visible).

In two cases, we found what may be qualified as talk page archaeology (see example in Figure 7). A user re-posts an old message or discussion that had been deleted or lost in the restructuring of Wikipedia. The reason for this is apparently not to answer the initial question or to correct a statement, but simply to preserve a trace from previous efforts. This preservative attitude has even led to keeping the very first versions of Wikipedia accessible in a dedicated website named *Nostalgia Wikipedia.*[7]

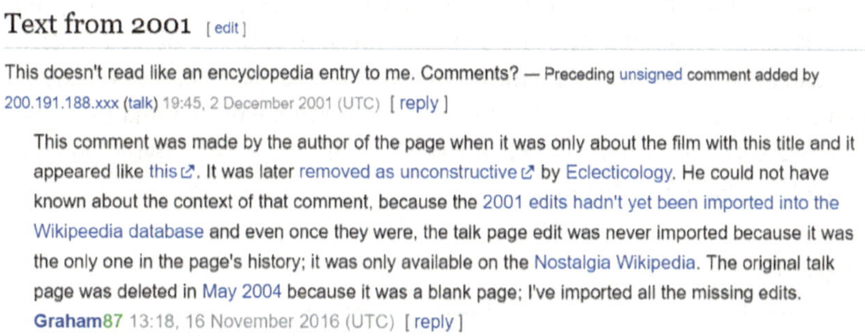
Text from 2001 [edit]

This doesn't read like an encyclopedia entry to me. Comments? — Preceding unsigned comment added by 200.191.188.xxx (talk) 19:45, 2 December 2001 (UTC) [reply]

This comment was made by the author of the page when it was only about the film with this title and it appeared like this. It was later removed as unconstructive by Eclecticology. He could not have known about the context of that comment, because the 2001 edits hadn't yet been imported into the Wikipeedia database and even once they were, the talk page edit was never imported because it was the only one in the page's history; it was only available on the Nostalgia Wikipedia. The original talk page was deleted in May 2004 because it was a blank page; I've imported all the missing edits. Graham87 13:18, 16 November 2016 (UTC) [reply]

Figure 7: sample thread restoring a previous comment
https://en.wikipedia.org/wiki/Talk:Casablanca#Text_from_2001 (last accessed 14 February 2025)

Although these temporal behaviours have not been formally described before, they confirm the specific position of the Wikipedia project as a global memory as expressed by Pentzold et al. (2017).

3.4 Longest single-user threads

Our last study focuses on single-user threads. In our dataset, 53% of all threads are authored by a single user, primarily due to them consisting of a single post. However, 6.9% of threads with 2 or more posts are entirely written by a single user. These "monologues" can grow to be quite extensive, reaching up to 150 messages. Similar to our previous analyses, we examined the 100 longest single-user threads (with 12 or more posts) and identified two main configurations.

7 https://nostalgia.wikipedia.org/ (last accessed 14 February 2025).

A significant majority of these threads (88) are lists, as we had observed in some of the longest threads (§3.2). The messages within these threads can take the form of paragraphs that include comments, remarks or suggestions.[8] These cases typically result from a review of the article, or a series of proposals and suggestions for rewriting or expanding it. Of course, these items can sometimes receive comments or extensions in the form of nested messages by other users as noted in §3.3.

But long lists of another kind contain only simple informational elements relevant to the article, such as products, dates, characters, users... In most cases, the thread lacks an explicit communication goal and appears to function as a logbook or to-do list for the author. A thread of such "grocery list" type can include check marks or crossed out items, indicating that they have been processed (e.g., proofread, referenced, integrated into the article...). In only 12 cases of such lists we could find explicit invitations from the author to others to contribute by extending, commenting or correcting the items, although in our sample these remained unanswered. Figure 8 shows such an explicit checklist with the author giving potential helping hands precise instructions.

Ship checklist

Each ship will be crossed out as its entries in the timeline are referenced. You can help with this work to improve the verifiability of the timeline. Entries in this list are alphabetical by country then ship, with earlier ships of the same name listed first. I will enter the ship's names first and then as time allows I will wikilink them here, before I attempt to start the work of referencing.**Nick Thorne** *talk* 10:58, 12 September 2008 (UTC)

Argentina

- ~~ARA *Independencia* (V-1)~~ **Nick Thorne** *talk* 22:14, 13 September 2008 (UTC)
- ~~ARA *Veinticinco de Mayo* (V-2)~~ **Nick Thorne** *talk* 07:44, 14 September 2008 (UTC)

Australia

- ~~HMAS *Melbourne* (R21)~~
- ~~HMAS *Sydney* (R17)~~
- ~~HMAS *Vengeance* (R71)~~ **Nick Thorne** *talk* 23:23, 12 September 2008 (UTC)

Brazil

- ~~NAe *Sao Paulo*~~ **Nick Thorne** *talk* 13:57, 14 September 2008 (UTC)
- ~~NAeL *Minas Gerais*~~ **Nick Thorne** *talk* 13:57, 14 September 2008 (UTC)

Canada

- ~~HMCS *Bonaventure* (CVL 22)~~ **Nick Thorne** *talk* 13:12, 16 September 2008 (UTC)

Figure 8: sample list thread by a single user (extract) https://en.wikipedia.org/wiki/Talk:Timeline_for_aircraft_carrier_service/Archive_1#Ship_checklist (last accessed 14 February 2025).

8 https://en.wikipedia.org/wiki/Talk:Timeline_of_the_Irish_War_of_Independence#Doubtful_edits (last accessed 14 February 2025).

Professor Mersini Radio Broadcast [edit]

Here is Dr Mersini's second paper which predicts the second void of one degree http://arxiv.org/abs/hep-th/0612142. Notpayingthepsychiatrist (talk) 16:21, 22 March 2008 (UTC). In that paper the writers refererence this paper as indicating the small void in the southern hemisphere http://arxiv.org/abs/astro-ph/0602478. Notpayingthepsychiatrist (talk) 16:36, 22 March 2008 (UTC) This paper attributes assymetry, planarity and alignment in CMB power between hemispheres as explained by assymetry of voids between hemispheres which seems to be were the prediction of a small void in the opposite hemisphere comes from. Notpayingthepsychiatrist (talk) 05:04, 23 March 2008 (UTC) [reply]

It seems the large void near the horizon of the universe verified predictions of the string theory landscape high scale inflation birth of the universe where, I think, long waveforms of different universes entangled and decohered http://wunc.org/tsot/archive/?b_start:int=42 (understandable radio broadcast as at 23-03-08) http://arxiv.org/abs/hep-th/0612142, radio broadcast archived as at 07-04-08 http://wunc.org/tsot/archive/sot0221b08.mp3/view?searchterm=mersini and the small void is simply to understand the CMB power. Notpayingthepsychiatrist (talk) 08:10, 23 March 2008 (UTC) [reply]

As yet the theory has not been adopted by high impact magazines like Science, Nature or PNAS. Notpayingthepsychiatrist (talk) 19:49, 29 March 2008 (UTC) The significance of Laura Menisi-Haughton's prediction can't be understated, the cold spot could have been dark matter. Notpayingthepsychiatrist (talk) 06:58, 5 April 2008 (UTC) [reply]

But the Wikipedia article doesn't give any competing theory Notpayingthepsychiatrist (talk) 10:47, 31 March 2008 (UTC). A competing theory was proposed on 5 March, where the cold spot is regarded as a gateway to extra dimensions: http://209.85.173.104/search?q=cache:2IABbS94HuEJ:export.arxiv.org/abs/0803.0694+arxiv+cold+spot&hl=en&ct=clnk&cd=5&gl=au Notpayingthepsychiatrist (talk) 23:46, 6 April 2008 (UTC) [reply]

At http://209.85.173.104/search?q=cache:ph3Xluba9Q8J:www.hr-online.de/servlet/de.hr.cms.servlet.File/08-022.pdf%3Fws%3Dhrmysql%26blobId%3D6423810%26id%3D33781304+susskind+mersini+void&hl=en&ct=clnk&cd=7&gl=au three physicists are commended for using mathematical proofs. This is a translation from the German using AltaVista Babel Fish: Are there infinitely many beside our universe still different university verses, possibly? The answers to this question are speculative - and most disputed. There are proofs none. But one must admit one: Researchers such as Alex Vilenkin, Laura Mersini and Leonard Susskind do not establish her theory buildings PAGE 10 page 10 by any means on that to nothing. They quite move with their computations on the ways its that is mathematically possible. — Preceding unsigned comment added by Notpayingthepsychiatrist (talk • contribs) 09:14, 6 April 2008 (UTC) [reply]

This report dated December says it is actually a group of extrema and not one, prefers not to use wavelet analysis as a measure of Gausinnity and also examines whether there are other cold spots. http://front.math.ucdavis.edu/0712.1118. (They conclude - using their different technique - that: "clustering of the extrema of the ILC III and WCM signals is a typical feature of the morphology,..." (p9) Notpayingthepsychiatrist (talk) 00:52, 7 April 2008 (UTC) [reply]

Here are the title of the article, it's authors and their positions:

Title: The mystery of the WMAP cold spot Authors: Pavel D. Naselsky (1), Per Rex Christensen (1), Peter Coles (2), Oleg Verkhodanov (3), Dmitry Novikov (4,5), Jaiseung Kim (1) ((1) Niels Bohr Institute, Copenhagen, Denmark; (2) School of Physics and Astronomy, Cardiff University, Wales, United Kingdom; (3) Special astrophysical observatory, Nizhnij Arkhyz, Russia; (4) Imperial College, London, United Kingdom; (5) AstroSpace Center of Lebedev Physical Institute, Moscow, Russia) —Preceding unsigned comment added by Notpayingthepsychiatrist (talk • contribs) 03:39, 8 April 2008 (UTC) [reply]

However, does this refute figure 5 in http://arxiv.org/abs/0704.0908 (which is quoted in the Wikipedia article itself)? Notpayingthepsychiatrist (talk) 04:10, 8 April 2008 (UTC). This study was designed, presumably, on radio waves, while the other one mentioned by Wikipedia on background temperature.Notpayingthepsychiatrist (talk) 05:17, 8 April 2008 (UTC) [reply]

However, the wikipedia article is not entirely easy to follow, as the article on detection by radio telescope proposes "modest redshift" objects lying they are further away? - eliminating the need for Gaussinity. But isn't it true that the smaller the redshift, the slower and closer the y? I now understand it is the integrated Sachs-Wolfe effect (of a hot spot before a void in the line of sight), which is why the article mentions modest red shifts, but doesn't change the size of the void. Notpayingthepsychiatrist (talk) 11:21, 8 April 2008 (UTC) [reply]

Figure 9: Example of a long monologue in which the user "thinks aloud" as he investigates a topic. https://en.wikipedia.org/wiki/Talk:CMB%20cold%20spot#Professor_Mersini_Radio_Broadcast (last accessed 14 February 2025).

The 12 remaining long monologues contain heterogeneous posts, which can consist of larger text segments such as problem analyses, reviews, suggestions, hypotheses, reports of actions taken, steps in an investigation and more, to various combinations of such messages within the same thread.

Figure 9 shows such a thread, in which the user reports his investigation of an issue which requires him to read additional sources, confront views and finally explicitly leads to an understanding. This thread has 13 messages, spans over a month and clearly shows the linguistic marks of an academic argumentation ("here is", "it seems", "but the article", "however" etc.). At no point can we identify an address to an interlocutor nor any asking for advice, opinion or help: the whole thread can be considered as a diary or a "thinking aloud" process. It also corresponds to the extended notion of dialogism theorized by Bakhtin (1994), which explains why monological genres show such traces of an interlocution. This is the case for all 12 such monologues in our sample, and it has been confirmed that there are many more cases with fewer messages – in other words, that monologues or single-user threads are a significant phenomenon in Wikipedia talk pages (see Tanguy et al. 2024 for a more detailed analysis).

4 Conclusion

Our study of extreme cases in a dataset of over 3 million discussions from the English Wikipedia talk pages has allowed us to identify several specific behaviours:

- For the most active users of Wikipedia, editing the encyclopaedia articles and participating in talk pages may be considered as separate or at least decorrelated activities. This would require additional efforts to investigate specific individuals' habits and propose a more precise profiling, but we were able to find prolific editors who do not discuss in talk pages, as well as users whose activity is more prone towards discussion.
- The threads involving a large number of users are mostly polls or series of polls, a known and common habit of the Wikipedia community to reach consensus.
- Very long threads can consist of poll series, but can also be genuine discussions between a small community of users. The length is mostly justified by conflicting views on a topic, but we have observed that the users give these discussions some value and make efforts toward a better readability.
- Talk pages may also be used as tools for other activities than communication between contributors: they can consist of logs, lists or diaries, mostly maintained by a single user as they perform some important editing work or inquiry.

- Wikipedia talk pages, as well as the articles themselves, are technically endless, leading to discussion lasting several years, potentially including long periods of silence.

The flexibility of the platform plays a crucial role in enabling these behaviours, as users can reshape and reorganise the posts in ways which are not possible in the other online discussion environments. The ability users have to freely insert or reorder messages in a thread facilitates the emergence of new forms such as organised polls, sectioned long threads and the use of threads as checklists. In some cases, these possibilities may induce a shift away from the supposedly central communicational goal of the talk pages, such as monologues and threads used as log books or diaries. However, interaction remains possible even in these cases.

Our observations of long-lasting discussions confirm the objective of the Wikipedia project to create a cultural monument and testimony. Talk pages, as the main articles of the encyclopaedia, are considered permanent documents. Therefore, it is not a problem for a Wikipedian to reply to a message 15 years later, with the response being primarily directed towards the community rather than the original user. In a few cases we could also witness the explicit unearthing of old discussions. These behaviours related to the passage of time seem to converge with our observation of the care some users make in organising long discussions and making them readable. These users consider that discussions are important traces or even sources of knowledge on a topic, or on the different views on a topic. This may also explain why the logbooks used by some users are made publicly available as discussions instead of remaining in a private storage, and why some users take the time to express their chain of thought and evolutive investigation.

From a methodological point of view, we consider that our mixed approach has been fruitful. Selecting items of interest on the quantitative basis based on the extreme values of their features, and examining them with a qualitative approach was both satisfactory. It is both reproducible and, as expected, the extreme cases were easier and richer to examine. For example, restructuring efforts in long discussions are more obvious when there are several of them, although we could later confirm that they can appear in a more isolated manner, and the "thinking aloud" monologues could be easily ignored or misinterpreted when they spread over only one or two messages. As a lighter note, extreme cases also were in many cases more pleasant to examine than random threads.

It was not our aim to investigate the specific topics or domains in which certain types of discussion take place. During our observations we did not identify any particular area of knowledge that would correlate with specific behaviours. However, it is evident that popular topics such as pop culture, sports and geopolitics tend to attract a larger number of participants. Nevertheless, impressive efforts to gather information from a single individual can be found across various subjects, including niche areas.

On the methodological front, our approach needs further completion by exploring the extent to which these newly identified phenomena appear in less extreme cases. Preliminary surveys have shown, for instance, that polls and single-author lists appear at much smaller scales (2–3 voters, a few items in a list, short monologues) and, therefore, occur more frequently.

This naturally calls for further investigations, including a more systematic corpus search of local configurations in order to estimate the frequency of these behaviours, and to enable cross-lingual comparisons. It should be noted, however, that Wikipedia talk pages cannot be regarded as typical CMC data without taking these specificities into account.

References

Bakhtin, Mikhail. 1994. *The dialogic imagination: Four essays.* (Michael Holquist & Caryl Emerson, eds.). Austin: University of Texas Press.

Beamish, Paul W. & Vanessa C. Hasse. 2022. The importance of rare events and other outliers in global strategy research. *Global Strategy Journal* 12 (4). 697–713.

Chen, Katherine K. 2015. Using extreme cases to understand organizations. In *Handbook of qualitative organizational research*. 33–44. London: Routledge.

Denis, Alexandre, Matthieu Quignard, Dominique Fréard, Françoise Détienne, Michael Baker & Flore Barcellini. 2012. Détection de conflits dans les communautés épistémiques en ligne. *TALN – Actes de la Conférence sur le Traitement Automatique des Langues Naturelles*.

Ferschke, Oliver, Iryna Gurevych & Yevgen Chebotar. 2012. Behind the article: Recognizing dialog acts in Wikipedia talk pages. In *Proceedings of the 13th Conference of the European Chapter of the Association for Computational Linguistics*. 777–786.

Flyvbjerg, Bent. 2011. Case study. In Norman K. Denzin and Yvonna S. Lincoln (eds.), *The Sage handbook of qualitative research*, 4th edition. Sage.

Ginzburg, Carlo. 2014. Microhistory: Two or three things that I know about it. In Hans Renders & Binne De Haan (eds) *Theoretical discussions of biography*. Leiden: Brill.

Gómez, Vicenç, Hilbert J. Kappen & Andreas Kaltenbrunner. 2011. Modeling the structure and evolution of discussion cascades. In *Proceedings of the 22nd ACM Conference on Hypertext and Hypermedia*. 181–190.

Kaltenbrunner, Andreas & David Laniado. 2012. There is no deadline: Time evolution of Wikipedia discussions. In *Proceedings of the 8th Annual International Symposium on Wikis and Open Collaboration (WikiSym)*. 1–10.

Kopf, Susanne. 2022. *A discursive perspective on Wikipedia: More than an encyclopaedia?* Cham: Springer International.

Herzberg, Laura & Harald Lüngen. 2024. Investigating reply relations on Wikipedia talk pages to reconstruct interactional strategies of Wikipedia authors. In Céline Poudat, Harald Lüngen &

Laura Herzberg (eds.), *Investigating Wikipedia: Linguistic corpus building, exploration and analyses*. Amsterdam & Philadelphia: John Benjamins.

Ho-Dac, Lydia-Mai. 2024. Building a comparable corpus of online discussions in Wikipedia: The EFG WikiCorpus. In Céline Poudat, Harald Lüngen & Laura Herzberg (eds.), *Investigating Wikipedia: Linguistic corpus building, exploration and analyses*. Amsterdam & Philadelphia: John Benjamins.

Hobman, Elizabeth, Prashant Bordia, Bernd Irmer & Artemis Chang. 2002. The expression of conflict in computer-mediated and face-to-face groups. *Small Group Research* 33, 4. 439–465.

Laniado, David, Ricardo Tasso, Yana Volkovich & Andreas Kaltenbrunner. 2011. When the Wikipedians talk: Network and tree structure of Wikipedia discussion pages. In *Fifth international AAAI Conference on Weblogs and Social Media*.

Lüngen, Harald & Laura Herzberg. 2019. Types and annotation of reply relations in computer-mediated communication. *European Journal of Applied Linguistics* 7 (2). 305–331.

Mehler, Alexander, Rüdiger Gleim, Andy Lücking, Tolga Uslu & Christian Stegbauer. 2018. On the self-similarity of Wikipedia talks: A combined discourse-analytical and quantitative approach. *Glottometrics 40*. 1–45.

Osborne, Jason W. & Amy Overbay. 2019. The power of outliers (and why researchers should always check for them). *Practical Assessment, Research, and Evaluation* 9, Article 6.

Pentzold, Christian, Esther Weltevrede, Michele Mauri, David Laniado, Andreas Kaltenbrunner & Eric Borra. 2017. Digging Wikipedia: The online encyclopedia as a digital cultural heritage gateway and site. *Journal on Computing and Cultural Heritage (JOCCH)*, 10 (1). 1–19.

Poudat, Céline & Marie Chandelier. 2024. Disagreements and conflicts in Wikipedia talk pages. In Céline Poudat, Harald Lüngen & Laura Herzberg (eds.), Investigating *Wikipedia: Linguistic corpus building, exploration and analyses*. Amsterdam & Philadelphia: John Benjamins.

Schneider, Jodi, Alexandre Passant & John G. Breslin. 2010. A content analysis: How Wikipedia talk pages are used. *Proceedings of the 2nd International Conference of Web Science*. 1–7.

Tanguy, Ludovic. Céline Poudat & Lydia-Mai Ho-Dac. 2024. Talking to oneself in CMC: A study of self replies in Wikipedia talk pages. *Proceedings of the Conference on CMC and Social Media Corpora*, Nice, France.

Index

https://doi.org/10.1515/9783111434018-020